THE NEW ENGLAND MIND
From Colony to Province

From the *American Magazine,* March 1745, reproduced through the courtesy of The Houghton Library.

THE NEW ENGLAND MIND: *The Seventeenth Century*
(Volume I)

THE NEW ENGLAND MIND: *From Colony to Province*
(Volume II)

THE NEW ENGLAND MIND

From Colony to Province

By PERRY MILLER

BEACON PRESS BOSTON

International Standard Book Number: 0–8070–5191–8

9   8   7   6   5   4

For
HARRY AND ELENA LEVIN

FOREWORD

This book stands, I trust, upon its own feet, and asks to be read as a self-sufficient unit. At the same time it is also a sequel to *The New England Mind: The Seventeenth Century*, published in September 1939. In that year I assumed that the next work would be quickly completed, but the situation proved not propitious either for scholarship or the dissemination of scholarship. I entered the Armed Services persuaded that my book had fallen on evil days and had failed to make any mark upon its generation.

However, since the end of the war *The New England Mind: The Seventeenth Century* has geen gratifyingly studied, and there appears to be warrant for reprinting it. Most of what a decade ago seemed novelty in the treatment has become accepted; many of the deficiencies have been remedied by other students, and on several topics—especially the academic curriculum and the Ramist dialectic—younger scholars like William Costello and Walter J. Ong have gone far beyond it. But for better or worse the book is obliged to reappear as it first came out, and I can only express my gratitude to the Harvard Press for undertaking the reissue, planned for 1954.

If the earlier book has any merit it arises from the effort to comprehend, in the widest possible terms, the architecture of the intellect brought to America by the founders of New England. Hence that book was organized by topics, treating the entire expression of the period as a single body of writing and paying little or no attention to modifications forced upon the mind by domestic events. The method could be justified because throughout the century, and down to the first decades of the eighteenth, the official cosmology did remain more or less intact. Such developments as took place affected the lesser areas of church polity, political relations, or the contests of groups and interests. These could be, and indeed as I believe this narrative demonstrates often were, intense and shattering experiences without causing any alterations in the doctrinal frame of reference. Therefore *From Colony to Province* may be imagined as taking place, so to speak, inside *The Seventeenth Century*. While the massive structure of logic, psychology, theology stands apparently untouched, the furnishings of the palace are little by little changed, until a hundred years after the Great Migration the New England mind has become strangely altered, even though the process (which, all things considered, was rapid) was hardly perceptible to the actors themselves. A hundred years after the landings, they were forced to look upon themselves with amazement, hardly capable of understanding how they had come to be what they were.

Consequently the focus of the study is narrowed down to a merely provincial scene, and much is made of events which, in the perspective of American—not to say of world—history, seem so small as to be trivial.

Frankly, did I regard this investigation as no more than an account of intellectual activity in colonial New England I would long since have given it over as not worth the effort. But the fascination of this region, for the first two hundred or more years of its existence, is that it affords the historian an ideal laboratory. It was relatively isolated, the people were comparatively homogeneous, and the forces of history played upon it in ways that can more satisfactorily be traced than in more complex societies. Here is an opportunity, as nearly perfect as the student is apt to find, for extracting certain generalizations about the relation of thought or ideas to communal experience. I believe profoundly that the story herein recounted is chiefly valuable for its *representative* quality: it is a case history of the accommodation to the American landscape of an imported and highly articulated system of ideas. We have a chance to see exactly how this process, which began the moment the ships dropped anchor in Boston harbor, was driven by local influences, and yet was constantly diverted or stimulated by the influx of ideas from Europe. What I should most like to claim for this study is that it amounts to a sort of working model for American history.

Circumstances and a lack of clear foresight betrayed me into composing things in the wrong order. In 1933 I published *Orthodoxy in Massachusetts*, which gives my version of the first two decades of the New England enterprise; I worked then under the delusion that it would serve as prologue to *The New England Mind: The Seventeenth Century*. But the research itself at length taught me that the second book was in reality the introductory exploration; *Orthodoxy in Massachusetts* constitutes the first chapters of a tale which *The New England Mind: From Colony to Province* resumes. For the establishing of continuity I have reached behind the year 1648—the formulation of *The Cambridge Platform*—to catch up hitherto unannounced themes, but have not reviewed all those which culminated in that document. I am obliged to pretend that this chronicle commences from a hypothetical starting point, from the vast literature of what I have called Non-separatist Congregationalism. Assuming that *Orthodoxy in Massachusetts* has stated its case, and further postulating the existence of *The New England Mind: The Seventeenth Century*, I now attempt to get on with an analysis of events as they befell.

As far as possible I have again employed the premise of my general title, that "mind" means what was said and done publicly. Therefore I have made sparing use of diaries or private papers, and have, on matters of larger concern, taken my illustrations indifferently from whichever writer seemed most to the point. But since this is a chronological story, and in it there is conflict, I have allowed sections to deal with personalities like Gershom Bulkeley, Solomon Stoddard, or John Wise apart from the over-all configuration. To save space and expense, I have not cluttered my text with specific annotations; where an utterance has special importance I have treated it at length, giving the title in the text and assuming that the readers will perceive that the following quotations come from it. All titles are listed in the Index under their authors (or by name, if anonymous); hence a combination of the Index and the Bibliographical Notes comprises a list of the major "sources." I have printed quotations as they appear in print or in manuscript, except that I have left out the italics which at the time were generally arbitrary ornaments and are peculiarly distracting to the modern eye.

Students of early New England know that I could not have written this book without the help of Thomas J. Holmes's monumental *Bibliographies* of the Mathers or of Clifford K. Shipton's continuation of *Sibley's Harvard Graduates*. I owe much to present and former students, especially Edmund S. Morgan. I. Bernard Cohen acted over and above the call of friendship by reading and criticizing the manuscript. Most of the work was done in the Houghton Library of Harvard University, where I added to the debt of gratitude I have long owed Miss Carolyn Jakeman; in the Massachusetts Historical Society, where I had the invaluable help of Stephen T. Riley and Warren G. Wheeler; and in the Boston Public Library, where I enjoyed the hospitality of Zoltán Haraszti. The volume has profited immeasurably from the expert assistance of Chase Duffy. Elizabeth Williams Miller worked with me in every stage of the research and writing.

PERRY MILLER

Cambridge, Massachusetts
December 10, 1952

PREFACE TO THE BEACON PRESS EDITION

With the reprinting of this volume I have the immense satisfaction of beholding all of the parts of my saga in paperback version, arrived at, as I endeavored to explain in 1952, in a disgracefully clumsy sequence.

I find a particular gratification in the reappearance of this final installment because it was a challenge — as much as I could make it one — to modern scholarship about what constitutes "intellectual history," and wherein it differs from, or should be set apart from, the "social." At one point, however, I incautiously remarked that by the close of my century the chronicle of New England's "mind" was being as much written by the actions of men of business as by theologians. That proved a gaff. I was soon appalled by the eagerness with which academic reviewer after reviewer seized upon this unfortunate passage as a welcome release from the burden of ideas which my treatment had imposed upon them, and by the glee with which they demanded of the book, where was the account of these actions? When they could triumphantly announce that it was conspicuous by its absence, they could comfortably dismiss this sort of history as irrelevant. They could then resume their researches, with a clear conscience, on such topics as ship, trade routes, currency, property, agriculture, town government and military tactics.

PREFACE

I still maintain, and want this reprinting to insist, that while indeed these kinds of activity require an exercise of a faculty which in ordinary parlance may be called intelligence, such matters are not, and cannot be made, the central theme of a coherent narrative. They furnish forth at their worst mere tables of statistics, on the average meaningless inventories, and at their best only a series of monographs. The most charitable of my critics paid me a dubious compliment on my ability "to extemporize" the history of New England society, but he intended this courtesy to be a rebuke to the profession for not having yet built the foundation on which my account ought, by rights, to have been based. He implied that therefore that construct was floating in thin air, like some insubstantial island of Laputa.

My unrepentant — or should I say defiant? — contention is quite the reverse. The terms of Puritan thinking do not progressively become poorer tools than were the concepts of the founders for the recording of social change. On the contrary, they are increasingly the instruments through which the people strove to cope with a bewildering reality. Unless we also approach that buzzing factuality through a comprehension of these ideas, it becomes even more a tumultuous chaos for us that it was for those caught in the blizzard. Unless we can do this, the writing of history ceases to be a work of the mind. But to proceed successfully from the intellectual to the social pattern requires of the historian — and the reader of histories — a sensitivity to the nuances of ideas at least as delicate as that of the best intellects in the period.

PERRY MILLER

February 25, 1961

CONTENTS

PROLOGUE

And the Lord put forth His hand, and touched my mouth. And the Lord said unto me, "Behold, I have put my words in thy mouth. See, I have this day set thee over the nations and over the kingdoms, to root out, and to pull down, and to destroy, and to throw down, to build, and to plant."

JEREMIAH 1:9–10

PROLOGUE

RICHARD MATHER'S FAREWELL

JⓞⱧⓝ Winthrop, Governor of Massachusetts Bay, died in 1649, as did Thomas Shepard, most eloquent of preachers, relentless searcher of souls, and acute divider between the states of grace and reprobation. Two years before, Thomas Hooker, magisterial founder of Connecticut, who could put a king in his pocket, preceded them. In 1652, John Cotton, foremost scholar and official apologist of the New England Way, died in Boston, his name a mighty one wherever Protestant learning and erudition were revered. These had been the spokesmen, and with them a generation ended.

There was still John Davenport in New Haven, but he had withdrawn into peculiarities which even to Puritans seemed excessively rigorous. Children of these Plutarchian fathers began a lament they could not restrain:

> *Shall none*
> *Be left behind to tell's the Quondam Glory*
> *Of this Plantation?*

By the sixth decade of the century only one remained from the pantheon of great founders—Richard Mather of Dorchester. Only he, principal architect of *The Cambridge Platform* (by which in 1648 orthodox New England published to the world its distinctive constitution of church government), only he could pronounce the admonition and benediction of the fathers.

By the tenth of April 1657, almost deaf and blind in one eye, he felt the time had come to speak *A Farewel-Exhortation To the Church and People of Dorchester in New-England.* (Actually, he was to live until April 1669.) He and his colleagues had invested property, energy, life; now others must carry on, children who, like his youngest son Increase, knew nothing of heroic days in England when King Charles darkened the skies by dismissing Parliament and when Laud's "visitors" told Richard to his face that he had better have begot seven bastards than to have preached without a surplice. Into this valedictory, Richard Mather poured the experience of a generation, strove by main force to warn of what in their eyes, despite the miraculous achievement, were evident dangers.

As we might expect, Mather exhorted the progeny to hold fast to the

theological propositions arrayed in *The Westminster Confession*, which he
had persuaded the Synod of 1648 to endorse, and urged upon them fidelity
to the scheme of ecclesiastical polity he had carried through that assembly.
But in his principal instruction he made a statement to which we may attach
special significance, all the more as it betrays uneasiness about something
that had not, in the infinite wisdom of the fathers, been foreseen. It reveals
a belated awareness of one factor in the developing economy with which
neither the *Confession* nor the *Platform* had dealt:

> It is true the condition of many amongst you . . . is such as necessarily puts
> you on to have much imployment about the things of this life, and to labour with
> care & paines taking in the workes of husbandry, and other worldly business for the
> maintenance of your selves & your families, the Lord having laid this burden on
> man . . . & experience shews that it is an easy thing in the middest of worldly
> business to lose the life and power of Religion, that nothing thereof should be left
> but only the external form, as it were the carcass or shell, worldliness having eaten
> out the kernell, and having consumed the very soul & life of godliness.

Mather admitted—as Puritans always did acknowledge—that these concerns are necessary, but New Englanders must, above all people, make them
virtuous, must be concerned not so much with "the things of this life" as
with "the heart wherewith they are done," for if there be no heart, even
preaching and praying, let alone husbandry and fishing, "will be no better then acts of profaneness & ungodlyness, and in the issue be charged
upon the doers as so many sinns." With his last voice, Richard Mather
laid upon the society this injunction, that it exhibit the life and power of
religion, no longer in defiance of king and bishop, but in earthly and civil
employments.

The posterity of American Puritanism have devised nothing that would
more shock their fathers than their inquiry into the comparative force,
among motives which impelled the settlement, of the economic as against
the religious. The coincidence of a crisis in the wool trade of East Anglia
with the Parliamentary débacle of 1629 was comprehensible: it signified,
as Winthrop recognized when he drew up his list of inducements, that
God was employing diverse arguments to persuade Puritans to get out of
England.

These Puritans never intended that their holy experiment should eventuate in a conflict, let alone a contradiction, between the religious program
and civil employments. They did not suppose that conditions in the New
World would make it any more difficult than in the old for virtuous men
to turn necessities into virtues: because—we cannot too often remind ourselves—they did not think of New England as being "new." It was going
to be the old, familiar world of sin and struggle: it differed only in that
it was vacant (except for a few Indians), that therein men might draw
breath to resume the fight, at that moment discouraged in England, against
sin and profligacy. This is what John Winthrop meant when, on the deck

of the *Arbella*, he said we "seeke out a place of Cohabitation and Con-. sorteshipp vnder a due forme of Government both ciuill and ecclesiasticall." The migration was no retreat from Europe: it was a flank attack. We are to be a city set upon a hill, the eyes of all the world upon us; what we succeed in demonstrating, Europe will be bound to imitate, even Rome itself. These were not—despite their analogies with Moses and the tribes of Israel—refugees seeking a promised land, but English scholars, soldiers, and statesmen, taking the long way about in order that someday they, or their children, or at least their friends, might rule in Lambeth. They knew that they would have to take pains in husbandry and business; since the fall of Adam such diligence was obligatory, but it was unthinkable that children conceived and educated in Massachusetts and Connecticut would become preoccupied, not with universal Christendom, but with provincial merchandise.

While the city was building upon its hill, citizens would have to live. This, of course, would be but a means to an end; whatever prosperity they achieved would serve to persuade opponents that their civil and ecclesiastical governments were good. But on the other hand, no activity could be in itself so meaningless as to serve merely as a means to an end. A man was doing the will of God when farming or trading as much as when preaching; none could give himself to commerce under the convenient rationalization that he was licensed to concentrate his whole soul upon that pursuit in order to strengthen a national economy—even a holy economy. All things are temptations: a man must labor in his calling as though all depends upon his exertions, but must remember that reward is given by God. Every citizen would have to make the wilderness supply food and clothing, to make it bloom, but he must exert himself not in order to vindicate propositions to which the society was dedicated, but as a consequence of his personal and prior dedication to them.

In other words, economic prosperity would be not a cause but a result of piety. Yet anyone who knew the history of Europe, particularly in the last two centuries, knew that men were prone to transpose cause and effect. Experience showed that they might come imperceptibly to derive satisfaction less from their piety than from the wealth which was its visible symbol.

John Winthrop was not dismayed before the economic task: as the fleet approached the scene of labor, he knew the danger to be not failure but success. Even in anticipation, what struck dread into his heart was a fear lest we should "fall to embrace this present world and prosecute our carnall intencions, seeking greate things for our selues and our posterity." The American problem was not to be different from the European: a vacant continent might offer greater scope for enterprise, but this made a difference in degree, not in kind. In either continent, diligence in a man's calling gave recompense, leaving the laborer with a torturing question about his spiritual motive.

Leaders of the first generation were participants in a great world. Not,

I mean, that they were courtiers or patrons of the Mermaid Tavern, but they were figures of weight and influence, both in their own and others' estimation, in a vast complex, compared with which court and tavern were frivolous byplays. They were performers in the main action, in international Calvinism, in Protestantism. They were not colonials, and never would become colonial; though they died in America, they were never to be Americanized. They were too old, had been exercised too deeply ever to learn provincialism. They came of age and to their convictions in a world where the shaping influences were the war in Germany, Richelieu's foreign policy, Buckingham's plots, Eliot's oratory, immense tomes on the cosmic structure of the liberal arts, and razor-edged arguments against Arminianism. Isolation is not a matter of distance or the slowness of communication: it is a question of what a dispatch from distant quarters means to the recipient. A report from Geneva, Frankfort, Strasbourg, or Leiden might take months to reach John Cotton or Thomas Hooker, but either comprehended it immediately, not as a tale from foreign parts, but as something intimately concerning them—exactly as Milton readily understood the significance of bulletins from the Piedmont.

The major events of the first decades in the history of these plantations were not the developments which now interest our historians: such mechanical adjustments as the land system or the bicameral legislature. For the leaders themselves, the important episodes were those in which they acted out their consciousness of filling roles in the over-all strategy of Protestantism. Suppression of Anne Hutchinson and the Antinomians; banishment of Roger Williams; tricky diplomacy with King, Parliament, Presbyterians, and Oliver Cromwell; adroit maneuvers to defeat the "Remonstrance" of Dr. Child; formulating *The Cambridge Platform:* these actions were guided not by domestic considerations but by their sense of New England's part in the Holy War. Learned books contributed to the fundamental issue of the age: Hooker's *Survey,* Cotton's *The Way of Congregational Churches Cleared,* Shepard's *A Defence of the Answer,* and Richard Mather's *Church-Government* were not written for home consumption but for an audience stretched across half Europe. These came out of a scholarship immense and sophisticated, and distinguished the particulars of New England only in so far as they had reference to the universals of Europe.

Naturally, even in the midst of this holy war, food, clothes, and utensils had to be produced and exchanged. Economic life was not something apart from the Christian: it was one among the multiple aspects of existence. With no sense that he was adding merely subsidiary arguments, Winthrop in 1629 included, among his reasons for migrating, the reflection that England was overpopulated and growing weary of her inhabitants, along with the plea that the move would perfect the Reformation. Even while laboring or trading, men's minds would be occupied not only with search of soul but also with the victories of Gustavus Adolphus or the agonies of La Rochelle. Christian men, working in the world, had daily experience of the conflict; though they did not get their news hourly or in screaming headlines, they got it eventually, and tension was unrelieved. Experience showed that amid worldly business a man might lose the power of religion, but if there was one thing Winthrop and the signers of the Cambridge Agreement could say, in all honesty, about themselves, it was this: men of affairs they were, but they conducted their businesses and built their estates without for a moment forgetting that they aspired to godliness. Precisely because they had come to the conclusion—after, as Shepard said, "many serious consultations with one another"—that hope was now dim in Europe, they resolved to go to America, knowing that to worship the Lord according to His will would involve "their toylsome Labour, wants, difficulties, losses." They were incapable of conceiving that their earthly employments might be tabulated on a separate ledger from their acts of godliness. Work in one's calling and a reformation of the church had one and the same goal in England. Why should it not remain the same in New England?

How deeply this conception was rooted in the minds and hearts of the pioneering generation—and revealing how little they were, in the ordinary sense, pioneers—one instance out of a hundred will show. On January 6, 1647, Samuel Symonds, magistrate in Ipswich, wrote to Governor Winthrop when the agitation instigated by Dr. Child's appeal to a Presbyterian Parliament threatened to destroy everything for which the founders had labored. In this dark moment, Symonds was reporting on the countermeasures adopted in Ipswich; signing the letter, he turned over his page: "I thought good to add a little more." In this moment of danger, something compelled him to take stock anew of why he was in Ipswich, why the enterprise had been launched in the first place. He could give seven reasons— "whatever more there be which tyme may yet discover"—why we came here and shall fight to stay here. These testify that pioneer experience had not dimmed the original notion of the "great adventure" as a deployment of shock-troops in a world-wide conflict.

Conversion of the Indians is, inevitably, one of the seven purposes; by 1647 there was not much to show for it, but should success come, it "will make vs goe singing to our graves." Another combines religion and mercantilism: "To make this place a Rendezvou for our deare english frends when they shall make their voyages to the west Indies to dry vp that Euphrates." But four of his conclusions belong to the larger strategy: God has peopled New England in order that the reformation of England and Scotland may be hastened, to prove to "the episcopacy" that true polity and good government may stand together, to provide a "hiding place" for those not destined to be sacrificed in the Civil Wars, to train up soldiers for the great war yet to be waged against Rome, to which New England may contribute godly seamen, "formerly rare in the world." But there is another reflection—actually the third in his enumeration, amid, and on an equality with, his theological calculations—that in this enterprise the richer. sort have had their grace tried by sinking their estates into the plantation, "And that the poorer sort (held vnder in Engl:) should have inlargement." For Samuel Symonds, all was of a piece—imperial, economic, religious. It was enough that all hung together; after sixteen years of settlement, he could reassure himself (and so encourage Winthrop) that were the government's proceedings against malignants frankly related to the people, "they are soone satisfyed when they are rightly informed."

Hasty as is Symonds' postscript, no passage in the literature leads us so directly and artlessly to the purpose of the founders, all the more because it was not composed, like Winthrop's sermon aboard the *Arbella,* in the first flush of devotion, but in a moment of anxiety after sixteen years of hard work. The sense of the great world is still there, is still the great idea. The economic interest remains what it was at the beginning: the wealthy must pay for the privilege of serving; the poor have a chance to serve simultaneously God and their prosperity, for which they could not have hoped in England. All this is so clear—even if a nervous magistrate needs to tell it over to himself—that it "causeth the solid christians to prize the rare and rich liberty and power which god hath given them, and they have deerly purchased (viz. in respect of men, in this their great adventure) at a very high rate." As long as men like Symonds, Winthrop, Hooker, and Cotton lived, this cost was calculated, paid not for New England or for America but for Christ. Within this frame farms were ploughed and nets lowered into the sea.

And yet, by the time Samuel Symonds was thus exhorting Governor Winthrop, it was also clear that Winthrop and Symonds were suffering from a grievous miscalculation. They started with the assumption that they in New England were about to attain what all Calvinist churches—Continental as well as English—believed in theory but were prevented by European conditions from achieving. In an empty continent, these Protestants could do what all Protestants, in their heart of hearts, wanted to do. On the *Arbella* Winthrop predicted that what "the most" maintain as truth only in profession, "wee must bring into familiar and constant practice." To comprehend America, you have to comprehend this sentence. Americans would be Englishmen who attained in America what their English and European brethren were seeking. America meant opportunity because there potentiality might become act. That purification for which Calvinists on the Continent and Puritans in England had striven for three generations was to be wrought in a twinkling upon virgin soil.

What tormented Winthrop was not that New England failed, but that the brethren in England rejected the lesson. Independents—fellow Congregationalists—deserted the high ground of a due and an intolerant form of government; they elected to defend a Congregational or voluntary polity by extending toleration to heretical opinions. In the ranks of the New Model Army, English Congregationalists learned to live and let live, while New Englanders were busy expelling Williams, Antinomians, and Anabaptists. Despite confident expectations of an indissoluble unity between saints in New England and at home, in the 1640's they became estranged. As soon as English Independents entertained a policy of toleration—well before the deaths of Winthrop and Cotton—New England became, not the vanguard of Protestantism, but an isolated remnant.

The settlement had been undertaken within a predictable pattern of history, the objective of which was capture of the Church of England. But instead, just as the hierarchy was crumbling, partisans of the true church admitted that Anabaptists had a right to be Anabaptists because on this condition they fought in Cromwell's army. New Englanders, having left England to become the mentors of Europe, found themselves with none to instruct. From their point of view, which had suddenly become merely an American viewpoint, they were forced to think that history had taken a wrong turning. With the dawn of that suspicion—although most of the founders died in the belief that Independents would repent—the isolation of New England commenced. New England Puritanism had become, by remaining faithful to its radical dedication, a stronghold of reaction.

As a starting point for this present volume, one passage will serve: in June 1645 thirteen Independent divines, including Goodwin, Owen, and Nye, names held in highest reverence in Boston, wrote to the General Court that the colony's law of November 1644, banishing Anabaptists, was endangering the cause of Congregational polity in England. People were saying "that persons of our way, principall and spirit cannot beare with Dissentors from them, but Doe correct, fine, imprison and banish them wherever they have power soe to Doe." Independents pled with Massachusetts: those who admire such severities "are utterly your enemyes and Doe seeke your extirpation from the face of the earth: those who now in power are your friends are quite otherwise minded, and Doe professe they are much offended with your proceedings." New England replied to these remonstrances by trying all the more to suppress heresy. Nathaniel Ward, taking upon himself to be herald of New England, warned schismatics to stay away.

The victory of Cromwell, even though a triumph for tarnished principles, at least left New England in peace; he was too much occupied in Europe to reduce the colonies to toleration. Most of the founders died without conceding anything, and in the monument of their triumph, in *The Cambridge Platform* of 1648, enshrined the doctrine that civil authority must restrain and punish corrupt and pernicious opinions. Nine years later, thinking himself the last voice of the founders, formulating their bequest to posterity—aware that he was beseeching their children to abide by what was now a peculiarity—Richard Mather, in his second exhortation, called upon New England to disregard those who "think a man may be saved in any Religion, & that it were good to haue all Religions free, and that opinions haue no great danger in them." These, he said, "are but the devises of Satan, that so pernicious errours might more easily be entertained, as not being greatly suspected." Hence, in this admonition, as in his exhortation not to let worldly business eat out the kernel of piety, we find a theme for the unfolding history of a people who had become, without quite knowing how or when, colonial.

Leaders resisted pleas of their erstwhile friends not, it seemed to them, out of obstinacy but out of courage. They had attempted the impossible and had done it: they had created an order upon a Congregational basis, on the proposition that a major part of the inhabitants should be excluded from church membership and from government. In the face of all common sense, they had made this restriction work; they had proved that a dictatorship of the visible elect could subdue dissent, conduct war and diplomacy, enlist the loyalty of a people, and vindicate God's laws to man. The principle of exclusion was not negative but positive; for it saints examined their souls, for it they endured all affliction.

What spirit stirred them may be illustrated in one of the few outbursts of irritation the immense reserve of John Winthrop ever permitted him. In the summer of 1643 he pushed a majority of the General Court to intervene in the civil war then being fought between two factions of the French colony of Acadie. Or at least he allowed the weaker of the two French leaders, La Tour, to hire ships and recruit "volunteers" in Boston, arguing that this was no violation of neutrality. (The whole episode has a modern ring; it was the one out-and-out blunder Winthrop ever made, and it cost him the governorship in May 1644, as well as the chagrin of having events prove that he backed the wrong man.) Three members of the Board of Assistants (including Samuel Symonds) and four ministers wrote a protest which stung him—perhaps because he knew he was mistaken—into an angry reply. They objected to his act as unconstitutional, but more cogently because it was imprudent; the conflict cannot be localized in Acadie, they said, because France will react to Winthrop's *démarche:* "The Daggers we draw here may happily prove swords in Christendome for ought we know." Furthermore, La Tour's opponent has the troops, artillery, and supplies; it is "dangerous" to risk a war with him ("Soe that we feare, our sheepe haue hastned to their slaughter"). Winthrop's nerves were on edge: letting La Tour raise volunteers in Massachusetts was "no vndertaking of warre, nor Act of hostility, but a meere Liberty of commerce," and then, inconsistently enough, he cried out, what if there be danger? Who are we, founders of New England, to be intimidated?

When we first set up Reformation in our Church way, did not this expose vs to as greate an hazard as we could run both from abroad and at home? Did not our frends in England many of them forewarne vs of it ere we came away? Did not others send letters after vs, to deterre vs from it? Did not some among our selvs (and those no meane ones) inculcate our inevitable dangers at home from no smale Company left out of Church fellowship, and Civill Offices, and freedome hitherto? Yet we trusted in God (though there appeared no meanes of safety) and went on our way: and the Lord hath still preserved vs, and frustrated all Councells and Attempts against vs.

Passions deep in the Puritan soul swirled into flame as Winthrop called the list of dangers Puritans had vanquished:

The Lord hath brought vs hither through the swelling seas, through perills of Pyrats, tempests, leakes, fyres, Rocks, sands, diseases, starvings: and hath here preserved vs these many yeares from the displeasure of Princes, the envy and Rage of Prelats, the malignant Plotts of Jesuits, the mutinous contentions of discontented persons, the open and secret Attempts of barbarous Indians, the seditious and undermineing practises of hereticall false brethren.

There is no more stirring passage in the literature here, for once, logic and decorum gave way to experiential utterance.

The time is not long but the cry is far from this revolutionary spirit to Richard Mather's oblique confession, in his third exhortation, of the effect of that revolution on a population who had grown up with victory already accomplished and institutionalized:

In these dayes and in this country, profession is somewhat common, Authority through the goodness of God countenancing Religion, and ministring Justice against all known ungodliness and unrighteousness of men. You have therefore so much more need to take heed and beware, least your Religion reach no further but to profession and the external form thereof.

New England was no longer a reformation, it was an administration. It was no longer battling for the principle that most of the populace should be left out of church-fellowship, but was striving to keep church-fellowship alive.

The future of the system was, obviously, up to the children. It will be a testimony of your love "to his Majesty," said Mather in his fourth and longest reprehension, "if you be carefull to train up a posterity for the Lord." Early in the 1640's ministers began to complain that sons and daughters were not exhibiting zeal. The basic assumption of Congregationalism was that it would be difficult, not to get people into the churches, but to keep them out. Hence only those who could demonstrate their title to the Covenant of Grace would be admitted, and with them their children: these, being baptized, were sealed into the Covenant and therefore, according to promise made to Abraham, would grow up to become saints. What Richard Mather in 1657 had to press upon these children was not tempests, fires, rocks, and starvation, but the argument that they were under an obligation: "Tell it them as soon as they shall be able to learn, what a solemn Covenant there is between the God of heaven and them, whereby the Lord takes them to be his." The glorious blessings of the Covenant, in which the founders had reveled, would also be theirs—"If it be not through their own default." (Remember, these were Calvinists, who professed predestination and reprobation!) If they do not keep their baptismal covenant, Mather had to say, they will be no better than

Turks or Indians or other "pagans"—nay, they will be worse, because they sin against mercy. "Tell them seriously of these things," he pleaded, "and press upon them the remembrance, consideration, and conscience of their Baptism and Covenant, and the great engagement that lyeth upon them thereby."

Twenty-seven years after Winthrop's sermon on the *Arbella*, with its abounding confidence, Richard Mather, speaking for Winthrop's generation, was forced to rally the second generation with solemn confirmations and seals, with the threat that if they failed their obligation, they would bring upon themselves "sorer and more dreadfull judgments." He was trying to give them the impact of Winthrop's inspired catalogue, telling them that in entirely altered circumstances, where profession is common and where authority countenances religion, they must rise to such intensities as had exhilarated their fathers when profession had been agonizing and perilous, when authority itself was ungodly and unrighteous.

Richard Mather, along with all the other founders of New England, was a disciple of Petrus Ramus, a practitioner of the plain style. In this aesthetic the primary function of speech was, as Michael Wigglesworth put it, "readily to express in words what the mind in thought conceives." Although Puritans understood that rhetoric appealed to emotions, they strove by might and main to chain their language to logical propositions, and to penetrate to the affections of auditors only by thrusting an argument through their reason. The practice—of which Mather's valedictory is an example—was constantly governed by a fear lest eloquence rape the will before the understanding be persuaded; yet the finest of their rhetorical theorists, Alexander Richardson, had pointed out that "inartificial arguments" are phantasms. By inartificial, Ramists meant those things an auditor receives at second hand, upon the testimony of others, as opposed to those he takes from primary sensation, from objects themselves. According to this doctrine, inartificial reports will tend to excite the emotions more than the intellect because they are bound to stimulate feelings not controlled by first-hand experience. The only way a preacher, even in a dramatic farewell, could summon people to a recognition of their predicament was by patiently spelling it out in logical detail.

Richard Mather strove to make his points with the force of logic; at the same time, in his anxiety over declining morale, he endeavored, as far as Ramist and Puritan rhetoric would let him, to arouse his people. Taking advantage of the federal theology, he addressed baptized children as persons already within the Covenant of Grace, who therefore possessed an ability to respond. But he was limited to the logic of that Covenant, to deducing consequential obligations; it would have been out of order for him to use such an incantation as had Winthrop in his exacerbated letter. Everything depended upon logic, upon the "invention" of the arguments, not upon elocution.

We know that the founders studied Francis Bacon. Indeed, the chief architect of their ecclesiastical theory, William Ames, cited Bacon with approval. In the sixth book of *The Advancement of Learning* they would have found a statement which they could endorse: "The duty and office of Rhetoric, if it be deeply looked into, is no other than to apply and recommend the dictates of reason to imagination, in order to excite the appetite and will." But we may wonder whether Richard Mather had ever looked further into that chapter, wherein Bacon—whom no one can accuse of being a Calvinist—criticized several seemingly self-evident arguments in the service of which rhetoric was often employed, and demonstrated that in these cases rhetoric was bound to fail because the propositions themselves were sophistical. For instance, it would seem to be a logical thesis that what we gain by our own merit and industry is a greater good than what we get from fortune or favor. If we can win something by our own efforts, we ought to be confident about the future; what we have done by ourselves we can do again, maybe even better. But against this, he pointed out—reaching deep into the constitution of man, to which the Ramist and Puritan rhetorics addressed themselves—that the other sort of "felicity," which is evidently a sign of divine favor, "both creates confidence and alacrity in ourselves, and wins obedience and respect from others." The founders of New England were favored of divinity, which had created in them confidence and alacrity. But how could their children, out of mere volition, copy them?

Furthermore, Bacon continued, the deeds of virtue and industry are imitable, but the felicity itself—that "is inimitable, and a kind of prerogative of the individual man." Hence, he said, "we generally see that natural things are preferred to artificial, because they admit not of imitation; for whatever is imitable is potentially common." Winthrop's fervid array of dangers overcome did not spring from the potentially common: it was a towering pride speaking out of felicity divinely given, and an ecstasy not to be imitated. What of all this could Mather's argument—his caution against the corroding effects of business, his exhortation to remain intolerant, his warning that external conformity must not be mistaken for real piety, his urging upon children that they assume an obligation to which they had been committed without knowledge of natural things—what of the inimitable felicity could these demonstrations convey to those who had never known London, never been sneered at by a courtier, never fled a pursuivant, never dined in Emmanuel College, and never even seen a Catholic (except for the brief moment when Winthrop's diplomacy allowed Monsieur and Madame La Tour to lodge in Boston)? Mather was trying to supply them with an experience they had missed; he was exhorting them in the stark rhetoric of the plain style to attain the passion which in Winthrop's letter exploded into figures and alliterative imagery. When he reminisced with survivors of the migration, he could speak arguments which, in Bacon's language, would be called natural, or, in the terminology of Ramus, artificial—*in fabrica rei;* but when he told these things to the rising generation, they became altered into arguments which Bacon called artificial and the Ramists inartificial. An apologist for the New England ecclesiastical system only a decade before had told a Presbyterian that he would eschew all such persuasions, since they "are onely inducements, not convincements, being onely inartificial Arguments."

In *The New England Mind: The Seventeenth Century* I set forth the massive cosmology within which, to the mentality of the founders, the settlement was undertaken, within which it had more than a merely colonial significance. This framework was to stand, without serious modification, for the remainder of the century and well into the eighteenth. It organized and classified all existence; its compendia answered all questions, laid out in systematic array all arts and sciences; in "technologia," its science of the sciences, it set forth the enduring and indestructible pattern of the universe. Within this scheme, by logical deduction could be resolved such matters as the form of church polity, the employment of metaphors in sermons, the baptism of children, or the reasons for migrating to Boston. The scaffold was immense, comprehensive, and consistent; basically scholastic and medieval, it also incorporated the learning of Humanism and the erudition of Renaissance Protestantism. It was European, it was static, architectonic, and formal. It presided over the story I am about to tell, framing and delimiting the intellectual amphitheatre, confining actors to certain methods and procedures. It restricted Richard Mather to a logical statement of enumerated points, here and there embellished with a rhetoric which took care not to lay too direct a hold upon emotions lest it become enthusiastic. With this instrument he was endeavoring to prove that the children were required to know anxieties which nothing in their life, except their parents' tales, had ever conveyed to them.

The four themes of his admonition furnish the motifs of this volume: the balance of economic life with the spiritual; preservation of the New England Way, both civil and ecclesiastical, in its indubitably colonial status, with its peculiarities of restricted membership and intolerance; transmission of the basic psychological experience of the founders; and perpetuation of the church order through a succession of converted children. These themes were thrust upon Richard Mather; they were unprovided for in that immense and supposedly definitive organon of knowledge with which the founders had been furnished. The first Puritans did indeed succeed in impressing upon the *tabula rasa* of America a European and a Protestant seal. With their articulated sciences of theology, psychology, logic, and rhetoric, above all with the three-fold doctrine of the covenant—the Covenant of Grace, the church covenant, and the social covenant—they possessed coherent answers to all conceivable contingencies. But the one thing they had not foreseen, nor could their compendia possibly have foreseen, was that experience in the New World might pose problems not on the schedule, which appeared to have no rationale whatsoever.

Mather's dying (as he supposed) injunctions are significant because they are recognitions of native forces. That they appear thus shyly, in the guise of developments to be resisted or deplored, should not lessen their value to the historian. The word "vicarious" was familiar to him, at least as associated with the doctrine of the atonement. The proposition that Christ had vicariously suffered for mankind brought out an affection of gratitude and adoration, but what Mather could not understand—how could he?—was that he spoke of this doctrine out of an ordeal that meant England and Holland, not Dorchester and Northampton. Only with the passing of his generation can we find something that really is colonial in thought or provincial in undertaking.

This something emerges not as an American revolt against the European heritage, but as a list of miserable and regrettable failures. Every one had to deplore them, and all confessed that America was not living up to expectations. Only with the second generation, and then in terms not of achievement but of shortcoming, does New England begin to be local and domestic, does it even commence to be itself. For that generation, the sufferings of the founders were remote and truly vicarious, but meanwhile certain facts—hard work, threat of English interference, administration of church and state, rearing the children—these were daily perplexities. They had become perplexing not because they were new obligations but because they were old ones in a new setting. A Winthrop, amid the perils of tempests and pirates, the rage of prelates and the mutiny of Antinomians, had taken them in stride; but the people of Dorchester and of every other New England town in 1657 had to perform the duties—as Richard Mather recited the catalogue to which Winthrop's had given way —amid "your eating & marriage . . . your buying & selling, your plowing and howing, your sowing & mowing and reaping, your feeding cattle and keeping sheep, your planting orchards & gardens, your baking and brewing, your building houses or outhouses, your fencing in ground or other business what ever." These, not what Symonds called "the great adventure," were the conditions of religious experience.

BOOK I

Declension

Also I set watchmen over you,
Saying, "Hearken to the sound of the trumpet."
But they said, "We will not hearken."
Therefore hear, ye nations,
And know, O congregation,
What is among them.
Hear, O earth!
Behold, I will bring evil upon this people,
Even the fruit of their thoughts,
Because they have not hearkened unto my words,
Nor to my law,
But rejected it.

JEREMIAH 6:17–19

CHAPTER I

THE WRATH OF JEHOVAH

the federal covenant

THE
first thanksgiving, held at Plymouth in 1621, has
become enshrined in an American institution. In the seventeenth century,
New England observed many days of rejoicing, but none in imitation of
this original; all were ordered "pro temporibus et causis," according to the
manner in which providence was dealing with the land. Accordingly, it
observed mostly days of humiliation; over the years there were more
chastisements than blessings. For the Puritan mind, to fix thanksgiving
to a mechanical revolution of the calendar would be folly: who can say
that in November there will be that for which thanks should be uttered
rather than lamentation? By the time ceremonial gratitude can be chan-
nelized into an annual festival, calculated in advance, society is rewarding its own well-doing, not acknowledging divine favor. When this happens, Calvinism is dead; though the society doggedly persists in giving
autumnal thanks, it no longer has a mechanism for confessing its shortcomings and seeking forgiveness for its trespasses.

From the Puritan point of view, an event occurred at Plymouth in July
of 1622 which, much more than the thanksgiving of 1621, ought to be
remembered by posterity. The colony was suffering a terrible drought,
crops were despaired of: when the situation became desperate, the authorities appointed a day of humiliation. Whereupon rain fell. The colony responded with a second ceremonial—a day of rejoicing and gratitude.

Nothing in the doctrine governing these observances can be attributed to
American experience. Even before the advance guard of Massachusetts Bay
reached Salem, in 1629, ships were saved from storms, passengers from
seasickness, whenever the Reverend Mr. Higginson held a fast. The procedure worked a dramatic result in February of 1631: the canny Winthrop, realizing in the previous June that there would not be sufficient
provisions for the winter, had despatched the *Lyon* back to England; when
stores were almost exhausted, the magistrates called for a day of humiliation—upon which the *Lyon* hove into view. The colony immediately decreed a day of thanksgiving—but not to John Winthrop, who was only
an instrument of providence. The Lord of Hosts brought the *Lyon* into
Boston harbor, beyond all doubt in response to the day of humiliation.

The success of these early fasts left upon the New England mind an
impression in which we may locate minute beginnings of adaptation to an

American situation. For the moment, however, events had merely fallen out according to imported doctrine, and the only question was from which authority should the summons issue. Ideally the call should come from the churches, because there men confess their sins and pray for relief. In the Bay, churches did in fact originally decide; whenever the General Court took the initiative, they expressed no more than a "generall desire," leaving the churches theoretically at liberty. For years many congregations went proudly through the form of voting whether they would concur. Yet gradually, because public distresses afflicted all alike, legislatures confidently assumed the function of summoning to repentance. The Massachusetts General Court first acted entirely on their own by voting a fast for January 19, 1637; since Antinomianism was a threat to the entire body politic, the central government had to take measures for common safety without standing upon constitutional scruple. Of course, churches were always free to observe fasts according to local circumstances. During the Civil Wars, when the governments had to walk warily to avoid openly offending either King or Presbyterians, they ordained few observances, discreetly allowing particular churches to set aside days for praying that their enemies be undone.

Thus a ritual—or at least a ritualistic response to events—took shape. Whatever afflicted the colonies became the occasion for a day of humiliation; whatever rejoiced them evoked a day of thanksgiving. In either event, worldly pursuits were laid aside (being inquests upon the significance of such work as the community had done in its various callings, these observances could not be distracted by work itself); the people gathered in their churches, either to acknowledge their sins and promise reform, or else to thank God for the favor He had shown and to assure Him of continued obedience.

Before long, it became apparent that there were more causes for humiliation than for rejoicing. Fasts had to be proclaimed because of dissensions and evil plots, "to prepare the way of friends which wee hope may bee comeing to us," for lack of rain or too much rain, for snow, cold, or heat. They were held in the face of smallpox, hailstorms, fires, winds, plagues, pests, tremblings of the earth, or witchcraft, and of such ominous prodigies as eclipses or comets; for years before Richard Mather gave his sermon to Dorchester, many of them lamented the passing of great founders.

In later days, responses were neither so prompt nor so unequivocal as in earlier times. The fast held on December 13, 1638, to assuage grief caused by the necessity of banishing the Hutchinsonians, produced a tempest in which several lives were lost. This seems to have been the first moment doubt stirred: some even ventured to ask whether there were no better way of seeking the Lord, "because he seemed to discountenance the means of reconciliation." The General Court turned to the elders, who deduced that a second day should be kept "to seek further into the causes of such displeasure." In King Philip's War, repeated humiliations were followed by disasters, but the clergy had a ready explanation: the people had not sufficiently humbled themselves. Thus early, the first episodes began in retrospect to take on symbolic value: they had been answered because the society, as compared with now, was then virtuous. Therefore the present society, by repeating a once magical incantation, was trying to recapture something it had lost. The ministers' cry for more and more days of humiliation had reached a crescendo when, in June 1676, as the Indians were at long last checked, a secular insight proved to be in closer rapport with the will of God. Defying the advice of Increase Mather, the general courts of Connecticut and Massachusetts demanded a day of thanksgiving instead of contrition. Immediately victories increased, and by August, Philip was dead!

The previous part of this study endeavored to show how the conception of a covenant was to certain English Puritans, above all to those who populated New England, the master idea of the age. That the illimitable sovereign of the universe should relate Himself to His creatures not only as absolute power but as voluntarily abiding by the stated rules of His regime offered a solution to all difficulties, not only theological but cosmological, emotional, and (most happily) political. This idea was the basis both of church polity and of social theory. Starting from the premise that a regenerate person, entering the Covenant of Grace, is taken into legal compact with God (this being available to him because God and Christ had, in a previous compact between themselves, the Covenant of Redemption, provided the foundation), federal theologians worked out a corollary that God likewise enters into covenant with a group as a unit. The two covenants—personal and public—were "branches" of the same, and yet distinct: saints dwelling alone may be in the Covenant of Grace without participating in a pledged society; a society may achieve this honor even though many (or most) of its citizens are not gracious. Over and above His contracts with persons, God settles the social terms with a band of men, which thereupon becomes committed, as a political entity, to a specifically enunciated political program.

This philosophy of the national covenant was not only a logical deduction from the Covenant of Grace, but also the theme of the Old Testament: Jacob wrestles in solitude with Jehovah, but Israel make their cohesion visible in an external organization—a church, a corporation, a nation, even a plantation. In their corporate capacity, saints stand, as long as they hold together, in a relation to God separate from (although bound up with) their spiritual salvation. As a people they are chosen because by public act they have chosen God. The prerequisite is not, cannot be, a flawless sanctity of all citizens, but a deliberate dedication of the community to a communal decision, like a declaration of war.

Theorists recognized at once that there are at least three respects in which a national covenant necessarily differs from the Covenant of Grace. A group exists only in this world: it does not migrate *in toto* to heaven;

both saints and sinners leave their earthly community behind, along with their clothes and property. Hence the relation of God to a community is not internal but external and "foederall." It has to do with conduct here and now, with visible success or tangible failure. Secondly, since a society cannot be rewarded in heaven for its obedience (whereas an individual may suffer torments here, but receive endless compensation hereafter), and cannot be punished in hell (a reprobate may prosper all his life, but suffer throughout eternity), it must perforce contract with the Almighty for external ends. Its obedience, in short, means prosperity, its disobedience means war, epidemic, or ruin. "What concerns such a People as they are a Body, or a Company of Professors standing under the Obligations of such a Covenant, referrs unto this life and the Affairs of it." In the third place, a community is not joined to God by so irrevocable a contract as will endure no matter how depraved it becomes. (A saint is at best imperfectly sanctified, but his sins have been atoned for; nothing he does, even the worst enormity, breaks the bond.) If a society, no matter how many saints may still be in it, sinks so deep into corruption that its abominations call for destruction, then the national covenant is ended. "It is true," said Thomas Shepard, "the Covenant effectually made, can never be really broke, yet externally it may."

An ironic, or rather agonizing, paradox lies at the heart of this doctrine. In the course of nature (of "common providence") any nation will have good or bad times; even Philistines wax before they wane. But a company received into the federal covenant has consciously accepted certain obligations: it *knows* that its successes in war or business do not arise from accident, from industry or ingenuity or opportunity, but that they are given. "For the substance the gist is one, both to the Iust and vniust: but in respect of the cause, possession and vse, there is great difference: which is discerned by faith, though it cannot be seene with the eye." Wealth, for both the covenanted and uncovenanted, seems to flow from natural resources, from inventions and policy; but the gains of the chosen are "gifts" of the national covenant.

Therefore it followed that for them afflictions are reprimands, entirely dissimilar to reverses which befall, by chance, right or left, a natural corporation. France and Spain are unlucky, or they miscalculate, or smallpox ravages them, and that is that. But a nation in covenant is systematically punished, the degree of affliction being exquisitely proportioned to the amount of depravity. While thus being chastised it is still in covenant— or, at least, as long as it has not committed the unpardonable sin which conclusively severs the covenant. Until that moment, no matter how bleak the prospect, there is always hope: if it reforms, it will recover the blessing. But where is that point of no return? On the one hand, a succession of disasters may be a sign that the nation is still chosen; on the other, a misery indefinitely prolonged may mean that it is forever lost. Was New England to say that defeats in Philip's War were no more than severe judgments upon an extreme decay of public morality, or was it to conclude that it had degenerated beyond recovery and been cast off?

Long before Winthrop and his Company assembled in Southampton Water, federal theologians had supplied him with an answer to this problem; aboard the *Arbella*, before setting foot in America, he employed it:

> Thus stands the cause between God and vs, wee are entred into Covenant with him for this worke, wee haue taken out a Commission, the Lord hath giuen vs leaue to draw our owne Articles we haue professed to enterprise these Accions vpon these and these ends, wee haue herevpon besought him of favour and blessing.

His Christianity permitted him—indeed, obliged him—to define the purpose of this expedition as a set of articles drawn up by the adventurers themselves, which the Lord *thereafter* (in point of time) accepted. Whatever doubts or homesickness might trouble particular passengers, one thing was certain: the communal responsibility could be defined; the society might thereafter go terribly wrong, but it would always know what was right.

The articles being thus definite, the sanctions become automatic. If the Lord has accepted our terms, He will seal the contract by bringing us to New England and prospering our settlement; if then we fail to observe them, "the Lord will surely breake out in wrathe against vs [,] be revenged of such a periured people and make vs knowe the price of the breache of such a Covenant." We must on this account "be knitt together in this worke as one man"—because in the federal covenant a people are treated (externally) as one. This band was not as others, who sink or swim according to the hazard of wind and weather, but one that should be delivered by "foederall right" as long as it remained federally righteous. In the worst of times, this company would have a resort not permitted ordinary nations, the chance to bewail its transgressions. Thus it could always (by mending its ways) recoup its losses.

The New England mind, at the moment of the founding, did not regard the federal theology and Calvinism (or more accurately Protestantism) as distinct systems. True theology was so thoroughly articulated in the language of the covenant that the founders had become as little conscious they were talking a peculiar doctrine as was M. Jourdain that he spoke prose. The physical universe is under the continuous control of providence, so that whatever comes to pass—rainstorm, smallpox, earthquake—is not mere natural law but judgment. Afflictions do not just happen, they are, literally, acts of God. In that sense, uncovenanted nations, dwelling in the realm of nature, are also subject to divine regulation; in theory, they may pray to God for deliverance, and He may be pleased to grant them succor if they reform. But they have no promise; their best endeavors may prove unavailing. A plighted community can interpret events, and so take appropriate measures with the assurance of success.

"As all good things are conveyed to Gods people, not barely by common providence, but by speciall Covenant," said Shepard, "So all the evils they meet with in this world . . . upon narrow search will be found to arise from breach of Covenant more or lesse." The federal covenant does not shield a federated people from the wrath of God: it makes that wrath intelligible. Public humiliation was the only sure method of relieving public misfortune, not only because it sought for mercy, but because it translated misfortune into a common resolution to do something about it.

The doctrine of the national covenant was therefore of greatest value to New England as a more accurate way of searching social conscience than was permitted other nations, including England. Other communities, containing good and bad, cannot comprehend wherefore they are punished; because the righteous suffer along with the unrighteous, confusion is confounded. The godly can do nothing but go aside, pray in their secret chambers, and condemn the administration. But in a covenanted condition, the virtue as well as the ability of saints is put to work. Success or failure is not sporadic, not fragmentary, but universal. "Deliverances from common providence are common to all, even Pagans, but not such as spring from the vertue of the Covenant." Both deliverances and trials become measures of fulfillment, and to the covenanted disclose what others can never perceive. For a dedicated people, seeking the Lord on a day of humiliation thus becomes a redefinition of the common purpose; a thanksgiving is a reaffirmation of it.

To our ears, the proposition held forth in Winthrop's *Modell* may at first sound like what Francis Bacon labeled a sophism, that felicity is most admirable when gained by merit. True, the promise of blessing was attached to performance, but the Puritan Jehovah, even when tied in a covenant, was still inscrutable. The principal effect of distinguishing the federal covenant as a separate transaction from the Covenant of Grace was not to assert that public prosperity could be earned whereas personal comes only by election, but merely to mark off the public realm from the private, and to specify the difference in the respective terms. A prospering people would not relax in self-congratulation but would, as Winthrop told them, "see much more of his wisdome power goodnes and truthe then formerly wee haue beene acquainted with." A communal thanksgiving, recognizing that felicity was a sign of divine favor, would therefore, in Bacon's phrase, create confidence and alacrity. So a day of humiliation would be a device both for regaining confidence and for reasserting, in the face of adversity, an assurance that felicity exists. John Cotton thus expounded the theory:

> To shew you how God is wont to expresse himself to his people, when we have broken Covenant with him, God will say, he will not look at us any more, he will never protect us more, he will neither meddle nor make with us, but will expose us to all evil; now if hereupon we return and bewaile our breach of Covenant with God, how little good we have done, and how little serviceable we are, he is then wont to let us see, that his Covenant was never so far broken, but he can tell how to be good to us, for the Lord Jesus Christs sake.

There was consolation in the worst of afflictions; a suffering individual knows he is being tried, yet must endure in silence and secret prayer; but something more is required from a trial imposed upon an entire people. Because outward afflictions signify the presence of God, a people need not despair: their sins, the stupidity of their politicians and generals, even their most furious dissensions, cannot destroy the body politic so long as they retain a sense—periodically reinvigorated—that their material welfare, although depending upon their own exertions, depends not entirely upon them.

A writer does not come to so succinct a statement of a body of thought as Winthrop achieved in *A Modell of Christian Charity* unless he has re-thought and digested the speculations of his predecessors. The decision at Cambridge on August 26, 1629, to transport the charter of the Massachusetts Bay Company to America was reached in fear and trembling. Behind Winthrop's exposition lies a deep conviction: the heroic attempt of two generations to bring England into federal covenant had failed; the nation seemed too far gone in depravity ever to be reunited to the bond. By the 1620's those Englishmen who found in the covenant a key to the universe had no other choice but to form themselves into smaller societies; they could prove that units might observe the external terms, even if England did not. Though the external covenant was called "national" it was not a nationalistic conception; Winthrop did not conceive of the migrants as a nation, but as a "Company," a "Community." Nor did he conceive of the federal covenant as being made with the soil of New England: he did not say that God had taken this piece of terrain and all upon it into the treaty. God was covenanting with the band, who had to foregather in some one "place of Cohabitation and Consorteshipp." Theoretically, this group might stay in England, as did many of their comrades, and still collect themselves into a covenanted society; they were simply convinced that it could be better done elsewhere.

The Great Migration thought of itself as achieving corporate identity by the act of migrating, but it did not identify the covenant—its promise of good to virtue and of evil to vice—with the opportunity of America. Any place in the world would have served. Massachusetts was only a convenient (not too convenient) platform on which the gathering might be enacted, so that the city upon a hill would be visible to Europe. The doctrine was developed as a way of finding hope for England, but had to be tried out in Massachusetts. This is what Winthrop meant by carefully selecting a title for his mid-ocean discourse: it was a "modell" of that to which England might yet be reclaimed, and of "charity," which meant, not giving alms to the poor, but the knitting of individuals together as one man in order to obtain the prosperity of all. The federal cast of mind could conceive of charity only in a social context, requiring the reduction of complexity to a single rationale. Were this model ever to triumph in England, the founders might well go home.

John Cotton had preached in Lincolnshire, "Where ever Gods servants are, because of his Covenant with them, where ever they crave a blessing, and mourne for the want of it, God will provide it shall be stretched forth upon the whole Country they live in." When he said this, he was trying to tell English Puritans that they did not need to be a majority, or to control the economy, before they could be of some effect in saving their country. Since the reward was not to be earned but given, they could, in a comprehensible way, become the occasion for it. What was necessary in 1629 was an organization of the saving remnant, which was not a geographical designation. In order to rescue England, that remnant had to demonstrate by a strict performance of articles in a covenant how a society thrives. This was what Winthrop meant by a city set upon a hill; he did not mean what today we call Boston.

Because those who came to New England had decided that there was slight hope for the covenant at home, they brought it about that a new land became the setting for experiment. Winthrop did hope "that men shall say of succeeding plantacions: the lord make it like that of New England," but he was not voicing incipient patriotism. New England was not an allegiance, it was a laboratory. The theory of feast and of fast days was already complete in every detail: it had not been invented as an engine of Americanization.

Yet that is what it became. John Cotton may have meant, even after he removed to Boston, that because the blessing would be stretched forth upon the land of the saints, they in New England would obtain it for England. In England, as in all Europe, while victory seemed impossible, still defeat was inconclusive. But failure in America would be clean-cut. Here the inhabitants were no longer, Winthrop told them, scattered and oppressed cells, "absent from eache other many miles, and had our imployments as farre distant," but were now in the "good Land" which they had passed over the vast sea to possess. They did possess it. To confess through formal lamentation that they had not come up to European expectation now amounted to a confession of American shortcomings. It might be failure, but it was theirs. So, by an exceedingly oblique device, the more these people accused themselves of having shirked their covenant, the more they asserted that they had not lost confidence.

After the isolation into which New England was driven by the Civil Wars, that faith perforce became one with the possibilities of New England alone. Imperceptibly the cry became less "the sins of the people," and more often "the sins of the land." Public purgations on days of humiliation, after experiences of divine wrath, became a method of recognizing, if not quite of becoming reconciled to, the actualities of American life. This was not a logical development: it was a matter of having lived long enough, deeply enough, in this particular country.

CHAPTER II

THE JEREMIAD

FOR twenty years the fast day functioned, on the whole,
as the founders anticipated. To survivors of those glorious decades, as John
Hull recollected, "The Lord . . . was wont to hear before we called,
when we did but purpose to seek God." He kept His rein upon them,
"chastening and trying, nurturing, lopping, and pruning his poor children,
by his own fatherly hand, for their good, from one year to another." All
this was to be expected: events are significances, and the moment they
become a pruning, a day of humiliation must be appointed—whereupon
misfortune is rectified. The procedure quickly became standardized, the
formula appearing, for example, in the call issued by the Massachusetts
General Court in 1648. First, a recital of afflictions: distractions in England
and an unfamiliar disease in New England, a drought, and the mortality
of our countrymen in the West Indies. (The collocation itself shows how
Massachusetts conceived itself one among the family of Protestant communities, how difficulties in London or St. Christopher were emotional
concerns in Boston.) Then follows the prescription: the General Court
resolve that these matters be forthwith "intimated" to the churches, and
that April 20 be appointed: "all persons are hereby required to abstaine from
bodily labor that day, & to resort to the publike meetings, to seeke the Lord,
as becomes Christians in a day of humiliation." As for New England health
and weather, this observance worked the customary relief. (Of course, as a
contribution toward the prosperity of England and the Indies, it could be
no more than an assistance, for those people would have to secure their own
deliverances.)

What should be noted in this proclamation is the scrupulous distinction
between physical afflictions—the disease and the drought—and sins. There
is implicit recognition of a causal sequence: the sins exist, the disease breaks
out; the sins are reformed, the disease is cured. The founders regarded the
Antinomian frenzy not as in itself a sin but as an affliction because of sins.
"Our wise God (who seldome suffers his own, in this their wearysome
Pilgrimage to be long without trouble) sent a new storme after us which
proved the sorest tryall that ever befell us since we left our Native soyle."
In this case the method was not, as we have seen, immediately efficacious,
but, severely tested through two intense decades, it still proved reliable.
The Lord blessed His people "with great prosperity and success, increasing

and multiplying, protecting and defending from all mischievous contrivances, supplying and furnishing with all necessaries, maugre all adversaries."

We may look upon October 19, 1652, as crucial in American history. On that day the General Court ordained a fast, and again listed the reasons (most of them conventional, such as storms and rains, wars in England) but also, for the first time, included the provoking sins—"the worldly mindedness, oppression, & hardhartedness feared to be among us"—among the afflictions. Corruption itself now appeared not as a cause but a visitation of wrath.

At the beginning, shift in emphasis was so imperceptible that it might have been merely careless phraseology—except that the tendency, once started, gathered momentum. At this point the people began to turn from external to internal: instead of looking upon sensible deprivations as retributions for crimes already committed, they confessed that their consciousness of sinfulness was itself a curse upon the body politic. Within another ten years the formula was completely transformed; proclamations concentrated more and more upon the sins themselves, reducing the resulting distresses to footnotes. By the time Richard Mather spoke, the orders usually read, "the great security & sensuality vnder our present injoyments, the sad face on the rising generation." Although such calamities as Philip's War, or droughts and tempests, received due notice, still the summonses of the seventies were expanding recitals of spiritual failures and moral deficiencies rather than catalogues of misfortune.

Hard-heartedness, security, sloth, sensuality, lack of zeal among the children, declension from "primitive affections," formality, hypocrisy—these took the place of caterpillars, shipwrecks, mildew, and the more visible "tokens of Gods displeasure." The subjective preëmpted the objective: a universal anxiety and insecurity had become no longer something which, being caused, could be allayed by appropriate action, but rather something so chronic that the society could do nothing except suffer—and perpetually condemn itself. In the thirty years after 1660, the conception of the relation of society to the divine was unwittingly (and unintentionally) transformed into a thesis which positively reversed primitive doctrine. The mental anguish of the second and third generations was intensified because, while recognizing that somehow they had declined, they had lost the measure by which to decipher exactly how much or why. And so the day of humiliation became, not a blood-letting and a cure, but an increase of appetite that grew by what it fed upon.

The ceremonial of the fast day—the whole town gathered in the church—inevitably centered upon the sermon. The ministers were, on these occasions more than on any other, the voice of the community, articulators of its awareness and spokesmen for its resolve to reform. They quickly devised a special kind of sermon for these convocations. Instinctively they responded to the demands of the situation: they arraigned sins that had caused the judgments, and pointed out what other terrors would descend unless repentance were forthcoming. The founding clergy had had many other topics to occupy their minds: the problem of church polity—which was not, as is witnessed by the treatises of Cotton, Hooker, Richard Mather, and Davenport, a merely organizational question, but one of vast philosophical range—and also the task of expounding the whole of life in the rhetoric of the plain style; hence the poetic and metaphysical sweep of discourses by Hooker or by Shepard. After 1660, those great issues were, for the New England communities, resolved. The doctrine of the Congregational church was settled, to its farthest implication; a library containing the works of the founders, along with those of the great Puritan theologians of England, made the cosmos comprehensible—upon the premise of the covenant. For epigones the duty was no longer speculation: it was to perform, and to see that the people performed, what was demanded of them.

Hence the one literary type which the first native-born Americans inevitably developed, into which they poured their energy and their passion, was the fast-day sermon. On annual days of election, in the spring, after officers were installed and oaths taken, before turning to business the General Court regularly listened to a sermon which, under the circumstances, was bound to be more a review of recent afflictions than an exposition of doctrine; ministers chosen for the occasion would try then to be their most impressive. Thus they developed, amplified, and standardized a type of sermon for which the rules were as definite as for the ode. Where the most characteristic creations of the founders were subtle explorations of the labyrinth of sin and regeneration—employing, as did Shepard and Hooker, a complex psychological doctrine, full of shadow and nuance— for the second generation the dominant literary form, almost the exclusive, is something we may term, for shorthand purposes, a "jeremiad." Although the practitioners themselves never quite distinguished it by name from the sermon in general, it quickly became so precise a formula as to be immediately recognizable to the student of types—as, no doubt, it was to the audiences at the time.

"First American kid"

The structure of this jeremiad was prescribed by the theory of external covenant. Perforce it addressed mankind not as beings of a complicated psychology, but as creatures governed by a simple calculus. The "doctrine" must be some proposition that they are pertinaciously pursued for their sins; any of a hundred verses in the Old Testament would supply the text, especially in Isaiah or Jeremiah. The "reasons" would then become expositions of the national covenant, its terms, conditions, and duties. But the real substance of the discourse came at the end, in the "applications" or "uses," where the preacher spelled out the significance of the situation. Here he enumerated, in as much detail as he had courage for, the provocations to vengeance, proposed a scheme of reformation, and let his imagination glow over the still more exquisite judgments yet in store unless his listeners acted upon his recommendations. A minister's reputation for eloquence came to be based upon the skill with which he could devise

Edwards

prognostications of a mounting disaster, by contrast with which the present suffering dwindled into mere annoyance.

The second generation, between 1660 and 1690, could not so easily send manuscripts to London as had Hooker and Cotton, or be so assured of a publisher there; they had to depend mainly on the creaking little presses of Cambridge and Boston. Notes taken by faithful attendants show that ministers did expound the more abstract themes of Protestant theology; Samuel Willard worked his way, on successive Sabbaths in the 1690's, through the entire system, leaving at his death the *summa* of New England doctrine, *A Compleat Body of Divinity*. But in the middle decades of the seventeenth century, virtually the only works for which there was a domestic sale were jeremiads—either a particularly brilliant one at some local ceremony or those officially pronounced before the General Court.

We can trace the forming of the jeremiad as early as the late 1640's, in the last publications of Shepard and Cotton, but the theme was first fully set forth by Michael Wigglesworth in 1662, in a verse meditation which may lay claims to poetry, entitled (as all jeremiads might be) *God's Controversy with New-England:*

> *Ah dear New England! dearest land to me;*
> *Which unto God hast hitherto been dear,*
> *And mayst be still more dear than formerlie,*
> *If to his voice thou wilt incline thine ear.*

Thanks to the passion which Wigglesworth put into these strophes we commence with a certain insight into motives that glow less conspicuously in his prosaic followers. In his senior year at Harvard, 1650, he had written, "Doth it affect with grief? why to be so grieved is no grievance. Doth it kindle coales, nay flames of fiery indignation? why those flames burn not, but rather cherish." Without this psychological clue, the student finds the form barren indeed; it was intended to draw tears from the eyes, but it also implied, in Wigglesworth's terms, "why even tears flow with pleasure."

Higginson's election sermon of 1663, *The Cause of God and His People in New-England,* approaches the pattern which achieved definite outline with Jonathan Mitchell's *Nehemiah on the Wall* in 1667 and William Stoughton's *New Englands True Interest* in 1668. Later practitioners, paying deference to these as their models, could ring no other changes except to add to the increasing array which the General Court catalogued before every order for humiliation. The foremost published utterances of the 1670's were all jeremiads, some of which made so deep an impression as to be cited down to the Revolution. These were Samuel Danforth's *A Brief Recognition of New England's Errand into the Wilderness* in 1670, the younger Thomas Shepard's *Eye-Salve* in 1672, Urian Oakes's *New England Pleaded With* in 1673, William Hubbard's remarkable *The Happiness of a People* in 1676, Increase Mather's bid for ascendancy among the New England clergy, *The Day of Trouble is Near* in 1673, and the election sermon which marked his attainment of it, *A Discourse Concern-ing the Danger of Apostacy* in 1677.

By calling the jeremiad a literary type I mean that it was more than a rhetorical exercise. Its hold upon the New England mind for four or five generations is an instance of the tyranny of form over thought. But there is a vastly more important consideration: art requires conventions which emphasize the relevant aspects of experience; a new convention, says W. H. Auden, is a revolution in sensibility: "It appeals to and is adopted by a generation because it makes sense of experiences which previously had been ignored." For the second and third generations of New England, the jeremiad was the one appropriate convention because it made sense out of their unique experience. After a time, it became stereotyped; after a century we may well call it, in Auden's language, "reactionary," but in the beginning it was, however manufactured according to formula, a vision. It was a way of conceiving the inconceivable, of making intelligible order out of the transition from European to American experience.

How profoundly the conception gripped the minds of these generations may be seen in its effects upon other utterances beside the fast-day sermons. Proclamations of the General Court and Wigglesworth's verses are cases in point, as also are the most deeply felt of Edward Taylor's secretive lyrics. A more public example is the composition of history. During King Philip's War, Increase Mather kept daily notes, and immediately after the victory made out of them *A Brief History of the Warr with the Indians in New-England,* for which he secured in 1676 a publisher in London. Histo-rians of literature have lumped this together with chronicles of the immi-grant generation—Bradford's, Winthrop's, Johnson's—as one more illus-tration of how the Puritans conceived history to be a record of divine providences. They fail to see the vast difference in structure between an account like Bradford's, which moves serenely from point to point, morally improving each incident, and Mather's conscious organization of his story into a dialectic of decline and recovery, which he thus imposes upon history. Bradford tells of pilgrims undertaking a long, winding journey, who con-stantly lift up their eyes to heaven, "their dearest cuntrie"; Johnson enu-merates a succession of "wonder-working providences" which ripple along for the duration of the book. Even Bunyan's *Pilgrim's Progress*—which is also a history—gets its coherence from the flow of the standard phases in the process of conversion; the direction of the narrative is steadily forward, even the deviations returning, another step along the way, into the pre-destinated path. The plan of Mather's history is neither succession nor progression: it is a fall and then a recovery of society. As events pile up, the descent accelerates, so that the outcome is for long in doubt. The se-quence is not one thing after another, but an agonizing drop, a crisis, and then the dramatic ascent. In that sense—because this is what happened to a visible people, within the frame of their external covenant—the story itself contains its only meaning; Mather's history is not allegory, as Bunyan's explicitly is and as the histories of the immigrant Puritans implicitly are. This fact marks a revolution in sensibility, enacted by the first generation born in America.

Mather concluded his book with "a serious Exhortation to the Inhabitants of the Land"—this he says was "the thing which I mainly designed." He resolved "to Methodize" his notes; the thesis controls the composition, so that episodes are strung upon it and do not give rise, as in the Interpreter's House, to random moralizations. This drama opens like a classical French tragedy with an intelligible theme: precisely on the evening of a day of humiliation at Swansea, Indians attack the homecoming congregation, "the Lord thereby declaring from Heaven that he expected something else from his People besides Fasting and Prayer." The logic of the narrative is controlled by a precise calculation: defeat must be measured out until the amount of present distress becomes equal to past transgression. In the swamp fight of July 19, 1675, had they pressed the attack, the colonists might have destroyed Philip, "But God saw we were not yet fit for Deliverance, nor could Health be restored unto us except a great deal more Blood be first taken from us." When it seemed that no more could be endured, the General Court, on October 19, called a committee to frame laws for the reformation of manners; that very day "the Lord gave success to our Forces" at Hatfield. At last, on May 9, 1676, a really immense and impressive day of humiliation was held in Boston by all magistrates, elders, and people, and a sincere repentance and reformation were sworn to. Thereupon the bottom was sounded, the crisis was over. "There are [those] who have dated the turn of Providence towards us in this Colony, and against the Enemy in a wonderful manner, from this day forward." Concealing the fact that he himself had miscalculated, Mather now locates the day of thanksgiving on June 29 at precisely the right moment for the upswing of action, and crowns the design of his history by showing ·that immediately after the proclaiming of a second day of thanksgiving, so that a chastened and now reformed people might see the coherence of their drama, God delivered Philip into their hands. The entire history— using the word in a Shakespearean sense—with its sweep of declension, its abrupt reversal, and its swift denouement, hinged upon the "wonderful success against the Enemy, which the Lord hath blessed them with, ever since they renewed their Covenant with him." This is patently no mere progress nor simple chronological collection of providences: this is social adventure within a schematic framework, with a definite resolution: "Therefore have we good reason to hope that this Day of Trouble, is near to an end, if our sins doe not undoe all that hath been wrought for us."

Remarking that a convention emphasizes certain aspects of experience, Auden also notes that it must perforce dismiss others to the background. What has been dismissed by Mather's treatment is the over-all theological concern of Bunyan (although Mather is still an orthodox theologian) and the cosmic perspective of Bradford or Johnson (although Mather still believes in the same sort of cosmos). What has happened is a concentration of emotion upon the destiny of a group, so that forms of thought and of speech are organized about this center, while other modes of discourse, even though kept up in ordinary Sabbath sermons, persist only as mementos of a vanished past. This form alone could draw out the energy and imagination of the Americanized Puritan artist. The greatest effort in the century to organize the experience of this people, Cotton Mather's *Magnalia Christi Americana*, throughout its 1400 pages—from the opening bar, "I write the Wonders of the Christian Religion, flying from the Depravations of Europe, to the American Strand," to its final coda, "Do we dream that the Almighty hath spent all his arrows?"—is a colossal jeremiad.

Increase Mather's *Brief History* illustrates one technical problem inherent in the convention: the jeremiad could make sense out of existence as long as adversity was to be overcome, but in the moment of victory it was confused. It had always to say that now the day of trouble may be ended, that God has thus far "answered us by terrible things in righteousness"—if only our sins do not again undo us. It flourished in dread of success; were reality ever to come up to its expectations, a new convention would be required, and this would presuppose a revolution in mind and in society. Mather was proud to relate how in 1675 the Assistants undertook something more serious than fasting and prayer, that they legislated actual reforms; he was happy to demonstrate that the maneuver succeeded, but he could not become confident that victory was final, even with the death of Philip. A few months consoled him: fires, shipwrecks, and epidemics increased. By the summer of 1679, the General Court were resolved that something radical had to be done; they issued a call to the churches to assemble in Synod and to give, once and for all, an answer to the two questions which had become the main, indeed the only, concern: "What are the provoking evils of New England?" and "What is to be done, that so those evils may be reformed?"

The jeremiad would be obliged to comment on the social scene in terms recognizable to those who knew it, but the remarkable fact about the succession of sermons is how stylized became the categories under which defections were grouped and arranged. As with "arguments" in logic, data were ordered according to Ramist "method." The *Result* of the Synod was not so much a fresh survey as a digest of previous inventories. As long as we understand that it was bound to be cast into a now stabilized mold, we may cautiously read it as a description of society. But properly to interpret it, we must remember how the *Magnalia* betrays the actual situation by confessing that the people had not really sunk so far into corruption as in other places; it was only that New England, being under the greatest "obligations," was to be held criminal for "omissions" which in other countries were more or less normal "commissions"! The *Result* must not, therefore be taken too literally, but rather construed as the climax of an emerging ritual. It was not sociological investigation, it was purgation by incantation.

Fortunately for us, the authors of the *Result* (the chief penman was Increase Mather) were students of Petrus Ramus and therefore knew that first things should be put first. Hence they systematically enumerated the causes of God's displeasure. Number one on their list was "a great and visible decay of the power of Godliness amongst many Professors in these Churches." This was the heart of the matter: there are too many, said the Synod, who commit apostasy "especially in Secret." It was not a question, as Urian Oakes had made clear in 1673, of professors making "any notorious and scandalous Digression and Diversion from the good waves of God"; it was merely their "drudging and plodding on in a visible regular course of Obedience and Profession." Then he added: "Yet behold, What a weariness is it?" Revealing phrases were heaped up: "a careless, rimiss, flat, dry cold dead frame of spirit"; security "in this Land of Rest, Quietness, and Fulness of Spiritual Enjoyments"; many have gone "a great way by civill honesty and morality, and if one be gone so far, he is accounted to be in a state of salvation." By 1674 a generation had arisen, said Increase Mather, "who give out, as if saving Grace and Morality were the same." This was the ultimate in confusion. Of course, Increase added—lest confusion be confounded—morality is all very well: "such persons are nearer to conversion than prophane ones are." Still, "this may be without Grace." New Englanders could not rest in being, according to William Stoughton, "empty outside Custom born Christians." But for lack of sound principles, "the Profession of so many hath run it self out of breath, and broke its neck in these dayes." The second generation, we are delighted to perceive, still had something of the rhetorical precision, the concreteness of imagery, of Hooker. Many have grown, said Oakes, "Sermon-proof."

We had as good preach to the Heavens and Earth, and direct our discourse to the Walls and Seats and Pillars of the meeting house, and say, Hear, O ye Walls, give ear O ye Seats and Pillars, as to many men in these Churches, that are deaf to all that is cried in their ears by the Lords Messengers, and are indeed like Rocks in the Sea, not to be stirred and moved by the beating and dashing of these waters of the Sanctuary, or by the strongest gust of rational and affectionate discourse that can blow upon them.

As time went on, it must be said, such dramatic imagery dwindled. It survives in William Hubbard's sermon of 1676, but Increase Mather had already reduced it to the balder sort of proposition which thereafter became the norm: "How hath the Lord been disappointed in his righteous and reasonable Expectations concerning us?" So it behooved the Synod to pass on to point number two, the most flagrant manifestation of this decay, which could be summarized by a single term: pride. Under this rubric were grouped three manifestations which might seem to any but a federalist theologian disparate: contention in the churches, disrespect of inferiors toward superiors, and extravagance in apparel. On second thought, the logic of the grouping becomes apparent: if a people committed in a national covenant begin to slacken in devotion, they will rebel against their federation by several seemingly unconnected forms of self-assertion. They will insult their betters, or dress beyond their means, or quarrel with their brethren; in every case, they are trying to escape their pledge. The Synod noted that servants and "the poorer sort" were notoriously guilty, but also, like the preachers, commented upon "such excess, gaudiness & fantasticalness in those that have estates." Leaders were persuaded in the darkest days of Philip's War that defeats in battle could be attributed to "monstrous and horrid Perriwigs, . . . Borders and False Lockes and such like whorish Fashions." These could thus be denounced as private indulgences which, by infringing the national covenant, endangered the lives of others. Likewise within the churches, a humbling of pride would restore harmony. "Strict and impartial Examination would yield large matter of uncontrolable Conviction as to such as these." Instead, said the Synod, there are "Sinful Heats and Hatreds, and that amongst Church Members themselves, who abound with evil Surmisings, uncharitable and unrighteous Censures, Back-bitings, hearing and telling Tales." Here we note the completion of the process by which external misfortunes were merged into internal accusations: these disasters were acts not of God but of the people against each other.

The remainder of the Synod's catalogue, which again was a condensation of charges already formulated in the jeremiads, consists of a more detailed enumeration of crimes, treating them not as causes of affliction but as disasters in and of themselves. The third heading was heresy, not only that imported by Quakers and Anabaptists but that emanating from professors who "hearken & adhere to their own fancyes and Satans delusions." The fourth was swearing and sleeping during sermons; the fifth was Sabbath-breaking, and especially that outburst of depravity which came at sundown on Sunday, when the Puritan Sabbath ended. ("There is more wickedness committed usually on that night, than in all the week besides.") The sixth was a decay of family discipline: parents becoming "cockering," letting children "have their swinge, to go and come where and when they please, and especially in the night." Number seven was an increase of angry passions exhibited not only in church strife but in the growing number of lawsuits. (The jeremiads, clinging to the original Puritan conviction that litigation could be settled by the Bible and common sense, steadily called for the suppression of attorneys, who "will for their own ends espouse any Case right or wrong . . . such as care not who loses, so they may gain.")

The eighth head of the Synod's *Result* was devoted to sins which loomed large in the jeremiads, sex and alcohol. According to the ministers,

militia training days were rapidly losing any semblance of what is cus-
tomarily called Puritanism: "Every Farmers Son, when he goes to the
Market-Town, must have money in his purse; and when he meets with
his Companions, they goe to the Tavern or Ale-house, and seldome away
before Drunk, or well tipled." During the war against Philip, preachers
first discovered—or first confessed discovering—that traders in the back
country were debauching the Indians with rum; this of course was a crying abuse of the national cóvenant, because the founders had sworn to
convert heathens, but it was still more terrible because it was a perfect
illustration of how sin becomes its own retribution: drunken Indians, or
Indians wanting drink, run amuck. As for sexual morality, the jeremiads
record a thriving promiscuity. In 1672 one Alice Thomas made what
appears to be the first attempt in Boston to operate, in the language of
the General Court, "a stewe, whore house, or brothell house." She succeeded so far as to give frequent "Entertainment" to persons of both sexes,
until she was taken and whipped through the streets. The ministers were
convinced that if so much fornication was discovered, "how much is there
of secret wantonness & wicked dalliances?" For the Puritan always knew,
in theology or in manners, "that which is seen is nothing in comparisón
of that which is not."

The ninth in the Synod's tabulation was a brief note on the want of
truth among men (in 1673 Oakes had declared that too many Yankees
"have gone to School to Machiavel"), but we are most arrested by the
peculiar grouping of enormities which the Synod put under its tenth heading, "Inordinate affection unto the world." For what it here described,
drawing again upon the jeremiads, was nothing less than mercantile,
capitalistic, competitive New England. This tenth chapter is the first systematic description of State Street.

The sermon which fixed the type of the jeremiad, John Higginson's of
1663, said that the Lord had not stirred the founders by the promise of
wealth. "Nor had we any rationall grounds to expect such a thing in such
a wilderness as this." (That use of "rationall" is notable.) God has blessed
certain of us, who therefore "have encreased here from small beginnings
to great estates"; nevertheless, New England was originally a plantation
not of trade but of religion—"Let Merchants and such as are increasing
Cent per Cent remember this." If the *Result* of 1679 is to be believed,
they had just about forgotten, but still they were increasing cent per cent.

The founders, of course, wanted land; they tried to parcel it out carefully in town grants. But as early as 1642 John Cotton found many disposed to cry, "If we could have large elbow-roome enough, and meddow
enough, though wee had no Ordinances, we can then goe and live like
lambs in a large place." He told them severely that if this was their frame
of mind, "you may have part in Reformation of Churches, but no part in
the resurrection of Christ Jesus." The jeremiads chronicle the augmenting
lust to live like lambs until, as the Synod put it conservatively, "There hath

been in many professors an insatiable desire after Land." In 1676 Increase Mather could not be so temperate: "Land! Land! hath been the Idol of many in New-England." The first settlers considered themselves rich with an acre a person and twenty acres for a family, but "how many Men since coveted after the earth, that many hundreds, nay thousands of Acres, have been engrossed by one man, and they that profess themselves Christians, have forsaken Churches, and Ordinances, and all for land and elbowroom enough in the World." Thus the real-estate speculator makes his entrance into American literature, as the second and third generations grew longer and longer elbows.

As the frontier expanded and ships put further out to sea, trade increased. In 1639 Robert Keayne was fined for buying as cheaply as he could and selling for the highest price he could get; even then, his fellow merchants protested on the ground that "a certain rule could not be found out for an equal rate between buyer and seller." Only the authority of John Cotton could force them to accept the rule of the "just price," but with his passing the records show a steady deterioration of regulatory efforts; while ministers repeated Cotton's dicta, the people did not obey.

Still more ominously, the lower orders began to reply in kind. If in 1673 Oakes could complain of much "Griping, and Squeesing, and Grinding the Faces of the poor," what wonder that by 1679 the Synod should have to bewail that "Day-Labourers and Mechanics are unreasonable in their demands"? Charles Chauncy had said in 1655 that if a poor man wanted a pair of shoes, or clothes to cover his nakedness, "truely he must be fain almost to sell himself, to get some mean commodities"; by 1674 Increase Mather could give a more penetrating description of the economic process: "A poor man cometh amongst you, and he must have a Commodity whatever it cost him, and you will make him give whatever you please, and put what price you please upon what he hath to give too, without respecting the just value of the thing." Two years later, with the bluntness that was always his most engaging quality, he exclaimed, "And what a shame it is that ever that odious sin of Usury should be pleaded for, or practised in New-England, especially by such as should give a better example?" John Dunton is not always a reliable witness, but he reported that in the New England of 1686 the art of cheating had become a "piece of Ingenuity" called by the genteel name of outwitting. The ministers possessed a somewhat larger frame of reference, and measuring facts by the original economic code, they again were able to gauge the curve of evolution along which the society was being carried by forces it could not resist.

The final two chapters of the Synod's discourse portrayed an unwillingness of the people to reform their evil ways and a corresponding disintegration of "publick spirit." By this were meant specifically reluctance to support the ministry and neglect of education; the ministers were fighting not only for their salaries but for the Puritan ideal of intellect and scholarship.

Urian Oakes hated to bear "too hard in this Case upon the people, that are generally poor and low enough," but the slenderness of ministers' maintenance in many churches was becoming alarming. Without a supply of learned men, support at a decent level of subsistence, "who sees not what Ignorance, and Rudeness, and Barbarism will come in like a Floud upon us?" True, Samuel Willard said, we "do not think the Spirit is locked up in the narrow limits of Colledge Learning," but on the other hand, ministerial gifts are not ordinarily "acquired in a Shoemakers Shop." Hubbard's oration of 1676 was the first clear enunciation of a theme which henceforth was a constant in discussions of the intellectual life, that "in other Nations" men of education and study have the chief management of affairs, and the like should "be necessary for the better ordering the affairs of Israel."

The Synod did not pretend that its digest was original: "The things here insisted on, have . . . been oftentimes mentioned and inculcated by those whom the Lord hath set as Watchmen to the house of Israel." Although the second half of the *Result* offered a program of reformation, still it did not breathe an overwhelming confidence of success. Two decades later, Cotton Mather ruefully, yet with a certain air of relief, acknowledged that it had always been "a matter of most sensible observation" that a reforming synod could not accomplish universal reformation. But if it could not, by curing the vices, make the jeremiad obsolete, it could do the next best thing: supply preachers with the subject matter of further jeremiads. Or as Cotton Mather put it, "Faithful ministers were thereby strengthened in lifting up their voices like trumpets." They had merely to review the Synod's twelve headings, keep the list up to date, and then deduce their exhortations.

The *Result*, by its very existence, further forced upon the content of the jeremiad an additional theme: open admission that the form had become a stereotype. In the 1680's appears the first intimation that listeners were getting a bit bored with the business; many, said Willard, suspect that these warnings are "nothing else but the mistakes of an irregular (though well minded) zeal, or the dumps and night visions of some melancholick spirits." Yet, even knowing that jeremiads "have been condemned by some, contemned by many more, scarcely believed by any," ministers continued to preach them. What else could they do?

The most conspicuous works of the 1680's continued the pattern: Willard's *The Only Sure Way to Prevent Threatened Calamity* in 1682, Samuel Torrey's *A Plea for the Life of Dying Religion* in 1683, and William Adams' *God's Eye on the Contrite* in 1685. Then came the loss of the charter; New England was rudely subjected to the "despotism" of a royal governor, of Sir Edmund Andros, and for the moment jeremiads ceased. For three years New England was held up to standards not of its own making, to the requirements of an imperial administration which had nothing to do with any sort of covenant. For the moment, New England could hardly pretend that it was a peculiar people. But in April 1689, by revolution and violence, it overthrew Sir Edmund, broke up the "Dominion of New England," and setting up again the government of the charter (while awaiting news from Increase Mather, their agent in London), put itself once more under the dominion of the external covenant.

As Cotton Mather tells it, "the compassion of God, by strange providences, fetched the country out of that condition"; whereupon the General Court, "returning to the exercise of their former authority," issued a proclamation advertising anew the ritualistic catalogue of corruptions, calling in the old tones for a backsliding people to recover themselves. Coming together to deal with the emergency, they first sat down to listen to Cotton Mather, filling in for his father, deliver a rousing jeremiad. Having suffered the intrusion of foreign tyranny and an alien ideology, having expelled the invader by an act of will, now resuming the direction of their own affairs, the Court found something infinitely reassuring— what reëstablished continuity with the past—in a rehearsal of the comfortable array of defects, phrased out of their own experience and in the accustomed language of their own judgment.

CHAPTER III

THE PROTESTANT ETHIC

WHEN
delivering jeremiads, a worried clergy were per-
forming, under compulsions they only half understood, a ritual of confession. Hence these ceremonial discourses do provide, taken in sequence,
a chronology of social evolution; in them everything the historian pieces
together out of records and documents is faithfully mirrored. They tell
the story, and tell it coherently, of a society which was founded by men
dedicated, in unity and simplicity, to realizing on earth eternal and immutable principles—and which progressively became involved with fishing, trade, and settlement. They constitute a chapter in the emergence
of the capitalist mentality, showing how intelligence copes with—or more
cogently, how it fails to cope with—a change it simultaneously desires
and abhors.

One remarkable fact emerges: while the ministers were excoriating
the behavior of merchants, laborers, and frontiersmen, they never for
a moment condemned merchandizing, laboring, or expansion of the frontier. They berated the consequenecs of progress, but never progress; deplored the effects of trade upon religion, but did not ask men to desist
from trading; arraigned men of great estates, but not estates. The temporal welfare of a people, said Jonathan Mitchell in 1667, required safety,
honesty, orthodoxy, and also "Prosperity in matters of outward Estate and
Liveleyhood."

In fact, in the ecstasy of denunciation, Jeremiahs enthusiastically in-
dorsed those precepts of pious labor which from the beginning had been
central in Calvinism. Merchants, farmers, and shipbuilders increased "cent
per cent," and the consequence appeared to be a decay of godliness, class
struggles, extravagant dress, and contempt for learning; New England
seemed to be deserting the ideals of its founders, but preachers would have
deserted them even more had they not also exhorted diligence in every
calling—precisely the virtue bound to increase estates, widen the gulf
between rich and poor, and to make usury inevitable.

That every man should have a calling and work hard in it was a first
premise of Puritanism. The guidebook for earthly existence, William
Ames's *Conscience with the Power and Cases thereof*, confirmed his authoritative summary of theology, *The Marrow of Sacred Divinity*, that
even the man who has an income must work. Everyone has a talent for

something, given of God, which he must improve. Although poverty is not a sin if it be suffered for causes outside one's control, for any to accept it voluntarily is utterly reprehensible. God has so contrived the world that men must seek the necessities of life in the earth or in the sea, but the objects of their search have been cunningly placed for the finding. Coming to his momentous decision, Winthrop had reflected, "Whatsoever we stand in neede of is treasured in the earth by the Creator, & to be feched thense by the sweate of or Browes." Ames worked it out syllogistically: God is absolute lord of all things; hence private property is only a temporary "dominion"; therefore the temporal possessor must enhance what is entrusted to him. Division of property "is founded, not onely on human, but also on naturall and divine right." The laborer is worthy of his hire, and fidelity in one's occupation, if performed in the fear of God, must lead to reward. Employing an estate so that it should become a larger estate was the inescapable injunction. Even in a jeremiad, William Adams remarked that while of course a believer must be crucified to the world, still he is not to be literally crucified: he "hath much business to do in & about the world which he is vigorously to attend, & he hath that in the world upon which he is to bestow affection." Ames's teaching was repeated in Samuel Willard's *summa:* "Man is made for Labour, and not for Idleness"; ergo, God has not given possessions to be held in common, "but hath appointed that every Man should have his Share in them, wherein he holds a proper Right in them, and they are his own and not anothers." This principle, Willard pointed out—as did all Puritans—has nothing to do with the spiritual condition; a right to property, exercised within civil propriety, is as valid for the pagan or idolater as for the saint.

Max Weber has taught us to call this configuration of ideas the "Protestant ethic." The finest exposition in New England literature occurs in John Cotton's volume of 1641, *The Way of Life;* his is the classic demand that men devote themselves to making profits without succumbing to the temptations of profit, that a believer be drawn by his belief into some warrantable calling, "though it be but of a day-laborer." Here is the ringing and abiding conviction of the Puritan, for whom civil life no less than the religious is lived by faith: "If thou beest a man that lives without a calling, though thou hast two thousands to spend, yet if thou hast no calling, tending to publique good, thou art an uncleane beast."

The peculiarly English note in Cotton's presentation is the strong emphasis upon "publique good." The Puritan's thought was so far from any suggestion of individualism that his exhortation to money makers was, in his mind, not incompatible with enforcing the just price. Furthermore, every laborer must remember that even as his gifts were from God, opportunities for employing them were opened by providence; the rewards of industry were not consequences of industriousness, nor of the state of the market or of rates of exchange. Knowing this, a saint in his counting house would patiently suffer loss as a trial of faith, but would also take good fortune "with moderation" and never be corrupted by success. No matter how much he outstripped his fathers in wealth, he would, by remaining an ascetic in the midst of prosperity, abide by their covenant—especially by the external covenant, within which the management, for public good, of external possessions so largely fell.

The Puritan mind, as we know, found allegory congenial. As Bunyan implores us, "Do thou the substance of my matter see, Put by the curtains . . . Turn up my metaphors." In 1657, twenty-one years before *Pilgrim's Progress*, one "N. D." published in London an allegory for which the curtains require less putting by; it was reprinted at Boston in 1683, and again as late as 1763. According to *A Rich Treasure At an easy Rate: or, The ready Way to true Content*, Poverty lives at one end of town with his wife Sloth, "in a sorry ruinous Cottage; which shortly after falls to the ground, and he is never able to repair it." At the other end dwells Riches, with his servants Pride, Oppression, Covetousness, Luxury, and Prodigality. Of his two sons, Honour died young, Ambition came to an untimely end; one daughter, Delicacy, has a bastard child Infamy, and the other, Avarice, gave birth to Misery. Into town comes Godliness, with a retinue of servants—Humility, Sincerity, Repentance, Experience, Faith, Hope, Charity, Temperance, and Sobriety. He tries to live beside Riches, who insults him; he tries Poverty, who raises a hullabaloo by coming home drunk every night from the ale-house. Godliness is tempted to retreat to the cloister, and then—being a Protestant—bethinks himself, "Man was made for Society." Upon the advice of Gravity, he settles in the middle of town, halfway between Riches and Poverty, beside old Labour, the best housekeeper in the parish, and his wife Prudence. We note—remembering how Riches has been repudiated—that Godliness proves a great help to Labour, assisted by Labour's attendants, Forecast, Diligence, Expedition, Cheerfulnes, and Perseverance, "early Risers and at their work." After Godliness teaches him to pray, Labour's estate increases, until Content comes to live with him, bringing in his train Justification, Adoption, Assurance, and Sanctification. At the end, Labour's happiness knows no bounds: "he had never prayed before, but now Godliness had thoroughly instructed him, and taught him a better Art, and the way of thriving."

John Hull, the greatest Boston merchant of the mid-century and the legendary mintmaster, was no child of Riches; his father was a blacksmith, and he himself had but little "keeping" at school; he hoed corn for seven years, until "by God's good hand" he was apprenticed to a goldsmith. He joined with Godliness at the age of twenty-three, for the Lord made the ministry of John Cotton effectual unto him, whereby he found "room in the hearts of his people," being received in the fellowship of the First Church of Boston. Thereupon the economic virtues waited upon him; he was an early riser and at his work, "and, through God's help, obtained that ability in it, as I was able to get my living by it." He kept his shop so well that shortly it kept him, yielding a surplus to invest in ships and land. But always, whether tradesman, merchant, or banker, he went in the fear of God. When the Dutch got his ships, he knew consolation: "The loss of my estate will be nothing, if the Lord please to join my soul nearer to himself, and loose it more from creature comforts." However, when his foreman at Point Judith Neck stole his horses, a Puritan saint knew what to say: "I would have you know that they are, by God's good providence, mine."

Hull's instructions to his ship-captains mingle piety and business without embarrassment; the Lord should be worshipped in his vessels, Sabbaths sanctified, and all profaneness suppressed. "That the lords prescence may be with you & his blessing upon you," he wrote, and added with the same pen, "Leave noe debts behind you whereever you goe." He told his skippers to follow their judgment, knowing that businessmen must take their chances: "but indeed it is hard to foresee what will be & therefore it is best willing to submit to the great governing hand of the great Governor of all the greater and lesser revolutions that wee the poore sons of men are involved in by the invoyce you see the whole amounteth to £405:16:3." There may be little punctuation, but every threepence is accounted for! Hull died worth over six thousand pounds, but would have been worth twice as much had he not supported the colony's treasury out of his own pocket.

In his old age he declined a venture to the Canaries because he had become desirous only "to be more thoughtfull of Lanching into that vast ocion of Eternity whether we must all shortly bee Carried." Still, it would be stretching the term to call him "otherworldly." To him, religion included seizing the main chance, and sin was synonymous with wasted opportunities. Into his shop he took two apprentices; one of them, Jeremiah Dummer, was a good boy (who became also a wealthy merchant and saint, and the father of—well, not exactly a saint), but the other, Samuel Paddy, was a wastrel. In the heart of John Hull there was little mercy for the Paddys of this world; after he had turned Paddy out of the house, he wrote him: "Had you abode here and followed your calling you might have been worth many hundred pounds of clear estate and you might have enjoyed many more helpes for your sole. Mr. Dummer lives in good fashion hath a wife and three children and like to be very useful in his generation." Was not life itself almost too transparent an allegory?

In 1683 Samuel Willard preached Hull's funeral sermon; taken in conjunction with his jeremiad of the year before, it demonstrates how innocently praise of the merchant and denunciation of commercial sins flourished side by side. Hull "was a Saint upon Earth," and "lived like a Saint here, and died the precious Death of a Saint." But he was no Papist, and so did not flee into desert or cloister: he did live "above the World," and did keep "his heart disentangled," but meanwhile was "in the midst of all outward occasions and urgency of Business." Parson Willard saw nothing incongruous in advancing among Hull's claims to veneration, along with his being a magistrate, church member, father and benefactor, the fact "that Providence had given him a prosperous and Flourishing Portion of this Worlds Goods."

Thanks to this spirit in the covenanted community—there were possibly more Paddys than is generally imagined, but there were several Hulls and Dummers—providence blessed New England with a flourishing portion of worldly goods. As Higginson said, on any rational calculation of the natural resources no one could have expected such success; it had been won despite reason (to the extent that all depended upon the favor of God), and yet in an eminently rational way, to the extent that the hard work of the saints, their leaving no debts behind, had served as "efficient cause." There were occasional bad years, upon which John Hull would moralize; he found in 1664, for instance, a smite upon all employments: "at least in general, all men are rather going backward than increasing their estates." Yet in that year he also noted that about one hundred sail of ships had come into Boston harbor, "and all laden hence." Laden ships meant profits for somebody.

For the first ten years, Massachusetts Bay and Connecticut lived happily off immigrants, who brought in foreign goods and specie, and so furnished a market for local produce. The New England Way, having been established during the "golden age" of 1630–1640 when the economic problem took care of itself, could never thereafter comprehend how economics might dilute religion. The golden age came abruptly to an end when the English Wars stopped immigration. Then New England found itself with little money and no markets; it had to have wares it could not manufacture, but it had little or nothing to peddle in England. Colonists had to find some way of converting their fish, lumber, wheat, flour, and livestock into English cloth and tools. For reasons best known to Himself, God had not laid before His saints the easy opportunity He gave Virginians, who found at their doorsteps a crop marketable at five shillings the pound. New Englanders had to learn commerce or perish.

They learned it. The "sacred cod" became a symbol second only, if that, to the Bible. "When the first way of supply began to be stopped up, God in his merciful providence opened another, by turning us into a way of Trade and Commerce, to further our more comfortable subsistence." But commerce is no half-time occupation. When a man spends all his waking hours amid—as an almanac jingle had it—"Heaps of wheat, pork, bisket, beef and beer; Masts, pipe-staves, fish, should store both far and near, which fetch in wines, cloths, sweets and good tobac," he will hardly have leisure for meditating upon the close distinction between works as a condition of the Covenant of Grace and the conception of works in the Arminian heresy. "Our Maritan Towns began to encrease roundly," the historian of 1650 could already say. The Resoration was a grievous setback for Puritan orthodoxy, and John Hull was most depressed as he saw "the face of things looking sadly toward the letting-in of Popery." Yet

economically he had no cause to complain, for the Navigation Acts and
the exclusion of the Dutch offered merchants in New England a truly
golden opportunity. Through the instrumentality of King Charles, master
immoralist of the age, divine providence arranged compensation for the
ravages of King Philip.

Whenever preachers of jeremiads answered outside criticism, they put
aside denunciation and resolutely boasted of how the people had demonstrated "that Necessity and Freedome could do wonders." Thus wealth
did accumulate, which could not be anything but a sign of divine blessing. Men started as millers and were paid in grain; thus providentially
invited to find buyers, they grew to be traders. Others started as artisans,
took apprentices, and shortly were capitalists. Merchants imported the
necessary stocks, advanced them to farmers and frontiersmen on credit,
and so became bankers who, in the name of honesty, cracked a whip over
their debtors. Was John Hull grinding the faces of the poor when he wrote
to a borrower, "I am afraid lest by keepeing a drinkeing House you learn
to tipple yor selfe and thereby stifle the voice of yor Conscience that else
would call upon you to bee Righteouse me thinks some fruits might have
come to mee last winter"? As soon as God made clear the market value
of the cod, pious citizens, acting from both necessity and freedom, bought
up the fishing fleet, and by the end of the century a few rich men dominated
the industry. By then, New England merchants had taken hold of their
opportunities with such diligence, expedition, and perseverance that they
succeeded the Dutch as the principal competitors of merchants in London
and Bristol; at the same time, they were steadily draining the back-
country and Newfoundland of specie, bringing in cargoes from southern
Europe, diverting the coinage of the Caribbean into their pockets, earning
freight-charges on everything they handled, and then—to cap the climax
—selling their very ships at immense profit!

Statesmen who led the migration of 1630 lost so much that if their
estates, at their deaths, were a thousand pounds, God had been merciful.
But merchant Robert Keayne, even though prevented by theological fiat
from charging all he could, left £4,000 in 1656. John Holland, by fitting
vessels for the cod-fisheries, had that much by 1653. Though Increase
Mather cried that land had become an idol, many church members were
accumulating titles. By 1670 there were said to be thirty merchants in
Boston worth from ten to thirty thousand pounds. By the end of the century the great names were not only Winthrop, Dudley, and Mather, but
also Lillie, Faneuil, Belcher, Foster, Phillips, Wharton, Clarke, Oliver,
Sargent—and Hutchinson. "In the Chief, or high Street," said Ned Ward,
"there are stately Edifices, some of which cost the owners two or three
Thousand Pounds." He thought that these illustrated the adage of a fool
and his money being soon parted, "for the Fathers of these Men were
Tinkers and Peddlers," but he did not comprehend Puritan ethics. Few
built bigger houses than they could afford; Prudence was still their wife.

But that the fathers of many had been tinkers and peddlers was well enough known.

An intellectual historian must detect the workings of change, but no preternatural astuteness is required to decipher the trend when Joshua Moodey in 1685 declared that salvation yields a hundred per cent clear gain and that therefore "It is rational that Men should lay out their Money where they may have the most suitable Commodities and best Penny-worths." Samuel Willard's *Heavenly Merchandize* in 1686 was exactly what the title indicates. Hooker and Shepard often took their illustrations from industry and business: in meditation, said Hooker, a man beats his brains "as the Gouldsmith with his mettal." However, their metaphors did not control their content. (As Jonathan Edwards was later to say, truly spiritual rhetoric mentions these things as illustrations and evidence of the truth of what the preacher says, not of his meaning.) But in Willard's sermon the merchandising metaphor governs the thought; the author never steps out of it: "A prudent buyer will see his wares, & try them before he will buy them." That men naturally try to haggle with God over the terms of salvation is thus conveyed: "He that really intends to buy, will first cheapen; every one hath such a principle, that he could buy at the best rates; to have a thing good, and have it cheap, is most mens ambition." Willard concluded that Christ was a good buy, and that those who can purchase had better pay the price.

Thus we are again confronted with the question of why New England in the second half of the century expressed itself most comprehensively in stylized self-denunciation. Why did spokesmen for a people who triumphed over forest and sea, who were piling up sterling and building more stately mansions on the high street—spokesmen proud of these achievements—call upon their people to abase themselves before the Lord as guilty of the Synod's twelve offenses? Why did they fill their diaries with self-con-demnation? Why did a John Hull or a Samuel Sewall accuse himself, even while hastening along the road to wealth? Why, when they assembled together, did they hunger and thirst after a methodical analysis of their imperfection?

Had the jeremiads been directed only at those outside the churches, expla-nation would be easy. Occasionally we do find an offender galled by his exclusion from the corporation of the saints; modern sympathies instinc-tively go out to one Peter Bussaker, who in 1648 was whipped in Con-necticut because he profanely announced "that hee hoped to meete some of the members of the Church in hell err long and hee did not question but he should." In 1673 Increase Mather intimated that non-members took delight in luring church members into taverns and getting them drunk, and in 1682 Urian Oakes let slip the admission that there were New Englanders weary of "theocracy." (This is one of the few usages of the term in the century, but Oakes was reduced to employing it, as we shall see, for political reasons.) In 1691 Joshua Scottow tried to tell himself that most of the enormities were committed by that mixed multitude who had not come with the saints.

All such excuses were in vain. The *Magnalia,* with disarming honesty, confesses that the real issue was the prodigious and astonishing scandals of those "that have made a more than ordinary profession of religion." The heart of the problem was the riddle of Protestant theology: "Why mayn't I, as well as David?" David sinned, to put it mildly, but nevertheless went to heaven; in the external covenant his example was more difficult to discount than in the internal. "Perhaps in his fall, and not in his rise again, David has been sometimes too much followed by some eminent professors of religion in this land; and the land has been filled with temptation by so venomous a mischief." No, the declension of New England was not entirely the fault of the vulgar: it was defection among the children of the covenant.

Whereupon a second hypothesis suggests itself: did anybody really believe in the declension? Was there a confession of sinfulness on Sunday, followed on Monday by the foreclosing of a mortgage? The modern temper finds this explanation plausible, and delights to quote, out of the *Magnalia,* the fishermen of Marblehead who announced that they came to America not for religion but for fish. But the problem for our culture is that the weight of the dilemma was felt not by such care-free fishermen, but by orthodox leaders of the community. The mixture of business and piety in Hull's instructions, though to us it seems quaint, is far from a keeping of the left hand in ignorance of the right; the jeremiads came from something deeper than pious fraud, more profound than cant: they were the voice of a community bespeaking its apprehensions about itself.

The cultural and intellectual problem becomes more complex when we ask whether there really was so awful a deterioration. Comparing the Synod's indictment with the recorded facts, Thomas Hutchinson, judging by the standards of an eighteenth-century gentleman, said "we have no evidence of any extraordinary degeneracy." We have heard Cotton Mather admit that the situation was not always so bad as painted. One can indeed cull from the records of the county courts an amusing array of thefts, bastardy, incest, and sheer filthiness, but the mass of the people, whether church members or inhabitants, were hard at work, clearing the land, attending sermons (and taking notes), searching their souls, praying for grace, and humbling themselves for their unworthiness. Above all, following the injunction to increase and multiply, they were begetting children, between-times garnering the rewards, in material recompense, of pious industry. No doubt, Hutchinson was basically correct.

But if, as we measure facts, New England was not declining, it was certainly changing. The orthodox colonies were originally medieval states, based upon a fixed will of God, dedicated to the explicitly just, good, and honest. Men were arranged in hierarchical ranks, the lower obedient to the upper, with magistrates and scholars at the top. Things were right or wrong intrinsically, not relatively, so that the price of a piece of cloth could be determined by theologians. It shall be lawful, said Cotton, for the judges in any town, with the consent of the town officers, to set "reasonable rates" upon commodities; at the end of the century, Willard was still contending for such "Equity," declaring that employers may not take advantage of the laborer "and beat him down so as to enjoy his Labour underfoot, for that which is next to nothing." Gradation in costume according to rank was the visible sign of a social philosophy based upon the law of nature and further sanctioned by revelation. "One end of Apparel is to distinguish and put a difference between persons according to the Places and Conditions." The code resisted change, and therefore changes became declensions; the jeremiads recognized the facts, but refused to accommodate theory to them.

William Hubbard's sermon of 1676, *The Happiness of a People*, is a most interesting memorial to this internal conflict, not only for its eloquence but also for the fact that its author was not in full sympathy with those determined at all costs to make a stand for the charter. On every page, Hubbard betrays his awareness of the changing conditions, and so pleads the more fervently for "unity" and "order." The Creator made the universe of differing parts, "which necessarily supposes that there must be differing places, for those differing things to be disposed into, which is Order." Especially must this "artificial distribution" be observed in a political structure, and "whoever is for a parity in any Society, will in the issue reduce things into an heap of confusion." Just as the angels in heaven are not all of one rank, and in "the pavement of that glorious mansion place," we shall see one star differ from another in glory, as the eagle surmounts "the little choristers of the valleys," so "it is not then the result of time or chance, that some are mounted on horse-back, while others are left to travell on foot." The Lord appoints her "that sits behind the mill" and "him that ruleth on the throne." The greater portion of mankind are but "tools and instruments for others to work by" rather than "proper agents to effect any thing of themselves"; left to themselves, they "would destroy themselves by slothfulness and security" were they not driven and supervised by their betters. Nothing is more remote from right reason, Hubbard continued—contending with peculiar vehemence against that stubborn egalitarianism which is seldom entirely banished from Christian piety—"than to think that because we were all once equal at our birth, and shall be again at our death, therefore we should be so in the whole course of our lives." Of course, Hubbard delivered this sermon when the war with Philip was still going badly, and it may be read as a covert expression of dissatisfaction with the administration. In any event, he asserted the principle of subordination as resolutely as Winthrop and Cotton. "In fine," he concluded, "a body would not be more monstrous and deformed without an Head, nor a ship more dangerous at Sea without a Pilot, nor a flock of sheep more ready to be devoured without a Shepheard, than would humane Society be without an Head, and Leader in time of danger."

If, as I believe, Hubbard spoke for the band of merchants who had already decided that repeal of the charter was inevitable, it is all the more remarkable that he should invoke the hierarchical conception of society. By this ideal all preachers—whatever their sentiments concerning the charter—were bound to judge the society. The jeremiads therefore testify to a grief that was not merely distress over a failure of reality to conform to theory, but unhappiness about theory itself. Class lines drawn upon the basis of inherited status might have a semblance of eternal order. When new families, such as the Brattles or the Whartons, forged ahead and then availed themselves of the philosophy of social subordination, the metaphysical dilemma became acute. In vain Samuel Willard reminded the new generation of merchants that civil deference ought to be paid to gentlemen, "tho' the Providence of God bring them into Poverty." Cotton Mather could only shake his head: "If some that are now rich were once low in the world, 'tis possible, more that were once rich are now brought very low."

Nor did a family have to rise to the very top of the scale, like the Brattles, in order to upset the hierarchy. It was enough, for instance, if a Robert Turner, admitted as an indentured servant to the church of Boston in 1632, should become master of a tavern, "The Sign of the Anchor," and die in 1664 with an estate of £1,600. Or if a John Kitchin, starting as the servant of Zachery Bicknell, should have a grandson Edward, who in Salem became the equal of Endecotts and Crowninshields. Samuel Shrimpton set up as a brazier, but at his death in 1698 he owned most of Beacon Hill and was inventoried at £1,800. John Harrison bargained for a monopoly of rope-making in Boston, out of which he built a great house on Purchase Street. Thomas Savage, son of an English blacksmith, began as a tailor, erected wharves on Fleet Street, and ended worth £2,500. The social structure refused to stay fixed, and classifications decreed by God Himself dissolved. Pious industry wrecked the city on a hill, in which it had been assumed men would remain forever in the stations to which they were born, and inferiors would eternally bow to gentlemen and scholars.

Had economic development merely recruited a few additions from the commercial classes to the Puritan oligarchy, the ideal would not have been endangered, but it played havoc not only by making some rich but by reducing many to poverty. John Josselyn observed in 1675 that while diligent hands had prospered, those of a "droanish disposition" became wretchedly poor. If there were Shrimptons and Savages, there was also Thomas Turvill of Newbury, whose entire estate consisted of: "An old worne out coat and britches with an old lining £0 6s 0d; A thread bare, tho indifferent close coat and doublet with an old wast coat, 1:00:00; Two shirts and a band, 11s; a pair of shoes, 4s; An old greasy hatt, 6d, a pair of stockings, 1s; An old doublet, an old wast cote and a pair of old sheep skin briches, 0:04:00." There had been a moment when it seemed possible that in New England the poor would not always be with us; by 1700 they were numerous. Had the process brought down only drones, it could have been admired: the problem was that it worked hardship upon yeomen farmers of virtue and industry, whose estates at most never got beyond two or three hundred pounds. They found themselves paying tribute to merchants, millers, and shipbuilders. After their little store of cash had flowed into Boston coffers, they went into debt for imported goods, and even then, since they had to pay with produce, received only the first cost. In rural districts trading was reduced to a commodity basis, wherein what was called "country pay" figured prices at a higher rate than the goods would fetch in sterling; but all this while, merchants tried to collect their debts at the hard money rate.

As the lines became more sharply drawn, even the upper class of inherited position, the sons and daughters of Winthrops, Nortons, Dudleys, Saltonstalls, Bradstreets, became less the dedicated leaders of a religious movement and more a closed corporation of monopolists. They married among themselves—Winthrops with Bradstreets, Dudleys with Saltonstalls—while the ministerial families also intermarried so extensively as to become within three generations a distinct caste, which Dr. Holmes was later to call, not quite realizing the full implications, "Brahmin." The church, it must be said, still did offer an avenue of escape for abler youths of the lower orders, to such as John Wise, son of an indentured servant, or Thomas Barnard, son of a maltster in Hartford; but the exceptions were few, and by 1700 the clergy no less than the merchants were a vested interest—which was not what the founders had envisaged.

New men of wealth came up by a different ladder from that by which Winthrops and Saltonstalls had ascended, and showed the effects of their training. Even in 1650 Edward Johnson was horrified to discover that merchants and vintners "would willingly have had the Commonwealth tolerate divers kinds of sinful opinions" because they wanted more immigrants "that their purses might be filled with coyne." Thirty years later merchants were the most ready of any group to surrender the charter, but whether loyal or disloyal, they and the tradesmen either would not or could not abide by the regulations. Laws fixing wages and prices, prescribing the amounts to be spent on dress and luxury, became dead letters: "Those good orders were not of long continuance, but did expire with the first and golden age in this new world." In 1639 to seek a profit "above 33 per cent" had been to invite condign punishment, but "since that time the common practice of the country hath made double that advance no sin." The records show little prosecution under the sumptuary legislation after about 1675; John Dunton seems again to have spoken truth: "The Laws for Reformation of Manners are very severe, yet but little regarded by the People, so at least as to make 'em better, or cause 'em to mend their manners." Increase Mather had denounced cards and dice in 1674 because, by the original philosophy, "If a man get anothers Goods at under price, this is Injustice, it is Theft, and a Transgression of the Rule of Righteousness." Subsequent jeremiads had to face the fact that not only did cards and dice abound, but that the economic philosophy by which Mather had condemned them became an embarrassment when employed by farmers to make Mather's merchant parishioners pay for produce at the country rate. At every point, economic life set up conflicts with ideology. It was defeat for the plan of New England that frontier towns should be settled without a ministry and a school, but, said Cotton Mather in 1690, the insoluble problem was how "at once we may Advance our Husbandry, and yet Forbear our Dispersion; and moreover at the same time fill the Countrey with a Liberal Education."

The husbandmen and traders were doing nothing but what they had been told to do. They worked in their callings—and brought multiplicity out of unity. There were perceptibly "more divisions in times of prosperity than in times of adversity, and when Satan cant destroy them by outward violence he will endeavour to undo them by Strife and variance." Saints waited upon God for the reward—and became social climbers. The more everybody labored, the more society was transformed. The more diligently the people applied themselves—on the frontier, in the meadows, in the countinghouse or on the Banks of Newfoundland—the more they produced a decay of religion and a corruption of morals, a society they did not want, one that seemed less and less attractive. From the beginning, the city on a hill was to have social classes, but status ordained by God should not become the prize of competition; the jeremiad could not arrest the process in which names rose and fell, but by grieving over the incomprehensible it provided a method of endurance.

Hence we may see in the sermons more than ministerial nagging of worldlings, more than hypocritical show, more than rhetoric. They were releases from a grief and a sickness of soul which otherwise found no surcease. They were professions of a society that knew it was doing wrong, but could not help itself, because the wrong thing was also the right thing. From such ceremonies men arose with new strength and courage: having acknowledged what was amiss, the populace could go back to their fields and benches and ships, trusting that a covenanted Jehovah would remember His bond. When again they grew apprehensive, they could look into their own hearts, find what was festering there, and hasten once more to cleanse their bosoms of poisonous stuff by public confession. Although jeremiads and the Reforming Synod called for an alteration of social habits, the result was only more days of humiliation. Knowing their impotence, the people needed a method for paying tribute to their sense of guilt and yet for moving with the times. Realizing that they had betrayed their fathers, and were still betraying them, they paid the requisite homage in a ritual of humiliation, and by confessing iniquities regained at least a portion of self-respect.

A literary form does not come into flower unless it answers some deep necessity of the time and the place. As drama was the ideal articulation of Elizabethan London, the jeremiad was for the tiny communities of New England. The form suited their needs, on the one hand satisfying a passionate desire to remain faithful to the Puritan inheritance and on the other inculcating the ethic which was steadily undermining that heritage. Devotion to business, accumulation of estates, acquisition of houses and lands: these were the duties of Christians. What they gained of elegance or luxury was the just reward of blessed diligence, yet business and riches meant devotion to the world, and luxury meant pride. The sins paraded in the sermons were not so much those of the notoriously scandalous but such as were bound to increase among good men. They thus had to be all the more vigorously condemned because they were incurable: after proper obeisance to the past, the society was better prepared to march into its future.

CHAPTER IV

THE EXPANDING LIMITS OF NATURAL ABILITY

WHEN
John Winthrop committed Massachusetts Bay to
the external covenant, he was not troubled because a majority, as many
as four-fifths, were not saints, even "unto visibility." In all Protestant
theology, there was a realm of conduct over which purely "natural" considerations held sway. The flight of every sparrow, let alone every motion
of man, was governed by providence; nevertheless, in politics and public
morality, laws were enforced and penalties exacted on the assumption that
ordinary men are responsible for such things as fornication, debt, and murder.

A nation in the federal covenant differed from the uncovenanted, not
because all citizens were holy, but because therein saints administered the
laws according to the covenant. Since a national covenant ran no further
than outward rectitude, and since natural inhabitants could be incited (or
compelled) to obey, the saints did not need to be a majority if only they
held the power. The covenant came into being as a consequence of their
internal pledge; the others were merely carried along; to keep the covenant alive, a core of saints was necessary, but a saving remnant was enough.

Had the founders been uncomplicated Calvinists like the Scotch-Irish Presbyterians, the intellectual history of American Puritanism could be briefly
told. But by retaining the scholastic liberal arts, and then by rephrasing
Calvinism in the language of the several covenants, New Englanders managed to bring to the wilderness a complex system (which they innocently
supposed was simple). As jeremiads multiplied, the complaint mounted
that sound conversions were few, and even of these, many were of so
insipid a sanctity as to cause doubts of their authenticity. Bit by bit preachers raised a suspicion that the remnant might have become too small any
longer to save. It became increasingly imperative, therefore, that prophets
urge upon the unconverted no less than upon the converted the necessity
of doing something. Since the national covenant demanded an effort by
all, mere natural ability gradually was deemed adequate (if commanded
by a few saints) for outward compliance. A whole town or colony recorded their vow of reformation on a day of humiliation, but the gesture
would remain empty unless everyone did have a power to keep his promise without first having to undergo the elusive rite of regeneration.

The task might well seem hopeless. Although in their academic physics

Puritans analyzed man into Peripatetic faculties, treating reason and will as
"powers," they were nevertheless determinists. Masters of their thinking,
like William Perkins, said that anyone who seeks in men the cause of predestination, as though God chose them only upon foresight of their ability,
is a Pelagian. The chief architect of the federal theology, William Ames,
agreed that God's determination could not be founded upon foreknowl-
edge; John Preston established out of the Covenant of Grace that men
are justly condemned for not doing what they can do, but he also declared,
"God hath kept it in his power to draw whom he will, to sanctifie whom
he will." "It is not," he added, "in any mans power to beleeve, to repent
effectually." The offer of the Covenant was genuine; therefore if a man
decried it because he could not accept it without grace and called it a
"giftless gift," he was perverse and unthankful.

New England theologians echoed their teachers. Cotton said that God
could and does pour His grace upon the most abominable sinner; nothing
can hinder Him. Thomas Hooker seemed no more helpful: the darkness
in man is unalterably opposed to the light that is in God, and "Thou canst
resist a Saviour, but not entertaine him, doe what thou canst." While
calling upon the nation to reform, the Synod of 1679 also demanded
renewed allegiance to *The Westminster Confession,* which declared, "God
from all eternity did by the most wise and holy Counsel of his own Will,
freely and unchangeably ordaine whatsoever comes to pass," and that therefore until grace visits the natural spirit, it must be wholly "passive." With
what right, then, could divines press upon ordinary men the obligation
of an external covenant? Were they not impotent? If men may sit all
their lives as obtuse as the walls and pillars to which Urian Oakes declaimed
—as Samuel Willard later testified, "woful experience tells us that there
are a great many that do so"—with what face could ministers blame sinful people for afflictions, or treat sin as avoidable?

The fundamental problem of life for English Puritans was not social:
it was salvation of the soul, out of which would flow a purification of the
church and a regeneration of the state. Perhaps precisely because the concern with polity and politics was a consequential rather than a primary
issue, Puritans devoted their energies to reform and revolution. Or perhaps
it is more accurate to say that the energy was there, to be utilized in subsidiary matters. Exactly because public morality would not contribute to
election, the founders were the more ready to let compulsion rule. Yet,
on the other hand, Puritanism called for exertion; preachers, for example,
cultivated the plain style because they must be understood and so work
an effect. The sense of solidarity exemplified in the town system owes
much to centuries of English communal life, and is not to be attributed
solely to the creed, but for that very reason reveals the inarticulate premise
of this creed. When Puritans preached that man was made for society,
they were not combating individualism, but recognizing what was and
always had been the order of things.

In the line of covenant theologians we can trace the growth of an idea, at first no more than a manner of speaking, which discloses their awareness that the doctrine of absolute predestination had to be worked out in a social context. They early began to speak about a stage of "preparation," a period in time when a saint, working at his calling and listening to sermons, would suffer preliminary motions which sooner or later would eventuate in conversion. It would consist mainly in secret meditation and perturbation, but would require conversation with others, with a man named Evangelist to ask "Wherefore dost thou cry?" If the pilgrimage from then on was largely solitary, the point at which the scheme of salvation and the institutions of society came closest together would actually be this moment of preparation.

By urging the people to rededicate themselves to the *Confession*, the Synod was asking them to recollect that natural man has lost ability to will spiritual good, that he "is not able by his own strength to convert himself, or to prepare himself thereunto." But the *Confession* was written by Presbyterian Calvinists, not quite sophisticated enough to grasp the subtleties of the Covenant. Formulators of the federal theology were indeed Calvinists; in casting their thought in the terminology of a covenant they were only using a metaphor. Nevertheless, by putting the relationship between God and man into contractual terms, they found themselves blessed with the corollary that the terms could be known in advance. If a Sovereign proposes conditions, there must be a moment in time, however infinitesimal, between absolute depravity and concluding the bond. If election be a flash of lightning which strikes without warning, men cannot place themselves in its path, nor cultivate anticipatory attitudes, but when it comes as a chance to take up a contract, they must first of all learn what is to be contracted. By treating with men through negotiation, the Almighty seeks "that we might know what to expect from God, and upon what termes." A phenomenon of Calvinism everywhere in the century was a tendency to analyze the process of regeneration into a series of moments, but that strain which invented the federal theology was impelled, by the nature of the metaphor, to set off an initial period wherein he who is about to believe begins to learn what to expect.

In William Perkins, the widely studied (by Puritans) theologian who first definitely propounded the federal conception, preparation is little more than a conventional admonition that preachers spare no pains: "This preparation is to bee made partly by disputing or reasoning with them, that thou mayest thorowly discerne their manners and disposition, and partly by reproving in them some notorious sinne, that being pricked in heart and terrified, they may become teachable." In the 1620's John Preston said that the worst of sinners may sometimes be summoned without any antecedent humbling of the heart, just as a sick man does not need a sense of sickness in order to be cured, but notwithstanding, "if he be not sick, and have a sense of it, he will not come to the Physitian." This coming will not of itself work the cure, but it may be "a preparative sorrow." It is not to be confused with faith; the reprobate may attain it, "It hath his originall from nature." Yet by 1630, the particularization of a stage of behavior which is not the work of the spirit but may well lead to it, which is within the compass of natural men, had become familiar.

It was not—it never did become—what one might call a doctrine. But as a descriptive term it came into increasing prominence in federal eloquence, because theologians of the covenant were most obliged to distinguish and divide the temporal sequences of regeneration. They had a devotion to dissecting the psychology of conversion so intense that it recalls St. Bernard; just as he took delight in rhetorically tracing the twelve steps of humility and the three stages of truth, they luxuriated—the word is not too strong—in fine discriminations of preparation from humiliation, of vocation from implantation, and all these from exaltation. Loyalty to the root principle of Protestantism required them to preach salvation by faith; all the more was a state of preparation—not being a saving act, nor a meritorious work, but a preliminary rumble before the storm—a useful gambit for men named Evangelist. Had the mechanism of regeneration been phrased exclusively in the blunt language of Calvin, as a forcible seizure, a rape of the surprised will, there would have been no place for a time of preparation when the saint would say with Thomas Shepard, "Although I was troubled for this sin I did not know my sinfull nature all this while." Regeneration through covenant meant that men could make themselves ready, at least by studying the nature of covenants. Though God might do as He pleased with His own, it was a matter of empirical observation, the Synod of 1637 told Hutchinsonians, "In the ordinary constant course of his dispensation, the more wee indevour, the more assistance and help wee find from him." So the clergy organized their astute analyses of "indevour," and composed discourses upon preparation.

They found at once that the conception had social bearings. A man undergoing a work of preparation, in the hope it may be followed by the successive works, will endeavor to perfect external behavior. He may finally go to hell, but if in this world he lives by endeavor, he automatically fulfills the national terms. As Puritans perforce became more concerned with power than with purity, they labored to make the moral incentive of the national covenant do what the founders had gratuitously assumed would be done by regulation, fines, and the stocks. What for Winthrop had been in the background, the inarticulate premise of solidarity and subordination, for the second generation became the foreground: how to arrest a splintering of society into groups and competing interests. All men could be called upon to prepare themselves, and so to exert themselves toward exactly that obedience required by the nation's covenant, which then would ward off tempests and plagues, which would—through the engine of the jeremiad—redress the evils of inordinate dress and tavern-haunting.

Thomas Hooker, dictator of Connecticut, one of the most socially minded of the clerics, was also the greatest psychologist. His consummate probings of these preliminary motions, in *The Soules Preparation for Christ* (London, 1632) and *The Unbeleevers Preparing for Christ* (1638), were intensified by Thomas Shepard and Peter Bulkeley—these three being, significantly, the most vindictive prosecutors of Mistress Hutchinson. All three scrupulously maintained that "Natural and corrupt actions cannot prepare immediately for Supernatural Grace." Sorrow in preparation is a work wrought upon us; calling election a covenant does not infringe this principle, Bulkeley explained, because "first the Lord doth dispose us and fit us to a walking in Covenant with him, by putting into us his own spirit." The Puritan Jehovah was unconfined, nor did His favor follow upon any virtue in man; no, said Hooker, in a characteristic image, "it hangs not upon that hinge."

What, then, did Hooker and his disciples gain by their elaborate study of preparation? They established what to the Puritan mind was all-essential: there is an "order" in God's proceedings. Hooker marked off chronological phases, demonstrated the factual existence of a probationary period, in order to prove that regeneration was not a precipitate or instantaneous frenzy—with disruptive social consequences! As soon as he could show that God first takes away the resistance of the soul by an irresistible operation, whereby the soul "comes to be in the next passive power," and is disposed to a spiritual work—*"vult moveri"*—Hooker could then persuade his people that "this consent is not from ourselves, though not without ourselves." The last was precisely the effective clause.

If all this seems at first sight abstract, it had practical bearings, for preparation is the hidden issue in the Antinomian crisis of 1637. Because it was not a consolidated doctrine, like the Trinity or perseverance, but only a manner of speaking, it figures deceptively as an incidental term in the technical disputations; yet all the argument with Mrs. Hutchinson boils down to her denial that such a phase of conversion exists. Because she was smashed, the New England mind was thenceforth committed to it irrevocably.

New England's determination to hold it at all costs was strengthened by attacks emanating from England. William Pemble, for instance, was a federalist, but Hooker's line smelled to him of sophistical Arminianism; the amount of ability which Hooker attributed to preparation, said Pemble, could be performed by the unregenerate, and instead of elevating natural abilities, he was cheapening grace. "They are not antecedents, but consequents and parts of true conversion"; preparatory gestures of the sort unassisted faculties might enact are "no efficient causes to produce grace of conversion." As late as 1670 Giles Firmin was denouncing Hooker and Shepard for polluting doctrine and causing seekers unnecessary anguish by casting distrust upon the first true motions of the Spirit. In their effort to entice men into action, said Firmin, these New Englanders demand more of men than God requires, calling upon them not to repent but to go beyond repentance, whereas the battle should be considered won as soon as men can lament their sins.

Most of the New England leaders followed Hooker—with one ominous exception: John Cotton. By virtue of his post as "Teacher" of the First Church in Boston—it was held open for him until he could get away in 1633—he was a sort of dean of the sacred college. (I am convinced that Hooker left for Connecticut because Massachusetts was not big enough to hold him and Cotton.) In the 1640's he became the best-known expositor of the New England Way, so that he is conventionally remembered as the chief "theocrat," though this estimate forgets that the influence of Hooker and Shepard upon the living thought of New England was infinitely greater than his, that Edwards renewed the vitality of their tradition rather than Cotton's, and that in 1637 Cotton came so close to disaster that he lived thereafter on sufferance.

The full story cannot be reconstructed because most of it was deliberately concealed. But the theological ears of a heresy-hunter like Robert Baillie were acute enough to catch the overtones in the muffled syllables that reached England in the form of Winthrop's account, *A Short Story*, brought out in London by Welde in 1644. This did, said Baillie, all it could "to save Mr. Cottons credit," but so inexpertly that it let "the truth of Mr. Cottons Seduction fall from their Pens." The halting sentences with which Cotton endeavored (eleven years after his ordeal) to answer Baillie, in *The Way of Congregational Churches Cleared* (1648), are confirmations of his utter defeat upon the issue of preparation.

Cotton was the pure scholar who sweetened his mouth every night with a morsel of Calvin; he was caught among idealogues, beaten down by practical men who could show—to his sorrow—that disinterested scholarship played into the hands of subversive radicals. He believed it obvious that the gulf between nature and grace is absolute: "A man is passive in his Regeneration, as in his first generation." Only when the spirit has burned up, "root and branch," our legal righteousness are we "fit for any duty." There might be something called a "saving preparation," but as Pemble had said, this was not an antecedent but a consequence, and "for our first union, there are no steps to the Altar." "Drowsie hearts" do not open upon the knocking of Christ "unlesse he be pleased to put the finger of his spirit into our hearts, to open an entrance for himselfe." A blind man cannot prepare to see, and the supreme refinement of false faith is the self-induced resolution to stand ready: "Here is still the old roote of Adam left alive in us, whereby men seeke to establish their own righteousnesse."

In Hartford, Calvinism was more realistic: "Know therefore, that desires and love are of a double nature," that some are observed in preparation and others in sanctification. With Hooker's empirical temper poor Cotton could never grapple. "Looke by what right and reason many judicious Divines of late yeares," said Hooker, "having by experience observed it in their owne spirits, and judiciously scanned and delivered it, that there is a saving desire, by which God brings in and breeds faith in the soule." Listening to this doctrine, and comparing it with Cotton's uncompromising separation of faith from works, Anne Hutchinson decided that Cotton alone was preaching the authentic Covenant of Grace, and so rent the society apart by accusing all others of purveying a Covenant of Works.

Certain historians, distrusting the intellect, like to quote Winthrop's passage that once emotions ran high, nobody could understand what the dispute was about; actually, the line of division was clear: Mrs. Hutchinson made it so when she said that she came to New England "but for Mr. Cotton's sake," and "as for Mr. Hooker . . . she liked not his spirit." Out of Cotton's radical disjunction between nature and grace she derived her assertion that no works could have anything to do with justification, that they could not be offered as "evidence," that a true saint might consistently live in sin, and finally—what destroyed her—that saints could receive direct revelations from the Holy Ghost. All of these theses amounted to one thing: a denial of preparation. The rock upon which the Antinomians stood was this: a man, "for his part, must see nothing in himselfe, have nothing, doe nothing, onely he is to stand still and waite for Christ to doe all for him." It was wrong to call the elect to their duty, because those concerned about conduct are under the Covenant of Works. Election admits of no degrees; justification is absolute, in and of itself.

Upon sentencing her to banishment, the General Court of November 1637 said that Mrs. Hutchinson's teachings "tend to slothfulnesse, and quench all indevour in the creature." All this while, until the bitter end, she wrapped herself in the mantle of John Cotton, protesting that she had merely repeated his sermons. Thus Cotton had to be dealt with, for a party in power cannot allow its high priest to deviate—either to left or to right. The elders brought Cotton to a conference, "drew out sixteen points, and gave them to him, entreating him to deliver his judgment directly in them." Winthrop concedes that copies of his reply "were dispersed about"; seven years later, Francis Cornwell published in London *Sixteene Questions of Serious and Necessary Consequence*, which purported to be a verbatim report; the book was dedicated to Sir Harry Vane, that friend of Mrs. Hutchinson being by then a power in the land. It was so popular among "sectaries" that two more editions, under other titles, came out in 1646 and a fourth in 1647—to the chagrin of Massachusetts. Winthrop tried to protect Cotton, as is evidenced not only by his *Journal* but by his high-handed action as presiding officer in the trial of Mrs. Hutchinson. Yet even he has to say that though at this conference Cotton cleared many doubts, "in some things he gave not satisfaction." In Cornwell's version he gave none at all except, when hard pressed, to cry, "Let Calvin answer for me." Which is to say that Cotton tried to adhere to the Protestant line until his colleagues forced him to recognize that he, for all his great position, would be sacrificed along with Mistress Hutchinson unless he yielded. As many another man in a similar predicament, Cotton bent.

According to this surreptitious report, the issue was clear: it was preparation. The clergy, professing Calvinism, "would not believe themselves justified, no further then they could see themselves work; making their Markes, Signes, and Qualifications, the causes of their Justification." The Antinomians upheld the pristine thesis that justification is discerned "onely by Faith in the Free Promise." The text shows Cotton doggedly standing this ground. Asked whether there are any conditions in the soul before faith "of dependence unto which, such promises are made," he replies: "To works of creation there needeth no preparation"—here the uncompromisable issue stares us in the face. Further along, in this volume, Cotton is represented as declaring that to see in sanctification an evidence of justification is "such a Faith as a practicall Sillogisme can make," which is not faith wrought by Almighty power; that a conviction engendered even by evangelical preaching should not be confounded with an action of faith; that God does not give grace upon the condition of our becoming prepared, because "it is not his good pleasure to give us our first comfort . . . from our owne righteousnesse." New England was plagued with Anne Hutchinson long after the Indians beat out her brains; in England, where the new-fangled heresy of toleration permitted Antinomians freedom of the press, as had been pled for by John Milton, Protestantism was invited to judge between the ways of Hooker and of Mistress Hutchinson, for whom the still breathing John Cotton had proved a feeble reed.

Anne Hutchinson said that her brother-in-law, John Wheelwright, was the only minister beside Cotton who preached grace; on the fast day appointed to bemoan these dissensions he preached an "incendiary" sermon, for which he was banished. Wheelwright later repudiated the Hutchinsonians and is supposed to have told them that "whilst they pleaded for the Covenant of Grace, they took away the Grace of the Covenant." Yet in 1637, he, like Cotton, was hostile to the notion of preparation. "To preach the Gospell, is to preach Christ . . . & nothing but Christ . . . so that neither before our conversion nor after, we are able to put forth one act of true saving spirituall wisdome, but we must haue it put forth from the Lord Jesus Christ, with whom we are made one." Hooker and Shepard were bending their energies to a discrimination of the successive periods of conversion; Wheelwright said that when the Lord works upon a man, He "revealeth not to him some worke, & from that worke, carieth him to Christ, but there is nothing revealed but Christ, when Christ is lifted vp, he draweth all to him, that belongeth to the election of grace." If men think they are on the highway after they have traversed the first mile but are not yet united to Christ, "they are saued without the Gospell." "No, no," he exclaimed, "this is a covenant of works." If so, Thomas Hooker knew on whose foot the shoe was intended to fit.

Wheelwright's letters show him a man of integrity and stiff courage.. He must have known what he was doing when he introduced, as a possible objection to his doctrine, "this wil cause a combustean in Church & comanwealth," and answered that it would indeed do precisely that—"but what then, did not Christ come to sende fire vpon the earth?" Therefore Wheelwright had to be expelled. But what of Cotton?

Winthrop managed to save him, but it was a near thing. Just how near depends upon which account we credit, Cornwell's or Cotton's own in *The Way* eleven years after the interrogation. Cornwell has Cotton presented with sixteen questions (all of them hinging on preparation), Cotton says he was asked only five (much more general). The fourth, Cotton says, was whether some saving qualification might not be a first evidence, to which he says he replied, "A man may have an argument from thence (yea, I doubt not a firm and strong argument) but not a first Evidence." There can be no doubt, whichever story is correct, that Cotton was subjected to a humiliating cross-examination "in preparation to the Synod," in which his colleagues vigorously searched his writings "to inquire in a brotherly conference with mee, how far I would own them."

Winthrop admits that his replies were not satisfactory; the Synod assembled with a stalwart group resolved to break him. Depending years later upon the report of a "gratious Preacher who was present," Baillie said that Cotton's brethren severely admonished him, bringing him "to the greatest shame, confusion and griefe of mind, that even in all his life he had endured." Cotton could truthfully say that nothing quite so terrible happened, but even he acknowledges that the conference came close to an impasse, "taken up in disputing and arguing that Point with mee." He saved his skin by coming to see that the apprehensions of the majority were suitable to certain phrases of Scripture: "I the next morning did of my self freely declare to them publikely, my consent with them in the point, which (as they professed) they gladly accepted." One feels certain that Master Cotton had slept but little that night.

Cotton Mather had access to reports never written down, which he, assuredly, would have been the last in the world to make public. One of the joys (it is not widely shared) of reading the *Magnalia* is to admire its fast footwork. Not that Mather is dishonest—he manfully faces up to distressing realities when he has to—but with his italics and exclamations he often distracts attention from admissions he hopes the reader will not notice. He admits that "there was a *dark day* in the synod" when John Cotton seemed positively to deny that the first motions of faith are preparatory to justification; the arguments used against him are transparently those of Hooker, but Cotton Mather is happy to record that "Mr. Cotton the next morning made an excellent speech unto the assembly, tending towards an accommodation of the controversie." The paragraph then ends, in Magnalian opulence, "An *happy conclusion of the whole matter*"; but in the middle, without italics or emphasis, the formula of concord is briefly passed over: the Synod would concede to Cotton that the qualifications of grace "must ever be coexistent, concurrent, co-apparent," if Cotton would agree for his part that a soul's apprehension of Christ "is in order of nature before God's act of justification." By heightening the beginning and end of his narrative, Cotton Mather averted his gaze, and tried to draw ours aside, from his grandfather's abject surrender.

All New England knew what had happened. Mrs. Hutchinson hopelessly threw herself away by declaring that a special revelation promised her deliverance. The glee of the majority, as recorded in the stenographic transcript of the trial, is all too evident: now Cotton was caught, he had either to condemn her or go with her. Like the good man he was, he tried to get her to distinguish between such a Christian hope as anyone might legitimately entertain and a false revelation. Winthrop's *Short Story* tried to minimize Cotton's part, but had to notice that he "being present" was set to questioning his too ardent admirer; he had no choice but to bring her to her defiant assertion that it was supernatural intervention she counted on. Winthrop's account immediately drops Cotton, exults that the Jezebel delivered herself out of her own mouth, showing "that she walked by such a rule as cannot stand with the peace of any State," since she believed in bottomless revelations above reason and Scripture, not subject to any control. Thus he presents the New England Way as having come at once to a happy and orthodox concord.

The transcript, however, tells a more dramatic story. Cotton clearly was trying to save Mrs. Hutchinson; when she refused to coöperate, the others could see through his game. By the time rumors of this episode reached England, they had it that Cotton was then admonished; he was not, but in a sense the facts were more harrowing. "I desire Mr. Cotton," demanded Dudley, "to tell whether you do approve Mrs. Hutchinson's revelations as she hath laid them down." Cotton evaded and made logical distinctions: "Good Sir," Dudley kept pressing, "I do ask whether this revelation be of God or no?" With Cotton sweating in the toils, Dudley would not let up: "Sir, you weary me and do not satisfy me." Endecott and others joined the chase; the game was treed when Winthrop called them off: "Mr. Cotton is not called to answer to any thing but we are to deal with the party here standing before us." With that sentence Winthrop saved Cotton, and so was able to publish his account with the certification, "Mr. Cotton had in publique view consented with the rest."

In a volume published after his death, Cotton says that Grace "is not of our will but of the Lords, that takes away our strong heart, and gives us a soft heart before any preparation." This may have been written before 1637, or it may show that even after that day Cotton had not really given up his conviction; but he made no more trouble, instead performed immense service for the regime. To Baillie and Williams he insisted that he had always been in perfect harmony with his brethren, and that it was sheer slander for the Antinomians to have said that no matter "what he saith in publick, we understand him otherwise, and we know what he saith to us in private." Because of this false report a "jealousie" spread in the country "that I was in secret a Fomenter of the Spirit of Familisme, if not leavened my selfe that way." He does tell Williams that he seriously contemplated leaving Massachusetts because in the opinion of many "such a Doctrin of Union, and evidencing of Union, as was held forth by mee, was the Trojan Hourse, out of which all the erroneous Opinions and differences of the Country did issue forth." But "private conference with some chiefe Magistrates, and Elders" discovered the agreement, and in the Synod and at the trial of the heretics in the First Church he paid full measure: "I bare witnesse against them." Naturally, as he presents his own case, he had not been recovered from error: it was "the fruit of our clearer apprehension, both of the cause and of the state of our differences, and of our joynt consent and concurrence." Therefore, Cotton could with a clear conscience say to Baillie, "All of us hold Union with Christ, and evidencing of Union by the same Spirit, and same Faith and same holiness." But what he could not say to either Baillie or Williams was that henceforth, whenever he touched upon the subject of preparation, he was obliged to preface anything he would say with "Reserving due honor to such gracious and precious Saints, as may be otherwise minded." In his last years Cotton would still insist that the first work of conversion be of God and not man, and then add, "There are many sins which a man lives in, which he might avoid by very common gifts, which would he renounce, God would not be wanting to lead him to further grace." That was all Hooker meant by preparation, all that he forced John Cotton to confess.

When he undertook to defend New England polity against Presbyterians, Cotton found the doctrine of his fellows a better bulwark than his own. When Baillie accused the ministers of neglecting conversions, Cotton told him to read the works of Shepard and Hooker and then declare whether "of all that have crossed the American seas" these can be thought lacking in such exertions. True, he inserted, these writers "sometimes declare such works of Grace to be preparations to conversion, which others do take to be fruits of conversion," but still, preparation was now the peculiar badge of New England's theology: "Yet they all agree in this, that such works are found in all that are under the powerfull and effectual saving work of the Spirit."

In spite of Cotton's effort to drape the mantle of unanimity over the memory of this conflict, the scars remained. To the end of the century, even up to the *Magnalia*, the clergy keep rebutting Baillie and Williams —thus proving how deeply those barbs had struck. In 1700 Higginson was still haunted by the business, and compulsively went over the ground again: Cotton had "differed from some of his Brethren in The Souls Preparation for Christ," and had accused them of taking those deeds for preliminaries which he thought were fruits, but, insists Higginson, this was never a serious issue because Cotton agreed that the deeds themselves were requisite. "And so the Difference is but Logical, and not Theological." But 1637 had certainly shown that those who would dispense entirely with preparation were at odds with the regime, not merely logically and theologically, but socially: "The difference between them and us is (as they say) as wide as between Heaven and Hell." Hooker thoroughly understood what he had won, and pressed his advantage; he spoke and wrote much on preparation, introducing his remarks, in striking contrast to Cotton's apologies, with: "I shall not only speak mine own Judgment, but the Judgment of all my fellow Brethren, as I have just cause, and good ground to beleeve." As for the charge of Arminianism, Hooker disposed of that by flatly saying he was no Arminian. The last embers of heresy had to be beaten out: "The soule of a poore sinner must bee prepared for the Lord Jesus Christ, before it can receive him." People must exert themselves: "he watcheth the time till your hearts be ready to receive and entertaine him." When—with the help of Hooker's preaching—the soul perceives it cannot save itself, it falls at the feet of the Lord, and although at that moment it has not yet any mastery over sin, "yet it is willingly content that Jesus Christ should come into it." A sharp sauce, said Hooker, never at a loss for metaphor, will not "breed a stomacke, yet it stirres up the stomacke"; so preparation, if sharply applied, stirs up the stomach of faith—and of external conduct.

Shepard capitalized no less than Hooker upon the triumph of the preparatory doctrine. He denounced as the worst of heretics those who teach that authentic grief can come only after the soul is safely in Christ by faith; a man who has not yet given thought to his sins is in no position to receive grace, even irresistible grace. It would be, he agreed, Pelagianism to say that a man disposes himself of his own power; nevertheless, an antecedent disposition is required; a form cannot be joined to matter until matter is "made such a vessel which is immediately capable" of the union. For ordinary minds this is difficult doctrine, and even angels may be "posed" by trying intellectually to expound it, but the practical consequence was obvious: before a soul can be changed it must learn to "lie like wax" beneath the seal.

The real tendency of a Puritan discourse is seldom to be found in its "doctrine," nor even in its considered "reasons," but entirely in its "applications." Hooker and Shepard shamelessly improve the concept of preparation to mean that every man can perform the requisite actions. The soul cannot choose Christ "out of the power of nature"—but an inn must be prepared to receive the guest, else He will go to another lodging! Or, as with a woman in childbirth: "when her throwes come often and strong, there is some hope of deliverance; but when her throwes goe away, commonly the child dies, and her life too." Let predestination be what it may, the world calls him mad who argues, "I can do nothing for my self, therefore I will take a course that no man shall do any thing for me." The conclusion is inescapable: "Therefore I must attend upon God in those means which he useth to do for all those he useth to do good unto." It may not be in your power to make the Gospel "effectual"—but "it is your power to doe more than you doe, your legs may as well carry you to the word, as to an Ale-house." You can sing the Psalms as well as idle songs, "you may read good books, as well as Play-books." In short, then, New England, following the lead of Hooker and not of Cotton, having weathered the storm of Antinomianism, could insist, "doe what you are able to doe, put all your strength, and diligence unto it." "We must fight for it, and wage the battels of the Lord," was Hooker's cry, because "it is possible for any Soule present (for ought I know or that he knows) to get an humble heart." Bulkeley put it in the less vivid but controlling imagery of the covenant: because a man can humble himself before God and entreat for a chance to enter it, "you see the way to enter into Covenant with God."

This conclusion, even though it can be found potentially in European drafts of the federal theology, was forced into the open by American experience. Hooker's last sermons (his most enduring prose), *The Application of Redemption*, were published in 1657 by Goodwin and Nye, who, not having participated in the struggle of 1637, could appraise the direction Hooker's thought had taken: he has been accused, they said, of "urging too far, and insisting too much upon that as Preparatory, which includes indeed the beginnings of true Faith." But by this time England had also encountered the Antinomian frenzy during the anarchy of the Civil Wars, and so welcomed this American assistance; Hooker was particularly of value because he most thoroughly set to right "those that have slipt into Profession, and Leapt over all both true and deep Humiliation for sin, and sence of their natural Condition." With this approbation, the concept more than ever became a prized possession of New England orthodoxy, something that they above all others had tested, that they had vindicated.

By 1657 Antinomianism had run rife in England and, in the form of "Quakerism," seemed again invading New England. John Norton wrote *The Orthodox Evangelist* in order to systematize Hooker's teaching against this newest wave of enthusiasm; stripping the doctrine of Hooker's rhetoric, he uncovered further meanings. Distinguishing between works which are preparatory in the sight of God and those which may be evaluated by men, he put all his emphasis upon the second sort. The period of preparation became, in his treatment, a half-way station, neither sin nor virtue: "By preparatory Work, we understand certain inherent qualifications, coming between the carnal rest of the soul in the state of sin, and conversion wrought in the Ministry." It is a "common work of the Spirit," putting the soul into "a Ministerial capacity of believing immediately." In the work of grace, "as we ordinarily see in the Works of Nature, God proceeds not immediately from one extream unto another, but by degrees." John Cotton had acceded to the formula that the stages of conversion were chronologically separate and sequential; what then was to prevent the process from being so extended as to leave a long duration, and so a more critical importance, to the period of preparation?

In fact, Norton managed to subdivide preparation itself into a series of distinguishable moments: believing in the holiness of the law would come first, then realizing the nature of sin, learning the message of Christ, comprehending the need for repentance, and at last waiting upon Christ in the use of means under the Gospel Covenant. All these actions, mind you, while remaining passive! Preparation does not work a change of heart, "yet there are in it, and accompanying of it, certain inward workings, that do dispose to a change." Arminians and Pelagians allow too much to preparation—we may wonder what more they could allow!—but clearly all fanatical enthusiasts are wrong when they deny reality to the chain of antecedents. The moral is clear: "It is the duty of every one that hears the Gospel to believe, and that whosoever believeth shall be saved; but also it ministers equal hope unto all (answerable to their preparatory proceeding) of believing, and being saved." This is the most helpful, as well as the speediest way, even though the minute subdivisions appear so cumbersome. This is the way to rescue and preserve a covenanted people.

Increase Mather fled from England of the Restoration back to Massachusetts in 1661, filled with the resolution to uphold at home the primitive faith of the founders in all simplicity. At first he preached Cotton's views about preparation. Soon after, he began to hint that while the gate is indeed strait, yet God requires that men strive for entrance, and consequently that "they should do such things as have a tendency to cause them to Believe." Others in the second generation went more easily with the tide. Samuel Willard found it one of Satan's most subtle cheats "to tell us we must wait before we resolve." In *A Compleat Body* he summarized, as always, a century of experience: in preparation the soul stands in "a posture and readiness for the exerting of the act of Faith, which follows thereupon."

As late as 1690 there was still considerable confusion, and a few earnest believers even yet hankered after Cotton's rarefied doctrine. In the lull after the Revolution, a committee of ministers attempted to organize the New England tradition by a clear and concise statement of what the society theologically stood for: *The Principles of the Protestant Religion Maintained* (Cotton Mather wrote it, but the Boston ministers signed it) said that even though men are saved by the will of God, nevertheless there are "some previous and preparatory common works" which may be done by all, though in those who afterwards fall away these are not to be regarded as the beginnings of justification—except that only afterwards can anyone tell! From then until Jonathan Edwards delivered his Boston sermon in 1731, most of the clergy spoke with a single voice. How may I know that I am saved? the people would ask; Samuel Mather would answer, "As your Conviction is, such your faith is: as is the preparation work, such is the closing with Christ." For this reason we press the work upon you, "And there is more preparation needful, than many think for."

The culmination of this development, as of many others, can be found in the writings of Cotton Mather. At the beginning of his literary career he was already so heedless of ancient scruples as to represent his brother Nathaniel entering into covenant with God *before* his regeneration, which transaction then became "an influence into his Conversion afterwards." He always conceived of grace as a graduated process—which could be "cherished and promoted." There was no harm in trying—"You must make a Tryal." He was persuaded, from the commencement of his ministry, that "never any Soul miscarried, that made such Applications," and, although God is not bound to those who seek Him, " 'Tis many ways Advantageous, for an Vnregenerate Man, to Do as much as he can." In all probability God intends to help him, "so that he shall do more than he can." In the ecstasy of freedom—driven by the need of keeping the faith alive under a royal charter—Mather could cry at last, "Try whether you can't give that Consent; if you can, 'tis done!" By a long road, through a thicket of scholastic distinctions and metaphysical dispute, the leaders of New England came to this highly pragmatical—and socially advantageous—injunction.

Some philosophers—although not all—have remarked that the human mind does not operate in a vacuum. Theologians who devised the idea of preparation had been concerned not to enlarge the ability of unregenerate men, but to vindicate a divine order; a century later clerics still felt this concern: there is "an order in which he brings them to a participation," said Willard. But a new accent was developing, as in the language Cotton Mather freely used by 1702: because we are capable of "treaties, of proposals, of overtures," God exhorts us and employs arguments; He deals with us "as Rational Creatures." The phrase was even older than the usage of Preston and Ames, but they had put it in the center of the federal theology; when we hear Cotton Mather insisting upon it, although he has changed no syllable in the assertion, we perceive that the history of the notion of preparation has carried us from the medieval universe of Protestant scholasticism to the very threshold of the Age of Reason.

CHAPTER V

HYPOCRISY

T HE
brave spirits at the English Cambridge in August
1629 pledged themselves to migrate with the charter, their families, and all
their worldly goods, "having weighed the greatness of the worke in regard of the consequence, God's glory and the churches good." As John
Cotton later explained, since Christ had instituted no ordinance in vain,
we dare not "so farre be wanting to the grace of Christ, and to the necessity of our own soules, as to sitt downe some where else, under the shad-
owe of some ordinances, when by two months travayle we might come to
enioy the liberty of all." To fall short in any particular of instituting every
ecclesiastical command would be a deficiency of sincerity and a cause for
self-distrust.

The essence of the Congregational idea was the autonomous church,
limited to visible saints and founded on a covenant of their profession, which
meant deliberate exclusion of the townsfolk who submitted to (and paid
for) the rule of the righteous. Presbyterians not only denounced the church
covenant as an artificial notion foisted on the Bible, but predicted civil war
for any society that dared "unchurch" the majority. In reply Congregationalists first offered proof that the covenant was both Scriptural and rational, and then demonstrated at length that it was a feasible method of
government.

As soon as debate was joined, Presbyterians and Continental Calvinists
grew alarmed at what appeared the most sinister tendency in the Congregational plan—"perfectionism." By delimiting churches to visible saints, it
pretended to such excellence as the world had not witnessed since Christ
culled the Apostles out of it. Sober theologians knew how grievously Christendom had suffered from visionaries who usurped His powers of discrimination, who then tried to purge the body and to inaugurate the communion
of saints: the result had generally been such massacres of the ungodly as
the Anabaptists perpetrated at Münster. All Christendom clung to the
teaching of Augustine that in this world the congregation of saints is scattered among reprobates. Calvinists treated regeneration as a sensible experience, but would not allow any man, even the most skilled divine, to
say to another, "You are infallibly elected." They did not believe that on
this earth—where hypocrisy is rife and where for every true convert there
are a hundred deceivers—the fact of predestination could serve as a basis

for polity. With the New England success, Presbyterians, who had already accused Congregationalists of Anabaptism, became exceedingly apprehensive and so insisted all the more that the colonists were deluded perfectionists.

However, virtually all Protestants agreed that the regenerate could become, despite the remaining stains of sin, capable of obeying the law not out of fear but out of positive freedom. Said the *Confession*, "Whenever God converts a sinner, and translates him into the state of grace, he freeth him from his natural bondage under sin, and by his grace alone inables him freely to will and to do that which is spiritually good." Although a man during preparation is technically "passive," once he has progressed to vocation, he may do wonders: "A Christians real Work begins when he is Converted," said Willard; faith is not an idle habit: "It is a principle of spiritual life which must have some act & exercise & that is doing the will of God"—whether in pulpit or countinghouse. Infallible assurance is not essential to this unleashing of activity; a believer may wait long and confront many difficulties, but faith in the least degree is "different in the kind or nature of it . . . from the faith and common grace of temporary believers." Antinomians rushed to the conclusion that the grace of believers could not be distinguished from that of hypocrites, but all Protestantism endorsed the Synod's assertion that saintly virtues are fundamentally different from pretenses. If, then, redeemed believers are not merely liberated (to some extent) from sin, but can know that they are free, what is to prevent them from combining to make pure churches and a holy commonwealth? Would they not thus carry the logic of the Reformation to its ultimate goal by creating a society truly dedicated to the glory of God?

Against this argument, more cautious Calvinists had to object that regenerate freedom was not easily recognized—not because, as Antinomians held, there was no real difference from ordinary ability, but because techniques for examination are fallible. However, the founders were not only Calvinists but federalists, and so believed that ascertainable evidences existed: the convert feels not only inward exultation, but a resolution to engage himself. "Because he is most free and willing to be the Lords . . . therefore he voluntarily binds himself to him." This very willingness, accompanied with power, to take up the church covenant—a disposition which could be tested by elders and the congregation—became presumptive proof of experience, and a workable basis for the order.

William James said that no formalized theology is ever an adequate translation of what goes on in the private man as he "livingly" expresses himself. Puritans would not have understood him: in their plan, a religious heart inevitably translated itself into the formulae of theology; to them the conception of private experience was real, but not of private expression—wherein they differed from modern poets. By the same token, a regenerated will would translate itself immediately into ecclesiastical and political action, upon which self-evident proposition they founded their churches. Their axiom put it: "The Covenant of Grace is cloathed with Church-Covenant in a Political visible Church-way." Their churches were born from liberated powers of consent and were not founded upon the fiat of governors, still less upon the custom of the country. To swear to the obligation of membership "is an evidence that God hath chosen us, entered into covenant with us & taken us to be his"; for according to federal logic, "all real hearty acts in us of chusing & engaging our selves to God . . . flow from the instinct of Gods spirit toward us & from that impression which like acts of his hath made upon us." Congregationalism was not Anabaptism, but a reasonable and sober program which could safely be put into practice as long as a civil authority guarded the churches' right to exclude the incompetent. It would not produce chaos, because those who called themselves saints would bind themselves, through the church covenant, to sobriety.

However, the objection of Presbyterians, having behind it the weight of centuries, had to be treated with respect. Being good Protestants, the founders knew that full assurance and perfect holiness are never obtained; sanctification is always imperfect, and the elect do not entirely free themselves on this side of the grave from the flesh. No man, even though a member of the church covenant, is above temptation.

Were not New Englanders then in an untenable position when they founded churches upon profession? Were they not sophistically disguising their perfectionism? Were not Antinomians more consistent in deciding that if the institutions were pure, members need not worry about their own impurities? With what face could the Synod say, "A man may truely feare God (therefore truely converted) and yet walke in darknesse, without cleare evidence or full assurance"? The colonial clergy were sifting out saints from sinners while insisting that saints could not even recognize themselves. How could they tell one from another if the true believer walked in a darkness more impenetrable than sin itself?

The founders might have ridden roughshod over this objection by asserting that their techniques were infallible—but that would indeed have been perfectionism. They always predicted that even the closest examination would not distinguish all the elect. The federal theology never denied, it positively insisted that man is a creature without rights or certainties, with whom God deals as He pleases; but thereupon it whispered that God has been pleased to deal through specified terms. Conversion works by degrees, from preparation through calling, faith, justification, adoption, sanctification, up to, at the end of the long process, assurance. The last may for some time be wanting to those who have true grace in their hearts; possibly they may never come to it. The spiritual life, said Hooker, is "partly collied and bemired with corruptions," and to go no further than outward judgments, saints "are the most forlorn, despicable Persons upon the face of the Earth." God may especially withhold assurance from them lest they should become proud "and pranke up themselves in regard of their priviledges, and be carried with contempt of the weakness of their fellow brethren." Because, as Hooker most profoundly understood, the stages of conversion are many and difficult, we seldom know with absolute certitude who are members of the invisible church, "for the truth of grace is invisible to man."

The first generation never forgot this clear-sighted theology, and never claimed that gracious power would in every case automatically flow into ecclesiastical behavior. Because a man might be converted without ever coming to assurance, much less to a demonstration, they never expected the circle of the church to coincide precisely with the Covenant of Grace. Eternal life is promised to the elect, but church membership only to those who exhibit signs of election. When Presbyterians accused Congregationalists of trying to track down the untraceable, of building upon uncertainties, they replied that their churches were founded upon firm manifestations of ability. "Christ believed on, is the Foundation, or Rock of the Catholick invisible Church: But Christ believed on and confessed, is the Rock whereupon a particular visible Church is built." A man of faith, lacking knowledge, may have fellowship with God, but he must have both in order to enjoy church fellowship. These societies were constructed on open covenants, openly arrived at.

That there were hazards in administration, the founders admitted; that government requires skill and tact, they boasted; but an occasional discrepancy—the exclusion of an authentic saint unable to profess—did not invalidate the system. And by the same logic, the inclusion of some who mistook natural conviction for a work of grace, who in false strength swore to the covenant and later proved unable to live by it, did not destroy the covenanted society. As the metaphysical distinction between the two aspects, internal and external, of the Covenant of Grace was widened, the founders showed themselves sober realists, not distracted idealists. Therefore they were prepared to rest much of their case upon a frank admission that many of their visible saints were hypocrites, and that hypocrisy had a positive function in their system.

At the heart of it, this ecclesiastical theory was an effort to reconcile a basic conflict: it would carry out the Reformation by a voluntary purification of the churches, but at the same time take account of sad experience and exact nothing beyond human possibilities. The civil arm guarded the fold, but no will was coerced. Among non-members there might be precious souls to whom the New England Way was ready to extend the hand of fellowship "in case they shall desire it," but they had to express the desire. Surely this was not too much to demand? "Seeing such are not liable and subject to the Churches censure, it is not meet they should partake of the Churches priviledges, therefore we have hitherto forborn it until further light shall appeare." By the present light, a man who convincingly yielded himself to the censure was capable of the privileges. Ergo, only those should be lawfully received who would before the Lord and His

people "professe their repentance, and faith in Christ, and subjection to
him in his ordinances: and do not scandalize their profession, with an un-
christian conversation." Such was the eminently practical utopia which
signers of the Cambridge Agreement undertook to set up in America—
in their forewarned innocence.

To expound the relation of inward to outward covenant, the Congregational theorist resorted, as with every vexing question, to the logic of
Petrus Ramus. He found a satisfactory solution to any problem as soon as
he could define the nature of a relationship; once he could show that the
terms were in disagreement with each other, he had demonstrated a law
of God no less than when he proved them in agreement. Once all forms
of connection are specified and named and then ranged in schematic series,
man has a logical transcript of the wisdom of God in so far as that is manifested in creation. An effect, for example, is tied to its cause by the rule
of "consent," but black stands toward white by the equally satisfactory
principle of "opposition." What applies to one set of terms does not have
to preside over another. Disjunction is as much a law of God as harmony,
and because men come upon a contradiction in their thinking, or in the
working of their polity, they are not to surrender to "epicurean" skepticism, but to study the nature of the discrepancy, and give it the proper
habitation and name. When experience shows a deviation from doctrine,
the latter is not to be discarded; instead, the exact form of the deviation
should be established, and then fitted to that particular concept of relationship which, in the hierarchical structure, describes it.

So with the problem of the inward and outward covenant. At first sight,
logic would assume that men who subscribed the first would for that reason take up the second. The latter is, as Hooker put it, "within the verge
and contained within the compasse" of the former. Nevertheless, what
gradually appeared was that the two allegiances were not related as cause
and effect, but as discreet "modes." Which meant that each could be separately described without the one necessarily and always presupposing
the other.

Not that the two lost all connection. The inner might still serve as cause
for the outer effect, but when, for the purposes of logical analysis, the two
became "distributions" of the same thing "into divers Adjuncts of the same
Members of the same Church," then each acquired a life of its own, each
could be discussed as though not attached to the same member, as though
each was the adjunct of a member entirely separate from the other. Two
distinguishable "arguments" which in some cases are united by the rule
of agreement may, in other instances, be connected, just as indissolubly, by
the rule of "partial dissent." God may interrupt any sequence, or put a
different cast upon it, having in view some larger purpose. By confronting
dislocations in his formulated scheme, man is forced to search out higher
consistencies; and to discover, under the stress of American experience, that
inner and outer were joined together under more headings than he had at

first supposed would be to strengthen rather than weaken Congregational dialectic.

Therefore when Hooker said the church was contained within the Covenant of Grace, he acknowledged that "in Propriety of speech" they were not identical. A man might be gracious, and yet be cast among Mohammedans or into a desert where he could not gather with others to form a church, yet he would be saved. A higher concern would take precedence over the ordinary: God would wish to try the believer by an extraordinary ordeal, or to raise up a martyr—reason enough for abrogating the rule of agreement and substituting that of partial dissent.

But if, when the two covenants thus partially dissented, men could be received into the internal without enacting the external, did it not follow that others might come into the external without a previous reception into the internal? Could one achieve terms satisfactory to the church who had never been delivered from sin? If the external order has its own rules, would not conformity be enough for external sanctification? Since the one can exist without the other, would not hypocrites be satisfactory members of an externally covenanted church?

Congregational theorists had fully anticipated these questions. William Ames early explained that when men gather to hear the Word, they are illuminated by the offer of the Covenant of Grace; only the elect receive the offer, but the illumination "is sometime, and in a certaine manner granted to those that are not elected." The church must accept them, for Christ has ordered it to receive all who profess Him; all such, "so long as they remained in that society are members of that Church as also of the Catholick Church as touching the outward state, not touching the inward or essential state." The settlers conned this lesson. Davenport said that the blessings of the Covenant of Grace "are limited to the persons of true Believers in the sight of God," but the blessings of the church "are given to a society of true Believers, in the account of the Church." Since the two are separable, said Hooker, "The wicked are in Covenant with the Lord outwardly, but not inwardly." Even when the church is vigilant, there are bound to be more outward than inward saints: "This outward is more large, the inward is more sure; the outward is larger, and may issue from false grounds." Hooker prefaced *The Survey of the Summe of Church-Discipline* with a warning: "A man may be in the Covenant of grace, and share in the benefit thereof, who is not in a Church state; and a man may be in a Church state, who is not really in the Covenant of grace."

Hooker was the "most melting," in Cotton Mather's phrase, of all the founders, and, as we have seen, most positive about the validity of preparation. He recognized how secret was the operation of the Holy Spirit, but would also exclaim: "Give me a Christian that God doth please to worke upon in this extraordinary manner, and to breake his heart soundly." Such a one could learn to walk with care, whereas a doubting and distressed spirit—for whom Hooker was so solicitous—"doth but little good in his place, and hath little comfort coming to him." He found it "to my blinde judgement incredible, that the soule of a man in faith shall fall upon the promise, and leave it selfe there with contentednesse"; yet he knew that this happened. He, more than any other, labored not to confuse an influx of the Holy Ghost with "federal holiness" ("Therefore covenant grace is one, and saving grace is another"), yet he more than any other refused to arrogate to himself that judgment which must be left to God:

> Now federall grace is such as all false hypocrites have, federall grace they have enough to shew, and may receive the seals . . . We cannot say this man is one sealed for salvation, and here is one sealed for perdition; no man can say this child or this man shall be damned: I cannot say, this or that man is a reprobate, if all the Churche on earth were together; there are many that shall be damned, yet I cannot say this man or that shall be damned.

Hooker so impressed this warning upon the Connecticut Valley that it blossomed in the teaching of Solomon Stoddard, and later bore strange fruit in the mind of Edwards; meanwhile, the churches were in substantial agreement. The Covenant of Grace was twofold even while single. Those were externally within it "who expressing their repentance, with their profession of the truth, ingage themselves to walk in the waies of God, and in the truth of his worship, though they have not for the present that sound work of Faith in their hearts, and may be shall never have it wrought by Gods spirit in them." Shepard put it that all are not Israel who are of Israel, and frankly announced, "It is clearer than day that many who are inwardly, or in respect of inward covenant, the children of the devil, are outwardly, or in respect of outward covenant, the children of God." Willard explained that while the Covenant of Grace is indivisible, it admits of a "double consideration," and in its outer aspect "extends, or bears a relation, not only to such as are true Beleevers, but others also, viz., Unto all those that are in the Visible Church . . . professing Obedience to Gospel-Order and Ordinances." Calvinists came to New England in order to establish churches limited to the elect; at the same time they publicly admitted, "It is not real, but visible faith, not the inward being, but the outward profession of faith . . . that constitutes a visible church."

Ramists held that logic was derived from experience by "invention." Therefore, logic had to remain faithful to reality: it could not create fanciful constructions, but only make replicas of that pattern of ideas embodied in creation. If God so desired, He could call His saints by an audible voice, or by investing them with a halo visible to the naked eye. Instead, He had chosen to deal with them as with rational creatures, to offer persuasions and inducements. Were He to distinguish the elect by physical stigmata, they would flow into the church as readily as water runs down hill. By such means, God might insure the purity of the church, but only by turning saints into automata. Eschewing such compulsions, He has provided that the Word should come to men's ears externally and sensibly, "containing letters and syllables." Since fallen man remains incapable of responding unless grace accompanies the syllables, in every evangelical appeal there is a double striving, or rather, on the part of the listener, a double apprehension. "Gods Spirit doth not alwayes accompanie the Preaching of the word by its efficacious workings; God many times strives onely by his word, and by the common workings of his Spirit, by instruction, by conviction, by correction." The word is two words: the internal, "which secretly speaks to the heart," and the external, which "only speaks to the ear."

By choosing the method of rational address, God runs the hazard of employing devices which permit certain of the reprobate to imitate the true response. By summoning the elect, not with a voice from heaven, but by letters and syllables, He allows the unregenerate to overhear the call, and to act as though it were meant for them. So, said Cotton, "To distinguish in men between that Sanctification which floweth from the Law, and that which is of the Gospel, is a matter so narrow, that the Angels of Heaven have much adoe to discern who differ"—wherefore a mere parson can hardly "cut the scantling in it." A clergy obliged to admit only those veritably sanctified would face the impossible. But again God adapts His method to humanity. Covenants require men to accept an offer, and therefore willingness to accept may be adjudged a criterion of inward consent. The consequence is ineluctable: willingness to take up the ecclesiastical obligation establishes qualification for membership, and those who so engage "become the People of God, by an outward Denomination," no matter how they may be listed in the secret book of judgment.

In each "consideration" the pattern of freedom is respected: as an inward summons without response does not constitute the invisible church, "so neither doth an externall calling constitute a visible Church, without an externall answer of that call." The church inspects only what it can inspect. We do not inquire into the invisible church, said Hooker, because that body is "not to be seen by sense." And yet it is reasonable that the visible should be founded upon that which cannot be seen: "The Politicall body or Church visible results out of that relation, which is betwixt the professours of the faith, when by voluntary consent they yield outward subjection to that government of Christ, which in his word he hath prescribed." If this seemed difficult to the contemporaneous mind, as it may to ours, George Phillips made it crystal clear to the former by drawing on the terminology of physics: in so far as members are related to Christ internally, they cannot be the "form" of a church; "the manifestation of these maketh them to be fit matter for a Church, which yet cannot be a church without the form added to the matter, and that is a covenant."

Thus armed by logic and physics, the founders set up purified churches which admitted impure persons. Since the elect are mingled with the wicked world, men can judge only by evidences, wherefore Christ "hath bestowed these offices as a royal gift upon the visible Church." As an instrument for the dispensation of grace, the church must be kept as pure as possible, but because it can determine only by sense, it is not to aim at unearthly perfection. Critics did not understand the logical distinction of the twofold holiness, of the intimate but discrete connection between the internal and the "foederall." The saints of New England were holy men, but their inward condition was suspect even to themselves. They were absolutely certain only of their federal status, and upon that—and that alone— they erected a city upon Beacon Hill.

The founders were so intent upon the success of their enterprise that they were ready to take the cash and pray for the credit. The success or failure of their regime became the criterion of their reasoning. In England, they had been so passionately committed to the struggle that they never took thought for what their problem might become in the face of triumph. Inevitably they believed that all would be well once abuses were abolished. But success in New England altered cases. In America they made the will of God prevail; there were no more crusades, and the only problem was how to stabilize victory. Having mastered their world, Puritans had to live in it. The subtle shift in fast-day proclamations from sensible judgments to the ravages of sin is a measure of the process by which Joshuas and Aarons were transformed into magistrates and parsons. The latter found themselves, greatly to their surprise, driven to advertising their church polity less as a perfect exemplification of the New Testament model than as an instrument by which men might observe the laws of God and of man.

The first symptom of accommodation was an effort to lower the standards for church membership. Leaders soon were acknowledging that in the flush of the first days they employed "unscriptural severities," and by 1640 or shortly thereafter, they were proclaiming that they did not exact impossible measures. Cotton professed a preference for admitting ninety-nine hypocrites to excluding one humble soul: "It is one thing to be satisfied in judgment of Charitie; another, in truth of sinceritie." Davenport, the most severe, would give those "weake in Faith" the benefit of every doubt; Shepard confessed that since by rule we never know the reality of a profession, "so long as the rule be attended, we leave every one to the wisdom of Christ." In the *Survey* Hooker defined the qualifications for federal holiness with a latitude unthinkable twenty years before: if a man professes faith, does not live openly in sin, has some knowledge and can give a reason for his hope, "These be grounds of probabilities, by which Charity poised according to rule may and ought to conceive, there be some beginnings of spirituall good." The records do not always tell how rapidly particular churches lowered the bars, but by the end of the century the teaching had become almost everywhere that words and deeds were enough, "to the Judgement of rational Charity," to determine the marks of federal holiness.

A further and even more striking development appears in the writings of the 1640's: a manifest willingness, which increased after the Antinomian affair, to take federal holiness at face value, and to accept it as sufficient for the purposes of earthly society. Objections have been made, said Shepard, on the ground that federal saints "have no saving grace many times . . . and many of them degenerate and prove corrupt and wicked." To which he answered, "Suppose all these, yet God may take them into outward covenant (which is sufficient to make them the church seed, or members of the church) although he doth not receive them into inward covenant." After all, the Lord is in some sense engaged to them; promises belong to those of the church—"among whom usually and ordinarily he works this great work, leaving him to his own freeness of secret mercy, to work thus on whome he will, and when he will"—so that the chances of their eventually becoming actual as well as official saints were great. We should not despise or cast off an ordinance because there may be "many weaknesses" in it. Of course, Shepard, having publicly fought the Antinomians, could well afford to amplify the external covenant; when we find Cotton also actively engaged in doing so, we may suspect that he was trying to cleanse himself of the taint of suspicion. Men are indeed carnal, "but what is all this to prove that such as are carnel by naturall generation, cannot be holy by the grace of the Covenant? or that it may not please God to admit them to the outward dispensation of his Covenant, whose inward spiritual estate hee is not pleased with?" Even though all they have is "an historical and temporary faith," they can do the duties of the church. Though a congregation be full of offenders, it is still beautiful in the sight of God—provided it be in covenant. Once received, "at least in outward profession, of the fundamentals of sound doctrine and pure worship," it is a true church and will remain true, "though they or their children may afterwards degenerate, and go on whoring from God in doctrine and worship." Surely these assertions ought to be enough to exonerate New England (and incidentally John Cotton) from the charge of Antinomian perfectionism.

Unfortunately, they were not. The leaders might widen the doors and disavow all aspirations beyond federal holiness: nevertheless they restricted the membership. They would not open the gates to all inhabitants, and they would still require that candidates show more than a halting familiarity with the catechism. These demands remained, despite their glosses, severe enough to exclude the majority even in the dedicated communities of Massachusetts and Connecticut.

And then in the England of the Civil Wars three developments took place which left the New England theorists bewildered and dazed. First of all, old England swarmed with visionaries and perfectionists: Anabaptists, Muggletonians, Antinomians, Quakers, and—worst of all—Levellers. All these groups began as "Independents"—that is, with the Congregational principle of a holy church membership. Yet, instead of heeding the precautionary intricacies of the American order whereby the principle was

defended even while fallibility was recognized, every one of these compa
nies let the conviction of a peculiar purity run away with it, until each
ended by arrogating unto itself all virtue and truth. This travesty of Congregationalism was bad enough, and should have called for repressive measures from the civil authority. Instead, New Englanders' own brethren
used their authority to extend toleration to these same rampaging Independents. Instead of standing firm upon restricted churches that were yet
skeptical about bringing a heaven on earth, Cromwell allowed these mani-
acs to call themselves the city of God. Whereupon, a third result appeared:
the Presbyterians—who were at one with the colonists in theological orthodoxy and political philosophy—blamed the whole shambles upon Congregationalism, and traced the source of all anarchy to New England!

New Englanders could not but abhor the sects, who seemed to them
perverters of the divine polity. They could not but be shocked at the
political treason of the Independents, as they could not but be grieved by
the charges of the Presbyterians. The world had gone mad, and left
them stranded. Only one thing could they do: in order to repudiate the
sectaries, maintain intolerance, and refute Presbyterians, they had no
choice but to make positive capital out of the fact that they suffered and
utilized a fair number of hypocrites. They had to say that while indeed
they had hoped to confine the outward to the inward covenant, they had
never expected—or really never wanted—to succeed so marvelously but
what their churches would still be imperfect and therefore subject to regulation. They were obliged to widen still more the disjunction of the two
covenants.

The great Scottish Presbyterian, Samuel Rutherford, sneered at them in
the name of all the Calvinist theologians—Beza, Peter Martyr, Piscator,
Pareus, Zanchius—each of whom held that every citizen except those specifically excommunicated should be within the church, so that "our brethren cannot build their new Churches, but be loosing the foundation stones
layed by these worthy builders." Since Congregationalists confess that they
cannot decipher the inward faith, they too "admit without sinne, multitudes,
who eat and drink their own damnation." Why then should they not
receive all the damned? Why select only a few? Had New England
claimed that its churches were one with grace, they would have been
foolish but at least consistent; by admitting that they judged only according to the rules of charity, they convicted themselves of absurdity. Even
Christ admitted Judas, whom He knew was no saint; what possible sense
could there be in setting up qualifications which any hypocrite could meet?
"By our brethrens way, workers of iniquity, and those that are never
known nor chosen of God, but are exactly gilded hypocrites . . . are visible Saints, not because they are so, but because they are falsely esteemed
by men to be such." The New England Way put a premium upon hypocrisy; it was "not a whit a cleaner visible Church then our way." Another

Presbyterian leader, Samuel Hudson, seized upon the admission that men must judge by appearances and pulled New England's logic apart; obviously whatever coherence there once was in the effort to administer the Lord's Supper exclusively to the godly had collapsed, and "I fear the Elders in New-England do not in their consciences judge so of all their members." If the colonial clergy have come to the point of unanimously proclaiming that visible instead of true faith is their requirement, asked still another Presbyterian, Daniel Cawdry, then "what degree of visible Saintship is required to make men members of a visible Church?" He was amused to note that the standard had already been lowered—"if they be grown tenderer since, it is well"—but once started along this road, should they not better hasten to the end of it, and resolve "for charity to proceed by negation, rather than affirmation?" This would mean admitting everybody except those expelled for censurable offenses.

There is no greater irony in the history of Protestantism than the defense which these Americans put up. Fifteen years after the founding of the city on a hill, the clergy were expending their dialectical skill in proving that it was riddled with imperfections. The New Englanders' plan, said Davenport, was to go as far as they could, "with due moderation and gentleness, to try them, who offer themselves to fellowship, whether they be Believers, or not; refusing known Hypocrites; though when they have done all they can, close Hypocrites will creep in." Upon John Cotton fell the chief responsibility for presenting the official thesis. He had to twist the case of Judas into a Congregational reading: Christ "made as good choyce as choyce could be made, and yet hee would have us see, what we may not unjustly expect in the like case." Invoking again the logic of Ramus, Cotton said that to speak of members as regenerate is to speak of what they "ought to be *de jure* . . . rather then what they are, or are want to be *de facto*." Anyway, at the end of it, "hypocrites in outward profession and appearance, go for faithful and godly." Samuel Willard again codified a century of experience: profession "may be Hypocritical, the Experience of discerning Men, hath sufficiently proved."

The experience of discernment! The professions of hypocrites may be insincere, but what they profess remains true. Though they have no real sanctification, they have "gifts" which cannot be entirely "meer counterfeit pretences." The motive for this expansion of New England thought is not far to seek. When Sir Richard Saltonstall, having returned to England and moved with the Independents into toleration, wrote to Cotton that for New England to force non-members to attend ordinances was to make them hypocritical, Cotton came back with: "Hypocrites give God part of his due, the outward man, but the prophane person giveth God neither outward nor inward man." As long as hypocrites keep up their hypocrisy, they are "serviceable and useful in their callings"—which is an immense help to the national covenant. Thus they "become very serviceable sometimes in the Commonwealth, sometimes in the Church." A man's evident lack of regeneration remains a just cause for refusing him admission to the church, but after he is in, even if the lack becomes equally evident, it "is not a just cause of casting him out of the Church, after he be received." While he is in, he may not be saved, but he can be put to work.

In the first drafts of Congregational doctrine there is a buoyant optimism, an assurance that saints could be gathered into holy fellowship, that the purity of the New Testament could be realized in New England villages. But a decade after the fathers had migrated, they were outdoing Presbyterians in what sounds like cynicism. Rather than admit that they were wrong—rather than go back to Presbyterianism or open the churches to the mass of inhabitants—they sicklied over the enterprise with the pale cast of metaphysics and special pleading, until it lost all other name for action than maintaining the forms.

Yet there are, of course, qualifications. In the first place, while generously admitting the existence of hypocrisy, the leaders were still pressing upon auditors the necessity for sincerity, and making the life of hypocrites as uncomfortable as possible. "It is not enough to bee Churchmembers, or visible Saints," said Charles Chauncy, "but wee must be sanctified in truth and reallity." Secondly, their defense of hypocrisy was a determined effort of the clergy to guard, even unto formality, the vital principle of consent, for hypocrites did give at least the semblance of an act of will and were in the churches not by compulsion but by choice. And thirdly, the clergy felt it all to their credit that they did not aim at the impossible, and that they could profit from American experience to lower their sights. The Antinomian notion that men in the Covenant could give over all doubts showed a blindness, according to the Synod, to the immensely human fact that the best of men will always be "exercised with sweete doubtings and questions." The difficult lesson of life is to learn how to do the will of God without expecting too much. The true temple of the Holy Ghost is hidden and invisible; if we preach that churches or political parties should be what none ever shall be—not even in America— will not men abandon society entirely "to seek Christ (where he is found in true spirituall life) in deserts and secret chambers?" By accepting the hazard of hypocrisy, by refusing to pretend that it did not flourish, the Puritans were in effect accepting the responsibilities of living in society— even though they found these more complicated and more frightening than they had anticipated.

Thus the mind of New England became committed to a proposition of which it never thereafter lost sight: the land is full of hypocrites, but they have their uses. "This," said Shepard, "serves to clear us in this country from a foul aspersion that is cast out of the mouths of pulpits upon us, that we hold the churches of Christ to have no hypocrites in them." If to Europeans this seemed such a condoning of hypocrisy as would belie the American profession of unique virtue, in America the recognition marked a stage of self-knowledge. It was not a confession of failure, but a discovery of uses to which an unforeseen development could be put. The city on the hill quickly began to prove one in which hypocrisy itself could be employed for the benefit of society.

CHAPTER VI

Even
in the first decades of practicing their polity rather
than theorizing about it, New Englanders discovered that, divinely commissioned though it was, it could not be kept frozen. Still, they could assuage misgivings by the reflection that they were not altering any particulars, but with the help of logic were drawing out of the Testaments "further light." As the external covenants of the nation and church developed a greater degree of "partial dissent" from the Covenant of Grace than they had foreseen, they found themselves free to treat each as a separate domain with laws of its own. Thus preparation could sustain the nation and mere profession the ecclesiastical contract.

Very shortly the theorists had impressed upon them a further respect in which, externality being described externally, both hypocrisy and profession radically dissented from the Covenant of Grace: they required continuity. Faith is an "eternal" union, but the believer carries his portion of it out of this world; a supply of saints is replenished by a series of discrete conversions, no one of which has an organic connection with its predecessors. But churches and nations do not die, or must not be allowed to; obligations accepted by one generation must be passed on to the next. Children must be inserted like replacements in a regiment, the cadre must be kept up to strength. Outward covenants remain viable as long as their particular terms are met.

In England, Hooker had said, "If that a people doe outwardly worship God, and sincerely mend things that be amisse, they may continue"; even Sodom and Gomorrah, had they only "legally" repented, would have stood. Cotton assured the departing fleet that security would cease only when ordinances failed. Hooker and Cotton were not excusing formality but heartening devout and sincere pilgrims: "If God plant his Ordinances among you, feare not, he will maintaine them." The least of doubts was that there might be no supply of converts down the generations, not because the ordinances would raise them up, but because the Almighty, according to His covenant, would pour forth the blessing where the external conditions were maintained. "It stands in reference to the covenant with God, and also the engagement of God to entertaine such as are rightly disposed and fitted for a covenant-holinesse." Starting with a superabundant stock of inherent godliness, New England could organize its churches on a federal principle, confident that "the soul that engaged it self, he set himself for God to attend upon him, and his posterity to do so."

Had they not been supremely assured that among their successors the preponderance of converts would never shrink below the danger point, the founders would not have undertaken the venture. They rested this expectation upon two securities, their doctrine of the sacraments and the federalist exegesis upon Genesis 17.

In sacramental theory Congregationalists modestly claimed that they alone of all Protestantism exorcised the last vestiges of Catholic "superstition." They alone allowed to these observances no slightest inherent efficacy. Federal logic enabled them most roundly to define the sacraments not as "means" but only as "seals of the covenant," stamps of approval placed upon a transaction previously consummated. The Lord's Supper was given to none but those who had made a profession; baptism was bestowed, not on all children, but exclusively upon those whose parents had been professing Christians.

Calvin had said that the most diabolical stratagem of Popery was its "representing the sacraments as the cause of justification," for thus they envelop the minds of men, "naturally too much inclined to the earth, in gross superstition, leading them to rest in the exhibition of a corporeal object rather than in God himself." New England stood firm—very firm —upon his teaching, and so put into practice, as he himself never quite did, his assertion that since the two rites have no "perpetual inherent virtue, efficacious of itself to the advancement or confirmation of faith," they can profit only those whose hearts are "already instructed." Because God is not confined to corporeal mechanism, participation in seals must come to men only *after* regeneration; otherwise, those who venture to receive them succeed only "in eating and drinking damnation unto themselves."

If it were true—as all Protestants declared—"that except a man be in Christ, he must not, hee ought not to apply to himself any of these spiritual priviledges that wee have by him," then Congregationalists had the courage to draw the conclusion which scandalized all other Protestants. Why encourage unregenerates to eat and drink destruction? Presbyterians vehemently objected that the church cannot tell who in this life already has faith; Ames and Preston announced that it is visibly manifested in a readiness to take the covenant. There must be, as Preston put it, a double act, "one on our part, another on Christs part," wherefore there must be something in our hearts and deeds to show that we have done our share. "Now if thou finde in thyself these two things . . . then certainly thou art in Christ; and if it be so, all the priviledges belong to thee; if not, thou hast nothing to do with this Holy Sacrament."

John Preston, Master of Emmanuel College, was a consummate politician who ventured to sup with a short spoon, if not with the Devil, then with the next devil to him, the Duke of Buckingham. Even as his editors, after his death in 1628, were preparing his manuscripts for publication, the political hope was waning in England. If any Puritan party should yet win the state, it would clearly be the Presbyterians, who had every intention, once in power, of baptizing everybody and forcing all except the openly scandalous to take the Supper. But true reformation, Preston had predicted, would come only when polity conformed to theology, and ordinances were not expected to serve as instruments for working upon a multitude. "Consider what the Gospell is, and the Covenant, and you shall know what this is, for it is but a Seale." To make his point, Preston hit upon a metaphor that was to be worked to death in America.

As among men, when a man conveyes either land or money, to another man, they use to confirme the bargain with seales or with some signe or memorial, that when they forget the bargain, or deny it, or goe about to breake it, it may be said to them, this is your hand and seale, the thing is done, you have past it, it cannot be recalled.

He who has put his hand to the bargain of grace seals his consent by taking the Communion, which thereafter is a witness against his defalcations. By thus eschewing the efficacy of the sermon, the sacraments acquired a new—curiously enough, a more compelling—power over the saints, "Presenting that to the eye, which the Gospel presents to the eare." The Supper was no longer a miracle, but still more marvelously had become a platform of "security" whereon God and His creature could meet, knowing what to expect from each other. Upon both was the covenant binding; hence this seal "that gives Title to the thing, that conveyes the thing to us, that binds the owner perpetually to the performance of the thing."

Administering the Lord's Supper according to this philosophy was eminently feasible: "Those only ought to be admitted to partake of the Lords Supper, who doe hold forth Repentance and Faith, with an ability to examine themselves and discern the Lords body." Being founded "not for Regeneration, but for nourishment and confirmation," it could nourish those alone who possessed the spiritual stomach. Only adult believers might approach the table without profanation, and lest the others heap curses upon themselves (and the land), churches should keep them off and the civil arm restrain them.

At first sight, the practice of baptism seemed entirely similar. When Parson Eliot converted an Indian, he would baptize him, then let him confess once more, then admit him to the Supper. An adult unbeliever had the steps to the temple cut out for him: he would undergo preparation, humiliation, exultation, and sanctification; when he had run that gamut and professed his faith, when the minister was satisfied of his sincerity, he would be baptized; he would then swear to the covenant of the church, be given the right hand of fellowship, and finally awarded the accolade, admission to the Communion.

The next question—which had arisen in the earliest drafts of the polity

—was whether baptism should, like the Supper, be reserved for adult professors. Was this not the inescapable consequence of federal thinking? There were several in England who felt that it was, who then decried infant baptism, and acquired the dreaded name of Anabaptists. Often they proved to be Antinomians, or worse; always they were enthusiasts and perfectionists. The founders had no intention that Congregational doctrine should become so perverted, and, convinced that Christ suffered little children to come unto Him, were determined to practice infant baptism. But if they also held that a sacrament does no more than confirm a faith already attained, if they asserted that he who receives it without having first experienced regeneration confirms not faith but his own damnation, how could they baptize an infant whose mewling and puking in his mother's arms were the sole expression he could give of his living hope?

They were certain that Christ commanded them to baptize the child, but unfortunately the New Testament was not too explicit, and interpretation required the help of logic. "This proving of things by Consequence," Cotton Mather was to sigh, "methinks, is not so Satisfactory." Mere logic, trying to extract the warrant out of Scripture, encountered the gravest obstacles, as Presbyterians were to learn when in the 1640's they confronted a monstrous outbreak of Anabaptism, but federalist theologians had what seemed a tremendous advantage: they had something upon which logic could hang. The covenant made a rational framework within which the baptism of infants became the inescapable conclusion of an invincible syllogism.

If any chapter of the inspired text might be said to be more important than the others, in federalist eyes Genesis 17 was the one, for there God explicitly promised Himself not merely to Abraham but to the "seed," to Isaac and Jacob and Joseph: "And I will establish my covenant between me and thee and thy seed after thee in their generations for an everlasting covenant, to be a God unto thee, and to thy seed after thee." Had God picked, here and there, this man or another, He would have recruited the Covenant of Grace, but humanity would have gained nothing more than a naked decree; but in stooping to the capacities of man, which He did by offering grace in the form of a covenant, the federal Jehovah also gave mankind something more predictable: He adopted both the saint and the progeny still unconceived in the saint's loins, taking in the children by extending absolute forgiveness through the line of generation. "Behold, my covenant is with thee, and thou shall be a father of many nations." This was the "pedagogie" of the Old Testament, which the New did not repeal but reaffirm, and the covenant made with Abraham is "in substance" that for which Christ served as mediator, that into which the children of New England were received.

This ingenious—not to say human—doctrine is the essence of the federal system; fully worked out by the English architects, it needed little addition by New England disciples. "The covenant in which the faithful are now

contained," wrote Ames, "is the same with that covenant which was made
with Abraham," and as that "did expressly extend unto Infants," so does
this. Peter Bulkeley argued it thus: "If both these things be true, first that
the old and new Covenant be·in substance the same; and secondly, that
children are within the new, as they were within the old, then there can
be no sufficient reason, to deprive children of the seal of the Covenant
now." Those who deny that the covenant extends unbroken—even through
the long night of Anti-Christ and superstition—from Palestine to Boston
would, said Cotton, "leave no more grace to the children of believers then
of Pagans," and New Englanders were certainly not going to permit that!

However, the New Testament had introduced a slight but reasonable
alteration in the administration, although not in the substance, of the covenant. Abraham had been father not only of a family but of a nation, and
his progeny constituted a "national" church, its boundaries coincident with
a territory; but after Christ, churches must be "Congregational," founded
on covenant and their limits determined not by geography but by profession. This modification of "mode" did not break continuity, but it did
change the form of the sacrament. Since God treated with Abraham not
only as first in the church "but as a Father of many nations, and as a
multitude vertually," He gave him circumcision "for the visible signe and
seal of it." After the Jews were cast out, and "we and our children were
engrafted into their roome and estate," baptism was substituted for the national rite. It seals the same covenant, and so the first remains a "com-
munum persona," pledging, like Abraham, his progeny as well as himself.
"The Covenant now under Christ," ran the finished argument, "is the
same with that before Christ, with Abraham and his posterity in the flesh:
Therefore as Infants were then in the Covenant, and signed with circumcision, so are Infants now in the covenant, are to receive baptisme the signe
thereof." This argument, "drawn from Circumcision to Baptisme," said
Bulkeley, "will stand against all the batteries which are made against it"—
which was the sort of argument the New England mind prized above gold
and rubies.

Even in the seventeenth century there were critics who accused Congregationalism of a species of spiritual snobbery: their children were holier than
others because they chose the right parents. The theorists answered that
this was not true; the children would not receive favor because of their
parentage—for "generation does not convey grace"—but because of the
Covenant of Grace: "God hath engaged himself to doe good unto them,
when they are propagated by vertue of the covenant." Bulkeley explained
the mechanism in detail: the fathers take hold of the Covenant of Grace
but it "takes hold of their seed after them." The original convert must be
an adult, but his children, and their children, can be baptized in infancy,
not because they "are first converted, and so come under the Covenant, but
are first under the Covenant, and so come to be converted." God does not
say to Abraham, "You must bee, or are circumcised, and therefore I will

bee your God," but rather, "I will be a God to thee and thy seed, therefore thou and they shall be circumcised"—and so they, a thousand years or a hundred generations later, are still as Abraham was. And therefore New England children were baptized.

Other Calvinists, notably the Presbyterians, were obliged to baptize indiscriminately because they had no method for discriminating; besides, all children, including those of saints, were conceived in sin. The Congregational notion, the Presbyterians declared, was a cruel deception, pretending to bestow sacraments only upon saints and so putting upon inarticulate children an insupportable burden. There was so much force in the objection that a few Congregationalists, especially Thomas Hooker, were troubled by it: he ingenuously confessed that he longed to baptize all babies he could lay his hands on: "I shall nakedly professe, that if I should have given way to my affection, or followed that which suits my secret desire and inclination, I could willingly have wished, that the scale might have been cast upon the affirmative part, and that such persons (many whereof we hope are godly) might enjoy all such privileges, which might be useful and helpfull to them and theirs." But the New England mind was guided in the first generation not by utility and humanitarianism but by logic: one insurmountable consideration deterred Hooker from his inclination, the dialectic of the covenant. "After all the stones I have turned, and the thoughts that I have spent in this kinde," he could find no way around "the nature and truth of Church-Covenant, in which I must professe freely, I am yet more confirmed, as I have been constrained to take it into more serious consideration." No federalist could baptize children of the unfederated, and Richard Mather proclaimed the solidarity of these colonies on the basis of the baptismal covenant: "We do not believe that Baptisme doth make men Members of the Church, nor that it is to be Administered to them that are without the Church, as the way and meanes to bring them in, but to them that are within the Church, as a seale to confirme the Covenant of God unto them."

The Congregational system embodied, as we have seen, the principle of voluntarism, but it was not what we should call liberal; instead, it required rigid subjection to the logically defined and authoritatively stated good, just, and honest. In its theory of baptism consent and authority seemed perfectly harmonized, and children were taken into the church not as inert lumps but as intelligent beings. At the moment they did not know what they were doing, but someday they would; now they were "capable," later they would become "able." Because they were "fideles" they were also "rationalls," and so could be treated in advance as responsible agents —in their very childhood be held amenable to ecclesiastical censures! Cotton was so keen upon this point that he came as near to sentimentality as a Puritan could come: children of the covenant are capable of gracious acts "sooner then we discern," and even in their cradles, "something they have in their hearts which pleaseth them, though they know not what it is," which they express "in their silent thoughts." What thoughts the children of non-members have Cotton did not inquire, but let himself be persuaded that these particular ones were "professors of ye Faith parentally, as well as personally." Upon others, church discipline would be wasted, but these could be instructed and admonished.

A few years after 1640, the New England Way, to its consternation, found itself accused in England not only of inspiring a rage for perfection but of stimulating a sacramental doctrine that inevitably resulted in an increase of Anabaptism. According to Presbyterian accounts, the Independents said, "No Children but of members confederate in the Church-Covenant with a particular Church," and the Anabaptists said no children at all "because they are not confederate, nor capable of the Covenant of the Gospel"; assuredly, the Presbyterians concluded, "the difference is not great." As long as both insisted that the baptized must be real converts in order to be church members, it made little difference at what age the ceremony was enacted. The colonial clergy advertised that they would not "put the seal to a blank"; it seemed to Rutherford that therefore they must either give up baptizing children or else "with monstrous charity they must believe all baptized Infants are regenerate." It was really a monstrous dilemma, arising out of the infatuated notion that the church can discern between regeneration and reprobation, which was a presumptuous usurpation of the will of God—and everybody in Christendom knew what that delusion signified.

New Englanders answered that they were not Anabaptists, and outdid the Presbyterians in expressing their detestation of the heresy, sublimely assuring themselves that if infant baptism could be made good by deduction from God's Word, then it was securely founded. But were they really so "monstrous" as to presume that they could tell which of the silent infants were saved and which were not? The founders left at least a little leeway; they would say, if pressed, that a baptized child was presumably a saint, but that he could not be publicly recognized until he made a profession. Baptism did not give a right to the Supper: experience must (as it would) intervene. This, Richard Mather explained, was Congregationalism's guard against Anabaptism: children born when their parents are church members are in covenant with God from their birth, but notwithstanding their "Birthright," they must make a personal profession when they come of years, "for without this it cannot so well be discerned, what fitness is in them for the Lords Table." New England's charity was great but not monstrous, and a child of the church could turn out a sinner. "Ordinarily" he would not. The first command was that the church be a communion of saints; it could not, said Cotton, "be thought unreasonable" to require the baptized to make such a statement as "others made in the Primitive times before Baptism." Here was the positive guarantee against degeneracy: as long as children were baptized, a supply of converts would continue; but if the children were severely tested, only those among them truly regenerated (along with a negligible number of hypocrites) would administer those ordinances upon which the life of the community depended.

And then, just when the Presbyterian attack was most threatening, the founders began to realize that their children were not living up to the expectation. Not that they committed flagrant sins, but the grace, amid their faithful callings, was not forthcoming. They wanted to renew their baptismal covenants but they could not: "They could not come up to that experimental account of their own regeneration, which would sufficiently embolden their access to the other sacrament." By 1645 a horrible prospect opened: the churches of New England would be filled with baptized adults, virtuous in the extreme, who stolidly lacked the rudiments of even visible holiness.

Also, holy or not, they went on propagating: should these grandchildren be baptized? In 1643 Richard Mather told a Presbyterian critic that these were not received, for to go one degree beyond the next parents, "we see not but we may go two, and if two, why not . . . 1000?" In 1645 he took that back, bethinking himself, in the face of diminishing churches, that the Covenant of Grace is eternal and so must extend through the generations to all progeny who have not, by sins of commission, annulled it. "I conceive this needs not to hinder their Infants from Baptisme so long as they, I mean the Parents, do neither renounce the Covenant, nor doth the Church see Cause to Cast them out from the same."

But some in New England quickly regarded such logic as a betrayal of the city on a hill, and wrote back to England; Presbyterians exulted at this news of divided counsel. The system pretended to admit none but saints: will the clergy then "excommunicate all persons out of their church that live without scandall, and yet are not convincingly gracious?" But if they retained the children and grandchildren, will they not have to embrace the doctrine of "baptismall regeneration"? And if they cut them off, will they not have to acknowledge that saints do not persevere, "for our brethren tell us, it is not lawfull to put a seale upon a blank"? New England had walked into a trap; could it get out?

In the spring of 1646, a Presbyterian triumph in England seemed assured; the General Court of Massachusetts had to take action, and on May 22 summoned ministers from all the colonies (except, of course, Rhode Island!) to meet in a synod and to settle the problem. It cost the magistrates much to let the world know of internal differences, but they had no choice. Most churches, the General Court complained, baptize only children whose nearest parents, or at least one of them, are in full communion, but some accept grandchildren, skipping the intermediate generation; others now question the entire doctrine, while a few—most shocking to relate— "doe thinke that whatsoeuer be ye state of ye parents, baptisme ought not to be dispensed to any infants whatsoeuer." It was just as bad in Connecticut: "We are at a Loss in our parts about members of Children being received into Communion," wrote Henry Smith from Wethersfield, reporting that they were applying themselves to a renewed scrutiny of Genesis 17.

The Synod failed abysmally. It did indeed, in its third meeting of 1648, complete *The Cambridge Platform,* which seemed a mighty vindication of the New England Way, but on baptism it shamefully hedged. Richard Mather arrived with a prepared clause extending baptism to all children born in the church whose parents were not openly scandalous, and ran head-on into furious opposition led by Charles Chauncy. Oliver Cromwell saved the Synod by turning the Presbyterians out of power, but he left New England alone with its gnawing problem. The clergy invented the stratagem of pretending there was no problem, and let the *Platform* say that members are to be visible saints, along with "the children of such, who are holy"; but they said nothing—for they dared not—about those children who had proved unable to profess, and less than nothing about the children of such children. Their cowardice is the first evidence that they had encountered in America an unexpected experience, and because of it had become something other than the men who in 1630 left England armed with an infallible prospectus.

However, apologists for the inclusion of the grandchildren could argue that they were only drawing upon the prophets of Congregationalism. William Ames had specifically insisted that baptized children are "in the Covenant of Grace by externall profession," not because the faith of their parents was necessarily sound. Indeed, they might well be hypocrites; yet the seal, being applied only to externals, was still valid, and the children retained their membership as long as there were no public violations: "It crosseth the nature of all Covenants in the world, for to dissolve the Covenant without the Consent of the other." With this warrant in hand, Cotton most vigorously refused to rest upon the generalities of the *Platform;* having bowed to the will of the majority in 1638 and conceded that externality was enough for external purposes, he now went the whole way and declared that while God takes an elect seed into the Covenant of Grace without reservations or qualifications, "the carnall and unfaithfull seed he taketh them also into his Covenant of Grace, yet giveth them not the sure and saving mercies thereof, but the common graces onely, and the outward dispensation of the Covenant." As for grandchildren—well, grace might skip a generation: though the church be corrupt and the parents also, yet "the Faithfulness of God who keepeth Covenant and mercy to thousands, supplies the effect of the Faith of the next Parents, and maketh good his Covenant to the Children of their former Ancestors in Elder Age." Baptized children, their legal title clear, belong to the church "though destitute of spirituall grace," and so may present their progeny.

One is tempted to read into Cotton a wry determination to let externalists have the best of it. Even Thomas Shepard, who never wavered against the Antinomians, let a note of disillusion enter his defense: "What Churches we may have of these, even heaps of hypocrites and prophane persons!"

But being a good soldier, he did not shrink from even such bitter consequences; we need not worry, he said, "for suppose all these, yet God may take them into outward Covenant (which is sufficient to make them the Church-Seed, or Members of the Church) although he doth not receive them into inward Covenant, in bestowing upon them saving Grace, or power to profitt, nay though they degenerate, and grow very corrupt afterward." Dr. Holmes grossly misrepresented the New England system in his allegory of the Deacon's One Hoss Shay, for he comprehended little about the connection of ideas and society. Originally, indeed, the vehicle was designed to be as strong in every part as in all, but when the Deacon attempted to enlarge it so as to carry his grandchildren to the meeting-house, a few joints had to be altered; a few hand-hewn additions had to be made, and the whole did not go to pieces all at once, as bubbles do when they burst, but bit by bit. Twenty years after the Great Migration, responsible spokesmen for the city upon a hill were already reconciling it to perpetuation by a succession of formal and possibly hypocritical generations.

By 1654, Henry Dunster, worried over that prospect, came to the conclusion that no children ought to be baptized; the Boston elders had only one argument against him: "soli visibiliter fideles sunt baptizandi." Dunster's conscience demanded that "fideles" ought to be something more than "visibiliter," for which scruple he was deprived of the Presidency of Harvard College—a large price to pay for a qualm which the guardians of the New England conscience were now ready to call a trifle.

Most of the founding fathers lived no longer than to suggest the outlines of this solution, but several of them commenced to realize that were it employed the theory of the sacrament would need restatement. For children about whom there was doubt, baptism did become—at least in a manner of speaking—a "means of conversion." A rigid holding of the first conception would mean that these persons were doubly damned; hence it was no longer sufficient to argue that the grandchildren had a legal title to baptism, but it had to be proved of some good to them.

Puritan theology always regarded baptism as putting the recipient under an obligation. If a man finds that, after receiving it, he has no increase of faith, Perkins had written, "he may well suspect himselfe, whether he did euer repent or not; and thereupon is to use means to come to sound faith & repentance." Thus, if not itself exactly a means, it might serve as a means toward using the means; it might become, as John Ball said, "a spurre and prouocation." In New England, non-members were presumed to have paralyzed wills, and upon them no obligation could be placed; but a baptized child, even if he appeared deficient, was not quite in the same plight. He was "in the Schoole of Christ and in peculiar fellowship with the other Schollars there"; he would listen carefully to sermons and so be "sought after by these means." Or, as Hooker put it, baptized children are kept in the church for "Manuring": God has them "in his hands as plants of his embracing in the means of grace." Like the children of the Jews, they remain "the true Olive, that grew not wild." In some sense, God stands peculiarly bound to them, as they are to Him.

For one thing, obviously the parent was committed to educating his children; knowing that nothing was wanting but the youth's consent, "he so trains it up, as that it may not fail of its consent in due time." Secondly, these children can be told that they have assented: "You have given your consent to what God hath done for you in Baptisme, and you desire it may for ever stand good in heaven." Others could be exhorted only to preparation, but these to full exertion. If a person becomes truly repentant years after his initiation, Anabaptists argued, this must show that the sacrament had been null and void at the time given; not at all, replied New England, because while then he may not have received saving faith, the rite had obviously proved "profitable" for him as it never could for those "not partakers of that grace offered and sealed." Because from the beginning of time "God ordered all good to be conveyed to us in a way, and by virtue of his covenant," the means can hardly reach, not "so much as externally," those outside it. Anabaptists would put all children "in an estate of persons that are without God in the world," but the heirs of the church "by this means may be distinguished," and upon them ministers could work without giving a second thought to strict predestination.

"Not," Cotton hastened to add, "that any can come when they will as by the power of their own will." Yet if they do not come, they can be blamed: "if the receiver hinder and stop the benefit, it is his fault, the sacrament is the same." These children, distinguished from those of mere townsmen, could be admonished "as they grow up, what a Covenant of Grace and Testament of peace it is, which God hath entered into with them in Baptisme: and by what promise of gratitude they have likewise obliged themselves unto Obedience to God." In his last days, Cotton was telling them, "If you can say, you have known some of your ancestors in this Covenant, and you have not refused it, but laid claim unto it, when you understand your selves, it is a certain signe this Covenant reacheth to you." If the obligation excited no positive conversion, it inspired "at least to knowledge and outward conformity in divers," which was enough to preclude despair—"as experience hath proved in New England."

Thus far along the road the founders themselves had come by about 1650. For minds like theirs, it was a long journey beset with dangers. They had to defend their program against enemies from the outside—Antinomians, Anabaptists, Presbyterians, and tolerating Independents—but they could not allow it to collapse from within. They had to maintain predestination and limited atonement, to eschew sacramental regeneration, and yet find a way in which successive generations in the church might be, as Hooker had it, "inserted by a way of nature." In their extension of baptismal theory, they were endeavoring to preserve the holy church of voluntary participation and of exclusion, and yet adjust it to what experience had demonstrated in New England.

CHAPTER VII

HALF–WAY MEASURES

THAT commandment which bids the chosen people increase and multiply was most congenial to New Englanders. Despite an appalling infant mortality, they begot so many children, who proceeded to beget so many more, that within three decades the problem of baptizing them became critically urgent. Many churches tried to solve it individually by extending the privilege, but often, as in Salem, encountered opposition within their own congregations. Roxbury in 1653 asked the advice of Jonathan Mitchell, already considered the rising hope of the second generation, who found himself still "in the dark about it." In 1655 Richard Mather needed all his diplomacy to persuade his people that the children "were members and that haveinge children, they should have them baptized if themselves did take hold of their fathers Covenant," but he could find no agreement upon what "that takeing hold of Covenant is." Following Congregational custom, Dorchester asked advice from its neighbors: Dedham had no light, Boston asked time to consider, Roxbury feared an onset of "the Corruption of old England which we fled from."

In 1653 the church of Hartford was riven by one of the most vicious quarrels of the century, a quarrel not at first about baptism but about finding a successor for Hooker; yet quickly the rights of children became involved. In May 1656 one faction demanded help from the General Court, which got in touch with Massachusetts; that General Court named thirteen ministers (taking care to pick both Mather and Chauncy) to meet with delegates from Connecticut and New Haven. John Davenport, jealously guarding what he considered primitive righteousness, objected that a synod "may prove dangerous to ye puritie and peace of these churches and colonies." He was persuaded that the Connecticut petitioners aimed at so enlarging baptism as to let in newcomers from England without any profession. Plymouth also held back; so on June 4, 1657, the thirteen Massachusetts divines met in Boston with four from Connecticut in what they preferred to call an assembly rather than a synod.

They drew up a report, undoubtedly written by Richard Mather, copies of which were sent to the churches. Increase Mather carried one copy to his brother Nathanael in London, where it was published in 1659 under the title, *A Disputation concerning Church-Members and their Children in Answer to XXI Questions*. Several churches felt justified by it in proceeding to baptize grandchildren, but still the report could not be regarded as official. By 1660, with Cromwell dead and Charles on his throne, the need for colonial unanimity was imperative. On December 31, 1661, brushing aside constitutional scruples, the General Court of Massachusetts commanded a full-dress synod "to discusse & declare what they shall judge to be the mind of God." For years the legislators had been including, among the causes for humiliation, the plight of the rising generation; now they had to know, once and for all, "Who are the subjects of baptisme?"

Meeting on March 11, 1662, the Synod resumed where that of 1648 had left off, Charles Chauncy, now President of Harvard, receiving yeoman support against Richard Mather from Richard's son Increase, just returned from England. When the Synod adjourned without result, the politicians exerted pressure through what had now become their favorite device: a summons to humiliation, "our spirits many ways exercised as to events & vnsetled as to trueths of great consequence, the cleernesse of judgment being greatly advantageous not only to churches but the good of familyes," wherefore prayers should be offered for "the synod now shortly to be assembled." Thus prodded, the Synod reconvened on June 10, to find itself still deadlocked. Before the third session in September, Increase Mather secured, through his brother Eleazar of Northampton, a letter from Davenport which he tried to read aloud, but he was squelched. Overriding opposition, the majority composed their report and submitted it to the General Court on October 8, where Increase Mather also appeared, prepared to renew the debate. The court had had enough: grudgingly admitting that dissenters should not be coerced, they ordered publication of the document. Mitchell, no longer "in the dark," wrote a preface, and it was finally printed at Cambridge, *Propositions Concerning the Subject of Baptism and Consociation of Churches.*

The Synod of 1637 achieved unity by exiling dissenters, that of 1648 by evasion, and this of 1662 by the brute force of majority vote; whereupon New England discovered, to its consternation, that it had no machinery for silencing an enfuriated minority. "All dissenting," wrote Eleazar Mather to John Davenport, "is esteemed intollerable & dissenters are accoumpted & charged to be the Breakers of the peace of the churches, Adhaerents to the Brownistical notions, & what not." Never one to endure aspersions quietly, Charles Chauncy composed an attack upon the *Propositions,* which he entitled *Anti-Synodalia Scripta Americana,* sent copies of both to London, where they were published, proclaiming aloud the shameful fact that the city on a hill was sundered by dissention over a fundamental tenet.

In New England the majority commissioned John Allin of Dedham to refute Chauncy, but even as he was at work, Increase Mather wrote a preface to Davenport's letter and pushed it through the Cambridge press as *Another Essay for Investigation of the Truth.* Jonathan Mitchell, with the help of Richard Mather, set himself to answering, meanwhile sending to the press a posthumous paper of Thomas Shepard's, *The Church-Membership of Children*, thus invoking a great founder against Davenport. Mitchell and Richard Mather's booklet, *A Defence of the Answer and Arguments of the Synod*, appeared in 1664, as did Allin's *Animadversions upon the Antisynodalia Americana.* Nobody can figure out how typesetters and equipment in Cambridge kept up with the schedule, and heaven only knows to what lengths the dispute might have gone had not Increase Mather in 1671 gone over to the majority and so wrecked the clerical opposition. In 1675 he sealed his conversion by publishing an anthology of passages from the founders to prove that they had all anticipated the opinion of 1662, *The First Principles of New-England*, as well as his own apology—the most able statement for the majority—*A Discourse concerning the Subject of Baptisme, Wherein the present Controversies . . . are enquired into.*

These publications, we must remember, were only the public manifestations of a dispute which raged for twenty years or more within the churches. "O! when," cried Allin, "shall we see Brethren manage such Disputes with that Brotherly Love, Ingenuity, and Endeavours to find out the Truth, as becometh the Cause of Christ and without such harsh reflections upon mens persons!" However, one fact is clear: the minority was led by survivors of the first generation, whereas the most active of the majority (with the sole exception of Richard Mather) were of the second —Mitchell, Allin, John Higginson of Salem (son of the pioneer). With the death of Eleazar in 1669 and the defection of Increase, opponents of the Synod commanded only a slight following among the younger ministers, while the few die-hards clung precariously to New Haven.

The year of the Synod was also that of Wigglesworth's *God's Controversy with New England*, after which the jeremiads took shape, so that throughout the 1660's and '70's these two topics, baptism and lamentation, constitute the intellectual expression of New England. Questions of church polity may be, the proponents recognized, of "a lower rank" than those of abstract theology, but in these realms the English genius peculiarly excelled all other Protestants—"which do also at this day exercise the most searching thoughts and ablest pens that are amongst us." They did not feel, as we may well feel, that they were constricting their energies to a pitifully narrow field; in their language, they were assured that they were further working out a European generalization in the specific terms of an American society.

The Synod's proposal was quickly dubbed—as it still is known, to fame and infamy—the "Half-Way Covenant." The issue was clear-cut: "The children of the parents in question, are either children of the covenant, or strangers from the covenant," to which the answer was equally direct, that since children and grandchildren are alike within the covenant, all should be baptized. The majority could reach such a decision because by now they had at hand, in the tripartite philosophy of the national covenant, of preparation, and of hypocrisy, a perfected rationale of externality: they merely extended these criteria to the covenant of the church. In one sense, there was nothing "half-way" about the solution, for the infants of baptized members were declared to be members, and so under "the watch, discipline, and government of the Church." But in a more important sense, the decision meant not half a way but a double way: the external and internal covenants, the covenant of the church and the Covenant of Grace, being now so drastically separated, were separately hypostatized.

Even so, the two could not be entirely divorced. Advocates of half-way paid the sort of tribute which external must always render to internal by requiring that a baptized but unconverted child, upon becoming an adult parent and presenting his own child for baptism, must publicly profess his assent to the covenant made in his own infancy, must solemnly renew his allegiance, not in order to partake of the Supper, but in order that his offspring might be externally sealed to the church.

As Increase Mather's anthology was to show, many of the clergy had long been working their way toward this ingenious compromise. The Synod gathered up their endeavors, and thus rejected what obviously would have been the easiest way out—namely, to allow baptized persons of decent conversation merely to have their children received. By obliging these citizens formally to renew their allegiance even while holding against them doubts about their inward conversion, the Synod forced them to go through motions theoretically within the compass only of the elect. Against this device, opponents bent their fullest energies, persuaded that it was far less dangerous to baptize grandchildren than to accept as a token payment from the children an act which could not possibly be meaningful.

It is hard, Mitchell grieved, "to finde and keep the right middle way of Truth in these things," but the alternatives, said Allin, were "an overloose Dispensation" or "the Rocks of Rigid Separation, Anabaptism, and the like." Actually, there can be no doubt about the motive, which Cotton Mather blurts out: "The good old generation could not, without many uncomfortable apprehensions, behold their offspring excluded from the baptism of Christianity." Or, as Allin put it, we did not come to New England to leave our posterity "at a loose end without the Discipline of Christ." We have all agreed that baptized children receive, so far as we know, only "Foederal Holiness," but if that endures no longer than their youth, how can church discipline "reform such great, many, and prevailing corruptions of Youth?" How indeed, unless the youth should renew their federal compact? And what greater instrument of compulsion could be imagined than concern for their children? To neglect this "means"— as Cotton Mather was later to explain—"would quickly abandon the biggest part of our country unto heathenism." In these terms, one may say that the Half-Way Covenant was an effort to salvage the imported civilization in an American setting.

However, there was one obstacle to be overcome, a chronic difficulty for the American mind. Puritans did not believe in "tradition," which they identified with Popish "superstition"; but on the other hand, they did believe that the founders had been inspired men, and the second generation—the Harvard-educated—were as uncomfortable under the charge of deviation from the founders as members of the Supreme Court of the United States accused of flaunting the fathers of the Constitution. Hence we may perceive in these technical disputes an early exemplification of a basic pattern in American thought, a struggle with self-imposed limitation. The insurgents, even though a majority, had to justify themselves by pleading that innovation was not innovation: "this is onely a progress in practising according thereunto, as the encrease of the Churches doeth require." America is not so much promise as fulfillment; but the criterion of accomplishment constantly becomes something different from the first formulation. "It is the way of Christ in the Gospel," said Allin, "to set up the practice of his Institutions as the necessities of the people call for them."

The dissident minority had on their side all of Europe's logic, against them all of New England's experience. By standing firm to a strict construction of imported theory, they wanted to declare these unresponsive children "felones de se"—automatically excommunicated for failure of will. However decently the children conduct themselves, said Davenport, "these despise the Church of God." Dismayed already by 'the tendencies of life in America, the "conservatives"—if that be the name for them—anchored themselves to an uncompromising standard. Philip said to the Eunuch, according to Chauncy, "Unlesse thou believest with all thy heart, thou mayest not be baptised," and upon this rock he and his colleagues would forever found the American churches: "This is all that we contend for in persons that are of age." But in the Synod he confronted other considerations, which to him seemed irrelevant; many of the delegates, educated in America, were "no Logitians," were "unable to answer Syllogisms, and discern Ambiguities," with the result that however clear the straight and logical way, they went with the mob, "especially when persons that are eminent in place and power, and learning and piety, are so linked together."

While still his henchman, Increase Mather reported to Davenport, "You may see which way things are like to be carried." But no Puritan society could embark upon a novel policy solely and simply out of considerations of utility; the majority had to make a case for themselves, exhibiting at least some show of consistency with primitive doctrine. However, at every point their abstract reasoning runs into the concrete. They insisted, for example, that they were safeguarding the essence of Congregationalism by inhibiting half-way members from the Lord's Supper and from the privilege of voting until after a satisfactory profession; the principle of exclusion was not infringed, because half-way membership was not offered to those outside the church, and both the sacraments remained, not instruments for regeneration, "but for nourishment and confirmation." Their opponents' position, they said, with its "curtailing the covenant," was dangerous precisely because it would tempt churches to admit more persons to full communion, without adequate testing, in order to extend the baptism; thus they would in time become governed by the "unqualified or meanly qualified." On the face of it, the Half-Way Covenant, instead of being a concession to worldliness, purported to be a device for preventing worldly children from invading the sanctuary; yet underneath, the real motive was, a determination to keep the actual control a monopoly of those who could be relied upon.

Having thus protected the Supper, the Half-Way advocates proceeded to exploit that line of thought which denied that Congregationalism aspired to perfection. True, they would say, in order to become a full member the half-way candidate must hold forth not merely "historical faith" but an ability to examine himself "and to discern the Lords body"; on the other hand, it is a great mistake "to apply that which is spoken of the saving Benefits of the Covenant, to the outward Priviledges thereof." New England had long since revised its incautious boasts, and no longer pretended that even the most convincing profession was an infallible sign of true salvation; it was at best only a qualification for the external covenant. If, then, even visible saints were sanctified only unto externality, where was the heresy in retaining their grandchildren in a merely external covenant? The issue was not whether the infants had true faith, but whether they could be admitted to the church: "This sufficeth, though they have no Faith or Grace really."

In other words, then, a metaphysical distinction between the inward and outward covenant was fundamental to the advocates' argument; their solution demanded that the church covenant be no longer viewed as a direct' manifestation of spiritual conversion, but that it be considered entirely on a par with the national covenant or the covenant of hypocrites. "Meer membership is separable from such ability," declared the *Propositions,* and then revealed the premises of this logic: "as in the children of the Covenant, that grow up to years, is too often seen." Where their opponents wanted to keep the two dispensations identical, the majority, having learned that the outward suffices for civic purposes, were prepared to let the internal look after itself. As Richard Mather emphatically put it:

It is one thing to be in the Covenant and in the Church, in respect of external state, and another thing to enjoy all the spiritual and eternal benefits of such a relation; and though this latter be the portion of none but such as come to be truly regenerate, yet the other is, and so continues, the right of all that have once had it.

And a covenant, especially an external one, endures as long as neither party specifically denounces it—as had been discovered in refined speculations upon the national covenant. Hence if these children behaved themselves, while we might not say that they were saved, we could say that they should not be cut off. Once properly in, a member "cannot be outed, till God out him."

The inner compulsion of the apology is revealed also by frank borrowings from the logic that protected hypocrites, by an unabashed cry that this solution alone could stave off Anabaptism. Allin quoted from Hooker to prove that "it is the Interest in the Outward Covenant that giveth right to Outward Priviledges of the Church," and proclaimed this "the Foundation of the Doctrine of the Synod." The dissenters shrieked that the Synod was in effect branding the whole generation as hypocrites and was tamely surrendering the city on a hill to dissemblers. But by now New England had become inured to that prospect: Mitchell could calmly remark that even if these children were no better than hypocrites, what of it? "May not such as come into the Church by the fairest Profession of Faith, prove so vile also?" Meanwhile, was it not evident that the rigidity of their adversaries' stand would, in practical administration, shut the door against all infants whatsoever? After he had crossed the line, Increase Mather looked sadly back upon his former associates: "I find that there is hardly an Argument proclaimed against such Inlargement, as is by the Synod asserted, but what the Antipaedo-Baptists make use of it to serve their turn." The dissenters might object that this sort of pleading was highly unfair, that the question should be settled by logic and not by experience, but already such men belonged to a former age.

And then, having come this far, apologists found themselves in possession of a delightful reflection: was it, after all, necessary to account these children no better than hypocrites? Was it not possible to account them as good as anybody? Once the external and internal were so far separated that profession was no longer a certain link, then the probabilities that those in the external might also be in the internal increased rather than diminished. Since all visible believers are only presumptive believers, why not presume for the children? The want of ability, said Richard Mather, need not "argue want of the very being of Faith." Granted that there are more convincing evidences which churches must demand before admitting the baptized to the other sacrament, still, if these persons were christened in their minority, if they understand the doctrine and are not scandalous, if they solemnly own the covenant of their infancy, "is all this nothing for Charity to go upon in accounting them Believers? no, not in the least degree?" Surely, Mitchell added—no longer hesitating to employ the *argumentum ad hominem*—the Lord does not make so light a matter of His holy covenant as to enter into a solemn pledge with these children, "and then let them goe out so easily, or drop off we know not how." It was not necessary to expect only the worst from our progeny. Of course, no Puritan could yield to downright optimism, and proponents of the Half-Way Covenant were, even while arguing for it, threatening dire judgments upon the entire community; yet, just as the jeremiads do not always mean exactly what they seem to mean, so these intellectuals responded to the promise of America by venturing to hope that their children might not be so bad after all.

At any rate, there was no necessity to bewail, with John Davenport, that the spirit no longer blew toward this posterity and so do nothing. In strict theology, a man had to be passive before his regeneration; in the ecclesiastical covenant, the more it was externalized the larger became the sphere of action. For ecclesiastical purposes, half-way members could be treated as enabled: they could be exhorted, censured, or excommunicated. They were, as the *Propositions* stated, "in a state of subjection to the authoritative teaching of Christ's Ministers, and to the observation of all his commandments . . . and therefore in a state of subjection unto Discipline." The only possible alternative was universal self-distrust: "otherwise Irreligion and Apostacy would inevitably break into Churches, and no Church-way left by Christ to prevent or heal the same," which would be terrible not only for the corporate health but for the individual, because it "would also bring many church-members under that dreadful judgement of being let alone in their wickedness." For the security, or at least the sanity, of believers, who had every reason constantly to reexamine their belief, it was necessary that the benefit of the doubt be attributed to an earnest but still unconverted posterity.

Factually speaking, the decision of the Synod was no more than that the non-regenerate children of the church were sufficiently in church covenant to transmit a like degree of membership to their children. Actually, the root of the problem was that the churches, little by little, had become convinced there is "no certain, but onely a probable connexion between federal Holyness . . . and Salvation." Why not make the best of probabilities? How can the Synod's doctrine, cried Mitchell, confirm the unregenerate in complacency when they are told, "over and over," that outward advantages alone are sealed to them, that the saving conditions are sealed merely conditionally—that is, on condition that they go to work? Especially when the work required was of parents upon children? "Should the Church-education of your children be by the want of your hearty concurrence, rendered either unseizible or ineffectual . . . we beseech you to consider how uncomfortable the account hereof would be another day." In the *Modell* Winthrop had said that we professed these actions upon these and those ends, that if we do our part, the Lord will signify His acceptance by giving us the reward; in the logic of 1662, the gamble was not upon whether He would or would not accept our invitation, but upon whether we could make good what He had agreed to accept. The difference in formulation was more than verbal, for the second opened up a larger field for ordinary human endeavor. But, on the other hand, nobody could deny that the founders had immensely exerted themselves.

Chauncy and Davenport could make nothing of a state of grace which never became evident. How, they asked, could sheep be separated from goats if all sheep look and act like goats? Only one conclusion was possible: "The Children in question, are in a state of Neutrality for the present, and such Christ accounts to be against him." If neuters are given baptism, why not go the whole way and give them Communion? Could the majority not see what they were doing? "It is apparent unto all what a corrupt masse of Unbelievers shall by this change throng into the fellowship of Gods People, and the children of strangers, uncircumcised in heart, shall be brought into Gods Sanctuary to pollute it." Why administer ecclesiastical censures upon those who will surely—not being converts—disregard them?

I have called Chauncy and Davenport—as have other historians—conservatives. The term may stand if we comprehend that they clung to what had been extreme radicalism in 1630, the principle of regenerate membership. Seen in that light, they illustrate the recurrent problem of the conservative in America: by older standards the innovation was wrong, but they had no alternative program. They were sufficiently aware of the facts to agree that the churches should take the children under watch and government; whereupon Allin rested his case: "the whole Cause was given up in that Proposition." In the preface to his father's book, the younger Thomas Shepard showed the folly of the dissenters' notion that a grown child becomes *felo de se* by the eminently practical consideration that this would "take away the use of a Ministerial Judge in the Church." Clearly, "this frustrates Church-discipline." Conservatism might be, as it often is, pure in heart; it was consequently the less capable of coping with realities.

John Drury spent his life in an effort to unite Protestantism, in the course of which he urged the clergy of New England to subordinate their private interests to the larger concern. Appeals for participation in world government are often countered by localities with an explanation of their uniqueness. John Norton (who had been the tutor of Increase Mather) was commissioned to reply; his Latin letter, translated into English, was also printed by the overburdened Cambridge press in 1664, and was designed more for home consumption than for Drury. By using Drury as an excuse to defend the Synod, Norton added to the defeat of Chauncy and Davenport. He said that he and New England welcomed communion with Protestant churches of Europe in order to reprove those who, through a "preposterous Zeal," are unwilling "to have any of the common Priviledges of the Church of God bestowed upon any, whose effectual Sanctification may be questioned," thus presenting the Synod of 1662 as the Massachusetts contribution to international solidarity! He could even go so far—farther than any other apologists dared—as to say that the great line of New England theology, from Perkins and Parker through Preston and Ames, was always resolute against "separatists," but that "it came to be the fate of these Churches in America, to verge too near them in their Primitive Administrations." Thus the Half-Way Covenant became a rectification of the founders; by endorsing Drury's vision of Protestant unity,

Norton let fly at those nearer home who, in the local view, seemed the threat to concord: he characterized Chauncy and Davenport, so that the Protestant world should know them, as those who say that they so "stand for Truth, that by too tenacious insisting upon Doctrine, we make no reckoning of the Rights of Society." To behave thus, he continued, "is to be carried with the study of Parties, not of the Truth; and to undertake the Patronage of an Opinion, rather because it is our own, then because it is true." Even after digesting this paragraph, John Davenport would not give up his persuasion that truth is truth, but Norton injected openly into the debate the premise which informed the whole defense: namely, that holding a truth in defiance of the rights of society becomes arrogant self-righteousness.

The power of this existential logic was vindicated in the career of Increase Mather. Having fled the Restoration because there was no longer in England any prospect of success, he came back prepared to fight for the purity of the New England churches, all the more because he knew the cause lost in Europe, and so joined Chauncy against his own father. Possibly his father persuaded him, but more likely it was Jonathan Mitchell; beyond any doubt, a few years of adjustment to the American scene added point to Mitchell's arguments. Chauncy made a mistake in trying to fit the Synod into the pattern of the jeremiad: he said that after 1662 afflictions upon New England increased, to which Allin replied that actually the next years were prosperous: "I had thought that Gods gracious answer to the Prayers of the Synod of 1662 in sending Rain so speedily and sweetly, might not onely have taken off that Imputation of the Drought unto the Synod," but have warned dissenters against applying providences to private ends. Experience, then, and an Americanized sense of the "rights of society" did their work on Increase Mather, who transferred his energy and his immense common sense to the Covenant, and then out-apologized the apologists. The question now became a purely ecclesiastical business: "That Faith which giveth right to Baptism . . . as to us is not invisible faith. But the visibility of faith is that which we must proceed upon." He told his erstwhile allies, "In the way your self and some others go, the bigger half of the people in this Country will in a little Time be unbaptized." With the fury that comes only to those who have given up absolutism, he rent the errors he had upheld: it would be "subversive to Religion," it would be "absurd," that a people "of a more reformed temper then ordinarily the world hath known . . . should so soon be the body of them unbaptized, as if they were not a Christian, but an Heathen People." Norton's line became the line of progress; the more delicate expositions of Mitchell and Allin were left behind. Mather's argument is entirely *ad hominem*:

There are many godly Souls in New-England, that the great motive which prevailed with them to come into this wilderness, was that so they might leave their Children under the Government of Christ in his Church . . . Have we for our poor Childrens sake in special, left a dear and pleasant Land, and ventured our Lives upon the great waters, and encountered with the difficulties and miseries of a wilderness, and doth it at last come to this, that they have no more Advantages as to any Church care about them, then the Indians and Infidels amongst whom we live? O this is sad!

In fact, Increase so eloquently and incessantly proclaimed this sadness that it became a permanent part of his son's mentality; for Cotton Mather the dramatic moment in the story of the Half-Way Covenant was not the Synod itself, but that in which Mitchell so worked upon Increase that Increase hailed him both as opponent and conqueror, and applied to him the words of Beza upon Calvin: "now he is dead, life is less sweet, and death will be less bitter to me." Cotton Mather does not, of course, point out that with the death of Mitchell, Increase Mather became the recognized leader of New England intelligence; he does manage to make a virtue out of his father's change, on the ground that most of the dissenters came in time "to see that the rigidity of their former principles had been a failing in them." Except for one or two passages of this sort, where the narrative required explicitness, Cotton Mather does not confess, what to the careful reader is everywhere evident, that the *Magnalia,* in addition to being a gigantic jeremiad, is a sustained reinterpretation of New England's past in order to support the decision of 1662, so that his father's tergiversation comes out with all the weight of history behind it.

We should not forget that the issues in this debate arose out of Protestantism, for which the dilemma is, as Luther said once and for all, that if works are sought after as a means to righteousness, they subject man to necessity, and so "freedom and faith are destroyed." What man does because he is required becomes "this perverse leviathan," from which no man can escape, as Ahab could not escape from Moby-Dick. This may give the individual a workable scheme of life, but always, when the proposition of freedom is confronted with a body politic, it runs up against some things that must be enacted and enforced. A people dedicated to God, even though made up of dedicated individuals, finds that such a general election cannot, in the nature of society, always be effectual; whereupon the hidden meaning of the Old Testament begins to appear. Calvin himself had seen the problem: "the external call without the internal efficacy of grace, which would be sufficient for their preservation, is a kind of medium between the rejection of all mankind and the election of the small number of believers." There seems to be no way in which the freedom of the individual—which consists in doing good as a consequence of faith rather than under compulsion—can be reconciled with the welfare of the community except by regarding society as something intermediate between the realms of sin and of pure salvation. Therefore the code of civic morality ever threatens to undermine that freedom upon which Winthrop and his colleagues founded New England.

Apologists for the Half-Way Covenant stumbled into this problem when they attempted to draw an analogy between baptism and circumcision. This, of course, was a standard Protestant argument, which Calvin used to confute Anabaptists. With the help of the federal theology, New Englanders were prepared to treat each covenanted church as a miniature tribe of chosen people; but instead of circumcising its children, it would baptize them. Mitchell thought he was on firm ground when he said that exactly as in the Church of Israel, "the Parent might want actual fitness for the Passover, by manifold Ceremonial uncleanness, and yet that hindered not the Circumcising of the Childe"; just so, the parent's lack of regeneration should not prevent his conveying the rite of baptism. Genesis 17 was still the authorization: "for so in the Old Testament, this was the ground of title to Circumcision."

"The similitude runs not upon four feet," said Chauncy. A church, he insisted, is not a nation; even in their apostasy, the Jews, like New England, might still be the Lord's people, but baptism is limited to believers. This cogent argument failed because the majority in New England·had in fact come to regard each particular church, with its external administration, as a nation. In the first theorists, in Preston and Ames, the substitution of baptism for circumcision was no more than a metaphor, a rhetorical trope, but in America the language of the external covenant— whether of the nation or of the church—became, as it could not in Europe, a description of reality. These people were in covenant in order to accomplish designated ends; their church covenant was founded upon Luther's proposition that regenerated men do good works freely as a consequence of faith, not under the necessity of leviathan. Yet it was also an assembly of citizens and their progeny for whom the external call, even without the internal efficacy of grace, kept them in a peculiar medium between reprobation and election.

Therefore, in the arguments over the Half-Way Covenant there first appears a problem which has been with us ever since, and to which the New England mind has for three centuries been particularly devoted. The nation (or the church) is in external covenant with the divine, whereby it is favored above other societies, being punished not by chance but by a specific bill of indictment. Successive generations inherit this obligation and this favor. What, then, do children and grandchildren do? Does the covenant mean a manifest destiny, and do they yield their wills to God, letting Him accomplish their fate? If so, they become listless. But do they, to avoid this deterioration, take up the burden of the covenant, and fulfill its ethical requirements? If so, do they not become enslaved to the leviathan of moral necessity? What guarantee do they then have that the favor of God will still be theirs?

CHAPTER VIII

REVIVALISM

HISTORIANS
critical of, or outraged by, what has been called the
filio-pietistic school of New England eulogy, in going to the other extreme
have declared that by resisting the Half-Way Covenant the clergy revealed "the extent to which liberal opinion had developed among the mass
of the laymen." In fact, as Hubbard's *History* understates the business, the
mass of laymen "were very scrupulous about any innovation," fearing that
the Covenant would "abate, if not corrupt," the purity of the churches;
or, as the *Magnalia* says, although the pastors "were generally principled
for it," the brethren were "stiffly and fiercely set the other way." If, then,
the Covenant was "liberalism," the clergy were liberals, while the laity
fought tooth and nail against this extension of the benefit of baptism.

The people took up the cry of the clerical minority, accusing advocates
of apostasy and betrayal; how reckless were their charges, said Mitchell,
"I had rather they would seriously Consider between the Lord and their
own Souls, then I go about to determine." The chief insinuation was a
lust for power: "We have been reflected upon by some as seeking our
selves, and driving on I know not what design," though to Mitchell it
seemed obvious, "I cannot readily Imagine, what Self Interest or Self End
we should be led by in this matter." The masses insisted there was such a
design, even though most of them, said Increase Mather, "never read the
Book, much less have they read other things written in defense thereof."
Perhaps we today may understand better than the unhappy clergy could
at the time what they were up against: the opposition was an uprising of
the crowd against the majesty of scholastical learning.

The real lines of conflict can be seen in Connecticut, where the situation
was particularly delicate because the new charter, secured by the skill and
tact of John Winthrop, Jr., in 1662, forcibly united New Haven to Connecticut. In 1666 the Church of Hartford tried to heal its schism by electing two ministers, one for each faction; when one of these proclaimed the
Half-Way Covenant, the other denounced it, and the neighboring churches,
trying to intervene, found themselves likewise torn. Just at this moment,
William Pitkin and six inhabitants of Hartford presented a petition to the
General Court, complaining that though they had been baptized in England, they were not therefore admitted to Connecticut churches and could
not secure the privilege for their children. Panicky lest this accusation be

carried to London, the General Court begged the churches to consider enlarging church covenant not only as far as the Synod had proposed but so as to include Pitkin. Thereupon the storm really broke. One result was that Abraham Pierson of Branford indignantly gathered his flock and —declaring New England lost beyond hope of recovery—started the process of expansion by retreating into the unsullied West, to Newark, in New Jersey.

In desperation, politicians called for a Connecticut synod, meanwhile ordering the churches "to suspend all matter controuersall"—which was to heap fuel on the flames. Opponents contrived that the Commissioners for the United Colonies should call for an intercolonial synod—hoping for support from the stubborn opposition in Massachusetts and Plymouth, but the General Court and clergy of Massachusetts refused, fearing a spread of Connecticut's disorder. Left to themselves, the Connecticut General Court dragooned a committee of ministers into determining how far the churches might walk together "notwithstanding some various apprehensions amonge them in matters of discipline respecting membership and baptisme." By an inspiration of fatigue, this body recommended, and in May 1669 a wearied legislature voted, to allow both ways. How far, by that time, excitement had passed beyond the original and scholastic definitions appears in Hartford, where seceders, forming the Second Church, decided to institute the Half-Way Covenant, against which they had begun their revolt!

For the original conception of the polity, this compromise, although it brought a modicum of peace, spelled a fatal defeat: the Word of God, being clear, was supposed capable of clear and unanimous interpretation by assemblies of sanctified divines learned in logic and rhetoric. The aftermath of confusion in Connecticut was sundered churches and rancor, with opponents of the Covenant calling it "Presbyterian" and advocates beginning to wonder if perhaps, after all, Presbyterianism might not better deal with anarchic propensities. To the Lords of Trade and Plantations in 1680, the General Court had sadly to say that, as for their religious complexion, "some of them [are] strict Congregationall men, others more large Congregationall men, and some moderate Presbyterians." The Reverend Gershom Bulkeley of Wethersfield, who served in the abortive synod and later on the committee of ministers, was disgusted; and in Northampton, new thoughts began to work in the mind of Solomon Stoddard, summoned in 1669 to succeed Eleazar in a valley reverberating with Connecticut's quarrels.

Bad as all this was, the next stage proved even worse, for controversy now flared up in Boston itself. Indeed, considering the principles professed on all sides, there is nowhere in the annals of New England a more sordid story than that of the fission of the First Church in 1669. In a half-hearted way, the congregation had accepted the Half-Way Covenant, but in 1668, upon the death of Pastor Wilson, Cotton's colleague, the church voted for seventy-year-old John Davenport. He had no business to accept: not only was he old, but his people in New Haven, having stood by him, did not want to lose him, and in Congregational theory no minister should leave his church unless released. Davenport's motive was obvious: he wanted to mount the throne of Cotton and from it condemn the Synod of 1662. Anticipating his move, supporters of the Covenant demanded to know whether New Haven had really dismissed him; a letter was read to the congregation which seemed conclusive, but before long it was discovered that the leaders of the church had deliberately suppressed crucial portions. As Hutchinson later enjoyed remarking, "There does not seem to have been that fairness and simplicity in their proceedings which the gospel requires." Opponents of Davenport, enraged at the deceit, withdrew in anything but a spirit of Christian charity, and formed themselves into the Third, or as it ultimately was more familiarly known, the Old South Church.

Congregational theory had never permitted a dissident minority, upon any provocation, to walk off by themselves; in moments of parthenogenesis, both doctrine and custom decreed that a "council" of neighboring churches should be called. In this case, the seceders, knowing that most of the ministers were advocates of the Covenant, called for a council, whereupon the First Church defied the entire polity by saying "that to grant a Councill tends to overthrow the Congregationall way." Seventeen ministers in the area of Boston gave their blessing to the Third Church, and, having discovered how the First had bowdlerized New Haven's letter, added insult to injury by testifying "against these deceitful and false ways." By this time, there were families in Boston, the city on a hill, who no longer spoke to each other.

Governor Bellingham and two Assistants were of the First Church, suspected, in fact, of being the chief falsifiers; a majority of the Deputies —representing the rank and file of the churches—were ardent opponents of the Covenant. Seven of the Magistrates were avowed half-wayers, who could not prevent the Deputies from voting in May 1669 that the last survivor of the founding clergy should give the election sermon. Davenport told them how he had been one "by whom the Patent, which you enjoy, was procured"; wrapping himself in the mantle of this primordial authority, he exhorted the General Court to give no help "in such things to whom Christ never gave such power," especially not to further "mens opinions" even though these be "consented to by the major part of a Topical Synod." An ecclesiastical council which accepts such opinions "is an abuse of Councils." Then he shot his final bolt: "The Synod in England under Prelacy, published Superstitious Ceremonies; against which many godly learned Ministers wrote, and were silenced; who are, to this day, called, The good Old Nonconformists."

It was Davenport's last act (he died within a few months), but it was his most effective, and nearly destroyed New England. Determined to show themselves also good old Nonconformists, the Deputies brought in a report accusing the Half-Way Covenant of innovation and of provoking judgments of God upon the land. The majority of Assistants refused to concur, but the infatuated Deputies plunged ahead, drawing up another paper against the Third Church, charging it and all its supporters with usurpation, subversion, turning the garden of Christ into a wilderness, extirpation of the Congregational order—with being gangrene, infection, provoking images of jealousy and causes of divine wrath. To Josiah Flint the insensate Deputies seemed possessed by "a spirit of division, persecution and oppressing Gods ministers and precious saints"; let us also remark that they were upholding what James Truslow Adams called, assuming that they were against it, the "conservative" position!

However the clergy managed it, in the winter of 1670–71 they went to work upon the country; at the election of May 1671 fourteen Deputies (all opponents of the Third Church) were defeated, nineteen (all "safe") were reëlected, and thirteen new names were chosen (all amenable). This seems to have been the first organized campaign in America to elect an entire ticket. At least five new representatives of interior towns were actually members of the Third Church. When he came to write the *Magnalia*, Cotton Mather acknowledged that New England had indeed been disfigured by violent quarrels, and that one of them, producing the Deputies' indictment of the clergy, was the worst; thereupon he turned his face in horror away, leaving us to guess at what means the clergy employed to pack the General Court with friends of the Half-Way Covenant.

They wanted their pound of flesh. Presenting the General Court with a petition in which they spelled out their triumph, they demanded vindication. To the credit of the legislature, the Deputies insisted that their acts were not open to question and that they had the right of free debate, but then paid their debt: they suppressed previous papers, exonerated the clergy of all charges, and voted the Third Church innocent and unjustly calumniated.

The censure had called the ministers "the Achan, the chiefe incendarjies of wrath & procurers of judgment on the land"; the new General Court publicly agreed with the elders "that we doe adhere to the primitive ends of our coming hither, reteyning the sober principles of the Congregationall way, & the practise of our churches in their present & most athlettick constitutions." By clear implication, this was declaring the Half-Way Covenant no innovation, and so writing it into the constitution of New England.

In 1671, interestingly enough, Increase Mather also learned to embrace the Covenant; whereafter there was no leader of the opposition, which died down, albeit slowly and sullenly. The jeremiads tried to stamp out smoldering suspicions. "Truly," said Samuel Torrey in 1674, "it is much to be feared, that we shall so long doubt and dispute the Interest and Right of such Children, and controvert, and neglect our duty towards them, untill the holy Seed will be wholly corrupted." By the last decade of the century, Cotton Mather was happy to report that most ministers had obtained from their people not only to forbear "all expressions of dissatisfaction at the baptism of such as the synod has declar'd the subjects of it, but to concur with them." He brushed aside, as mere frivolity, George Keith's assertion that New England, having forgotten inwardness, now held that "nothing can constitute a Visible Church, but that which is only or merely Visible"; he ended his account of the Half-Way Covenant with the conversion of his church, the Second, in 1692. The brethren supported it by a vote of twenty to one, but still more gratifyingly, the few not yet entirely divested of "anti-synodalian scruples" signified "that it should give no uneasiness unto their minds to see the desires of their pastor accomplished; which was done accordingly."

Though the victory of 1671 was smashing, the ministers never relaxed their pressure, from which fact we may calculate the doggedness of the opposition; they could not completely triumph until practically all second-generation antagonists had died off. The implication of Urian Oakes's sermon to the Artillery Company in 1682 is unmistakable: "Obey therefore such as the Lord Jesus hath set over you in the Lord, if you mean to please him." "If the Ministry stand for the government of Christ in his Church," asked the younger Shepard, "must they be now Presbyterian?" In many places, he broadly hinted, "two or three men . . . continue to disturb the peace of a whole Congregation." Installed at the Third Church as a Half-Way Covenant man, Samuel Willard began his long career with dark insinuations against those churches that "exalt themselves above the Civil Magistrate" and so renounce "Consociation." Our form of government, he pointed out, "is partly Democraticall"; hence, if it descend toward anarchy, the fault lies "upon the people, especially if persons in Office and Place do their endeavour to rectifie and amend them, but are overpowered." Oakes's jeremiad of 1673, *New-England Pleaded With*, frankly exhibits a tension between ministers and people, and is haunted by the accusations of 1670. It is a denunciation of demagogues who, under the cloak of liberty, would subvert all order; their devices are not only the work of "petty politicians and little creeping statesmen," but "the very Gunpowder Plot that threatens the destruction of church and state." Nothing is more usual for such ambitious men than an affectation of "Popularity," of seeming to sympathize with the people and complaining "of the Defection, Apostacy, and evil Intentions of their Governors":

Take heed of such Imposters, though Religious in pretence and appearance, Acting all with a Theatrical Gravity. . . . In Popular States the great danger is of a Licentious, Factious, Ungovernable Spirit, that kicks and spurns at Authority; and this makes way for Anarchy and Confusion, and that for Tyranny.

Was this merely rhetoric? Or was there a real crisis in the society? If we look ahead to the little book of a distressed layman, published in

1684, Daniel Denison's *Irenicon,* we find a clue: opposition to the Half-Way Covenant, balked in the General Court, retreated to the towns, and carried on the contest within particular churches. In 1630 bishops and Presbyterians had predicted that Congregationalism would "moulder away, not having, or not acknowledging any way to determine our differences." On the record, Denison notes, the four New England Synods had succeeded, but in the wake of 1662 grew up a tendency which by the 1680's was a serious threat to unity: a faction had arisen among the members who contended that "the major vote of the Brethren is conclusive, and makes a Church Act, though the Elders consent not." Some even insisted that though a majority of the congregation agreed with the minister, his proposal should not prevail if resisted by "considerable persons."

Congregational theory assumed—having behind it the prestige of learning and a European conception of intellectual authority—that in a covenanted church the minister would be, not one among the membership, but a separate power, holding a veto upon the people. ("A speaking aristocracy," Samuel Stone had called it, "in the face of a silent democracy.") But after the ministers' sweep of the election of 1671—which they achieved not so much by aristocratic speaking as by political management—they returned to their churches armed with the endorsement of the General Court, to find that a core of the membership refused to surrender to a rigged decision. At first these recalcitrants tried to make the minister's vote count as only one, but when they found themselves in a minority, often a band of only four or five out of some fifty or sixty, they demanded the right, because of their standing in the community, to block the minister's followers. They threatened to become, in modern terminology, "bosses." The European conception had been that men of influence, creditors or employers, would serve as lay elders or deacons, and thus become meek lieutenants of the educated cleric; now these men were employing their power to direct the church behind the parson's back. The democracy might still be silent, but it was no longer submissive.

In 1673 Urian Oakes could barely keep himself to the generalities of the election sermon; no work of the period leaves a better, or more bitter, characterization of the boys in the smoke-filled room than does *New England Pleaded With:*

> Many of those Brethren that give out themselves to be the great Assertors of the liberties of the Church, that make such tragical complaints of the Presbyterial Usurpations and Encroachments of their painful, faithful Officers, that oppose them in their Government, and bind their hands that they cannot act according to their Commission from Jesus Christ, under pretence and colour of securing the Churches power and priviledge, and liberty: It is but that they may grasp all the power in their own Hands and in effect Lord it over Gods Heritage, and that the church may in truth and reality be governed by three or four Ruling (you may call them, if you please, Presbyterian) Brethren, rather then by the Officers that the Holy Ghost hath made Overseers and Rulers.

We think ahead to Edwards or to Theodore Parker: "Do but open your eyes," cried Oakes, "and look about you!" Tell me, he begged the General Court, whether if in many churches "a few Pragmatical and Loquacious Men" are not exercising real power, while the constituted authority is helpless? And still worse, "many of our Brethren (such is their weakness, and the power of prejudice) will never come humbly and kindly to submit themselves in the Lord to the Government of Jesus Christ in his Church, till they have been soundly scratch'd with this Bramble-Government of some aspiring and domineering Brethren." We have not changed the form of our polity, but a horrible thing has happened within it; the rule of the clergy has become a shadow, "and three or four heady Brethren lead the Church and rule all."

It would be rash indeed to call these heady brethren "liberals," or to conclude out of hand that the ministers were hypocrites in conceiving themselves true champions of the people's liberty. In these extra-legal combines of pragmatical politicians Oakes could perceive a more ominous form of "Presbyterianism" than that against which the founders had fought in England. The new pragmatical would be writ larger than the old priest, "there will be an Oppression of the liberties of the people." Let them have control, and the criterion for admission would become not sanctity, not even hypocritical righteousness, but "Adherence to a party, or to be a Darling of the Faction." The question, "Who are you for?" would become "in reality the only Test and Touchstone of the sufficiency of persons for Communion with us in Church Ordinances."

What the aspiring practitioners of "Bramble-Government" were actually up to in 1674 is difficult to say, since we have to make out their movements through the haze of clerical denunciation. But this much seems evident: within the congregations was shaping a struggle for power—not so much between clergy and laymen as between the European constitution (slightly but legitimately modified by the Half-Way Covenant) and the impulses of a new society. The inherited, dialectically articulated order made no provision for the fact that a man might carry weight in the community because he had character, ambition, or property. When strong men wanted certain things in the community—call them liberal or reactionary —they found that they had cut across the niceties of scholastic legalism; they also discovered that, despite it, they could get results, not by occupying office, but by manipulating the community.

Were the ministers to stand idly by "whilst power and Government hath been fixed in those that should be ruled, and only a liberty to lift up their hands left to the Rulers?" What had started as a debate about baptizing grandchildren had become a life-and-death struggle between those who clung to consistency (even if that required the tenuous logic of the Synod for proof) and a newly arisen, American-born tribe of pragmaticals who would bow to the parson in public but behind closed doors use their power to run the churches according to their own lights.

Against these major-domos the ministers had only one weapon: such authority as still adhered to the designated prophet whose function was to summon the populace to repentance. For them, exhortations were—now more than ever—instruments of ascendancy. At which point they began to appreciate, as they had not fully realized even in 1662, the advantage of the Half-Way Covenant: not only could they call upon all New England to submit to the national covenant, but more particularly they could thrust upon pragmatical brethren an obligation to walk according to their own baptismal covenant—the first requirement of which would be a cessation of pragmaticalness. Exhortation thus meant more than the inculcation of morality: it was a counterattack upon anti-ministerial sentiment. Enshrined in his pulpit, high above the heads of his congregation, the minister could still press upon the pragmaticals their precommitment to be other than they were. He could at least make insurgents squirm. Thanks to 1662, the clergy were able not only to impose a duty, but to allocate an ability to behave respectfully which aspirants to respectability would find difficult to deny.

Hence the clergy enlarged, expanded, extended the responsibility of the baptized. "I tell thee, when God shall come forth to execute his Judgments upon sinners, thy Church-membership, thy priviledges shall not save thee, God will no more regard thee for all this then if thou wert an Indian; except it be to punish thee the more because thy sins have been greater." Faced with this explication, would the most loquacious of pragmaticals (be they grandchildren, or, as was soon the case, great-grandchildren) have the gall to persist in schemes for usurping prerogatives? By carrying the war into the pews, the pulpit won the battle, and, for the moment, shackled the opposition. Increase Mather, as might be expected, was the most aggressive:

Did not our Fathers come hither in hope that they should leave their children under the Discipline and Government of the Lord Jesus in his Church? Hath not Christ owned the application of solemn publick Admonitions, &c to some of them that have been Children of the Church (tho not in full Communion) even so as to convert souls thereby? Why then should disputes about the mode wholly evacuate the Thing, when so much of the welfare of souls and the interest of Christs Kingdom is concerned therein?

Granted that most ministerial exhortations were aimed at the shortcomings of the faithful; yet we note that the vices which gradually become central in these catalogues were those of merchants and land speculators, most of whom were pledged to avoid them by a baptismal covenant not of their own making, and so we comprehend why the onslaught of the jeremiad acquired such vehemence. When children of the covenant fail, this "is their own fault in a great measure." To check their arrogance, the threat that unless they heeded the warning they would be damned far more terribly than all others became the most effective deterrent.

But could this net of obligation be further extended? Were there not pragmaticals outside the covenant who also should be reached? These questions determined—as would no purely theoretical consideration—the next step in social evolution. Apologists in 1662 kept up a show of logic when extending baptism only to the grandchildren of professing members; around 1680 (in some localities even earlier) leaders of the half-way principle found themselves prepared to accept into half-way membership persons hitherto outside the covenant—persons formerly considered unregenerate but who now were ready to make the same acknowledgment of obligation as was demanded in an "owning of the covenant." The tentative recommendation of Connecticut's General Court, which in 1664 seemed too shocking even to contemplate, was imperceptibly accepted by church after church, until by 1684 the general practice had become to receive into half-way status any who were of decent conversation and showed a competency of knowledge, who would join the inferior segment of the ecclesiastical society in order to gain baptism for their children.

This was as wrong—theoretically—as wrong could be; it was a complete betrayal of the argument of the Synod. As late as 1679 Increase Mather was hewing to the old line: the "vein of Election" runs only "through the loyns of godly Parents," and although some regenerate parents have reprobate children, "yet God hath seen meet to cast the line of election so, as that generally elect Children are cast upon elect Parents." Yet the curious fact is that, while busy denouncing pragmaticals, the clergy —including those most explicit in protecting the exclusiveness of the *Propositions*—found ways to extend a half-way status to many who never had been in church covenant at all, who were good citizens, who prized the baptism of their children. And all this with little public comment except from some such rank and negligible outsider as George Keith!

Explanation is obvious: the ministers so succeeded, with the charter government on their side, in browbeating opponents of the Half-Way Covenant into silence that around 1685 these persons were diverted into other enterprises. Meanwhile, the ministers were obliged, despite theological consistency, to fill up the churches with obedient citizens, even though they had to search for them outside Israel. They have been accused, by nineteenth-century purists, of cheapening the ordinances; actually, they were caught in their own logic of the distinction between external and internal, and so had no choice but to go all the way with their dialectic of the external. A volunteer to the half-way congregation, even though he had no vote in the church, would be a make-weight in the town meeting against pragmaticals.

Nevertheless, logic was maintained: even by the strictest Congregational reasoning, said Mitchell, there is no proving out of the Bible that adults "understanding and believing the Doctrine of Faith, and publicly professing the same, not scandalous in life, and solemnly taking hold of the Covenant . . . may be denied or debarred from Church-Membership or

Baptism upon their desire thereof." Of course, he meant only children of members: but what—upon more mature consideration—was to prevent this measurement from applying to persons outside the church?

In 1677 Increase Mather was still steadfastly warning against admissions to the church and to the Supper of those who could offer no more than "an Historical Faith"; in 1702 his son reported that by then (meaning long since established) the custom of the churches was to receive adults "who had never been Baptised in their Infancy, yet are awakened unto a Desire after Baptism for Themselves, and come up to the Terms of it, giving Rational Hopes, that they have truly Begun to Believe on Christ." These may not apprehend themselves fit for the Lord's Supper, but even so, "Our Churches do receive These (and the Children of These) unto Baptism, and Shut them not out of Doors, because they press not much farther than the Porch of Initial Christianity." In the 1660's a cautious, logically supported proposal to extend a partial membership to the grandchildren of the founders excited ferocious opposition; by 1700 the New England Way was little bothered with ancient scruples, and was pressing visible membership, including the precious rite of baptism, upon all who would own the external covenant.

By the end of the century, therefore, this was roughly the situation in almost all communities: there was still, at the theoretical center, the "church"—consisting either of the children of founders who had fully renewed their spiritual covenant and made a profession, or of those who had somehow been converted from the outside. Surrounding these was a circle of half-way members, already distinguished from the church and called the "congregation," consisting either of those who, inheriting their position from an ancestral professor, remained content with their baptismal obligation in order to gain baptism for their own children, or of those who entered directly from the outside through owning the external covenant in order to bring *their* children within the pale. On the outer circumference, surrounding both sorts of members, was the town, consisting of inhabitants who had no professing ancestors or who would not make even the half-way profession. By the end of the century, these inhabitants, assembled in town meeting where they voted taxes for the minister's salary, were showing an interest in his character and his doctrine, and daring to voice their opinion upon the choice of his successor.

In the town meeting full communicants were definitely a minority, and a dwindling one at that. Theoretically they alone should vote admissions or censures, or choose a successor, but actually they were helpless. The ministers could win a political victory in 1671, but could not comprehend why thereafter hordes were content to remain, and let their children remain, half-way members. "All the Priviledges," complained Oakes, "are so charged with duty, so clogged and encumbered with service, they set at so great a rent of service, and pay so dear (as they think) for their Priviledges, that they are weary of them." Formerly the "generality" of the people were church members, moaned Increase Mather, "but how much otherwise is it now?" It was otherwise because to many it seemed enough: "if they can but get Baptisme for their Children, (tho they never had any right unto it in the sight of God) they look no further." The ministers were prisoners of victory: "What," they demanded, "are you afraid of being holy, afraid of being happy?" Solomon Stoddard watched this development with increasing disgust, reminding his brethren that in several towns scarcely five or six any longer attended the Supper. The Half-Way Covenant promised to enlarge the congregation, which is exactly what it did—at the cost of diminishing the church.

In their astonishment and their consternation, intellectuals set themselves to reëxamining their premises, hoping that in the once logically perfect doctrine they could discern answers to this impossible predicament. Empirically considered, the problem was clearly that the half-way members were not active enough: if you rest upon the security of your parents' covenant, Willard said to them, "you are deceived: you may be the natural Children of godly Parents, and yet the spiritual Children of the Devil." Increase Mather could see, by 1679, that the conversation of the congregation differed so little from that of the town that men could rightly say, "there is nothing in being in Covenant with God, nor is it any mercy to be born of parents that fear the Lord." The need was thus designated: was there anything in Congregational polity and federal Calvinism that could be put to work for exciting the will power of half-way Christians?

The Synod of 1662 required the half-way member, upon presenting his child, to "own the covenant." This, its most contested article, had to be redrafted three times: at first the subcommittee said that adults should understand the grounds of religion, to which Chauncy objected that such an understanding required no knowledge of sin; they then phrased it that the parents should exhibit a sense of a need for Christ and a desire for Him, which Chauncy still contended could be attested by devils in hell. Finally they hit upon what, in the light both of Congregational and federal reasoning, seemed the perfect solution: "understanding the Doctrine of Faith, and publicly professing their assent thereto . . . and solemnly owning the Covenant before the Church." This was more than a mere understanding of abstractions, more than vague desire: it was explicit *assent*, and it was public—exactly those signs of an act of voluntary commitment upon which a Congregational church was constructed. This was the very heart of federal theology.

Opponents cried, with Davenport, that such an owning was no more than "a Parret-like saying the Doctrine of Faith," but they could never deny that it did require a form, even if a ghostly one, of active assent, that it took on the nature of an oath administered before witnesses, requiring henceforth fulfillment of terms from those who thus acted of themselves.

If then, fifteen years later, these covenanted children had not sufficiently responded to their commitment, how better bestir them to the enterprise than by making them renew their renewal? Since they had all done it individually when each had come before the church with his infant in arms, what was to prevent gathering them all together—along with the now adult infants—upon some stated day of humiliation, and, following a jeremiad sermon, require them in unison to repeat what they had already said? Would this not reinvigorate the zeal of all, but especially of that portion of the community which had become a congregation rather than a church?

Institutional historians have, it seems to me, failed to appreciate the importance of that moment in New England's history when renewal of external covenant ceased to be a particular and individual recitation, when it was transformed into a communal chant. Adumbration can be found even before 1675, but the agony of King Philip's War made the practice general. The Church of Norwich seems to have been the pioneer, where on March 22, 1675, Pastor James Fitch got a vote from the congregation that all baptized children should be required to "take hold" the covenant of their fathers on threat of excommunication. But the action of Plymouth, as in the method of thanksgiving, fixed the pattern: at the worst moment of the struggle, on July 22, 1676, according to a vote of all the church and congregation, the entire body stood up and "did solemnly renew their Covenant with God and one another." While Fitch modestly took credit for the idea, Increase Mather seized upon it before his father's people at Dorchester in March 1677, asserting that "Renewal of Covenant" is "the great Duty incumbent on decaying or distressed Churches." What church could pretend, even if not altogether decayed, that it was not distressed? The two General Courts publicized the method, and the "Reforming Synod," faced with the question of what should be done about its catalogue of afflictions, answered in the language of Increase Mather. At the second session, in May 1680, he was running a fever, but "he forgot his Illness" and from the moderator's chair so harried the delegates that in two days they published his resolution: "Solemn and explicit Renewal of Covenant is a Scripture Expedient for Reformation." It was not enough that on days of humiliation an "implicit" renewal be assumed, or that individuals perform the oath on particular occasions: there must be a clear and public acknowledgment, "that so all the Churches may agree," and such a general awe be laid upon all consciences, even upon hypocrites, "as to enforce them unto outward Reformation, and that doth divert temporal Judgements."

Cotton Mather notes that a few churches—"from I know not what objections"—questioned the Scriptural warrant, but most fell rapidly into line. Even at New Haven, with the installation in 1685 of James Pierpont, Davenport was forgotten. "For us to covenant and ingage the Lord," became the standard plea, "is the best way in the world to cause designs which may be against us to prove abortive." As the design of the Crown against the charter became more evident, mass renewals multiplied. They had little effect on Crown lawyers, but, once started, they did serve to fill needs closer home. For John Preston and the theological founders, one consequence of the covenant in federal theology had always been that a particular saint, whenever sorely tried, might "for his owne particular" renew his covenant, "for I finde," Preston had added, "that in all times when the Lord hath stretched forth his hand against a Church and Nation, that this hath beene required, that they should come and enter into a Covenant with God." Throughout the development of this idea, New England theorists insisted, as Increase Mather said, that "a work of this nature should be done not in our own strength, but humbly depending upon Christ, and with all possible seriousness, since it is a most dreadfull thing to transact personally with the holy, and infinitely glorious Majesty of heaven and earth." Yet in this most "particular" act there was a deliberation and a decision. "Choice," as Samuel Willard remarked, "is a judicious and voluntary act, it is the act of a cause by Counsel, acting according to the dictates of right reason and freely resting in the conclusion." If men were thus to resolve with themselves in order to save themselves when the Lord stretched forth His hand upon their nation, with what greater effectiveness might the nation itself, assembling all its particulars into one common personage, save itself against further judgments by a unanimous renewal of the national covenant?

For a Puritan in the England of Preston's day renewal had been a secret means of steeling himself against Laud and Wentworth, but for the American community, the question had become, "What is done by a People in their Renewing of Covenant?" to which Willard could reply, "They doe deliberately chuse God, and strongly oblige themselves to serve him." Some might object that when thus obliged to participate, they swore the oath not out of conviction but out of conformity; but the act still remained, said Willard, a voluntary assumption of the obligation: "You shall also have this advantage by it, that you shall have it as a perpetual monitor, gravely and seriously to advise you of, and excite you to your duty, if you do not wilfully or carelessly put it out of your mind."

Thus renewals of covenant became, in the 1680's, a joyous feature of New England life, usually attended, as Cotton Mather proudly relates, by "a vast confluence of other neighbours." After a day of fasting and prayer, and a sermon on the sins to be repented (the Synod's "catalogue" with local additions), came the ecstatic pledge. Some churches permitted only communicants to pronounce it, but in most the children of the church were also "actively concerned in these transactions." The great thing was that there be activity.

Promoters of these ceremonies still studied Hooker, Shepard, and Stone, still recited the definition of a Congregational church as consisting in an aristocracy that spoke and a democracy that kept silent. But from conflict, dissension, self-distrust and from an urge to hang together, a new phenomenon emerged. It was utterly unlike anything provided for in the original constitution: upon this festive day of renewal (the neighboring confluence looking on) the aristocratic minister spoke, but he begged the democracy not to remain silent. He was not so much instructing them, he was presiding (hopefully) over a movement from the ranks; they, rather than he, were promising "that they will serve God, and Endeavor to perform whatever his Covenant requires of them." At a renewal of the Second Church, Increase Mather explained that it was not a new covenant but a resurrection of the old covenant within which, should any members do or speak evil, "one Brother or other would soon help them to see their Error." On this day the preacher laid aside the prerogatives of Hooker and Cotton, while the congregation took their destiny upon themselves. The clergy had won their fight against pragmaticals, or at least forced them to recede before the Half-Way Covenant, but they could no longer put a king in their pockets. They depended now, though still retaining the prestige of learning, not upon a scholastic definition of their place in the hierarchy of being, but upon a revived community, upon the ability to evoke from year to year an answering chorus.

CHAPTER IX

INTOLERANCE

B_Y
starting with the proposition, "the Magistrate hath
a coactive power to compel the Church to execute the ordinances of
Christ," the founders aligned themselves with the then universal premise
of Europe. As a matter of fact, their peculiar ecclesiastical program obliged
them to give to this thesis a heightened and sharpened prominence. They
did not want to dissociate themselves from the Protestant internationale,
yet in European terms Congregationalism was "radical" (not in our sense
of "liberal") because it strove to institutionalize salvation by faith in a
covenanted church from which most of the population were excluded. The
scheme of "partial dissent" might satisfy metaphysical objections, but the
fact remained that the civil governments of Massachusetts and Connecticut aspired to a tighter control than any European duchy or monarchy
was able (though all tried) to impose. The effort to realize a church of
pure saints demanded actually an even greater concentration upon the
political problem than was demanded of those who acceded to the comfortable formula that a region's religion should accord with the sovereign's.
The attention given in Congregational writings to the external, national
covenant is a sign of how conscious the founders were that they had to
justify, not intolerance itself, but the way in which they could be intolerant.

By emigrating before 1640, these Englishmen missed a vital chapter in
English history. The ideals they had come to vindicate in America—
which they did vindicate—underwent a drastic overhauling at home. Re-
currently the mind of America falls into such isolation: axioms brought to
this country—Puritanism, the social contract, Romanticism—and here successfully tried out, have, by the time the American experiment is completed, ceased to be meaningful in Europe; America is repeatedly left, so
to speak, with an institution on its hands.

In this case, New Englanders won the case for the Independent theory
of 1630; they reported their result at the moment their former colleagues
repudiated its fundamental contention. The English brethren learned revision in an ordeal which Americans could not share—just as, let us say,
they did not share in the Napoleonic struggles, in the slaughter of Verdun,
or in Nazi concentration camps. By 1648 English Independents had become greater strangers to *The Cambridge Platform* than were all those

enemies against whom New Englanders believed they both waged common war.

Being "Independent" in theory, the founders were convinced that the dilemma of Protestantism could never be solved so long as all society was included in the church; they reconciled faith and power by limiting the church to men of the spirit, by entrusting government only to them. These chosen leaders had the responsibility, as did every civil power, of restraining human depravity through the ordinary regulations, but they also had the more positive function of leading (or driving) a whole community up the heights of purity. And all this without becoming "perfectionist," without letting their feet get off the ground! The first and foremost requirement of their program was the suppression of schism and heresy, of all distraction, whether natural or spiritual.

Roger Williams is regarded today as a prophet, and I admire him inordinately; still, we need to remember that he repudiated the persecuting power of the civil arm not because, like Jefferson, he was religiously indifferent, but because he took Congregational purity with dreadful literalness. He was a perfectionist, saved from dogmatism by his realization that perfection is unattainable; nevertheless, he demanded that saints become so holy as to render political regulation superfluous. He became so infatuated with justification by faith that he lost the concomitant sense of innate depravity. He really had little in common with Cromwell and the New Model Army, who came to similar conclusions on different grounds, more properly termed "liberal," that they could not keep regiments in the field if good troopers were to be cashiered for purely speculative opinions.

Wherever, in either the seventeenth century or the twentieth, the idea appears that government should be concentrated in a select few, a coercive imposition upon the majority is inevitable. John Cotton in 1636 made clear to Lords Say and Brook that such a principle cuts across conventional classifications: none should "be appointed and chosen by the people of God, magistrates over them, but men fearing God." Carnal men often have useful abilities—"gifts" as soldiers, architects, merchants—which may be employed, "but yet are men not fit to be trusted with place of standing power or settled authority." An ability to command troops or to make money, although respected in a non-perfectionist order, is not in itself a Christian virtue. Even a hereditary title, including the King of England's, is not a qualification for church membership; nobles, like cobblers, must submit to the test of sainthood.

Cotton was not arguing democracy, he was bidding for power. The noble lords understandably decided not to migrate, but the glory and wonder of New England was that, without titled assistance, it maintained intolerance. The theorem of rule by men "fit to be trusted" became one and the same with orthodox uniformity. To most Protestants, the Congregational proposals of Ames and Preston had seemed as fantastic as the dictatorial visions of Karl Marx were to appear to nineteenth-century socialists; but New England proved that a church order composed only of those visibly justified could also organize and administer a state.

Dr. Robert Child was no champion of religious liberty; he was a Presbyterian who calculated, once his petition of 1645 was rejected, upon bringing a Presbyterian power into Massachusetts. To the Massachusetts authorities, his design was transparent: his complaint that godly men, "members of the church of England," were barred from the sacraments because "they will not take these churches covenants, for which as yet they see no light in Gods word," was an attempt to break the Congregational monopoly. He was clever enough to argue that rule by a minority was civil tyranny, an invasion of "our due and naturall rights, as freeborne subjects of the English nation," that it meant taxation without representation and an administration not bound by law, "which is the true interpreter of all oathes to all men, whether judge or judged," but he was not a martyr for constitutionality; he was using constitutionalism as the weapon of a competing interest. New England's order was not based upon a charter of rights and liberties; it was founded upon the conviction that only men fearing God could and would properly administer rights and liberties. The authorities understood all too well Pascal's observation that the art of revolution consists in upsetting established customs by accusing them of injustice, in wilfully refusing to see in their revolt "the fact of usurpation." Congregationalism was the one society in a Protestant world prepared to give short shrift to rebels who cloaked insurrection with a specious legality.

The General Court did not prevaricate when telling Child that a nonmember had "all the priviledges of a freeborne English subject," even "without right of election of publick officers," or that the only reason inhabitants were excluded from citizenship was that, even though they might have faith, "they doe not manifest the same by any public profession before the church . . . and so it is not knowne that they are thus qualified." But as for compelling non-members to attend services and to pay rates—well, objection to that requirement was obviously an attempt to excuse such disgruntled persons "as are tainted with corrupt opinions as doe cause them to cast off all publick ordinances of Gods worship." Child's attack, in the name of equity, upon exclusion was countered by the doctrine of the external, national covenant set forth in the *Laws* of 1648:

> Wee answer that a subsequent, or implicit consent is of like force in this case, as an expresse precedent power: for in putting your persons and estates into the protection and way of subsistance held forth and exercised within this Jurisdiction, you doe tacitly submit to this Government and to all the wholesome laws thereof, and so is the common repute in all nations, and that upon this Maxim: Qui sentit commodum sentire debet et onus.

The founders did not rationalize a lust for power, but having control, they resolved to hold it, and so put together a political theory as fully coherent as their ecclesiastical doctrine. It was an intellectual registration of that act of will which came to unalterable decision in the Cambridge of August 1629.

"Hence it is," Cotton wrote, "that we plead for this order to be set in Civil Affairs, that such a course may be taken as may best secure to our selves and our posterities the faithful managing of Civil Government for the common welfare of all, as well in the Church as without." Not that church members had any peculiar economic or legal advantages: should "none have Lots in due proportion with other men, nor the benefit of Justice under the Government where they live, but onely Church-members," this would indeed be tyranny; the record bears Cotton out that these commodities were dispensed without regard to ecclesiastical status. However, the doctrine did openly and intentionally hold that not only law and order, the distribution of land and enforcement of civil peace, but also the spiritual purpose of the community would best be secured "when the publick Trust and Power of these matters is committed to such men as are most approved to God." Nothing could be more frank. Therefore, "that Form of Government wherein the power of Civil Administration is denied unto unbelievers, and committed to the Saints, is the best Form of Government in a Christian Commonwealth." There was no doubt that this "Theocratie," with all its guarantees, empowered the government to say to heretics, as did Winthrop to Anne Hutchinson, "We are your judges, and not you ours, and we must compel you to it."

The shock of the Independents' perfidy did not shake the confidence of the regime in the rule of intolerance, but rather hardened its resolution. Thereupon colonials acquired a sensitiveness to external criticism entirely lacking in the first philosophy; they could not understand the very words Henry Vane used to Winthrop: the "exercises and troubles" of the kingdom, he said, had taught the Independents forbearance, "which makes me hope that, from experience here, it may also be derived to yourselves." But how could experience be shipped across the Atlantic? In fact, Vane's contention that the example of New England inspired Presbyterians to extirpate Congregationalism "from its owne principles and practice" was an invitation to colonial authorities to redouble repressive measures. The only restraint was a fear lest, if they went too far, Cromwell might intervene; but when it became clear that he was too much engaged elsewhere, and when the contagion of toleration, in the form of Anabaptists and Quakers, approached these sacred shores, the regime, led by Endecott and Norton, lost all sense of proportion. Williams addressed *The Bloudy Tenent of Persecution* to an English audience which, in 1644, included most Independents, but Cotton's reply, *The Bloudy Tenent, Washed, And made white in the bloud of the Lambe*, shows how, by 1647, American Congregationalists were approaching a state of hysteria because their best friends had gone over to Williams' heresy.

Thus the New England mind was condemned to an even greater stress upon doctrinaire intolerance than it had originally intended. The most lively contribution was Nathaniel Ward's *The Simple Cobler of Aggawam in America*, also published in 1647, the conscious point of which is that American experience had come to mean, or rather remained, something different from England's: "I dare take upon me, to be the Herauld of New-England so farre, as to proclaime to the world, in the name of our Colony, that all Familists, Antinomians, Anabaptists, and other Enthusiasts, shall have free Liberty to keep away from us, and such as will come to be gone as fast as they can, the sooner the better." Precisely because he no longer expected the approbation of the world (or at least of that part of the world which really mattered), Ward gave all the greater precision to his defiance: "Morall Laws, Royall Prerogatives, Popular Liberties, are not of Mans making or giving, but Gods: Man is but to measure them out by Gods Rule." He then asserted the further corollary that America no longer signified a universal but rather a peculiar destiny, "which if mans wisdome cannot reach, Mans experience must mend."

Other leaders joined the cry: Thomas Shepard, for instance, declared toleration "the foundation of all other Errors and Abominations in the Churches of God, if it once be attended among any People of God." In 1658 Edward Holyoke of Lynn discussed the problem more allegorically in *The Doctrine of Life*, representing King Solomon as lecturing the Queen of Sheba (after she had given him "all the best content she could") that man is by nature a wild colt, "and there is no taming of corrupt nature but by a strict course of holy Laws, which to a regenerate and godly soul is an easy Yoke." Unfortunately, the Queen had "orient eyes, damaske rosie cheeks," along with "cherry lips, and all festivity and grace of speech," being endowed with "what may give a man content (I speak simply of man and woman)," with the dreadful result that, the morning after, she lured the wisest of men into tolerating paganism. To forestall her charms, the General Court of Massachusetts ordered in May 1658 that no person should be allowed to hold forth in any town where the churches, a council of state, or the court themselves disapproved.

The temptress came to New England, not in the luscious form of Sheba's Queen, but in the grimy guise of a handful of Anabaptists, and then of a company of Quakers, among whom appeared that same Mary Dyer who had walked out of the First Church with Anne Hutchinson. The three Anabaptists came to Lynn to comfort a dying colleague, were arrested, and arraigned; John Cotton preached a sermon before them, proving that by rejecting infant baptism they overthrew all churches, then Endecott shrieked at them, and Pastor Wilson struck them. Surprisingly enough, sympathizers paid bail for two of them, but Obediah Holmes was given thirty lashes with a three-thonged whip. The Baptists further asserted that a witness who murmured against this treatment was sent by Endecott to jail with the injunction, "we will deal with you as we have dealt with him."

One of the three, John Clarke, in 1652 published their story in London as *Ill Newes from New England.* The Quaker story was similarly broadcast in 1661 (with an appendix in 1667) by George Bishop of Bristol, *New-England Judged, Not by Man's, but the Spirit of the Lord.* Whether or not these narratives are accurate—assuredly both authors have a sense for drama—is of less importance than the fact that they made effective propaganda against New England. An Anglican Restoration was delighted to make much of them; upon New England, their effect was to stiffen the determination to resist by fair means or foul.

According to Bishop, the means were foul to begin with, and his description of Endecott is a masterful portrait of the reactionary driven to frenzy by the refusal of history to support him. The Quaker version is more fully substantiated by other records. On October 19, 1658, the Court promised death to those who returned from banishment, under which law William Robinson and Marmaduke Stevenson were led, along with Mary Dyer, to the gallows on October 27, 1659; she was reprieved, the authorities waiting until the last moment to inform her, on condition that her husband take her back to Rhode Island. Stevenson and Robinson perished in the grand manner of the *Book of Martyrs:* "for to me to live is Christ, and to Dye is Gain; and truly I have a great desire, and will to dye herein, knowing that the Lord is with me, whatever Ignorant Men shall be able to say against me." After Mary Dyer had voluntarily stood up with Anne Hutchinson, she was delivered of a premature fetus (one may understand why); in a Calvinist universe such monstrosities were signs of divine counsel, and the great Winthrop himself eagerly inquired after the goriest details. Despite this early miscarriage, Mary Dyer subsequently produced several children of her body, from whom many Americans today have descended. Her husband could not restrain her, and she came back, to be hanged on June 1, 1660. William Leddra was executed on March 14, 1661, before an order arrived from King Charles forbidding Massachusetts Bay to kill his subjects.

"So Death was the Thing ye aimed at, and their Blood ye would have, and their Blood ye had," Bishop proclaimed to the same world Nathaniel Ward had also addressed. In 1657 Commissioners of the United Colonies tried to force Rhode Island (which was not, of course, in the Union) to banish Quakers; that colony replied with the curious observation that Quakers had proved, when tolerated, to be hostile only against persecutors: "Surely we find that they delight to be persecuted by civill powers, and when they are soe, they are like to gain more adherents by the conseyte of their patient sufferings, than by consent to their pernicious sayings." Roger Williams was shocked by the doctrines of George Fox and wrote against them, and the colony's authorities assured the Commissioners that Quaker teaching did indeed threaten the overturn of all civil government. But Rhode Island found itself obliged, by its previous declarations, to tolerate differences of opinion, and so made this astounding discovery.

For the rest of New England, Quakerism was one more, and apparently the most vicious, eruption of perfectionism, which would indeed nullify all laws and ordinances: Quakers "have no need to purify themselves dayly, as all Christians should, for they are perfectly pure already." Apologists for the regime try to defend it on the plea that Quakers did things which, as Henry Martyn Dexter said, would invite arrest "even in the brightest light of this nineteenth century," as, for example, when Lydia Wardwell and Deborah Wilson paraded naked in the streets. Critics answer that such gyrations were not so serious as to call for punishment in the form of whippings through several towns in midwinter. Both arguments forget that there was nothing in the philosophy of the communities enabling them to regard these offenses only as disturbances of the peace or indecent exposures; they had no way of knowing (neither did Cromwell) that this pacific kind of perfectionism was not the old Anabaptism of Münster.

Only one thing could check the orthodox regime, some brutal imposition by an outside force, such as the King's command. The Restoration made no sense in any Protestant conception of history; yet there it was, "as if," mourned Hull, "when they had now twenty years of conflicting, and a great part of them in bloody war, for reformation, they should all upon a sudden be sent back again." Within a matter of months New England learned that not only "they" in England but they in the colonies were caught in the meshes of this reversal. New England faced the problem of coming to terms with a universe completely altered from that with which the founders had supposed themselves in perfect accord.

In the election sermon of 1661 John Norton tried to tell the society what it had now to attempt: on the one hand, to recollect that it was loyal to the Crown ("It is not a Gospel-spirit to be against Kings: 'tis neither Gospel nor English Spirit for any of us to be against the Government by Kings, Lords and Commons"), and on the other to justify its peculiar system. The pressing question will now be "whether the Congregational-way be practicable, yea or not?" Here was the dilemma, sharpened beyond anything Richard Mather in 1657 had imagined at Dorchester, by its very insistence bound to start new lines of thought.

The first maneuver was inescapable: the General Court professed their absolute fidelity, explained their treatment of Quakers, defended their seizure of Maine lands, and, for good measure, bethought themselves to pass laws enforcing the Navigation Acts. They then asserted their view of legality: any government under such a charter as theirs has power over all its peoples, "without appeal, excepting law or laws repugnant to the laws of England." Less publicly, they instructed their agents to block any suggestions that colonial laws could be reviewed in London, for this "would render authoritie and government vaine and uneffectual, and bring us into contempt with all sortes of people."

As a chapter in intellectual history, this part of the narrative falls short of precision for one sufficient reason: the government of Charles II was inefficient, dilatory, absent-minded, inconsistent, and in general stupid. For two decades it did not press its advantages, did not complete motions it inaugurated, kept up a threat it never got around to executing, and so gave New England time to adjust piecemeal, allowed die-hards to die, and a faction to emerge which, wearying of the dispute, grew into readiness to give up the charter. Because King Charles could not keep his mind on colonial business, and preferred to chase moths in Lady Castlemaine's apartments even while the Dutch were in the Medway, let alone while Norton, Endecott, and Davenport were expiring in New England, he permitted the New England mind to struggle through the first and most important stages of a mental revolution in splendid isolation.

Assuredly, had the government struck in 1661 with anything like the force Laud had contemplated in 1636–37, American history would be another story; we owe an incalculable debt to the bungling of English officialdom. The situation was ripe for intervention: belated efforts to conform to the Navigation Acts, or a sullen leaving off of hanging Quakers (upon the first hint of royal indifference, Massachusetts commenced a new series of whippings, some of them almost unto death) were empty gestures. But instead, the Crown gave Connecticut a charter in 1662, uniting it with New Haven and virtually conceding local sovereignty. To Simon Bradstreet and John Norton, arrived in London as agents, King Charles in that same year graciously gave a letter calling for things he could have extracted only by force; by telling them what England would demand if it ever mustered enough energy, the letter plainly informed the colonists that they might get their way indefinitely if, instead of meeting charges head-on, they essayed diplomacy, pious misunderstandings, evasions, and half-truths. For two decades thereafter, the conduct of public affairs was for New England a thorough schooling in duplicity. This fact has to be connected with the flourishing of the jeremiads, with the doctrine of renewal of covenant and the emergence of community revivalism. Time gained by ruse and by stratagem was time acquired for institutional evolution. Not until the end of the century could any in the region even commence to comprehend that the long training in protraction undergone between 1660 and 1685 imparted to the Puritan mind qualities which it had not possessed—or at least brought forward some which had hitherto been recessive—at the foundation. Read with this thought in mind, the *Magnalia*, while seemingly a lament over the decline of New England or purportedly an elaborate defense of the Half-Way Covenant, becomes a shrewd analysis of intellectual change: "But whether New England may Live any where else or no, it must Live in our History!"

The king's letter of June 28, 1662, while confirming the Massachusetts charter (but saying nothing about appeals), demanded that the Common Prayer should not be denied those who desired it, that persons of honest lives be admitted to the Lord's Supper, and that freeholders of competent estates be admitted to citizenship. Nothing could have been more grandiloquently pronounced, in utter ignorance of reality. At that very

moment, King Charles's government was limping along by grace of the
Clarendon Code, with the result that the great issues among the Dissenters
were being reduced from a high and mighty clash of absolutes to squalid
haggling among sects. The royal letter was not, as interpreted in New
England, an invitation to toleration: it was a bid for Anglican supremacy.
The New Englanders had no choice but to treat it as such, and to fend
it off; by doing so, they tacitly demoted themselves from champions of a
city on the hill to an idiosyncratic congregation, protected merely by distance from the confusions of their former brethren. In that case, distance
became such a bulwark as Scriptural conviction had once been.

At last, in 1664, when a Royal Commission was on its way under orders to investigate how far the king's commands had been obeyed, the
General Court of Massachusetts rushed through a law ostensibly extending the suffrage to freeholders who had estates paying a ten-shilling tax—
or to those who presented a certificate from their minister that they were
orthodox and not scandalous. To which the General Court innocently
added, "or that they are in full communion with some church among us."
Since the time of Hooker, the certificate system had been followed in Connecticut; it achieved the same results as Massachusetts' legislation, and
now enabled the Connecticut General Court to tell the Royal Commissioners that the franchise was not ecclesiastically limited. The Commissioners quickly discovered that the Massachusetts law was a farce: scarcely
three in a hundred paid as much as ten shillings, whereas any church member, "though he be a servant and pay not two pence," was a freeman. But
the General Court were learning audacity: their new law, they said, complied with the king's request "as farr as doth consist with conscience of our
duty towards God, and the just liberties and priviledges" of the charter.

The Synod of 1662 was positive that half-way membership should not
convey a franchise either in state or church, and for years there was no
linking of citizenship to the covenant. But shortly after 1665 an awful
result became evident: because citizenship meant obligation, masses of good
people found themselves content to stop with the half-way position in order
to evade it. This was nothing less than a silent revolution worked by prudence; in the shifting context, citizenship had ceased to be the prized possession of an elite: it had become an onerous chore.

Coincident with this discovery there appears the first division within
New England society that was not a local quarrel (as was Winthrop's
with the Hingham militia) or a theological issue (like the Antinomian dispute), but a calculation of policy. An opposition party took shape, at first
not hostile to the regime itself but composed of such pious citizens as John
Hull, convinced merely of the folly of opposing English might. These men
urged, and raised the money for, Norton and Bradstreet's mission in 1662
against the intransigence of Endecott and Bellingham; among the subscribers appear many "new" men, mostly merchants. In 1666, while the
General Court procrastinated about answering still another royal letter,

petitions for a more complaisant response came from Boston, Newbury, Ipswich, signed by men of substance, frankly confessing that they did not want the king angered because of "the interest of their persons and estates."

Thus we perceive the hidden background of the jeremiads. Mitchell's *Nehemiah on the Wall* bemoaned "discontents and divisions" in such pointed terms as to make clear that he was striking in 1667 at what had already become a party of appeasement: "Yea, there were among themselves that [were] helpers to their Adversaries, and complied with them, even some chiefe men . . . Yea, there were some of the Prophets." Neither he nor his followers could bring themselves, in public, to name names, and therefore the workings of the moderate group remain, to this day, obscure. Leaders of the dominant and vocal faction affected to be so shocked at the very existence of such persons in Israel as to be without words. But the evidence is clear: by 1670 the holy society had become like any other society outside the national covenant, sundered into two opinions, not over a basic theological or even ecclesiastical question, but over one of political expediency.

For ten years after the Royal Commission, Whitehall left New England alone. Yet in that decade of salutary neglect, the wall of intolerance steadily cracked. On May 28, 1665, Thomas Gould of Charlestown, who had long suffered doubts about infant baptism, gathered with eight others (five of them freemen) to form a Baptist Church; try as they might, the authorities could not suppress it. Gould and one of his colleagues were imprisoned for nearly a year; a public disputation was held at the First Church in April 1668, which was supposed to convince the Baptists, but did not; whereupon Gould and his fellows were sentenced to banishment. They refused to budge. The old magic that had worked against Antinomians, Roger Williams, and Dr. Child was no longer effective. The General Court had to receive a remonstrance they could not disregard, signed by James Oliver, by Edward and Elisha Hutchinson, Usher, Shrimpton. Soon came a letter from thirteen of the most respected Nonconformists in England telling the General Court what unfortunate effects their action would have "at home." In the language of the past, the court tried to explain that to allow Gould his church would be to set up a school of seduction, to open a door for abominations, "to the disturbance not only of our ecclesiastical enjoyments, but also contempt of our civil order & authority here established." But news of the outside world kept flowing in: in 1667 the second part of Bishop's *New-England Judged* was published, and in 1672 William Coddington, years ago banished as a partisan of Mrs. Hutchinson, sent a letter to Governor Bellingham (that worthy burned it unread, but Coddington printed his copy): "You may as well withold the flowing of the Tide into the Massachusetts Bay, as the Workings of the God of Truth in the Hearts of his People in the Massachusetts Jurisdiction, or to limit the holy One to a Company or Tribe of Priests, who make a trade of the Scriptures, keeping People always under their Teaching, that they may be always paying of them."

King Charles was, we know, anything but an apostle of toleration, but he was working that effect in his dominions beyond the seas. By 1672 Coddington's letter could not be dismissed as merely the ranting of a Rhode Islander; Gould and his Baptists could be neither banished nor silenced, but kept their church in being on Noodles Island until Governor Leverett, elected in 1673, gave up as a bad job any further attempt to torment it. The next year John Hull shook his head in sorrow: "This summer, The Anabaptists that were wont to meet at Noodle's Island met at Boston on the Lord's Day." Also, he noted, there were now several Quakers living unmolested in the town, and—most inconceivable—some magistrates would "not permit any punishment to be inflicted on heretics as such." In 1678 Gould and his brethren built a meeting-house in Boston, and, though they had something of a struggle to occupy it, they prevailed. Ecclesiastical uniformity was visibly crumbling. Two decades later, Cotton Mather told the story of Gould with the utmost distaste for all its aspects, and passed over these "contentious matters" as quickly as possible with the *Magnalia's* summation: "Thanks be to God we have done with them; and all the foam whereinto we were chafed by them, is now comfortably wiped off."

CHAPTER X

PROPAGANDA

BEFORE
getting down to business with the Royal Commission
in 1665, the General Court tried to arouse public opinion with a proclamation of how much prosperity "hath its dependence, vnder God, vpon the benigne aspect of our soueraigne lord the king towards us." After they had, by barefaced tactics, thwarted these investigators, they declared exultantly that we must all lie low before the King of Kings, just as we have been casting ourselves at the feet of King Charles "for the continuance of his royall favour towards vs, & exerting of it in such a way as may establish our all vnto vs in this our time of tryall." Dismissing for the moment the myriad afflictions so frequently tabulated, the General Court solicited the people to remember that they had been "singularly exempted from his sharpened stroaks, wherein so many abroad haue had so deepe & peirsing a sense," and in that thought to beseech the Lord to preserve "our sweete union." The technique of supplication, addressed either to the King of Heaven or the King of England, professed to be an efficient means, by exhibiting sorrow for past transgression, of softening a royal demeanor toward the community; but it served locally to mobilize energies which, in the act of humiliation, would flow into unanimity.

Meanwhile, as encouragement to those energies, the leaders, both lay and clerical, raised the spectre of the bishops, dread ogres of the founders' fireside reminiscences. They had to do so without antagonizing the restored prelates, but explicitly enough for the people to understand. If you do not stop fighting over the Half-Way Covenant, Oakes warned, then "your differences will make way for those that will make no difference between Synodists and Antisynodists, Old or New-Church men." Against the menace of such tyranny, there was only one protection: "Keep to your PATENT!" Whereupon a subtle shift in emphasis was bound to appear: this charter, which had originally signified, as against Anne Hutchinson or Dr. Child alike, a "Christian liberty" in the sense of a willing subjection to authority, had now to be presented as a bulwark of constitutional liberties (including the ecclesiastical) against encroaching despotism. "Reced from that one way or other, and you will expose your selves (for ought I know) to the Wrath of God, and Rage of Man"; by holding firmly to it, you will retain "the Liberties and Immunities conferred upon you therein." In this strength, you "may with good Conscience set your Foot

against any Foot of Pride and Violence that shall come against you."
Obliged to gird the people for resistance in order to make the day of
humiliation an instrument of unification, the preachers were further compelled to identify the cause of the charter primarily with civil rights; whereupon the stress became the reverse of that employed against Dr. Child.
Were their exhortation heeded, the effect would be, not so much to encourage reformation of sins, but to make anyone who whispered a word
against the charter an enemy of the people: "A Mutinous Army and a
Divided People are easily made a prey to their Enemies," a statement for
which Oakes found proof in Scripture, but more cogently in "Reason
and Experience."

To master this argument required skill, because on every public occasion
the leaders had to protest an absolute and undying allegiance to the Crown,
and yet in the same, or next, breath, to show that "the Government set-
led here by the Charter of this Colonie is a subordinate Government"
which provides us not only with the true church order but also those rights
which had suddenly assumed such vital importance as that of "the people
here to chuse their own Magistrates." All this made for a complicated predicament: the "theocrat" was still beholding his vision of a city on the hill
—"I looke upon this as a little model of the Glorious Kingdome of Christ
on Earth, Christ Reigns among us in the Commonwealth as well as in the
Church, and hath his glorious Interest invoked and wrapt up in the good
of both Societies respectively"—but those advantages which wrapt up the
interest of the secular Commonwealth would rally more persons than
merely church members to a defense of the model. Thus the ministers
became progressively victims of their own propaganda as they subordinated the ecclesiastical cause to the civil. If you quit your liberties, Oxenbridge said in 1671, you will get such magistrates as please neither God
nor yourselves, "but other men will be your masters, for servants, yea,
slaves must you be." "This your day of free Election is preforable before
all your own dayes," Oxenbridge continued, hardly realizing the implications: "There is no such day in other Colonies abroad." Thus, little by
little those who sought to preserve the charter, by force if necessary, in
order to save their spiritual administration, came to present it as worth
fighting for on the grounds of prescriptive rights: "Your civil and your
religious liberties are so coupled here, that if one be lost the other cannot
be kept"; yet in order to make the appeal work, they had to put the civil
before the religious. The elders themselves betrayed the drift when advising the General Court of 1672: "It being the great liberty of an English
subject to be tryed by his peers, before whom he hath free and full libertie
to plead law for his endempnitie and safety," a reflection that had not figured so prominently when men fearing God had dealt with Mrs. Hutchinson, Obediah Holmes, or Robinson and Stevenson.

But this liberty of an English subject would hardly be worth preserving
if, by maintaining it, New England lost its own spiritual administration.

Loyalty had to be aroused to the privileges of the charter, under which the regime had been able to execute, or at least not to tolerate, Baptists and Quakers. As Higginson said, even as he warned the merchants who increased cent per cent, the cause of New England is "Not a toleration of all Religions, or of the Heresies & Idolatries of the age we live in," for what is contrary to the Gospel "hath no right, and therefore should have no liberty." Because there is, or is professed to be, trial by jury, the laws *therefore* profess subjection to the Gospel—which means "your non-toleration of that which is contrary thereunto; this will be a name and a glory to New England so long as the Sun and Moon endure."

Year by year, election sermons show an increasing confusion. Stoughton in 1668 confessed that the problem was full of knots and intricacies, but pulled himself up with the certainty that "true Christian Gospel-Liberty, was never unto this day a Womb big with Licentiousness." The connotations (and soon the denotation) of liberty shifted with every utterance: in 1671 Oxenbridge, comparing the uniformity which bishops would impose with Congregational discipline, went so far as to wish that "forbearance may be exercised to all sober people, so it be not against piety or peace," but had to note in the printed text that this passage "did not sound well in the ears of two or three persons whom I honour." The next year, the younger Shepard pleased those persons better by saying that the Lord had blessed exercises of coercive power in New England by crushing "in the very Egg" what would have become a brood of "poysonful, fiery, stinging Serpents." Yet, he had to observe, many are now saying "this is but persecution, and better let all alone, these things will dye of themselves." The more, as we have noted, a vice is denounced in the jeremiad, the more we assume it prevalent; hence Shepard tells us much by distinguishing, as one sign of perilous times, the fact that the "swaying part among a professing people" could see charms in "such a Syncretisme in Religion as takes in all perswasions (without regard to that spiritual chastity and virgin spirit, which . . . ought to be in all true followers of the Lamb)."

Preachers of the 1670's and '80's—their brains working as hard as had their fathers' when first devising the church covenant—wove together, into one conglomerate appeal, fear of bishops and political tyranny, an identification of liberty with the charter, and religious intolerance; and then declared that the incongruous collocation of these three tenets was the basic condition of social survival. So they achieved such mosaics as this of Oakes in 1673:

God hath delivered you from the Paw of the Lion and of the Bear, so that you have not known by woful experience to this day, what a wicked, oppressing Ruler means, nor seen one of these cruel and imperious Beasts among you. God hath not given us Rulers that would fleece us, that would pull the bread out of our mouthes, that would grinde our faces and break our bones, that would undermine and rob us of our Liberties, Civil and Religious, to the enslaving of this people and their children.

Liberty, prosperity, religious independence, and intolerance thus became (in contrast to Winthrop's) their little model of the Kingdom of Christ —"not in the wild sense of those that are called Fift-monarchy men, but in the sober sense of many of our Divines." Yet at the moment this intellectual synthesis was achieved, the church order had barely escaped disaster over the Third Church, and the ministers had been so accused of arrogance that their counteremphasis upon intolerance has a visibly frenetic quality. Theirs was not, like Winthrop's, an assertion of the ideal society, but a lash with which to whip unruly congregations and pragmatical Deputies into line.

Of course, said Oakes, Englishmen are tenacious of their rights, and religious ones "are wont to be as stout Asserters of their Liberties as any men," but for persons then to cry for liberty of conscience as a right is "to fling open the great Gate for the ready Admission and Reception of all Abominable Heresies." Samuel Willard laid bare the motive behind such pleading when denouncing, in the same year, those who still opposed the Half-Way Covenant: the sinews of civil order will be destroyed "by reason of the necessary evils incident to a declining Popular Government." Not all the Deputies who in 1670 arraigned the ministers were necessarily enemies of the charter, but they surely struck at the one interest most resolved to fight and die for it. The clergy had thus to double and redouble their efforts to convince the masses that the preservation of the regime was one with the cause of freedom, and then to incite this regime to deprive large numbers of them of religious freedom. The danger, increasing every moment, was that such dissidents would begin to look toward the threatened English intervention as a promise of relief. At the Reforming Synod, where the clergy made a supreme effort to retain their power, they also impressed upon the civil authorities the lesson that no reformation ever succeeded without vigorous assistance from magistrates.

Several developments in the succession of jeremiads which otherwise might seem merely rhetorical take on more precise meanings when linked with these political tensions. The national covenant, for instance, was so exploited as to become the bond that included all the population; judgments of God could then be presented as provoked by universal corruptions, and the obligation to reform—having become an obligation to accept the dictates of authority—could be pressed remorselessly upon both half-way members and natural inhabitants. So, too, greater and greater weight was given to the argument that rewards of the external covenant are "temporal"—wherefore merchants should remind themselves of what they owed to government under the charter. God "brought us into a wealthy place," said the Synod's preface in 1680; nowhere else on the face of the earth have a people come "to such perfection and considerableness, in so short a time." James Fitch in 1676 devised an interesting twist to this consideration: he was willing that the unregenerate should be less disturbed in their sins as long as they supported the government, because "if the ruling and carrying party do shine in Grace and Godliness, this will argue for that People." Sinning merchants would not provoke so much vengeance (and financial loss) if only they would not coöperate with Royal Commissioners.

Philip's War gave a wonderful opportunity to pronounce judgment on the entire people, since the tomahawk observed no distinction between saints and reprobates: "because of the provoking of his sons and daughters, the Lord hath moved us to anger with a foolish Nation, and moved us to jealousie with those which are not a people." The summons to reformation here merged with that to political allegiance: will you, asked Samuel Hooker in 1677, still drink, swear, and "scoffe at the wayes and servants of God?" Then beware lest "the names you bear, the houses you dwell in, the estates you inherit, and places you sustain, rise up in judgment against you." Yet with every such utterance, the fact came closer to the surface: the jeremiad was not succeeding in gearing ancient names (Dudley and Denison) or houses and estates (Wharton, Brattle, Sergeant) into the united front. In 1682, as the cause of the charter drooped, Willard sounded another of these exhortations, but as much as admitted, in *The Only Sure Way to Prevent Calamities*, that the device was growing stale.

In addition to the national covenant, there were other instruments of excitation to be tried—preparation, for instance. "The unpreparedness of this or that people for a full Scriptural Reformation many times is a great Clog and Remorce to pious Rulers and Ministers that are vigorously pursuing it." In order to make these clogs the more inexcusable, some exhorters, employing the Peripatetic doctrine of psychological faculties, found themselves depicting the mechanism of preparation in such manageable terms as to put it at the disposal of all but the utterly besotted. Man being a rational creature, Allin explained, his "understanding is the guide of the will, the will hath command of every other faculty"; consequently, one who understands the value of reformation (how could he not comprehend after decades of jeremiads?) will command his affections to make a try. But how does one come to understanding? Not alone through knowledge of good and evil, but through experience of them; there must be not only a discovery of evil, "but an experience of it that it is so." Had not New England, with plagues, wars, and now internal dissensions, had enough experience? In such discourses the conventional reminder that before the spirit assists us we are impotent becomes perfunctory, often being omitted; the more usual application takes the form, "Would we be free from misery, would we be happy, make this Our business."

Allin explained, in the language of the faculty psychology (which, as a subsection of physics, was taught throughout the century at Harvard), how an outward stimulus is received by the senses as an image, is stored in the memory, whence it can be summoned by the reason, "causing the will and affections of the Soul to live and walk in the strength of it." If the people were to be invigorated into acts of will, their memories and imaginations had to be filled with images of the pristine virtue, of the success—and the unity—of the original New England. Hence in the jeremiads of this era, particularly after 1676, a theme receives literary formulation which henceforth was to be a staple of the New England mind: ancestor worship. Virtually every one who migrated as an adult before 1640 was gone; in order to lay the covenant of the golden age upon their descendants (and incidentally to prove to those who bore such a name as Dudley that they were a lesser breed than their fathers), the spokesmen called for such a veneration of progenitors as is hardly to be matched outside China. When God first "began to keep House in this Wilderness," said Stoughton, "it was furnished with the choicest Household-stuff"; or, as he put it in another metaphor that quickly became the classic statement, "God sifted a whole Nation that he might send choice Grain over into this wilderness." Soon emphasis upon this theme was carried to such lengths of abjectness ("I should rather suspect my own judgment in Scriptures, then theirs about that case") that we marvel how any Protestant culture could so abnegate its Christian liberty, until we remind ourselves that the preachers were fighting tooth and nail for what they considered survival, that these gestures were not so much humble submissions to the past as a discharge of heavy artillery against their antagonists. Increase Mather was the foremost artisan of this appeal, and his son grew up in a household where it was the daily topic of discourse, so that the *Magnalia* ultimately was to become, under the guise of history, a sustained chant to the glory of mighty and already misty ancestral heroes. But Solomon Stoddard, looking on from the safety and distance of Northampton, was obliged to notice that despite all this Matherian eloquence, the posterity seemed little disposed to emulate their fathers; he wondered if there were not better ways to subjugate pragmatical merchants.

In March of 1676 the newly organized Lords of Trade dispatched Edward Randolph to Boston, ostensibly to present the claims of Mason to New Hampshire and of Gorges to Maine, but actually to prepare for action against the charter. While he was still on his ten-week voyage, and while the war with Philip hung in doubt, William Hubbard of Ipswich delivered at the election in May *The Happiness of a People in the Wisdome of their Rulers Directing And in the Obedience of their Brethren Attending*, the finest prose of the decade, which rises into a lofty hymn to order: "It was Order that gave Beauty to this goodly fabrick of the world, which before was but a confused Chaos." At first sight, it appears a repetition, in more poetic vein, of Winthrop's conception of a hierarchy of mutual obligation, concluding, like the *Modell*, with the social moral of "Unity, Love and Peace"; yet on second reading it reveals, in the name of these slogans, a lesson distinctly counter to that of Shepard, Oakes, and Increase Mather. As openly as possible, Hubbard pleads for toleration. The end of government, he says, is civil peace and honesty, which does indeed require enforcement of the "First Table," but peaceable dissenters in religion will not be recovered by excessive severity, nor should we be too eager to attain unanimity in opinions of lesser certainty for which the wisest of men have always demanded latitude. While the liberty of choosing our own rulers is a high privilege, yet "it may become an occasion of the greatest bondage; as hath been too sadly verified almost in all elective states and kingdoms in the world." With calculated effrontery, Hubbard says he will not reprove those who have fulminated against toleration "lest it should be an insinuation, that some here present are inclined that way," but will remark that when we have to deal with mistakes not seditiously or blasphemously maintained, "there seems neither rule from the word of God, nor reason from the nature of the thing, why any should undergoe capital punishment." The Netherlands, he ventures to remind the General Court, strengthened themselves by softening "the sharpness of all differences about religion found in other places so troublesome." Just as magistrates should not, "Gallio like, let truth and errour run together in a race, catch it who can; no neither should they Gyant-like strain up all under their power to their own measure, or bringing them down to their owne size, as was said of Procrustes, that used so to deal with his Guests."

Unfortunately we know little about Hubbard. The General Court commissioned him to write a history of New England, which he finished in 1682, but it displeased certain elements (particularly, it seems, Increase Mather) and so was never published. When news of the abrogation of the charter arrived in 1685, Hubbard wrote the General Court a counsel of moderation, whereupon several ministers violently protested that he spoke not for them. Thus Hubbard seems clearly to align himself with those Randolph called the moderates, an impression somehow confirmed by the fact that at the ripe age of seventy-three he scandalized the respectable by marrying his housekeeper. Certainly the jeremiads contain dark references to the awful fact that even "elders" were in the opposition; while Hubbard's sermon of 1676 is no mighty blast for religious liberty, it represents the sort of caution that was dawning upon men like Simon Bradstreet and Major General Daniel Denison—both of whom, incidentally, were married to sisters of Joseph Dudley. Small as it may seem to us, the gulf was in fact immense between the enraged lashings of Urian Oakes and this serene sentence of Hubbard's: "Or to what end should men be put to produce either Scripture or reason to confirm the Religion they profess . . . if they can expect no other Answer, then from the executioner or officer of Justice?"

The next year, 1677, Increase Mather gave the election sermon, and *A Discourse Concerning the Danger of Apostacy* is manifestly a rebuttal of Hubbard: "The Toleration of all Religions and Perswasions, is the way to have no true Religion left." For the supreme demonstration of this rule, Mather cited the crushing evidence of the founders: "If your blessed Fathers and Predecessors were alive, and in place, it would not be so: If Winthrop, Dudley, Endicot were upon the Bench, such profaneness as this would soon be suppressed." By threatening the General Court, he forced the division into the open: "God will change either you, or your Government ere long."

This was frank speaking—too frank. Hitherto the General Court had regularly voted the printing of election orations, but this time they pointedly baulked. Mather waited two years, then published his sermon himself, but took off some of the sting by half-concealing it amid three moralizing sermons in a volume labeled *A Call from Heaven*, explaining the delay on the ground that he suffered from an inability to perform good works—a humility which nobody in the colonies took seriously. By 1679 Mather had also triumphantly managed the Synod, and was issuing its resolutions with a blistering preface, *The Necessity of Reformation*, which, in the vehemence of its excoriation, reveals how much the effort to excite a moral renaissance was in fact an attempt to mobilize the community against England, against toleration, and above all against those in its midst who would surrender to both. At this moment, Cotton Mather says, the "adversaries" began to call his father "the Mahomet of New England"!

Randolph was a fussy, devoted, unimaginative and exasperating man, one of those who want to tidy up the universe and who therefore expend a lifetime of energy on the first detail they find amiss. He tried to make good Englishmen out of New Englanders, for which most of them hated him —"blasted wretch," Cotton Mather cried—as cordially as he did them. He was coolly, not to say rudely, greeted by Governor Leverett, but he soon detected the existence of the two parties, his reports dubbing the one "moderates" and the other, that which, led by Increase Mather, clung to the charter, the "faction." The shrieks of the faction cannot be explained unless we remember that from 1676 to 1684 a group of solid and influential citizens actually abetted Randolph to an extent which patriotic members of the faction could regard only as treason. In this decade was introduced into history a division of Americans into two basic types, each legitimately derived from the founders, but irreconcilably opposed over their conception of the destiny of America.

Nothing, from this point of view, is more instructive than the reception which greeted, upon their return to America, successive "agents" sent by the colonies to Europe. John Winthrop, Jr., coming back in 1662 with a veritable triumph of negotiation in his Connecticut charter, had the Devil's own time convincing the colony of its advantage and was accused, of course, by New Haven of having been corrupted and seduced by wily diplomats in Whitehall. Simon Bradstreet and John Norton brought back, in September 1662, the king's letter that enabled the General Court to renew persecutions of Quakers, but because these patriots could not get everything their constituents wanted, they were execrated; Norton died of chagrin, and Bradstreet rapidly became what Randolph called a moderate. In 1676, in reply to Randolph's first demands, the General Court sent William Stoughton and Peter Bulkeley to London, where they had to answer several pointed questions. They tried to contend that the law of 1664 had enlarged the franchise, and that a later one, in 1673, had fully opened it, although the Attorney-General had been informed by Randolph that both were ineffective. But, though they thus resolutely carried out their instructions, and for the moment staved off action against the charter, they too came home to murmurs of a mission unaccomplished, whereupon both became moderates. Bulkeley's action is not difficult to understand: he was in business. But Stoughton, who had graduated from Harvard in 1650, had seemed up to this point another Increase Mather; he had gone to England, become a Fellow of New College, and then a curate in Sussex until ejected in 1662 by the Act of Uniformity, when he, like Mather, retreated to New England. For some reason he did not take a pulpit, but turned to the study of law; at the election of 1668 he spoke for the orthodoxy when he said that God winnowed all England to select the choicest grain for this wilderness. Yet from London in 1677 he began to write home that colonial evasions of the Navigation Acts had become a serious offense, for which he was branded a traitor. Under this treatment, he who in 1668 was an extreme asserter of American exceptionalism by 1679 became an ally of Randolph.

In February 1680 the General Court was ordered to send new agents. Stoughton was elected, but begged off—he knew the penalty. In March of 1682, John Richards and Joseph Dudley were finally sent; in the history of American embassies none is more prophetic, in the fullest sense of the word, than this one. As was frequently to be the case, Europeans were warned in advance: Richards, wrote Randolph to the Secretary of State, belongs to the faction but is of mean extraction and should be kept "very safe till all things tending to the quiett and regulation of this government be perfectly settled." The English took such good care of him that he figures not at all in the negotiations, and so came home as much a faction man as ever. But Dudley, son of Winthrop's severe lieutenant, "hath," said Randolph, "his fortune to make in the world," and could be bought.

While Dudley was being bought, the General Court proclaimed day after day of humiliation, praying God to continue "our libertjes, civil & sacred, and in his good time, to returne our agents, & saue his deare people in the land of our fathers sepulchers." After failing to keep Gould from occupying his church, they repealed their laws against Quakers and instructed Richards and Dudley to tell the Lords that Anabaptists "are now subject to no other penal statutes then those of the Congregational way" (although in 1680 Increase Mather had published a denunciation of that "blasted Error"). They also told the agents to assure the home government that all laws restricting the citizenship were removed, though with a last whimper of defiance they humbly conceived that by the charter they might admit whom they would. In this year, 1682, someone who signed himself "J. W." printed in London *A Letter from New-England*, which Dudley found in the stalls upon his arrival. It shows what the jeremiads were contending with behind the scenes: New Englanders pay no attention to the king; their religion consists in cheating; they deny baptism to any but the children of their churches, "looking upon all but their own dear Cubs as the Seed of Pagans and infidels"; they are fornicators and adulterers, and "the worst of Drunkards may here find Pot-companions enough, for all their pretences to Sobriety." They reveal their disagreeable character in a thousand ways: a vintner put up a sign with two naked boys upon it, "their Nudities Pendent"; when reproved, he replaced it with "two Chopping Girles with Merkins exposed," for which he was dealt with by a local sessions gravely determined "(to keep the Girles from blushing) they should have Roses clapt upon their Merkins; which is the original of our new Proverb, Under the Rose a Merkin."

Dudley worked under difficulties, not the least of which was his attempt, under pious instructions, to bribe Lord Hyde with two thousand guineas. Country boys play in London the game either of bribery or gallantry at their peril; Dudley made a mess of it, and wrote to Bradstreet, "Truly, sir, if you was here to see how we are ridiculed by our best friends at court . . . it would grieve you." This was a danger his father and other builders of the city, being members in good standing of the Calvinist internationale, had not contemplated—that they should be ridiculed as boorish provincials. From this humiliation Joseph Dudley never recovered, but when he came home in January 1684, he received the ultimate insult from his own countrymen: at a Boston town meeting Increase Mather aroused the citizens with glowing pictures of how their fathers had purchased this vineyard, and in the excitement of the moment got from them a resolution condemning Bradstreet, Stoughton, Dudley, and Bulkeley as "Enemies of the Countrey." That the foremost spiritual leader of the regime should thus rouse the rabble against those who temporized in the slightest degree with internationalism is in itself a final commentary on the course the social evolution had followed since the time John Winthrop crushed the Hingham rebellion with an implacable disquisition about the nature of civil liberty.

To the bitter end the General Court kept appointing days of humiliation "in respect of our sacred, ciuil, & temporall concernes, and more especially those in the hands of our agents abroad, as also for those kingdomes vpon whose welfare our oune doth so nearly depend, & for the Protestant churches and interest elsewhere." To the last the court kept up their semblance of unity, instructing Richards and Dudley in February 1683 to preserve at all costs "our liberties and privileges in matters of religion and worship of God, which you are therefore in no wise to consent to any infringement of." Because it appeared that despite such exhortations Dudley responded to European blandishments, he became the scapegoat for outraged domestic virtue, and so, pilloried as a traitor, the most resolute foe of the regime of his father.

Randolph exaggerated the numbers and influence of the moderates, but they were formidable: Dudley and his brothers-in-law, Bradstreet and Denison; Stoughton and Bulkeley, the discredited agents; William Browne, Wait Winthrop, Samuel Shrimpton, Bartholomew Gedney. Correspondingly the faction waxed more positive, better organized, some of its leaders —like Elisha Cooke and Elisha Hutchinson—taking their stand not as convinced theocrats but simply as enemies of Dudley. To support this band, preachers of jeremiads arrayed the cosmos on the side of the charter. When at last it was annulled, and a majority of the Assistants were prone to surrender, the combination of ministers and political agitators proved still strong enough to carry the "popular" House of Deputies—that organ which in 1670 had accused the clergy of subverting the order!

Were we to judge from printed survivals, we should suppose all New England united at this moment in detestation of some unnamed and lurking enemy in its midst. The moderates worked under suspicion, by word of mouth or through papers quickly burned; but one or two utterances can be found, and they give us essential clues. Governor Bradstreet's son wrote him from New London:

> Better the ruin, if it must be so, under other hands than yours. Time will make it appear who have been the faithful and wise conservators of New England's liberties, and that the adored saviours of our interests, many of them, have consulted very ill the interest espoused by them.

An intransigent defense of the charter—let the federal theology be what it may—seemed to such realists no way to advance either the prosperity or the freedom of the colonies. Therefore, by opposing the logic of the jeremiad—which was the logic of the covenant—they in effect were obliged to depart from the ideal of intolerance; somewhat to their own surprise, they had to suggest that allowance of religious difference was compatible with the welfare of the land.

Daniel Denison died on September 20, 1682; Hubbard preached his funeral sermon (conclusive proof that he was in the moderate councils). On June 24, another day of humiliation, Hubbard had carefully prepared *The Benefit of a Well Ordered Conversation,* but not until 1684 dared print both the sermon and the funeral discourse. His point, as when speaking on Denison, was sufficiently clear:

> If we cast an eye upon all the following Histories of the Church, in succeeding Ages, we shall find, that much of those sufferings which have fallen upon the Generation of the just, might either have been prevented or much abated; if they had governed their affairs by a suitable measure of Wisdom in their concerns with themselves or others.

Lest this should appear no more than abstract rhetoric to honor a distinguished magistrate, Hubbard appended Denison's own last word of advice to his country, *Irenicon, or a Salve for New England's Sore.* A neglected book, it is a wise, sane, level-headed plea for toleration written by an orthodox New Englander (and thus to be distinguished from the inspired works of Roger Williams). Men are forced to associate, Denison mused, but it is possible, within the general body, that diverse groups remain separate "and following their Laws and Manners to flourish in wealth and peace." Because God has given men reason, well-meaning persons may manage to live side-by-side "without submitting themselves to the common reason of others combined in a body politick"; civil order is important, but Denison wished that we might still reserve "to our selves those natural powers by liberties which God and Nature hath betrusted us with as men." Slowly emerging from the moderates' stand against the die-hards were tentative outlines of a conception of freedom of conscience as a right based upon immutable nature; they may have been helped, here and there, by the news that this idea was on the march in Europe, but most immediately they were led to it in order to gain ground against the jeremiad, according to which no rights existed except those that had been specifically covenanted for, the definition of which depended upon authoritative decision of experts in federalism, upon the clergy and their synods.

Here we find ourselves amid a confusion of labels. A patriotic nineteenth-century version of colonial history held that Dudley and his friends were despicable Tories; in 1864 John Gorham Palfrey (himself untroubled by lack of income), noticing that the moderates were generally rich men among whom noble sentiment is timid, announced that "the instincts of wealth incline to the side of arbitrary power." Reacting to such pomposity, recent students perceive that the moderates were pioneers of religious toleration and so deserve the name of liberals; in this view, the faction becomes a hive of demagogues fighting, in the language of James Truslow Adams, "to perpetuate religious intolerance, and the intrenched privilege of a minority to tax an unenfranchised majority four times as numerous." All of which proves doubly confusing if we revert to the actual words (such as survive) of those who, both in Massachusetts and Connecticut, welcomed the English action: they were men disgusted with the arrogance and presumption of democracy. They were anything but libertarians; they were authoritarians, ready to give up the charter because, in their experience, it supported elected officers and rampaging parsons who could not keep the populace in order. Where in the civilized world, asked Denison, exist a people less respectful of their leaders, where "men of worth" weigh so little? The rabble, having only "some slender opportunities of the knowledge of some affairs in Church and state," are so puffed up with notions of their own importance "that they dare not only vye with, but contemn the judgements of those Grandees whose abilities and atchievements all wise and sober men have admired." What Denison meant by grandees is, to say the least, interesting: Calvin, Ames, Walsingham, Burleigh—and "Matchiavel." This opens up avenues of speculation concerning exactly what the moderates of the 1680's stood for: those who first moved, not like Williams out of faith but out of disillusion, toward toleration found moral support in Machiavelli! The clue is worth remembering, for, as we shall see, the figure of Machiavelli has a curious prosperity in the later life of the New England mind.

After the Reforming Synod, the clergy found themselves shorn of every weapon except moral persuasion and their threat of vengeance. Within a year, they had to perceive that the Synod was a failure: "Are not some weary of that Theocracy, or Government which God hath established amongst us, as to sacred and civil respects, willing for a change in both?" They could not admit that valid reasons for compromise on the charter— or on toleration—existed within the realms of reason and nature. Could they, by subordinating these sanctions to the covenant, find any more persuasive arguments for a final stand?

Increase Mather, having stood against the Half-Way Covenant on doctrinaire grounds, had learned how to behave when events were running against him. The passion with which he conducted the Synod of 1679–80 shows him aware of what was at stake: he foresaw that loss of the charter would mean not merely that his faction was out of power, but that the whole structure of colonial thought—the national covenant, the framework of the jeremiad—would be in jeopardy. If a society federated with Jehovah could have its form of government imposed by an unfederated Whitehall, New England would be reduced to merely one among the communities of this earth, its regulations amounting to nothing more than those of natural circumstance. Unless something were done to rescue the basic concept of a peculiar obligation—in some such fashion as might survive even an annulment of the providentially given charter—the cause of religion would be lost for a civilization where there was no other tradition to fall back upon. Without it, Christianity itself would become, like the political theory of the moderates, nothing more than a rationalized naturalism.

On May 12, 1681, Mather met with the ministers of the colony, and organized them to collect from their several localities all the "notable Stories" they could find; he edited their reports, and in 1684 published *An Essay for the Recording of Illustrious Providences,* the most successful of all his writings, a second edition being called for within a year and a London imprint quickly following. It has been studied by antiquarians, by students of science and of folklore; today it is as much alive as anything he ever composed.

He invited his colleagues to assemble "All, and only Remarkable Providences," those testifying the glory of God "and the good of Posterity"— by which he meant to exclude mere "common" providences and to reproduce "such Divine Judgements, Tempests, Floods, Earthquakes, Thunders as are unusual, strange Apparitions, or what ever else shall happen that is Prodigious, Witchcrafts, Diabolical Possessions, Remarkable Judgements upon noted Sinners: eminent Deliverances and Answers of Prayer." Increase patiently sorted out the accounts, improved the style, and classified them under subject-headings, such as sea-deliverances, preservations, "daemons," apparitions, and tempests.

To most modern readers, the book seems a collection of old-wives' tales and atrocity stories, at best hilariously funny and at worst a parade of gullibility. Charitable historians of science, recognizing that in 1684 the thesis of God's hand exhibited in strange events was neither abnormal nor absurd, lamely defend the work as an inductive investigation, data collected to support a hypothesis. Mather lends support to the latter view by advertising that he had achieved only a small part of what might be written about the "Natural History of New England" according to rules "described by that Learned and excellent person Robert Boyle Esq.," or by citing, from time to time, Digby, Sir Thomas Browne, and the *Philosophical Transactions* of the Royal Society. He did, indeed, try to check his facts, to present what he believed was accurate reporting. One is entitled to see in this assemblage of horrors an important advance in the Puritan temper, which always paid due regard to strange occurrences, as did Winthrop to the birth of Mary Dyer's "monster." After the Restoration, English Puritans, shut out of the government, concentrated their energies upon similar investigations, like Samuel Clarke's *Mirrour or Looking Glasse both for Saints and Sinners* of 1671 (upon which Mather drew). Indeed, Mather freely acknowledges that the nucleus of his project had been conceived in England twenty-six years before, and had been communicated to John Davenport, among whose papers Mather found the manuscript. Thus the *Essay* aligns itself with a venerable tradition stretching back to the medieval exempla, but also supported by the most recent scientific method. This interpretation allows us to suppose the incredible: that, at the moment Mather and his colleagues were engaged in a struggle for existence, they idly embarked upon a collection of curiosa!

They were doing nothing of the sort. The *Essay* is a concerted counterattack upon enemies, or at least skeptics, of the covenant theology. Even in his account of King Philip's War, Mather had implanted corrosive doubts about the doctrine because he recorded the failure of victory to follow the ritualistic humiliation, or the astonishing success of a thanksgiving he thought unwarranted. Since then, fervently repeated days of humiliation had led only to a diminished confidence in the charter, to the increase of moderates who muttered that it had outlived its purpose. An efficient cause could, in Puritan theory, determine an effect without invalidating the thesis of a final cause; but when the weight of English authority began to press upon local arrangements, skepticism concerning the national covenant was bound to increase. How could men continue to believe that New England enjoyed a peculiar and sanctified relation to Jehovah, or that He would come to their aid against King Charles merely because the people repented and reformed? And if Jehovah would not help them, why should they repent at all?

This background gives a special poignance to the publication in 1682 (with a preface by Increase Mather) of a sermon by Urian Oakes, delivered as long before as 1677: *The Soveraign Efficacy of Divine Providence.* Its subtitle, that omnipotence overrules human counsels, carried even more of hope—or desperation—when published than when delivered, because it seemed to assure the faithful that time and chance—although to them unpredictable—are governed by God, who does not stir up second causes (such as Crown lawyers) and leave these to their own inclinations, "whither they shall go, & what they shall do: but He leads them forth, and determines them to this, or that object." Because Oakes contended that this rule applied not only to natural agents (like fire or sea) but to "rational Agents, that act by Counsel," readers in 1682 would suppose that it might confine the Lords of Trade. His conclusion was vibrantly optimistic: "Chance is something that falls out beside the Scope, Intention, and foresight of Man, the Reason and cause whereof may be hid from him; and so it excludes the Counsel of Men; but it doth not exclude the Counsel and Providence of God." But, in 1682, did there seem much likelihood that the chance action of the Crown (it had so far been irrational enough!) was any longer to be directed into those channels which, viewed from New England, were counsels of God?

Mather's *Essay* was an attempt to show that the wisdom of God does prevail, if not in general, then in particulars. Thus it tried to redeem the vocation of New England, even after a series of agents who either failed their instructions or went over to the enemy. The faction would not yield an inch, either to nature or to toleration. God will regulate all instruments, Willard explained in 1683, "yes, though, as they are rational agents, and causes by councel of their own actions, they design nothing but mischief"; He will use them, "not to gain their own projected ends, but his, which they neither know nor design." Even as Mather brought out the *Essay*, he published *The Doctrine of Divine Providence Opened and Applyed*, in which he cast light upon the secret intention of the larger book: yes, wicked men do prosper in this world (New Englanders would think of Dudley), but God raises up His enemies in order to cast them the farther downward. At the back of his mind, as of Willard's and of others' in the faction, lay the seed of self-distrust Hubbard had gently sown in 1676: even amid the horrors of war, Hubbard suggested that while some saw therein punishment for a declension from the ways of our forbears, "It is two to one if some doe not say the contrary." The sailors had been overhasty in accusing Jonah: "We must not eye for God, and need be carefull we doe not entitle divine Providence to the mistakes of our minds, and make God speak that by his providence, which never entred into his heart." Should such a doubt get abroad, the jeremiad would collapse; the conception of special significance that had been the strength and sustenance of New England ever since Winthrop's *Modell* would disintegrate, and resistance to England's attack on the charter would evaporate. In order to prove that, despite the overbearing power of the home government, some fragments of the peculiar designation remained—to demonstrate, with the help of scientific method, that the covenant still prevailed, if not for the whole colony, then for innumerable particulars—Mather and his colleagues, confronted with political ruin, girded themselves to compose the *Essay*.

The book was a gesture against despair: it was a surrender of the idea of national covenant, a strategic retreat to an atomistic, fragmental version of divine regulation. The scale was no longer a coherent sweep of history, but discrete "magnalia"; not an over-all design working steadily through a predestined course, but simply this tempest or that shipwreck, a deaf person who learned to speak, or so-and-so who was possessed. The inclusive vision of Bradford, the systematic structure into which Winthrop's jottings fit, was not so much lost as broken up, so that now falterers were offered, not an inexorable dialectic of progress, but an array of occasional and private "special providences." Men in the community would no longer respond to blessings (or curses) upon their corporate interest; wherefore, let them consider that individuals suffer singular fates, wherein God frequently may do good specifically to one or another. Left to natural logic, men might conclude that because the charter was abrogated they should as well submit to imperial agents-by-counsel, but if God still worked upon New England through such illustrious providences as were collected in the *Essay*, then each pious citizen, in the citadel of his hearth, became a resistant against the temporarily overweening power of the Crown—against its treasonable allies like Dudley and its natural agents such as Randolph.

In no perspective of this guerrilla warfare could the acceptance of toleration be allowed: as long as illustrious providences supported one sort of men rather than another, no trust was to be placed in the professions of liberals. "Corrupt minds," said Increase Mather, "though they may plead for Toleration and Cry up Liberty of Conscience, &c., Yet if once they should become numerous and get power into their hands, none would persecute more than they." Even while the clergy were confessing that not half the freemen would come to the hustings for election of a Deputy, Willard was telling these debilitated saints that the design of the first planters had not been toleration, that they "were professed Enemies of it, and could leave the World professing they died no Libertines." The next year, Willard had to acknowledge, "I am not ignorant to how much calumny I expose my self in mentioning this point," but he was not deterred from speaking up for what, after all, was the essential (although not always so blatantly advertised) point of the jeremiads: "If men, upon pretence of Conscience (and who will not pretend it, if they may find it a shelter against Justice?) . . . may be suffered . . . without any restraint to run to and fro, Disseminate their erronious principles," then Christ would show His disapproval, if not through national, then through illustrious providences.

Willard's discourses show, as do others in these years, a realization that the Reforming Synod had failed to evoke popular response. Increase Mather further betrayed it in 1682, on receipt of news from France, by preaching on the doctrine that the true church must endure persecution. Had he had a united and resolute society behind him, he might have rallied it to defiance; all he could do, confronting the loss of the charter, was to tell Massachusetts that never did "degenerate Churches continue long without smarting under the Rod of persecution"—and hope that New England would submit as little as had Puritan England in the days of his father.

Thus, while a number of realistic (self-appointedly patriotic) citizens were considering that a reasonable deal could be made with the English government, intractable isolationists like Mather and Willard (reduced to this extremity only because the Europe of their inherited conception no longer gave them support) strove to convince the colonists that submission to their sovereign Charles II would be as fatal as yielding to Louis XIV. While the tide of politics ran against them, they turned in anguish to tabulating special and peculiar providences—not out of a devotion to science, but in the hope that science, by bringing home to the multitude the horrors and dangers of diabolical possessions and witchcrafts, would keep alive allegiance to the ancient ways of New England even after a foreign authority had commanded concessions to difference of opinion.

Despite the providential theory of the national covenant, despite the special providences, in the providence of history the charter fell. The Deputies were resolute to the end—their protests written by Increase Mather. Dudley, Browne, Gedney were not reëlected to the Board of Assistants, whereupon Bulkeley and Stoughton resigned; even though conducted to their homes by a mounted cavalcade, they were subjected to public insult. Internal dissension had, so it seemed, shattered the national covenant: were Jehovah any longer to maintain His controversy with these people, He would need to prod them, again and again, through particular trials, through individual deliverances.

In London, the charter was annulled on October 23, 1684. In Boston, the General Court designated October 22 as a day of humiliation "for the more effectual promoting of the worke of generall reformation, so long discoursed of among ourselues (but greatly delayed)." The delay had proved fatal, the propaganda offensive had failed.

For a while—British administration being British—nothing happened, and the General Court continued to function. An election was held in May 1685, for which the court asked William Adams to deliver the sermon; he entitled it, *God's Eye on the Contrite,* under which designation he addressed the court as those "that are from among ourselves"; but he reminded them that God, for His own inscrutable reasons, sometimes favors unrighteous men: "This is not so constant and perpetual, as that any man can merely from thence infallibly know love or hatred to be in God to him by all that is before him." This was for Joseph Dudley to consider. In Connecticut, where it was expected that the colony would soon be dealt with, John Whiting, in the election sermon of 1686, could take a more comprehensive view: bewailing, among other dark prospects, the increase of drunkenness, he summarized the mood of orthodox New England with, "It looks to me like the Approaches of a GENERAL DELUGE."

BOOK II

Confusion

Make ye mention to the nations;
Behold, publish against Jerusalem,
That watchers come from a far country,
And give out their voice against the cities of Judah.
As keepers of a field, are they against her round about;
"Because she hath been rebellious against me," saith the Lord,
"Thy way and thy doings have procured these things unto thee;
This is thy wickedness, because it is bitter,
Because it reacheth unto thine heart."

JEREMIAH 4:16–18.

CHAPTER XI

PROFILE OF A PROVINCIAL MENTALITY

THERE

being nothing else to do, the government of Massachusetts continued to function and that of Connecticut to tremble while Charles II died, Monmouth was subdued, and Catholic James was crowned. On May 12, 1686, Massachusetts held another election, but two days later Randolph landed with a commission that established a Council under the presidency of Dudley. In December came Sir Edmund Andros, with a comprehensive warrant making him Governor of the Dominion of New England (to which New York and New Jersey were added in 1688). He instituted proceedings against the charters of Rhode Island and Connecticut, whereupon, in October 1687, the regime at Hartford submitted with indecent haste. Dudley served as chief of the Council, but there was no elected legislature. In March 1689, intelligence reached Boston that William of Orange had landed, and on April 18 the town revolted. Andros and Randolph were imprisoned and then sent home to face charges of oppression, while the colonies quietly resumed their charter governments, Massachusetts awaiting what its agents could extract from the new sovereigns in London, whither Increase Mather had been smuggled in 1688.

In the history of British imperialism this experiment in consolidation is important, but for the New England mind it is, taken by itself, only an episode. The years of the Dominion were, measured by domestic publications, the most barren since the beginning of the Half-Way Covenant debate, amounting only to a few of the more innocuous or generalized sermons (except that, the presses being so little occupied, Solomon Stoddard was able in 1687 to print *The Safety of Appearing at the Day of Judgment in the Righteousness of Christ*, in which Sir Edmund would have seen nothing subversive). However, if for two and a half years thought and expression were arrested, the memory of this experience left an indelible impression: the Dominion endured as a symbol around which ideas had to be grouped. In that sense, the brief years are a tremendous gulf; after crossing them, the community emerged basically altered, radically transformed.

The most striking effect of the "tyranny" was a disintegration of the moderate party: no longer forced to stand together as an unpopular minority, they turned to knifing each other instead of supporting the regime.

Randolph picked the Council by hand: four of them—including Bradstreet and his son—refused to serve, suddenly and unaccountably calling the commission they had aided Randolph to secure "a thing contrived to abridge them of their liberty and indeed against Magna Charta." Randolph was still more dismayed to discover that the grandees, once assembled in the Council, could achieve unity only when blocking some administrative project; not only did the various colonies conspire against each other, but in each delegation, especially of the Bay, there appeared a fundamental conflict of interests, of real-estate men against merchants, of Dudley, Stoughton, Bulkeley, and the Tyngs against Gedney, Wharton, and Usher. They turned out to hate each other more bitterly than any of them did Increase Mather.

In a manner of speaking, they found themselves better Americans than they had supposed, and at the end of it a nauseated Randolph despaired of finding servants of the king among Yankees. He testifies, although with reluctance, to the fact that repudiators of the founders could no longer find their way back to becoming Englishmen: they wanted to get rid of what had become for them the disorder of Congregationalism, to escape from a teleological world into a universe of commerce and profit, and so to soften the notion that Jehovah visited their sins upon the community; but they had to find philosophical bases within their own experience, not in those supplied by Andros and Randolph.

The commissions issued to Dudley and Andros required extensions of religious freedom, but Randolph was never able to get substantial help from the Council, even from the most moderate. Dudley, in fact, so fawned upon Increase Mather and showed so little enthusiasm for the Church of England that Randolph had to report his crony "treacherous" and to declare his rule "still but ye Govr & Company." Moderate Puritans would not assist the Rev. Robert Ratcliffe, whom Randolph brought over to conduct Anglican services and who became the center of violent scenes when Andros tried to force the Third Church to lend itself to his necessities for half the Sabbath; the few Anglicans were soon reduced to undertaking the construction of King's Chapel. All accounts agree that vices denounced in the jeremiads—particularly drunkenness and street fighting, as well as the wearing of wigs—increased. The experience helped to impress upon the colonies a realization that they would have to come to terms with the idea of toleration, that they could not henceforth publicly treat the Church of England as though it were Rome; but even those who, a few years before, had pled for moderation, showed no enthusiasm whatsoever toward these innovations.

The Revolution of 1689 completed the break-up of the moderate alignment. Those who, like Stoughton, came through without being ruined played the turncoat, and only a handful—Dudley in Massachusetts, Gershom Bulkeley in Connecticut—had enough conviction to stay with the sinking ship (or were too deeply committed). When Dudley was arraigned before the Lords of Trade, the charges were prepared by his onetime associate, Wait Winthrop. Home-grown conservatism learned in 1689 that the problem of keeping businessmen loyal to their professedly conservative principles is every bit as difficult as that of restraining the disorderliness of democratic congregations.

It is, as we have seen, juggling with words to call the moderates "conservative." In one perspective, we may behold in them ancestors of the Tories of 1776, and so trace a line of descent from Dudley to Governor Hutchinson; however, as Oscar Handlin says of the effort to detect party continuity after the American Revolution, we must take into account the social mobility and such realignments as are bound to occur in revolutionary years. Granted that 1689 produced no such convulsive realignments as 1776, and that the social mobility of 1690, compared with that of 1790, was relatively constricted, still, in the scale of things as conceived by the New England mentality under the old charter, the effect of the Dominion and of its overthrow was shattering. Such social philosophy as the moderates had achieved consisted mainly of an aversion to strict intolerance; as long as they were contending with Increase Mather they might as justly be called liberals as conservatives, but when revocation of the charter destroyed the legal foundation of Mather's regime, and Mather himself became, overnight, the apostle of religious liberty, they found themselves without a cause. Their devotion to the Crown was in reality no more than impatience with local restraints; once the charter was gone, they had everything in common with the Mathers.

If there was anything more in the way of a political philosophy burgeoning in their minds, it may be called an incipient royalism, a pale manifestation of that spirit which in England became a passionate return to the throne as the refuge from religious and republican anarchy, and so inspired the Tory doctrines of non-resistance and the rejection of reason in religion. No New Englander went quite so far as to say with Dryden, "common quiet is mankind's concern," but Hubbard's hymn to "order" points that way. Dudley may already have concluded that a vigorous imperial administration was the only possible corrective of colonial particularism, but he was so much the careerist and egotist that one hesitates to assign to him any coherent theory. The rest of his party had veered so little toward Toryism that, when the Glorious Revolution knocked the props from under them, they could hastily shift over to ardent Whigism and commence to seek their ends under shelter of the Bill of Rights.

However, even in provincial New England, there was one remarkable exception. Whether Gershom Bulkeley should be seen as an extrapolation of ideas momentarily entertained by men like Hubbard, Stoughton, and Dudley can hardly be asserted, since they never committed themselves beyond the possibility of retreat, whereas he did. I think it worth noting that he, like Dudley, was a favored child of the charter regime and that by all the laws of heredity and environment he too ought to have followed the standard of Increase Mather. What is it, we are obliged to ask, in American life that makes the difference between a John Wise and a Bulkeley? If today we still are unable to answer that crucial question, we should not be surprised that the New England mind, recovering from the shock of the Dominion, was unable to supply an answer the first time it was posed, and that consequently the figure of Gershom Bulkeley remains obscure and puzzling. In *Will and Doom* he wrote a minor masterpiece, but it was utterly without effect (being printed only in 1895) and my narrative might legitimately pass him by. If it did, it would miss a key to the comprehension of many subsequent and apparently unconnected phenomena.

Gershom's father was Peter Bulkeley of Concord, one of the foremost theologians among the founders, a vehement prosecutor of Anne Hutchinson. Gershom thus was born to the Puritan purple, and accordingly graduated from Harvard in 1655, but immediately he exhibited an inability to get along with his congregations. He preached for a while after 1661 in New London, moved to Wethersfield in 1666, and seems to have been more interested in medicine and surgery than in his father's theology. He served in Philip's War, nominally as chaplain but effectively as physician, was wounded and received New England's equivalent of a citation, a vote of thanks from the General Court of Connecticut. Assuredly, he was a brave man. When Connecticut supinely surrendered to Andros, Bulkeley accepted a commission as justice of the peace for Hartford county, and so ate the King's bread. But the moment tidings of Andros' overthrow reached Connecticut, the old government (legal proceedings against its charter never having been completed) resumed their power, pretending that nothing had happened. Bulkeley called them cowards, hypocrites, and time-servers; in order to stigmatize them, he composed a little pamphlet, *The People's Right to Election*, which he had to get printed in Philadelphia, for no Boston press would touch it.

Showing himself more the lawyer than the theologian, Bulkeley argued that by their own act the Connecticut government had committed suicide, wherefore they could no longer pretend (even though the suit in London was not yet finished) that the charter was valid—despite the legend of its being hidden in the hollow of an oak! What burns fiercely in this booklet is Bulkeley's utter contempt for his fellow countrymen, whom he brands as guilty of "Tumults, Insurrections, rebellious Riots, Sedition, Rebellion, Treason, &c." Having gone thus far, he could not well sit down and let traitors rule; evidently he set forth a paper of "Objections," which had a wide circulation, and which he rewrote in 1692 as *Will and Doom, Or the Miseries of Connecticut by and under an Usurped and Arbitrary Power.* The General Court, acting now in the name of English liberties, had ordered the collection of taxes, declaring that any who refused should be rated "will and doom." In Bulkeley's eyes this tyranny made Andros look like an amateur.

His book, the first explicitly anti-democratic utterance in our literature, is one of the most vigorous and best written productions of the era. Energy and incisive language can, after all, flow from a reactionary pen. In the General Court, "what is wanted in authority is supplied by ferocity"; hence, "being angry with themselves for this supposed wrong, they wreak their spleen upon us, as if we had done it." "We must call a spade a spade, and rebellion by the name of rebellion, tho' some masters of rebellion may call us Tobiahs and Sanballats for so doing."

The thesis is that of the 1689 pamphlet: the government of Connecticut is illegal because these cowards abjectly yielded in 1687 and so exist at the moment merely on royal sufferance. But what Bulkeley is really driving at, with all his scorn, is the spirit that motivates them: "A levelling, independent democratical principle and spirit, with a tang of the fifth-monarchy, which is a very churlish drug." They cry up their loyalty to King William and their love for the good old liberties, but in reality they trample upon the laws of England, indeed upon all law "except the forgeries of our own popular and rustical shop and the dictates of personal discretion." To show what he means by the horrors of their "nomothetic power," Bulkeley points to the miserable condition of England between 1642 and 1660; this son of Puritanism regards the Puritan uprising against Charles I as the unforgivable sin against justice, King, and God; in remote Connecticut he condemns it with a passion as infuriated as the most irate Cavalier returning with Charles II to wreak vengeance on Noll's damned troopers.

There is a peculiar kind of vehemence, a main ingredient of our literature, which can be achieved only by Americans disillusioned with America. Bulkeley came out with a program frankly authoritarian and arch-Tory; one has to go to contemporaneous pleas for subordination such as those of Dryden in order to find a parallel; yet Dryden's development into a social and theological conservative is, naturally, more explicable in London than is Bulkeley's in Wethersfield, Connecticut. Nevertheless, Bulkeley's assertions are as uncompromising (because the text is hidden in the *Collections* of the Connecticut Historical Society, I may be forgiven for quoting several of the more pungent aphorisms):

That authority of government is a right of ruling over others.

That civil government is the ordinance of God . . .

Monarchy is the best form or kind of civil government.

The king of England is (as was said of Solomon) the chief or supreme governor in all his dominions, over all persons and in all causes.

The king is the minister of God for our good, and the fountain of all lawful civil authority within all his dominions.

The royal power is so far [from being] the creation of man as that it is still, and firstly, the ordinance of God, to whom it belongs to limit and set bounds to it; and that degree of authority, and that prerogative which God hath by his ordinance given to the king as king, to accomplish him for the better attainment of his end, ought to be ascribed and yielded to him without limitation or restraint, else we resist the ordinance of God . . .

No man hath authority to abuse his authority . . .

All lawful authority being of God is therefore sacred, and ought to be obeyed, may not be resisted: he that resists lawful authority resists God, and therefore we would take heed of that . . .

Rebellion against the king is a mediate rebellion against God, and is like the sin of witchcraft.

It requires, at least of most Americans, considerable exercise of a nice feeling for theological consistency to understand why Archbishop Sancroft and five other prelates whom James II accused of malice and sedition because they would not read from their pulpits his Declaration of Indulgence would thereafter give up their livings and voluntarily consign themselves to the desert of Nonjuration rather than acknowledge William as King. Even at the time, and even to many Tories, that dialectic became altogether too complicated and curious wherein a passionate devotion to the doctrine of non-resistance was consistently manifested as a refusal to obey. However, behind the Nonjurors lay a rich literature in which the duty of conscience to maintain both the Church against an erring king and an erring king against a usurper who pled natural right had been fully elaborated. Possibly Bulkeley knew something of this literature, but nothing in his social experience would accustom him to living, day-in and day-out, with such exquisite refinements. At this remove, and in his isolation, he could not denounce the Glorious Revolution in England. But where Nonjurors had complete handbooks on the casuistry of non-resistance to guide them, their lone New England analogue had nothing but his profound disgust with the gang who were ruling his community. Since the new cant had suddenly become "liberty and property are natural rights," he would go along, only pointing out that these rights were grounded upon the individuality of the king; then, by the same token, he would declare that slavery is contrary to nature, that "the desire and endeavour of the recovery of lost liberty cannot be blamed," and so come round to his conclusion that the most abject kind of slavery is that yielded "to base men"—meaning, palpably, the General Court of Connecticut. This colony, he contended, is as much subject to the Crown as London or Oxford: "The realm of England is the mother that bare us: we are a swarm out of that hive." We are indeed remote from the king, lamented this American, and the farther we are removed, "the nearer we are to violence and injustice." The hope for America was that Their Majesties would extend the reign of justice to this land, so as to deliver men like Bulkeley from monsters "whose mouth speaks vanity and their right hand is a right hand of falsehood."

In 1704 Joseph Dudley, still consistently trying to get Connecticut's charter revoked, sent a copy of Bulkeley's manuscript to London, where Sir Henry Ashurst commended it to the Cabinet as saying "all the malicious things he possibly can invent, with great cunning and art." But England being England, some clerk filed it in the Public Records Office, and Gershom Bulkeley, having begged off from his ministry on the plea of a weak voice, lived out his life until 1713 in obscurity as a physician in Glastonbury. In 1692 he had coupled rebellion with the sin of witchcraft, and in passing made an observation which, that very year, had for the first time (though not for the last) become a startling insight into American society: "A denial is as good as an accusation, which without proof is but a calumny."

The Revolutions of 1689 meant, if only by their coincidence, that communication was reëstablished with England; because it was with a Whig England, the course of New England history perforce took a sudden and new turning. The Mathers were not only agile enough to go with the reversal of direction, but resolute enough to attempt to direct it; a number of other intellectuals were driven back upon themselves, into seclusion and meditation. These were the years in which Edward Taylor, Harvard class of 1671, was serving as minister and also, like Bulkeley, as physician in his western town, Westfield. He took no part in politics, and was not, as was Bulkeley, a rebel against the Congregational order; but in some deeper sense, he too was out of touch—and consciously—with the system that emerged from the Revolution. He too turned inward, pouring out his anxiety in a verse technique that Puritans considered suitable only to the sensualities of the Church of England:

> *Shall I not smell thy sweet, oh! Sharons Rose?*
> *Shall not mine Eye salute thy Beauty? Why?*
> *Shall thy sweet leaves their Beautious sweets upclose?*
> *As halfe ashamde my sight should on them ly?*

In seclusion he composed the finest American poetry of the century, as also in seclusion Bulkeley wrote some of its best prose; while his neighbor Stoddard and both the Mathers expended their energies upon what had become the pressing problem of how to adjust the ecclesiastical order to the new political situation, he alone raised his eyes to the universe and asked the stupendous question of who, in this cosmic bowling alley, bowled the sun? At his death in 1729 he left orders that his manuscripts should be destroyed. We need seriously to ponder the spectacle of such different but authentic talents as Bulkeley, Taylor, and Wise living withdrawn and private existences—today we can discover little about any of them except their writings—while the Mathers, Colman, and Stoddard held the center of the stage. Yet only with the help of these recluses can we detect the subterranean currents that flowed between the era of Andros and that of Jonathan Edwards.

The other figure whom the crisis of the Dominion summoned from what seems to have been contented obscurity was John Wise, and he, oddly enough, stood for everything in New England which Gershom

Bulkeley most despised. Andros shouldered immense—probably impossible—responsibilities, and he needed money; he tried to get it from quit rents, by demanding a registration of titles to lands long since distributed by unincorporated towns, and by seizing the yet undistributed common lands. These actions were more than any moderate had bargained for. In 1687, his needs being great, Andros had the Council vote a tax levy (several Councillors were later to plead, not too convincingly, that they refused to vote); most towns gave in, a few demurred, but in Ipswich (Hubbard's town) resentment found a leader and became revolt.

We know so little about John Wise that we are bound to make much of the fact of his father's coming to America as an indentured servant. He was born in Roxbury and somehow went to Harvard, where he was involved in a surreptitious and scandalous feast of turkey; other undergraduates got into similar scrapes, but there seems something peculiarly symbolic in the earthiness of this imbroglio. Wise was a big man, and was accounted a superior wrestler. Graduating in 1673, he was installed in a newly formed rural church outside Ipswich, generally referred to as Chebacco parish; there he disappeared during the hectic disputes over the Old South Church, the Reforming Synod, the fall of the charter—publishing nothing, evidently never giving so much as a lecture in Boston—until Andros' attempt to collect taxes by fiat aroused him.

In August 1687 (he was thirty-six years of age), Wise stampeded the town meeting with a harangue which, as it is reported, was decidedly non-theological. Several of the "principal inhabitants" had drawn up a protest, saying that Andros' levy abridged them of their liberties as Englishmen, and that "that was not the townes Duties any wayes to Assist those ill Methods of Raising money without a General Assembly." Apparently there was hesitation among the citizens, but Wise carried the vote by proclaiming "we had a good God, and a good King, and should do well to stand to our Priviledges." He and five leaders were arrested (a strange colonial premonition of the seven bishops at Lambeth: "This is a standard of rebellion," King James was to shout), and brought to trial before Joseph Dudley, who then uttered words as fateful as his king's: you "must not think the laws of England follow us to the ends of Earth"; "you have no more privilidges left you, than not to be sold for Slaves." Dudley told the jury, "we expect a good Verdict from you," and they, under the circumstances, gave him what he wanted. From jail Wise wrote an apology to Andros, acknowledging the folly of his action and begging for release, because he could get "But Little Sleep Sinc I have Been your Prisoner Here in Town the place being so full of Company." The six heroes were fined £185 and costs, and Wise was suspended from his ministry. Although Andros soon restored him, by then the damage was done, and Dudley had done it.

What he had done, in short, was to give to his fellow Americans an entirely new sense of the value of the rights of Englishmen; in a flash he set these privileges (which to the founders were incidental to the pursuit of holiness, no more than instruments for obtaining it) in a wholly secular light, as matters pertaining to prescriptive right, grant, and precedent—entirely political in character, and to be maintained not out of Scripture but out of law, or else by stratagem. Furthermore, he instilled in the New England mind the henceforth unshakable conviction that any party which, like the moderates, invokes English support for domestic ends is inviting a foreign tyranny. In short, he made certain that the whole moderate position as of before 1684 should collapse, that every faction in America—except for that minority of one who was Gershom Bulkeley—would hereafter have to concede that particular forms of government are not ordinances of God, that resisting lawful authority for the sake of protecting rights, whether prescriptive or "natural," is no rebellion at all.

And precisely at this moment—which otherwise could have become for the colonial mind an insoluble dilemma—came the Revolution that for New England even more than for England was truly "Glorious." Back in 1637, when Winthrop disarmed the Antinomians and was accused of tyranny, he replied that his measures prevented a rising of the disaffected: "The wellfare of the whole is not to be put to apparent hazard, for the advantage of any particular members." Bulkeley and Dudley might regard themselves as the inheritors of this conviction: by this token the Ipswich protest, at a time when frontiers were ablaze, was a particularist assertion that deserved to be put down for the welfare of the whole. New England Puritans, it must be stressed, were not originally admirers of revolution; they were legitimists, as their effort to prove their churches not Separatist testifies. The colonies never openly supported the revolt of their fellows against Charles I—as they were careful to stress in 1660. But in 1689 they could greet a Revolution as nothing less than divine intervention (in London, Increase vaunted that Bostonians revolted for William "not knowing that He was then King"), and from that time on, the respectability of revolt in the name of those principles asserted at Ipswich was something no true New Englander could call in question, even though, within a few decades, there were to be some who cursed the day it became written into the tradition.

For a century thereafter the New England mind could never cease marveling that just at the moment its burden had become insupportable, revolutionary England came to its aid—not, that is, until this wonder could be replaced by the still greater marvel that the New England and Virginian mind should jump together! The sense that they had put William on his throne, that old and New England had shared in "the common Deliverance," made such a difference in the attitude of New Englanders toward the Crown as in itself to constitute an intellectual revolution. "Indeed," as Cotton Mather delighted to say, "nothing in the World could more exactly imitate and resemble the late circumstances of our Mother England than the Revolution here, in all the steps thereof and this, though we understood not one another." In fact, out of this consideration it could finally be argued—at least in Boston—that the Revolution of 1689 was not revolutionary, that it was a spontaneous and instinctive, yet divinely guided, imitation of a "Noble and Heroick" example. Thus any discomfort caused by recollecting the founders' suspicion of rebellion could be quieted.

For there was a larger issue at stake than even taxation or the rights of Englishmen, one that both Dudley and Bulkeley failed to appreciate: Protestantism itself. William of Orange saved the true faith from Louis XIV and the Pope. Actually, although the apologists presented Boston's outburst on April 18 as a popular movement, it was carefully planned and skillfully managed, to the point of having well in advance prepared its manifesto. *The Declaration of the Gentlemen, Merchants and Inhabitants of Boston, and the Countrey Adjacent* is the first of those transparent masquerades in which Cotton Mather descended from the realms of the spirit to take a guiding hand in the sinful world of politics—little realizing that he might not be able to reascend. He hit upon the one cunning device which could both reëstablish a show of continuity with the past and yet present the uprising as an ultimate proof of New England's loyalty to the Crown: the whole sad friction that had come between the colonies and the mother country, from the Restoration to Andros, could now be interpreted, not as England's effort to bring recalcitrants into line, but as a plot inspired "by the great Scarlet Whore." The overthrow of Andros was, therefore, simply a rejection, in the venerable English spirit, of Popery; it was in fact a deed of sheer patriotism to prevent New England from being "given away to a Forreign Power."

The great virtue of this device was that it expunged from memory every consideration which had obliged the English government to vacate the Massachusetts charter and to attack that of Connecticut. If everything New England had suffered was not a castigation of its arrogance but a Catholic plot, then nobody need any longer heed the charges of Randolph; every accusation of insubordination, every infringement of the Navigation Laws, now became a Jesuitical lie—and the community could pick up where it had been interrupted in 1684, with the advantage of now serving under a monarch it adored. It could once more regard itself as a special people, distinguished above all others by having been the target of conspiracy; its destiny could again be presented as pertaining, not to the field of mere imperial policies, but to the exalted region of God's "controversy." New England could once more become the theme of jeremiads.

In this sense, recent history could be made intelligible: the humiliation of New England under Andros was a covenant affliction, while William and Mary were a providential deliverance, according to the promise. Of course, with experience of the Dominion so fresh in mind, there was bound to be one emphasis in the account that had not previously figured so prominently: in this case, the restoration was not so much to orthodoxy as to the rights and privileges of Englishmen. No matter: if the liberation could be proved a simultaneous overthrow of both Popery and tyranny—so much the better, so much the more legitimate, so much closer the tie that would now bind New England to the Crown!

Working with yet imperfect reports of events in Boston, Increase Mather in July of 1689 cast off all recollection of what he had preached five years before, and forecast the next phase of colonial history by asserting the intimate dependence of New England upon the Crown precisely because "both the Charters in England and New-England, were taken away by the same sort of Men, and on the same Grounds, viz. in order to the Establishing of Arbitrary Government." As soon as he was fully informed, he rushed into print to link Boston's action with William's; when Palmer tried to assert Dudley's doctrine that the colonies are not parts of England and that therefore English liberties do not extend to them—so that a Boston revolt cannot be defended in the same terms as one by Parliament—Increase fell back upon a version of New England history which, after the two revolutions, appeared to be the real meaning of even the Great Migration: in 1630, no Englishmen in their wits would have ventured their lives to enlarge the king's dominions "if their Reward after all must be to be deprived of their English Liberties." No, he said, fashioning on the spur of the moment the song which neither he nor his colleagues could, for the rest of their lives, stop singing—or resist incorporating into their jeremiads—"the New-Englanders in their late Revolution did but act in a Quarrel wherein they and all English-men had an Interest." Hence this "Happy REVOLUTION," as Cotton Mather termed it, was, to say the least, no innovation; instead, it made recent events intelligible, fulfilling the wonderful and secret design of God, wherein New England could enact a peculiar role in history, no longer at odds with the Crown, but having fully digested those elements of the Whig philosophy that triumphed with the Glorious Revolution.

In this fashion—in Increase Mather's telling the world that Andros' rule was at one and the same time a "Treasonable Invasion of all the rights belonging to the English nation" and "a Government under which Wickedness would be sure of countenance and Piety be as sure of the utmost discouragement"—the leaders in effect incorporated the right of revolution into their creed without, as far as they could see, ever having resisted an ordinance of God. Ipswich, electing John Wise to the General Court, voted that the aggrieved selectmen should get revenge upon Dudley, an assignment which Wise cheerfully accepted. In all their charges against Andros, the colonists radiated a serene confidence that hereafter any who opposed them would be the veritable revolutionary, and a Tory!

It all amounts to a complicated feat of the intellect, as ingenious as anything the founders devised when proving that Congregationalists were not Separatists. But it could be achieved only because of the great and central fact that William and Mary did save the Protestant succession, and in the glory of that achievement, lesser concerns of ecclesiastical polity could be

relegated to details. By harping upon this interpretation, the Congregationalists of 1689 could bury unpleasant memories; the "Envenomed
Arrows" that had been shot against New England's tranquillity could be
attributed to the "squinting malignity" of "the Frogs of the Romish
Egypt." If the sole meaning, or at least the only one worth talking about,
of 1689 was that a profligate Charles II and a Papist James II were
miraculously replaced by a Protestant, uxorius and serious William, New
England could go—or at least ought to be permitted to go—its own way
unmolested.

There was, however, one condition that had to be not only fulfilled
but repeatedly met, for otherwise the entire effort would collapse as
fatally as had that of the moderates when confronted with Andros: New
England's case would hang together only if at every point it contended
that "there is nothing more to be demonstrated, Than that the people
of New-England are the most Loyal People in all the English Dominions."
The founders had professed loyalty; but before 1689 nobody believed the
profession, or was expected to. If the protestation which now became the
basis of communal integrity was to serve its purpose, it had to be sincere.
Or rather, it had to sound immensely sincere. For this reason, because
actions speak louder than words, the liberated colony of Massachusetts,
having resurrected the government of the old charter, and while awaiting the grant of a new, threw itself with unprecedented vigor into mounting an expedition against Quebec. Our service to William and Mary,
preached Cotton Mather, must be demonstrated not only by securing
their interests in this land, "but also by making a brisk Salley forth upon
the French Territories, which must else be a Perpetual obstacle to the
thriving of these Plantations." It eluded him, as it did his hearers, that in
reëstablishing self-respect upon the basis of loyalty to William and Mary,
he had also tacitly shifted the main inducement for fighting the French
from the true order of the Gospel, or even from the survival of the saints,
to a "thriving."

The clergy beat their drums, sounding alike upon the appeal to Protestantism and to patriotism. In their relief at being able for the first time
to identify the two, they did not perceive that by inciting this crusade they
were accepting their role in the altered political order: they were assuming
the function of advocates for causes already determined, and were no
longer themselves formulators of objectives. To compare jeremiads delivered during Philip's War with Cotton Mather's exhortation to the
departing troops is to get a glimmering of what the Revolution had really
wrought. "Certainly, My Countrymen," he cried, " 'Tis Time to Look
about us, We are driven upon a purely Defensive War, which we may
now make Justly Offensive to the first Aggressors in it." It was no longer
enough to say, as had Bradford, that the grace of God will sustain saints
amid hardships; loyalty to the Protestant Crown had to be more aggressively demonstrated:

You are Fighting, that the Churches of God may not be Extinguisht, and the Wigwams of Heathen swarming in their room: You are Fighting that the Children of God may not be made Meals or Slaves to the veriest Tygers upon Earth.

Thus an extended form of the jeremiad took shape in Mather's decision that we might repair many of our sins not merely by repentance but more cogently by conquering Canada; hence "we should forsake our soft Beds, our full Tables, and our Fine Houses." Prosperity would be less deplorable if employed in William's just war.

But alas the gulf that lies between just causes and their military fulfillment! The expedition was a dismal failure. To reward John Wise for his work against Andros, the General Court had made him chaplain. We do not know whether he shared Mather's certitude that if all New England would pray, French devils would run, but when he got ashore with the second wave and found the men utterly disorganized, he blamed not the inadequacy of prayer but the incompetence of New England generalship. Finding one company mired in a swamp, and telling them, "Gentlemen you are out of yor Witts we did not come hither to drive a parcel of Cowardly Frenchmen from Swamp to Swamp but to attaque Kebeque," Wise hunted out General Walley, a saint from Barnstable, and "was affected when I first saw him for to me he seemed very much down in his Spirit to say no worse." In the dismal annals of the American militia, including Bull Run, there is perhaps no more pathetic wail than that of Walley: "Saith he, I cannot rule them." And never from an American chaplain was there a less theological retort: "To whom I replyed Sr you must not expect when men are let loose upon an Enemie that they should attend all the Ceremonies martial and that are in fashion on a field of Peace." This was the rural agitator of Ipswich, and in his prescription we find an utterance which further demonstrates how inapplicable the old-fashioned jeremiad had become to the actualities of the community; Cotton Mather certainly had his work cut out for him as he dedicated himself to confining this kind of New England to the ancient pattern.

I doe professe had we had a man that would have ventured his Life, his way had been to have stilled all noyse got himself and army into a few hours Sleep sent on board and had ready one bisquet cake pr man and a good round Dram and have put these into their bellys the next morning & in the heat of it marcht up to Towne the Army would I am satisfied by their Valour have payd him his Kindnesse in good Roast meat for Supper by the next night and a good feather bed to have layn on instead of Boards or Straw.

It is a far cry from Mather's exhortation to leave our sinful tables and houses to Wise's hearty acceptance of a dram in the belly and roast meat for supper; complexity and common sense had somehow emerged out of the simplicity and intellectualism of the covenant.

Wise was given three hundred acres, whereupon he went back to Chebacco. But the new rationale of colonial existence, in the name of which the expedition had been launched, now faced the highly practical ordeal of paying its soldiers. The provisional government had no more money than had Andros. Since it could enforce no tyrannical levies, it resorted, on December 10, 1690, to issuing promissory notes, "bills of credit," to the amount of £40,000, which it ordered should pass at face value. Thus the reconstituted Puritan commonwealth plunged into the un-Puritanical realm of finance, and immediately confronted a law that had not figured in federal theology: paper money, backed by no security, depreciates.

For Cotton Mather, events between 1689 and 1692 moved fast. Having started down the road toward secularization by preaching this Canadian crusade, he had further to divert his attention from the state of his soul by composing (although anonymously) a defense of the bills, thus finding himself appealing to criteria not so concrete as Wise's but hardly less profane. It now appears, he said, that we cannot keep silver in the country (what had this to do with the sins of New England?); are we not then better off to have, and to honor, a currency of our own, which will be kept here "where it will (or at least) ought" to be accepted as legal tender? That he should have to distinguish, even parenthetically, between a "will" and an "ought" was, in 1691, a cloud no bigger than a man's hand on the intellectual horizon; still, it was one thing to exhort New England yeomen to refrain from rum and fornication, and another to ask them to receive payment for scanty crops in money not worth its announced value. Moral persuasives had to come to terms with social fact: because we do not yet know whether we have a charter or not, the people imagine that we "are Reduced to Hobs his state of Nature," in which the strongest take all; but the bills are a draft upon the whole community: "All the Inhabitants of the Land, taken as one Body are the Principals, who Reap the Benefits, and must bear the Burdens, and are the Security in their Publick Bonds." The pull of this sort of argument was reflected in Mather's very language; profiteers who buy up the bills will finally lose everything: "Thus the woman shook her Dog by the Collar, till she made him Disgorge again all her Puddings." Thomas Hooker might well have used such an image in a sermon; Mather could resort to it only in an anonymous deviation from his pulpit manner, speaking as "A well wisher to New-England."

Though the invasion of Canada miscarried, the effort still had an immense propaganda value: New England had proved its loyalty. Biding his time in London, Increase Mather used it to plead for generous terms, because if "his Majesty shall graciously please to restore his Subjects in New-England to their ancient Priviledges," they will undertake a second venture, and should they succeed, "that would be worth Millions to the English Crown and Nation"—not, let us note, in terms of Christian virtues, but in "Bever-Trade," fisheries, and the "encreasing of English Sea-men." For the next generation, and indeed down to the Stamp Act, the memory of this gratuitous display of loyalty was assiduously kept alive by New England's apologists, although it never greatly impressed cabinet ministers. Year by year the contention grew that it should be accounted to New England for righteousness, until in 1721 Jeremiah Dummer brought the plea to a magnificent climax: yes, the expedition was a failure ("who can answer for the fortune of war?"), but it cost the colony £150,000 and 1,000 men; nor, he added, were these forces vagrants and such as in England are picked up in disorderly houses, "but heads of families, artificers, and robust young men, such as no country can spare, and least of all new settlements, where labour is the dearest thing in the world, because nothing so much wanted as hands."

As the years unrolled, it was found that the substance of the covenant doctrine, indissolubly wedded to a conception of the inherent rights of Englishmen, could be salvaged if only it could be dissociated from the self-government of the old charter and firmly attached to the Protestantism of the English Crown. William and Mary were thus not only instruments of a providential deliverance from Popery, they were moral sovereigns who recovered "the Married State, from all that Infamy, which the Debaucheries of the Two last Reigns, had been trying to cast upon it." By 1701, William III had come to figure in the New England mind as its appointed champion, for thanks to him "we are not Priest ridden by the Janizaries of Antichrist," and do not have "Nonsensical Figments thrust down our Throats with Burning Fire brands." When he died, every minister in the colonies climbed to the pulpit ostentatiously to lament the first sovereign to whom New England had been able to be loyal, for, as Wadsworth put it, he came to save this people when they "were in languishing circumstances; almost quite depriv'd of Liberty and Property; having their Religion, Laws and Lives in utmost hazard; sinking under Arbitrary Power and Tyranny; almost overwhelm'd with Popery and Slavery." And what made gratitude all the more heartfelt was, as Cotton Mather could gloat, "You, O dear People of New-England, have your Share in this amazing Deliverance"—in this single but manifold rescue of liberty, property, and religion.

The chant was not only renewed but enlarged upon the accession of Queen Anne, and was still more vociferously raised when Bolingbroke was thwarted and George I mounted the throne. This succession, Cotton Mather exulted, definitely proves the existence of divine providence and foretends that Louis XIV shall never "arrive to the Universal Empire of Europe"; the death in 1715 of that "most Finished Representation of Satan that was to be seen on the Face of the Earth" again increased New England's already utmost devotion to Hanover, through whom we are secure "from a Despotick or Arbitrary Government, or having our Liberties Invaded by Papal Usurpations and Tyrannie." By 1716 Colman could see in the rule of George I a distinct covenant blessing specifically contrived by a providence "concerning it self for and exercised towards the

Professing and Covenant People of God." Upon that king's death in 1727, New Englanders mourned in language which makes strange reading to those acquainted with his character: "comely, florid Countenance, like David"; a man of wisdom, courage, resolution, steadiness, integrity, clemency! On and on the refrain was carried: "For what Province, subject to the British Crown," asked Samuel Fiske in 1731, "more values the Royal Family and Succession?"

Today we may too easily doubt the sincerity of these patriotic professions since all the while they were being uttered, the House of Deputies was refusing to pay the governor's salary; also, many of the loyal citizenry were piling up fortunes by smuggling. Be that as it may, a society's (like an individual's) image of itself does not stand in so simple a relation to how it behaves. The long-sustained rhetoric of excessive loyalty served between 1690 and 1730 deeper needs than excusing the General Assembly or concealing smugglers: it enabled a society which, upon the revocation of the old charter, needed to establish its identity anew, to avoid intellectual suicide and to reconstruct its personality. For one of the reasons why New Englanders could hail William III was that by the Act of Toleration he seemed to tell them that they could be let alone with their church system and all its problems. The deliberate obtuseness their public utterances thereafter displayed toward religious strife in England, the calculated omission from their panegyrics of any mention of the Occasional Conformity Act or the Test Acts (about which they were well informed) reveals that the extravagance of their profession sprang from uneasiness: the more they praised the tolerance of the Crown, the less likely the Crown would be (or should be) to interfere in their ecclesiastical affairs. Every praise of William, the deliverer from Popery, every condemnation of the "Tory-Sachims," every identification of the House of Hanover with the House of David, only meant (it was to be hoped) the more "security of the true knowledge and worship of God among us." To praise the Georges for their "Catholic Spirit," for defending "a Righteous Liberty of Conscience," would be a way of warning bishops and governors that "we still enjoy those precious Charter-Privileges, for which our Fore-Fathers left their Native pleasant Land, and came over hither into a miserable Thicket to procure." As Thomas Prince was at last to make absolutely clear, while bowing from his pulpit before the ascending glory of George II, our charter privileges and the Protestant succession "Both come and stand on the same Foundation."

The Act of Toleration ought to have settled the religious problem: Congregationalists could avail themselves of the same terms accorded Dissenters at home. Indeed, as a matter of plain factual record, this is about what the next forty years amount to. But the intellectual problem was not so simple, and here again we have to distinguish between literature and life. Should the New England Way accept the status of a dissenting sect, should it settle down to enjoy this dispensation, it would admit such a defeat as even a regaining of the civil rights of Englishmen would not recompense. This was not a conclusion to which inheritors of the Non-Separatist logic could comfortably bring themselves, nor did they ever quite do so—a fact in the realm of the mind which explains much in that of politics. Even while the new charter was pending, Charles Morton in Charlestown tried to send over assistance to the negotiators by advertising that New Englanders are "of the Church of England"; lest this sound too grotesque to English ears, he quickly added, "in that they acknowledge the Doctrinal Articles of Religion" and do not, like so many who get preferments, preach Pelagianism, Arminian and Socinian heresies, or a spice of Popery. He may not have assisted Increase Mather's diplomacy, but he was serving notice that New England would not abandon that logic of the founders by which, as the "true" Church of England, they virtually excommunicated nine-tenths of the institution. In the *Magnalia* Cotton Mather carefully documented this contention, never letting on that in the course of time it had become absurd. Yet on the other hand, neither he nor his colleagues wished to forgo the advantages offered by a tolerant Crown, and by 1715 he managed to reinforce his declarations of loyalty with the assurance that a Protestant succession, being on principle devoted to toleration, was the best guarantee of New England's ecclesiastical security: a king so beloved will ever give "the Best Friends of His House" cause to rejoice, "Among whom, it is incredible, that the DISSENTERS who have been so Universally true to that, and His Interest, should not be regarded as a Body of People, too true Britons and Christians, to be Excluded from a Share in the Common Joy of their Fellow-Subjects." Thus by not quite admitting that they also were Dissenters, but rather by attaching themselves to the Crown through innumerable oaths of loyalty, the New England clergy contrived that a royal indulgence should serve their churches in place of that bulwark their grandfathers had erected out of Scripture.

But as early as 1690 one thing was clear. Both Mathers, although separated by the breadth of the Atlantic, had the wit to see it: New England could not take advantage of the Act of Toleration without proclaiming, along with its allegiance to William, its acceptance of the theory of toleration. Writing in 1724, in the biography of his father, Cotton was to say that both Mathers began to change their minds during the 1680's—a statement I do not believe. But it is a fact that in 1690 Increase—whose ideas six years previously we have heard—did present himself before Queen Mary blandly explaining that New England heartily concurred with the Acts of Indulgence and Toleration. Son Cotton got the cue, and in the same year, with equal blandness informed the provisional government, "For every man to worship God according to his Conviction, is an Essential Right of Humane Nature." We should note this interesting use of "humane nature."

Throughout his negotiations, Increase had a bad time explaining away the record of New England. He had to confess it a fault in the people "that in some matters relating to Conscience and difference of opinion, they have been more rigid and severe than the Primitive Christians or the Gospel doth allow of." Quakers and Baptists shrieked in all the byways of London that this was classic understatement. Increase was driven further to explain that fundamentally the churches of his country were one with the reformed orders of Scotland, France, Holland, Switzerland, except that New England "chooses to do that more Explicitly, which is done Implicitly in all those other Churches." He was saving what he could of the vision of a city on the hill; at the same time, confronting a government that had declared itself ready to tolerate dissent, he was suggesting that Congregationalism be regarded a local and harmless crotchet which might pretend that it was the fulfillment of the Reformation, but which a Protestant king could allow to have its dream. In all the history of Western Europe, there is hardly to be traced in so short a compass such a gigantic reversal as Increase Mather's repudiation of his father's farewell principle for the sake of preserving as much as possible of mere self-government.

How did Increase Mather find the gall to say that admission to Congregational churches was so wide in 1690 that many Presbyterians, Episcopalians, and even Antipaedobaptists were members? Well, he said it, and he published it. He also said that New England had, "long before the Questioning of their Charters," come to "an Intire Tolleration" of dissenters. In 1686 he had written, and Cotton had surreptitiously circulated, *A Brief Discourse Concerning the Unlawfulness of the Common Prayer Worship*, at a time when it seemed that Randolph might force them to use the Prayer Book; after the flight of James II, Increase hastily brought out (though still anonymously) a London edition. This proved an embarrassment, but Increase was up to explaining it away: there is nothing in that book, he said, but what every Nonconformist holds; it is "A placid and modest account" of a belief dear to thousands who support King William!

Increase was moving in a world where inconsistencies could be explained away, but the issue was more squarely put up to Cotton by George Keith (then a Quaker), who took advantage of the situation to publicize the record. He smote the established order on the hip not only by retailing the hangings and whippings, but by calling the "narrow-spirited party in New England" the "Brownists" of Queen Elizabeth's days, who therefore were not and never had been qualified to speak for Luther and Calvin. Furthermore, to cite their own account of themselves, they "have not a little degenerated, both in Doctrine and Life." Whatever Increase might be saying in London, he had been a persecutor; his son, by striving to exonerate him, "doth the more lay open his Fathers Nakedness."

Cotton Mather was feeling the pinch; he mobilized three other ministers to issue with him a reply to Keith, and when Keith answered with still another attack (published in Philadelphia), calling their pretended antidote a "Poyson," Cotton himself was forced to disavow the actions of thirty or forty years past: "Tell them, That New England has Renounced whatever Laws are against a Just Liberty of Conscience." Thus Cotton Mather prepared himself—or was obliged to prepare himself—for the provision that any charter issued by William III was bound to contain, a requirement that liberty of conscience be allowed in the worship of God to all Christians except Papists. As soon as he learned of it, Cotton saw the point: "I feared, that the Zeal of my Countrey had formerly had in it more Fire than should have been; especially, when the mad Quakers were sent unto the Gallowes, that should have been kept rather in a Bedlam." Whereupon he resolved with himself, saying (not quite accurately), "I think, I am the only Minister Living in the Land, that have testifyed against the Suppression of Haeresy, by Persecution."

Even so, we must give credit where credit is due: on Thursday, June 9, 1692, Cotton Mather preached before the governor his father had elevated, Sir William Phips, and committed the new regime to tolerance. A civil magistrate must not compel men to a way of worship to which they are conscientiously indisposed; he must say, "as the King now on the British Throne," that he will not become a persecutor. A ruler is most properly "the Officer of Humane Society," but a Christian who does not conform to an imposed way of worship does not therefore break the terms on which he enjoys the benefits of that society. "A Man ha's a Right unto his Life, his Estate, his Liberty, and his Family, altho' he should not come up to these and those Blessed Institutions of our Lord."

These are splendid words. We should not forget that Cotton Mather spoke them, but neither should we forget that he had come face-to-face with a dilemma from which he and other orthodox leaders were never, in his lifetime, to escape: they detested heresy, but could no longer persecute it; they could take refuge behind the new charter on the ground, as Increase said, that "Your religion is secured to you," but they simply could not use it, as they had used the old charter, to condemn Anne Hutchinson or the Quakers. They would survive and would rule only if they learned, however reluctantly, to regard themselves as no more than a majority of Dissenters within the most loyal of all British provinces.

Nothing in all this means that the dominant clique suddenly became whole-hearted libertarians; in 1708 Samuel Sewall refused to sign a warrant for a Quaker meetinghouse: "said I would not have a hand in setting up their Devil Worship." For a long time—a very long time—Cotton Mather's brave words served mainly as a political device: they proved that New England was theoretically tolerant, but not that it actually tolerated. However, if only as a stratagem, the gesture served its purpose, as when Increase in 1699 assured Governor Bellomont that any godly man could honor another, "Suppose him to be Episcopalian, Congregational, Presbyterian, Antipedobaptist." The next year, Increase also asserted that there exists no Protestant sect but what "amongst them all, some with whom Godliness in the Truth and Power is to be found." By 1718 Cotton Mather could outdo even himself in writing to Lord Barrington, brother of the new governor (with each arrival, the protestations were intensified), that just as the people's welcome to Colonel Shute witnessed New England's allegiance to "our Lawful, and Rightful, and Invaluable King GEORGE," so also its churches, above all others upon earth, make the terms of their communion run parallel with those of salvation: "And Calvinists with Lutherans, Presbyterians with Episcopalians, Pedo-baptists with Anabaptists, beholding one another to fear God, and work Righteousness, do with delight sit down together at the same Table of the Lord; nor do they hurt one another in the Holy Mountain." Had this boast corresponded to reality, New England in the eighteenth century would have outrun the aspirations of Roger Williams. But as Cotton Mather knew only too well, this sort of talk had several uses, the least of which was to bring about a happy communion with lesser sects; in brute fact, its principal utility, year after year, was to retard, as much as was compatible with the payment of such lip service, the increase of "dissent" inside New England. With 1689 the philosophy of intolerance collapsed, nor could it be revived; the Mathers demonstrated their perspicacity by becoming the first to renounce it. But in its place survived a determination to procrastinate extending actual freedom to Baptists or Quakers, or even to the Church of England, not because Congregationalism was any longer identified with an absolute divine prescription, but because it was a bond of union. The "standing order" henceforth was of value not so much because it was Christ's but because it was New England's "Way."

Thus 1689 meant that two obligations were laid upon the New England mind: it had to incorporate into its social theory a fulsome declaration of loyalty to the Crown and to accommodate itself to the idea of toleration. Several decades were required for working out the task, although even in April of 1689 anyone could see that these were to be the conditions of survival. But also, the one great lesson of the Andros regime had been the preciousness of "Civil Liberties." After the revolt, while Massachusetts still had no legal status, there was every temptation to derive these liberties from "the light of nature," but considering how apt depraved humanity is to pervert the notion of natural right (as Cotton said, some in New England took it in the Hobbesian sense!), Puritan leaders during the interregnum made a concerted effort to found them upon English legal tradition. Thus by proclaiming their utter dependence on "that brave Nation," they could all the more appropriate "those Liberties which are a rich Inheritance." They prostrated themselves before the throne, assured that they would not be left "without our share in the Universal Restauration of Charters and English Liberties." If loyalty and toleration were the two principal gifts of 1689 to the body of New England thought, they were impositions from without: from within came the third acquisition, a much enhanced veneration for the prescriptive rights of Englishmen, never to be forgotten so long as memory survived of tyrants who had declared us "a People fit only to be Rooted off the Face of the Earth, and who might have been in Forwardness enough to accomplish That Rooting Business."

Considering how little he had to bargain with—beyond the argument that Boston helped enthrone William or that because the planters had enlarged the king's dominions at no cost to the Crown they should "enjoy those Priviledges which by their Charter were assured to them"—Increase Mather achieved a spectacular success. True, a governor was imposed (Increase softened that blow by managing that the first one be his creature), and the franchise was extended, regardless of church membership, to all freehold estates to the value of forty shillings a year, but there was once more an elected General Court, with the House of Representatives having the great privilege of selecting (subject to the governor's veto) members of the Council, and the priceless privilege of controlling the purse. For this confirmation of civil liberties, conceding the principle of toleration was a small price to pay.

Nevertheless, many New Englanders believed Mather had conceded too much. Whether the opposition arose from the new-found enthusiasm for civil liberties or merely out of jealousy of Mather's power, it took the form of an attack upon him and his charter for having sacrificed, not religion, but freedom. Increase came home to encounter the proverbial fate of the Massachusetts agent, to be reviled for his failures and given no credit for his successes. He set himself to defending his work with the help of his faithful Cotton.

Knowing in advance that he would have a fight on his hands, Increase took the precaution of getting an endorsement from twelve English Nonconformists—names greatly revered in New England, Bates, Howe, Mead, and Alsop—who declared that minor inconveniences should be accepted as the best obtainable under the circumstances because the main object was secured, "Liberty and Property, the fairest Flowers of the Civil State." On this ground Mather prepared his line that the charter was "a MAGNA CHARTA" whereby English liberties "and all Mens Properties, are Confirmed and Secured." He did regret that the governor should have a negative upon the choice of Councillors and upon acts of the lower house, for this, he confessed, makes the government "more Monarchical and less Democratical than in former Times," but still the people have a negative on the governor, and New England is more "Privileged than Ireland or than any other English Plantation, or than even England itself." Whatever his misgivings, when he could again use his pulpit for a sounding board, he insisted that the great point of the charter was that "a Governour with a Juncto of his Council cannot (as of late they did) make Laws, and impose Taxes on you, without your own consent, by your Representatives." Cotton Mather regularly seconded him: "We have a Royal Charter, which, Effectually Secures unto us, all Christian Liberties, and all English Liberties," and in 1700 was still exclaiming over the "Matchless Favour of God unto us, that we have our claim to English Liberties (though our

Task masters Twelve years ago, told us we had None!)." Dudley's sneer would never cease to rankle; Sam Adams would know how to use it, and Thomas Hutchinson would find that he could make no headway against it. One does not exaggerate when saying that in 1776 New Englanders could take up arms against George III because in 1689 they had sprung so alertly to the side of William III.

Much of the writing of both Mathers in the 1690's, and above all the *Magnalia*, is a sustained propaganda offensive to make the charter, with all its liberties, the standard of a new conservatism—of the only "orthodoxy" that could be salvaged from the wreck of the old charter. If sober demonstration of advantages would not silence detractors, then the Mathers would heap ridicule upon them for rewarding the instrument who saved their lands, lives, and liberties with the "cruel Malice and Slander . . . commonly known by the name of Country-Pay," or would lecture that a "Murmmuring Spirit" is not the way to get more, or at last circumvent the intransigent with an appeal to loyalty: "Although the Governour and Lieutenant Governour are not chosen by our selves; yet we have the Consolation and Satisfaction, that they are chosen by the best King upon Earth." Very quickly it became apparent that the most telling argument for the charter was not so much habeas corpus and religious freedom as security of property: "And is this nothing," demanded Increase Mather, "that every Man may sit under his own Vine, and his own Figtree?" The Revolution of 1689, and more specifically the identification of the new charter with English rights, set this seal firmly upon the New England mind, that government is, as every election sermon was sure to assert, "the great Buckler (when rightly managed) both of Religion and Property." The marriage of these two words became so close that one suspects they were fast becoming interchangeable. The founders had not been contemptuous of property, and had supposed that they could deal with it at no cost of holiness. By the beginning of the eighteenth century, as New Englanders more and more linked religion with property, the second inevitably became the great concern which the first had been for Winthrop or Hooker.

How rapidly the New England mind was moving into this new universe Cotton Mather himself made evident in 1692 in his major effort to assist his father by adventuring into a literary realm even more remote from the sermon than his tract on the bills of credit: he composed and circulated in manuscript four bestiary allegories, *Political Fables*. They are not literary masterpieces, but the point is that they tried to be; they aimed at, if they did not quite attain, wit and urbanity, and deliberately sought to be amusing. They were an effort to bring the manners of London to solid Boston, and if they are innocent of the deftness of *MacFlecknoe*, their spirit is as worldly. In the first, the inhabitants of New England are birds: "some catched fish, some lived upon grains; the woodpeckers also made a great figure among them; some of them scraped for their living with their claws," and "Geese you may be sure there were a good store, as there are everywhere." Increase is the eagle, who flies to Jupiter's palace to get a new "settlement," and comes back with guarantees that all strange birds shall be kept out of their council and that none shall disturb them "in singing of their songs to the praise of their Maker, for which they had sought liberty in the wilderness." In the second, Phips is a good elephant; and in the third, the party of Elisha Cooke become ungrateful sheep to whom Mercury (Increase again) brings privileges above those of any other part of the English nation. In the fourth, French wolves discover with glee that New English dogs are too busy snapping and snarling at each other to bother them. "This is a story so old, that, as the good man said, I hope it is not true."

When we reflect upon Mather's *Political Fables*, upon both their content and manner, the real thread of the story of late seventeenth-century New England becomes not, as in so many accounts, a growth of toleration, but rather a shedding of the religious conception of the universe, a turning toward a way of life in which the secular state, even when embodied in a provincial corporation, has become central. In New England we can see as clearly as anywhere how Protestantism was imperceptibly carried over into the new order, not by turning from religion to an absolutist state, but by translating Christian liberty into those liberties guaranteed by statute. Which is another way of saying that religion became the support, not of Winthrop's ideal city, but of property. Long before the conception of uniformity was shuffled off, that of economic regulation and the just price had been let go. Soon afterward, the philosophy of social status yielded to the ethic of success, and merchants who took advantage of the market learned to control congregations despite the clerics; the prestige of ministers still was great, but they would need every bit of it were they still to dominate. The Mathers could say that government should not consist of a party or a faction; this was all that remained, a ghostly survival of Winthrop's doctrine that all should be knit together as one man. The clergy could preach the ideal of unanimity, but what could they do when their supporters became divided into furiously warring camps over such a question as the land bank, or when they themselves had to take sides? And what were they to do when others of the diverging interests accused them of serving the ends of only one element in a violently competitive economy?

It is not fantastic to see in Gershom Bulkeley the last of the theocrats. He had become disillusioned with Puritanism and with Congregationalism, but only because they had moved away from the original ideals of subordination and submission. He turned, therefore, to the throne, believing it the only power capable of arresting centrifugal tendencies. Yet Increase and the other spokesmen also turned to the king—not to Bulkeley's sort of monarchy, but to one who dispensed charters and liberties. No synod could ever again speak with the voice of God, as Increase had almost made that of 1679 speak; such assemblies could no longer be anything but arenas for debate and compromise. By the same token, government under a royal charter could not exercise the majesty of a Winthrop; it would have to be an affair of expedience, haggling, and of sparring with royal governors. The ultimate criteria would have to be, not the rule of Scripture, but of efficiency and diplomacy.

The society of New England was no longer simple and uniform; by our standard, it might superficially appear in 1700 still uncomplicated, but relative to what it had been (or had thought itself to be), a culture that contained a Bulkeley, a Wise, and two Mathers was already sundered. Parties and alignments were not drawn, as in the Antinomian crisis, on doctrinal issues; they arose out of social conflict. The vast inclusive framework of the New England mind, spread out in architectonic perfection, which supplied the pattern for the earlier part of this history, disintegrated speedily after 1690, and by 1730 was virtually dead. Up to 1690, although the intellectuals had been learning from experience, they had been pouring their experience into literary forms—such as the jeremiad—originally devised to accord with the now vanishing cosmology. Henceforth, they would have to rescue what they could of religion and morality by modifying those forms, or by finding others more pertinent to the social reality. Loyalty to the Crown, toleration, and constitutional liberties—these were the preconditions of provincial culture. As for the churches, Cotton Mather in 1692 foresaw the issue: the primitive church, he said in his oration before Governor Phips, cut off a thousand Hydra's heads without any help from penal laws; "it was by sound Preaching, by Discipline, by Catechising and by Disputation, that they Turned to flight the Armies of the Aliens." These words were still more prophetic than Mather may have realized, for they delimited the array of weapons with which, once the charter was established, in even a society so religious in character as New England, the religious authority could any longer effectively wage its several campaigns.

CHAPTER XII

SALVAGING THE COVENANT

professional pessimist obliged to confess that things
are not so bad after all is in a predicament. Up to 1688 Increase Mather
had preached an already classic series of jeremiads, much imitated by young
men at Harvard; yet in 1690, in his effort to persuade the British government that it should resuscitate the "good and easie Government" of the old
charter, he said that under it the country, far from presenting a bleak spectacle of degeneration, had prospered to a degree unparalleled in history, that
never in so short a time had a region been brought from a howling wilderness into a "pleasant Land, wherein was abundance of all things meat for
Soul and Body."

Before 1684 the communities had been so self-centered that they never
stopped to think how their self-denunciations would sound to non-New
England ears. They got a rude shock when Quakers like Keith and
Thomas Maule, taking the jeremiads at face value, proclaimed New
England a sink of iniquity. Therefore it had to be explained that the
jeremiad was a rhetorical exercise, not to be tampered with by "designing
persons that are not great friends to holiness and righteousness," who, being
ignorant of the innermost meaning, wrest the utterances beyond the authors' intentions, and so "that hath past for their Opinion, which only was
intended by way of Admonition." Parson Nicholas Noyes of Salem confessed the basically literary rather than sociological character of the type:
some "well meaning holy men, being of dark melancholy Spirits," little
acquainted with parts of the world where atheism and iniquity actually do
exist, had magnified the pecadilloes of New England, witnessing by the
very disproportion of their distress the relative innocence of the whole society—"It cannot with truth be asserted, that as yet we are as bad as bad
can be; for there is real danger of growing worse." Even Cotton Mather
had to check himself with the distasteful reflection that there was "propor-
tionably" more piety here than anywhere else under heaven; in order not
to supply the enemy with ammunition, he made the litany of afflictions become so rhapsodic a witness to "our being those Children, whose Nurture
the Great God is very careful of" that it became a catalogue of blessings.
For a Puritan to boast was considered bad form, but at the risk of incurring
divine correction, Samuel Belcher in 1707 asserted that the colonial ministry was godly, learned, painful, and "Condescending," and that even in

Boston, where there was a deal of vanity, there was also a great deal of
godliness.

Thus after 1689, and especially after the charter, spokesmen for these
provinces found their task complex: how could the jeremiad be so recast as
still to serve the old needs, and yet be accommodated to the altered political
situation? One answer might be to dispense with it entirely, to cease thinking of New England as a peculiar people in a special covenant, and to devise other literary forms in which the issues of the society could be phrased.
To some extent, as we shall see, the most astute intellects between 1690
and 1730 were to do precisely that; but for certain purposes, no other
form would serve, or rather the jeremiad was the only one available. New
England could not be expected, just because the Bay had a royal governor
and the Crown could disallow its laws, suddenly to root out the conviction
that it was the object of a most peculiar solicitude in heaven. The people
could not jettison their experience and commence overnight to look upon
themselves as just another group of provinces, no different from Virginia
or Barbados. No man—and no society—so disowns the past, even though
in 1697 it might seem that in its degeneration New England had become
worse than "those parts which were at first Peopled by the Refuse of the
English Nation." Thus the jeremiad had to be refurbished; it had to be
brought up to date on the matter of toleration and kept from encouraging
the region's enemies, but at the same time it could not let go the delights of
ritualistic condemnation.

Increase preached cautiously to the first Assembly, explaining how they
might still be intolerant in the midst of toleration: "You may by Laws not
only Protect, but encourage that Religion which is the General Profession
of the Country." The Assembly dutifully responded by enacting that idol-
aters, blasphemers, and incestuous persons be punished as capital offenders,
and provided that taxes be collected for ministerial salaries. For a moment
the Mathers persuaded themselves that they were actually better off under
the new charter than under the old, and in that mood spoke such praises of
it as they could never take back. There was indeed "A Righteous and Generous Liberty of Conscience Established," but the legislature might nevertheless give a "Distinguished Encouragement" to the dominant churches,
in fact possibly a more effective encouragement, "As far at least, as the
powers of a Province Exceed those of a Corporation." It now wonderfully
appeared that the Assembly would severely punish all the sins enumerated
in 1679 and since then woefully increased, which would not be an invasion
of civil liberties but a happy exercise of the greatest of all the rights of
Englishmen—"That the People are to be concerned in the making of the
Laws whereby they must be Governed."

The Matherian scheme suffered a serious setback when the Crown disallowed the capital punishment act (London was astute enough to appreciate that under the heading of subversive idolatry and blasphemy Quakers
or even good Anglicans might find themselves, in the provincial sense of

the terms, guilty). It was further handicapped by the strenuous opposition of an anti-charter party which so hated the Mathers as to resist any recommendation they supported. Some in this group were originally die-hard theocrats who should have supported the program of strict moral regulation, but they were so set against the charter that they tried to prevent it from succeeding, even in the direction of their hopes. Other elements, chiefly Elisha Cooke, were inspired less by religion than by love of power; inevitably they would contest the Mathers in the name of rights and liberties. Once these became the slogan, the party offered a refuge for a few survivors of the pre-1684 moderates, because resistance to Increase and Phips now became a defense of native liberties against foreign aggression! At the first free election, in 1693, the House left out ten of Increase's Councillors, and put in men like Danforth, Addington, and Browne; it tried also to put in Elisha Cooke, but Phips invoked the power Increase had attempted to keep from him, and negated Cooke's election. Thus, within a short two years, the internal situation took on a novel and ugly configuration: the parties became those of the Governor and of the House, the former centered in the eastern merchants, the latter relying upon the back-country. This alignment was thoroughly secular and cut across all religious concerns; it was enough to reduce the Mathers to despair, yet it marks, if only for that reason, a momentous shift in the intellectual history.

To the Mathers, as Cotton had remarked, there remained but one weapon with which to check these developments—the jeremiad. After Phips failed and was recalled in 1694, and after Stoughton, as Lieutenant Governor, admitted Cooke to the Council, they could do nothing but raise the ancient cry that "faction" is a sin, and sneer at Cooke's followers as "secret Enemies to all the Good Order, which the Ancient Constitution of New-England has moulded us into." By taking special pains to prove that they, champions of the charter, did not "go to set by an English Tenderness of our Liberties," they managed again and again to demonstrate that the opponents were the ones not "Tender, and Tenacious of such precious Liberties, as the Country is, by a Royal Grant, at this Day, priviledg'd withal," and therefore "cannot be True to the Interest of the Country." By this logic, the best friends of the community were demonstrably "those, that most Vigorously Endeavour to Restrain, and Redress, and Reform, that Liberty of Sinning, which men are too ready to give unto themselves" —or, in short, those who encourage and protect that order which is "the general Profession." By pleading for unity upon such indisputable propositions as that drinking houses should be supervised, or family government encouraged and "oppression" redressed, the jeremiad could present Elisha Cooke as both profligate and unpatriotic, as one who brought down upon all the people both divine and political retribution.

This being the most effective means the clergy could devise, for the remainder of our period they employed it, explaining constantly that while the charter regime holds dear our liberties and estates, "yet in themselves considered, and as they relate to us, they are a very Trifle, in comparison of the Object of divine Worship." Whatever furthered "due execution" of laws already made on behalf of the churches would be a service to God: "I beseech your Honours in your Wisdom to meditate it, and by your Authority to see it done." Increase managed to inform even that easy-going Anglican, the Earl of Bellomont, that he should administer Massachusetts in the interest of Congregationalism; Cotton called for "a General Consultation, upon the Methods of Reformation" because "Conformists"— who of course had full liberty of conscience—"are in New England, Dissenters." Where sin is tolerated, any ruler, charter or no charter, becomes infamous, and the principle of liberty of conscience did not mean that the civil magistrate had nothing to do with matters of piety.

That the clergy were obliged to harp constantly on this theme, especially in election sermons, suggests that legislatures and governors failed to oblige. Even in Connecticut, where officials were all of the people's own choosing, the proposition had to be vigorously defended that active political support of the instituted worship is not incompatible with the theory of toleration or a respect for English liberties. The state might still enforce support of ministers and pass laws for the reformation of manners, see that true doctrine was taught and the sacraments rightly administered. If in virtually independent Connecticut the civil power fell short of ministerial expectations, perhaps in both communities this fact is historically of less importance than that the intellectual leaders could still continue calling upon it to act. Continuity with the past was thus maintained, so that even fatal concessions to constitutional rights and to toleration would not appear fatal. There was no open disagreement among the ministers upon this philosophy; in the most acrimonious phase of his controversy with the Mathers, Solomon Stoddard came out of the wilderness to deliver the election sermon of 1703, and made Increase's point for him:

> Rulers are to be keepers of both tables; and as they must practice Religion and Morality themselves, so they must take care that the people do it; they must use all proper means, for the suppression of Heresy, Prophaness & Superstition & other Corruptions in Worship.

Neither did Benjamin Colman, who figures in history as a "liberal," neglect in 1707 to affirm this sentiment. Cotton Mather held firmly to it, although he was to make greater and greater allowances; in his last days, as he trembled for the future, he left his testament in the biography of his father, which codifies this fundamental law of the provincial mind: if the magistrates do not keep religion flourishing in the hearts of the people, "the Fault will not be in the New-Charter, but in Themselves."

In 1692 Increase entertained high expectations of the Council, the upper chamber in the legislature which, by the charter, replaced the old Board of Assistants; he considered the finest stroke of his diplomacy to be his securing for the House of Deputies the privilege of selecting it. He entitled his election discourse on May 31, 1693, *The Great Blessing, of Primitive*

Counsellors ("primitive" meaning as in primitive New England!), and by
so expounding the charter as to make the Council the hinge of all recovered
liberties, tried to bully the House into reëlecting his choices. Councillors
should be pious, faithful, and wise persons, who "will concern themselves
to uphold Religion in the Truth, Purity and Power of it." There would be
no danger of "Apostasy" so long as the Council was orthodox, let the
House become what it might; thus "the Word of the Lord does Instruct
this General Assembly, whom they ought to Choose or Confirm this Day."
He told Phips frankly that the power to veto elections was something the
governor would not possess "if any Interest that I was capable to make,
could have prevented it." Whereupon the Assembly chose such "rash,
heady, unthinking" men as Increase said would endanger the public weal,
and so Phips employed his power. Henceforth the Council could not be
relied upon.

Generally they fulfilled one part of Increase's prescription: they were
"men of Estate, and of some Port in the World," and were "advantaged
by Liberal Education"; but only of a few could the Mathers say, as Increase did of John Foster, that he was both "an hearty Revolutioner" and
also "a friend to the Churches of the Lord Jesus Christ, and Zealous for that
Holy Order of the Gospel which has been Professed and Practised among
them." In an astonishingly short time, Increase was appalled to discover
that the rage of party conflict thrust upon Councillors a policy, as Hutchinson later said, of keeping their seats by becoming of no importance. Nevertheless, if the Council largely failed him, the fact that it was there, and
that it was elective, helped Increase to insist that the regime was of the
people, and therefore was duty bound to enforce religious laws on pain of
offending that God who was still—although through the medium of
William III—in covenant with them. The ministers could still agitate for
their candidates lest the Lord be provoked to let prevail those wicked men
who were plotting to deprive the House of its privilege and to put the choice
of Councillors in the hands of a tyrannical governor.

The great point repeatedly gained in these dialectical maneuvers was
that 1684–1692 had not been a break. The wound was healed. New England was not after all like other nations, but veritably a chosen people,
even though the terms of union now incorporated clauses inserted into the
covenant not by Scripture but by the Privy Council. Connecticut, naturally, had less difficulty (despite Gershom Bulkeley) in carrying over the
doctrine intact, and moving with it into the eighteenth century:

Remember that there is a Solemn Covenant between God and this his People;
God hath taken them to be his, and they have owned themselves to be the Lords;
upon this Foundation stand all our Mercies, Priviledges, Enjoyments, and whatsoever can contribute any thing to our present or future Felicity: and therefore
the recovery of us from all our Apostasies, and the maintaining and promoting of
serious Godliness among us, should and will be the chief Scope of such Rulers, as
make Conscience to Serve either God, or his People.

But the life of the conception in both Connecticut and New Hampshire —perhaps even in Rhode Island!—depended on the success with which it could be supported in the Bay. In 1704 Samuel Willard took as his text, "we are a People in Covenant with God," and explained that he meant the people of all New England. As applied to the entire region, not to just one colony, the familiar logic was again spelled out. By the covenant "God makes over him-self to a People," so that they know the ways wherein "they may expect all outward, spiritual and eternal blessings." Because they live in the bond, they—and they alone—enjoy the Word and worship which are the means of grace, leading to their final fellowship with Him. They could be assured that God is faithful to His engagement, and break forth anew into hymns of religious patriotism: "O New-England, thou art a Land of Vision; and has been so for a long time. The Sun for one day stood over Gibeon, so has the Sun of the Gospel been standing over us for Fourscore years together."

Furthermore, if the charter had not ruptured the covenant, even though the civil authority was not so pure an ordinance as hitherto, the obligation continued to rest upon the people themselves. Nothing would be further from the truth than to insinuate that the Mathers moved consciously toward "democracy," but in these circumstances, all the more because of their exasperation with the Council and the politicians, they were obliged to give to the national covenant a social implication that was a large step toward an identification of the voice of the people with the will of God. The whole populace "have deliberately bound themselves to a constant, faithful Compliance with these Terms"; hence the concern affects all classes "in their several Stations and Capacities." Obedience will engage God's blessing, and from every ill of the society or from every economic misfortune there is only one escape: the people must put away their iniquities and set about the work of reformation "in good earnest." Sabbath after Sabbath, at lectures, elections, and conventions, even at funerals, the doctrine was reiterated. In 1730 it was being pronounced with all the solemnity of 1692; that the repetition became progressively mechanical, the phrases stereotyped—that in every exposition the preacher spared no detail, as though the audience had not already heard it a thouasnd times—does not mean that the philosophy ceased to be useful. As long as it could stand, progress was possible. The social structure and the mentality, shaken by the Dominion and the Revolution, continued to absorb more shocks and to change at an accelerating pace, but while the over-all conception could be retained, even though only verbally, intelligence could cope with events. To out-and-out dissenters from the Congregational order, to Quakers and Episcopalians, to royal governors and to the Board of Trade, to a Jeremiah Dummer fled to the more genial world of London coffeehouses, the rationale of the covenant was nonsense. That did not matter; these communities preserved their personalities as long as they possessed a framework which validated their reason for being.

The tyranny of Andros was, as we have seen, a punishment for breach of the religious covenant. An unshakable conviction gripped the New England mind (a conviction reinvigorated in 1776) that political liberties must be defended on both religious and political grounds together, largely because the jeremiads for decades hammered upon this as the moral of the Dominion. The day of humiliation thus became more and more an engine for mobilizing social forces. The provisional government, recognizing its efficacy, at once seized upon that most congenial form for celebrating the liberation; it issued a proclamation calling for a "Public Work of Reformation," and everything seemed back to normal when the ministers could again denounce the population for falling short: " 'Tis you, that bring whole Armyes of Indians and Gallic Blood Hounds in upon us; tis you that clog all our Councils with such Delay and Slowness, or terrifies us in our most Rational Expectations." The people had lost "the most happy and easy Government in the world" because they frequented taverns; the possibilities of divine correction now included, in addition to plagues and crop failures, such a political regime as Andros', which "has by the most impartial men been confessed to have become Intolerable." The way hereafter to resist tyranny would be to heed the Synod of 1679.

To keep the appeal alive, there would have to be a succession of further evils, and these were furnished in gratifying abundance: Indian wars, decay of trade, party squabbles. However, most of these were already familiar; the jeremiad labors under an inherent necessity to pile up its tale of woe. Cotton Mather, most expert of the practitioners, was driven to uncover fresh material; in the years after 1689, he added, for instance, the dwindling state of the Protestant interest in Europe, and called upon farmers and merchants to reform their manners in order to rescue Huguenots from French dragoons or to save the Palatinate. And at this point, searching for more and more effective lashes, he realized that there was one horror above all others which had not yet been adequately exploited—witchcraft.

There were sporadic cases of witchcraft in New England before 1688, and some ten or twelve executions. The wonder is that there were no more, for it was axiomatic that the Devil would try hard to corrupt regions famous for religion. As Mitchell said in 1677, though we may have supposed that he could not reach so far, "New-England is but Earth and not Heaven; No place on Earth is exempted from molestation by the Devil and his Instruments." Perhaps the reason there were so few witches in New England during a century when hundreds were being destroyed in England and thousands in Scotland, Germany, and Scandinavia, is the same reason that, after 1637, there was so little Antinomianism or native Quakerism: the people were good enough Calvinists to resist temptation. They might not always be able to refuse an extra tankard of rum, but this sin— although it was the most plausible and the most enticing—they withstood. Of course, as a crime it was, I need hardly remark, as definite and tangible as is treason today, and for rules by which to prosecute it, the New England mind accepted a vast body of accumulated precedent exactly as it did in trials for murder or theft.

Increase Mather gave a new emphasis to the subject in his *Essay for the Recording of Illustrious Providences:* employing scientific methods to support the covenant thesis, he showed that a federated people are bound to suffer such afflictions as floods, tempests, and diabolical possessions. The book could also lay claim to a special modernity: several of the most progressive intelligences in England, many associated with the Royal Society, were striving to mobilize all Christians, regardless of sect, against the common enemy of all churches, atheism. Whatever Increase may have owed to the manuscript of Davenport, he owed even more to Joseph Glanvil's *Sadducismus Triumphatus* (1681) and to the writings of Henry More and Robert Boyle; he demonstrated that New England was not behind the times, but was keeping pace with an enlightened movement that deliberately attacked the "Sadduces of these days" by proving the truth of witchcraft. If witches exist, atheists are refuted. Mather's diplomatic success was materially assisted by the fact that in the *Essay* he had joined himself to such leaders as Baxter, to men trying to persuade Dissenters to stop quarreling among themselves and to unite on broader principles of piety, such as a stout insistence upon the reality of witchcraft.

Hence Increase devoted great care to setting up rules by which satanical possessions might be distinguished from natural distempers. A mistaken prosecution of the latter for the former would, of course, play into the hands of the enemy. As a tactical device, he showed the largeness of his view by acknowledging that sometimes innocent persons have been put to death, or that there are instances of confession which are not to be credited, springing from "the deluded imaginations of mind and melancholy persons." However, there were trustworthy records of authentic confessions by persons "whose judgment and reason have been free from disturbance by any disease" (as in the twentieth century there were to be confessions of espionage upon which authorities act). He could not certify that any in New England had yet seen a specter, since every narrative suggested that the apparition might be no more than "phansie." He was alert enough to insist that demons may transform themselves into angels of light and thus impose upon the credulous, and he perceived that devils most easily work upon those suffering the disease of melancholy, so that a course of physic—"emetic medicines, clearing them of these melancholy humors"—is a preventive; but the best of weapons—this was Mather's thesis—is repentance and a confession of sins, exactly as called for in the jeremiads.

Here, then, in 1689 was a sanction of the covenant that had been allowed to languish, but which might be invoked for rallying shattered morale. Cotton Mather studied his father's hints as a lover does the whims of his mistress: the *Essay* called for further investigations. In the summer of 1688, the children of a mason, John Goodwin, were afflicted with what was evidently a diabolical persecution; having in mind his father's researches, as well as the "pains Mr. Baxter, Mr. Glanvil, Dr. More, and several other Great Names have taken to publish Histories of Witchcrafts & Possessions unto the world," Cotton took one of the children into his house, and, at great inconvenience to himself and his domestic arrangements, not only accumulated data for a case history but cured the patient. The witch, Goody Glover, was quickly apprehended; conclusive evidences were found—images of rags and goat-hair which she had stroked by a finger wet with spittle—and she was promptly hanged. Andros and Dudley could offer no objection to these activities, so that when Mather's narrative appeared, Charles Morton, James Allen, Joshua Moodey, and Samuel Willard signed a prefatory endorsement, making the book a manifesto of the orthodox.

Mather's motive in writing *Memorable Providences, Relating to Witchcraft and Possessions* was twofold: on the one hand to disprove New England's provinciality ("Go then, my little Book, as a Lackey to the more elaborate Essayes of those learned men"; Richard Baxter willingly composed an endorsement for the London edition of 1691), and on the other to show that the afflictions of New England were augmenting because of its sins. Only when seen in the light of the situation of 1689 does this, one of the most notorious productions of the New England mind, make sense. As Cotton's colleagues put it, the book, by proving that there is a God, a Devil and witchcraft, thereby demonstrates that "There is no out-ward Affliction, but what God may (and sometimes doth) permit Satan to trouble His people withal"; thus it summons us to the only possible remedy, to prayer and reformation, the never-ending inculcation of the jeremiads.

To comprehend the *Memorable Providences* objectively—a difficult feat, because opponents of Puritanism have poured their scorn upon it and would-be defenders have aggravated the problem by trying to defend it— we need to remember that it was published two months after the rising against Andros, and that it was as much directed against his regime as the Revolutionary tracts. Mather gleefully reported that the bedeviled Martha Goodwin could easily read in the Prayer Book except when she came to direct quotations from Scripture; he said he would make no reflection upon this diabolical phenomenon, but then suggested that if any "inconsiderable men" were offended because he reported this fact, they should blame the Devil and not Congregational polity. Furthermore, he was careful to advertise that the "Magistrates"—meaning the town officials— had proved faithful to the Puritan code and had applied themselves with vigor to getting rid of Goody Glover. The moral for any chartered regime would be obvious.

Lest the provisional government should miss the point, Cotton enlarged for the next three years upon the increased threat of witchcraft. Because the country had weathered the assault of Andros it was not to assume that it would no longer be assaulted: "we have lived in the Territories of our Enemies; and we can scarce take a step without Annoyances from the bloudy Murderers of our Souls"; all our sins have been "at least Implicit Witchcrafts." But while Increase was negotiating in London, there were other miseries to add to the roll call: disaster at Quebec; Indian outrages at Amesbury, York, Wells, and then at Groton, only forty miles from Boston. The charter, when it arrived, was a covenant blessing, although the failure to recover full independence was a chastisement; the strife that ensued was all too evident a curse. Thenceforth the enumeration grew by leaps and bounds: more massacres—Oyster River, Lancaster, Andover, Haverhill, and in 1704 the most frightful, Deerfield; Dudley, who came back as governor in 1702 and promptly exhibited ingratitude to the Mathers (in which they saw one of the clearest signs of divine displeasure); military failures; violent controversies over Dudley's salary; attacks on the charter in Parliament; a steadily depreciating currency; terrible passions aroused by the land bank; real estate speculation. And all this while, the customary crop failures, epidemics, and shipwrecks. In 1697 two students were drowned at Cambridge and an eight-year-old child accidentally killed his baby brother: "Is there not a voice of Heaven in these things?" Good men, like Foster, died; every funeral became an occasion to foretell more fearful deprivations. There were great storms, such as have generally proved "the forerunners of greater Calamities immediately following them." And on October 3, 1711, Boston was half destroyed by a fire which consumed the First Church. Seen against the backdrop of all this misery, witchcraft at Salem was but an episode.

In the 1690's a certain caution was imposed upon the Jeremiahs by their awareness that harm might be done abroad. Samuel Willard delivered three judicious discourses (*Rules for the Discerning of the Present Times Recommended*, 1693; *Reformation the Great Duty of an Afflicted People, Setting forth the Sin and Danger there is in Neglecting of it, under the continual and repeated Judgments of God*, 1694; and *The Peril of the Times Displayed*, 1700), in which he prescribed a technique whereby, under the royal charter, threatenings could be employed. The sequence of his titles furnishes the main heads of his revision, and the contents reveal that henceforth the emphasis would have to fall, not so much on sorrows already endured, as upon a prophecy of worse yet to come. When a nation enters into covenant with God, the scheme of history becomes a crescendo. Willard could not but recognize that a long succession of jeremiads had so far failed to work a reformation; however, in dealing with a whole people God works (as He may not with individuals) by degrees, because He must impress upon them that in public matters they constitute a single entity. The punishments affect "the body of a people"—famine, pestilence, sword, captivity, bondage. The sin of an individual needs must "have a common influence, when it is a growing and prevailing malady among a people," because "every man as he is a member of the whole, and hath his outward concerns in the life involved with them, cannot but be touched and afflicted with the evils which come upon the places they live in, and will, without doubt, feel much of the smart of them." This administration, being agreeable "to the common sentiments of humane reason," requires a consistent policy, which takes the form of a gradual multiplication of evils, increasing in severity as the reformation fails to materialize. Otherwise, the lack of success of the Reforming Synod would recede into history, leaving serious doubts as to the method; but in such a perspective, that very futility became part of a divine plan, pointing to the inescapable conclusion that the ills of this society would have to grow worse until it at last would reform itself—an act it is fully capable of, whether or not it can elect its own governor.

In this conception, not only was the augmentation of disaster welcome, but it would serve as a spur to still more doleful predictions. For this kind of oratory, the frenetic genius of Cotton Mather was ideally suited: "Methinks I feel the sad Presages of it; I see the multiplied Invitations and Introductions leading to it." The sense of mounting intensity, of a drama annually becoming more critical, bore him ever upwards: "The Curse is not yet Executed on you; God waits one year after another, to see what will prove. But the Execution of the Curse, it is Nigh, it is Nigh, to you . . . It won't be long before you are thrown into the Fires for which the Tares are to be burned." The more it became evident that a chartered government, even though the House and Council were made up of church members, would not or could not take the holy initiative, the more it became necessary to pitch the responsibility upon "the People of New England." The shift in emphasis was gradual, but by 1708 it had become the norm, as when Samuel Danforth defined sin as a "Common Enemy" of "all our Communities and Societies; a publick and open Enemy to us, and an Enemy to the publick interests of a People, as well as to the interests of private men."

However, the preachers knew only too well that audiences, even of Puritans, can be bored by too much repetition. At the election of 1708 John Norton confessed that his *Essay Tending to Promote Reformation* could claim no more than a tendency: "I have said nothing, as to the Substance . . . that hath not been before said." The jeremiads of 1710 to 1720 are (except for some of Cotton Mather's) the dullest in the entire progression, and the most wooden seem to have been spoken in Connecticut, where, for instance, Samuel Whitman ponderously proved *Practical Godliness the Way to Prosperity:*

> If Religion do not Revive, the Land will become more Wicked: The Hand of God will ly heavy upon it still, and many of our Hearers will go to Hell. If Religion Revive, many of our Hearers will be Converted and go to Heaven; but if it do not Revive Multitudes of them will Perish for ever.

Around 1720, as a new generation came into the pulpits, and as the children of a provincial rather than of a theocratic New England took up the chant—especially those disciples of Cotton Mather who captured the Boston churches, Cooper, Joseph Sewall, Prince, Foxcroft, Webb, Gee—the clerical temper began to show signs of impatience. "The longer we stand it out, the greater will our Charge and Trouble be." By then there was clearly need for a rhetoric which would achieve what academic rhetoric had so far failed to achieve; there was wanted someone who could make language convey the terror which a jog-trot "We are all very Sensible of the Decay fallen on Religion" would not. In the 1720's, Cooper, Sewall, and Prince were striving manfully at the task.

During this period the provincial jeremiad developed two further assertions which were to play a part in the intellectual future. By its very nature, the jeremiad is under obligation to look simultaneously backward and forward—back to the purity from which the people have degenerated, ahead to the ultimate vengeance. The founders had displayed, as did Richard Mather, a disposition to treat their colleagues as Christian nonpareils; to rally the second generation by the standard of an absolute perfection incarnated in their fathers was natural for Increase Mather. But after 1689, idealization of the founders became an obsession, and from the first decade of this provincial regime we must date that species of ancestor worship which some believe is today the only surviving vestige of Puritan piety.

Joshua Scottow, not expecting much from Increase Mather's exertions in 1691, published *Old Men's Tears for their own Declensions*, and in 1694 *A Narrative of the Planting of the Massachusetts Colony*. These are charming elegies: "The Lord took delight in our Fathers, and they in him"; they were partakers of the Divine Nature, and served God "without Large Chambers, or Windows Cieled with Cedar, or painted with Vermillion." And what have we to show for our advances in interior decoration? "Now the Scene of Affairs is turned, we are made a Spoil to our Haters, to our Popish and Pagan Neighbours, a Derision, we are sold and scattered among the Heathen." Afflictions might be borne were we half the men our fathers were; but the explanation for our miseries is all too evident: "Whatever Piety your Fathers pretended in the *Pia Mater* of their Brains, to be sure it is Ardled into impious matter of Devilism, in their Childrens crack'd Crowns." Old Joshua is welcome relief from the more clerical accounts, if only for the liveliness with which he describes the provoking sins: "strange and fantastick Fashions and Attire, naked Backs, and bare Breasts and Foreheads, if not of the whorish Woman, yet so like unto it as would require a more than ordinary Spirit of Discerning to distinguish."

The Mathers avoided such anatomical references, but found the temptation irresistible, after Cooke began badgering Increase, to thrust home the declension thesis by comparing the present epigones with "that Greatness, and Goodness, which adorned our Ancestors." Ringing his peculiar changes on Stoughton's dictum, Cotton descanted upon the "Visible Shrink" from "the First Grain, that our God brought from Three Sifted Kingdoms." By 1700 Increase, being one of the few survivors of even the second generation, virtually put himself in the posture of an ancestor, regularly predicting his own death and calling upon younger people to emulate his resignation. By this time, a standard paragraph in every jeremiad reminded New Englanders that they were the posterity of magnificent ancestors, but that they were a disgrace to their derivation.

Well then, at the other end of the spectroscope, how far could they descend? By 1700 the jeremiad threatened to become a sterile form because it could contemplate nothing but an indefinite declension—which, in a sense, was effectively to discourage anybody's bestirring himself. A society accepts the fact that there is a great deal of ruin in it—unless the threat of cataclysm comes too near. Could this society continue interminably under the prediction of greater and greater judgments without confronting the greatest of all? Was not the only resolution for the ever-expanding jeremiad the actual end of the world itself? If these predictions were not to fall of their own weight, would not that end have to come within a calculable future?

Several preachers were carried by such logic into proclaiming it: when persons or provinces have contracted the guilt of so many provocations, said Peter Thacher in 1708, "they must justly fear their next shall be their last." But one of the clues to this difficult period is the fact that practically all spokesmen held back from naming too precisely the day of doom. There were two exceptions: Increase and Cotton Mather. They took the leap, and by 1710 were regretting that "this Doctrine is no more inculcated by the present Ministry."

Increase always insisted that the doctrine of the millennium was a teaching of "the first and famous Pastors in the New-English Churches." This is one of those half-truths of which he was so prolific that several of his contemporaries preferred to call him a liar outright. In Calvinist circles of 1630, speculation about the end of the world—particularly as to whether the second coming of Christ was to precede or follow the millennium—had become highly suspect. Protestants had discovered, as Augustine in his day had learned, that both opinions are easily translated into revolutionary action; the subtlety of Satan, as Increase put it, had cast the blemish of "the wild Phansies of Enthusiasts" upon all Chiliastic opinion. Increase had to separate himself from those "late French ecstaticks and Enthusiasts" who recently in London ran wild with their expectation of the final catastrophe (the same whom Charles Chauncy was to invoke against Edwards). Increase Mather knew all this, yet there was something in him and in his son that impelled them along the dangerous road. Increase's first book, in 1669, was an investigation into the conversion of the Jews, which in the traditional Chiliast mythology is to inaugurate the last days. The two Mathers were, in this respect at least, peculiar in New England; possessed by the true apocalyptic spirit, they marched into the Age of Reason loudly crying that the end of the world was at hand.

However, outside New England they were, as they knew, in good company. One of the more curious phenomena in Western thought is the assiduity with which, in the late seventeenth century, leaders of the new science devoted themselves to proving that modern physics not only confirmed but actually contrived a final conflagration. Three years before the Great Migration, George Hakewill, in a work known at Harvard, *An Apologie or Declaration of the Power and Providence of God in the Government of the World*, had tried to rally all good Aristotelians against the new science on the grounds that it was raising a horrible belief in the "perpetuitie and continuance" of the world. But even he was so much infected with the heresy that he made haste to extricate himself (as did Wigglesworth in New England's first best-seller, *The Day of Doom*) by falling back upon a faith in sheer arbitrary intervention—the light and the blast that shall break forth upon an unpredictable midnight. But in 1681 Thomas Burnet came to the rescue with an impressive demonstration that destruction of the globe could be put upon a scientific basis; *The Sacred Theory of the Earth* provided a physical explanation, fires at the center of the globe, for both the Deluge and the Judgment. In the 1690's John Ray accounted for both dread occurrences on a still more persuasive hypothesis, a shift in the center of gravity; in 1696, William Whiston, Lucasian Professor of Mathematics at Cambridge, in *A New Theory of the Earth*, conclusively raised the flood and consumed the earth through the agency of a comet. The greatest intellect of the age, Sir Isaac Newton, allowed that either Ray or Whiston might be right.

All these works were perused in America. Increase respected Burnet's great learning, and felt that Ray "Answers Dr. Hakewills objections"; at the Harvard Commencement of 1717 President Leverett made a Latin speech "taking the Whistonian Notion about the Flood." If there was the least suspicion that these investigations were unbecoming the dignity of scholars, there was always the example of "the Incomparable Sir Isaac Newton," who, after writing the *Principia*, devoted the second half of his life to studying the fulfillment of Biblical prophecies, and so came to a firm conclusion, "the last age is now approaching." Yet there was always a danger in these conjectures of that distemper which Cotton Mather named "Hypothesimania"—that is, that they might altogether exclude God from the action. The Mathers were probably not familiar with William King's "The Battle Royal," but they would have agreed with him (and with wits like Jonathan Swift) that both Burnet's and Whiston's physics implied

> *That all the books of Moses*
> *Were nothing but supposes;*
> *That he deserv'd rebuke, Sir*
> *Who wrote the Pentateuch, Sir,*
> * 'Twas nothing but a sham.*

It might be but a short step to declaring openly,

> *That as for Father Adam*
> *And Mrs. Eve, his Madame*
> *And what the devil spoke, Sir*
> *'Twas nothing but a joke, Sir*
> *And well-invented flam.*

Cotton's way of putting it was to cite the musician who defined the soul as a harmony, which hypothesis "had a Tincture of his own Profession in it"; likewise were the theories of physicists tainted. Therefore it was deemed necessary in New England to insist that whatever "second causes" were to be involved, there was still sufficient power to bring about the event in what Blackmore called "Heav'ns Mighty Voice."

We utterly misunderstand the age if we suppose that for the Mathers this meant a surrender of the scientific intellect. On the contrary, theirs was a concerted effort, as Increase said in one of his finest sentences, to keep up the conviction that the Deluge and the end "are things intelligible." Wherever in history the conception of the termination is taken seriously, there is always the insistence that events are purposeful. Whenever it is also attached to the doctrine of the millennium, it becomes, by defining the corporate goal, a judgment upon society. A purpose and a judgment were what New England desperately required; Increase found them in what his son aptly termed "Sober Chiliasm." This was not, let us be clear, a form of fideism; it meant:

> Look as God hath stretched the Firmament over this natural World, and hath placed the Stars there to be for Signs as to Natural Events in the ordinary course of Providence; so hath he stretched out the Expansum of his Word over the Rational World, and therein set his Statutes and his Judgements, from whence the wise-hearted may conjecture what is like to come to pass.

Life in this America, so the Mathers perceived, could not be carried on without at least some reasonable assurance of what was likely to happen.

The opinion to which the Mathers subscribed is generally known as "pre-millennialism"; that is, Christ will physically appear, the earth will be refined but not consumed by fire, and for a thousand years paradise will reign. Satan with all his power and party (i.e., Rome) will be "Chased off the Face of the Earth," and the remaining society will be everything to which the jeremiads summoned New England. As a young man at Harvard, Increase, like the other Puritans, had not been a Chiliast, but he came to it (significantly enough after the Restoration of Charles II) by what Cotton described as "the Delectable Study of the Prophecies." He was further confirmed by discovering the doctrine of the millennium to be that for which Satan has a peculiar spite, and "that but few Papists have been Chiliasts." But the great effort which both of them invested in this conception is not to be ascribed to their scholarship or even to their peculiar temperaments: it arose out of their experience, and may be called the supreme symbol of their patriotism. The only check upon approaching disaster was reformation, which did not come; even had it come, it would have been at best a temporary halt on the road to destruction. Therefore the ultimate goal of the jeremiad, pushed to the limit, would have to be the Judgment, when the complete and enduring reformation would be wrought—and this would require divine aid. Then, only then, would the jeremiads secure their objective: then devils like Louis XIV and Elisha Cooke would be bound, and "there shall be only Good men Entrusted with the Government of their Neighbour-hood."

If, on the one hand, the doctrine supplied the Mathers' jeremiads with the threat above all threats—"They shall be Sentenced to be burnt to Death, and that with an Everlasting Fire, ten thousand times hotter than Nebuchadnezzars Furnace"—on the other hand, Cotton said that his father (and by implication himself), through much meditation upon it, "sailed so near to the Land of Promise, that he found the Balsamic Breezes of the Heavenly Country upon his mind, which, where they come, usually Refine and Sweeten, and Marvellously Purify the Souls that are Favoured with them." In these moments, the discomforts and imperfections of America dropped away—"But, How Long, O Lord, Holy and True; How Long, How Long!"

Out of that cry was born the impulse—for the Mathers as for Newton—to prove by all close computation that there "are more than Twelve Hundred and Sixty Reasons to make One think, that the Century is begun which must see this amazing Revolution." (Can one indeed begin to comprehend the eighteenth century, with its ultimate revolutions, unless he recognizes the apocalyptic spirit in which it was conceived?) From 1693 on, the Mathers hourly expected the day; like Newton, they were convinced that most of the prophecies had been fulfilled, that the new century was bound to be "the most wonderful Age that ever was since the World began." By 1710, in the finest of his Chiliastic hymns, *A Discourse Concerning Faith and Fervency in Prayer*, a long-drawn-out dramatization of his death, Increase cried, "I Dye in the Faith of the Speedy accomplishment of those glorious Things." A year before his own death, Cotton Mather said that the coming of Christ is not "a Metaphor"—it is "the Next Thing that is to be look'd for."

The Mathers made this doctrine so prevalent, at least in Boston, that in 1708 Mr. Pemberton's maid, seeing the light of a burning warehouse reflected on a black cloud, "came crying to him under Consternation; supposing the last Conflagration had begun." For ordinary homiletic purposes, it led logically to the exhortation that New England should "Antedate" the millennium as far "as may be Consistent with our present Circumstances." But the final purpose of the entire doctrine was to give meaning, cosmic meaning, to precisely those distressing circumstances. While preaching the millennium, as at no other time, Increase would look down upon the banterers and scoffers who jeered at New England as the self-styled New Jerusalem: let us strive after a conformity to it, and "let the Ishmaelites of the world Mock on." For as Cotton said, according to sober Chiliasm, "AMERICA is Legible in these Promises."

This pattern of the jeremiad, reworked to fit the circumstances of a province, informs at every point the most imposing of them all, *Magnalia Christi Americana*. It is the fullest assertion of colonial loyalty, accepting completely the fact of toleration; it stands firm upon English liberties and fights unremittingly against the enemies of Increase's charter; it defends the virtuousness of New England and condemns New England's depravity; a massive appeal to the government (especially the Council) to implement the public reformation, it nevertheless places the responsibility squarely upon the people; the most unflinching chronicle of New England's woes and sins, it is a monumental piece of ancestor veneration, full to the brim of "Hero's worthy to have their Lives written"; and it is, finally, fraught throughout with a sense of the impending destruction of the world—wherefore these things must be so quickly recorded. It is a summation and synthesis of the New England apocalypse; it took three years to write, but all the country's experience to produce. The author lived in an agony of anticipation while his Gargantuan manuscript, too large for any American press, was shipped to England; he committed it to the Lord, and received back special assurances that the Lord would accept it, "and preserve it, and publish it, and that it shall not be lost." ("But, if it should miscarry after all, O my God, My God, what Confusion would ensue upon me!") The Lord disappointed his "particular faith" that his wife would live, but even while she was sinking, He delivered into the hands of Cotton Mather the first copy (with all its misprints), who thereupon set apart a day of thanksgiving for "the Harvest of so many Prayers, and Cares, and Tears, and Resignations." To the end of his life he felt it no violation of modesty to quote the opinion of the great Alsop that the work would not admit of abridgment, for "No man that has a Relish for Piety or Variety can ever be weary of Reading it."

Although, as Increase bemoaned, most of the clergy would not venture with him into Chiliastic regions, Judge Samuel Sewall was also a profound, if amateur, student of prophecies; he too had suffered when Andros humiliated New England, and had grieved over the sins of the land. In 1697 he felt that upon certain difficult passages in Revelation he had acquired light, and so published a few lines "toward a description of the New Heaven." The jeremiad, with its arraignment of defects and blemishes, hardly seems a suitable vehicle for celebrating a sensuous love of the land; yet when resonant enough, linked to the cadences of the millennium, denunciation revealed its real tonality. The most renowned of New England poets, Anne Bradstreet, being an immigrant, wrote only of English streams and English birds; but while meditating as one who stood entirely "upon the New Earth" about the part New England should play in the new heaven, Sewall bethought himself of Mary Brown, the first-born of Newbury, who still lived as the mother of many children on Plum Island, where he as a boy had played; he yielded—as no Puritan could have contrived to do without subsuming his love under a millennial destination—to that delight in the American prospect which for over half a century had been perversely nourished under the canopy of the jeremiads:

As long as Plum Island shall faithfully keep the commanded Post; Notwithstanding all the hectoring Words, and hard Blows of the proud and boistrous Ocean; As long as any Salmon, or Sturgeon shall swim in the streams of Merrimack; or any Perch, or Pickeril, in Crane-Pond; As long as the Sea-Fowl shall know the Time of their coming, and not neglect seasonably to visit the Places of their Acquaintance: As long as any Cattel shall be fed with the Grass growing in the Medows, which do humbly bow down themselves before Turkie-Hill; As long as any Sheep shall walk upon Old Town Hills, and shall from thence pleasantly look down upon the River Parker, and the fruitfull Marishes lying beneath; As long as any free and harmless Doves shall find a White Oak, or other Tree within the Township, to perch, or feed, or build a careless Nest upon; and shall voluntarily present themselves to perform the office of Gleaners after Barèly-Harvest; As long as Nature shall not grow Old and dote; but shall constantly remember to give the rows of Indian Corn their education, by Pairs: So long shall Christians be born there; and being first made meet, shall from thence be Translated, to be made partakers of the Inheritance of the Saints in Light.

If our patience be large enough—it requires much!—we may come, through this astonishing paean of Sewall's, to a divination of the hidden import of the sermons. It is a revelation of what, in America, happened to the covenant theology. In the guise of a millennial faith, it became possible—at least this once—to embrace Turkie-Hill, the barley-harvest and the twin rows of Indian corn. Even as Sewall was singing these words to himself, and scrupulously scoring their melody with his punctuation, Cotton Mather was bundling up the bale of manuscript that constituted the *Magnalia* and entrusting it to the Atlantic Ocean. This, the most sustained of jeremiads, resounds from beginning to end with "the Wonders of the CHRISTIAN RELIGION, flying from the Depravations of Europe, to the American Strand."

CHAPTER XIII

THE JUDGMENT OF THE WITCHES

THE
most curious of all the facts in that welter we call
Salem witchcraft is this: if you expunge from the record those documents
that arise directly out of the affair, and those which treat it historically,
like the *Magnalia* or Hale's and Calef's accounts, and a few twinges of
memory such as appear in Sewall's *Diary*, the intellectual history of New
England up to 1720 can be written as though no such thing ever happened. It had no effect on the ecclesiastical or political situation, it does
not figure in the institutional or ideological development. Aside from a few
oblique lamentations in election sermons (briefly noted amid the catalogue
of woes), for twenty-eight years this cataclysm hardly appears in the record—until summoned from the deep by opponents of inoculation as a stick
to beat the clergy for yet another "delusion." Only in 1721 does it begin
to be that blot on New England's fame which has been enlarged, as much
by friends as by foes, into its greatest disgrace.

To this statement, there is one qualification: after 1692, not only is
the episode seldom referred to, but the very word witchcraft almost van-
ishes from public discourse. While the clergy were steadily expanding the
list of possible afflictions which would surely befall the community, the
place reserved by Cotton Mather's *Memorable Providences* for the threat
of demonic intervention is suddenly vacated. This silence speaks volumes:
although new and fascinating abuses are relentlessly explored, no one any
longer tries to induce a confession of sinfulness by predicting a spate of
witches.

I do not need to demonstrate that belief in witchcraft was, for the
seventeenth century, not only plausible but scientifically rational. No more
tedious pages exist than those devoted to the thankless task of exonerating
the Puritans, on this score, from the charge of superstition. Despite such
efforts, thousands of Americans are still persuaded that Cotton Mather
"burned" witches in Salem; further refutation becomes a bore. Still, it
is difficult to see clearly and objectively just what was involved; language
itself proves treacherous, and analysis rebounds upon the analyst. Critics
of the Puritan priesthood—often children of that caste—have wrenched
the story from its context; sober historians, trying to restore the true setting, slide into the accents of apology and gloss over a crime. One may
appreciate that witchcraft was as real an offense in 1692 as murder or trea-

son and yet remain profoundly convinced that what went wrong at Salem is something for which Puritanism and New England are justly to be indicted, not in terms of a more "enlightened" age, but specifically in their own terms—in those of the covenant.

I dislike dissociating myself from previous scholarship, but many students, including some who strive to place these occurrences within the intellectual frame of the period, fail to consider them in relation to the whole scheme of thought. They have read the contemporaneous literature of witchcraft, but not the weekly sermons. We shall avoid confusing ourselves by an irrelevant intrusion of modern criteria only when we realize that what struck Salem Village was intelligible to everybody concerned—instigators, victims, judges, and clergy—within the logic of the covenant. That in the end the irruption nearly wrecked this intellectual structure—that it left the scaffolding dangerously shaken and out of kilter—is its deepest meaning in the actual language of the community.

Let us remember, without concerning ourselves about the psychosis of the hysterical girls who precipitated the panic by their reckless accusations of an array of tormentors, that an appearance of witchcraft among the afflictions of New England was from the beginning as much to be anticipated as Indian raids; by 1692 several instances had been encountered, and a more organized assault was altogether predictable. Some in Salem Village may have read *Memorable Providences*, but they needed no book to set them off. Accusations and interrogations were already in·train when the former minister, Deodat Lawson, came back to the town from Scituate to deliver a Thursday lecture, on March 24; he knew something of what was going on, and had even heard that victims complained of being tormented by specters of his wife and daughter, both three years dead. Charles Upham, writing from the point of view of 1867, felt that Lawson must have prepared his sermon in advance and have come to the village deliberately intending to blow up the flames. But Upham had not studied the jeremiads. Lawson did not require preparation: the formula, with its neatly boxed heads of argument and application, with its rhetorical tags already minted, was as ready to be wheeled into action as a loaded fieldpiece. Of course his sermon did nothing to allay the panic, but what Lawson applied to the situation was not malicious incendiarism; it was traditional federal wisdom. What other wisdom was there?

He made the standard points: afflictions come upon a people from God (or by His permission) because of their sins; the only relief is prayer and repentance, to be manifested by confession of the provoking deeds; meanwhile, the duty of civil magistrates, in the interest of public welfare, is vigorously to suppress disorders and to punish criminals, above all those who refuse to repent and confess. He used customary artifices of style to "improve" the present distress, exactly as every preacher enhanced military disasters or epidemics. In the light of accumulated experience, his discourse was no more "irrational" than the speech of Edward Everett at

Gettysburg. So recognizable an exercise of the type was Lawson's *Christ's Fidelity the only Shield against Satan's Malignity* that upon its publication in Boston, masters of the form—the Mathers, Willard, James Allen, Baily, Charles Morton—happily endorsed it. That it reënforced the resolve of the magistrates to ferret out evildoers cannot be questioned: since 1689 clerical leaders, worried lest the royal charter should prevent magistrates from coöperating, had redoubled the effort to exhort them; Lawson followed precedent, and besought Hathorne not to bear a sword in vain.

But, as we know, the list of sins and their afflictions was long and daily becoming longer; no single offense stood by itself, for all were interconnected. The pattern of depravity was so subtle that an exclusive concentration upon one vice easily became encouragement of another. Lawson knew that already the specter of his dead (and sainted) wife was being accused; this was a highly suspect piece of witchcraft which might the more readily be explained on the grounds of a disordered "phansie"—as Increase Mather in the *Essay* had accounted for previous apparitions in New England. For decades the ministers had been denouncing—without effect—an increase of backbiting, talebearing, and rash censuring; Lawson recognized that a vigorous prosecution of real witches might offer the temptation, to a people exacerbated by a series of peculiarly acrimonious village quarrels, to imagine that the specters of any or all their neighbors were let loose. So, even thus early, he delivered the momentous caution: the Devil may represent good and decent citizens as afflictors of others; therefore, to accuse any without sufficient grounds will have a pernicious influence, will bring in confusion and an abundance of evil.

This much we may say the jeremiad (as developed up to 1692) could do: on the one hand exhort to action and on the other caution against headlong zeal. But what Lawson saw with his own eyes, the day before he spoke, was as real as any Indian rush upon a frontier town; the situation did not require subtle discriminations concerning the role of specters. Gestures of the accused produced physical and visible effects upon the afflicted, "so that they are their own Image." This was as welcome to the investigating authorities as first-hand evidence would be to a modern prosecuting attorney eager not to have to rely on circumstantial testimonies.

Through the next weeks and months doubt spread, more slowly than we might wish, but at about the pace we ought to expect. The Court of Oyer and Terminer, with Stoughton presiding, and with Sewall, Richards, Gedney, Wait Winthrop, Sargent, Corwin on the bench, was trusting far too much to "spectral evidence." It was not insisting upon the solid common-law principle that an act must be seen by two witnesses. The doctrine of the specter was as old as the science of witchcraft itself: as Cotton Mather summarized it, once a witch signs the book and covenants with hell (the special heinousness of this crime was the fact that it, like regeneration, took the form of a covenant), Satan delegates to him a devil who, taking on the likeness of the witch, executes his behests, such chores as pinching his enemies, blinding them, burning their houses or wrecking their ships. True, the specter, like the sorcerer's apprentice, might gain mastery over the master and compel him to molest those with whom he had no quarrel; but still, the specter belongs to the culprit and, if seen, is a fair presumption against him, just as a dog may lead the police to its owner.

Nonetheless, experience had shown that spectral evidence must be handled with care. New England intellectuals probably had not heard, "The spirit that I have seen may be the Devil"; but in more authoritative works they had learned that he might assume a pleasing shape and abuse the credulous in order to damn them. Wherefore not every specter was to be taken for the person he resembled. But the court at Salem—mainly because of Stoughton's conviction—committed itself to the proposition that no innocent person could, under the providence of God, be represented by a specter, and that therefore those who were manifested were guilty. That the accused should deny their confederacy was only to be expected: having become the Devil's children, they could confess only with his permission. Upon these (as Cotton Mather called them) "philosophical schemes of witchcraft," they proceeded, as juries have been known to act upon a settled pre-conviction that no white woman can possibly offer sexual provocation to a Negro.

There is no evidence that any minister ever taught this doctrine, or that more than three accepted it; both Mathers, the principal theorists in the country, had explicitly warned against it. As early as May 31, Cotton was begging John Richards not to lay too great stress on this sort of testimony, because—here was the issue—"It is very certain that the divells have sometimes represented the shapes of persons not only innocent, but also very virtuous." Indeed, the riddle of Cotton Mather's part in the business is bound up with his prophecy that if once unrestricted credit were yielded to diabolical representations, "The Door is opened!" Had the court heeded his recommendation, there would have been no executions; if, having made it, he had thereafter kept his mouth shut, he would be a hero today.

By June 15, doubt was spreading rapidly, and a puzzled Phips, trying his level best to be a pious magistrate, asked advice from the local association of ministers. In the *Magnalia* Cotton says, with that unction which infects even his most worthy actions, that the answer "was drawn up at their desire by Mr. Mather the younger, as I have been informed." *The Return of Several Ministers*, by whomever written, is a significant document in the history of New England because, first, it acknowledges that the ministers were in a quandary of their own making, and, second, it shows that even in a regime where they had contrived to seat their own governor and a Council of their own choosing, and where the court at Salem was made up of professing brethren, they really no longer had any power. The court was proceeding on a principle of its own; the clergy might counsel otherwise, but were prisoners of their own reiterations; they were obliged by their previous utterances to conclude with the familiar exhortation that civil authority should press forward to a vigorous prose-cution of the obnoxious—which Stoughton was heartily doing without their encouragement. At that moment, nobody quite heard the crash, but a central pillar of the jeremiad, shored up after 1689, tumbled to earth. This was the last time that a ruler of Massachusetts, in an hour of hesi-tation, formally and officially asked advice of the churches.

In the eyes of posterity, *The Return* is vitiated by its concluding para-graph. This must be read as a formality which the ministers were obliged to observe. The really important paragraph is the sixth, which asserts positively that a demon can appear in the shape of an innocent person, and that therefore a mere charge of representation does not constitute adequate grounds for conviction. On August 17, Cotton Mather was again insist-ing, this time to John Foster, that spectral evidence is fallacious; during the summer he so far admitted his awareness of the court's incompetence as to propose the remedy he had proved efficacious in the case of Martha Good-win: he offered to take six or more of the afflicted into his house and cure them by prayer, without any trials or executions. Finally, on October 3 Increase Mather—and he alone—brought the murders to an end by issuing *Cases of Conscience*, which so unequivocally condemned spectral evidence that Phips at last saw his duty clear and terminated the court—although by that time twenty persons had been executed and a raging Stoughton, as his final gesture, signed a warrant (which Phips annulled) for eight more.

We may imagine—though there is no way of telling—that had *The Return* spoken as emphatically on June 15 as *Cases of Conscience* did on October 3, the frenzy would have been arrested. Lacking such guidance, between these dates the madness had to work itself out: a reckless use of spectral evidence gave rein to the seething passions and festering animosi-ties of New England. Prisons became crowded, every man's life lay at the mercy of any accuser, brother looked sidewise at brother, and the friend of many years' standing became a bad security risk: said Gedney from the bench to John Alden, "that truly he had been acquainted with him these many years; and had always accounted him a good man; but indeed now he should be obliged to change his opinion." If the ministers are to be blamed—as they must—for not aggressively combating Stoughton's in-sensate dogmatism, still only three let themselves become open supporters: Samuel Parris (who appears utterly contemptible), Nicholas Noyes of Salem (who lived to repent), and John Hale of Beverly, who abruptly altered his mind when his wife was accused. Otherwise a fair number of them ventured at least as far as offering testimonials to the good character of several of the accused—an act which required courage. We become convinced that behind these attestations lies more than readily meets the eye when we find a petition from Chebacco parish on behalf of John Proctor headed with the name of John Wise. The mania had, to almost everybody's perception except Stoughton's, run its course when at last

Samuel Willard of the Old South was cried upon. Out of the dungeon of the condemned, John Proctor sent an appeal to Increase Mather, Willard, Allen, Baily (endorsers of Lawson's sermon), which told them of the "Popish cruelties" the court was employing in order to extract confessions; the ministers were the last hope. And Thomas Brattle is convincing proof that, aside from the misguided three, throughout the country the elders were dissatisfied, and that, above all, Increase Mather and Samuel Willard were aghast.

Thomas Brattle's *Letter*, purportedly addressed to someone in England, is dated October 8, five days after Increase's *Cases*; that it was ever sent is doubtful, and the presumption is that, like Cotton's *Political Fables*, it circulated through the proper quarters in manuscript. Phips put an end to the court because Increase gave him the signal; Brattle's *Letter* was not a factor in that decision, but it represents a response to the deteriorating situation which, independent of the ministers, was in step with them—although chronologically no earlier. Brattle was a merchant, a mathematician, and an amateur astronomer whose contributions won him the gratitude of Sir Isaac Newton. The *Letter* is a milestone in American literature if only for its free-and-easy, its highly literate and satirical tone; in New England it is the first treatment of disaster that steps outside the scheme of the jeremiad. Considered merely stylistically, it may be interpreted as a more open expression than any provincial had yet undertaken of the mentality that had slowly been taking shape in "moderate" circles. Certainly its style was the more accessible to Brattle because, after 1689, through contact with the capital New England had become aware of the revolutions wrought in prose discourse since the days of Cromwell. He did not trouble to wrestle with the problem of how a covenanted nation could make so manifest a gaff as that at Salem. Striking a new note in American polemics, he plunged directly into ridicule of the court, calling its doctrine not a "new philosophy" but "Salem superstition and sorcery." If rhetorical tricks would serve, he would goad his countrymen into the Enlightenment with the sneer that such nonsense was "not fitt to be named in a land of such light as New-England is."

Hence it is all the more instructive to discover Brattle's reason for delaying until October his blast against Stoughton's court: he was reluctant to besmear authority. He did not want to appear as one notoriously given to a "factious spirit." In 1692, this meant only Elisha Cooke's anti-charter party (one has to remember that the witchcraft issue did not, at least at this time, become entangled in the acrimonious political division, and that Cooke's "patriots" did not use it against the Mathers—which shows that they were no clearer in their own minds, and that at this moment no such charge against the clergy would have stuck). But now, as bitter experience made clear that the court, through its fanatical adherence to an idiotic principle of jurisprudence, had shed "the innocentest blood imaginable," Brattle excoriated the "Salem Gentlemen" because, having submitted to the Devil's stratagem, they imperiled that "liberty" which "was evermore accounted the great priviledge of an Englishman." At no point suggesting the slightest disagreement with Increase Mather—rather making clear his full accord—Brattle concluded his *Letter* with one of the great sentences of the time, which, eschewing the jargon of the covenant, reveals how much the theme of the jeremiads had become, if only through the discipline of disillusion, a secular patriotism: "I am afraid that ages will not wear off that reproach and those stains which these things will leave behind them upon our land."

Perhaps I make too much of Brattle's omission of any covenantal consideration. Nevertheless, brief as his *Letter* is, not only does it fail to summon up that conception, not only does it take the land to be simply "our land" instead of one plighted to God, but it assumes two radical positions: it declares that the (by then) glib confessions of guilt are not to be trusted; and it flatly asserts that the court has perpetrated a disastrous mistake.

One fact the record does indeed make clear: in this situation that very course of action so resoundingly trumpeted in the jeremiads as the only remedy for social ills—confession and repentance—became a dodge. It did not heal the grievance, but compounded the evil. For decades the logic of the covenant had been clear, whether applied to individuals or to nations: one enters into the bond, he sins, and is afflicted, according to explicit terms; he confesses his sin, the affliction is removed, he is restored to the covenant (as a church member under censure is fully restored to the church after public confession). But on August 20, Margaret Jacobs, who had acknowledged the crime and whose accusations hanged her grandfather, recanted her admission, "Having, through the magistrates' threatenings, and my own vile and wretched heart, confessed several things contrary to my conscience and knowledge." At Andover, whither the accusations spread, the whole mechanism became a shambles as six women promptly confessed, only to explain that they had not known what else to say. By the time Brattle and Mather wrote, the jails were full of confessors; several fled, but others confessed wholesale—and were safe. The hunt could have become such a horror as to outrun the worst imaginings of the time had not the very weight of the confessions broken down every effort to secure them; their value depreciated spectacularly (as did the bills of credit) as they became patently devices for eluding what Brattle called the "rude and barbarous methods" of the court. But in this case, what was left, in the midst of such merely politic humiliations, of that sincere repentance called for in the enduring covenant of Abraham?

According to federal theory, an afflicted but unrepenting people invite further affliction. In the opinion of many unprejudiced spectators, said Brattle, the condemned "went out of the world not only with as great protestations, but also with as good shows of innocency, as men could do." By strictly and conscientiously applying the doctrine of the jeremiad, the court created a situation in which meretricious confession went free and

sincere denial automatically became guilt. There is no more poignant testimony to the hold of the conception upon the minds of ordinary New Englanders than the fact that those who died because of it remained to the
end faithful to it. Records of the court were not published, and so few
actually heard the words of Mary Easty, but such "considerate" observers
as Brattle were bound to sense the logical impasse to which she had come:

> I petition to Your Honors not for my own life, for I know I must die, and my
> appointed time is set; but the Lord he knows it is that, if it be possible, no more
> innocent blood may be shed, which undoubtedly cannot be avoided in the way
> and course you go in. I question not but Your Honors do to the utmost of your
> powers in the discovery and detecting of witchcraft and witches, and would not be
> guilty of innocent blood for the world. But, by my own innocency, I know you
> are in the wrong way.

Her dilemma was precisely her inability to do what, had she been guilty,
she would gladly have done; and she could not, like so many others, pros-
titute the federal theology by cynically confessing. "They say myself and
others have made a league with the Devil, we cannot confess." Hordes
of reformed witches, instead of testifying to the mercy of the covenant,
were becoming an embarrassment, while Mary Easty simply said, "I cannot, I dare not, belie my own soul." Good citizens, caught in the mesh of
accusation, had no way to escape except by a deed more evil than any bargain with the Black Man, while repentant witches could smear whomever
they pleased with impunity. In a remarkably short time (all things considered) it was borne upon even John Hale that had all twenty of the
executed ("some of them were knowing persons") been guilty, a few of
them would surely have saved their lives by doing the expected. Whereas
for the mass who did confess—"we had no experience whether they would
stand to their Self-condemning confessions, when they came to dye." For
Mary Easty, having worked herself through the labyrinth with no other
guide than her native wit, said to the court, "I would humbly beg of you,
that Your Honors would be pleased . . . to try some of these confessing
witches"—which the court never dared do. Indeed, had it come to that
extremity, there was reason to suspect that many of them, instead of standing to their profession of evil, would have recanted to virtue!

Cases of Conscience is as important a document in the history of the
American mind as Brattle's *Letter*, not so much because it was effective
as because it sprang from the same recognitions. Fourteen ministers signed
the preface, making it even more a manifesto of solidarity than Lawson's
sermon; they showed their comprehension of the issue by declaring that
unless there was convincing proof for any crime, whether witchcraft or
murder, God does not then intend that the culprit be discovered. Whereupon Increase denounced spectral evidence, and skillfully turned the possibility that a good man should be so represented into a trial of faith. Those
who supposed that the malice of Satan is so constrained that he is incapable

of this feat were now accused of being the Sadducees! Confession itself, at least in these realms, was no longer a safe rule; the only reliable ground was such as would obtain "in any other Crime of a Capital nature"—the credible testimony under oath of two actual witnesses.

But—and it is a large but—Increase added a postscript: he did not intend any reflection on members of the court! "They are wise and good Men, and have acted with all Fidelity according to their Light, and have out of tenderness declined the doing of some things, which in our Judgments they were satisfied about." He himself had attended the trial of Burroughs, and could declare it fair. The judges must be believed when they say that none was convicted "meerly on the account of what Spectres have said." Without the postscript, *Cases of Conscience* would be a bold stroke; with it, the book is a miserable species of double-talk.

We grasp its import only to the extent that we appreciate the habit of speech that grew up in New England as an inevitable concomitant of the jeremiads: references had to be phrased in more and more generalized terms, names never explicitly named, so that we are obliged to decipher out of oblique insinuations what to contemporaries were broad designations. When ministers denounced "oppression" and "luxury," they meant certain people whom they did not have to specify. The controversy between moderates and the charter party must be deduced from what seem like platitudes in election sermons, where minor shifts of emphasis betrayed party maneuvers. This habit of ambiguity, developed out of New England's insecurity, out of its inability to face frankly its own internal divisions, out of its effort to maintain a semblance of unity even while unanimity was crumbling—which became more elaborate and disingenuous as internecine passions waxed—was to cling to the New England mind for centuries. We look ahead to the decades in which an emerging Unitarianism swathed itself in terms of studied vagueness; even after the split, the habit clung especially to the Unitarian pulpit, many of whose brightest lights were proud that their sermons never indicated any awareness of controversy. In Boston society today, matters may be fully discussed which, to an outsider, seem never to be mentioned at all. Such tribal reticence only an occasional Thoreau was to defy or an Emily Dickinson to turn into secret triumph.

Hence, for contemporaneous ears, *Cases of Conscience* was actually a blast against the court. Early the next year, Increase was circulating a letter from an English correspondent expressing surprise that so learned a man as Stoughton "should take up a persuasion, that the devil cannot assume the likeness of an innocent, to afflict another person." Increase Mather would stand in American history with a Zenger or a Lovejoy had he said what was in his mind, had he publicly repudiated the court. But neither he nor any of the clergy could do so—the friendship of the judges and all they stood for was too valuable. A modern political party will write into its platform a plank which in effect disowns the conduct of Congressional leaders—and then support the reëlection of exactly those discredited members. The virtuous act would be to split the party, but Increase shrank from that nobility. He wrote a treatise which by every implication—and in historical fact—proscribed the court, but which still preserved a show of unity among leading citizens by praising what it censured. He may honestly have persuaded himself (as at the trial of Burroughs) that the court was not sentencing "meerly" on spectral evidence, but he could not have written the *Cases* had he not known otherwise. It is a carefully designed book—courageous but also dishonest. Once his arguments were accepted, the court became (as Increase knew it would) infamous; group loyalty—or, if you will, class loyalty—kept him from saying so outright, and still more distressingly, kept him trying to avoid saying so for the rest of his life. Still, there is honesty in his book, enough to make it a matter of record that the supervisors of the covenant—the ruling class of Massachusetts—had been stampeded into a barbarism as gross, fundamentally, as anything they charged against Louis XIV. And as he defined it, the error consisted not in any charge which later generations would levy, but solely in violation of the standards professed by the Puritan jeremiad.

Increase had long since become a tactician: he had learned much in London that he had not known when preaching on the woes of Philip's War. He was capable of writing his postscript to the *Cases* even while acknowledging to his journal that innocent blood had been shed. His son Cotton never left the vicinity of Boston, never served apprentice in a wider, a less scrupulous world. Upon him fell the weight of contradiction, and we must say to the credit of provincial morality that he was the one to suffer. Pressed into service by those already apprehensive that things had gone wrong, he was commissioned to absolve them; to his undying infamy, he accepted the assignment. He knew of only one device through which the deed might be justified—the theology of the national covenant. If the Salem Gentlemen (which meant all gentlemen) were to preserve their self-respect—or their solidarity—they must have not so much a defense as a demonstration; whatever had happened had still, by some stretch of ingenuity, to be translated into a proof that New England was the chosen people. He undertook the task when he knew better, and composed that apologia for insincerity which, entitled *The Wonders of the Invisible World*, has ever since scarred his reputation, even among those who have no notion wherein its actual dishonesty consists.

He had put himself into the position from which he could not retreat by becoming the peerless penman of the colony. In the middle of September, poor Phips was under fire from the home government; he needed help. He asked—Cotton says "commanded"—that Mather prepare a plausible record of some, if not all, of the trials. On September 20, Cotton, who seems not to have known exactly what his father was pondering, wrote an abject letter to Stephen Sewall, brother of Samuel, clerk of the court in Salem, beseeching a transcript of the record; even then he betrayed the paralyzing doubt that hung over the composition of his most deplorable utterance. "You should imagine me as obstinate a Sadduce and Witch-advocate as any among us," he begged of Sewall: "Address mee as one that Believ'd Nothing Reasonable." Propagandists put to an impossible task commence with the prayer that they may first of all manage to propagandize themselves.

On September 22, the final day of the court, after the last executions, Samuel and Stephen Sewall, with Stoughton and Hathorne (who had conducted the high-handed preliminary interrogations), rode down to Boston; they met with Cotton Mather and sealed his fate. Stephen promised to go back to Salem and get the records; Stoughton and Sewall promised to stand by him; Cotton went to his study and, in fear and trembling, began to write. Leaving a blank page for the endorsement Stoughton was to supply him, this tortured soul blurted out his first sentence: "I live by Neighbours that force me to produce these undeserved Lines." If ever there was a false book produced by a man whose heart was not in it, it is *The Wonders*.

Once started, this man whose pen raced across blank paper at breakneck speed could not stop. His mind was bubbling with every sentence of the jeremiads, for he was heart and soul in the effort to reorganize them. And for days Stephen Sewall did not send the records. Cotton might have waited; a man secure of himself would have waited; he was insecure, frightened, sick at heart (at the end of his manuscript he was again to betray himself: he had done "the Service imposed upon me"). He wrote an introduction, hoping that it would anticipate the records; like a criminal who protests his innocence, the more he scribbled, the more he disclosed. Still no word from Salem: he put in an extract from Perkins; he redacted a sermon (in the vein of Lawson's) he had delivered on August 4; he devised a further jeremiad-like address to the country—and still nothing from Salem. He ransacked his library for stories of apparitions, hoping that they might substantiate what he was about to receive. The book was already swelling much too big—he had to admit—and he had just transcribed the report of a trial before Sir Matthew Hale, when, to his immense relief, Stephen's packet arrived. He worked out a version of five of the twenty trials, wrote a few wearied and confused observations, and rushed the monstrous collection to a printer. The book was on the streets about October 15. (Meanwhile, Increase had read *Cases of Conscience* to the associated ministers on October 3; though it was not published for another month, Phips and the General Court had acted upon it; and Stoughton, who raged against Phips and was never to retract his conviction that a specter is proof of witchcraft, had written his foreword of full approbation for Cotton Mather's zeal and vigor—which he would never have done had the book managed to convey, except by its utter confusion, what Cotton Mather had really believed about spectral evidence.)

Cotton evidently finished his redaction of Stephen Sewall's notes on October 11, for on that day Stoughton and Samuel Sewall attested that it was a true report of matters of fact and evidence. Why did the poor devil not leave well enough alone, publish the reports, and throw into the fire everything he had poured out during the days of waiting? He suffered from a monstrous lust for publication, that much is certain; but the fuller explanation, accounting for the discharge of both his conscious and unconscious motivations, is the compelling force of the jeremiad. He had to find a rationale for his country's ordeal and at the same time a modicum of peace with himself; he did both by forcing this wretched business into the traditional scheme of sin and retribution, which to him was the only form that would give conceivable significance either to New England's tragedy or to his own comprehension of it. He could not let a word he had written out of his trance go to waste; hence he, a stylist who kept even the sprawling *Magnalia* under some coherent control, published the most incoherent jumble he ever allowed to appear between covers.

In the helter-skelter of prefatory material he made once again every point which in the previous two chapters have emerged as themes in the reconstituted jeremiads. The first part—a good two-thirds of the book—is an epitome of all pronouncements since 1689. We New Englanders, he says, are the most loyal of subjects: hence Their Majesties' people should not be tormented by witches. We fully accept the principle of toleration, and make no distinction among Christians, whether Congregationalists, Presbyterians, or Episcopalians. Somehow at stake in all this are our "English Liberties" and our charter, which is attended "with singular Priviledges," such as choosing our own Council. Cotton could not cope with witches unless he first explained once more that New England was not so bad as the jeremiads had sometimes said: the body of the people were honest and industrious, multitudes here grew ripe for heaven, and were such as could make a right use of stupendous and prodigious occasions. Therefore New England should not have "an Unsavoury and a Sulpherous Resentment in the Opinion of the World abroad." At the same time, this community—founded by a chosen generation of saints and at first "a true Utopia"—was abysmally degenerated; it had become a nest of swearing, Sabbath-breaking, whoring, drunkenness. Consequently it had suffered in increasing severity a series of judgments—Antinomians, crop failures, sickness, revocation of the charter, Indian wars, fires, losses at sea, and now this climax, a descent of devils *in propribus personibus*. There is something both appealing and repulsive in Cotton's frantic clutching at the old array of sins in order to explain this affliction, at those village vices so long since arraigned: back-biting, scandal-mongering, talebearing, suits-at-law—precisely that cave of winds into which anthropologists of today would search for "causes" of the saturnalia that overwhelmed Salem Village.

Cotton Mather made all he could of the manifest stepping up of the scale of suffering, which would in itself certify New England's special position in the universe: "A Variety of Calamity has long follow'd this Plantation," even unto "a more than ordinary affliction." Against all these there was in 1692, as from the beginning, only one preservation: "REFORMATION! REFORMATION! has been the repeated Cry of all the Judgments that have hitherto been upon us." But, according to formula, because we have hitherto been as deaf as adders, "the Adders of the Infernal Pit are now hissing about us." Here at last was the long-sought, the long-desired consummation of the catalogue.

Except that there was—or there might be—a climax beyond even this: that dreadful culmination which for the Mathers (if not for all their colleagues) would be the truly final resolution. We cannot begin to comprehend this curious volume without perceiving that on page after page, whenever the tension becomes unbearable, the discourse plunges into Chiliastic ecstasy. The witches are signs of the times, of the death-pangs of the Devil; mischievous powers prevail for the moment, but only because his rule is nearing extinction. "The Devils Whole-time, cannot but be very near its End."

In the pressure of these packed moments, on the tenterhooks of anxiety, Cotton Mather made a syllabus for the new jeremiad. In his feverish concentration, everything pointed to one conclusion—the one he had striven for three years to make—that because Satan was gathering his forces for the ultimate assault, the civil magistrates were especially required to suppress any and all disorders, to punish every offender. (However, oddly enough, even in his delirium he kept his recently acquired sense of proportion, and though he termed New England the "center," hastily added, "and after a sort, the First-born of our English Settlements.") Whatever cautions he had studied during the summer, in throwing together these words he went with the tide of his rhetoric and found himself exhorting the magistrates "to do something extraordinary in promoting what is laudable, and in restraining and chastising of Evil Doers."

All of this was in the pattern; and Salem judges, having done their duty, endorsed *The Wonders*. There was only one hitch, and Cotton revealed it: the convictions had been secured "notwithstanding the Great and Just Suspicion, that the Daemons might Impose the Shapes of Innocent Persons in their Spectral Exhibitions upon the Sufferers (which may perhaps prove no small part of the Witch-Plot in the issue)." Every day he waited for Stephen's transcripts, Cotton heard that this had become "a most agitated Controversie among us," until he was shrieking that the Devil has pushed us "into a Blind Mans Buffet, and we are even ready to be sinfully, yea, hotly, and madly, mauling one another in the dark." This sentence is, obviously, a prime example of that peculiar kind of revelation without explicit admission that had become an acquired characteristic of the New England mind.

What he could not conceal from himself was that the formula of covenant reformation had miscarried. As all good jeremiads had said, the preliminary to release from affliction is confession; now there were confessions aplenty, the jails were full and "there is extream Hazard, lest the Devil by Compulsion must submit to that Great Work, may also by Permission, come to Confound that Work," lest he "intertwist some of his Delusions." Knowing that every moment he delayed, "a common Stream of Dissatisfaction" was mounting to which Phips would have to yield, putting the best face possible upon that prospect by prophesying that a wise magistrate may leave undone things he can no longer do "when the Publick Safety makes an Exigency," Cotton salvaged what defense he could for a court in which he did not believe by the pitiful remonstrance: "Surely, they have at worst been but the faults of a well-meaning Ignorance." We avert our gaze while he, having made what he could of Stephen's notes, fled up the ladder of the jeremiad and soothed himself with fresh dreams of the New Jerusalem, "from whence the Devil shall then be banished, there shall be no Devil within the Walls of that Holy City."

Mather did all this harm to himself after the trials were over, at the very moment sanity was returning. There is no need to apologize for him, for what he did deserves no apology; but we need accuse him only of what he actually did do. He is not responsible for killing Rebecca Nurse or George Burroughs. But he tried to make those killings legitimate when he knew they were murders by dressing them in the paraphernalia of the federal doctrine ("When this is done, Then let us own the Covenant"). He tried it even though he knew that the covenant remedy of confession had become a farce. By gathering the folds of that prophetic mantle around the gaping hypotheses of Stoughton's court, he fatally soiled it. The consequences were not to be fully realized for several years, but the damage was done. Samuel Eliot Morison says that Robert Calef tied a tin can to Cotton Mather which has rattled and banged through the pages of superficial and popular historians. My account is not popular, and I strive to make it not superficial; assuredly, if by tin can is meant the charge that Mather worked up the Salem tragedy, it does not belong to him; but what Calef was actually to charge was that he prostituted a magnificent conception of New England's destiny to saving the face of a bigoted court. In that sense, the right can was tied to the proper tail, and through the pages of this volume it shall rattle and bang.

Sometime during this fatal week, while Increase Mather was seeking a way to stop the court without discrediting it, while Cotton was being forced into defending the indefensible and Thomas Brattle was sickening of the Salem Gentlemen, a wit in Boston wrote a sixteen-page dialogue between *S* (obviously Salem) and *B* (by the same token, Boston), entitled *Some Miscellany Observations on our Present Debates respecting Witchcrafts*, and got it printed as though by William Bradford in Philadelphia. It purports to be issued for Hezekiah Usher, and to be written by "P. E."

(everybody knew this meant Philip English) and "J. A." (John Alden)—three of the accused who had fled instead of confessing. Scholars say that the type bears no relation to anything in Bradford's cases. A remarkable achievement of the native intelligence, this neglected essay is perhaps a greater indication of the tendency of the society than either of the Mathers'.

Who wrote it? Immemorial tradition says Samuel Willard; in 1695 Calef addressed him as "the suppos'd Author." He has a good record: at Groton in 1671 Elizabeth Knapp put on an exhibition which anticipated the antics of the possessed girls in Salem Village, and Willard (then the pastor) stifled the furor and wrote a clinical report which, had it been studied, might have cured the Salem wenches. He helped Usher, English, and Alden to escape, and he signed Increase's *Cases*. True, he also signed Lawson's tirade, but, as we have seen, early in the business that had seemed just another jeremiad. At his funeral, in 1707, his successor said that he should be honored for discovering the cheats and delusions of Satan—which undoubtedly meant something more specific to a congregation in the Old South than it does to us. It is difficult to recognize evidences of Willard's Style in the *Observations*—unless, under the pressures of this terrible moment, and writing secretly, he divested himself of his polemical mode and addressed himself to a more conversational manner.

For the *Observations* is a masterful analysis of how, in this model for all witch-hunts, confession became acquittal and an opportunity to besmirch others, while denial *ipso facto* became guilt. *B* does not doubt the existence of witches; neither does he deny that magistrates should hang them—but cautions should be observed: there must be clear proof. Whereupon *S*, good federal theologian that he is, asks the crucial question: can you maintain the "Rectoral Holiness" of God in governing the world if the specter of an innocent person be allowed to make mischief? *B* replies that God in His infinite wisdom may permit even this. Step by step, *B* drives *S* to conceding that the evidence of a renegade witch is not to be taken seriously, because even if he be sincere, he cannot be trusted. But when rational argument has all but stripped *S* of his defenses, he turns upon *B* with a snarl which comes down the years like a bullet: "You are an admirable Advocate for the Witches." After this, it becomes indeed difficult for *B* to protest that he is sound on the subject.

For modern ears, an equally dramatic moment comes when *S* protests that if a trial is to be hampered by too many safeguards, no witches will ever be caught; hence, he says, it is better to convict upon presumption. To which *B* replies,

This is a dangerous Principle, and contrary to the mind of God, who hath appointed that there shall be good and clear proof against the Criminal; else he is not Providentially delivered into the hands of Justice, to be taken off from the earth. Nor hath God exempted this Case of Witchcraft from the General Rule. Besides, reason tells us, that the more horrid the Crime is, the more Cautious we ought to be in making any guilty of it.

One's admiration goes further out to *B* (who, let us remember, signifies Boston) as he explains, in the face of spectral accusations, "This is no light matter to have mens names for ever Stigmatized, their Families ruined, and their Lives hazarded," and so concludes that if such creatures as specters are to be believed, then the Devil himself has turned informer, and all good men shall forever be hoodwinked.

To comprehend the predicament of the Puritan intellect in 1692, we should note that earlier in the crisis Cotton Mather preached one of his most stirring jeremiads, *A Midnight Cry*, in which he trounced New England with the gory threat of Indian atrocities: they "have taken our Brethren, and binding them to a Stake, with a Lingring Heat, Burned and Roasted them to Death; the Exquisite Groans and Shrieks of those our Dying Bretheren should Awaken us." In the intoxication of such external dangers, he publicly committed himself to the thesis that internal traitors had been convicted "by so fair and full a process of Law, as would render the Denyers thereof worthy of no Reasonabler Company than that in Bedlem." But his *Diary* shows him wrestling with the doubt that corrodes the pages of the *Wonders*; by June 7, 1694, he had openly to declare that the affliction consisted not so much in a descent of evil angels as in "unheard of DELUSIONS." At the election of May 27, 1696, he was simply nonplussed: "It was, and it will be, past all Humane Skill, Exactly to Understand what Inextricable Things we have met withal." In 1697 he had the honesty in his life of Phips (and later the integrity to incorporate the passage into the *Magnalia*) to acknowledge that the court had operated upon an erroneous notion; he still, though lamely, insisted that there had been other proofs, but in a last agony could not prevent himself from recording: "Nevertheless, divers were condemned, against whom the chief evidence was founded in the spectral exhibitions."

In the privacy of his *Diary*, Cotton Mather could simultaneously tell himself, even in 1692, that he always testified against spectral evidence and that the judges were "a most charming Instance of Prudence and Patience." Because he spoke "honourably" of their persons (at least according to his own account), "the mad people thro' the Countrey . . . reviled mee, as if I had been the Doer of all the hard Things, that were done, in the Prosecution of the Witchcraft." Considering that there is ample evidence in the *Diary* (all the more remarkable because it is studiously composed) that he never succeeded in persuading himself he had done the right thing (in 1697, after Sewall had repented, he grew panicky lest the Lord take revenge upon his family "for my not appearing with Vigor enough to stop the proceedings of the Judges"), it is the more striking that there are no respects in which one can say that the clergy suffered any immediate diminution of prestige or influence because of witchcraft. Nor did the judges lose standing in the community: neither Stoughton, who never admitted error, nor Samuel Sewall, who, in one of the noblest gestures of the period, took the shame of it upon himself before his church. The real effect of the tragedy is not to be traced in the field of politics or society, but in the intangible area of federal theory, and in the still more intangible region of self-esteem.

Henceforth there was, although for a time desperately concealed, a flaw in the very foundation of the covenant conception. The doctrine that afflictions are punishments to be dispelled by confession had produced at least one ghastly blunder; repentance had been twisted into a ruse, and the civil magistrate, by a vigorous exercise of his appointed function, had become guilty of hideous enormities. Nineteen years later, Cotton Mather was still keeping vigils to inquire of the Lord "the meaning of the Descent from the Invisible World," and was obliged repeatedly to discharge his sense of guilt by advertising, as a fundamental tenet of New England along with liberty of conscience, "That Persons are not to be judg'd Confederates with Evil Spirits, meerly because the Evil Spirits do make possessed People cry out upon them." The meaning of New England had been fixed, by Winthrop and the founders, in the language of a covenant; if henceforth there was so much as a shadow of suspicion upon that philosophy, in what realm of significance could the land hold its identity?

John Hale, we have seen, was one of three ministers who committed themselves; in his revulsion, he went so far to the other extreme that Sewall feared he would deny witchcraft itself. He wrote *A Modest Enquiry Into the Nature of Witchcraft* in 1698; it is a sad, troubled, and honest book, which he could not bring himself to publish, so that it appeared two years after his death, in 1702. It passed unnoted, and is of importance mainly for the light it sheds upon the working of many minds obliged to live with perplexity. For the fact could not be got round: Hale had been trained to a belief in certain articles, and precisely these fundamentals "I here question as unsafe to be used." Nobody in New England had yet uttered such a sentence. Once the process of "a more strict scanning of the principles I had imbibed" was started, once it led to a rejection of any of the principles of aged, learned, and judicious persons, where would it stop? We followed (with a "kind of Implicit Faith") the "traditions of our fathers," and now see that they, "weighed in the balance of the Sanctuary, are found too light." The whole edifice of the New England mind rocked at the very thought that it might be based, not upon a cosmic design of the covenant, but merely upon fallible founders; yet Hale forced himself to recognize the power of conditioning: "A Child will not easily forsake the principles he hath been trained up in from his Cradle."

Frightened by his own audacity, Hale turned back at the end of his soliloquy: because our fathers did not see deeply into these mysteries, let us not undervalue the good foundations they did lay. They brought the land into an engagement with God, and He may even yet not entirely "cut off the Entail of his Covenant Mercies." In 1720, Samuel Sewall had his memories come thick upon him as he read the account in Neal's *History*, and cried out, "The good and gracious God be pleased to save New England and me, and my family!" The onus of error lay heavy upon the land; realization of it slowly but irresistibly ate into the New England conscience. For a long time dismay did not translate itself into a disbelief in witchcraft or into anticlericalism, but it rapidly became an unassuageable grief that the covenanted community should have committed an irreparable evil. Out of sorrow and chagrin, out of dread, was born a new love for the land which had been desecrated, but somehow also consecrated, by the blood of innocents.

CHAPTER XIV

THE DILEMMA OF THE SACRAMENT

IN
1692 Salem witchcraft was a peripheral episode,
during which the New England mind was engrossed with its real problem:
how, under the terms of the new charter, could it survive the disintegrating
and seemingly irresistible consequences of the Half-Way Covenant?

Even while the hierophants were hailing William and Mary's charter as
a victory, they betrayed the fullness—and bitterness—of their realization
that because of it their future depended more than ever upon their producing a succession of pious children. At the acme of his success, as he came
home with his puppet governor in tow and his nominations to the Council
secured, even as he pretended that civil authority had once more become
the handmaiden of primitive polity, Increase Mather knew that this administration was not to be relied upon. New England's system rested upon
covenant: a Congregational society expected more from officials than that
they enact moral legislation, suppress vice, collect tithes, and even frankly
(with concessions to liberty of conscience) favor the standing order. An
Anglican or Presbyterian system might get along with this kind of support,
but Congregationalism required something more positive. It presupposed
that power arose out of society's federated will, that it should be not merely
well intentioned but actively conscious of what Winthrop called "our Commission and Community in the worke." The new charter, with all its advantages and privileges, was by its very nature primarily concerned with
either constitutional rights or with the Navigation Laws; by no exegesis
could it be transformed, as the founders had transformed the first charter,
into a scaffold for a city of righteousness. Even with the best of intentions,
a royally appointed Phips (bewildered in a dignity that was none of his
choosing) was anything but a Winthrop; after him, the governorship was
foreseeably bound to degenerate from the pinnacle of ultimate adjudication
into a merely administrative office, and so to lie at the mercy of conflicting
interests.

If these churches were to continue, they had not only to remain dominant
but to fill up their ranks with saints. They had to create in each community
a core of members who voluntarily took the covenant, who would attend
the Lord's Supper as a symbol of free choice, who would be there not because they lived in the parish or were obliged by custom and law, but because they made and recorded a decision. Anything in the way of ecclesiasti-

cal legislation that could be got past a royal disallowance was indeed to be enacted, but even so, the principle of voluntarism had to be preserved. The magnificent scheme of the founders called for willing subjection to the inherently good, just, and honest; now, with no more to be expected from the state than, at best, a half-hearted tagging along, the ministers had to evoke this willingness. The very day they rid themselves of Andros, they perceived that they still possessed, in addition to the jeremiad, one further device for mass persuasion: they could still press home the obligation of the baptismal covenant.

Hence, during the terrible summer of 1692, Cotton Mather was unable to concentrate his whole mind upon the distressing business in Essex County. He was too much preoccupied with the larger strategy: church fellowship must be enlarged, the ministry better paid, ecclesiastical discipline stiffened, the Lord's Supper extended, and—most essentially—baptism be "improved." This last was the hinge of the whole campaign: unless it were dispensed to more persons, and all these galvanized into following its injunction (of their own volition!) into becoming professors, the New England Way would perish.

Mather showed his preternatural sense of what the liberation of 1689 really meant by issuing, within the year, *A Companion for Communicants,* of which the point was that the baptized (however they came to be baptized) have engaged themselves to qualify for the second sacrament. There was no longer a political inducement; therefore Mather resorted to the one incentive he could yet employ: he threatened "baptistes" with a supernatural vengeance infinitely worse than any in store for ordinary sinners. "The Waters of Baptism, will prove more bitter and baneful than the waters of jealousie to the guilty Souls of them that forget what engagements are by their Baptism laid upon them." Willard joined him in 1691 by publishing *The Barren Fig Trees Doom,* wherein, says the title page, "is set forth the woful danger of all who abide unfruitful under the Gospel-priviledges, and God's husbandry." Membership in the merely visible covenant does indeed have value, but—here Willard tried to arrest New England's history, to call a halt to the march of hypocrisy and preparation—men do not become intrinsically better because of it: "Church-Membership is not only a title of dignity, but also an obligation to Service." Those who luxuriate in the one without assuming the other provoke the Lord most grievously.

In short, this American system could not work upon anybody unless he were first got into covenant—so that he could then be presumed capable of action. Inert citizens can no more make a church than a water-logged vessel can obey the helm. In New England, by the doctrine of national covenant, by the fact that all had come (either of themselves or through their fathers) because of an act of choice, a certain rudimentary ability could be attributed even to the meanest inhabitant. All were immigrants, and to them could be assigned (what could not be presupposed for Euro-

peans) enough power to reform their external manners: "Children born in
New-England, if they dy in their Sins, will fall under an heavier Condemnation at the Last Day, than if they had been born in Sodom." But for
New England itself, still more was demanded: there had to be a willingness
within the will, a covenant beyond the covenant; therefore a larger freedom
had to be placed at the disposal of the baptized (the favored children of a
favored land), who then could be addressed as though entirely capable of
performing or not performing, and consequently be berated for their failures. The last enemies of the Half-Way Covenant were dying off; few
were left to accuse Cotton Mather of sophistry when he argued that the
two factions should now come together. Opponents might as well admit
that some may "do that as a point of pure Morality" which others had
wished "to do as a point of Institution." "The Statute-Law of Discipline"
might still be silent, but the churches had safely proceeded upon "the Common-Law of Reproving." In either view there was adequate warrant for
"thus dealing with such as have been Baptised in their Bosoms." Why keep
up a lingering scruple against applying the force of ecclesiastical discipline
to half-way members when that was what the country needed?

If so, those addressed on a point of morality should not only be reminded, Sabbath after Sabbath, of their obligations, but be periodically
quickened. Here Cotton Mather perceived the great possibilities of renewal
of covenant: *A Midnight Cry* told how he listed the sixteen common evils
of the land and then had his church testify against them while "renewing
our Covenant." Speaking to the country, out of the fears and doubts that
haunt the *Wonders,* he could think of no better way for the churches to
assist in the cure of witchcraft than "to do something extraordinary, in renewing of their Covenants, and in remembring and reviving the Obligations of what they have renewed."

The decade of the 1690's witnesses the full flowering of this ritual. At
Hartford in 1696 the universality of the pledge constitutes what in later
parlance might be called a "revival." Yet while there was no longer substantial opposition to the Half-Way Covenant, there was stubborn objection (a small cloud on the horizon) to this extrapolation. Cotton Mather
defended it, arguing that communal reaffirmation was no violation of pre-
destinarian theology because such a mass surrender was, on the part of the
people, a renunciation of their own strength: possibly it might be something
beyond "what is to be found in the Old Way of Returning to God," but it
still could be justified as an "Expedient circumstance of Explicitness, dictated by the very Light of Nature, for the better doing of it." If there was
an incipient antagonism between his two sanctions of God and nature,
Mather tried not to notice it. The published literature amounts to an expanding plea for more and more experiment with this natural means, exhibiting an astonishing sophistication about stagecraft. By 1696 Mather described it in detail, calling it "a very special and Important Expedient of
Reformation," showing that it had become not an occasional resort in

desperate times (as in Philip's War), but a standard feature of the social pattern:

> Let them that have Enjoy'd the Seals of this Covenant, again and again, with all possible Solemnity, Repeat the Consent of their Souls thereunto. Syrs, A most wondrous Reformation would follow hereupon Immediately.

Here indeed was an expedient ready at hand!

However, expediency calls for whatever will expedite. In this decade sermons unmistakably tend toward increasing emphasis upon the threat of hellfire, the flames blown with a special bellows to receive the baptized who die unconverted: if plants in Christ's vineyard will not serve for fruit, preached the gentle and moderate Willard, "they will do for burning." The torments of these children will more glorify God than shrieks of the reprobate "by so much as these have had more cost and pains laid out upon them." In this period we may precisely locate the beginning of a rhetorical gambit which quickly became a regular feature of the oratory, an exquisite calculation, moment by moment, of the mathematical infinity of torture. It appears, for instance, in Cotton Mather's preface to Lee's *Great Day of Judgment* in 1692:

> Suppose an heap of as many Little Poppey-seeds, as according to the old Ptolemaick System, would fill the whole Machin of the World, and no more than one of them in a Thousand Years fetch'd away, but the Sinner in Anguish till the heap were all wasted so; behold, and be amazed! All this Long while would be as a Drop to the Ocean, Compar'd with that Forever! that horrible Forever! whereto the Torments of the Damned shall be Lengthened.

Increase made it more clear than Wigglesworth had done in *The Day of Doom* that "some will have a more intolerable Hell of it than others shall" —a reflection in which the New England mind now took a satisfaction it had not known or needed in the first days. From here it was a short step for Benjamin Wadsworth to commence his ministry at the First Church with a half-conscious revelation of the hidden drift of the conception: since a person in such inconceivable misery will be no nearer the end after millions of ages, the law of self-preservation, "originally Imprinted on the nature of man," indicates his duty to avoid it. On days of public renewal, the fires of hell burned most brightly, so that by their glare the baptized might read the law of nature. (*The Westminster Confession* did indeed say that there was enough light in nature to render the unconverted "inexcusable," but the demonstrations of a scholastic physics were of a different order of persuasiveness from these economical calculations.)

In this decade appear several further rhetorical tropes which also are transparent efforts to play upon an enlarged range of emotions. About 1695 Increase Mather began to announce his impending demise and to urge listeners to take advantage of his preaching while there was still time: "I have more reasons then I shall express, to believe that my Opportunities of

Serving any . . . in New-England, are very near unto their end." So theatrical a gesture John Cotton would have scorned; it recalls John Donne's preaching in his shroud, and just as Donne made himself one of the sights of London, so Increase's long-drawn-out dissolution (continuing for twenty-eight years) became the major histrionic spectacle of Boston. The fervid style of Cotton Mather led the way from the plain manner of the seventeenth century to the sentimentalism of the eighteenth; to appreciate the unique and not entirely enviable place he occupies in the history of American prose, we must realize how he launched upon his career deeply convinced that he had to "bestow a few Joggs and Pulls upon my Sleeping Hearers." From the beginning he labored for a jogging technique, wherefore many of his inventions sound to us as though derived, not from the sinuous rhythms of Hooker and Shepard, but from those of Pyramus and Thisbe:

Let us Beware of every Sin, for Sin will Turn a Man into a Devil, oh! Vile Sin, horrid Sin, Cursed Sin; or, to speak a more Pungent word than all of That; oh, Sinful Sin; how Pernicious art thou unto the Souls of Men!

Along with a schematic enumeration of the units of eternal torment, he refined his calculus of the approaching end of the world—"we are doubtless very near the Last Hours of that Wicked One"—and of the nearing conflagration, when this stage upon which the sinner enacts his crimes shall appropriately become "the Scaffold of his Execution." Drunk with the fumes of Chiliasm (and little noting that he and his generation were drifting into a purely lineal conception of time, in which the possibility of any sort of end was becoming remote), Cotton Mather began to proclaim that already accomplished which he shortly expected, and so mounted to his most rapturous flights in a confidence that he had not long to wait for his triumph:

I do firmly expect, a NEW REFORMATION to be begun; a REFORMATION more Glorious, more Heavenly, more Universal far away than what was in the former Century; together with most formidable Desolations to be Hail'd from Heaven, upon those that shall incurably retain an Antipathy to this REFORMATION.

On the brink of so magnificent a chasm, what else could New England do but "go forth to meet this Blessed Reformation"?

In the rush of eloquence there was no time for pausing over scholastic distinctions between natural and spiritual abilities. And precisely here, in the absence of such circumspection, we perceive the direction of the process, intellectual as well as social. For more than a generation after 1689, no New England writer except Stoddard produced anything worth remarking in the way of a purely theological treatise. True, through two hundred and fifty lectures Samuel Willard undertook a systematic review of the colony's theology, and left behind him an immense manuscript, *A Compleat Body of Divinity*. This is indeed New England's *summa*, but it codifies the system imported in 1630 and since then become rigid; it is not at all modified (as is the *Magnalia*) by any American experience. Otherwise the clergy published little (and preached little) beyond what we may roughly call "practical theology"—which in this context meant incessantly calling the people to reformation and thundering at the lassitude of the baptized. The key works are *A Midnight Cry* and *The Barren Fig Trees Doom:* the emphasis is upon the summons to action, let theology define capability as it may. Of course, all these preachers were loyal to *The Westminster Confession*, nor did they in any explicit particular renounce the intellectual architecture that formed the first part of this study: they simply stopped talking about it, while concentrating upon getting results. They would not understand what I mean, but actually in this fashion they were becoming Americanized—all the more speedily because, not obtaining the results they desired, they had to redouble their endeavors.

One remarkable consequence of this exertion was the unabashed mobilization of the concept of preparation into the service of Mather's "REFORMATION," whereby the obligation that legitimately rested upon the baptized was extended to all inhabitants. Cotton Mather always declared that regeneration comes from above, but his life-long message ran, "You may make a Tryal. There can be no hurt in trying, whether you can turn and live, or no." An unregenerate creature does not prepare himself; nevertheless (the number of sentences in Cotton Mather's writings which turn, diagrammatically, upon this crucial "nevertheless" are legion), "If he do what he can, there is a probability that God intends to help him, so that he shall do more than he can." By 1699 Mather had his theology wonderfully simplified: "Try whether you can't give that Consent; if you can, 'tis done."

Here, then, we are at a crisis in American cultural history. It was indeed Arminian heresy to suppose that the talent of common grace might be improved by unassisted nature into a claim upon divine grace; nevertheless (again!) in the attempt there is "a Vital Efficiency." Before they cross the threshold of election, "Men have a Natural Power, as to the External part of Religion." And it stands to reason—or at least to what stood for reason after the old charter was lost—that if they do all they can out of natural power, "there would be a greater Likelihood (I say not, a Certainty, but a Likelihood,) that God would grant them that Higher Power." The parenthesis preserved technical orthodoxy, even though by the skin of the preacher's teeth; yet when consigning the qualification to a parenthesis, he signified that at the end of the century any one in New England who wanted baptism could, regardless of ancestry, have it for the asking.

Considering toward what renovations this argument was tending (the ghost of Mistress Hutchinson would be regarding it wryly, as would also the specters of Davenport and Charles Chauncy), it seems the more remarkable that leaders never asked themselves how they reconciled what they were doing with their Calvinism. Yet to raise this question is to forget how fundamental changes in a society do come about, how imperceptibly alterations of custom infect the ideology, or how ideology, submitting to unforeseen pressures, yields up novel warrants. The ministers copiously denounced Arminianism even while expanding the covenant in every direction, and they could continue to do so, until one should arise to accuse them of having become, to all practical purposes, Arminian—although by that time they would no longer be capable of understanding what their accuser meant.

Thus the day on which a church renewed its covenant became an occasion for numbers of townspeople to petition for baptism. Theoretically the rite remained a seal upon the Covenant of Grace, administered only to converts or to the seed of converts, but during the 1690's it became in actual fact a certification of natural abilities which might in all "Likelihood" be elevated. In 1705 Samuel Danforth conducted what his peers regarded as an eminently successful renewal at Taunton, giving liberty to everybody "from sixteen years old and upwards to act with us"; Cotton Mather, using terms carefully, noted that Danforth thus brought several hundred "Inhabitants" to enter (cheerfully!) into the engagement, and complimented him upon "bringing that popular and vicious Town to a wonderful Reformation."

In 1689, while busily setting these mechanisms to work, the clergy, happy in their regained freedom of action, yet apprehensive lest some sort of charter should curtail it, were listening attentively for any suggestion Increase Mather might convey, through his mouthpiece in Boston, as to further instruments. Soon the signal came: there are ways in which the old, the not only detrimental but now meaningless schism of Congregationalism and Presbyterianism can be healed. In the mother country, such accommodations are actually under way, and these would be immensely assisted were New England to imitate them; there would also be an added advantage that the colonies could thus create a further agency of control, and so would need to rely even less upon the civil magistrate.

After thirty years of the Restoration and the Clarendon Code, of James II and his Declarations of Indulgence, English Presbyterianism, hastening into the shelter of the Toleration Act, was no longer the haughty exclusiveness that Dr. Child almost brought down in wrath upon Winthrop's enterprise. Driven underground, it had survived by breaking into congregations; out of that ordeal, it emerged with a chastened realization that a solid theological front was more important than uniformity of polity. After all, New England (protected by its charters) had achieved just about everything to which Presbyterianism aspired: was there any longer reason for splitting the forces of Nonconformity over academic distinctions between classis and synod—when synod had proved every bit as effective as classis? Might not men of good will contrive a politic definition in which both could be reconciled, and so stand against either Lambeth or a Quaker meeting?

Increase Mather reached London at the fortunate moment when the two segments of Dissent had learned through adversity that the issues of polity no longer mattered; they were eager to come together on fundamentals, but needed the help of a neutral whom both could respect. Mather was received in complete amity by Presbyterians—by Baxter and John Howe, by Dr. Daniel Williams—and actually found himself more at home among them than with the ragged survivors of Independency, albeit one of these was his brother. Smuggled out of Andros' Dominion, he was ideally suited to serve as broker for the shattered ranks of Cromwellian Puritanism, and his mission succeeded where Franklin's eighty years later could not, because he could present himself in Whitehall not so much as an agent for America as the plenipotentiary for English Nonconformity. No wonder, therefore, that the cause in whose name he won the charter should inspire in Boston corresponding efforts to show how, despite long and regrettable struggles, Presbyterianism and the New England Way were basically in accord.

The Toleration Act was passed on May 24, 1689. Within a matter of weeks, representatives of the two denominations met in London, and by July of 1690 progressed so far as to establish a common fund for the aid of impoverished churches, to be administered by seven Congregationalists under the leadership of Matthew Mead and seven Presbyterians headed by John Howe. In October, the ministers of Boston, Cambridge, and adjacent towns assembled at Harvard College to form the "Cambridge Association" (Increase Mather, although still abroad, was enrolled as a charter member). The sequence of events is explicable: Cotton was producing evidence to bear out Increase's claim that Congregationalism permitted governing bodies so closely analogous to a Presbyterian classis that further dissension was pointless.

New England could argue that in its history there was precedent for such associations; the pure fathers had set up regular conferences in the 1630's, and Roger Williams added to the head and front of his offense by accusing them of Presbyterianism. Whether or not because of his attack, these conferences had fallen into neglect by the middle of the century (after the Synod of 1662 they would have been impolitic), but this lapse could blithely be disregarded by the Cambridge Association when asserting that it embodied nothing more than the old Congregational principle of "consociation." For several years the ministers in the neighborhood had been coming to town for certain public lectures or for election sermons; now they simply organized themselves "in a more significant manner," out of a hearty admiration for "the UNION of their Brethren at London." Henceforth they would meet every month, "at the College in Cambridge, on a Monday at nine or ten of the clock in the morning." Inspired by their example, other regions formed associations, and by 1705 five of them were functioning. (On October 3, 1692, it was to the Cambridge Association that Increase Mather read *Cases of Conscience,* and by using it as the agency of informing and directing opinion, a month before the book was printed, he brought the Salem court to an end.)

At the first session in Cambridge, the role of synods was discussed; the decision—reflecting New England's disillusion with, or anxiety concerning the future of, autonomous churches—held that synods ought to be reverenced "as determining the mind of the Holy Spirit" and in that sense be acknowledged "decisive." Thus supported, Cotton Mather hastened, as quickly and emphatically as possible, to proclaim that "the differences between Independents & Presbyterians, are so swallowed up, as that only the Substantials of Religion are become the Terms of our Communion." Should Presbyterians still be suspicious, let them know that synods in New England, although theoretically limited only to the clarification of terms, "Rarely, if Ever, fail of putting an Issue to any Controversies, which they meet upon."

So Increase Mather could hold his head high amid English Dissenters: he had the formula of accord. Presbyterians ungrudgingly admired New England's record: men like Baxter and Dr. Williams knew how effectively the Synod of 1637 had squelched Antinomianism (whereas English Presbyterianism, at the height of its power, had not been able to suppress Quakers and Anabaptists), how the Synod of 1662 reconciled Congregationalism with the facts of procreation, how the Synod of 1679 magisterially set forth a program of reformation (such as they would have loved to prescribe for England). Consequently John Howe, foremost theologian among the Dissenters, who in his youth had been an Independent, appealed to the ambassador from New England. A Congregationalism that functioned like Presbyterianism was obviously the answer to Nonconformity's dire necessity (especially since few Nonconformists were any longer so confident about their readings of the passages on polity in the New Testament). These mighty figures of the capital, upon whose published words provincials hung for intellectual tutelage, turned to the provincial emissary for guidance through an enterprise for which his experience had been a better training than theirs.

On April 6, 1691, the two parties crowned their concord by issuing *The Heads of Agreement*, which Howe, Mead, and Increase Mather had composed with exquisite care. They showed how far the Puritan mind had traveled in the fifty years since Presbyterians and Independents sabered each other at Dunbar and Worcester by thankfully accepting "the favour of our Rulers in the present Established Liberty" and by disavowing all thought of coërcion. Let us also abandon, they exhorted each other, jealousies and carnal suspicions, and so "reduce all distinguishing Names, to that of UNITED BRETHREN." Mead preached a moving sermon on "Two Sticks made one." Increase Mather, who had cause enough to congratulate himself upon his charter, preened himself even more for the decisive part he played in negotiating this treaty: he dreamed that out of it would come not only a great, solidified Dissenting power in England, but a solution for New England's ecclesiastical problem.

Immediately upon receiving a text of the *Heads*, his enthusiasm set in motion, Cotton Mather preached *Blessed Unions*, dedicating the publication to Howe, Mead, and his father. He smugly boasted that New England, having long practiced "those very Principles upon which our European Brethren do now Unite," was a standing exhibition of the union toward which "your most Evangelical Souls have been aspiring." In the North Church (at least there, if not in others) "the Name of PRESBYTERIAN and CONGREGATIONAL (Yea, and EPISCOPAL too, when Piety is otherwise visible) and I may add, the Name of ANTIPEDOBAPTIST, Likewise, is of no Consideration; both, yea all together do, As one man carry on the Affairs of our Lords Ecclesiastical Kingdom." The implication was clear: let the rest of the country drop local jealousies and unite into associations; these would develop centralized powers, and then nobody need worry because the magistrate had become an official of the Crown rather than of the saints.

The Heads of Agreement, a masterpiece of diplomacy, seems at first sight more Congregational than Presbyterian. There is indeed no specific mention of the church covenant (had there been, Howe would not have signed), but it defines the church as a competent number of visible saints consenting together; it does not give authoritative jurisdiction to the classis (if it had, Mead would have refused), but it requires neighboring churches to be consulted about the choice of a pastor, and particular churches not to dissent, without explicit warrant from Scripture, from the advice of the surrounding pastors in all cases of internal dispute. Were this rule observed, New England would be safe. Should the association assume dictatorial powers, the cry would go up of treason and subversion; but could the people be persuaded to accept directives from bodies put upon a regular footing, the churches could rule themselves without the help of magistrates. So, disdaining George Keith's sneer that the once free congregations were "almost wholly degenerated, if not altogether, into a Presbyterian Laxness," Cotton Mather hailed the *Heads* by reciting New England's deep, long-held respect for such Presbyterians as John Howe and Dr. Williams.

Hardly had Increase come home, glowing with the satisfaction of one who has wrought a wonder, than distressing news followed him: the English Congregationalists were muttering that the Union was "a Verbal Composition" contrived "with great ambiguity," that it was at bottom a Presbyterian plot. They dug up the fact that John Howe had supinely yielded to the Five Mile Act, and whispered that the amalgamation was a trick to lure them all into "Sacramental Communion" with the Church of England. Ominously enough, this discontent was agitated by two scions of New England: by Increase's brother, Nathanael Mather, minister in Paved Alley, Lime Street, and by Isaac Chauncy, Harvard College 1651, son of that same President Chauncy who fought the Half-Way Covenant on the ground that it would lead straight to Presbyterianism. Then, at the worst

possible moment, Dr. Williams, whom many called "the Bishop of the.
Dissenters," elected to denounce in a sermon at Pinners Hall the recently
republished works of Dr. Tobias Crisp. Within two years the United
Brethren were divided more hopelessly than ever, and Increase Mather's
great work was ruined.

In other words, an institutional compromise that promised a political success which every participant desired was wrecked by the recrudescence of
the most divisive issue in seventeenth-century theology, which all hoped
was buried. The book that did the damage had been written in the 1640's,
at the moment English Independency lunged toward heresies as abhorrent
to American Congregationalists as to English and Scottish Presbyterians.
Tobias Crisp, who died in 1643, commenced, like Saltmarsh, as an orthodox federalist, basing the Covenant of Grace between man and God upon
an anterior Covenant of Redemption between Christ and the Father, in
which Christ had undertaken to fulfill the law in man's stead. But from
this premise, Crisp came to the conclusion, as did Anne Hutchinson, that
the Covenant of Grace had nothing to do with moral behavior, and that
therefore no ethical duty could be imposed upon, or any response expected
from, mankind. In New England eyes, Crisp figured as an arrant Antinomian; the founders had tried in vain to warn their Independent brethren
against tolerating him. Now in 1690 his son Samuel edited Tobias' remains
under the disturbing title, *Christ Alone Exalted*. The irenical movers of
the Union allowed themselves to become so intent upon their organizational
project as to forget theology, and therefore both Howe and Increase
Mather joined Nathanael Mather and Isaac Chauncy in attesting that
Samuel Crisp had accurately transcribed his father's manuscripts. On the
whole, Increase Mather made few mistakes; when he did, like the late
Mayor of New York, he perpetrated a beauty: his signing the foreword to
Crisp was perhaps his most unfortunate gaff.

Richard Baxter first took alarm; Howe begged him not to endanger the
Union, and he held off. But nothing could stop Dr. Williams: after two
years of sober consideration, he deliberately used the joint lecture to excoriate "Crispianism." Thereupon the flames that Howe and Increase Mather
believed they had smothered flared up as furiously as in the 1640's. Williams published *Gospel Truth Stated and Vindicated*, the first edition bearing an endorsement of sixteen ministers, the second that of forty-nine—all
of them Presbyterians. Nathanael Mather and Isaac Chauncy prepared a
"Paper of Exceptions"; the fund was divided, Congregationalists withdrew
from the Union, and in 1694 Williams, Bates, and Howe set up a separate
and strictly Presbyterian lecture at Salters Hall. For seven years raged one
of the bitterest pamphlet warfares in English church history—Isaac
Chauncy being the principal and most aggressive Congregational spokesman—to the great chagrin of the Cambridge Association in Massachusetts, which had been serenely dedicated to the proposition that Congregationalists and Presbyterians were brethren under the skin.

One gauge of what had happened to the New England mind since it let itself become so heedlessly concentrated on organizational matters, such as the Half-Way Covenant, is the fact that it could barely understand, let alone mediate, the controversy. Federal theology had always hypothesized the Covenant of Redemption as preliminary to the Covenant of Grace: it was "the Consultation that Passed between God the Father and the Son, at the Council-Table of Heaven, when there was none else present, but that Principal Secretary of State, the Holy Spirit of God, who has Revealed it." (The idea was much older, but in 1706 Cotton Mather thus phrased it—prefacing his sentence with an "as I may say"—indicating by his phraseology something of the effect which the incorporation of Massachusetts Bay into the British empire had upon the imagery, not to say upon the thought, of provincial Boston!) Because of this heavenly protocol, grace is "free"— that is, irrespective of human merit. In 1693, the thoughtful Willard, distressed by news from London, published *The Doctrine of the Covenant of Redemption,* hoping that it might help bring the factions together, or at least explain where New England stood. He was convinced that the relation of the two Covenants might still be so stated as not to mean that a sinner should give over all endeavor or that preparation was futile. Man is not to rest in security amid his vices, trusting Christ to do everything for him. Why, these colonials pleaded, could not their friends in England agree upon so simple a statement and not quarrel over words? If this sort of Calvinism had become plausible on one side of the Atlantic, why not on the other?

In England agreement proved impossible because the line of thought which Crisp embodied was too deeply embedded; it might have become equally rooted in New England had not the Synod of 1637 so ruthlessly exterminated Antinomianism, had not the conception of preparation been so subtly but decisively enthroned, or had not objectors to the Half-Way Covenant been so effectively silenced. America was difficult but relatively simple: in 1662 (or in the years thereafter) the dominant party was able to impose upon the land a single definition of the powers of the semi-regenerate; but England was hopelessly complex, nor, during the years of persecution, had Puritanism been able to maintain intellectual, let alone ecclesiastical, uniformity. Under the Restoration, too many of them felt the almost irresistible pull of the doctrine of "absolute" covenant, and improved their misfortune by pronouncing strictures against every semblance of natural ability. For instance, John Bunyan, no university graduate and therefore not skilled in those academic distinctions by which depraved inability could be transformed into an ability of some sorts: he said that the Covenant of Grace is not made with sinners at all, but reaches the elect only because God has previously consented with Christ in the Covenant of Redemption. Likewise, Thomas Boston fulminated against the slightest suggestion that the Covenant of Grace might be termed "conditional," and therefore insisted that there were no distinctions, not even verbal, between it and the Covenant of Redemption. Hence, when Tobias Crisp's exaltation of Christ alone reappeared in 1690, those closest to the Calvinism of early Puritanism—who like Nathanael Mather and Isaac Chauncy had never been obliged to dilute their absolutistic theology in order to keep children within the church—welcomed it as a banner of the good old cause. When Dr. Williams said that Crisp destroyed all morality and gave full license to blasphemers and murderers, they raised the ancient battlecry, and accused him of Arminianism, Pelagianism—or if those were no longer explicit enough, of what Chauncy called "Neonomianism."

In this renewed dispute, old stubble was thoroughly threshed anew, to the tune of vigorous insult and a most un-Christian calling of names. One fact is of supreme importance: the Presbyterians freely cited, as being wholly on their side, the record of New England—Increase Mather having placed it at their disposal. "My heart akes to think of the late stirs in the New-England Churches, occasioned by Master Wheelwrite, Mistress Hutchinson, and their followers, especially when I consider, that this very Tenent, No Condition in the Covenant, had a great influence thereon, if it were not the main cause thereof." Declaring their position "the general Tenent of our Brethren in New England," the Presbyterians adduced (almost too ostentatiously) not only the Synod of 1637 but Thomas Hooker, Peter Bulkeley, John Norton, and even those venerable architects of Non-Separatist Congregationalism, Perkins, Preston, and Ames, whose writings still furnished the content of Harvard's ministerial training. By asserting that the Covenant of Grace is not absolute—that it remains distinct from, although founded upon, the Covenant of Redemption—they capitalized upon what New England had come painfully to learn: the intrinsic worth of preparation and of such exertions of will as the colonial clergy demanded from the baptized. Denying that they preached salvation by works, English Presbyterians asserted that, through the atonement of Christ, man's imperfect deeds are accounted to him for righteousness—wherefore he should perform deeds. As against this imperfectionism, the world had learned how Crisp's kind of perfectionism opens the floodgates of depravity: "New England hath felt the Troubles it occasioned. And many places in Old England are now suffering."

For the provincial clergy to have their land made the vindication of the central paradox of Protestantism was flattering, but to have such praise heaped upon them at this particular moment was embarrassing. They had rallied to support the Union, proud that it imitated the New England system, and had out-done themselves in complimenting Presbyterians. For decades their every adjustment to circumstance had meant enlarging the sphere of preparation, of hypocrisy, of unregenerate liability, and now they were busily encouraging natural inhabitants to renew a covenant never heretofore sworn. But they were not, they could not become, Presbyterians. Their churches were particular, not national: they still guarded a sacred precinct (even though it seemed steadily contracting) into which no mere renewers but only visible saints might enter, not because of preparation but only because of a demonstrable calling and an act of liberated will. The clergy were haunted by the thought that possibly Nathanael Mather and Isaac Chauncy in London were more faithful to the precepts and the spirit of the founders than they in Boston who most extravagantly professed veneration of their common grandfathers.

Once the dispute in England got out of control, New Englanders had no choice but to keep from being involved. Increase signed a book by John Flavel which sought to prove that the differences between Dr. Williams' Neonomianism and Isaac Chauncy's Antinomianism were merely formal. Searching out what the founders had written, the ministers doggedly insisted that the Covenant of Grace "is built upon the Covenant of Redemption," and that further dispute was idle. At Willard's funeral in 1707, Pemberton reminded the Old South that Willard's treatment of the Covenant of Redemption gave them, at one and the same time, "the sovereignty and freeness of divine grace displayed, and the stability of the believers salvation asserted"—which answered the criticism of either side in England and so ought to be enough for America. What happened to the Union was, as Cotton Mather wailed, "no less Unaccountable unto us, than Uncomfortable." Years after *The Heads of Agreement* had become in England a dim memory, New Englanders kept on pleading for it as that which obliterated all reason for estrangement between them and the rest of Nonconformity; they enshrined it, along with *The Cambridge Platform,* among the symbols of the New England Way. Preaching before an undoubtedly astonished Bellomont in 1700, Cotton Mather held it a glory of the local system that it took neither side in an already defunct controversy:

> The Neonomian and Antinomian Errors, about that Great Point of A Sinners Justification before God, which have bred such a Scandalous Contention, among the Non Conformists beyond Sea, have not yet straggled over the Atlantic, among this People of God. The two Covenants, that of Works, and that of Grace, are not here so confounded, as in many other places.

This theological neutrality was not so naïve as we might suppose: if no rude questions were asked, there would be no necessity that enlargements of preparation and of hypocrisy, of the social obligations of the baptized, of the ritual of renewal, would have to be either defended against the charge of Arminianism or too closely reconciled with a doctrine of strict predestination.

Yet—if the English Presbyterians were using New England to bolster their arguments against Independents, was New England not then tarred with a Presbyterian brush? Isaac Chauncy was attacking the very same gentlemen for whom Cotton Mather had published his admiration, men who, said Chauncy, preach a "Grotian, Pelagian Divinity." In defense of his father, Samuel Crisp portrayed the citizen who "comes with his Gifts, good Nature to forgive his enemies," and plaintively whines, "I have lived well, and I don't doubt but God will have mercy on me when I die, for Christ's sake." Who was this creature if not both the target of all New England jeremiads and he whom Bunyan named "Ignorance" because his heart told him that his heart and his life agree together? And yet this person was performing everything the jeremiads meant by "REFORMATION," he who would never know, said Crisp, whether or not he was converted, who would never learn to work "from a Divine Principle, from the new Nature received, that is to say from Life." He "labours and toils all Night, and catcheth nothing." A national Presbyterian system might pardonably keep a visible church going even while admitting that most members caught nothing, but in order to perpetuate these American institutions, a considerable portion of the recruits had annually to demonstrate that they did work out of a divine principle, that they were not luxuriously crossing the river with the help of Vain-Hope. Because there had proved to be so many difficulties about detecting visible, let alone indubitable, saints, the easiest solution would have been to give over trying; but for better or worse, New England was what the founders had made it, and there was bound to be a point beyond which preparation, or venturing upon a trial, simply could not be pressed. There had to be some technique which, though it might make copious allowance for the guile of hypocrites, could still be confident of its grounds for discrimination. Unless such a technique did truly exist, congregations could no longer be urged to venture upon the second sacrament; without it, the baptized would live in perpetual doubt, amid increasing doubt, as to whether the proper qualification ever could be ascertained.

The literature of the 1690's shows the skepticism becoming endemic. The collapse of the Union, curiously enough, accentuated it: here, all had supposed, was the great chance for the colonies to rejoin the main stream not only of the British empire but of English theology and religious life; with the disruption, New England was thrown back upon itself, upon its narrow foundations, upon its inability to conceive of issues outside the rigid framework of a federal jeremiad. Had the Union stood, New England might have become a third force, equal in prestige with English Presbyterianism and Independency; but when the project failed, it was reduced to a mere frontier post, its doctrines and its history of no use to any but itself. For the next generation it would have to pick up such crumbs as, in Cotton Mather's revealing phrase, "straggled over the Atlantic."

Hooker and Shepard had searched the dark places of the soul with surgical skill, yet to the simplest of their listeners they imparted enough of that "particular certainty" which meant the life of their polity. Preachers in the 1690's had accumulated a more varied knowledge of the intricacies of the psyche: Cotton Mather's *Diary* is perhaps the fullest confessional any man ever recorded, especially as so little of it is, like Pepys's or Sewall's, unconscious; Willard was a tender doctor of melancholia, as in his *Spiritual Desertions Discovered and Remedied* in 1699 and *A Remedy Against Despair* in 1700. But as the decade wore on, such expert analyses excited

not particular certainties but confusion and distress. In the splurge of renewal, the sharp line between preparation or hypocrisy and genuine conversion became blurred, and renewers found themselves, the day after, once
more in the dark. Hence thousands preferred to remain transfixed, amid
perplexity, in their half-way status, expending their anxiety in repeated
commitments; they could not venture where more self-assurance was required. Willard consigned the barren fig tree to a heap of burning rubbish
—and in the next paragraph said that because God keeps the secret of
election to Himself, "therefore all our endeavours must needs be under
uncertainties, and the issue must be dubious to us." There seemed less and
less comfort in the right by inheritance: "If Godly Parents," said Cotton
Mather, "have many Children, it is very seldome seen that All of them
do prove Ungodly; but it is very often seen, that some of them do so."
Furthermore, it was sufficiently obvious that persons who once gained admission because they put on a good enough show to qualify, although there
might be reason to doubt their sincerity, became immune to the federal
threat: "when the necessity of Confession, repentance and holy life is
pressed, they regard it not, if Christ's love to them be thus confirmed & the
pledges of their Salvation by Christ be thus given them."

Here was a dilemma: on the one hand, sinners should not profane the
Communion, but on the other, "the best that come into the Church have
done worse then we know of or then we can oblige them to confess publickly." The people objected when ministers exercised too great charity, but
rebelled against strict measures. Cotton Mather could never get over the
prodigious and astonishing scandals occasioned by many who made a more
than ordinary profession, and in the *Magnalia* compulsively held them up
to public scrutiny. More and more he was obliged to lament how difficult
it is "to open and explain, even to a common capacity, all those Narrows
& Difficulties that be in the way to Life." "The best of Gods people have
been deserted," crooned Willard, while Cotton was explaining that "all
Externals of Religion may be done by a man, that has no right Principles
of Religion within him." How then could a man approve himself, either to
his examiners or to himself?

Associations might be formed, and might encourage themselves to think
that they brought to New England all the advantages of Presbyterianism
without sacrificing the virtues and guarantees of the covenant; but still
they confronted the seemingly insoluble antinomy of the Congregational
sacrament: unless more men were persuaded to take the Lord's Supper, the
churches would decay; but those who took it without assurance would be
undone "Totally, Finally, and very Terribly." Hypocrites, as the awesome
phrase had it, "eat and drink damnation unto themselves," and those who
approach the table unworthily "do but provoke Him to sanctify Himself in
terrible plagues upon them"—by which their saintly comrades also suffer.
For the founders, a world in which hypocrites would certainly be burned
as rubbish but in which we ourselves would never be entirely certain we

were not hypocritical conveyed a sense of high adventure that is the heart of the Protestant experiment; in the *élan* of it, they had built churches out of those whose sanctity was strong enough for the society to lay a wager upon. But to found churches in that spirit was one thing; to keep them going on a gamble became increasingly difficult, even enervating, when the demand for supplying a procession of communicants had become a constant social necessity. It was all very well for Cotton Mather to exhort, "Do not think now to mock the God of Heaven, by something that Looks like a Renewal of your baptismal Covenant, without seeking the Supper of the Lord"; even as he said this, he had also to declaim, "unworthy partaking at the Supper of the Lord hath been the procuring cause of Sickness and death among us." Max Weber contends that the Protestant ethic became an engine for the creation of the concept of "personality"; here in New England was an ethic presupposing a decision which presented personality with a choice that might well make it, but seemed more likely to break it.

The ultimate sacrament had, of course, been an ordeal for the founders, but men like Hooker and Winthrop took it in stride. In 1690, knowing himself on the verge of a new era, full of trepidation as to how his society might manage without the strong arm of a federated magistrate, Cotton Mather foresaw the blank wall at the end of a long vista of aids and devices: "It is a sin to come unworthily to, but it is also a sin to stay unworthily from, that Blessed Ordinance." While the masses stood in dismay, or expiated their sense of guilt by renewing their covenant and then frantically renewing their renewal, the old-line communicants were passing away. In the first years of the new charter, congregations were fairly successfully held up to strength, but the "church" shrank, and lay elders disappeared. The holy remnant of the righteous, without which no nation was ever saved or ever would be saved, but without which a covenanted nation would be plunged into inconceivable disaster, dwindled to so meager a proportion as to constitute a portent of almost certain destruction. "Lord," prayed Samuel Willard, "lead me through this Labyrinth."

CHAPTER XV

CONTENTION

FLEEING
in 1661 from England to the paternal study, In-
crease Mather was overjoyed to find his beloved brother Eleazar paying a
rare (because hazardous) visit "from a Remote place where he was now
Stationed in the country." The next year Solomon Stoddard was graduated from Harvard College; in 1669 he succeeded Eleazar—and Northampton was indeed remote, as far from Boston as Kansas City today.
Yet during the 1690's every thought uttered by members of the Cambridge Association on the questions of baptismal obligation, qualification
for Communion, the United Brethren, or the authority of associations, as
well as virtually every sentence of the *Magnalia*, was silently conditioned
by an uneasy consciousness of this man in his remoteness. What I have so
far described as the effort to salvage the covenant appears on the record;
within that record a secret is concealed: the Association was formed in fear
and trembling lest Solomon Stoddard should speak, but it was prevented
from attacking him lest it publicly jeopardize the pretense of New England's unity. In every Boston imprint, his is the invisible, uninvited, and
haunting presence.

In 1692, the year of witchcraft and of the debacle of the Union, Benjamin Colman took his degree. So astute a youth would have heard at least
whispers about Stoddard's frontier. In 1695, completing his advanced
studies, he went to England, and there prospered in the society of those
whom Independents denounced as Arminians. He conducted a sentimental flirtation with a minor poetess, providentially named Elizabeth Singer,
learned the best of manners, and lived with Sir Henry Ashurst near Oxford. The way is long from Oxford to Northampton, as far as from the
High Street to Main Street, but the two stations had one thing in common: they were outside the dominion of the Cambridge Association, and
in them two of the best minds of New England (if for the moment we
disregard the recluse of Chebacco Parish) could think other thoughts than
those suggested by Increase Mather.

Advocates of the Half-Way Covenant gave their sacred pledge that it
was no innovation, that it would never open the Lord's Supper to unsuitable persons or permit them to vote for officers. In that direction, said
Mitchell, lay "such a piece of ruining confusion" as would become Anabaptism; Oakes saw danger in an opposite quarter and warned against turning

"Councils and Synods into Clases and Provincial Assemblies," which would result in such "laxeness in Admission of Members to Communions as is pleaded for and practised by many Presbyterians." Scylla and Charybdis could be avoided if mere half-way members were resolutely barred from the Communion—even, declared the younger Shepard, "though they bounce at the door." On that understanding, Increase Mather came over to the Covenant—and thereafter was prevented from ever again changing his mind. He was obliged to hold fast this citadel, even while engaged with might and main in devising formulae whereby associations might exercise consociational powers, or by which baptized children might be induced to bounce.

Eleazar, settled at Northampton in 1659, was Increase's main support in his fight against the Synod; however, in the town itself, the usual situation was reversed, and the people were advocates. Eleazar held them off until the spring of 1669, when they voted for the measure in his despite; on July 24 he died, leaving his widow Esther, daughter of John Warham of Windsor, with three children and an estate of £524. While hunting for a successor, the church took no further action; in New England, there already existed an economical method for meeting this situation: leaving the young widow in the parsonage, the town picked an unmarried candidate, and let nature take its course. Solomon Stoddard came to demonstrate his prowess, and remained to marry Esther, on March 18, 1670. (Thereafter the Mathers must call him, even while hating and fearing him, "brother.") Esther bore him twelve children and outlived him by seven years; in her old age, although "lame of the Sciatica," she kept spinning "at the Linen-wheel" until she followed him in 1736, aged ninety-two.

Even while Stoddard was being tested, the town presented to the General Court the petition in favor of the Third Church of Boston which precipitated revolution among the Deputies. Ordained in 1672, Stoddard immediately put the Half-Way Covenant into effect: two forms were prepared, one "to be used in the admission of members unto state of education," whose children were baptized upon their owning the covenant; the other for admission "of members into full communion." Over a hundred promptly took up the Half-Way Covenant, and for five years Stoddard dutifully kept the customary double-entry ledger. Then, in 1677, without warning, without so much as a by-your-leave, least of all from Increase Mather, he closed the separate account of baptisms. Thereafter—secure in his Congregational autonomy but still more in his frontier remoteness—he baptized every adult who assented to the articles of faith, and admitted him to the Supper. He treated the congregation and virtually the whole town (there were still a few resolute sinners) as the church; at one stroke he cut his way through the maze of the covenants by identifying the church not with a society of saints but with the town meeting—where he himself was dictator. At first he could not carry all the people with him: there were times when he "knew not what to do with them," when the heat of their contention "was raised to such a degree that it came to hard blows"; but he soon won the title of "Pope" by forcing his will upon them. In his last years they were with him to a man.

He came of a stock that knew how to govern. His father, Anthony Stoddard, was the richest of pioneer merchants; his mother, Mary Downing, was niece of Governor Winthrop and sister to that accomplished politician who gives his name to Downing Street. At his commencement, he maintained the affirmative of "Utrum Deus puniat peccata necessitate naturae," and for three years thereafter was librarian of the College, although he appears to have spent two of them in the Barbados because of poor health. Northampton's committee of three made the long trek across Massachusetts to inspect the roster of unemployed Harvard graduates, but had no difficulty in selecting. They were the sort of men with whom Stoddard could work: Elder John Strong and William Clarke had come with the Great Migration, while Medad Pomeroy—who spelled himself as he was pronounced, "Pumry"—was born in Windsor, started life as a blacksmith, but was already well along the road to wealth, being a merchant, town officer, associate justice of the county court, and, after 1684, owner of the local monopoly on the sale of wine. At the moment they reached Boston, Stoddard was about to sail for England: this speaks volumes for his character, since few New Englanders were then deliberately putting their heads into the mouth of the Clarendon Code; rather, like Increase Mather, they were streaming back to colonial security. Dr. Williams lost an able lieutenant when Solomon Stoddard turned his face to the west.

Northampton was no place for a delicate scholar: Eleazar had been lucky to last ten years. Stoddard made it a fortress and then a throne; after 1700 he dominated the Connecticut Valley down to New Haven. Among the United Brethren, Increase appeared "the foremost American Puritan," but the English are not always informed about domestic American situations; at home, Mather's hegemony was already disputed by Stoddard, and within a decade leadership was divided between them. Even Indians went in awe of Northampton's Pope: during Queen Anne's War, as he paced in meditation by "Dewey's Hole"—where his grandson was also to exercise an inherited genius for rapt cogitation—he was ambushed; a Frenchman took aim, but an Indian knocked the gun down, saying that they must not affront the Englishman's God.

Much of his story is that of any country parson's—or of such a rare one as was able to rule his people—and must be basically similar to John Wise's. The town voted him a salary of £100, increased it, and gave him twenty acres; for twelve years he lived in Esther's house before he got around to building. Children came regularly, as did the "meazels." He was a partner with Joseph Parsons in running the sawmill, but later sold out and thereafter denounced ministers who diverted their holy thoughts into business. He had the usual difficulties about collecting his wages, but did better than most. He took the lead in civic enterprises—chiefly because of him, the province built a road to Boston wide enough for wheeled vehicles. Valley air agreed with his once frail health, and for fifty-nine years he missed no Sabbath or lecture except when on his journey to Boston.

> *He preach'd with strength of Voice and Memory,*
> *Near Sixty Years, and not a Note at's Eye.*

A servant in Boston cheated his master and brought the payment to Stoddard, who sent it up to town with the command, "I doubt not but you will be ready to passe by his offence & beg forgiveness of his sin from God." Many a son of Harvard was wrecked, once he got out of the calm of the Yard into the turmoil of a town, over the "seating arrangements"; but the Northampton committee charged with that ticklish mission, Elder Strong, Joseph Hawley, and Elder Clap, desired "Mr. Stoddard to assist 'em in said work," and nobody uttered a peep. Five of his daughters married parsons—one of them the widower William Williams at Hatfield, and another (named Esther for her mother) Timothy Edwards at East Windsor, to whom she bore ten tall daughters and one pale son, whom they named Jonathan. At his death in 1729, Stoddard's estate was inventoried at £1,126 exclusive of his library of 462 volumes and 491 pamphlets; it included ten knives and nine forks.

These local successes, however, do not explain why Timothy Dwight, grandson of his grandson, who knew the inner history of the Valley as none of us shall ever know it, said that Stoddard "possessed, probably, more influence than any other Clergyman in the province, during a period of thirty years." This is a large claim, for those thirty years (the first three decades of the century) were also the last of the Mathers' existence. Stoddard was on the frontier; when accepting their call, he told the church that "without eyeing that power and grace which God has treasured up in Jesus Christ, it were altogether vain for me to attempt such an undertaking," and proposed "that light, and peace, and the power of religion may be continued in this plantation." He brought the light and power, but the enemy no peace. He was the first to get wind of Philip's conspiracy, and wrote warnings to Boston which were not heeded in time. In 1676 the magistrates contemplated abandoning the Valley, only to receive a stinging rebuke from Stoddard: "we dare not entertain any thoughts of deserting this plantation." After the war, he demanded (and received) £20 for personal losses, since it would "not answer my occasions to have it paid little by little out of the rates of the town." Indians may have reverenced him, but he did not repay the compliment; the autumn before the Deerfield massacre (in which his stepdaughter perished) he argued with Governor Dudley to train big dogs for hunting down the vermin. Of course, did the Indians "manage their warr fairly after the manner of other nations," this would be brutality, but "they are to be looked upon as theives & murderers, they doe acts of hostility, without proclaiming war . . . they act like wolves & are to be dealt withall as wolves." Stoddard adjusted his conscience to a world where atrocity was met with atrocity; he became a power because he spoke for the Valley, in a forthright, plain style such as a neurotic Cotton Mather could never emulate.

This scion of Boston's merchant aristocracy, grandnephew to John Winthrop, asked "brother" Increase in 1685 to write an epistle for his manuscript, explaining, "I live in a remote corner & am much unknown." Increase, who was so misguided as to endorse Crisp, was stupid enough to refuse this service. Perhaps he was already annoyed because, even as he strove to utilize Philip's War to make himself the leader of reformation, Stoddard was writing him that the cause of the country's affliction was "that intolerable pride in clothes and hair; the toleration of so many taverns especially in Boston, and suffering home dwellers to lie tippling in them." It was one thing for Boston's foremost citizen to summon the colony to repentance, but another for a Valley parson to put the blame upon Boston. Nor did it help when Stoddard learned the next year that in the capital existed a Baptist church—which Increase had striven to suppress—and informed his exasperated brother, "I fear it will be a meanes to fill that Town, which is allready full of unstable persons, with error."

This man was a personality:

> *His venerable Looks let us descry*
> *He taller was than mean or common size,*
> *Of lovely Look, with majesty in's Eyes.*
> *From Nature's Gate he walk'd like King's on Earth*
> *There's scarce such Presence seen 'mongst human breath.*

At the Synod of 1679 a venerable delegate from Medway, Mr. Wheelock, said it was unjust that ministers should not be "rated" for taxation; Stoddard became, according to Peter Thacher, "high" and called Wheelock a liar. The next day, poor Wheelock apologized: "Mr. Stodder did something tho' very little" by him. The index to Stoddard's position in the community is that every year, at commencement time, he used his road to Boston, always delivered the public lecture on Thursday and sometimes the election sermon. In 1707, he spoke *plainly* (Samuel Sewall's italics) "in Several Articles against Superstition," and "against excess in Commencem't entertainments"; that night he stormed into Sewall's house, dragging along Governor Dudley, and roundly told the good judge that he as a magistrate should restrain sinful profusions in Cambridge. Their friendship stood such strains; year after year, Sewall sent back with him for Madame Stoddard a piece of "Commencement Cake," or two pounds of "Reasons" and almonds "in a paper bag," or "two half pounds of Chockalat." In 1717 a bereaved Sewall was "refreshed" by a letter from Northampton: "I soked it in Tears at reading." In 1721 Stoddard had to give over his journeys, but wrote Sewall he was still a "Well-Willer" to his Boston friends. In 1728 Sewall learned "that although you continue your Ministerial Labours on the Sabbath and Lecture, which is wonderfull, yet

now it is with much pain; and you hardly expect to live out the winter";
let Stoddard reflect on "the unparalleled constancy of Serviceableness,
which God has honoured you with, and the Blessings granted you in the
Serviceableness of your Children and Grandchildren." (Grandson Jonathan Edwards was now his colleague.) When the time comes, Sewall continued, "I hope you will be enabled joyfully to pronounce Simeon's Nunc
dimittis. 'Tis more accurately expressed in the Greek, than in our Translation. I pray you turn to it, for I cannot tell how to write it." But even for
old men, especially old Puritans, there were gratifications: Sewall reported
the death of his doctor and optimistically added, "I have buried very many
noble Physicians."

These invasions of the capital show that Stoddard was more than a
country parson. (We have no evidence that John Wise ever put in an appearance.) Upon Stoddard's death, Colman said, "Both Ministers and
People receiv'd his annual Visits with a peculiar Reverence and Pleasure,"
and Joseph Nash claimed that the Boston clergy lit their candles from his
flame:

> He much a Primate and a Prince among
> The Learn'd, who joy'd to hear his annual Song.

However, these estimates were penned when the tumult had subsided; for
many years after 1677, those who lighted their candles from Increase
Mather's torch were less respectful: but because Stoddard was so mighty
a figure, they had to be cautious. The Boston Weekly News-Letter of February 20, 1729, said that Stoddard was "well vers'd in the religious Controversies that relate either to Points of Doctrine or Church-Government,
and was himself a ready and smart Disputant, a wise and judicious Casuist."
Increase was then only six years dead, and Cotton but twelve months: it
was hardly fitting to note that upon them Stoddard had sharpened his disputant's claws and his casuist's teeth.

In 1677 Increase Mather received intelligence from the Valley, and, in
the roundabout manner already imposed upon the election orator, indicated that something was wrong: naming no names, because his auditors
knew the name, he piously hoped that no teachers in Israel espoused "loose,
Large Principles here, Designing to bring all Persons to the Lords Supper,
who have an historical Faith, and are not Scandalous in Life, altho' they
never had Experience of a work of Regeneration." Such a practice "would
corrupt Churches and ruin all in a little time." And then—having not yet
tested the metal of his opponent—he reminded the General Court "what
our Fathers have Taught concerning that matter," and assured them that
whoever betrays the principles "which they did with much cost and pains,
dig out of the Rich veins of the Scripture" is automatically reprehensible.
At this moment may be dated the opening of that vein into which the
Mathers henceforth, and much of New England after them, were assiduously to dig: not that of Scripture but of ancestral precedent.

Increase Mather was master of the Synod of 1679; he could not endure the affront of a Stoddard, who unrepentantly came from the Valley with two years of heresy behind him. He challenged Stoddard to debate, with Urian Oakes as moderator; Oakes was a cautious man, and as soon as the dispute grew hot, he managed to have it deferred, "& at present It was Eased." In the eyes of the world Mather came off victor, for he wrote the *Confession of Faith;* but Stoddard was on the drafting committee, and managed one verbal revision: Mather proposed that persons aspiring to the Supper should offer a relation of the work of the spirit; the committee changed his clause to read, "a personal and publick profession of their Faith and Repentance." Mather thought this still meant authentic profession; Stoddard, taking it to signify simply owning the Covenant, went back to Northampton unperturbed and ever thereafter contended, "I voted with the Rest, and am of the same judgment still." Years later, Increase cut a sorry figure as he insisted that Stoddard's version of "the blotting out" of the clause was wrong, and that the Synod clearly intended a work of grace to be required. Stoddard remained unconvinced.

In March of 1681 John Russell of Hadley sent to Increase Mather what must have been a galling letter: "Our good Brother Stoddard hath bin strenuously promoting his position concerning that right which persons sound in doctrine of faith, & of (as he calls it) a holy Conversation, haue to full Communion." Sparing Increase's feelings, Russell said it was now time for those "who were of the Synod in 62" to prove that their propositions really would secure the churches from pollution; as for himself, he did "everyday sorrowfully increase in satisfaction" that the Half-Way Covenant "doth tend in the end of the worke (how good soever the end of the workers was) to shake & undermine the fundamentall doctrine & practise of the Congregational way." But since Increase, by going over, had made himself the arch-apologist, then if anything were "doable," Russell could not resist saying, "I take the great care of that matter . . . to be upon your selfe."

And there the matter rested, for the charter was going down and Increase Mather was distracted; there already had been more controversy over the Covenant than the society could stand, and another split over anything fundamental would wreck it. For the moment, all Increase could do was to receive Stoddard's request about his manuscript—"it may be a few words from your selfe may gain it the greater acceptance"—and refuse to write a preface. But in 1687 even he could no longer bully the press, and Stoddard's *The Safety of Appearing at the Day of Judgment* was published. It was widely read and admired; a second edition appeared in 1729, and it was to be a powerful influence in the Great Awakening. As Colman was to say in his funeral oration, "among the worthy Remains of his Learning and Ministry in Print, the Mantle he has left us, his Safety of appearing in the Righteousness of Christ outshines all the rest." Stoddard's book is one of the ten or dozen key works of the period, and comes closer than any except Bulkeley's and Wise's to being what we might term "original." It is the only speculative treatise since the founders and before Edwards that makes any constructive contribution to New England theology.

Or rather, I should say not constructive but destructive: it is virtually the only work which, since the Synod of 1637, endeavors to call a halt to those tendencies that (in the perspective of time) we would call rationalistic. To modern eyes, *The Safety of Appearing* is difficult to interpret (as it was not for Increase Mather) because on the surface it appears to accept completely the reformulation of Protestant theology which, commenced by Ames and Preston, had become the distinctive badge of New England and which still purported to guide theologians amid the intricacies of the full covenant and the Half-Way Covenant. The great and magnificent discovery of the federalists, in old England or in New England, was what Willard summarized: "we conceive of God's decrees in a rational way . . . because else we could entertain no conceptions at all about this glorious mystery." Step by step, from Genesis through Hosea, federal theologians had interpreted the unfolding of the covenant, finding it progressively conforming to the canons of reason, so that at last in the culmination of God's agreement with man, through the office undertaken (also in a covenant) by the Savior, man could rationally consent to avail himself of Christ's performance: reason and arbitrary decree here coincided. Stoddard rejected this traditional exegesis; he went back to a bare, naked interpretation of the covenant with Abraham as being an imposition of command (such as he himself imposed on Northampton), and declared it no rational contract of a *quid pro quo*, but an absolute fiat.

Stoddard's strategy was to let the Boston federalists have all that they argued for (they, let us remember, had enlarged preparation into a claim upon the covenant, admitted hypocrisy to be an adequate qualification for external membership, and had received unregenerate children upon a mere parental "owning"). It has, he said, been God's manner to deal with men "in the way of a Covenant, to that end that men may be encouraged to walk in the right way to the obtaining of good." Yes, he agreed, "God engages himself by promise to give believers eternal life": He is bound by the covenant, and we do indeed know upon what terms salvation may be had. But in 1687 he strove to remind his colleagues (as had Anne Hutchinson in 1637) that the ability of man to conform to such terms depends not at all upon rational inducement: "The only reason why God sets his love on one man and not upon another is, because he pleases." All federalist rationalizations (especially those of apologists for the Half-Way Covenant) were wrecked upon this rock: "The will of God is sufficient to move him to choose one and refuse another." The covenant does not flow from the mercy of God, "but he exercises grace freely from His Sovereign Will and Pleasure." He would still be infinite in mercy, despite all forms of the covenant, "if it had pleased him never to exercise any."

It requires scrupulous caution to apply to one age the terms of another, but Stoddard may be described as an anti-rationalist—if we remember that the rationalism to which he objected was that tentative variety into which the Mathers and proponents of the Half-Way Covenant unwittingly drifted. Stoddard did not yet realize, as his grandson was to appreciate, that the enemy was a cosmic rationality, an identification of God with the laws of motion which, in that very year, Isaac Newton was making public. All Stoddard knew was that half-way members were not being converted. So he announced his theme: there is a persuasion arising from "rational conviction" which recognizes that other ways are frivolous, which intellectually concedes that only through grace is acceptance to be obtained—"but this perswasion is not sufficient to encourage a soul to venture himself on Jesus Christ." Thus advocates of the Half-Way Covenant (who also found virtues in preparation and in hypocrisy) magnified "common illuminations," forgetting that these cannot constitute a human claim upon the divine. Yes, the means are to be attended and preaching is a means—"periwigs are unlawful"—"but the way of reconciliation does exceed the discovery of reason." The light of nature—such light as had crept into the logic of the half-wayers—cannot confine the free and sovereign decrees of Jehovah.

The original federalists, whom New England revered, extracted from the doctrine of the covenant a method for provisionally determining the identity of saints: it all depended on their willingness. Ergo, willing saints could be distinguished from the unenabled, and churches should be limited to those assured (more or less) of salvation. But Stoddard—rigidly consistent logician that he was—employed an opposite reasoning: because the Covenant of Grace is dispensed by an inscrutable and unpredictable divinity, because it is *not* reasonable, it is open (in this life, and especially on the American frontier) to all men, since no man can tell for sure who is a saint. Individuals may attain inward assurance, but there is no objective standard. Conversion is a reality, but it "cannot be made evident by experience to the world, because the world cannot certainly know." An inevitable but curious corollary follows: all should strive to be the best they can. "The meer pleasure of God does decide it, who shall be the objects of his love and his hatred. You have no reason to be discouraged because you can find no reason in your self of God's love." That a child of godly parents will become regenerate is mere probability: "the free will of God is the only thing that does determine it; and therefore you have sufficient ground of encouragement to accept the offer of salvation." Why should the dictator of Northampton refuse anybody because of some fanciful qualification erected by a Massachusetts Synod—especially when, on the record, that qualification had become too complicated to be administered?

Remembering that Stoddard put his case within the conventional language of the covenant, and paid to it such obeisance that the Mathers could never quite accuse him of doctrinal heresy, we may then appreciate his role in New England's development: he used traditional logic to turn away from calculation and hereditary interest, from the pleasure-pain arithmetic of the jeremiads (he preached, therefore, extremely vigorous and effective jeremiads!) to sheer zeal and piety. He did this by reminding the New England mind that its theology was built upon the *Deus Absconditus*, upon Him who graciously utilizes the covenant to execute His unpredictable will. Yet the conclusion of Stoddard's treatise was dictated not only by theology but by the necessities of the society: as his title declared, all men should feel "safe" in coming to the Lord's Supper. "We may safely venture our souls upon his word. God assures us that it is so, and gives a large account in his word how the thing is brought about." A Christian may not know all the subtleties of theology, but he need not worry: he knows what "will satisfy his heart that it is sufficient: namely, that God gives this testimony to it, and invites him to venture upon it."

Had there been time and leisure in this American society for "pure" theology, the issue between the Mathers and Stoddard might have been debated. The former might have had to stand and deliver—in which case, our intellectual history would have gained in precision. For in the background of Stoddard's thought there looms a stark conception of irrational sovereignty which goes beyond anything previously entertained in New England, which recalls the ruthless pronouncements of Calvin himself, or perhaps those exaltations of the divine transcendence by which Arminius sought to establish morality upon arbitrary command. God has "absolute liberty," said Stoddard; He could have glorified Himself in man's ruin, and at no point should man listen "unto the cavils and pretences of reason." The most profound of questions was at stake, but neither the Mathers nor Stoddard were able to join the debate on intellectual grounds, for Stoddard's argument had an immediate, practical effect. Because the will of God cannot be translated into specific qualifications, he called upon every inhabitant of the town to venture upon the Lord's Supper: "The call is to every one that will . . . So that they that are at a loss about their present condition, have free liberty to come as well as others." God requires no more than effort; "There is no bar in any man's way." At this point, the Mathers and most of the clergy of eastern New England, as well as some westerners, like Russell, foresaw the end of the New England Way, and braced themselves for the struggle. Hence Increase Mather would write no preface to Stoddard's book, and bided his time against the conflict he feared, even while he knew that it must come.

So many pages in *The Safety of Appearing* sound like conventional doctrine that one wonders how, had the controversy centered on abstract propositions, the parties would have defined their real differences. But in the actual situation, the fact that loomed largest was Stoddard's indubitable success in bringing his community to such a general repentance as the jeremiads called for; having scrapped the Half-Way Covenant, he could achieve in 1679 and 1683 the first of what he called his "harvests," during which "the bigger Part of the Young People in the Town, seemed to be mainly concerned for their eternal Salvation." Boston could show nothing like them. Hence Stoddard threw down a gauge of battle in the prefatory address to his town (in the space where Increase would not write):

I have made it my business to gain Souls to Christ, and build them up in Faith and Holiness; principally insisting upon such things as have reached the heart of Religion . . . I meddle not with those false Doctrines that have been invented by men, in opposition to this truth: the Lord hath been pleased to keep these Churches sound in the Faith, and does not yet lay a necessity upon his Ministers to spend their time in the confutation of such erronious opinions; but I have made it my work to establish your hearts in this Truth.

At Stoddard's funeral, his eldest son-in-law, William Williams, said that at the time he had accepted the call to Northampton (which would have been when he was marrying Esther), the work of grace made so deep an "experimental" impression upon him "that he always remembr'd it, and often spake of it." *The Safety of Appearing,* in its grappling with the covenant theology, retains the freshness of this experience; so wonderful was Stoddard's sense of it that he was prepared to admit to the Communion not only those who made the relation of a similar work, but all those who by their good conversation were yet susceptible of it, in the hope that this sacrament might become for them an "effectual means."

While the charter fell, while Andros ruled, while Increase negotiated in London, there was none to prevent Northampton's going Stoddard's way. Cotton Mather's *Companion for Communicants* in 1690, asserting that only believers should enjoy the Supper, begged the reader's patience to let him "Contend earnestly against a sort of men, who tell us, That a bare Dogmatical or Historical Faith . . . together with a submission to the Government of the Visible Church will entitle a man to Sacraments!" He dared not identify this sort of men more closely, but he could deny emphatically that the Supper is "a converting Ordinance," and try to work on Stoddard's nobler nature by crying that, should we ever forget the old Protestant belief in regeneration as the necessary prerequisite, we shall "without a meer Fancy, over-hear the dolefull, wofull shout, which was audibly sounded from Heaven to Rome, when the Church-Doors began to grow as wide as Hell Gates themselves." Two years later, in the glow of great expectations aroused by the United Brethren, Cotton suddenly minimized the differences of New England, since Stoddard as well as he required some sort of preliminary action from candidates: "Behold then, a Temper, wherein we may, as hitherto we do, in this thing Unite!" But in 1693 he served notice that if Stoddard ever published anything, "we would as Publickly animadvert upon it."

The Mathers were in the toils: by enthusiastically supporting the United Brethren, by making that name a domestic slogan and flaunting it even after the structure had been shattered in London, they did their utmost to close the gap between Congregationalism and Presbyterianism. But now rumors of still worse developments came from the Valley: Stoddard not only opened wide the Supper on the theory that it was a converting ordinance, but was denying that churches were founded upon covenant; he was openly advocating Presbyterianism. With what face could the Mathers ever "animadvert" upon him should he appear in print as champion of the cause of Howe and of Dr. Williams? In the election sermon of 1696 Cotton revealed the depths of his insecurity by loudly proclaiming that those who upheld the first principles of New England were now being called apostates.

Meanwhile the Mathers had another and a growing worry closer to home. Increase's title, Rector of Harvard College, added to his dignity abroad; that he was a non-resident executive, who looked after the College only in such moments as he could spare from the Second Church and from his innumerable ecclesiastical concerns, did not detract from his stature. The College, after 1686, was in the hands of two able tutors, William Brattle and John Leverett, the latter a grandson of the great governor of Philip's War. It was Increase's responsibility to secure a charter for the institution as well as for the colony, since there was doubt about its legal status after the old charter was annulled: people were saying that the calf had died in the cow's belly. But he was exercised not alone over the constitutional footing: there was a terrible dread lest a royal charter should place the College under the control of royal governors, and so transform it someday into an Anglican school. While he strove to persuade the English government that it should provide by-laws for "an Able and Faithful Ministry," Increase also urged that the College "be Confirmed in such Hands as would promote virtue and learning"—meaning Congregational hands. Across the sea, Cotton stood up to exhort colonial authorities to support the "Arts"; let them go well, he said, and all things else will go accordingly.

Significantly enough, in these same years Cotton also began to utter his peculiar brand of ominous warnings against the spread among "our unwary Children" of an inclination toward those remainders of Popery "which the first Reformers were hindered from sweeping out of the English Nation." Andros was gone, but King's Chapel remained, and what was worse, attracted not only sightseers but converts. Thus there was all the greater urgency, since Increase had failed to get an authorization for the College, that he get one from the provincial legislature, and get it quick while he still had Phips and the Councillors he had chosen. So Increase jammed through a charter which pointedly omitted overseers or any visitorial power, for which the grateful College voted him the degree of Doctor of Divinity.

For the moment it looked as though all were well; the College made a strong team, especially in 1693 when Thomas Brattle joined the tutors as Treasurer. They and the Mathers stood firmly together in the witchcraft crisis, and no one can locate exactly when the break came. But in retrospect, it seems that a split was inevitable. Leverett and the Brattles admired what soon became widely celebrated as an "enlarged Catholic Spirit." Of course, the Mathers also, having been conspicuously converted to the principle of

toleration and having extended themselves in support of the United Brethren, had become as "Catholic" as possible, but these younger men entertained notions still more "enlarged." During Increase's absence, Brattle
substituted the logic of Descartes for the crumbling system of Ramus,
and a graduate of 1687 was later to say that Brattle and Leverett showed
the greatest hospitality to Anglican authors, especially to latitudinarian
theologians. And furthermore, instead of bringing peace, the new charter
brought contention, for the party of Elisha Cooke, smarting over what
they considered Increase Mather's concessions in London, began to pass
votes requiring him to reside at the College and devote his full time to it.
This would in effect exile him, remove him from that center of power
and propaganda which was the North Church. He refused, and a bitter
fight commenced.

If he had supposed that the Crown would let him have his college without supervision by the Crown's appointee, he was sadly mistaken. The
charter was disallowed; for the next eight years he and his son struggled
through draft after draft to get an establishment, agitating furiously by
every means they could muster to force the legislature to send Increase
back to England for negotiations on the highest level, and all the time resisting the demand that Increase pack up and go to Cambridge. The first
sign of real division in Harvard's ranks appears in 1696, when the Mathers
and their clerical colleagues protested, without being joined by the names
of Leverett and Brattle, against a legislative charter which provided for
visitation by the Governor and Council. At the ordination of Wadsworth
(their student and known to be their friend), Increase, who in the Council
had just exhibited an unprecedented "height of rage," spoke "notably" of
some young men who apostatized from New England principles, "contrary
to the Light of their education." He submitted a new form of charter in
1697; William Brattle was resigning his tutorship to become minister in
Cambridge (thus to be an even greater influence on the College) and
Leverett was turning to the study of law. Increase's nominations for the
Harvard Corporation did not include them, but the House of Representatives voted that John Leverett should be a member. In the midst of these
distractions (how he did it is a mystery of scholarship), Cotton Mather,
plugging away at his mighty *Magnalia*, at this moment completed his biography of Jonathan Mitchell, chief architect of the Half-Way Covenant; it
was ready for the press, and his father, at the height of his rage, sat down
on May 7 to dash off a preface for *Ecclesiastes*.

This remarkable document has been supposed, by students familiar only
with the eastern regions, to be directed solely against the tutors and their
friends. When William Brattle migrated from the hall to the church of
Cambridge, he preached his own ordination sermon (a shocking innovation, particularly as he should have shown proper respect by inviting Increase), but still worse, he induced his church to vote that the formal and
public relations of candidates might be dispensed with, that an examination

by the pastor and elders should suffice, and that the people would signify their assent by silence. This meant that, although yet in a mild form, the contagion of Stoddard was spreading. So Increase Mather's preface strikes in two directions (still observing, although barely, the convention of calling no one by name), both at Cambridge and at Northampton. It marks the point where the Mathers realized that the centrifugal forces of a society increasing in complexity, released and accelerated by the removal of the old charter and by divided political councils, were getting out of control. They fought hard, but their backs were against the wall and they could only lay about them on either side.

How the situation looked in Increase's view is shown by the fact that he commenced by attacking Stoddard, devoting most of his space to refuting him, and only then turned by natural progression to the College. Despite the state of his nerves, he tried to be temperate, although his tone probably reflects his dread of Stoddard's riposte. Unjustifiable severity, he told the churches, should not be used in admissions; candidates need not name the exact hour of their conversion, "such especially as have been advantaged with a religious education." But a full extreme of laxness is a damnable betrayal of the founders, of Mitchell, and of the country. Churches are absolutely obliged to inquire not alone into the knowledge and orthodoxy of those they receive, but into their spiritual estate. He could not pronounce Stoddard's name, but he indicated him clearly enough: "Above all, their notion is to be rejected, as a church-corrupting principle, who assert that the sacrament is a converting ordinance," for if it were, "then the most scandalous persons in the world—yea, heathen people—ought to have it administered unto them." This is dreadful "degeneracy from the reformation which we had attained unto." In a desperate and transparently specious effort to cover his flanks, Increase had the temerity to insist that Presbyterians concurred in these views, though his nerve so far failed him that he invoked only "some of those that are called Presbyterian," and concealed the weakness of this dodge by holding aloft the banner of the United Brethren—in whose name, deviation from the principles of Congregational fathers became demonstrably treason! Which brought him by a natural transition to the Church of Cambridge, to which he penned a little address that is a masterpiece of impotent rage expressed in circuitous irony. (There was obviously no reason for singling out Cambridge except Brattle's installation.) He reminded that body how five years before they had invited no less a person than himself, and so he could not but have a dear affection for them and hope that they "may be confirmed in those ways of the Lord which your fathers, and your selves too, have experienced so much of His presence in." He grimly told them that the Lord would require of him an accounting for his conduct toward the College, and he relied upon the church to help.

Then he turned to the College itself, without which, he declared, these churches cannot subsist: if it degenerates, we are indeed lost. "You that are tutors there, have a great advantage put into your hands (and I pray God give you wisdom to know it!) to prevent it." He told them in what was, under the circumstances, sheer insult that he had put them in office and that they should therefore behave as he commanded. They might see, in his son's biography, how Mitchell instructed students not only in tongues and arts but in things of the spirit; hence students should cultivate "the one thing necessary" in addition to knowledge: they should eschew Pelagian and Arminian principles, but not rest content with mere orthodoxy. Here was Increase's challenge: "If you degenerate from the 'order of the gospel' (as well as from the 'faith of the gospel') you will justly merit the name of apostates and of degenerate plants." Out on the frontier, Stoddard's neighbor at Westfield, Edward Taylor (who kept most of his thoughts to himself), grieved over the death of Samuel Hooker, and deciphered Mather's thinly veiled references:

> *Apostasy wherewith thou art thus driven*
> *Vnto ye tents of Presbyterianism*
> *(Which is refined Prelacy at best)*
> *Will not stay long here in her tents, & rest,*
> *But o're this Bridge will carry thee apace*
> *Into ye Realm of Prelates arch, ye place*
> *Where open Sinners vile vnmaskt indeed*
> *Are Welcom Guests (if they can say ye Creed)*
> *Vnto Christs Table.*

But neither Taylor's laments nor Mather's innuendoes had any effect on Pope Stoddard; one by one the towns of the Valley fell into line behind him, and as the fatal year of 1700 approached—which loomed portentously in the Mathers' Chiliastic calculations—his kingdom had become so firmly consolidated that he could take the field in open warfare.

After *Ecclesiastes* events moved, as they were bound to, very fast. Increase essayed charter after charter, while the patriot party forced residence upon him. He, Cotton, and six other ministers put through a bill in July 1699 which declared that none should be chosen to the Presidency or to the Corporation but those who declared their adherence to the principles of the founders. Lord Bellomont, supposing this provision directed against the Church of England, negated it; in his ignorance about New England factions, he did not comprehend that the real target was the Brattles, though he might have caught on had he noted that the Treasurer (Thomas Brattle) was excluded from the Corporation. By an adroit maneuver, wherein we detect the fine hand of Elisha Cooke, a temporary settlement was drawn up that left out the Brattles, but with it was coupled a request to Bellomont that he, and not Mather, obtain the King's consent. Mather's last hope being gone of ever again appearing at Whitehall as ambassador from this cave of the winds, he could do nothing but receive and, with the worst grace in the world, obey a peremptory order that he go to Cambridge.

John Leverett and the two Brattles were not the sort of men to sit idly by and let themselves be insulted. While Increase took the drowning of two students in the Charles to be a sign that ere long there might be no College at all, while he expanded his fears to the limits of creation and cried that in the glorious times promised to the church, "New England will be the wofullest place in all America, as some other parts of the World once famous for Religion, are now the dolefullest on the Earth, perfect Emblems and Pictures of Hell," while he made oblique references in similar rhetorical profusion to Stoddard, while he even achieved the distinction of informing the Anglican Bellomont that mortal disease fell upon the Corinthians because they approached the Table "after an unprepared manner"—while Increase thus wailed, the Brattles and Leverett met in January 1698 with the merchant John Mico and a few men of like-minded "Catholic" spirit (and of substance), and decided to found a church after their own instead of the founders' notions. Thomas Brattle contributed the land; upon further consultation the group unanimously agreed that the ideal choice for a minister would be Leverett's favorite student, the slender, delicate-voiced Benjamin Colman, who all this time had been imbibing the refinements of the Catholic temper in England. They also suggested that, since the plot deliberately contemplated "innovations," Colman might avoid trouble in Mather's Boston were he to secure ordination in London rather than face rejection by the local clergy. It was dead against a fundamental tenet of New England that a minister should be ordained by any other agency than his own congregation, but since Increase had become such a public advocate of the United Brethren, how could he object to an ordination administered by his friends the Presbyterians? On August 4, 1699, Colman was thus consecrated, and reached Boston on November 1. In a few days, the society published a *Manifesto* frankly declaring their intentions; the Matherian lions had been bearded in their own den.

It has become a cliché of historians that the innovations of the Brattle Street Church were not, after all, very radical, and that its importance in "liberalizing" the situation is easily exaggerated. This is true if we think ahead twenty or thirty years, in the course of which this church became an accepted member of the community, while its practices were silently imitated by others. In 1699 its proposals naturally seemed more momentous, not that they were in themselves so exceedingly sensational, but that when they were advanced, the black cloud of Stoddard was piling up on the horizon and Increase was being fought to a standstill at Harvard. This concatenation of events, especially when seen through Chiliastic eyes, could mean nothing less than an explosion into fragments of the once proudly unified New England society; it could foretend nothing less than that America was about to become hell on earth.

We approve and subscribe, said the *Manifesto*, *The Westminster Confession;* this was a disarming but honest statement, and there is no evidence that any of the Brattle Church promoters, although hospitable to latitudinarian writers and especially devoted to Archbishop Tillotson, ever entertained a single doctrinal dissent from the established creed. By no admission of their own—although William Brattle championed Descartes—did they ever become "Arminian"; and Colman was never to exhibit the slightest sign of being anything but a faithful Calvinist. Secondly, they spiked Increase Mather's guns by their stated intent to practice the true worship of God "conformably to the known practice of many of the Churches of the United Brethren in London." (Stoddard might have chuckled at this!) Then they announced their revolution: portions of Scripture would be read by the minister at his discretion, with or without comment (thus permitting what the Mathers called "dumb reading," which they considered Popish); baptism could not be refused "to *any* child," and, the administration being a ministerial act, all decisions would be left to Colman; "visible Sanctity" would be sufficient qualification for the Lord's Supper, and public relations could be dispensed with at the wish of the candidate; the pastor alone need examine him, silence of the brethren giving consent; the choice of minister was to be by election of the whole congregation, that is, by every baptized adult who contributed to the maintenance and not by communicants alone. A church should be founded upon mutual agreement, the *Manifesto* conceded, but it added insult to injury by deducing this necessity, not from Scripture or the first principles of New England, but from "the Law of Nature." This was a palpable hit, because in May Cotton Mather had mobilized the Cambridge Association to declare itself on *Thirty Important Cases* then bothering the country (such as usury, cards, dice, drinking healths), and had inserted some pointedly anti-Stoddardian decisions, such as that the church covenant is of divine inspiration even though, the Association added, it is also evident from "the Light of Nature." Taking a leaf from the Association's book, the undertakers of Brattle Street cheerfully declared themselves in favor of brotherly communion among the churches, and gracefully invited members of all other societies to communicate in Brattle Street as frequently as they wished!

Persons who estimate social complexity by, let us say, the example of a modern American Congress, with its factions and shifting alliances, would regard New England in 1700, could they behold it, as a haven of simplicity. These things are relative: if you started, as did New Englanders, from such a conception of unity as prevailed under the old charter (a period enhanced by the jeremiads into a veritable golden age), what happened between 1698 and 1701 would seem a convergence of devilish and disruptive forces beyond the ability of man to subdue. But the design in this carpet should be instructive to a student of American culture: it consists in the fact that during these years the society experienced simultaneously four separate crises, and that, though there are connections between the different developments, the one characteristic all had in common was a designation of the Mathers and the Cambridge Association as the foes of progress.

Even an abbreviated chronological sketch gives a sense of the rapidity with which blows were struck. In June 1698, just as the Council first rejected Increase's request that he go abroad, Cotton learned, through his spies, that "a sort of Saducee in this Town" had sent for publication to England a book full "of invented and notorious Lies" about the role of the Mathers in the witchcraft affair. "And now," said Cotton to himself, "I thought it, high Time for mee to look about mee." In July, the Mathers entered the lists to prevent the ordination of Simon Bradstreet at Charlestown because he had indicated adherence to Stoddard and William Brattle by calling the church covenant a human invention. For the first months of 1699, the situation simmered: no news of Calef's manuscript from London, no move from Stoddard, only rumors about a conspiracy in Brattle Street, while the Mathers' faction concentrated upon persuading Bellomont to accept their version of Harvard's charter. Within a month or two after Bellomont refused them, the *Manifesto* was out.

John Higginson, now the oldest minister in the colonies, was a son of the founder of Salem; Nicholas Noyes, despite his error at Salem, was almost as old and as much revered. In his exaltation of ancestors, Increase put a special halo around septuagenarians, and there can be no doubt that either he or Cotton persuaded these two to address, in December 1699, a letter to the "Manifesto Church" (as it was already called), expressing their shock and horror at its arrogant action, at the opening of the gates to promiscuous baptism, and above all at its advancing no other sanction for covenantal duties "besides the dictates of the law of nature." As for election of ministers by the baptized congregation, that surely will lead to chaos: "the females are certainly more than the males, and consequently the choice of ministers is put into their hands." Should this example be followed, every church in the land will be surrendered into the hands of non-communicants —who, Higginson and Noyes frankly admitted, are a majority! They accused the organizers of betraying not only the first principles of New England but also *The Heads of Agreement*.

Throughout this December, Increase Mather stood haughtily aloof; on the ninth, Samuel Sewall, who two years before had chastened himself by confessing the shame of witchcraft and who, although worried about Stoddard, did not need to wring his hands over Calef, received a visit from Colman and expostulated with him on the effrontery of certain expressions in the *Manifesto*. Sewall scored what he considered a hit by telling Colman that "Philomela" (the pen name of Colman's English enamorata) would have found out gentler words—"at which he smil'd." Sewall pressed upon Colman everything to which he objected and still more what he feared might follow; but to Sewall's eternal glory let it be recorded that as Colman was leaving, he brought himself to say: "if God should please by them to hold forth any Light that had not been seen or entertain'd before: I should be so far from envying it, that I would rejoice in it: which he was much affected with."

In areas where conscience was less refined, in those quarters which for long had served as targets of denunciation without having a chance to reply, a certain exultation sprang up over this conflict among the pundits, and upon the very door of the new building was found one morning a piece of verse which, full as it is of merely topical puns, conveys unmistakably the idea that some elements in the community found the whole solemn to-do highly comic:

> *Relations are Rattle with Brattle and Brattle,*
> *   Lord Bro'r mayn't command,*
> *But Mather and Mather had rather and rather*
> *   The good old way should stand.*
> *Saints Cotton and Hooker, Oh look down and look here*
> *   Where's Platform, Way and Keys? . . . .*
> *Our Merchants cum Mico do stand sacro vico*
> *   Our churches turn genteel,*
> *Our Parsons grow trim and trig with Wealth, Wine and Wig*
> *   And their heads are covered with meal.*

Not that this is great satirical verse—but the immense fact is that it was satirical at all. Five of the first twenty-six male communicants of Brattle Street were men of wealth—among them (let us remember his name) Thomas Banister.

Cotton Mather thought of the organizers as "Head-Strong Men . . . full of malignity to the Holy Wayes of our Churches." I suppose that as great a piece of dishonesty as any in his *Diary* is his attempt to consider them apart from Stoddard. On December 28, Increase and James Allen (of the First Church) addressed to "Mr. Colman" a nasty letter, telling him that would he lay aside the *Manifesto,* they might consider assisting in his installation, but otherwise they would not become guilty of condoning his "irregularities." Cotton Mather takes all the credit for bringing his father around, but the evidence (which is fragmentary) suggests that Stoughton and Sewall persuaded Willard, Danforth, and others of the local clergy that they should agree, so that ultimately both Mathers were obliged to come along. The forms of Christian fellowship were observed on January 31, 1700: Increase preached and Cotton prayed; Colman was installed, and peace might have been realized—if only there had not also been Harvard College, Stoddard, and Robert Calef.

As the spring wore on, two facts emerged: Elisha Cooke was perfecting his design to prevent Increase's mission to Europe, and Solomon Stoddard had definitely completed a manuscript which he was sending to London. The mainspring of Increase's action was fear of Stoddard, but there was no way he could move without breaking the truce established in Brattle Street. He characteristically took all challenges in stride, and in March 1700 published *The Order of the Gospel.* It was on the streets, said Cotton Mather, just before copies reached Boston of Stoddard's *The Doctrine of Instituted Churches,* and so could be said to have "anticipated it, with an Answer." But in Brattle Street, where it was politic to pretend that Stoddard did not exist, Mather's publication could be interpreted only as a stab in the back.

On July 4 (premonitory date!) Solomon Stoddard was in Boston on his annual visit, his book already circulating and Increase's anticipatory reply feeding the flames of Brattle Street's anger. He appeared before "a very great Assembly of Ministers," and Cotton Mather attacked him in the manner of a Cicero arraigning Catiline: "Among all the Attempts against the State of our Churches," he declaimed, "I know none more open, more daring or more explicit." Turning to the elders, "I beseech you Syrs, what you would be at! Your Attempts only furnish a profane Generation of People in the Countrey, with Cavils against the Churches . . . You cannot rationally imagine to attain any further Ends, but only to throw all into Confusion and Contention." There were some, he hinted, who were prepared to defend these positions—did he mean Colman?—but now that the master-traitor has appeared, they hold back: "for their Sake, Syrs, I do here make him an Offer of a Disputation; I say, I do offer him Disputation, when and where he shall please to appoint it." The insolent Pope scorned to debate with him whom the Quakers were already calling "the Colledge-Boy of New England," and the Mathers betook themselves, as of old, to the press.

Six days later, the General Court demanded that Increase go to Harvard or resign, and he, still smarting from Stoddard's contempt, could not surrender the College. He went to Cambridge, hated every moment, complained that the place was unhealthy, but stuck it out until October. Meanwhile, Cotton was, as usual—or more than usually—busy: he picked up an almost forgotten treatise by an obscure Presbyterian member of the United Brethren, John Quick's *The Young Man's Claim unto the Sacrament of the Lord's Supper,* which seemed to call, on Presbyterian grounds, for more of a qualification to admission than Stoddard any longer demanded, and in September published it with a preface which he and his father jointly wrote, but more importantly with an endorsement by old John Higginson and by the eighty-year-old William Hubbard, who back in 1676 had been Increase's major opponent. It was a calculated part of Cotton's tactics to turn back upon those "who most unjustly call themselves Presbyterians" the charge that they violated the standards of the United Brethren; wherefore they could be accused, without any sacrifice of the principle of accommodation, of betraying the witness "of many elderly Ministers, in the County of Essex."

At that moment, not only were hundreds of Stoddard's *The Doctrine of Instituted Churches* being sold (there was no authority any longer to prevent the sale), but the book was being reprinted. Worse soon followed: in November, "a Time of much Affliction in the Town, by malignant Colds, and Coughs," Cotton received news that Robert Calef's *More Wonders of the Invisible World: Or, The Wonders of the Invisible World, Display'd in Five Parts* ("wherein I am the cheef Butt of his Malice") had been printed in London and that shipments were on the way. Even as these were being unloaded, the town was also flooded with a forty-page pamphlet, printed by William Bradford in New York, entitled *Gospel Order Revived, being an Answer to a Book Lately set forth by the Reverend Increase Mather,* which was Brattle Street's reply to *The Order of the Gospel,* bearing an advertisement that, because the press in Boston stood in such awe of the tyrannical Increase, this piece of liberal journalism had to be published in New York.

The chief Boston printer, Bartholomew Green, retorted that he would have published the book if only the author had disclosed himself; he had refused, not out of awe of Increase Mather, but out of business scruples. This was a left-handed sort of defense, but Cotton made what he could out of it, and endorsed Green's statement with further references to "the Profane Scoffs and Scurrilities" in which the Catholic spirit indulged. "First Calf's Book, and then Coleman's," he grieved, "do sett the People in a mighty Ferment. All the Adversaries of the Churches lay their Heads together, as if by Blasting of us, they hoped utterly to blow up all."

Years later, Increase still harbored rancor because *The Order of the Gospel* was "received in New-England, but not in England, with Scoffs and Railery instead of a Solid Answer by Innovators." He was so involved with Harvard College, to which he was forced to return in February 1701, that he left Cotton to take on both foes at once: against what he supposed was Colman's pamphlet Cotton himself wrote and published (anonymously) *A Collection of Some of the Many Offensive Matters, Contained in a Pamphlet, Entitled The Order of the Gospel Revived,* while seven faithful members of his Church undertook, with his supervision and with a prefatory letter by him, to answer Calef in *Some Few Remarks upon A Scandalous Book.* In the midst of these efforts, he also compressed the Matherian position into a single sheet of paper, and published *The Old Principles of New England.*

By June 30, Increase could stand Cambridge no longer; on September 6, by a resolution of the General Court, he was discharged from the Presidency of Harvard, and Samuel Willard, to the fury of the Mathers, accepted the direction of the College under the title of Vice-President (which relieved him of the residential requirement). Stoddard went on conquering the Valley; Calef's book signified that anticlericalism was henceforth a factor in the society; and Benjamin Colman, his innovations secure, was proving by his eloquence and ease of manner that a new epoch had opened in pulpit oratory. Increase was out of Harvard College, while Cotton turned his irrepressible energies toward setting up a rival institution that should forever be kept out of the hands of such as the Brattles and Leverett: thus he became the chief begetter of Yale. In general, the culture of the region remained homogeneous, the people preponderantly of one stock, hard-working and Protestant; but the intellectual solidarity was gone, and now divisions of opinion represented not mere factional strife but fundamental cleavages.

In October, Sewall, learning that an English official had been appointed

Judge of Admiralty, in one sentence wrote the conclusion to this pathetic chapter: "Thus a considerable part of Executive Authority is now gone out of the hands of New England men." No such brevity was to be expected from Increase Mather, who on November 14 gave tongue to a jeremiad-to-end-all-jeremiads, appropriately entitled *Ichabod*. The glory had utterly departed: there was "Pompous and Superstitious" worship; unqualified persons were admitted to the Supper, and the College had become "a Seminary for Degenerate Plants." On the next May 27, Joseph Dudley was already appointed Governor, but was still on the seas; the General Court invited Increase (it was the least they could do for him) to give his fourth and, as it proved, last election sermon. He begged Dudley to let bygones be bygones, ran through his jeremiad once more, and published the text along with a sermon he had given at a Thursday lecture, defiantly called *The Righteous Man a Blessing*, in which he in effect washed his hands of further responsibility for New England: he had other work to do, he was getting old, and "the ill treatment I have received from those, from whom I had reason to expect better, have discouraged me from being any more concerned on such Occasions."

In 1703 the Brattles were reinstated on the Harvard Corporation (Sewall says that Cotton Mather, by staying away, simply "abdicated"), and the General Court, observing the custom of inviting foes to speak in alternate years, called upon Stoddard. The heart of modern man can hardly apprehend the glee with which this Puritan must have pronounced:

Many men have bad Principles respecting the Worship of God; some allow too much to the authority of men: and some allow too much to the judgments of men; as if they were in their Nonage or Dotage, that they don't know to chuse the good and refuse the evil . . . There are many ways whereby persons come to be ill Principled . . . some by being too tenacious of old Traditions.

Stoddard may well have taken a wry satisfaction in twisting the knife in the wound, because the Mathers—recoiling from the quadruple defeat of witchcraft, Harvard College, Brattle Street, and Northampton—had so lost their bearings as to turn, in their hour of need, to the most despised of their enemies: they not only connived at, they were actively instrumental in securing the selection of Joseph Dudley, in the fond hope that by controlling him they might yet win back the College and the power. Within ten years of the diplomatic triumph by which Increase Mather had apparently rescued the system and secured its future, to this miserable expedient had these champions of the pure and unified "Order of the Gospel" been reduced.

CHAPTER XVI

THE FAILURE OF CENTRALIZATION

THE
grief of such patriotic citizens as Judge Sewall over
the fragmentation of their culture was exceeded in 1701 only by their
bewilderment. In January, Benjamin Wadsworth preached at the First
Church on *Mutual Love and Peace Among Christians*, publishing the sermon (his second appearance in print) in the hope that it would allay the
"uncomfortable heats & contests" arising out of Increase Mather's *The
Order of the Gospel*. Wadsworth had already shown, since his ordination
in 1696, a superlative genius for stating the obvious, a gift that was to elevate him eventually, through a series of the dullest utterances in the
period, to the Presidency of Harvard College. He pleaded that the policy
of toleration, to which the Mathers had ostentatiously subscribed, ought to
be practiced among members of the same family; calling for meekness,
forbearance, good manners, Wadsworth said that were all things really
searched to the bottom, "we should scarce find two Christians in the whole
world exactly of the same mind in all particulars." He ventured to propose that the original assertion of New England—the pure Biblical polity
—was actually of less importance than the fact "that we are men, rational
Creatures of the same Species, or kind," wherefore we should be induced
"to live peaceably and quietly." With a simplicity which, in the circumstances, amounted to genius, he asked why "should any man impose his
particular notions or opinions upon mee, or I impose mine upon him?"

That man is a rational creature was not a novel theorem in New England's theology. Puritan scholasticism assigned him that rank in the great
chain of being, and the federal theology capitalized upon his prerogatives,
utilizing the rules of reason and rhetoric to extract from the Bible the
system of covenants. But Wadsworth was no longer trying to justify
those "powers" through which the founders had arrived at their definitions of polity; instead, he was bespeaking a mood that had become wearied
with "great contentions, shameful Strifes, grievous Divisions." No doubt,
when compared with the dissensions that rent the fabric of English Christendom, the internecine warfare of New England was relatively mild, but
measured against the background of the original expectation, it seemed
terrifying. There had not yet appeared such doctrinal divisions as those of
Calvinist and Arminian, Antinomian and Socinian, let alone of believer
and skeptic. So far, the disagreements were merely political or administra-

tive, but they threatened to raise, sooner or later, fatally divisive formulae. In an effort to forestall further strain, Wadsworth and his friends turned with the instinct of born moderates to a vague conception of "Reason," a maneuver which they could support by citing those English theologians, some of them Dissenters but most of them Anglicans like Tillotson, who, also recoiling from a century of profitless disputation, were celebrating the gentle charms of reasonable forbearance. However, we must not forget that the colonial version of this tendency, whatever it owed to foreign influence, acquired its peculiar impetus from the profound consternation arising out of a purely colonial predicament.

Wadsworth's sermon of 1701 suggests that those who studied at Harvard under Brattle and Leverett acquired there, under the conception of a "catholic" spirit, such a distaste for the regimentation of opinion as Increase Mather could only imperfectly share; the Mathers showed themselves no such catholics, and certainly did not turn the other cheek when assaulted by Calef in *More Wonders of the Invisible World*. Although Cotton insisted that the seven worties who signed *Some Few Remarks* wrote without supervision by him or his father, and that similarities to his own style did not mean that the good citizens were incapable of original composition, still, of the book's seventy-one octavo pages, five are taken up by this declaration, six by a letter from Increase, twenty-five by a statement of Cotton's, and twenty are a lamentation, unmistakably in his manner, that worthy pastors should have to bear insults. Precious space is devoted to refuting Calef's aspersions against the historical accuracy of *The Life of Phips:* the location in 1690 of the fleet off Quebec, and how many hits the flagship received. In all, only ten or twelve pages talk about witchcraft; the over-all effect is anything but peaceable and quiet, and there is more than a suggestion of a rage conscious of its impotence.

Calef was a dealer in cloth and described himself as a "Merchant"; Cotton Mather was so bankrupt as to sneer that he was a "Weaver"— "though he presumes to call himself a Merchant." Aside from expressing a holy horror that so "worthy Good man, a Scholar, and Gentleman" as Cotton Mather should be bespattered, or that judges should be called "the Unjustest, Cruellest and most Blood-thirsty men," the seven putative authors said nothing concerning witchcraft but that Cotton had been wary of the validity of spectral evidence as early as *Memorable Providences,* and that the ministers had spoken against it. Cotton's contribution shows how his conscience had been dealing with him; he had indeed written about the Salem court with honor, as any gentleman should: "This made people, who Judge of things at a Distance, to dream that I approved of all that was done." Devoting a weak paragraph to contending that the judges followed, to the best of their understanding, English and Scottish precedents, the book tried, as its main rebuttal, to call Calef a tool of Elisha Cooke (who, at that moment, was remorselessly compelling Increase Mather to retreat to Cambridge).

There is, however, one remarkable fact about *More Wonders of the Invisible World:* had the Mathers and their parishioners passed it by in silence, or did Cotton's journals not survive with their frenetic passages on it, we would have no evidence that anybody paid it the slightest attention. By 1700 witchcraft was a dead issue. Stoughton died in 1701, according to legend unrepentant, but Sewall had made his retraction in 1697; the society never gave decent recompense to the families of the victims, but it was on record as regretting its error. Calef had put his book together in 1697; three years later, when the printed text at last appeared, righteous citizens were striving to forget the miserable business, and thus managed to ignore one of the noblest, if also one of the crudest, expressions of the New England mind.

In the enlightened present it is highly esteemed, and justly. For one thing, by printing full transcripts of the trials (how did Calef get them?) it shows the inadequacy of Cotton Mather's *Wonders* (from Calef come the tremendous sentences of Mary Easty; not until 1700 did the community at large know what she had written—and then did not care). By publishing, without Cotton Mather's consent, the account of Mather's treatment of the possessed Margaret Rule (under the title "Another Brand Pluckt out of the Burning"), the book does confirm the sincerity of his efforts to keep another panic from starting, but it gratifies the instinctive suspicion of a later age that Mather's all too literal handling of the patient betrays a streak of pruriency. It also makes clear that in 1692 spectral testimony was the main evidence, and states emphatically the charge which posterity must hold against the ministers, that they did not object to this procedure "in such a publick manner as the case Requires." (As for the "advice" of June 15, 1692, Calef points out that despite their cautions about specters, the ministers exhorted the court to persevere, "and thereby encouraged them to proceed in those very by Paths already fallen into.") The portions of *More Wonders* in which these points are made are the ones generally reprinted; but in fact, if the book is looked at as a whole, the crucial section, to which the Mathers did not even dare reply, is Part II, a bumbling but sternly intense assertion that in the midst of such confusion as New England had come to, the only salvation lay in a return, in the spirit of primitive Protestantism, to stark Biblical literalism.

The cloth-merchant addressed letters to several ministers, to Cotton Mather, Willard, Wadsworth, and one presumably to Thomas Brattle (we have to take his word that the texts are accurate). They are turgid, repetitious, confused, but from them emerges a noble thesis: the Bible does indeed declare that witchcraft exists and should be punished by death, but nowhere enunciates explicit rules for detecting the witch; therefore all learned theories concerning the nature of the sin or its evidences are "humane inventions"—mere "traditions" of men foisted onto Scripture, exactly on a par with the superstitions of Rome. Above all, that assumption to which all theorizers subscribed, the notion that a witch enters into explicit "covenant" with the Devil, is utterly without textual foundation. Here Calef's attack struck at the very roots of New England society. Federal theologians had accepted the idea of a witch's covenant with the greatest of ease because it offered them an analogy in the diabolical realm for their central thesis: a deed becomes punishable after recorded consent (as in church and in state) has been given. But Calef now declared that the covenant theory was unscriptural, was a heathen fantasy affixed to Christian truth by Papists. We shall not have completed the Reformation, he cried, until we cast off this last vestige of Babylon, and as long as we retain it, we may anticipate more such pagan outbursts as swept over Salem Village.

More Wonders contains stirring statements about the laws of evidence which are even more worthy of respect today than when uttered. Calef saluted Willard, for instance, on the assumption that Willard was the author of *Some Miscellany Observations*, which had been very "serviceable," yet he had to point out that in this work Mr. *B* was allowed to say that an accusation upon merely spectral evidence might be entertained if the accused were already of ill-fame. No, exclaimed Calef, "Justice knows no difference of Persons," and a judicial examination should not be prejudiced in advance because the defendant is already indicted "by the Malice of Ill Neighbours." We are tempted to applaud Calef as a pioneer prophet of the great principle that no man is guilty until proved so, and to let our praise of him rest on this ground; however, closer inspection indicates that he came to his conclusion not out of a background of liberal jurisprudence but out of the jeremiads' own analyses of hypocrisy. Since, according to the official confessions, the land is rife with fraud, then open and dissolute sinners, convicted fornicators and disreputable tavern-haunters would be the last in the community to engage in secret transactions with Satan, whereas the "more Cunning, or more seeming Religious" would be most likely to yield, because witchcraft depends, as does hypocrisy, upon "Invisible Evidence."

There lay Calef's real contention, there he reinforced Stoddard and the *Manifesto:* the orthodox still insisted that the essence of witchcraft (even after they learned caution about spectral evidence) must of necessity be the supposed covenant between witch and Devil. Yes, said Calef, witches undoubtedly exist, but as for this covenant, there is no authority for it in Scripture. He may not quite have declared it, but the implication arises from every paragraph of his flamboyant letters: if there is no warrant for this sort of covenant, is there any for the other kinds?

Evidently Cotton Mather sent a letter to Calef, but did not allow him to make a copy, in which he tried to expound another possible mechanism of witchcraft: perhaps witches utilize the substance lately discovered by Henry More and the Cambridge Platonists, "the Plastick Spirit of the World." He also sent him Richard Baxter's *Certainty of the World of*

Spirits, telling him it was an "ungainsayable Book." Replying that "I know no ungainsayable Book, but the Bible," Calef insisted that nowhere in the Bible was there any such thing as a plastic spirit, and that Mather was overlaying the Word of God with absurdities exactly as when using the covenant delusion. Calef's point was not that witchcraft is a superstition, but that in dealing with it the New England orthodoxy had played fast and loose with holy writ. If they believed what they professed, they should stick to the limits of the Word and not suppose themselves "under a necessity of taking up with the Sentiments of such Men or Places that are thought worthy to give rules to detect them by."

The stalwarts of the North Church were so ill-advised, in *Some Few Remarks*, as to congratulate the booksellers that, being acquainted with the integrity of the Mathers, they would not "admit of any of those Libels to be vended in their Shops." This sentence came abroad at the very moment *Gospel Order Revised* was accusing Increase Mather of censorship. The threat of *More Wonders* was not that it fomented a reaction against orthodoxy's management of the witchcraft trials, for that had already become general—"Who is it," the book rhetorically asked, "that now sees not through it?"—but that Calef brought into serious question the whole apparatus of logical and rhetorical interpretation out of which New England had wrought its peculiar system. Calef was a Protestant, but no liberal; he went to his Bible with open eyes, and therefore declared that witch covenants are not to be found in the text:

If the law of God be perfect, and exceeding broad, as being given forth by the Omniscient Law-giver; it is exceeding high Presumption and arrogance, and highly destructive to the lives of Innocents, for any to pretend to give another, and a pretended better description of a crime made thereby Capital, with new rules to try such offenders by.

If this literalism were to prevail, what then would become of the complex machinery of interlocking covenants—the Covenant of Redemption, the Covenant of Grace, the church covenant, the national covenant, the Half-Way Covenant, the covenant of renewal, indeed, of the jeremiad itself? What verses of Scripture could then be marshaled against the deviations of Brattle Street or the still more destructive heresies of Solomon Stoddard? No wonder, therefore, that in replying to Calef the Mathers frittered away their ammunition on minor points, for they could not so much as mention the basic challenge. No wonder that they tried to divert attention by smearing him as a hireling of Elisha Cooke.

The great ecclesiastical discourses of the founders—Richard Mather's, John Cotton's, and above all Hooker's—set the system within a vast metaphysical, or rather cosmological, frame. Increase Mather's *The Order of the Gospel* reduces their immense conception to 144 octavo pages, to seventeen gnarled theses all directed specifically against Colman and Stoddard. Crying that apostasy from the original constitution would in New

England "be a greater Sin and Provocation to Christ, then in any Place in the whole world," he reviewed the generations: the first were gone, the second (his own) "are now in years," and of the third, while some are blessings, "many of them are not so." Certain "Young Divines" regard the sacrosanct practices of New England as "Novelty and Singularity." "Is there no one that will stand up for the Churches of Christ?" With a pointed prayer that the tutors at Harvard might remain faithful "and not Hanker after new and loose wayes," Mather's book so closely identifies the covenant theology and the jeremiad with his own faction that a defeat for him is bound to mean the destruction of the land. "As yet," he said, "the Declension is not gone so far but a Stop may be put thereunto." But to put a stop to it, if Mather's terms were to be accepted, would mean the suppression of Calef, the total submission of Colman and Stoddard, and the retention of Increase Mather in the presidential chair at Harvard.

Mather's dogged contention, throughout his various arguments, is that the Congregational church covenant is plainly derived from the New Testament. But on every page, as in all his disputation henceforth, he had to recognize how embarrassing was the part he had so proudly but incautiously played in the United Brethren, and how disconcerting the publicity Cotton had given his action. He had to weaken his position by maintaining that Presbyterian and Congregational churches could freely communicate, that "a moderate Presbyterian" and "a solid Congregational man" differ "in so few and small things" that there is no reason for them to quarrel; yet all this while, he was reviling Colman and Stoddard as apostates because they made a few gestures in a Presbyterian direction! Increase could do nothing but insist that in London Congregationalism might be compatible with Presbyterianism, but in New England the slightest modification of the church covenant was treason deserving the utmost vengeance of an outraged God.

He knew that not even he could any longer read the New Testament with the sublime certitude of the founders. They had had no difficulty in finding the covenant among the verses of the Apostles; but he, having listened to more critical examinations, was obliged to perceive that many of the proof-texts were, to say the least, ambiguous. He resorted for explanation to historical considerations: in the first century the very word covenant was obnoxious to the Roman authorities; hence the Disciples tactfully avoided using it, "but Established the Thing by Similitudes evidently implying it." The logic of Ramus and the rhetoric of Talon had enabled us to unscramble the apostolic anagrams. But was this not after all an admission that the covenant system rested not upon the Bible itself but upon a peculiar interpretation? And had not William Brattle hinted, when he introduced Cartesian techniques at Harvard, that the old logic and rhetoric were inadequate? Had not Colman acquired in England a prose style more attractive and more comprehensible than that of the founders by studying models who owed nothing to Talon? Suppose then that the Word were read, not in the light of Ramus, but in the more serene light of an enlarged Catholic spirit? Would it then yield up the idea of a church covenant any more surely than, according to Calef, it supplied the notion of a witch's covenant?

Because liberal historians have exaggerated the importance of Brattle Street, we must insist that the only really revolutionary proposition in *Gospel Order Revived* is its assertion that the doctrine of church covenant "is a stranger to Scripture, and has no foundation in the Word of God." Covenants may be used; a people may, if they wish, bind themselves to walk in the ways of the Lord ("This is the Covenant we own, and which we renew every time we attend the publick Worship of God"); they may covenant to reform their manners or to pay their pastor, but all such conventions come from the order of nature, not from the Bible, and are merely social or political conveniences. Brattle Street denied that the New Testament prescribes any such covenant as permits a minority of the society, "exclusive of the rest," to bring a church into being, or is so fundamental to the life of the society that those who scruple it should on that account be excluded. Once this premise was demolished, certain rational or natural consequences automatically followed: personal relations became superfluous, and the election of officers was seen properly to pertain to the whole number of financial supporters.

Gradually it became evident that the innovations of Brattle Street did not mean in practice marked differences from ordinary behavior. What is most important about the enterprise is the new tone it imparted to colonial controversy. *Gospel Order Revived* noted with amusement that Increase Mather filled up his pages, in the scholastic manner, with an array of authorities (although omitting those who did not support him); instead of mobilizing an opposing battery of citations, the book merely quipped, "This is a good way to amuse the Reader, and to cloud his mind, and to terrifie him, by mustering a legion of inartificial Arguments." The fact that in 1700 opponents of Increase Mather could toss back at him a term out of the Ramist logic, with the clear implication that the once vital distinction between real and secondary persuasions served now only to make fun of him, indicates the true nature of this intellectual revolution. Historically, this is a stupendous enough achievement, and needs no further enhancement.

Within these definite limits, the preface to *Gospel Order Revived* deserves a place in the unfolding of the American mind. Respectful of Increase Mather's reputation, it quietly asserts "that we are not over-awed by any Names," that the consciences of Christians will not be "imposed on by Men or Their Traditions," and inaugurates a new era by saying, "It appears very strange that those who fled from an Act of Uniformity, should presently impose on themselves, on their Neighbours, and entail the Mischief on their Posterity." Here, for the first time, a group singled out to be the object of pontifical denunciation had the courage—and the prestige—to rebut the accusation, to fling back the boast that instead of declining they were progressing: "Our dissent from any of them is so far from a going back from any Gospel Truth or Order, that it is rather a making progress, and advancing the Evangelical Discipline."

The gentlemen of Brattle Street had learned to make such a declaration out of New England's experience. They were accustomed to the distinction between external and internal covenants, but the effort to keep the two in alignment had become, in their eyes, futile. They knew by heart the rationale of hypocrisy; above all, they had seen the Half-Way Covenant expand, through renewals, into a membership that bore no relation to the original principle of exclusion. They reminded Increase Mather that in the 1660's enlargement of baptism had been cried upon as declension, "but the present generation feels the happy effect of it, and rising up at the Reformers names, do call them blessed." Also they called his attention to the fact that in London he was "esteemed more a Presbyterian than a Congregational man." If only he would show in Boston the spirit he had there exhibited, "we should be his easie Proselites too." Because at home he acted the tyrant, Brattle Street had to question his motives, and to answer not out of logic but out of realistic appraisal: "It would but cause us to suspect (what abundance of people have long obstinately believed) that the contest for his part is more for Lordship and Dominion than for Truth."

The chief undertakers at Brattle Street, we have noted, were men of wealth, such as Mico, Thomas Brattle, and Banister. It had not been a problem for business men like Anthony Stoddard or John Hull to combine profits with search of soul, or to humble themselves by public profession before the congregation; but by the time the Half-Way Covenant had obscured the distinction between profession and membership, men of this sort would no longer subject themselves to the indignity of a public relation of their sins. Too many of what nowadays passed for professions seemed to their refined taste "insipid, senseless things." Nor would they, simply because they scorned "to make a quaint Speech in the Church," be prevented from taking their proper place in it; since covenants are usually made "by the lesser part," why should the majority pay any attention? Increase Mather admitted that the founders had based the idea of the covenant not only upon the Bible but also upon nature and reason; the moment he allowed weight to those sanctions, the merchants seized upon them and opened the American eighteenth century by asserting that therein they found no justification for exclusion: "That which pertains to all is not valid, if some sorts have not a consent in it." In this sense (important it certainly is, but in this sense alone), Brattle Street made a contribution to what eventually could become democracy.

Because all three of the Mathers' opponents had to get their books published outside Boston, the impression is strengthened that the Mathers definitely represent at this juncture the forces of reaction and repression. Bartholomew Green's denial that they dictated his policy was not convincing when printed along with Cotton's imprecations, nor did the latter reassure his foes by displaying in *A Collection of Some of the Many Offensive Matters* an irate temper that patently would have used suppression if it could. Assuming that Colman wrote *Gospel Order Revived*, Cotton lampooned "the Weakness of the Arguing, the Romantickness of the Phrase, and the Air of the Author in vilifying his Superiors," and declared that even "a Moral Heathen" would not, like Thomas Brattle, have paid for the printing. Cotton Mather's blast is pure frenzy; he does not argue, he simply shrieks with horror at the very suggestion that church covenant is not explicitly commanded in Scripture, and counters Colman's adroit use of the United Brethren with the astonishing insult that "were this Young Pseudo Presbyterian really what he would be thought to be, Mr. Mather would not in the least discountenance him on account of Presbyterianism." He can only exclaim against "Bold Youths" who mock "the Aged Praesident of the Colledge," and predict that such monstrosities are so near to the superlative of sinfulness that the most dreadful of judgments must soon be upon us, possibly the end of the world itself.

But, although these samples of Matherian eloquence are at least pathetic where they are not comic, since we have raised the great word "democracy," we must pause to consider another dimension of the controversy. In passing, *Gospel Order Revived* did bow, although not very warmly, in the direction of Stoddard, and said of *The Doctrine of Instituted Churches* that it was "in most parts . . . a Mine of Gold, and a rich Treasury of right Thoughts." As far as I can make out, the two movements—Brattle Street and Northampton—were independent; Stoddard wrought his revolution as early as 1677, but there is no evidence that Leverett and the Brattles took their cue from him, although their awareness of the open secret may have encouraged their own thinking. Certainly in 1700 Stoddard denied the existence of church covenant in a much more emphatic fashion than they did: "There is no Syllable in the Word of God, intimating any such thing," nor, he added, "neither is there any need of it." The consent of visible saints cannot create a church, because bodies corporate are made either "by Law" or "by Charter"; as for individuals, their covenant "is no other, then what all Christians do make, when they make a profession of Faith and Obedience." Congregational theory tried to hold that a free Christian people could be bound together only by consent, and for decades labored to keep that principle alive in the pallid form of a ghostly owning of the covenant. The American frontiersman was bored with these metaphysics: it is not consent, he said, "that binds a free People in the same Town to mutuall subjection, to the Government of the Town" (had he been obliged to wait for the people in Northampton to consent, he would have got nothing done); it is the law of the land and the absolute command of *Deus Absconditus*.

If a Christian live in a Town, where there is a Church, he is immediately bound to joyn with that Church; and that Church is bound to him to govern him . . . but there is no occasion that every Member should Covenant particularly with the Church . . . This Doctrine of the particular Covenant is wholly unscriptural, is the reason that many among us are shut out of the Church, to whom Church Priviledges do belong.

The last sentence is the key. Seventy years of New England had demonstrated that even ostensibly holy men are not upright enough, responsible enough, to work a democratic system. If this argument prevails, wailed Cotton Mather, "all the Ungodliest Wretches that call themselves Christians, in the Town, are Church Members, even, whether they will, or no." Precisely, agreed Stoddard: the important thing was that they call, or be forced to call, themselves Christians. The neglect of "good Government of all Gods people, born within the Pale of the Church," was bringing "these Churches to a great defection." He was tired of distinguishing covenants, of attempting through jeremiad eloquence to stimulate a nonexistent freedom. The remedy was not to exhort, "not to deny them their right at the Lords Table, but to give them that, and a good and strict Watch over their Lives and Manners, together with it."

I am, of course, speculating, but the impression of Stoddard's personality is so vivid that one cannot help seeing in his doctrine the reflection of his surroundings; to these, rather than to any European or English influence, must be attributed his so-called "Presbyterianism." He did indeed advocate a national church and centralized control; but the source of his conviction was the fact that in Northampton all men, and not church members alone, worked shoulder-to-shoulder when raising the frame of a house or of a church, that so they fought against Indians. The conception of a national covenant which would bind all alike, which would provide him with an engine for controlling a tumultuous people—this was the only form of salvation that any longer seemed to Solomon Stoddard worthwhile. The simplest way of putting it—in which a century of American life is compressed—is that for John Winthrop it had been logical to conceive the whole migration as in an external covenant with God, having adventured upon these and those ends, and yet to believe that only a select minority of visible saints would guarantee the majority's performance; to Stoddard, it had become apparent that the majority must also be bound, and that therefore "the whole must have power over the parts, to rectify all Mal-administrations, and to see the Covenant kept." He did not, like some Scottish Presbyterians, repudiate the covenant; he merely decided that the national covenant was enough. "What is a National Church but a Professing Nation jointly bound to keep Covenant with God?" The seeds of all the difficulties which, over two centuries, New Englanders were to encounter in their efforts to come to terms with Presbyterianism were planted by this first native-born apostle of Presbyterianism: he would indeed identify church and town, but only on condition that there were someone like himself who would first harry the town into the church.

Still, we should not confuse the issue of 1700 by anticipating later complications. In that year, *The Doctrine of Instituted Churches* stated it with marvelous concision: if there be no national church, then every congregation is absolute and independent:

> This is too Lordly a principle, it is too ambitious a thing for every small Congregation to arrogate such an uncontrolable Power, and to be accountable to none on Earth; this is neither a probable way for the Peace of Churches, nor for the safety of Church Members; appeals are admitted in all Kingdoms; and it is more probable that in a whole Country, persons may be found that may rectify the Miscarriages of particular Congregations, then that particular Congregations will not miscarry; this absoluteness of particular Congregations is a dignity that the primitive Churches did not enjoy, this is not the common Priviledge of Gospel Churches.

How pedantic, how remote, sounds Increase Mather's *The Order of the Gospel*, with its "inartificial" arguments, alongside this frank speaking!

For Stoddard, a few organizational consequences were obvious: synods of elders should oversee the calling of ministers to particular churches; excommunications and censures should be reviewed by boards of clerical supervisors: "every Man must stand to the Judgment of the National Synod." Men ordained to the office may be ministers even when not connected with a particular church (Colman had availed himself of this thesis). Stoddard remained enough of a Congregationalist to insist that synods are not infallible, and drew upon his American experience when justifying a national church: "they that are one People, should Unite together in carrying on Gods Worship, and should have Power to regulate and govern the several parts of that Body." Satisfying himself that he had paid sufficient deference to the Bible by retaining the Hebraic conception of a nation in covenant, Stoddard shamelessly constructed the rest of his system out of brute fact, and called it "the Light and Law of Nature."

Since historians have incautiously saluted Stoddard's revolt as an assertion of democracy—on the grounds that it did away with restrictive membership—we should observe that by his explicit declaration the aim was to put dictatorial powers into the hands of ministers and elders. In every town, as New England had long since proved, there are many not to be confided in: "the Minister hath Power by Virtue of his Pastoral charge, to see that they Learn." Or, as he succinctly expressed it in 1700 and was to say until his death, "The Elders are to Rule over the Church, and therefore not to be overruled by the Brethren." Hence the pastor should determine who might be admitted or excommunicated—not the brethren. "It is not the work either of the Brethren or Ruling elders any ways to intermeddle in that Affair or Limit him"; for, as Stoddard wrote with a freedom which the harassed Mathers must have envied, "The community are not fit to judge & rule in the Church."

Let us be clear: here was no Populist uprising. This Puritan aristocrat was enraged by the leveling tendencies of the frontier; his reaction was to equate all persons in orders that they might the better be controlled by aristocrats. Matters of administration require wisdom, "but the Community are not men of understanding"; most of them "have not had the advantage of Reading & Study. Some of them are Men of very weak Abilities, some of them are rash, some of them are Young, hardly Sixteen Years of Age, some of them are Servants." It was against reason to suppose that Christ would entrust His government to men so "uncapable." Therefore Stoddard turned to the ideal of a national church; otherwise "every particular Congregation is absolute and independent, and not responsible to any higher Power." There had been too much liberty: America (or at least New England) cried aloud for centralization.

Thus it is worth our while to listen once more to the words of Cotton Mather, flung in the face of Stoddard before the assembly of ministers on July 4, 1700:

> The Liberty of the Fraternity, in things of common Concernment; for the Fraternity to be Governed, not as meer Bruits or Mutes: The primitive Churches, preserved it, for many Ages . . . Our Gentlemen do assay utterly to take away all manner of Liberty, from the Brethren in our Churches. Because it may be, in some Churches things may have been sometimes carried in a Strain too democratical, these Gentlemen will do well to remember, who they are . . . But they can't speak of the People in any other Terms, than the Pharisees did of old; Whereas, indeed, Syrs, this People, is the Lord's Heritage. They tell us, they will reform our Churches. And then they tell us, it shall be, by pushing them from the primitive Church-State, wherein they at present are, and by plunging them into the Church-State, which the Romish Apostasy, after some Centuries had brought all into. A goodly Reformation! Syrs, tis unintelligible, tis unaccountable.

Likewise against Brattle Street, Cotton Mather spoke most cogently when declaring that its reduction of all members to a passive participation made the condition of Christians "that of Souldiers in a Company." Not, of course, that in becoming tolerant the Mathers had also become democrats; but, hounded as they were from every quarter, they had the grace and the wit, in what otherwise was a confused and indefensible salient, to rally and to hold some of their forces on this ground: "we thought the Lord Jesus Christ had made them His Free men." Granted that the extreme of "Brownistical Anarchy" is bad, "Is not one Extream to be shunned without Running into another?" If credit is to be distributed—and who of us can withhold admiration from Stoddard, or do else but welcome the Brattles?—it should be recorded that in their desperation, while power was being shorn from them, the Mathers did manage to stand firm upon one root principle of Protestantism, that the consent of a believer is an essential part of belief.

Unfortunately for these most unfortunate of men, their hands were tied because of Increase's hearty participation in the United Brethren. Both Stoddard and Colman could point out that he had already so far compromised the notion of church covenant in order to meet the Presbyterians more than half way that he had no right to denounce Stoddard. The unhappy fact of the matter was that the Mathers were doomed to be thwarted in whatever event. Stoddard and Brattle Street flouted the majority opinion of New England: but what of the autonomy of individual churches? Besides, there had been no synod in New England since 1679–80, and such associations as that of Cambridge were not Presbyteries but merely social gatherings. Then Stoddard proceeded to organize his area into the Hampshire Association, and to encourage it to act like a genuine Presbyterian classis; Cotton Mather was left whimpering that while the associations in eastern Massachusetts "do not assume unto themselves all the power, which many Presbyterians can allow them," still they ought to be equally respected because they do not invade the constitution of our churches "without the Advice of Neighbouring Ministers." In this sense, they have done nothing—"(even in Print)"—contrary to the order professed in New England; whereas his enemies, preëmpting the name of Presbyterianism, were flagrantly defying the customs of the country in a manner which, in any Presbyterian nation, would have been censured by their fellows. It was after Cotton had repeated his charge of July 4, 1700, in the preface to Quick's *Young Man's Claim*; after he and his father had issued another (according to their definition) "Presbyterian" tract, Thomas Doolittle's *A Treatise Concerning the Lords Supper*; after they had prodded Higginson and Hubbard to issue a *Testimonial* to stigmatize Stoddard's defection from the founders; after they had taken shots at him in everything they published; after Increase in *Ichabod* had made his last gesture of despair—after all this, Stoddard came to Boston and delivered the election sermon of 1703, charmingly entitled *The Way for a People to Live Long in the Land that God hath given them*. He gracefully evaded any label, especially that of Presbyterianism, but he told New England that it had to rethink its basic propositions, and in so doing must not be bound by the example of the founders. Men run into great mistakes, he said, if their tender consciences are vitiated by false principles: those who judge licentiousness lawful have indeed lost the light of nature and so cannot distinguish between good and evil; but on the other hand, "Some run into the other extream, and make strict rules for themselves and others that God never made."

Every month, every week, the position of the Mathers became more difficult. In *The Order of the Gospel*, Increase laid down the points on which there could be no yielding: examination of candidates, explicit covenant, exclusion of non-members from the election of officers, baptism upon some fragment of hereditary right or upon public profession. He was clinging to the tattered remnants of Congregationalism; but he would not budge from the one great standard, that "The Lord has joyned the Exhibiting Sign, and the Grace Exhibited thereby, together." Cruel as it might sound, the sacrament could not be administered to any "to whom we cannot in charitable Judgement say, 'You are in Covenant with God.' " Granted that immense difficulties had developed in testing the proposition, one fact remained incontestable: "The Grace of God is a discernible thing."

Ever more frantic in the execution of his balancing act, Increase had to insist, in *Ichabod*, that to surrender these fundamentals would infringe both Congregational and Presbyterian tenets, that the innovators, "Yea and some who are not the Youngest men," have advanced notions "which our Presbyterian Brethren in England, & the Reformed Churches beyond Sea, have Condemned, & which the English Liturgy it self approveth not of." Hence he and his followers, while guarding the principle of consent, had to demonstrate that within the framework of *The Heads of Agreement*, even as Congregationalists, they could undertake measures that really would refute Stoddard; they had to show that they could go far enough toward the centralization of control to justify their allegiance to the United Brethren. They had to prove that they could rectify the disorders and insubordinations of which Stoddard complained. And by 1704 the compulsion was all the stronger because the civil government, under Joseph Dudley, would obviously be no help at all.

On June 1 a convention of ministers was called by the Cambridge Association, which issued a circular letter proposing several motions upon which all might easily agree (such as that pastors should be more "laborious" in their personal visits), as well as "That Associations of the Ministers in the several Parts of the Country may be strengthened." Willard was moderator, Cotton Mather, Wadsworth, Benjamin Colman, and twenty-three others signed the document (Increase Mather augustly held aloof). On September 11, 1705, delegates from the five associations met "according to former agreement," and on the thirteenth issued the *Proposals*.

The Mathers were not the prime movers, but since the opening of their controversy with Stoddard they had become the chief spokesmen for the point of view the document articulated. One might tell the history of the *Proposals* without mentioning Stoddard; in one sense they were an attempt to settle what from the beginning had been a problem in the ecclesiastical theory: the founders, basing their polity upon the Bible, declared that occasional synods, summoned upon particular emergencies, should exercise no other powers than those of advice and counsel, and their decisions should bind only those churches who accepted them. Was this an adequate system for maintaining uniformity? Upon this theory the Synods of 1637, 1646–48, 1662, and 1679–80 officially operated. To be sure, their "advices" had been supported by the civil government, but even though after 1692 that agency could no longer play its traditional role, the theory remained intact: synods do *not* have compulsive power. The primary assumption had been that they would never need it because, the Word of God being so clear, a judicious interpretation would carry its own credentials and convince every society of true saints. John Cotton had taken pleasure in telling Presbyterians, "no Church hath stood out so long in maintaining any offence found amongst them."

Furthermore, various practices had grown up which, to some degree, restrained a too free exercise of independent power, such as "consulting the neighboring churches" in difficult moments, until gradually the method crystallized into unwritten law. It was symbolized in ordinations, when near-by ministers preached the sermon and gave "the right hand of fellowship." Because New England succeeded with its theoretically "consultative" synods, which in effect wrought everything Presbyterianism desired, Increase had been able to play down their voluntaristic character, to insist that Congregationalists could join the United Brethren without violation of conscience.

Thus, in one point of view, formation of the Cambridge Association could be presented in 1690 as no innovation; it was simply a method for regularizing consultation among neighboring churches, and no voice was raised in protest. As other areas organized their own associations, Cotton Mather pointed to them as further reasons why Presbyterians and Congregationalists should come together. Since the government was a royal government, even in the hands of a Phips or a Stoughton, it could not be called upon to punish recalcitrant churches, so that little by little, the associations tried to keep order by themselves. In 1698, for instance, Cotton Mather went with the delegates of five churches to John Wise's Chebacco parish, there to cut off a neighboring but disorderly church from the communion of the faithful. All this while Mather was agitating for the formation of still more associations, assuring the people that these were not "Classical Combinations," that they threatened nothing against the "overwhelming Rights of particular Churches." He and the Cambridge Association, adjudicating on *Thirty Important Cases*, remained clear in their minds that synods, not only by Scripture but by the light of nature, might do no more than expound the mind of the Holy Spirit—although "it is but reasonable that their Judgment be acknowledged as Decisive in the affairs for which they are Ordained."

This much, on the surface, was orthodoxy, but already the test had come, and the Association had proved inadequate: Charlestown elected Simon Bradstreet in 1697, choosing him by a vote of the inhabitants, and then ordained this spokesman of the "Catholic" spirit in defiance of the Association (significantly, Bradstreet appears to have no connection with the *Proposals* of 1705).

By 1700, those who had joined associations on the supposition that they thus might remain good Congregationalists even while exercising Presbyterial powers were hard put to it, against the jibes of Stoddard, to explain how they slept at night. As if this were not enough, in 1699 Boston had its first experience with a clerical impostor: Samuel May for a while fooled even the Mathers, claiming to be a pious Presbyterian; he turned out to be a rascal, who gave himself away by delivering plagiarized sermons and launching into abuse of the regular pastors. His supporters grew insolent, and threw "libels" into the houses of other ministers, while he, if Cotton is to be believed, devoted himself to the seduction of converts; it was only God's mercy and the exertions of the Association that kept the young women of Boston from being "betray'd and debauch'd into fearful Whoredoms." The horror was that even after the Association exposed him, he took refuge in the Baptist church, whence nobody could dislodge him. If this was the consequence of accepting toleration, then clearly it was time that the Congregational order either go all the way with Stoddard, or prove against him that it could tighten its own screws of discipline. The laws, as Increase Mather had to confess, did not provide adequate security; realizing, as Pemberton put it, that "there is not sufficient provision made for the tryal of such," even "Catholic" spirits like Wadsworth and Colman found themselves, a few short years after the *Manifesto*, ready to sign the *Proposals*.

There were other worries, all of them arising from obvious failures of the original polity—or rather from the inability of that polity to function without the active coöperation of pious magistrates. There was, for example, the decay of the office of lay elder. By 1694 Joshua Scottow represented, in the language of the streets, what had happened: men of low degree say "they are of mean Estates, and low Capacities, their Counsel will not meet with acceptance, and some others might do," while the brethren of high degree beg off because "their occasions will not bear or admit of so mean an Employ as to be a Ruling Elder." In Northampton, Stoddard had no trouble in getting Pomeroys, Claps, and Hawleys to serve; but in the east, among churches founded upon covenant and upon consent, there were fewer and fewer Sewalls to take on the job. Sallow Harvard graduates found themselves in towns where they had not only to preach but to rule, and seldom were up to both requirements. They needed help, and turned in panic to the associations.

And finally, about the year 1700, the clerical leaders commenced to realize those awful consequences of the new charter which their own propaganda had for a time concealed even from themselves: they existed on sufferance, thanks to the Act of Toleration; the governorship would certainly pass into the hands of an Anglican (Bellomont had come and died, but he was a portent); there was every reason to foresee that their churches would have to resist the Church of England. For that, they would need to be united.

The news from London told them that even while the United Brethren were falling apart, powerful "high-flying" forces within the Established Church, having recovered from the Revolution of 1689, were

regrouping for more aggressive measures not only in England but throughout the Empire. They marked the skillful strategy of Francis Makemie,
who wrote from Barbados a book published in Edinburgh in 1699, copies
of which soon reached Boston, *Truths in a True Light;* Makemie had
been a gallant apostle of Presbyterianism in Maryland and Virginia, had
met Increase Mather in London and supported him in the United Brethren, and had disputed with the Quaker, George Keith (who also had annoyed New England). *Truths in a True Light* laid down for Dissenters
the line which seemed, after 1689, to be most promising: they agree with
the Church of England on all essential matters; therefore, differences
should not be magnified, and all Protestants should stand together. On
May 29, 1700, Cotton Mather appeared before Bellomont to deliver his
fourth (and, as it was to prove, his last) election sermon; with Anglo-
American relations momentarily uppermost in his mind, he forgot the
jeremiad pattern, quietly boasted that the Protestant faith has generally
made a nation great and rich "even in Temporals," and adduced the
prosperity of New England (which the jeremiads had pronounced at an
end) to prove that here the "Doctrinal Articles of the Church of England"
were more faithfully held than anywhere in the king's dominions. To
make sure that none should mistake, he aligned New England with the
Presbyterian element in the United Brethren by condemning "Neonomian
and Antinomian Errors," and assured Bellomont that there was not one
Socinian or Arminian among the colonial pastors.

This sermon, entitled *A Pillar of Gratitude,* was, according to its subtitle, "A Brief Recapitulation, of the Matchless Favours, with which the
God of Heaven hath obliged the Hearty Praises, of His New-English
Israel"; it contended that the Church of England should therefore let
this Israel alone. Cotton followed the effort with *A Letter of Advice to
the Churches of the Non-conformists in the English Nation,* published
in London in 1700, wherein he assured English Nonconformists that they
were the true Church of England and that by the Toleration Act they
had become "legal Parts" of it. They need pay no attention, therefore,
to "that Faction, whose Religion lyes in Sainting their Martyr Charles I."

Nevertheless, in 1701 the Society for the Propagation of the Gospel
was founded; the next year George Keith, now an ordained Anglican,
was on a scouting expedition for the Bishop of London, and was engaging
Increase Mather in controversy by declaring that there were six plain
rules which, if decently observed, would bring all Dissenters back into the
fold. In their role as advocates of the United Brethren, the Mathers had
lengthily insisted that Christian fundamentals were few and clear, but
still not those of Keith; whereupon this Anglican convert joined hands
with Calef and Stoddard by asking how the New Englanders could claim
simplicity as long as they preached the church covenant: "Thousands of
good Christians cannot find any Warrant for it in Scripture, by the best
Judgment of Discretion that we can make; but on the contrary, we not

only think it superfluous but more burdensome to our Consciences" than all the Canons.

And by this time, the fact was borne in upon New England that in England the United Brethren had failed; the extent of the demands being made upon the Mathers' energies is shown in the summer of 1699 when Cotton preached two sermons (published as *The Everlasting Gospel*) expressing New England's grief over the shocks given to the Union, and trying to prove that there was nothing for the English Dissenters to quarrel about, in which he as good as confessed that if he had to choose sides, his sympathies lay with the Presbyterians.

In this atmosphere of confusion and distraction, knowing that they had to cut their way out of the web, delegates from the eastern associations issued on September 13, 1705, the *Proposals*, and officially despatched them to the churches on November 5. These suggestions were grouped under two heads: under the first, it was proposed that the association be given the right to intervene in local disputes, that candidates for particular churches undergo a "Tryal" before it, and that it be empowered to recommend "such Persons as may be fit to be imployed amongst them." The second head went further: it recommended that churches within an associated area form themselves in a "consociation" (to consist of both clerical and lay delegates), which in turn should erect a "standing or stated Council" to determine all affairs within the geographical limit. These were to meet at least once a year; their determinations were to be looked upon as final, and any church that refused to be "Reclaimed" should be declared no longer fit for communion.

In Massachusetts Bay, nothing ever came of the *Proposals*. In 1726 Cotton Mather ruefully remembered that they were opposed by "some very considerable Persons among the Ministers, as well as of the Brethren, who thought the Liberties of particular Churches to be in danger of being too much limited and infringed in them"; out of deference "to these Good Men," the *Proposals* were never pushed. We do not know to what lengths they might have been had Governor Dudley been favorable, but neither he nor the legislature (too much engrossed in disputing with him about his salary or his conduct of the war) could be enlisted. There was no power in the colony that would make Simon Bradstreet or John Wise bow to a consociation. Cotton Mather should have known better; on July 4, 1700, he himself told Stoddard that the decisions of synods, even if any could be assembled, would signify nothing "except they have a civil Magistrate, that will make them cutt. Whereas they are not yett provided of a Magistrate, that will be their Tool; no, nor ever will be." In the Valley, Stoddard could look with pity upon the *Proposals* as a pathetic attempt to realize, under another name, his own conceptions; he pragmatically devoted himself, through the sheer force of personality, to making the Hampshire Association act, even without magisterial assistance, as though it were a full-fledged consociation.

One cannot say how much the influence of Stoddard worked upon Connecticut, but it is fair to surmise that the western regions felt his weight. While arguing against him in 1700, while declaring that even English Presbyterians would not support him, Cotton Mather cited Rutherford, and barbed his remark with, "to whom, we hope, you our Brethren in the Colony of Connecticut, that Exceed all the rest of New-England, for proclaiming your Indisposition to the Order wherein Your Churches have so long flourished, will above others attend." Clearly he associated the movement in Connecticut with Stoddard, but after the *Proposals* (one fascinating aspect of the Mathers' story is how wantonly they threw away their advantages) he was powerless to object if that colony acted upon them. In 1700 Stoddard based his "Presbyterian" doctrines frankly upon the *de facto* power of self-government; a conquered country, he said, does not choose its rulers, neither does one under hereditary control, but otherwise, "All the Power that Men have over a free People is by their own consent." Thanks to the inefficiency of the Board of Trade, Connecticut still had power over itself; it was also fully conscious of the reasons why the Massachusetts associations had launched their *Proposals*. In that colony there were even more dissensions, splintered churches, and insubordinations than Governor Gurden Saltonstall, translated from his New London pulpit to Hartford in 1707, liked to contemplate. Hence the legislature itself called for a synod, which met at Saybrook in September 1708 (eight of the twelve delegates being members of the new college), and there drew up *The Saybrook Platform*, which, although borrowing much of its language from the *Proposals*, institutionalized the ecclesiastical theories of Solomon Stoddard.

The Saybrook Platform organized the ministers of each county into associations and their churches into consociations; it ordered the councils to use the authority of these bodies to "see their Determinations or judgments duly Executed." The only sanction was the sentence of non-communion, but in Connecticut that would have a force infinitely greater than in Massachusetts. Although there was opposition to the *Platform*, though it did not bring absolute peace to the churches, still it was a formidable instrument for enforcing uniformity and obedience. The church remained, but the effective unit of communal life became the "Council of the Consociated Churches of the Circuit." This institution might or might not be found in the Bible; the founders certainly had not discovered it there in anything like the form set up by Connecticut; but its real source was neither Scripture nor logic: it sprang from the proved necessity for resisting those forces of disintegration which a purely Biblical polity carelessly encouraged.

The result of the Saybrook Synod was published at public expense in 1710, and 2,000 copies were distributed. The strategy of this volume is interesting: commencing with the sort of praise for the Toleration Act which had now become standard in New England, it reprinted the *Savoy Confession of Faith* and *The Heads of Agreement*. Thus proclaiming that

Connecticut, being "fully grounded upon the Holy Scripture," was a full participant in the ecumenical movement of English Dissent, the *Platform* could then insist that it was only "a more Explicate asserting the Rules of Government sufficiently provided in the Holy Word," even though acknowledging, in the same sentence, the actual motives: these rules were found necessary "for the healing of our Wounds," since "our difficulties have been of a long time troublesome." It was doubtless hoped that no one would notice the omission in both *The Heads of Agreement* and in the text itself of any mention of church covenant. Although the preface called upon the people to believe the *Confession* with more than "an Humane Faith," there was no emphasis whatsoever upon regenerate membership; the whole concern was for the efficiency of an administrative machinery.

For the future of America, this development has importance, because out of the Valley and out of Connecticut came the migration into New Jersey, and with it New England's contribution to the Presbyterian Church and to the College of New Jersey. Jonathan Dickinson is the embodiment of this penetration: born at Hatfield in 1688, he grew up in the kingdom of Stoddard, took his Yale degree in 1706, and settled in Elizabeth Town in 1709, where he needed eight years to persuade his congregation to join the Synod of Philadelphia. In the long run, the fact that the Presbyterian Church received, in its formative stages, this New England element, of which Dickinson is foremost, was to have repercussions felt even today; the immediate result was that in the center of the most powerful organization of the Middle Colonies stood a group who resisted the doctrinal mentality of the Scotch-Irish, who fought against slavish subscription to even *The Westminster Confession*. How do you know, Dickinson demanded of the Philadelphia Synod in 1729, that the *Confession* is contained word-for-word in Scripture? "I challenge you to bring one Word to evince your Certainty; that our Interpretations are agreeable to the Meaning of the Holy Ghost; and have the Divine approbation that any Sect under Heaven may'n't bring in the same Cause." These are momentous sentences which commenced a long campaign, but it has not always been realized that they are substantially what Stoddard had said about the church covenant: what is not explicitly disclosed in the Word of God is not needed in America.

Thus in the first years of the eighteenth century multiplicity continued to grow out of simplicity; the covenant theology, having conceived and cradled the principle of voluntary consent, set the New England mind at work destroying that theology. The whelps were eating up the dam. He among the offspring who appeared in the mantle of autocracy was the one most clearly to assert the right of man to read the Bible for himself, and to establish the social order upon reason and nature. The assurance that this process should not be reversed, that no interest could any longer enforce intellectual uniformity, came in 1707 when Willard died and

John Leverett was chosen President of Harvard. The charter of 1650 was resumed by a simple resolution of the legislature, and the "enlarged Catholic spirit" captured the school of the prophets.

The Mathers fumed, Cotton declaring that the College might as well be given to the Bishop of London. However, thirty-nine ministers (Colman the only one from Boston, but among others John Wise) assured Dudley of their satisfaction, noted that "the greatest part of the now rising ministry" had been educated under him and Brattle, and that they fully expected "to see religion and learning thrive and flourish, under Mr. Leverett's wise conduct and influence, as much as ever yet it hath done." Stoddard received his copy of the petition too late to sign (he was far away), but sent Colman his hearty approbation. "I desire you," said Dudley to the once mighty Increase, "will keep your station, and let fifty or sixty good ministers, your equals in the province, have a share in the government of the college, and advise thereabout as well as yourselves, and I hope all will be well." With the prospect that still more of the rising ministers might imbibe Leverett's spirit, there was no prospect that the councils of associations could impose upon the churches such persons as the Mathers judged "fit." While Stoddard prepared to renew the fight, to push his radicalism to even greater lengths, the *Proposals* gathered dust, except that in Chebacco Parish the man who had once defied Andros was troubled by their implications; like Stoddard, he commenced to ask himself upon what philosophical bases this covenanted society actually did rest.

CHAPTER XVII

THE UNRESOLVED DEBATE

WE want persons of your character," wrote John Leverett to Colman; at that moment, in Bath, Colman was proving his character by preaching upon the evidences of the Divinity to be derived from the beauty, regularity, and order of the visible world: from the sun, air, water, and earth, from the sensitive creatures, from the shapes and beauties of animal forms. From these data he proved the existence of natural conscience and divine judgments; he so celebrated the uses of the intellect —its searching into nature, soaring to the skies and bringing down the science of astronomy, constructing noble systems of ethics and politics— that he could happily arrive at the eminently emotional conviction that "the universe had at least a blunder without a humane mind in it."

That design was to be proved by natural evidences had always been a staple of Puritan theology, but Colman's technique radiated a new kind of serenity:

Without a summer, the earth would yield no Increase, but everlasting sterility would follow: without a Winter, the Earth would have no rest, but would bee too soon worn out . . . Without a Spring, the change from cold to hot would be sudden & very prejudicial to nature: & autumn again prepares for winter, making the passage gradual & tolerable from heat to cold.

The universe thus described remarkably resembles Benjamin Colman: everything gradual and tolerable, nothing sudden or prejudicial. Such was the irenical, the conciliatory insight he brought home from his sojourn among what were left of the United Brethren; he summarized himself in praising William Brattle: "wise and discreet; humane, affable, courteous and obliging; free, open, sincere and upright . . . a known peace-maker to persons or societies." Of another contemporary he could imagine nothing finer to say than that "he was no furious Bigot in Religion, but of a Spirit of Moderation." His sermons are filled with citations not only from Plutarch and such Dissenters as Baxter and "Mr. Milton," but also from tolerant Anglicans like Bishops Bull, Beveridge, Patrick, and above all Tillotson. His was not a profound or speculative mind, but it was graceful, and therein consists his importance.

He himself said of one of his disquisitions that he had nothing new to contribute "except in Method, Stile, Allusion, etc." In England he learned to adduce as a supreme proof of the divine authorship of the Bible its style: "it is not tumid & affected, but scorned the embellishments of fancy," and exhibited his own cast of mind by insisting that it is supremely natural. Scripture scorns "humane laws of Method," and nowhere descends into the pattern of such artificial discourse "as we in Sermons first propose a doctrine, & then explain its forms & then produce arguments for its proof." For New England, where the rigid scheme of doctrine, reasons, and uses had held absolute sway over the processes of the mind, this was liberation indeed, opening the road toward a discourse that might experiment with freer modes of address, that could approximate an Addisonian essay.

In 1715 (Benjamin Franklin was ten years old), Colman eulogized Thomas Bridge of the First Church because he "always cloth'd his Tho'ts in clean, decent and manly language." His own conception of elegance left him unresponsive to certain markedly manly writings in the Age of Queen Anne; when he argued that Boston should establish a market in order to keep country men from hawking and sauntering about the town, he begged forgiveness for "the coarseness of the Expression." But if his appreciation of the manliness in the Augustan ideal was somewhat deficient, he subscribed without reservation to its renovated conceptions of cleanliness and decency; from the moment he began to publish, the prose of Increase Mather, let alone that of Cotton, in fact of all the older generation, became antiquated. Even those in the younger generation who, like Thomas Prince or Joseph Sewall, were of Cotton Mather's party and therefore opponents of Colman owed their style to him rather than to their master.

Since Colman set the tone for the next decades, it is interesting to observe just what he did with the tradition of the "plain style." His two most important books both appeared in 1707, one indicating what he thought had become a major concern of the epoch, *The Government and Improvement of Mirth*, and the other *A Practical Discourse upon the Parable of the Ten Virgins*, deliberately inviting comparison with the treatment by Thomas Shepard that long since had become a devotional classic in both Englands. Shepard had formulated his "doctrine" thus: "All those that are espoused unto Christ ought to be in a constant and continual readiness to meet Christ"; Colman's runs: "An open visible Profession of Christianity is the Indispensible Duty of all to whom the Gospel comes." Shepard, defining his terms, said, "Virgins are such as are fit for marriage, and not defiled with any man," and declared those shut out of the ordinances who go "a whoring from God." Colman approached the metaphor in this wise:

I wou'd check the Exuberance of Sense and Fancy in so nice a Matter, remembring with what Decency the Subject expects to be treated and how ill I shou'd recommend Purity by trespassing on it through an unguarded Management. My Instances therefore in respect of Propriety of the Similitude shall be the fewer.

Where Shepard wrote, and the founders had exulted with him, "if love be great, there is little standing on terms—let me have him though I beg with him," Colman's boldness overcame his diffidence only this far: "At least Religious Love is decently free and open in declaring its regard to its glorious Object." In the *Discourse* he particularly leaned upon Tillotson, "the greatest Example of Charity and Moderation that the Age produc'd," who had remarked upon "the charitable Decorum" the Savior always contrived to observe in His most earthy parables!

In 1728 Thomas Prince had to acknowledge that Cotton Mather's style was "something singular, and not so agreeable to the Gust of the Age," but was to plead nevertheless that in his "very emphatical" manner "we clearly see the Beauty and Life of Religion, in the strongest Colours." By a studied avoidance of overemphasis, Colman softened the colors of both rhetoric and religious emotion, yet he liberated colonial prose for the expression of other emotions—indeed, taught it how to compose whole paragraphs where the passions were muted to gentle and gratifying feelings. Thus he was primarily responsible for bringing to New England a consciousness of "the Age," an awareness that the Enlightenment had dawned and that provincial imitators of the capital should hasten to become enlightened. He deftly showed by his example that the driving, narrow controversialism and intensity of the seventeenth century had become bad form. He was fully instructed that the spirit of this new age often found expression in skepticism, Deism, atheism, but he also knew that the forces of a sober and moderate, yet by no means ascetic, morality were mobilizing against these tendencies, and he specifically aligned himself with "Mr. Collier's" attack upon immorality in the drama. "The Humour of the Age is for a turn or two of wit"; hence he felt that he was indeed addressing himself to a central problem by treating in his first bid for fame not some abstract doctrine or problem in polity, not the soul's preparation or the Gospel covenant, but mirth.

Not that the result can in any sense be called hilarious; Colman pleaded for "sober mirth," and found nothing attractive in tavern boistrousness where "Drink has intoxicated men and banish'd Reason and Sobriety." But he did inaugurate a tradition of New England letters by recognizing, what no native had yet ventured to commemorate, something that had in fact become an amenity of society in Boston:

A great deal of Pleasantry there is in the Town, and very graceful and charming it is so far as it is Innocent and Wise. Our Wit like our Air is clear and Keen, and in very Many 'tis exalted by a Polite Education, meeting with good Natural Parts.

Hence Colman marked the cultural transition quite simply by contending that Christian virtue may "consist with Occasional Mirth, or with

Habitual Chearfulness," by asserting that melancholy people "commonly make drooping Christians, to the disadvantage of Religion." Thomas Brattle gave the Brattle Street Church an organ, the first such ecclesiastical instrument in the colonies, to which has been attributed the beginning of a much needed improvement in communal singing; while taking care not to approve "loose Sonnets," Colman glorified music, when "Address't with Art," as a means of working upon our souls "in ways adapted to our Frame and Nature." That indeed is the remarkable feature of this astonishing book, its justification of a modicum of joyousness as suiting with a faculty which "Nature" would not have put into us, or made so beautiful and so pleasing, without intending it to be used. For a people who had been fed a steady diet of jeremiads, it must have been a relief beyond our conceiving to hear from at least one pulpit: "Why shou'd not Holy Joy express it self freely? Why shou'd not the Brightness of the Face, and the Life in the Eye, speak it? and the Tone of the Voice be Natural?"

It would be entirely false to suggest that Colman was either a rationalist or a naturalist; the third of his most sustained works, *A Humble Discourse of the Incomprehensibleness of God*, in 1715, argues at length that the human understanding is disenabled and depraved by the fall of man, although after demonstrating the incapacity of the natural intellect to comprehend the Deity, for him the wonderful "use" of this demonstration becomes: "What is the duty of rational creatures as related to so glorious a Maker." The effect is not so much to render deplorable our limitations as to encourage us to live with them, enchanted that "the Understanding is the Superior Faculty in Man, by which he is raised above the Rest of the Visible Creation: And this Power is the Glory of Humane Nature." Regeneration remains an "act of Dominion," but it consists in bringing a reasonable creature to subjection through ways agreeable to its nature, liberty, and faculties; it is a "Rational Dominion," governing "by Law free & Intelligent Beings."

Once more, this proposition had been a teaching of the federal theology (in certain respects, the founders, with their utter devotion to logic, were greater "rationalists"—certainly vastly more "intellectualists"—than Colman). What made Colman's presentation striking was its context, which was not the covenant or the logical cosmology of technologia, but the universe of modern science. His emphasis upon the argument from design was inspired by thoughts of "The Discoveries of this kind made by Microscopes," or of the learned men who now believe. "from what they do see and know of the Creation by Tellescopes, that there may be and in probability are many such Worlds as this which we behold." The principle of plentitude excited his wonder more than definitions of covenant membership: the church covenant was so little a mystery transacted between God and man that it could be plainly derived from the law of nature, but how truly mysterious it had become that this globe should hang suspended in the ether, "How Unsearchable is the Law of its Center or Gravitation, wherein it is fixt!" Evidently he had heard of, if not altogether comprehended, Sir Isaac Newton.

To understand precisely the influence of Colman upon this provincial civilization, one must notice that while he points toward a freer and more rational theology, he also opens up a vein of rational emotionalism, of what may well be called a sentimentalized piety. Our labors, he said at the ordination of William Cooper in 1716, are of both head and heart; our pains require not only that we put our materials into due frame, but that we bring "lively Affection with us in our Work." His ideal of style meant shedding the archaisms of the Mathers, but it also designed a prose in which ordinary emotions were given greater play. If the tone of the voice were kept natural, then naturalness itself would produce its own sort of purple patches. His discourses on the natural universe delighted in pleasures of the senses: "the very Grass we tread on, and every Weed in the Field as well as the green Herb and painted Flower in the Garden." Or again, "What Beautie for our gazing Eyes? What Pleasing Sounds for our Ears? What Delicacy of Food for our Palates?" In a mood which associates him, even from afar, with such a poet as Thomson, Colman launched into rhapsodic panegyric of a universe which "speaks aloud the Pulchritude of its Maker."

Immediately after his ordination, when the furor over his *Manifesto* subsided, Colman applied himself to publication; presently he became Cotton Mather's nearest rival in productivity. The three titles already mentioned are his major efforts, but he poured forth the usual ordination and funeral sermons, advices to young people, pleas for reformation, lectures, artillery discourses, and election orations. In all this output, down to the Great Awakening he avoided controversy, entering into only one fray (that over inoculation, where he managed to be in full accord with the other clergy). Sometimes, when he provided instruction, he would realize that his reflections were "too general and lax," and try to give them more weight. To judge from surviving letters, he and Stoddard were on good terms, and Stoddard seems to have been most friendly in Boston with those of Colman's rather than of Mather's persuasion, with Wadsworth, William Brattle, Ebenezer Pemberton, Bradstreet, and, of course, Leverett. Stoddard knew nothing at first hand of London, Oxford, or Bath, but in his library, replenished by visits to Boston booksellers, were volumes of the "new" divinity. No more than Colman did he see any conflict between them and the positions he had taken in *The Safety of Appearing* (which Colman admired). Instead, he found in them encouragement to think for himself, to settle ecclesiastical problems on the grounds of common sense rather than of academic logic. He too began to elevate to an equal rank with reasonings from the Word of God those extracted from the order of nature: he commenced to preach that "the world is a glass reflecting the glory of God; and when men's eyes are opened, they may plainly see it." Without qualifying or in the slightest altering his Calvinism, he put especial emphasis upon the assertion, "Reason enlightened by the Spirit of God, teaches men convincingly what God is."

Meanwhile, the ability of the Mathers to concentrate upon matters theological was being distracted by Joseph Dudley, whom they had helped to put in the governor's chair. Although he gratified them by drawing the fire of Elisha Cooke, whose election to the Council he regularly set aside, and by keeping up his formal membership in the Church of Roxbury, yet he showed himself an Anglican at heart, and worse than that, a friend of Leverett and Colman. The character of Dudley is difficult for the modern American to comprehend; but, as we have seen, he must be evaluated in any history of the New England mind. In 1705 he found the road into Boston blocked by two Yankee farmers taking their produce to town; he berated them, even attacked them, with all the splenetic frenzy of a Squire Western, and poor Judge Sewall was much torn between his innate respect for authority and his sympathy with his countrymen, who conducted themselves with great dignity. The best defense for Dudley is that he had somehow acquired an understanding of the imperial interest; yet to say this is to pose the question of where or how he came by it: to which I can give no other answer but that like Gershom Bulkeley he learned disgust when trying to find his place in the New England society. Not that he and Bulkeley were bad Americans: considering the fact that so much of American literature consists of a critique of America by those in revulsion against it, we should not be put off because Dudley and Bulkeley were stigmatized as "Tories." Certainly the Dudley who returned in glory in 1702 was the same who uttered the insulting words to Ipswich, who executed Leisler's party in New York, who had nothing but contempt for colonial particularism. Yet the Mathers, who had perceived the significance of Bellomont, supported his candidacy because at least he was a New England man (that being, they were reduced to supposing, better than nothing); the name of Increase Mather still carried weight with the Foreign Office, and so Dudley got his job.

In 1706 one of his agents, Samuel Vetch, was accused of trading with the enemy, and the charge soon included Dudley as well. In constitutional history, this affair is important because the General Court (led by Cooke) fined Vetch and his associates, only to have their sentence annulled by the Privy Council; for this narrative, the noteworthy fact is that the fracas coincided with the election of Leverett, whom Dudley supported, as President of Harvard. That party in the House which pushed the investigation of Vetch had been hostile to Increase Mather; but both he and his son, smarting from their defeat at Harvard, flung themselves into the assault upon their traitorous ally. They addressed to him two of the most insulting letters in the literature of New England contumely, and because he would not heed them, published in November 1707 *A Memorial of the Present Deplorable State of New-England*. Such a controversy would be decided (if at all) not in Boston but in London; there Dudley printed his answer, *A Modest Enquiry*, and there the Mathers (Cotton no doubt the once again anonymous author) arranged for the publication of *The Deplorable State of New-England By Reason of a Covetous and Treacherous Governour, and Pusillanimous Counsellors*. To be sure, this was not a reply to Dudley, because it was sent off before copies of Dudley's broadside reached Boston, but it was another of those craftily inspired Matherian "anticipations," in this case taking advantage of the ignominious failure of the military attack, in May 1707, upon Port Royal, for which they gleefully assumed that Dudley could be blamed. While all this was going on, Colman continued to preach resolutely against envy and revenge, by which was reckoned, according to Judge Sewall, that "he lash'd Dr. Mather and Mr. Cotton Mather . . . for what they have written, preach'd and pray'd about the present Contest with the Govr."

In literary history the two letters and the three pamphlets are memorable not only because they display a few of the more opprobrious habits that had accrued (outside official speech) to the New England language, but also because indirectly they show that the frame of the jeremiad was broken by the obstinacy of Joseph Dudley. Cotton Mather realized that he and his father no longer enjoyed much esteem among the mass of the people, but he proposed nevertheless to fight Dudley in their name. Here the Mathers had to confess that what they had expected to be an instrument of orthodox supremacy, namely the Council, proved itself a feeble reed; but in the face of this admission, they still endeavored to excuse themselves by accusing Dudley of corrupting that body: "You hurry them; you force them; you chase them out of their pace; you drive them too fast"—wherefore these hapless senators have been "Trappan'd." Those contemporaries who in the same year availed themselves of Colman's permission to indulge in moderate mirth could hardly ignore the humor of a situation in which Cotton Mather turned to the House of Representatives, the preserve of Elisha Cooke, and exhorted them to stand firm upon their nominations to the upper chamber: "Should you be Negativated out of the Council . . . it would be a much greater Honour to you, than to be there." Ever since Dudley was installed, the recipients of this negativating treatment had been Elisha Cooke and his friends, the same insurgents against whom Increase Mather had allowed Phips first to exercise the power he had wished no governor to possess! How utterly, amid these shifting sands, the vision of a covenanted people had become obscured was revealed by Cotton's accusation that many Councillors outwardly complied with votes they inwardly disapproved, in the hope that their measures would be defeated in the House. Increase had gained for Massachusetts the inestimable privilege of selecting these magistrates; by 1707, said his son, all one could behold was "the Pusillanimity, and Unfaithfulness of their Governour's Counsellors, who will, too many of them, Consent to almost any thing he would have them." (They had just consented to the election of Leverett!)

At this late date, the Mathers recollected Dudley's career as a minion of Andros; they emerged as champions of liberty. It was indeed too late. They coined splendid slogans: Dudley exercises arbitrary power, the people are bought and sold, the faces of the poor are ground. Dudley may have been a rogue, but in his answer he struck hard at the hidden purpose of the Mathers' invective—and at their version of the jeremiad: they had formerly maintained "that Dominion is founded in Grace; and knowing themselves to be the elect people of God, they resolved to perfect what they had begun." Dudley delighted the sharp and clear wits of Boston by publishing the tale of a damsel of ill-repute who made an assault upon Cotton Mather's precarious virtue, and called him a would-be patriot who impressed only the inferior sort of people with his sanctimoniousness. Meanwhile, the Mathers rushed their second pamphlet to the press, for they learned that a petition of ministers had been organized in Dudley's favor. Cotton assured the world that the signatures of these rural pastors were obtained either by force or by circumvention, that not one minister in Boston would sign, that the petition meant nothing more than a vague endorsement of the principle of toleration. He told the endorsers that the governor's son Paul had been heard to say, "This Country will never be worth Living in, for Lawyers and Gentlemen, till the Charter is taken away," and he scolded them, "Your predecessors would not have done, as you have done." But nowhere in the Mathers' pamphlet does it directly appear what really infuriated them about this petition of the rural parsons: at the head of the list stood the name of Solomon Stoddard.

After his election sermon in 1703, Stoddard published nothing except, in 1705, a lecture he gave in Boston, *The Danger of Speedy Degeneration*, which took the noncommittal ground of a jeremiad. Publications of the Mathers and their friends kept up a steady denunciation of *The Doctrine of Instituted Churches*, concentrating their fire not upon its consociationalism (after the *Proposals* they dared not), but upon its heretical thesis that membership did not require a previous profession of faith. (Every dig at Stoddard was, by implication, a thrust at Brattle Street, but Colman was resolved upon silence.) Stoddard took his time, and chose 1708, just when the Mathers were in their rage against Joseph Dudley, to publish *The Inexcusableness of Neglecting the Worship of God, under A Pretence of Being in an Unconverted Condition*. Increase Mather promptly countered with *A Dissertation wherein The Strange Doctrine Lately Published . . . is Examined and Confuted*. He also brought out another edition of Thomas Doolittle's *Treatise*, with an "Advertisement Directed to the Communicants in the Churches of New England." The next year Stoddard came back with *An Appeal to the Learned*; whereupon a band of communicants in the North Church, remembering the strategy employed against Calef— undoubtedly because Cotton Mather similarly inspired their hesitant pens— issued *An Appeal, of Some of the Unlearned, both to the Learned and Unlearned*. Virtually every Mather imprint of these years contains some oblique, or less than oblique, reference to Stoddard: the tone is, to say the least, immoderate.

Events had deepened Stoddard's conviction, and he could now state his position succinctly: external duties are parts merely of the external covenant. Behind this assertion lies his immense persuasion that the reality of anyone's regeneration is never to be proved in this life. Therefore both the sacraments —the Supper as well as baptism—are designed not to nourish faith in those who already have it, but to be "converting" ordinances for the help, for the stimulation, of sinners. This confirmed, by a more profound analysis, his earlier thesis that no such thing as church covenant exists, or ever did exist, in Scripture or in nature; he refuted that error by appealing not to the Bible or nature, or even to reason, but to the lessons of history in western Massachusetts.

Stoddard's doctrine is actually the culmination—it seems almost inevitable—of that line of research set in motion by the founders themselves when they made their distinctions between outward and inward covenant, or when they tentatively found a place for hypocrites. He simply gives the final stroke to the wedge that had for so long been driven deeper and deeper between the two. His motive is clear: he wanted to solve the intolerable dilemma of the sacraments. The covenant which God makes with a visible people is visible, and does not require sanctifying grace; hence the people have "a natural power" to attend visible ordinances. Unregenerate men are not in the internal covenant, yet they may be in the external; and hypocrites, as long as they behave, do great service: "They help to maintain the Church and Ordinances of God, they do defend the Church, they do incourage the Church, they are Serviceable by their gifts, by their authority, by their prudence & zeal, by their Estates; and it would be exceeding difficult for the Church to subsist without them." Churches therefore judge only of appearances, not of realities; wherefore all those "that are in external Covenant with God, and neither Ignorant nor Scandalous may lawfully come to the Lords Supper." To stand upon the ancient (and mistaken) doctrine of New England, that men are commanded to come but damned if they come unworthily, is, said Stoddard, "unreasonable."

The New England mind dearly loved logic, but Stoddard's was a new kind of dialectic, the premises shot out of his experience like bullets from a musket, the syllogisms unerringly aimed at social realities:

The visible people of God are able to keep the external Covenant: It cannot be said to be lawful for them to keep the external Covenant, if it doth depend upon their Conversion which is indeed out of their power. But indeed there is no part of the external Covenant, that is beyond mens natural power, or their legal power.

It had now become abundantly evident that "saintship" might consist with considerable iniquity: why then keep up an artificial and unreal distinction? Visibility consists in saying "yes," and all yea-sayers—which would mean all the town except its idiots and most notorious sinners—should receive the Lord's Supper in the hope it might do them good. Sanctifying grace is indeed "an inestimable blessing," but it "is not necessary unto the Lawfull attending of any duty of Worship." All apologies for the Half-Way Covenant admitted that churches made mistakes, and of late years had admitted it generously; let us then give up the foolish pretense, recognize that the best we can attain is a "probable hope," wherefore "such persons may come as are not sincere." For decades the order had tried to attribute moral ability to those who merely owned the covenant; why not face the facts? "When such profess faith, they make a true Profession, they profess that which they do indeed believe, though their profession be not graciously sincere, & men are bound to speak the truth, though they do with a moral, and not a gracious sincerity." The people may be ignorant of the creed, but they "may soon be sufficiently informed." To suppose that men may be born into the covenant, and live from childhood to maturity as visible saints, and yet not be capable of coming to the Table because of some hypothetical lack of faith, is—once more—"unreasonable." With calculated irony, Stoddard appealed to the learned by a pragmatic recasting of the founders' doctrine: "All ordinances are for the Saving good of those that they are to be administered unto," and then left the learned to stew in the juice of their own erudition while advertising, "I dare not my self, as one of the Stewards in Gods House, refuse his Bread to such as regularly demand it." Thus he subtly concealed from view, yet allowed the realistic to perceive, that by putting himself in the public position of being prepared to dispense the bread to those who demanded it, he contrived that in a frontier community those who would not make the demand should suffer the consequences of self-ostracism.

Stoddard did not intend to be as "large" as most Reformed Churches or as the Church of Scotland; he wanted a power of debarring the scandalous, and he demanded that church members make at least as much of a profession as nodding their heads. Hence he was not a renegade from Congregationalism to Presbyterianism: he evolved his thought out of American conditions, realizing, first, that with the waning of political power, wider inclusions had to be allowed so that the churches might subsist without the help of dedicated magistrates, and, second, that the ordeal to which the doctrine of the holy sacrament subjected ordinary men was not only wasteful but excruciating. By it, "Sacrament Days which should be Days of Comfort, will become Days of Torment," because in the Matherian logic, a sincere Christian "is charged to come because of his hopes, and condemned for coming because he is unsanctified." By a curious analogy (to which, of course, Stoddard would never have confessed) to Calef's discovery in the realm of witchcraft, Stoddard found that in the church covenant men who aspired to sainthood were judged guilty of sinfulness by entertaining honest doubts about themselves. The presumption had become that if a man did not publicize his holiness, he was guilty of every enormity; hence many, as did Giles Corey at Salem, refused to speak at all. Forty years ago, said Stoddard, we yielded to the fact that multitudes were unbaptized and concocted the Half-Way Covenant; now we have a still more perilous problem: "To this day there be Four to One that do neglect the Lords-Supper; as if it did not belong to them to magnify God." And what wonder, when people were instructed by the Mathers? "It is a poor thing for men to be scared into Religion, but it is sad indeed for men to be scared out of Religion, & to neglect Gods Worship out of fear of God." If scaring there had to be, Stoddard would rather scare people in than out.

For, as he was able to show, the long succession of jeremiads, coming down since the first sermons on days of humiliation, were all attempts to frighten the populace, and had progressively become frankly so; they had not worked—had become, in fact, a bore. In the light of this fact, and not out of the splendid logic of the founders, the Bible should be read anew, in the *a priori* certainty that a deduction so unreasonable as that which discourages godly men from doing their duty is not to be found therein. By universal admission, these were "degenerate times"; the clergy were only adding to the momentum of declension by excluding moral citizens from the churches. "Staying from Ordinances is not the way to fit men for Ordinances; the neglecting of the Sacrament is the way to make the Country grow profane." (Could a culture which had achieved coherence on the assumption that the generality of men would always strive to fit themselves for the ordinances face up to the fact that in the very firmness of its assertion it had evoked its antithesis, so that a realist, even while remaining a Calvinist, could blame it for destroying itself?) The Mathers accused Stoddard of formalism, of sacrificing inwardness for outwardness, even of Popery; he retorted that their doctrine "has a tendency to nourish carnal confidence in them that are admitted, and to nourish Prophaneness in them that are excluded." It encouraged the presumptuous to suppose themselves converted; the bold are flattered "as if the bitterness of death were past," yet all this while the conscientious were aghast. His wife's father, the founding saint of Windsor, had, in his old age, so come to doubt his regeneration that in despair he withdrew from the sacrament. The man who wrote *The Safety of Appearing* understood the agonies and uncertainties of the soul, and in his forthrightness refused to add unto them.

On the intellectual side, Stoddard's argument embodies an element of skepticism, or at least a deep distrust of the power of the human mind to penetrate to this particular truth. He uses reason as a weapon to destroy what the Mathers considered infallible logic. He may be said to have brought into the open that strain of nominalism which always lurks in Calvinism, but he did it without becoming an Arminian (although the Mathers stooped to call him one). He definitely did not regard reason (no matter how many times he dismissed his opponents as unreasonable) as in any sense itself the giver or revealer of truth. By contrast with the Mathers he appears—strange as this may sound—anti-intellectual: they were insisting that a pattern does exist, that men do become regenerate and that of them churches can consist; they knew that in this world the pattern is difficult to make out, they realized that it had proved less easily translatable into practice than the founders had supposed; they had retreated step by step from the pure doctrine of John Davenport, back through the Half-Way Covenant, the jeremiads and the ownings, but now they stood at the last unsurrenderable bastion. Suppose it be true, as Stoddard says, that in many towns there are only two or three capable of demonstrating their regeneration: "Must we have Churches gathered, and the Body of the People admitted to the Lords Table, when there are but two or three among them fit to be there?" Because there are great difficulties in detecting the real saints, is this any reason for abandoning the effort? Especially when the judgment by "rational charity" allows for mistakes? Had Stoddard merely contended that visible saints are not always inward saints, "he would have affirmed, that which no body will contradict," but he was saying that saints by calling are to be accepted whether they be converted or no. "Did you ever hear," demanded Increase Mather, "of Unconverted Saints by calling before?" This notion "is *Contradictio in adjecto*, a notorious Contradiction of it self." His tirades are thus studded with terms of the old logic, with those turns of phrase by which disputants, not only at Harvard but more impressively at Oxford and Cambridge, gained momentous triumphs, the effects of which were to be reflected in the doctrinal formulations of every rural parson. Stoddard knew all that rigmarole, knew it by heart, and was through with it.

Increase Mather would make all allowance possible for failures of correspondence between inward and outward, but would never acknowledge that the outward could have any validity unless based upon the objective reality of the inward. He could never understand how much of an empiricist Stoddard had become; perhaps Stoddard himself did not comprehend, although he did amazingly develop a few of the implications in his position. Because he had to fend off the Mathers, he applied himself to proving by word and deed that his direct approach would get results denied to scholasticism. In 1712 and 1718 he had two more "harvests" which were the envy of all his colleagues. In 1714 he published *Guide to Christ*, which was to reach as large a public as *The Safety of Appearing* and which represents the farthest extension yet made of the concept of preparation. He found the area within which preliminary motions might operate so wide as to encompass virtually all human activity; this "we learn by Experience" and it "is very agreeable to Reason." He was infinitely less bothered than Thomas Hooker ever had been by Calvinist scruples: "Men are able to do many things in order to believing, and hereby they are put upon it to prepare for that." In these respects he furnished a model for hundreds of younger preachers; it would be difficult to overestimate the force of his example in the western regions or in early New Jersey, just as it would be hard to make too much of Colman's upon Harvard graduates, yet many historians, insufficiently skilled concerning the power of the word and the phrase, have given only passing mention to either of them.

Stoddard's son-in-law, William Williams, said that he was a grave man but also of a delightful conversation, "accompanied with a very sweet Affability & a Freedom from Moroseness." If given to mirth, Stoddard never laughed more heartily than at the self-confessed "Unlearned" of the North Church. They prostrated themselves before the titanic scholarship of Increase Mather and sneered at the "very little Reading" exhibited by Stoddard; they did "not think it any Answer to an Argument, to flout at the Author for being a Man of great Reading." Stoddard was secure enough in his own kind of scholarship; but he hammered insistently upon the theme which, as he pronounced it, was to have wide effect, that ministers ought not to carry their academic erudition into the pulpit. Increase Mather, fighting to keep the visible church in some degree of conformity to the invisible, had said in 1677 that the interest of religion and good literature was identical; Stoddard said, "Whatever Books Men have read, there is great need of experimental Knowledge in a Minister; many particular Things will occur that he will not meet withal in Books." He knew—none better—at what cost young men were sent to college: "the whole Family is fain to pinch that they may go through with it." Learning might be a help to civility and piety, but it could not engender either, and " 'tis not worth the while for persons to be sent to the Colledge to learn to Complement men, and Court Women." (It would be worth much for certain underprivileged members of this society who were learning from handbooks on manners, or from *The Spectator*, if not how to compliment at least how to court, to hear an old Harvard graduate thus tell off the society in which they were prevented from figuring solely because their fathers were not rich enough.) Such an investment, continued Stoddard, should "prepare them for Publick Service," which demands practical results.

As he saw it, "it is not enough for a Minister to be able to make some Edifying Discourses" (one thinks of Wadsworth), he must know how "to set those points that are more intricate in a true light." What he meant by casting a true light upon intricate points Stoddard showed by becoming the foremost New Englander in preaching, and advocating that others preach, the terrors of hell: "If men be thoroughly scared with the danger of damnation, they will readily improve their possibility, and not stand for assurance of success." Of a piece with his scorn for preaching from notes ("Experience shews that Sermons Read are not so profitable as others"), or for the use of historical arguments ("Men cannot believe them to be infallibly true upon probable Arguments; Probable Arguments must be looked on but as probable and not convincing"), was his contempt, in which the whole passion of the man appears, for those who spoke only to comfort and encourage, who talked about moral duties and awakened nobody. "The body of the People are in a perishing condition," and no gentle hint will awake them: "the threatnings of God had need ring in their Ears." Healing "plaisters" do not eat away proud flesh, and those who would convert others must use "piercing words." Too many are merely rhetorical, as if they were still in college: "this may tickle the Fancies of Men, and scratch Itching Ears; but we have Mens Consciences to deal with." Of course, he agreed, men cannot be frightened into the love of God, but "they may be scared into Reformation." Yet it requires a real man to frighten other men: "Experience fits men to teach others." In 1727 he told Northampton (by then they did as he commanded) to select, out of his grandsons, the child of Esther Edwards to be his colleague and successor; to him he bequeathed these admonitions.

It is of the essence, in order to appreciate Stoddard, to comprehend that he was not rationalizing conversion; on the contrary, in contrast to Colman, in his preaching the experience figures as a cataclysmic flash, a convulsion. Though he expanded the period of preparation, he contracted the crisis to a brief moment of ecstasy: "This change is made at once on the Soul, it is wrought in the twinkeling of an eye." It is not a gradual awareness, it is violent: "and tho' men never forget it, yet they cannot call to mind all that they were convinced of." The images Stoddard used were startling, and upon his grandson their lesson was not lost: "So, if a man should caste his eye upon a beautiful Person, he is much affected with his beauty; but he can't give a particular account of all his features, the comeliness of his forehead, eyes, cheeks and lips, nor give a description of them." It would be a mistake to suppose that Stoddard's reforms in polity came from a lessened rather than from a heightened sense of the reality of conversion; although historians have made this error, Increase Mather did not: he argued that Stoddard was led to abolish public relations because his own experience had been of "such notable Operations of the Holy Spirit" that he let himself set too high a standard for lesser Christians, and so dared not impose it. Were we to measure ordinary men by a Stoddard, said Increase in one of his few handsome passages, "there will not be in a whole Town, Regenerate Persons enough, to make a Church," whereas by the milder criterion of Boston, "a Judgment of Charity would find a considerable Number." But there was exactly Stoddard's point (which neither of the Mathers was capable of grasping): if the experience is so mighty and so shattering, then it is better that all men be brought to face it, and none coddled into supposing it easy. His last works—*Three Sermons Lately Preach'd at Boston*, 1717; *A Treatise Concerning Conversion*, 1719; *The Defects of Preachers Reproved*, 1724—are as searching investigations of the religious psychology as any published in New England between the analyses of Hooker or Shepard and the *Religious Affections* of his grandson (much in the latter being, in fact, indebted to them).

Considering, then, what a turn Jonathan Edwards was to give to the Stoddard tradition, and at what cost to himself, one does well to remember that from the beginning to the end of his own career, Stoddard's idea was that man does not know for certain about salvation. If true regeneration be utterly impossible to ascertain—contrary to the founders' courageous confidence—then to admit that fact became for the Mathers a final defeat; by deliberately contending that no one ever is assured, Stoddard turned defeat into victory. "Men don't know who are blessed," but "this uncertainty of Election is no discouragement." By surrendering to skepticism, by rediscovering that the Almighty, as approached from Northampton as from Geneva, is inscrutable, Stoddard faced unflinchingly what the Mathers could not contemplate: "There is no infallible Sign of Grace, but Grace. Grace is known only by Intuition. All the external Effects of Grace may flow from other causes." There simply was no absolute rule in Scripture for distinguishing between saints and hypocrites—any more than, according to Calef, there was a rule for detecting witches. All we know is that saints, hypocrites, and witches exist. "There is not knowledge enough upon Earth in order to the practice of it"; upon this, in the last analysis, clerical humility was founded the conduct of the proudest ecclesiastical autocrat of his generation: "The Church through their ignorance must wholly forbear acting, for their knowledge of other mens Piety is but a supposition." He went so far that he would not dogmatize about the inward state even of those cast out for the worst offenses: "the reason of their rejection is because they are obstinate in Scandal." In him appears that admiration for the likeness to Omnipotence discernible in the darkness of sin which for the greatest of theologians, from Augustine to Kierkegaard, has proved an instrument for the humbling of spiritual pride.

Or, to put it another way, Stoddard made it possible, for the first time in America, to talk about "varieties" of religious experience. The Mathers had been forced to acknowledge the variety, but held that all manifestations are resolvable into a single archetype. Stoddard gave up that effort, and erected a new coherence, adapted to frontier society, in which men could be different from one another and the church freed from an impractical formula. Out of his initial skepticism, Stoddard inaugurated the era of revivalism, which his grandson was to bring to a climax. He surrendered Winthrop's vision of a city on the hill, and used other means to gain his own ends; he bullied town officials and rigged the election of legislators, and he refused to wax hypocritical about hypocrites. "All that are taught by the Father will make a Profession of Christ: but there be many that make that Profession, that are not taught by the Father. There is a great difference between the visible Church and the invisible."

If the Mathers were left defending a beleaguered fortress, it must be said that in eastern New England they held it. "Stoddardeanism" proved unsuitable for import into the older areas, although it flowed across the Hudson into New Jersey. Henceforth neither the Mathers nor their fellows in the Cambridge Association have anything new to contribute to ecclesiastical doctrine; they remain fixed on the system of covenants, committed to the ideology of the jeremiad. They lament declension, threaten affliction, deplore the paucity of converts, try to improve the baptismal covenant and to stimulate owning of the covenant in order to baptize a few more. They have no other resource but the stereotyped procedure: they call for a reformation of manners, and nothing happens—nothing, that is, to be compared with Stoddard's harvests. They lament their plight, but will not attempt to achieve those ends at the cost of *The Cambridge Platform*. In 1708, Increase tried to cow Stoddard by calling him a false Presbyterian; he certainly was not like those "of the Union in London," of whom every one testified "against that Error of the Sacraments being a Converting ordinance." Yet all the Mathers' attempts to reinforce this charge, as in their issuing such Presbyterian writings as those of Quick and Doolittle, affected Stoddard as little as pebbles bouncing off a man-of-war. Obviously the solution in eastern New England was no solution: the community merely got along with what it had. The *Proposals* failed; a large number of the published titles thereafter, by the Mathers, by Colman and most of the eastern ministers, are pleas for making the old system work, and represent no advance over themes codified in the 1690's. Until the end of our period—and beyond it, even down to the Great Awakening—the topic of ecclesiastical polity, although much bewritten, remains a barren branch.

But during these years in the Valley, town after town went over to Stoddard, and so took a new lease on life. Some ministers, like Edward Taylor at Westfield, held out as long as they lived, but Stoddard survived most of them; at his death in 1729 only three (Enfield, Pelham, Belchertown) resisted, and his heir entered easily into a vast demesne. The Mathers kept up a mild fire, but their later lamentations are more whines than assaults. Stoddard was so well entrenched that they virtually surrendered, and after 1710 made every effort to show they entertained no hard feelings. Increase, who in 1687 had loftily refused Stoddard a preface, did penance in 1714 by writing a glowing introduction to Stoddard's *Guide to Christ*, acknowledging that in some points (*not* fundamental) "I differ from this' beloved Author"; but as Jerome said that he could not but love Christ in his opponent Augustine, "so do I say concerning my Brother Stoddard." In 1722 Cotton quoted with approval a suggestion for revising *The Westminster Confession* lately put forth by that renowned servant of God, "daily waiting to be dismissed unto his everlasting Rest; my venerable Uncle, Mr. Solomon Stoddard." It soon became a part of the Mathers' strategy to play down the controversy; Cotton in the *Parentator* hardly mentions it, and Samuel Mather, in *The Life of the Very Reverend and Learned Cotton Mather*, manages in 1729 to omit it entirely. Historians have followed the lead, and even among chroniclers of the Congregational churches, this great debate is seldom accorded its due.

Yet there is no way in which the development of the American mind can be coherently told without an appreciation of the arguments. Because the contest resulted in a stalemate does not mean that it was without effect, although the more far-reaching consequences were to show themselves only in 1740. Even in more immediate terms, the impact was great: New

England was effectually divided into two realms. There were still, of course, basic habits maintained from Maine to New Haven, and in that large sense the cultural pattern remained a unity; yet within that frame, the ecclesiastical order was definitely split, east opposed to west. When one remembers how central in the life of that society was the church, and how about it were organized concepts that have immense implications for American social history, this division becomes truly momentous, not to say prophetic.

Increase Mather lived just long enough to hear that the Presbyterian wing of the United Brethren, the group with whom he had had the greater sympathy during those years "I reckon'd among the more signal Mercies of my life," was becoming notoriously tainted with Socinianism. Cotton lived five years more, to learn that Socinianism had indeed triumphed among the sons of his father's sometime allies. To the very end, as the political hope grew dimmer (alas, bewailed Increase at the funeral of John Foster in 1711, eighteen years ago the governor and four of the Council belonged to the North Church: "Now there is none remaining"), the Mathers had no ecclesiastical argument left but to urge the obligations of the covenant, to threaten punishments upon those who defaulted, and to lament "What multitudes, Multitudes!—turn their Backs" upon the Lord's Supper, contented with their placid half-way status. "Especially, Press them to Mind their Children of the Obligation which their Baptism has laid upon them"—here, in one sentence, is the burden of most New England imprints between the *Proposals* and the Awakening. Yet nothing more could be said, because the covenant was the way of the founders; those led by the Mathers could not see any other way, no matter how much they strove to make the baptism into an instrument of stimulation, to desert the twin principles of consent and of covenant.

In this light, then, perhaps the most important note struck in the long debate between Mather and Stoddard was precisely that of the prestige of ancestors. Against both Brattle Street and Northampton the Mathers shrieked, in holy horror, that we must "abide in those Truths respecting the Order of the Gospel, which our Fathers have left with us a Legacy." It were "better to Dy," proclaimed Cotton, than to become a discomposer of that sacred heritage. But Stoddard was a man who, as William Williams put it, "us'd a freedom in examining of Things, and confin'd not himself to the Opinion of others." The founders, Stoddard told a Boston audience, "were a very holy People that came into this Land, whatever mistakes they were under, in any particulars, their hearts were engaged to do the Will of God"; nevertheless, he implacably insisted, "it lyes upon us to consider whether we have not corrupted ourselves." So at last a voice was raised, stronger than Colman's, against the first assumption of the jeremiads, against the thesis that Americans were inferior to their progenitors. "The mistakes of one Generation many times become the calamity of succeeding Generations." When Increase persisted in declaiming against him as apostate, Stoddard answered with words that deserve to be fully repeated, for they constitute a turning point in colonial, indeed in American, literature:

> As the Renown of those Reformers is a bulwark against those Errors that were Exploded by them, so we find our selves embarrassed by their mistakes from proceeding in the work of Reformation: As if it were criminal not to mistake with them . . .
>
> Men are wont to make a great noise, that we are bringing in of Innovations, and depart from the Old Way: But it is beyond me to find out wherein the iniquity does lye. We may see cause to alter some practices of our Fathers, without despising of them, without priding our selves in our own Wisdom, without Apostacy, without abusing the advantages that God has given us, without a spirit of compliance with corrupt men, without inclinations to Superstition, without making disturbances in the Church of God: And there is no reason that it should be turned as a reproach upon us.
>
> Surely it is commendable for us to Examine the practises of our Fathers; we have no sufficient reason to take practises upon trust from them: let them have as high a character as belongs to them, yet we may not look upon their principles as Oracles . . . It would be no humility, but baseness of spirit, for us to judge our selves uncapable, to Examine the principles that have been handed down to us: If we be any ways fit to open the Mysteries of the Gospel, we are capable to judge of these matters: And it would ill become us so to indulge our selves in ease, as to neglect the Examination of received principles. If the practises of our Fathers in any particulars were mistakes, it is fit they should be rejected, if they be not, they will bear Examination; If we be forbidden to Examine their practises, that will cut off all hopes of Reformation.

William Ellery Channing could not be more precise, Emerson more self-reliant, Theodore Parker more resolute! What Stoddard here proclaimed is that royal right of judgment which has come to be supposed (nobody quite knows how) the essential meaning of Protestantism; however, there is nothing quite like it to be found among the great Reformers, certainly not in Calvin, nor among the Protestant founders of New England, not even in Roger Williams. Possibly there is inherent in Protestantism a mentality bound, sooner or later, to turn the technique of protestation against its own origins, but in this case the spirit of self-criticism was evoked out of dogmatism not only by the failure of jeremiads to produce the needed results, but by the Mathers' doctrinaire demand that no methods except those which could claim ancestral sanction ought to be applied to American conditions. Hence, when Increase indulged in eloquent hymns to the founders, proclaiming that never did a generation attain to such perfection, Stoddard sourly observed that he magnified the fathers into the Apostles, and that this sort of hyperbole "especially is his proper Element." When Increase moaned, "Would he bring the Churches in New-England back to the Imperfect Reformation in other Lands, and so deprive us of our Glory for ever?" Stoddard remarked, "Mr. Mather all along intermingles

Passionate Lamentations with his Arguments," which "serve to swell the Book and make it more in bulk, but not in weight."

Stoddard's irony did not prevent Increase Mather from continuing to call, in his peculiarly sepulchral tones, upon the perfect and flawless founders, from whom his audiences were supposed always to have degenerated. This, as Stoddard had said, was his element. But Stoddard lent heart to other spokesmen, and helped Colman assert that if some of the first customs too much restricted Communion or infringed "the Natural Rights of Men and the Legal Rights of English Men," then we had "done well long since to Abolish any such corrupt and persecuting Maxims." We may revere our forefathers without repeating their errors, and above all we should not be inhibited by their notions from doing something about the altogether too many unbaptized and unconverted persons we have among us. Thanks mainly to Stoddard, an occasional election preacher could rebel against a reckless denunciation of every difference of opinion as constituting apostasy and subversion. Thanks more to Stoddard than to the royal government, John Leverett at Harvard College could let students examine even the founders of Harvard College in a critical spirit, and could impart to them the excitement of a liberalized education. "There is," said Solomon Stoddard, "a necessity of vindicating the Truth, yet we cannot do it without making some disturbance."

T HE
Proposals, as sent to the churches, bore the date of
November 5; scorning fixed holidays, the orthodox signers may not have
noticed that this was Guy Fawkes Day, but among the people profane
memories persisted, and a man of the people would remember the anni-
versary of Gunpowder Treason. We have beheld John Wise at Ipswich
and at Quebec: if any cleric was of the people, or spoke their language,
assuredly it was he. We can recover nothing of how he lived or what he
preached after returning in disgust from Phips's mismanaged invasion of
1690; he appeared as a character witness in defense of at least one of the
accused in Salem, and signed a petition for restitution to heirs of the
slaughtered. Worth noting is the fact that, although the hysteria spread
from Salem Village to Andover, it did not infect Ipswich. In 1697 he
drafted instructions for a company intending emigration from Essex County
to South Carolina, which are notable for their concern with such practical
considerations as the nature of the soil and the manners of the population.

Undoubtedly a copy of the *Proposals* went to Chebacco Parish, as to all
established churches. Cotton Mather preserved his own manuscript, which
was printed in 1814, but all other copies of the text ultimately disappeared.
The movement was dead; why keep the thing around, or why give it
further thought?

Wise dates the preface of his answer May 31, 1710: we suspect that if
he sought a Boston publisher, he faced what Calef and Colman had confronted, but perhaps he was canny enough not even to try. For whatever
reason, *The Churches Quarrel Espoused: or, A Reply in Satyre, to certain
Proposals*, was published in 1713 at New York; this issue is today exceedingly rare, and there is no evidence that it had much circulation in New
England. But in 1715 a "second edition" did appear in Boston, prefaced
by a letter to Wise from Samuel Moody, stationed since 1698 in York, and
John White, minister since 1702 in Gloucester, husband since 1703 to
Wise's daughter Lucy. They begged him to reprint, professing that their
eyes had been opened by his transcendent logic, grammar, and rhetoric,
to see the value and glory of New England's privileges, and that therefore
his book might be of wonderful service to the churches; or at least, they
said, "it will be a Testimony that all our Watchmen were not asleep, nor
the Camp of Christ surprized and taken, before they had warning." They

seem to imply that the New York printing was not getting through to the people.

This edition could hardly be ignored. Evidently the Cambridge Association rebuked Moody and White for endorsing it, and on August 2, at a fast in Brattle Street, Colman in the morning "Censur'd him that had Reproach'd the Ministers as they were Gog and Magog," while in the afternoon Cotton Mather (this collaboration in 1715 of the opponents of 1700 is the true measure of Wise's significance) further censured him "that had reproached the Ministry, calling the Proposals Modalities of little consequence, and made in the Keys; call'd it a Satanick insult, twice," and lamented (according to Sewall's elliptical account) that the insult had "found a kind Reception." Sewall thought the whole proceeding excellent, although he himself "could wish the extremity of the censure had been forborn." On September 17, Cotton Mather wrote to Woodrow of Glasgow that there were no disturbances in the colonial churches except that "a furious Man" had published a foolish libel "against some of us, for presbyterianizing too much in our Care to repair some Deficiencies in our Churches." Then he who against Stoddard had delivered the resounding oration of July 4, 1700, dryly observed: "Some of our People, who are not only tenacious of their Liberties, but also more suspicious than they have cause to be of a Design in their pastors to make abridgments of them; are too much led into Temptation, by such Invectives." However, he thought Wise had not had, nor would have, much effect.

That he should affect to speak of Wise as some rank outsider was absurd: he had several times celebrated the Ipswich protest as a stroke for English liberties, and he knew Wise's part in it. The sentiments of Chebacco were familiar to Sewall, who in 1714 took part in the gathering of a church at Ipswich Farms, there to hear Wise give the right hand of fellowship, "much applauding the N. English venerable Constitution."

In 1717 John Wise, following this train of thought, boldly issued his second book, *Vindication of the Government of New-England Churches.* Cotton Mather felt the shock, and took thought with himself what he might do throughout the land "that the Poison of Wise's cursed Libel may have an antidote?" But he lifted not a hand; in the *Ratio Disciplinae,* published in 1726 but undoubtedly written in 1719, he recounted the history of the *Proposals,* explaining that they had been shelved out of deference to several "Good Men," although there was, he added, "a Satyr, Printed against these written Proposals, and against the Servants of God that made them," but these followers of the Lamb, remembering the maxim of "Not Answering" (a new weapon in the Matherian arsenal) and profiting by the example of the University of Helmstadt (which Cotton had already cited in his letter to Woodrow of 1715), retired into generous silence and pious contempt.

There the story seems to end, which is a puzzle. In relatively modern times, Wise's works have come into their own, first rediscovered by political scientists and then celebrated by historians of literature; if any writing of the period has an assured place in the canon of American expression, it is they. For a while, students assumed that such powerful attacks must have demolished the *Proposals*, but later investigation demonstrated that long before Wise published, the project was moribund. Aside from the few evidences of contemporaneous perturbation already noted, the books were swallowed up in Cotton Mather's generous silence. Samuel Moody, even then becoming the legendary eccentric "Father Moody," was a strict conservative in theology, later a resolute advocate of the Awakening; John White pronounced in 1734 a jeremiad, *New Englands Lamentations*, which deplored the too great individualism of Congregational churches and made the first public accusation that some among the clergy were Arminian (that very year, Jonathan Edwards was to commence his fatal feud with his Williams cousins by denouncing the spread of "Arminianism"). The mystery might be resolved if we had a single scrap of a theological utterance from Wise, but the efforts of countless researches have turned up nothing. The unwary might assume that he who radically expounded the authority of reason in ecclesiastical realms would also preach reason in religion, but to jump to that conclusion is to miscomprehend the first decades of the century. That Moody and White were Calvinists and denouncers of Arminianism is significant: there is no cause for supposing that the author of the *Vindication* did not preach *The Westminster Confession* undefiled, as also did Stoddard and Colman.

Hence the importance of Wise, great as it is, must be stated cautiously. *The Churches Quarrel* readily provides the clue: Wise was inspired by a tremendous passion for the rights of Englishmen, wherefore he was more prepared than most of his contemporaries to call them simply the rights of man. In his extravagant enthusiasm for the British constitution he hymns praises of the "Empire" that might have made Joseph Dudley blush, and cries up November 5 as "Blessed! Thrice Blessed Day!" trusting that if ever some monster shall threaten the nation's glory, on this day a hero will arise to confound him. So he overwhelms the absent-minded associations: "Why Gentlemen! have you forgot it? It is the day of the Gun-Powder-Treason, and a fatal day to Traytors." After all, he had been in 1687 the forerunner of that solemnization of the rights of Englishmen to which champions of the old charter learned to give voice in the 1690's. What could there be of revolution in his objecting, upon the analogy of the English Parliament, to consociations or standing councils? He was saying only what Mathers themselves had said: "In Honour to the New-England Churches, and with veneration for the English Monarchy, I dare assert, that there is in the Constitution of our Church Government more of the English Civil Government in it, and it has a better Complexion to suit the true English Spirit, than is in the English Church." The New England mind had not yet dared take the positive step of defending Congregational polity on the grounds of its affinity with the civil order of "the most flourishing Common-wealths" in the world, or of equating its basic principles with those which gave preëminence to the House of Commons or with the idea of judgment by one's peers, but the way for such an assertion had long been prepared by precisely those against whom Wise now rose in his anger and his contempt.

Cotton Mather therefore called him furious, but Mather would have a hard time, considering his own pronouncements, taking exception to such premises as that Englishmen live and die by laws of their own making, that their government is based upon a charter or a mutual compact, that "Englishmen hate an Arbitrary Power . . . as they hate the devil." Hence Mather could not but feel the sting when Wise concluded, out of these premises, that the *Proposals* "Out-King'd," "Out-Bishop't," and "Out-Pop't" all existing kings, bishops, and popes.

But the rights of Englishmen are more than sentences on parchment, more than devices by which a Puritan oligarchy might turn a royal charter to its notions of orthodoxy: they have a common-sense implication, they apply to real situations. Wise objected to consociations as invasions of English liberty, and reinforced his opposition with such utilitarian arguments as that they would squander the time of ministers in the deadly atmosphere of the committee room. They would keep a man from getting on with his proper work, and like all trappings of tyranny, their very superfluousness proved them false. The *Proposals* said that councils should answer questions of importance by due deliberation; Wise replied that there were no questions in New England so important as to require that much deliberation: "We must enquire, How many deep Questions can be found in our Country, grown mouldy with the Gibeonites Bread, for want of wise handling?" As for problems of moral regulation, every parson had on his shelves Ames's or Turretine's handbook of casuistry, which "for a few Shillings will do more in a month, for an Inquisitive Mind, than this Proposal can do in the tedious apprenticeship of many years." To a man who knew his rights and stood upon them, the *Proposals* were a confession of pusillanimity, of that shrinking from the rough facts of life which had aroused the contempt of Stoddard: the lily-livered were taking refuge in consociations, trying to support each other in actions likely to produce "Imbroylments." On this score Wise and Stoddard joined hands across the intellectual gulf: deeply immersed in their different communities, each of them knew that a minister worth his salt gets into "Imbroylments" and then gets himself out of them, not by crying for help but by being, like Wise, a man.

The most that we can make of it, is a Covering of Figg-Leaves, and may serve for a Harbour to Cowards and Fools but not for men of Spirit and Conduct. The Dream of an Imbroylment, can never Counter-Poize Duty; If men are Trusted with Duty, they must consult that, and not Events. If Men are plac'd at Helm, to steer in all weather that Blows, they must not be afraid of the Waves, or a wet Coat.

If, in their first conception, the works of Wise were defenses of the rights of Englishmen, they show how the exercise of those rights was being translated into the terms of his society: for him, the rights were not bulwarks of security but the prerogatives of forceful personalities, of leaders capable of creating disturbances and resolving difficulties, who could maintain their privileges in the sort of speech where, to use Colman's phrase, the voice is kept natural.

These works, as posterity has learned to appreciate, are important as much for how they speak as for what they say. They amount to a liberation of language, and their example, even if not noticeably felt by Wise's ministerial colleagues, could not be lost upon James Franklin or his little brother Benjamin, or upon men more concerned with the declining currency than with the declension of the spirit. Wise's books are truly forerunners of the literature of the American Revolution, first creating that symbol which then was to be so central of the square-toed, common-sense American who calls a spade a spade and does not manufacture pinheads.

This I am sure must needs stand for a verity, that the Judgment of a real honest and skilful Artificer (keeping close to his Shop) concerning the Nature and Qualities of an Edge-Tool which he hath wrought, and hammered on his own Anvil, out of its first Rude Matter, must certainly Excel him that hath been long from the Trade, that only takes it, turns and tries the Edge slightly, or has but a transient view of it.

We may rejoice that such prose now enters this narrative, but the real humor of the passage is even deeper: it is part of Wise's argument that the churches should depend, when selecting new ministers, upon the recommendation of "Harvards Commendamus" and not upon the opinion of an association; "the best and most Infallible Standard for the Philosophical Accomplishments of our Candidates, is the Judgment of the Honourable Praesident, and noble Fellows of our Famous Colledge." Thus John Leverett (who indubitably was F. R. S.) was pictured as an honest artificer who keeps close to his shop, while Cotton Mather was exhibited to the country as one long from the trade! What good sense Mather showed by deciding to remain silent now becomes apparent.

Wise's vocabulary is the man himself: "Where men are without the Law, and all hail fellows, not well, but badly met"; we shall only lose "by swapping Governments upon these Terms"; the *Proposals* are a "crude Dose." The councils were supposed to contain lay delegates; Wise the minister saw that this was a sacerdotal deception to fool the people into thinking the decisions were not merely clerical; but once the clergy have soared "above their proper Sphere," they will push the laity out by a "Back-door very Artificially finished and left upon Latch, for their execution." To illustrate the fate of these dupes, he used a metaphor which, in its outspoken sexuality, would be at once comprehended by every Yankee farmer:

It is an observation, on the Monarchy of Bees, that the Drones formerly sup-posed to be not only a lumpish, but a useless Bee, yet it is of that nature, and so Essential a Member of that Commonwealth, that it is Really the Male-Bee, and does Impregnate the Females, who are the Sole Labourers in that Kingdom, but when that Crisis is over, the poor Drones are by common Consent Banished, as a great Incumberment.

No American writer had yet managed so felicitous a handling of a single word as Wise bestowed upon his "crisis."

With the proposal that councils take upon themselves the selection of ministers for particular churches Wise made such sport as altogether to sur-pass the limits set by Colman to sober mirth:

It seems to me very Adviseable (if this Proposal may stand for a sound Precept) that forthwith another Office be erected, and put into the hands and under the Government of a few men, exactly skilled in Physiognomy, and deeply Studied in the Sympathies and Antipathies of Human Nature, with an absolute super-intending Power to Controul, and direct all Wooers in their Choice for the Mar-riage Bed; for that there is many a fond Lover who has betrayed the glory of Wedlock, by making an unwise and unfortunate Choice; And why may not par-ticular Beds be overruled, as well as particular Churches?

There are evidences (which we inordinately treasure) showing that the Puritans knew how to laugh. Cotton Mather is often funny, though seldom by deliberation (when he tries, he is generally labored); however, Samuel Sewall told of his courtship of Madame Winthrop with at least some aware-ness that he cut a ridiculous figure. But when Wise's lines were read around country hearths, we may be sure that a guffaw arose, after which New England would never quite be the same again. His son-in-law, John White, hardly impresses us, from his own publications, as a genial character, and we may even suspect that in the funeral sermon he pronounced upon Wise in 1725, which he entitled *The Gospel Treasure in Earthen Vessels*, he encountered a certain difficulty in getting the image of a Gospel message into the large and loose-limbed figure of the wrestling parson. (We should indeed note how eulogists of both Wise and Stoddard make much of their great height and their physical stamina.) It was a fact, said White, that no man ever went out of Wise's presence sorrowful. Words had to be chosen carefully in 1725, but White picked those which, in the context of the time, were revealing, at least to readers who had received the benefit of Colman's *Mirth:*

And some who had viewed him at a distance thro' a Glass, when they have Visited him, and familiarly Conversed with him, have been Charmed, and even Ravished. They have beheld Majesty mixt with Affability, Gravity with Facetious-ness, Charity and Severity; Charity to the Persons, and Severity to the Opinions of his Antagonists.

Gravity and facetiousness struck an alliance—although in contemporaneous eyes the charity was not so visible—when Wise informed signers that rather than try to subvert by despotic measures "an Empire and Province so Charmed with such Inchanting Liberties as ours are," they had better write words on the ground, "or with the famous Domitian, spend the time in Catching Flies." The student of American speech will find himself obliged to pause in the midst of the argument to note the prominence, both in Wise's statement and that of his son-in-law, of the words "charmed," "inchanting," and "ravished"—linked with "facetiousness." What sources in Puritan Essex County fed these springs of humor?

Wit had more scope in the "satyr" than in the *Vindication;* Moody and White asked for its republication out of admiration for its grammar and rhetoric as well as for its logic, since it chose to answer the *Proposals* by a device without precedent (unless Nathaniel Ward's might be so accounted, who, we should remember, found two comforts in Calvinism, the perfections of Christ and the manifold imperfections of Christians) in colonial literature. Like Ward, Wise assumed a masquerade (a more sustained jape than that of the simple cobbler, hence one that might give ideas to younger writers seeking a pseudonym for scoring unpopular points): he pretended to be a prosecuting attorney, "under Commission from Authority, to appear in Defence of my Countries Sacred Liberties"; hence he drew up an indictment, using as his model the speech of Sir Edward Coke "in the Arraignment of Sir Walter Rawleigh." This gave him a chance to depart, whenever he chose, from logic into rhetoric, to point out that only by an act of the government could consociations ever come into compulsive power, but that meanwhile ministers might freely gather in mere associations as often as they wanted, "for they are Masters of themselves, and no more accountable how they spend their time, than other men are." The masquerade also enabled him to give an historical analysis of how associations, formed under the necessities of 1690, had gradually come to think of themselves as possessing a power they had no right to, until at last "out come these Proposals, like Aarons Golden Calf, the fifth day of November, 1705," and then to tell the reader that here was the whole history, "like Homers Illiads in a Nut Shell." The pose further permitted him to stud his discourse with appeals to the jury, such as that they protect their "sacred liberties" and fight bravely "in withstanding vassalage or a servile State," in the name of those "liberties wherewith Christ has made us free, and be not entangled again with the yoke of bondage." The peroration asserted that *The Cambridge Platform* contained everything necessary for the prosperity of the churches, that it required no additions, and that stirring up the hearts of church members to live according to their professions was the only thing necessary.

This, amusingly enough, was the sustained message of the jeremiads, although in Wise's statement it sounded nothing like so ominous or strenuous. Obviously, it was not his real conclusion; irony and satire were all very well, but in the course of making fun of the *Proposals,* he called them unreasonable. This led him into a digression, wherein he defined

reason as "that great oracle in human affairs," that soul of man, sometimes sharpened by constitution, by grace or by study, "whereby man's
Intellect is inabled to take up (*pro Medulo,* or in a degree) the true Idea
or Perception of things agreeable with, and according to their Natures."
This sounds like orthodox Ramist doctrine, which Wise would have
learned at Harvard. Still—is there not a difference in the conception
of agreement between idea and thing when the idea is called upon to
correspond with the "crisis" of copulation among bees or with the marriage
bed among men, from what it had signified when the idea was a construct of artificial and inartificial arguments extracting a church covenant
out of the New Testament? If, as a common-sense man, basing yourself
upon the rights of an Englishman, you know what is true, might not
"Recta Ratio" signify even more than an ability to read the Bible? The
inner logic of the positions to which Wise's passion drove him then further obliged him to proceed from the satire of *The Churches Quarrel* to
the demonstration of the *Vindication;* the *Proposals* were quickly forgotten, nor did the censures of Colman and Mather much bother anybody in
Chebacco. The great fact was that rhetoric dictated to logic: a man could
not let himself playfully describe the *Proposals* as embryos "born out of
due times," nor could he draw upon his knowledge of bastardy among the
people in order to say, "there is no Statute to be found that will justify
the first Coitus of the Parents" and so slyly invoke the rule of Deuteron-
omy, "A bastard shall not enter into the Congregation," without having
to ask himself, in all seriousness, what after all is natural? An emanci-
pation of language meant, irresistibly, that the intellect must also liber-
ate itself, that resistance to the *Proposals* be vindicated not merely out of
the Bible or out of English constitutional tradition, but out of pure natural reason.

This is the achievement of the *Vindication,* to which it addressed itself
in the second and most copious of its five proofs by daring to defend the
order of the New England churches "fairly" out of the law of nature
alone, without any reference to revelation. Wise wryly protests that in
making this experiment he is merely gratifying his own curiosity, although
possibly diverting the reader; he acknowledges, "I shall go out of the Common Road, and take into an unusual and unbeaten Path," but hopes he
may thus open a road to knowledge and wisdom. Actually the direction
of the road to be explored had, as we have watched the signs emerging,
been prefigured; Wise was the first to realize its destination: the reason
for these churches' being what they are "is really and truly owing to the
Original State and Liberty of Mankind, and founded peculiarly in the
Light of Nature."

In the opinion of some scholars, Wise is not so great a figure as was
once supposed because whole paragraphs of this second demonstration
turn out to be paraphrases of Samuel Pufendorf's *De Jure Naturae et
Gentium.* The accusation is generally accompanied with a further deni-

gration, that he was ignorant of Locke; the curious supposition, peculiar to Anglo-Saxon scholarship, is that he would have been more original had he drawn upon the English Locke rather than upon the German Pufendorf. Basil Kennett's translation of Pufendorf had appeared in London in 1703 (the first printing in England of the Latin text was 1672); Wise may have used either it or the original, but he does acknowledge, "I shall Principally take Baron Puffendorff for my Chief Guide and Spokes-man," and so plunges ahead. Kennett's text has Pufendorf say that the law of nature consists of "the accurate Contemplation of our Natural Condition and Propensions"; Wise puts it, "The way to discover the Law of Nature in our own state, is by a narrow Watch, and accurate Contemplation of our Natural Condition, and propensions." This insertion of "narrow Watch" is typical of the redaction Wise gave to his source, even when following it most literally. In this fashion he presented a body of thought with which the colonies were not quite familiar, modulating it into a key they would comprehend. There are, as we know, differences between Pufendorf and Locke's *Treatises on Government,* but both arise out of the same background, out of the secularization of the Protestant conception of the state. Perhaps it is all the more to the credit of the rural intellectual in Chebacco that he did not yet know of the English theorist, and that somehow encountering the German philosopher, he seized as decisively as Locke himself upon the conceptions of social compact, natural rights, and right of revolution; just as Locke made these the rationale of the English constitution, Wise proposed that they rather than Scripture gave the *raison d'être* to Congregational societies.

At any rate, whatever he took from Pufendorf, he contrived to set it in a context purely New England. His first demonstration appealed to the "Voice of Antiquity" and relied, so pointedly as to be downright insulting, upon the works of Increase Mather. (He knew, as did his readers, that the author of *The Order of the Gospel,* deeply committed against Stoddard, had refrained from signing the *Proposals.*) Wise then made the transition to his rational demonstration easy by quoting "the London Ministers," thus placating in advance all champions of the United Brethren. From that point, it was clear sailing, so that, after finishing the proof from nature, he could add, almost as an afterthought, those demonstrations which the founders took from the Bible, and then reinforce them with practical considerations, such as the inherent "ballance" of the system and its affinity with English parliamentarianism. So the crux of his thesis, the point where he dug in his heels, is the second section, the unusual and unbeaten path; here, with or without the help of Baron Pufendorf, but with great help from his native wit, Wise commenced a new chapter in the history of the provincial mind—even though many of his sentences were in fact variants of venerable propositions.

The uniqueness of his treatment consists in his isolating the rational proof, of allowing it to stand entirely by itself; in daring to dispense, if only for the moment, with Biblical and historical evidences, he established the philosophy so firmly upon a secular basis of nature that all other testimonies were reduced to subsidiary confirmations. His heart was really in this portion of the book: the Congregational polity is the "Royal assent of the supream Monarch" to *previous* decisions of reason. "It seems to me as though Wise and Provident Nature by the Dictates of Right Reason excited by the moving Suggestions of Humanity; and awed with the just demands of Natural Libertie, Equity, Equality, and Principles of Self-Preservation, Originally drew up the Scheme, and then obtained the Royal Approbation." It was of course from God—"whether we receive it nextly from Reason or Revelation, for that each is equally an Emanation of his Wisdom"—but if it could be received in its entirety from reason, what need of revelation? So then, after the fiasco of witchcraft, after the *Manifesto* and Stoddard had cast grave doubts upon the Biblical source of the covenant, after Stoddard had concluded that a vigorous pastor would not let himself be hamstrung by the covenant when he addressed himself to the task of keeping his people in order, there arose a pastor who also was vigorous but not inhibited by the theory of the covenant, who in his heart was indifferent to the question of the Biblical warrant, but who was passionately devoted to the polity in and for itself, and for whom it meant, not an autocratic city on a hill, not Stoddard's or even Winthrop's contempt for the commonalty, but, by all the laws of reason and of nature, democracy.

Wise is indeed a riddle. We can trace with perfect consistency the evolution of political ideas through a sequence of (on the whole) conventional election sermons, wherein the Puritan conception of the Bible commonwealth was slowly, and never radically, transformed into the philosophy of a government limited by the law of the land and by the terms of its charter, until the ultimate deduction quietly emerged that a tyrannical invasion of this law may legitimately be resisted. But no thinker before the Revolution, not even Jonathan Mayhew, gave to this doctrine the democratic, egalitarian emphasis that Wise did. This element in his formulation he did not get from Pufendorf, but from (we must assume) his experience among a rural population, and that not on Stoddard's frontier, but in an older community where the way of life had subsided from the lofty vision of the founders into getting a living. His logic, which was not what the founders called logic but what was to have a wider vogue under the name of common sense, argued that men in a state of nature were in a condition of natural freedom and equality, that therefore they would preserve as much of nature as possible, and so in their first covenant would set up a popular government. By this insight, democracy is "most agreeable to the Just and Natural Prerogatives of Humane Beings," and that system is best which favors the natural equality of men; assuredly "Government was never Established by God or Nature, to give one Man a Prerogative to insult over another." All this, he said—here parting company not only from the Mathers but from Stoddard—"is as plain as day light."

Possibly the really revolutionary maneuver in the *Vindication* is not so much the assertion of democracy (for the word had not yet become a slogan) as those definitions of reason and of the law of nature out of which he derived his democratic conclusions. Wise's books were so little discussed at the time (at least in anything that survives) that we are not exactly sure what Cotton Mather meant by their "poison"—whether the democratic teaching or merely the derisive tone; but if he was (as seems most evident) deeply troubled and yet dared not attack Wise, knowing himself too vulnerable, then what most appalled him must have been the stark rationalism. During a later controversy, in 1772, one faction reissued Wise's volumes (curiously enough, there appears even then no connection between them and any theorists of the Revolution); Nathaniel Whitaker answered by reaching back into seventeenth-century technologia for his definition of reason, saying it is no more than the faculty which "draws inferences" from Scripture, that it may reject what is contrary to revealed rules, "but it may make no new institutions." Hence Wise was simply arrogant because he gave "large scope for such towering and self-applauding fancies in the breasts" of ordinary and unregenerate men. However, those closer to the seventeenth-century teaching were uncomfortably aware that technologia was not too consistent; there were many passages in Richardson and the Harvard theses which celebrated the intuitive rational truths which man, despite innate depravity, retains in his soul. By separating the self-evidently reasonable demonstration from the revealed, and allowing it to stand with no suggestion of outside support, Wise did not so much propound a novelty as extract out of the intellectual heritage a truism to which he could thus give a novel (and dangerous) implication: man "is the Favourite Animal on Earth; in that this Part 'of Gods Image, viz. Reason, is Congenate with his Nature." Then, because he was arguing (if only for the moment) in wholly secular terms, Wise went further than any colonial theologian had ventured, catching up with and even surpassing the most latitudinarian of English rationalists. He positively presented reason not merely as an instrument for interpreting Scripture, but as itself the giver of truth. "That which is to be drawn from Mans Reason, flowing from the true Current of that Faculty, when unperverted, may be said to be the Law of Nature." Furthermore, this authority is inward and so available to all men—not like the Quaker inner light a supernatural visitant, but universally "Congenate." By it "the Understanding of Man is Endowed with such a power, as to be able, from the Contemplation of human Condition to discover a necessity of Living agreeably with this Law." The understanding is able, as Wise asserted by his subtle but staggering addition to Pufendorf, to evolve political principles out of itself "by a narrow Watch."

To John Winthrop this would have been rank heresy. The human choice, as he described it in the famous speech of 1645, had not been between authority and reason, or between tyranny and liberty, but only between order and depravity. Hence he found it impossible to imagine natural liberty, outside the social condition, as anything but brutish, whereas there was nothing tyrannical in obliging the multitude within the covenant to submit to those set over them for their own good, compelling them by force to yield to what is, in itself, eternally good, just, and honest. The content of this goodness, justice, and honesty was not given by reason, but it was eminently rational. Wise drew out the revolution which had been implicit in Winthrop's federal authoritarianism to a conclusion that would have horrified every one of the founders, not only Winthrop but Roger Williams as well. He took as first premise an identification of natural liberty with "the Tyes of Reason, and Laws of Nature," and then exclaimed, "all the rest is Brutal, if not worse." In his argument, brutality became any attempt of the authorities to impose upon the population, by irrational compulsion, something which only the authorities had defined as good, just, and honest.

It seems significant that in the spring of 1719 Wise was at last invited to give the election sermon; the House of Representatives was possibly not so much interested in abstract theories of reason as in maintaining their privileges against the governor and Council, with whom the Mathers were once more in alliance. (In theology, the "Patriot" faction were arch-conservatives and regarded Cotton Mather as much too loose!) Whatever the motive, Wise was too judicious to engage in forensic combat and refused; whereupon William Williams, a devoted partisan of Stoddard (as well as a son-in-law), was summoned from Hatfield. Wise was not a man who went out of his way to make trouble. He approved heartily of Thomas Symmes's efforts to introduce a semblance of harmony into the communal singing, giving it "as His Judgment, That when there were a sufficient number in a Congregation, to carry away a Tune Roundly, it was then proper to introduce that Tune." Here again is the mark of the man: the good and just tune may be prescribed by the laws of music, but the propriety of introducing it depends upon the existence of a sufficient number in the democratic congregation. The fact that Symmes took such care to cite him shows that the yet unanswered Wise was a formidable figure and that his name carried weight; in 1721, when the ministers were at last united as one man in their advocacy of inoculation and Increase Mather needed to prove their solidarity, he deliberately associated with himself the names of those whom the community knew had been his two great enemies: "We hear that the Reverend and Learned Mr. Solomon Stoddard of Northampton concurs with us; so doth the Reverend Mr. Wise of Ipswich, and many other younger Divines." By indirectly confessing that Stoddard and Wise were separate powers, Increase was admitting that the effort to maintain a single ecclesiastical system had failed; he was conceding that both opponents had stood their ground, that the era of the founders, in which polity and the Biblical covenant had been the dominant ideas, was at an end, and that in the new epoch points of view which Stoddard and Wise had developed out of their ecclesiastical deviations had to be reckoned with.

One must guard against claiming too much for Wise, but it is impossible not to behold in him the first clear-cut spokesman for the farmer, the agrarian, the "native" American. In his sentences first clearly appears that contrast between the natural felicity of America and the miseries of artificial Europe which Crevecoeur, Tom Paine, and Thomas Jefferson were to make the main theme of American literature. Churches in Europe are corrupt, and there ecclesiastics get kings by the throat, wring vast treasures from the public coffers which should go to the public good, "and the People have no more wit but to Justifie and defend them in their Claims and Oppressions, and that till they themselves (in great Numbers) are as thin and ragged as Penury it self." But in New England the constitution "is very fair-mannered," and the clerical interest, "when it sits down to the stalled Ox," carries itself temperately, leaving the people's prosperity "to the Empire to make its Armies and Navies."

A careful reader of Wise—who will take the pains to consider him not in the light of subsequent "democratic" theory or even in that of the Revolution, but in terms of his situation, in those that had developed out of New England's apprehension of the real meaning of the Massachusetts charter, out of Dudley's efforts to extend the tutoring—must be struck by the cunning with which he contrives to argue for the limitation of ecclesiastical power in this community and at the same time shoves upon "the Empire" responsibility for the army and navy. I strongly suspect that political scientists who have written learnedly upon his debt to Pufendorf or debated the question of his knowledge of Locke have missed the point: he would use what he had found, but his tongue was in his cheek. What gives not only charm but vitality to his "poison" is just the passion at the heart of him, the same fanaticism which inspires Sewall's dithyramb on Plum Island: a love for the land and its people. His wits were sharpened by decades of dealing with country men, not with theories; he had learned tricks to catch the unwary, and had come to understand the church system in a frame of reference made up of such local considerations, to which the scholastic theses taught at Harvard College had, at best, a distant relation. When at last he laid his large frame upon his deathbed, he told his son-in-law (who probably modulates the speech) "that he had been a Man of Contention, but the State of the Churches making it necessary; upon the most serious Review, he could say he had Fought a good Fight: and had comfort in reflecting upon the same: He was conscious to himself of his acting therein sincerely." We do not need to detract from his peculiar genius by insisting that his special mixture of sincerity and facetiousness is a cultural as well as a personal triumph, and so to demand that any historical conception of the New England mind take stock of both him and his younger contemporary, Benjamin Franklin. The twinkle in his eye is visible even from this distance as he concludes the *Vindication* by reprinting that testimony to the order of the Gospel which Cotton Mather had extracted in 1701 from the venerable Higginson and Hubbard. Those saints were now departed, but the cream of the jest was that Wise should cite, in his defense, what they had painfully written in behalf of Increase Mather against Solomon Stoddard. By aligning himself with them, Wise had everybody at a disadvantage, and played upon this ludicrous situation (indeed, reducing Cotton Mather to silence) by printing these great names at the back of his book and then permitting himself a mock apology:

> For you must note; I am now Retreating out of the field of Battle, and I hope upon Honourable terms too; and then the Reer is the highest place in dignity; so that though they are bringers-up, its no diminution to them. And not only so, but out of Prudent Conduct; for though I presume the Enemy is fairly Vanquished, yet some forlorn party may rally, and to gratify their desperate fortune may disturb us, but I hope these valiant and wise Commanders thus posted, will secure our Reer, beat back the Enemy, and bring all off with Triumph.

Stoddard won his case by forthright scorn; Wise stood off Cotton Mather by employing the one weapon against which Matherian Puritanism had no defense: he laughed it out of court.

Increase had mobilized the holy and mighty weight of ancestral precedent, thus forcing Stoddard explicitly to reject that authority when he turned his church into a Presbyterianized autocracy. John Wise was no less emancipated from ancestor worship, but he saw in the polity of the founders aspirations which they perhaps had not recognized but for which they could even so be honored. Without overworking the appeal, and certainly not in the Mathers' hysterical fashion, he reminded the people what shiploads of blood and treasure had been expended to win for them "those Civil Things" which their fathers had bequeathed:

> And many of you being immediate Successors, cannot but be very sensible what these New-England Liberties have Cost your Progenitors, some of them having buried their Estates, and all of them their bones in these Foundations, and left you now in Possession, that if you should put Contempt upon their Adventures, their Courage, Wisdom, Zeal, and Self-denial, by Under-prizing these Inestimable Infranchizements, and slight them . . . God may then put you to learn the Worth of them at that School where they Learnt it; and I am sure you will pay dear for your Tutoring if it comes to that.

Thus Wise, like Increase Mather, fought to save the church covenant, but not on Mather's grounds; for him it was New England's way of life, it meant rationality and freedom, it was democracy.

Wise and Stoddard may be pictured as confronting each other across the grave of John Winthrop, neither of them (so far as I know) ever mentioning the other, but each of them, in a manner of speaking, striking at the other through the hapless Increase Mather. Neither could be disciplined or silenced, which was to say that thenceforward the task of keeping the New England mind unified and coherent could no longer be accomplished in the field of church polity. If the region was to maintain its personality, it would have to find symbols of unity in other spheres, in social or ethical theory, in politics, in literature. This would be a problem, for by the first definition, so strongly imprinted upon the mind, New England was dedicated to a due form of government both civil and ecclesiastical. Out of its very success in establishing that form had arisen confusion; out of the original premises had come, by equally legitimate lines of descent, the irrevocable contradictions of Stoddard and Wise, foreshadowing a division that would deepen rather than close throughout American history. Had these controversies been, as on the surface they appear, only parochial squabbles, they would today be of only antiquarian interest; but New England during the century following 1630 was part and parcel of Western Christendom, or at least of Protestantism. The lines of cleavage have larger analogies in Europe, and are prophetic. By the first decades of the new century, with the symbolic antagonism of Northampton and Ipswich marking the extreme right and left, with the North Church and Brattle Street variously placed in the center, with Leverett at Harvard and with Yale becoming a counterweight, with its original bases thus sundered, the New England mind set itself to search for new formulae of accommodation in the realms of a simplified piety, in a moral code and a scientific outlook, in a defense of political privileges, and in an assiduous pursuit of profits.

BOOK III

The Splintering of Society

"Oh that I had in the wilderness a lodging place of wayfaring men;
That I might leave my people, and go from them!
For they be all adulterers,
An assembly of treacherous men,
And they bend their tongues like their bow for lies:
But they are not valiant for the truth upon the earth;
For they proceed from evil to evil,
And they know not me,"
Saith the Lord.
"Take ye heed every one of his neighbour,
And trust ye not in any brother:
For every brother will utterly supplant,
And every neighbour will walk with slanders."

JEREMIAH 9:2–4

CHAPTER XIX

A MEDIUM OF TRADE

T_{HE}
moment Andros was overthrown, Cotton Mather
resumed, as we have seen, the litany of sins composed by the Synod of
1679. He commenced the applications of his sermons with, "Let us take
a Catalogue of the Iniquities, and the Transgressions wherewith our Congregation hath sinned." In 1729, Jeremiah Wise came down from Ber-
wick to deliver the election sermon his father had declined to give ten
years before, and announced that the very abuses enumerated in 1679
were still the procuring cause of God's continuing judgments—except
that to the original catalogue had been made innumerable additions.

Preachers felt most safe when reciting the familiar array. They were
on solid ground when lamenting infringements of the Seventh Commandment, "exceeding frequent, in the Land, notwithstanding the Care is taken
to prevent them." But the tabulation, which in 1679 had covered an entire civilization, was no longer adequate: not only had the proliferation
of standardized sins become luxuriant, but a host of new iniquities cried
aloud for classification—let alone for reformation. A whole realm of
abuses, some of which had once been subsections, now grew into major
topics: for instance, fragmentary recognitions of the effect of life on the
frontier needed to be recast into a more coherent picture. Upon these
"Pagan Skirts of New-England" people "Indianize" themselves, thus
developing depravities unknown to 1679: they become impudent liars
who "invent Reports and Stories at a strange and monstrous rate." They
dispense with ministers, neglect schools and family government, and fill
idle hours gaming, so that "If our Youth be permitted to run wild in
our Woods, we shall soon be Forsaken." By 1702 such ungospelized plantations had become, in the opinion of Cotton Mather, "The very Brothel
houses of Satan."

Although the frontier had not, as such, figured as a category in 1679,
still it was a conception within which manifold observations could be logically grouped. In the more cultivated areas, complexity augmented, and
the problem merely of organizing denunciations into a logical pattern required a gallant effort of mind to keep up with the march of society. What
had been deemed luxury in 1679 paled into sobriety as compared with
what was to be reported in 1710 or 1720. To the ever expanding catalogue were added such diverse items as wigs and then bigger wigs, "the

Rudeness and Lewdness of our Husking Times," "Christmas Revels," such pagan customs as Shrove Tuesday, and that "most horrid and Shocking Profanity" at launching of new vessels, "breaking a Bottle upon her." In the churches themselves, evenings after an ordination produced "preposterously" unseemly actions; weddings grew boisterous; court days, like Commencements, were turned into fairs. Jests and songs increased, as did the reading of romances which tainted the mind with "very false Notions of Love Honour and Vertue," and prevented people, especially housemaids, from studying the Bible or polemical divinity. Jeremiahs had to find a place in their scheme for even fortunetellers, astrologers, and palmists, to bewail a spreading indisposition to await events "in a willing and wholesome Ignorance." In 1728 the nadir seemed reached when a duel was actually fought on Boston Common, in which one participant was killed. Eleven ministers, Colman and Chauncy along with Foxcroft, were in despair over this latest addition to the mounting chronicle:

> That any of the sons of New-England, who have been born and educated in this land of light, should be so forsaken of God, and given up to their lusts and passions, as to engage in a bloody and fatal Duel, deserves to be bewailed with tears of blood.

The Synod, in its innocence, had supposed the land in 1679 to be at the bottom of the abyss, but it had been unable even to conceive anything so abysmal as this.

Furthermore, even the most conventional themes made constantly more exhausting demands upon descriptive powers. Drunkenness, for instance: not only was there more of it, there was less shame; numbers were to be "seen in the open Street, staggering and reeling," and by 1713 it had to be admitted that women were no strangers to the vice, "The Town has had cause to know the Truth of this." The vice itself became a more complex thing; in 1673 Increase Mather had addressed *Wo to Drunkards* to imbibers of wine, but in the preface to a revised edition of 1712 had to lament that so little wine was drunk. Instead there was "Cyder, and a Spirit Extracted out of it," and then that even more pernicious concoction "imported from the Sugar Islands" which both people and ministers, although in different moods, called "Kill-Devil." Rum, said Cotton Mather, was a greater disaster than a French invasion; in 1726 he and other ministers in the vicinity (ecclesiastical factions could present a united front while speaking through the jeremiad) issued a manifesto against it; yet even here, certain cautions had to be observed if that front were to be kept united: instead of unmitigated condemnation, the document had to concede that innocent diversions might enliven and fortify nature, that a bit of rum, "invigorating the Animal Spirits, and brightning the Mind, when tired with a close Application to Business," might be allowed to pious businessmen. The associated pastors had to adapt their tone to an objection offered by certain frequenters of taverns who now had the brashness to plead in their own behalf that this was "the Custom of the Place, and they wou'd not affect Singularity." The previous year in Connecticut an election preacher had confessed that many excuse themselves for sitting in the tap-room because "Ministers and Magistrates do now and then make an innocent Visit to the Tavern."

If so simple a rubric of depravity as intoxication thus raised internal difficulties, requiring more sophisticated or at least less dogmatic analyses, how much more complex was the task of dealing with that jungle which the Synod, in the naïve days of 1679, had lumped under its tenth heading as inordinate affection to the world. In pursuing this investigation, the clergy found themselves wading deeper and deeper into a morass of economics, until Cotton Mather had to exclaim, "This Variety, begins to grow into too much Acrimony." In despair of mastering it, he counseled his fellows to account themselves too ignorant "to pronounce any Judgment upon that Spirit of Over-trading and Over-doing that some suppose very much threatens us." When the businessmen themselves, including many professing Christians, divided into hostile armies, the clergy, who had once whipped a Robert Keayne into line, whose advice men like John Hull had sought and followed, had to stand helplessly by, begging both factions to remember charity. As times grew hard and prices rose, Increase wistfully wondered whether the government ought not revive the old law "That no Merchant should ask above Four Pence, or Six in the Shilling for what he sells"; when that code had prevailed, the clergy had been the economic arbiters, but in 1719 Mather merely sighed that he could no longer "meddle" in these affairs, and advised sufferers to seek consolation in prayer.

Yet neither he nor his colleagues could abdicate outright; they were still official spokesmen for the social consciousness, and through the jeremiad alone could that consciousness be expressed, although with increasing imperfection. They might be bewildered, and realize that they were unqualified to understand the world of business, but they could not escape the duty of denouncing, and so of tabulating, the outward and visible signs of prosperity and its abuses. In the 1690's, for instance, they commenced a rising lament over the conduct of women of wealth: "The Cards at which many Gentlewomen Play wickedly with their Hands" are infinitely more debasing than those "cards which fit the Wooll for the Wheel"; a painted face, Cotton Mather was declaring as early as 1692, is a sign "hung out for Advice to Strangers that they shall find Entertainment there." In 1695 Increase spoke of women in Boston who sported tinkling ornaments, chains, bracelets, and "changeable suits of Apparel"; by 1718, commenting on the complaint of New England's poverty, Colman must declare, "Look on our Cloathing, our Furniture; our Tables, our Children; and if it were not for shame I had said our Balls, and say if we be Poor." It had gone so far that Cotton Mather was reduced to pleading with "the richer sort" to set an example to the poor in order to "make all Goodness a Fashionable

Thing." We look back to the Boston of 1720 as to a charmingly provincial simplicity, but to measure it by the scale of the mid-seventeenth century is to behold an emerging Babylon. There is historical evidence that by this time culture, amenities, fine furnishings, and even handsome women were to be found in Boston houses, and funeral orations began spontaneously to include the adjective "affable" among the virtues of the pious; but the time had not come when these privileges of opulence could be relished without qualm of conscience.

This did not prevent men from struggling hard to acquire them. Here the conscientious analyst found himself indeed bogged down in an ethical quagmire to which ancient rules seemed every year less and less applicable. It had become, said Joshua Moodey, a lying and deceiving age, "Overreaching one another in Dealing, the weakest (though the honestest) goes to the wall." Not, it must be said, for a lack of realistic appreciation of the facts were the clergy nonplused; Cotton Mather could give this minutely objective description of commercial practices:

The fish is naught; the Tar has undue mixtures; there is Dirt & Stone instead of Turpentine; there are thick Layes of Salt instead of other things that should be there; the Cheese is not made as tis affirm d to be; the Liquor is not for Quantity or Quality such as was agreed for; the Wood is not of the Dimensions that are promised unto the Purchaser; or perhaps, there was a Trespass in the place of Cutting it; the Hay does not hold out Weight by abundance; the Lumber has a false Number upon it; or, the Bundles are not as Good Within as they are Without.

What made such a report depressing was not so much the extent of the corruption as the tendency from which it flowed: men used these tricks and cheats to rise in the world; they refused to abide patiently in the stations to which providence had called them. They could no longer bear the humiliations of a mean rank, and so ran into debt: "Those Flags of Pride, if I may be so bold," asked Mather, "are they paid for?" When finally pressed by their creditors, people—"Church-Members for ought I know"—escaped by "breaking." In all consultations for the general good, each thought only of himself, and "he who would make a Speech to the Men of Publick Spirit, must go into the Burying-Places, and Speak among the Sepulchres." Likewise in Connecticut: overreaching, defrauding, endless strife about "the property of Lands, which has brought such Confusion, Contention and Division among our selves." With all his great prestige, Stoddard could not check the ravages of ruthless competition among the settlements in his empire: "In Country-Towns, Men sometimes give a shilling for that, which at Market Town, might be had for six pence"; when a man goes to seek what is plentiful elsewhere, "the Seller takes that advantage to oppress him." The year before his death, Cotton Mather, always seeking for conceits on which to construct ingenious sermons, took the familiar list of shady devices in trade—by now commonplace to his audience—and "improved" each of them into analogous deceptions in the realm of the spirit. To this resort the New England mind was driven!

The last vestige of the scholastic objection to usury was gone; in 1699, considering the problem as one of *Thirty Important Cases*, the Cambridge Association calmly declared that "Humane Society, as now circumstanced, would sink, if all Usury were Impractable." While wringing their hands over declensions which seemed to them utterly destructive, the clergy took this shattering revolution in stride, and justified usury (within moderation) on three accounts, each of which had for centuries been employed to condemn it: by the law of equity, for a man should partake in that benefit which his estate procures another; by the law of parity, for "Money is really as Improvable a thing as any other," and there can be "no reasonable pretence that should bind me to lend my Money for nothing"; and, most wonderfully yet most rationally, by the law of charity, for a man may legitimately reap a benefit for his family from those things of which he is proprietor. Of course, the rate of interest should not become extortionate and he is to be reprehended who lives upon usury alone; but still, settling the procedure may be left to the consciences of good men. For the next thirty years, having thus opened the gates, the clergy had no resort except to berate (without affecting) those who, lending money, took the first year's interest at once, leaving the borrower insufficiently supplied; this, they would cry, "is a Biting Usury which cannot be Justified." But they quickly learned how irresistible was the increase of usury; by 1730 their constant complaint was that New England had become a region of "Men ready to take one another by the Throat, saying, Pay me what thou Owest."

Such men could, of course, still be threatened—as they were—with divine judgments; otherwise, they could be discouraged only by a pious exhortation to rest content with what they had and not to learn cheating and oppression in order to get what was beyond their station. After all, Cotton Mather tried to reason with them, great estates are not yet to be expected in this country; maybe in the future—since we do have harbors —but not now. As a method of dissuading men from the accumulation of estates, this argument was a characteristic boomerang: if wealth were eventually to be had, the time to commence was now. In the face of so empirical a logic, the dialectic of the covenant became constantly more academic.

The jeremiad might preach moderation and resignation, but it could no longer pretend to control a process it did not understand. Its technique, its very vocabulary, was limited to itemizing the surface manifestations of a reality which was not a matter of morals but of finance. In all innocence, Cotton Mather in 1691 had abetted the first motion when he defended the bills of credit. Every year the paper increased in volume, as it decreased in purchasing power—while gold and silver were drained off to England. Laws inspired by the philosophy of the founders—demanding that bills be accepted at face value or prohibiting the export of bullion—were dead letters the moment they were voted. By 1714, silver having disappeared and the cost of living doubled, the New England mind entered upon a new phase in its history when a group of citizens, all of Elisha Cooke's connection, issued *A Projection for Erecting a Bank of Credit . . . Founded on Land Security*.

It is, of course, an imperfect story of the New England mind which pays so little attention as I have paid to Elisha Cooke, to his son Elisha, and to their cohorts; however, this analysis is obliged to concentrate upon what the mind made out of events rather than upon the events themselves, and the Cooke faction wrote their opinions not in books but in votes. So far, since their opposition to Increase Mather, they had contributed no "ideas" to the community; their stock in trade was the rights of Englishmen. Under that banner they pressed nominations to the Council upon governors to whom they refused a decent salary. Yet, though they may have had no original thoughts, by their unending campaign they did prove that provincial politics were steadily becoming secularized. In 1714, when they had achieved the intellectual and literary power sufficient for formulating the scheme of a bank, they became the first authors in New England to argue a case with hardly so much as a genuflection in the direction of religion.

Paul Dudley, son of Joseph—inheriting from his father both a philosophy and a temper—replied with *Objections to the Bank of Credit;* one of the promoters answered in *A Letter From One in Boston to his Friend in the Country*, and at the end of the year nine of them—headed by the younger Elisha, John Colman, Dr. Oliver Noyes, William Payne—published *A Vindication of the Bank of Credit*.

These four pamphlets—nothing like so long or so ponderous as items in the Stoddard-Mather dispute—mark the beginning of an epoch, not only for their subject matter but even more for their language; they show how, behind the façade of the jeremiad, certain segments of the society, long excoriated but now grown strong, had become capable of thinking and talking about social measures without having to borrow premises from the covenant. Instead, the projectors commence from this proposition: "Without a Medium, the Trade must necessarily decay, to the unspeakable detriment of the Landed Interest as well as the Trading Party." Seeing no other way to produce a medium and not being content to sit helplessly down and bewail affliction, these gentlemen proposed to incorporate a bank on the security of land, which would then issue money; they expected to benefit the country but also to make a profit, and to show that their hearts were in the right place they offered to turn some of it over to charity and to Harvard College. On these grounds the debate was staged: Paul Dudley attacked the economic heresies, but no more than they did he bother with any theological aspects of this "Pandora's Box"; he denounced it chiefly because we are "a Dependent Government" and should

remember that the Privy Council will disallow any such scheme. The projectors intend, if they can set up so independent an institution, to get the
entire country mortgaged to them, and "so at length beard down the Government it self, and nothing be restrained from them." "Like a Fire in
the Bowels," their bank "will Burn up and Consume the whole Body";
it hopes to create "A Gulph of Misery by Stock-jobbing," it is "the Philosopher's Stone," and its clients will find themselves "Bubbled Borrowers."

The advocates cried out upon Dudley as a tool of "the Court Interest,"
and joined battle in purely political terms. His proposals were "Golden
Bait," intended to deprive the people of their liberties; the tone of the projectors was always, "I assure you Sir, I am the plainer on these Heads,
in that I value the Liberties of my Country so dearly, as never to esteem
such its best Friends, that are willing to part with them." The faction
did not conceal, they positively flaunted, their design: "An empty Treasury is very much our Security," because it "prevents many fine schemes
of Arbitrary Power"; all arguments for a sound currency mean merely
that the governor will have something to rely upon: "Will there be any
room left for Contests about settling Salaries?" Or again, "I never knew
that Governour and Government, were one and the same word." When
Dudley did quote a verse from Scripture, his opponents accused him of
abusing it; otherwise, that august authority was not invoked.

There was a small but hard-headed group of men—led by Thomas
Hutchinson—who thought the bills utterly bad and that the only salvation lay in returning to specie payment, let the people suffer as they might.
Dudley had sympathies in that direction, but considered the position doctrinaire; hence, if bank there must be, he proposed, as against Cooke's
private bank, to erect a public bank, through which the government would
continue to issue bills of credit under the supervision of solid citizens. By
charging a five per cent interest for them, it could keep the issue from
getting out of hand. This plan, supported by Hutchinson as the lesser evil,
was pushed through the General Court, and on November 5, 1715,
£50,000 were released, to be followed every year by larger amounts. The
Patriots still agitated for their notion; during the next generation, this
struggle over the bank became the secret of political alignment, wherefore power resided less and less in righteousness as it progressively became
identified with financial faction. Pure theorists of the covenant were left
standing helplessly by, reduced to the role of grieving spectators. They
might exhort the government "to find out a just Medium of Exchange,"
but the annual repetitions of their plea indicate how little effect they had.
"What must be the End of this at long run," asked Colman, "but great
damage, not to say ruine, to the Publick?" "The Blood in the Body Politick is depauperated, and has too Hectick a Circulation," exclaimed Cotton Mather as he begged "the Men of Thought" (to this dignity they
had been promoted) to devise methods of stopping "that Hemmorrhage."

In 1716 one nameless man of thought published *Some Considerations*

Upon the several sorts of Banks, and therein argued, like a provincial Keynes, that the way out was a public works program—"for building a Bridge over Charles River, cutting a Channel at Sandwich for safe and more speedy Passage of Vessels." He wanted government loans to encourage infant industries, such as iron and glass works, and even dreamed of granaries in which the state should store up corn for lean years; he alone in this controversy denounced large landholders and condemned usury itself.

These radical proposals went unnoticed, and in the year 1720 crisis came: trade was bad, the bills were depreciating fantastically, and the landbank men renewed their campaign with one of the most skillful compositions of the age, John Colman's *The Distressed State of the Town of Boston Considered.* Almost every week thereafter a new pamphlet appeared, the tone and treatment purely secular; yet a curious note which Dudley had first struck in 1714 is now sounded heavily, and offers, as it were, an economic parallel to the jeremiad: the root of our problem, Dudley said—and all had to agree—is that we import more from abroad than we can pay for out of our own produce; hence, whether or not we have sinned against the federal Jehovah, we have certainly sinned against the balance of trade: "the great Extravagance that People, and especially the Ordinary sort, are fallen into, far beyond their Circumstances, in their Purchases, Buildings, Families, Expences, Apparel, and generally in their whole way of Living." Were frugality and sober husbandry in fashion, there would be no lack of a medium; therefore, the aim of a good bank must be to keep the printing of paper to as little as possible.

Although they hated each other, both the parties had one thing in common, that they accepted as sufficient this diagnosis of New England's miseries and upon it constructed their opposing measures. The rich were told by either side to set an example to the poor; yet, as one writer put it, while luxury is indeed something for penitent reflection, "I'm now considering the matter, as to the Cost of such Imported Liquors." In what terms the New England mind was learning to think—and in which, more importantly, it was learning by leaps and bounds to express itself—appears as one runs an eye over these writings: "Let no Wool, Hides, Leather, Grain nor Candles be Exported"; "Let us be diligent and laborious, to raise, produce, make as much as we can for our own support, as to Food, Raiment, Tools, Utensils"; "We should raise more for Export than now we do . . . Fish, Oyle, Whalebone, Horses, Lumber." With every pamphlet, the litany becomes more explicit, until language itself proclaims the new century: "We in the Country think, that Plotting heads, Proud hearts, and Idle hands, will never maintain a People; and that a close following the Wheel within doors, and the Plough without are much better and stronger Politicks." The New England mind had needed three generations of first-hand experience before it could achieve such a sentence as this: "If I'm a Labourer and can have Four Shillings for a Days Work, and a few Years ago I could buy Wheat for Five Shillings a

Bushel, but now must give Ten; this shows that the Produce of my Labour is not above half the Benefit to me that it was."

The shift of focus from the theological covenant to staples was not, in these impassioned writings, a conscious literary revolution; still, with each word, a new frame of reference was established, within which for the first time colonial thinking adopted—and clearly expressed—what were to become classic counters for the American mind: debtor against creditor, farmer against merchant, poor against rich. John Colman, although a Bostonian and a brother to the genteel Benjamin, in his effort to enlist rural debtors to the mercantile side, found himself using language with a specification which entitles his pamphlet to a place in the development of American prose:

If we consider the Poor, we are promised a Blessing, and as it is most certainly the duty of every Man, according to his capacity to consider them, in such a distressing time as this; when good Honest, Industrious, Modest People, are driven to such streights, as to sell their Pewter and Brass out of their Houses, which is scarce worse for wearing, to Brassiers, at the price of Old Pewter and Brass to buy them food, as I have been Informed by the Brassiers, who spoke it with great concern to me.

In this state of affairs, it behooves the people to improve their interest with the government; opposed to them are only "some Country Gentlemen, who Live on their Farms, and others, men of plentiful Fortunes, who do not feel the Straits of the Times, and therefore cannot sympathize so feelingly with their Neighbours." Those who oppose the printing of more paper, wherewith poor men might pay their debts, are the same who oppose the land bank—not so much reprobate as wealthy: "but the Richest Men are not always beneficial to the Commonwealth." In 1690 the leadership of New England had striven to rally the community around the conception of English liberties; at that time they hoped that under this slogan they might protect Congregational polity, but by 1720 the slogan showed dangerous tendencies, which John Colman and his friends deliberately exploited, of becoming an instrument of the many against the few.

Colman artfully represented himself as a gentleman in town writing to a friend in the country. His opponents replied by adopting the role of countrymen; whereupon Dr. Oliver Noyes improved still further upon Colman's blunt speech. One of the answers he thought beneath notice, but he put it in his pocket, "thinking it might serve, (as dirty as it was,) for a necessary occasion." He deplored paper money, but clearly the society needed a medium and paper was better than nothing: £200,000 of it had been issued, yet "in this large Country," that "is but as a sprat in a Whales Belly." The hard-money men might temporarily put up with a public bank, but their real intention was to curtail credit, force the people to pay, and to wait for business to pick up; Dr. Noyes could suggest a speedier remedy, "and that is to leave off Eating, Drinking, and Wearing." This would assuredly put an end to buying and selling, and so deliver us from impoverished debtors. But Dr. Noyes's most penetrating charge was that the hard-money spokesman really intended the country to live on its own provisions and wear its own clothing: "so I find he is for having the Town and Country independent of each other; for he don't pretend they shall raise more than they use, & for us we may go naked and starve."

These little tracts are not profound sociological studies, but they do reveal what had happened to John Winthrop's conception of a community knit together as one man in a holy purpose, where civil liberty was to consist in submission to the inherently good, just, and honest. Colman and Noyes were pleading a special interest: they had plenty of land but little money, and so advocated a land bank; but at the same time they were insisting that the welfare of the whole should not be sacrificed to rigid conceptions of monetary orthodoxy. The conservative policy of returning to a currency worth its face value meant, in concrete terms, "that then a Man who hath Mortgaged an House for Two Hundred Pounds which cost him a Thousand, must be forced to let it go for the Two Hundred, because when the Bills are all sunk, he will not be able to get wherewith to redeem it." A mentality which had learned to reason in this fashion had left far behind the criteria of a jeremiad.

By 1720 the issue was squarely presented to the official guardians of the New England mind: if out of Christian wisdom they could not adjudicate between debtor and creditor, on which side would they align themselves? If they were to preserve the prestige of their corps, if they were to remain anything more effective than mere exhorters, would they not have to choose? Could they evade the challenge?

Most of them, so far as the public record goes, did evade. They restrained themselves to such noble pleas as that of Joseph Sewall in 1724: "That Publick Faith and Justice be preserved, relating to our Bills of Credit." But the implication in even the most generalized of these injunctions was hostile to the plan of Colman and Dr. Noyes. Those clerics who did dabble in support of the land bank quickly discovered the true nature of their interest. Of these, Cotton Mather is the most instructive: in 1714 he so far favored the project as to beseech an English correspondent to cast a "benign Aspect" upon it, but by November of 1716 he was rating Noyes, Payne, and Cooke as "unhappy Men." Noyes had heard "Intimations as if I declared some relinquishments of my former Thoughts, about our private Bank," to which Mather replied, "tis *cujus contrarium.*" Those who have become acquainted with the personality of Cotton Mather know that when he talks this way he is about to betray somebody; even as he wrote thus to Noyes, he was assuring Jeremiah Dummer (who in London fought consistently against the private bank) of his support, and by February was offering prayers for the redemption of John Colman, a creature "in whom the three parts of the Satanic Image, Pride, Malice and Falshood, are very Conspicuous." As was his customary procedure once he came thoroughly to hate somebody and be hated in return, on March 16, 1721, he purged his soul of all personal rancor by entrusting his case to the Lord, who within a few hours thereafter struck Dr. Noyes dead of an apoplexy. Thus rid of one "who has been and would still have been the greatest Hinderer of good, and Misleader and Enchanter of the People," Cotton Mather could "go on with my humble Supplications to the Lord."

However, a few of the caste chose to fight the enemy with less secret weapons. Edward Wigglesworth, child of the old age of the author of *The Day of Doom*, graduated from Harvard in 1710; in 1720 he was again living in College, having failed to impress himself upon any congregation to whom he exhibited his wares; he was a close friend of Benjamin Colman, and, admired of Leverett and Nathaniel Appleton, he was already being groomed to occupy the Professorship of Divinity which Colman was extracting from the bounty of Thomas Hollis. Intellectually he was far from sympathizing with the Mathers. Yet this theological "liberal"— whose influence upon the next two generations of Harvard men was to be profound—devoted his leisure to preparing and publishing on May 11, 1720, *A Letter from One in the Country to his Friend in Boston*. After Dr. Noyes declared that this looked "like a design to inslave a People and make a few Lord's, and the rest Beggars," and therefore decided it best employed in the water closet, Wigglesworth answered with *A Vindication*. By becoming propagandists for their bank, the agitators gave to New England not only a new type of expression, but one which barely concealed an antiministerial threat; hence they compelled the theological mind, whether Matherian or "Catholic," to match it, and to meet the attack in the manner and upon the grounds the enemy had chosen.

Wigglesworth therefore addressed his two pamphlets as much to the tone and style of the agitators as to their arguments: they have represented things "in such a smart and moving manner as (I fear) will tend much to stir & irritate men's Passions and revive those Heats and Animosities, which have done us too much mischief already." Employing his unheated intelligence, he could forgive the people: "when we have been dunn'd and worried by our Creditors, we have cry'd out for more money too," but obviously this was a sentimental and self-defeating resort. The grim law—more implacable to this enlightened mind than any rule of Scripture had been to John Winthrop—was simple: "For while more is imported from other Countries and consumed among us, than our own produce alone can ballance, we must continue growing poorer daily." Hence the people must be kept from running further into debt, which means calling in all bills of credit, let the consequences be what they may. "All this (I think) is as plain as a Mathematical Demonstration, and I challenge any man to confute it."

Wigglesworth contributed to the debate the most rigorously consistent statement (which must have delighted old Thomas Hutchinson) of what we are bound to call the conservative point of view—although historically he figures as a pioneer liberal in theology. He will have no sort of bank, public or private, to which the people, having spent all they earn, may "go and borrow more, to lay out for things they have no need of." He thinks it a responsibility of government to hinder "inconsiderate People from doing themselves harm" (officers are set over you, Winthrop had told the Hingham militia in 1645, for your own good), which in this context meant reducing wages. "The only way of doing this is, by shortning Credit, so that People may not be able to consume more than they earn." To this assertion, Noyes answered that the effect would be to sunder country from town; Wigglesworth's *Vindication* explained that he knew how ungrateful his proposal would seem, "But yet I am so satisfied of the safety of it above other Projects, and the good Effect it would quickly have upon us, that I could not choose but communicate my tho'ts upon this matter, and wish that they may take place." His father had written *God's Controversy with New England!*

His was the most serious challenge, outside pulpit lamentation, yet leveled against the party of Cooke; and Elisha the second, obliged in 1720 to vindicate his right to become Speaker despite Governor Shute's veto, turned aside in the second of his forays into literature to pay his respects to the incipient Hollis Professor. He represented a "Country Gentleman"—designedly!—asking a Boston gentleman why all these pamphlets? The Bostonian explains that because the province lacks a medium, the land is deluged by oppression (as the rural parson could tell him); hence schemes and projects, "almost an infinite number of Pamphlets dispersed thro' the Country." Of all these, those of Wigglesworth (of course, Cooke does not publish the name) are most remarkable for their "circular way of Argumentation," but perhaps that is explicable: "I suppose (being immers'd in more sublime Studies) he might imagine himself. on some lofty Topick in Metaphysicks, and so has at once been mistaken in his Theme, and his Notions of the true Interest of his Country." In his academic isolation, Wigglesworth supposes one can "force Men (by a fatal Necessity) to Industry, Frugality and Good Husbandry." Hence he would do away with both money and credit, and for this piece of abstraction claims the authority of mathematics. "Sir," the countryman asks— and Cooke knew how, in the House, they would talk—"don't you think Longitude, and a Communication between us and the Moon, will be found out quickly, and be made as plain as a Demonstration?" For the first time since Harvard was founded, a professor was thus publicly made fun of as incompetent to meddle in practical affairs.

One must take care when using such terms as country and town not to suppose that country, at this date, means everything west of Boston, or town merely Boston and Salem. Solomon Stoddard would twit the Mathers about the sins of the city or the riot of Harvard commencements, but in relation to the surrounding terrain, Northampton was town, not country.

There was nothing whatsoever of the frontier radical about the autocrat in his Connecticut Valley. He was a firm believer in private property and in 1722 felt called upon to assert it; the owners of parks in England would properly be offended if poor people plowed them up on the excuse that poverty gave them a right. Pious industry was all very well, but piety did not prevent a man doing what he would with his own. By the same token, Stoddard was consistently outspoken (in contrast to the vacillations of Cotton Mather) against paper money in all its forms. Certain people (for whom he would not conceal his contempt) were enabled by it "to help themselves, by getting greater wages for their Work, and advancing the price of what they bring to Market," but most had become "great Sufferers by this practice." In his denunciation of the bills he virtually aligns himself with Wigglesworth's program.

But in the beginning of 1721 another clerical voice was raised: *A Word of Comfort to a Melancholy Country* declared itself written by "Amicus Patriae," yet all New England knew, from the first paragraph, that only one stylist in the land was capable of such wit. It spoke as we should expect the author of *The Churches Quarrel:* in frank defense of paper money, in positive advocacy of inflation. As against Wigglesworth's mathematical demonstrations, in contrast to Cotton Mather's method of disposing of Dr. Noyes, he remarked that while love of money is indeed the root of evil, "The Paper Medium is easy of Exchange, and not so apt to corrupt the Mind." Not out of Northampton but from Ipswich comes the first American Populist; the manifesto was written by a minister and a Harvard man—although, of course, John Wise was not exactly typical of either category.

He did not much care which kind of bank was set up, "either under the Management of the Government, or in the Hands of Particular Gentlemen of Known Integrity and Estates," so long as there would be plenty of money, and that cheap. Yes, the Word of God does caution us against inordinacy in affection to the world, but at the same time we are expected "by no Means to slight the Comfort, and Outward felicity of our Wives and Families." Again employing that irony which had silenced the Mathers, he dedicated his book to the merchants of Boston; not that he was particularly a friend of the private bank, but that he would make of either bank something their promoters did not exactly intend: if city bankers will only keep enough money circulating, their colleague and brother, the farmer, will keep them in business. It was as clear to Wise in Ipswich as was a mathematical demonstration to Wigglesworth in Cambridge that if the country were abruptly restored to a metallic standard, farmers would have to pay their debts at once, they would have nothing left, and their creditors would therefore be bankrupt. Do you suppose we are so stupid as to believe that once we return to specie, we shall keep it? "No! by no Means! unless you will burn our Ships and knock all our Merchants on the Head."

Wise's real concern—in fact his only concern—was the farmer, "the great Studd and Strength of our Country." Keep him in a threadbare coat, Wise warned the metropolis, and you "dis-animate" not only the best servant of the king but the means of your own plenty (here joining hands with Dr. Noyes). A paper bill may depreciate, but what of that? It still keeps the farmer at his plow, "Brightens and inlivens all his Rurall Schemes; Reconciles him to all his hard Labour, and makes him look Fat and Chearfull." His comprehensive program, as opposed to Wigglesworth's contractionism, envisaged doing "something to purpose in Manufactures," but only because "the Bills will do it all."

Men like Hutchinson, Paul Dudley, and Wigglesworth were asking whether, were provincial bills to depreciate indefinitely, they would not soon mathematically demonstrate that zero is an easily approachable limit. Wise answered out of a deeper humanity: in Ipswich the paper was not yet, nor was it likely to come, "under so fatal Eclipse, as to deserve quite and clean to be made Extinct in Darkness, as some Men pretend to." Against such men, he took pleasure in cutting the Gordian knot of modern finance by appeals calculatedly human:

Gentlemen! You must do by your Bills, as all Wise Men do by their Wives; Make the best of them. It is an acknowledged Theorem, that there is no doing without Wives. The Lonesome and sower Philosopher would frankly confess, that Women, were necessary Evils: For without their Assistance the whole Humane Race must vanish; And unless they are Metamorphised into things called Wives, the whole Species would soon Laps into an unheard-of Brutified Animals.

This was hardly an argument to carry weight in King Street: economic skill is comparable to that of the countryman who, because he loves his wife, disregards the ill-conveniences he finds in her; but for Wise, this was the essence of sanity: "And thus you must do by your Bills, for there is no doing without them."

Wise knew it was Wigglesworth who had written the two pamphlets (if rumor had not informed him, Cooke's references would have); we may particularly relish the deliberate naughtiness with which he undertook to argue that inflation had worked wonders for Harvard College. And again his language, dipping into that frank sexuality which had so startlingly appeared in his pleas for church covenant, was designed to embarrass professors of divinity: do but compute, he asked, the size of our graduating classes in the last thirty years, and it will appear that since paper money was introduced our Alma Mater has renewed her youth:

Sometimes we were wont to have One, and sometimes Two, or Three at a Birth, with abundance of graons to bring them forth; and in some Years nothing but Dead Embrio's, or Abortions; so poor and insufficient was the Seminal Matter and Flames of our State, viz. Our Medium . . . But of late our Dear Mother brings forth Thirty or Forty at a Birth; And escapes not a Season, but makes a great Addition Yearly to her Numbers.

The literature of this dispute is memorable enough if only because it is the first extensive body of expression since Richard Mather's *Farewel* to escape from the formulae of the jeremiad; Wise capitalized upon that revolution to advance the thesis that more boys from the backcountry, and more poor boys, might use paper money to pay term bills at Harvard —"for Apparently this is the means that has awakened her Genial Powers." Throughout his plea shines that vision of a democratic culture of which he is preëminently the prophet: a system of barter is suitable only for those who dwell in the clefts of valleys and live upon acorns, but is incompatible with the life of a bustling people "that would spend their Life, to the height of Religion and right Reason." Nor had he forgotten what right reason signifies: "Its hardly possible to uphold Equality where there is no Common Medium known and allowed to be as a Rule or Measure." It was not a mathematical demonstration, it was common sense, and it meant equality.

By now, as far as we can make out, Wise had a following among the people; we should expect, therefore, that Hutchinson or Wigglesworth or some other pundit among the conservatives might have ventured to answer him. Whether they inspired the next move, we do not know; if they did, it was both adroit and contemptible. In the *Boston Gazette* for February 20 appeared an "Advertisement," dated from Castle William: it noted that Amicus Patriae is "a Worldly Wise Man," who speaks two words for himself and but one for the country, because having been for twenty years deeply in debt, he refuses to pay what he has borrowed either from private persons or from the government. His argument for "Miracle working Paper Money" is only a means of manufacturing enough paper bills "for every body to take what they please"; further than this, "his whole bustle of words" is nonsense.

Who wrote it? The town knew and Wise knew, but to us it is a mystery. An Anglican clergyman, a certain Mr. Ayers (who caused Sewall trouble during his aged courtships) was then stationed at the Castle; the rebuttals hint that someone of his character was responsible. But several things are clear: passions were now running high. Wise's pamphlet had struck its mark, and the government was anxious. In the next *Gazette*, on Monday, February 27, bookseller Benjamin Gray announced that in the afternoon he would publish *A Letter to an Eminent Clergy-Man*, along with a reply to the Castle William advertisement. The former did appear, and by the very next day, the twenty-eighth, the Council read it, voted that it contained scandalous reflections on His Majesty's government, and directed the Attorney General to prosecute Gray and every other person concerned in the publication.

Gray told the Council, and stuck to his story, that he did not know the author; the manuscript was delivered by hand at nine o'clock on Saturday, and was signed "Yours Unknown." Financial disputation had released a current of secular wit, but now the flow became a flood; attack-

ing all conservative financiers, this pamphlet refused to call them men.
"Ah shameful Metamorphosis! Do they not Degrade & sink themselves
below Humanity, and themselves fit for nothing but (with Nebuchadnezer)
to graze among the Beasts of the earth?" Wigglesworth and his party are
"the most Screwing Misers, who are for no Bank at all, but the Clam
bank," yet the public bank is little better. The whole province is ablaze,
"Every man's Hand is against his Brother: Bonds and Mortgages are
sued; and Men are pulling one another by the Throat." As for that ad-
vertiser from Castle William, he mutters nothing but impudence, tautology, and falsehood, and "is Desired to Imprison his forked Tongue within
his Teeth, and further to say nothing." The House is corrupted by bankers of either persuasion, representatives are led by the nose and have
become unfit for public trust; meanwhile usurers make fifteen or twenty
per cent by grinding the faces of the poor. Some recent writings may
seem "too Smart and Satyrical," but the most animated "(which is almost
a Paradox)" are the most true.

The Councillors were shocked by the language of this pamphlet—at
what they called its "many Vile, Scandalous and very Abusive Expressions"—but they had more cause to worry over what emotions might rally
round the figure of John Wise. The *Letter* clearly was addressed to him,
calling him a bright ornament "and in many respects a Father to your
Countrey." On this same February 27 was also published another anonymous reply to the Castle William advertisement which showed that Wise
had still other friends: *A Letter from a Gentleman in Mount Hope, to His
Friend in Treamount* celebrated Wise as the one who had shown himself
a patriot "when many Others (considering their Stations in Government)
were under stricter Obligations to appear, were afraid to be Gap-men,
and protest against the Gross Injuries, Arbitrary and Illegal Actions of
the then Government."

It was high time that the clergy demonstrate, if possible, that they
could still moderate the passions of the people. The parson in Weymouth,
Thomas Paine of Harvard 1717, undertook the thankless task by publishing *A Discourse Shewing, that the Real First Cause of the Straits and
Difficulties of this Province . . . is its Extravagancy & not Paper Money;
and also what is a Safe Foundation to Raise a Bank of Credit on, and
what not.*

It seems highly appropriate that the clergyman who took upon himself
this impossible assignment was not only the father of a signer of the Declaration of Independence, but also one of those parsons so occupied with
business sidelines that by 1733 he was to be dismissed from his pulpit, to
finish his days as a merchant and ultimately to die insolvent. In the light
of what was yet to come, we detect certain unministerial, or at any rate
fairly materialistic, accents in his argument; but in the context of 1721
he tried to bring economic disputation to order by translating the facts of
the situation into a jeremiad, to prove on this basis what the jeremiads had

always contended out of spiritual insight, that the root of all difficulty was a sinful lust of the people for expensive (and incidentally foreign) commodities. In almost the standard pattern, he berated the gentry but even more the commonalty for trying to dress like nobles, "nothing short of the finest of Broad-Cloths, Silk," so that however we lack money, we abound in luxuries, and "if we can't pay our Debts, we can as yet, by running into Debt, get and wear fine Cloths." He said that travelers arriving from Europe stand on the wharves "with open mouths drinking in amazement, to see the Grandeur (ah, empty Grandeur!) of New England"—buildings, equipages, servants, and balls. "Our Apparell, how fine and rich! Our Furniture and Tables, how costly, sumptuous and dainty! And our Funerals, how ample are they!"

But although Paine did reprimand the gentry, he heaped his fiercest criticism upon the inferior sort, who so aped the attire of the rich and honorable that in the churches, "were it not for the different Seats they sit in, One would scarce know Joan from my Lady by Daylight." Which brought him, inevitably, to confront that renegade from clerical solidarity, Amicus Patriae, who had actually contended that the fault lay not in the abundance of trade nor in a lust for articles, who argued that merchants should import as much as they could. "Are there no *Wise* skilful Merchants in the Province that have done so?" In Paine's view, John Wise deserved such sneers; his ascription of miraculous power to paper bills was the product of a too exorbitant imagination—this was the way to dispose of him!—and as for respectable economics, "I find no manner of Care taken in it either to support their Credit any further than Fancy will do it."

Thus Paine's conclusion was essentially that of the jeremiad, although he had enough wit to attempt teaching his lesson in the form of economic morality: what the country needs is industry and prudence, what the people must avoid is idleness and bad husbandry. Moral virtues will rectify financial difficulties. "I know Amicus Patriae will laugh at this, and tell us that their Credit may be kept up by the power of a Wise Imagination," but this sort of wishful thinking is as chimerical as the doctrine of transubstantiation.

One thing Paine's discourse does show—the laughter of John Wise was something to be feared. Governor Shute stood less in awe of it, and on March 15 addressed the General Court in support of Paine's thesis, telling them that frugality and industry alone would save them, "without which the Mines of Peru and Mexico wou'd not make you a Prosperous & Happy Community." He promised to assist them in everything that would keep the bills from further depreciation, and looked with no favor at all upon the prospect of issuing more.

John Wise was now sixty-nine; it was thirty-four years since he defied Andros. He took up his pen, to let fly the old barrage against the intruder from Castle William, and for a few sentences the wit sparkled:

Don't you see how Proudly he Rides in our Chief Harbour, with all his Colours abroad, and in the heart of the Country; and has Cast our Gentlemen hoarders into miserable Paroxisms in the Lower Bowels, that they are in hazard of falling into Old King James's Pickle; which will be a great Misfortune to their Ladies.

But even jokes involving the legendary diarrhea of James I were growing dim. Wise had no heart to go on with it; if anyone would write solidly against his monetary thesis, he would engage to own himself fairly subverted, but he was wearied at the prospect of answering the letter from Çastle William foolishly enough to show a fool his folly; but let the writer know that the country—John Wise's people—are alarmed: "They are fully Resolved not to be Hectored or wheedled into unsolvable Penury and Vassalage, for want of a Plentiful Medium [when] it is in their own Power to Remove those who stand in their way, and supply themselves." The nameless pamphleteer whom Gray published might be prosecuted for scurrility, but the paper money argument, in the hands of John Wise, showed its true bent: it contained the threat of revolution.

Dramatically speaking, this ought to be Wise's final word; or at least his opponents ought to have answered him, as he invited them, solidly. Only one of them, sheltering behind the anonymity of the *Gazette*, attempted it, and by a snide device; securing from Stephen Sewall of Newbury (who had supplied Cotton Mather with incomplete records of the witchcraft trials) a certified copy of a petition which Wise had presented to the Quarter Session on September 29, 1719, he ran it as an answer to Amicus Patriae. By that time, after a long struggle, Wise found himself, like most of the clergy, starving on the salary for which he had years ago contracted, his £70 per annum sadly depreciated. He told the General Court that it was "a poor business to maintain a Family Sick & Well" on such a pittance, and begged the authorities to persuade his good neighbors, with whom he was loath to contend, "that they must needs perswade themselves, that Bills are not Money." If they can pay him only in bills, then they must do it to his satisfaction. The correspondent who dug up this item hoped that it would receive "a very candid Entertainment, as well from Amicus Patriae, as his Imployers and Admirers."

It was a clever smear, except that it was not clever enough to comprehend the character of the man. Obviously, the intention was to suggest that Wise was a hypocrite in campaigning for paper money even when demanding more for himself; Wise was too old a fox to be taken in that trap, and on March 20 answered in the *Gazette*.

As to admirers, "if he has any, He the said Amicus, Admires them, for Admiring him." As for employers, he spoke only for free men, and "the State of his Country has lain as near to his Heart, as ever Calis did to Queen Marys." As for the petition of one John Wise, asking for more depreciated currency, so far was this from contradicting the doctrine of *A Word of Comfort*, it might well be interpreted as being, by a "Prelipsis," not only an anticipation, but a brief system of the book. He would play the game out and illustrate once more, both by style and by wit, what he had always intended, whether against Andros, the *Proposals,* or mathematically contrived theorems: "insomuch that he is ready to be Jealous, when the judicious shall compare the Petition, with the Book, that Amicus Patriae was John Wise, or that John Wise was Amicus Patriae." Whereupon he takes his leave in one of the finest of exit lines, begging those who believe the doctrine of metempsychosis, should they "hear that the said Wise is Deceased, they will surely conclude that by a Transmigration Wise's Soul is entered into Amicus Patriae."

In 1724 the General Court again invited him to give the election sermon and he again declined; Joseph Sewall spoke in his place, urging the country to maintain its credit. The next year Wise was dead. As no other theorist of the time carried the conception of social compact and natural rights to such democratic lengths, none so openly or cheerfully applied the criteria of educational opportunity and equality to the case of cheap money. And none since Bradford, if indeed even he, composed so graceful a sentence, with all its implications, as that in which the soul of Wise was committed to the spirit of Amicus Patriae.

The contrast between Wise on the one hand and the various shades of opinion represented by John Colman, Cotton Mather, Paine, Stoddard, and above all Wigglesworth, is a portent. Intellectuals were falling not so much into opposing camps as into splintered fragments, not over theological or abstract issues (all were nominally loyal to *The Westminster Confession*), but because they were identified with diverging interests. In the process, language was becoming freer, more vivid, colloquial; wit was sharpened and the life of the people directly expressed in the vernacular. On every side, speech vibrated with a new sincerity, because each man was learning to write not as an Englishman but as a lover of his own country.

Those of the intellectuals who tried not to take sides, who remained above the battle and hoped that religion would yet cure economic ills, may seem at first sight to have been less affected by the forces which made Wigglesworth a preacher of the gold standard and Wise of free coinage. In 1710, Cotton Mather discoursed on the golden streets of the holy city, and characteristically took refuge in his Chiliastic vision of the millennium; looking down from this vantage point upon the economic life of New England, he grieved over its cheats and its frauds, yet had to confess, "I am not versed in the Niceties and Mysteries of the Market-Place." He could only insist that the Golden Rule would, were it observed, rectify all our dealings. But he called this vision of the good society *Theopolis Americana,* and remembering Judge Sewall's paean on Plum Island, as well as all else the aging Justice had done for the people, forgetting the quarrels that sometimes had sundered them, he dedicated this book to him, as one patriot to another: "My Pray'rs and Hopes for America, are Yours."

T HAT
Cotton Mather should resort to private prayer in
order to kill Dr. Noyes, even while sadly acknowledging in his pulpit that
he understood little of finance, was in effect a confession that neither he
nor his colleagues could fit the currency issue into their frame of reference. Their idea—virtually their only idea—was that the land, the whole
of New England, stood in covenant with God, wherefore it prospered
when virtuous and suffered when sinful. If inflated currency was an affliction, then in the logic of the covenant relief would come only when the
people should repent: in this context, repentance meant labor and frugality. By the wisdom of the covenant, the only way to beat the rising cost
of living was pious economy. Yet even these prescriptions had a different
implication when advocated by Paul Dudley and the hard-money men on
purely economic grounds, for thus they raised the specter of popular opposition, of which John Wise was the portent. There was every danger
that, should the clergy express their hostility to paper money in terms
more explicit than some generalized exhortation to maintain the colonies'
credit, they would excite a reaction with which they were woefully unprepared to deal.

Therefore they studied caution. Yet even that soon became an untenable line: on the larger issue, preachers might be reduced to neutrality
because they were unable to take sides, but one specific working of the process did bear so hard upon them that there was no keeping silent. As money
depreciated and prices rose, the majority of parsons, trying to live on a salary for which they had contracted, found themselves, like John Wise,
unable to make both ends meet. So, though the ministers were not altogether clear in their minds as to whether specie, a private bank, or a public bank was the way to relieve the people's (and their own) distress,
they were obliged to denounce their people for allowing the purchasing
power of the minister's shillings to shrink, and to call for repentance in
the form of higher wages. When churches, congregations, and especially
towns demurred or refused, the clergy found themselves face to face with
a widespread, a sullen resistance.

By 1706 someone who advertised himself a friend to the churches
published *A Plea for the Ministers of the Gospel,* in which, despairing of
extracting more money from the people's bounty, he advanced the thesis

that according to Biblical rule a minister is entitled to a tithe of the community's income, be the currency what it may. The author perceived that unless the clergy were paid enough to keep them in the style to which they had become accustomed, their prestige would decline; they should have as much right to grow substantial as merchants or tradesmen. Hence the rate should not be determined by mere willingness, by reason or by the light of nature (because if left to such guides, the brotherhood will skimp), but by divine "Institution." Unless this is done, he concluded, the society will be cursed with still more disasters, for a low-spirited and underpaid clergy will not reprove sinners, wherefore sin will augment, and with it judgments.

Increase Mather was loyal enough to the spirit of Congregationalism to see the heresy in this proposal; he was also sensitive enough to public opinion to know how angrily it would be taken. In the midst of his defense of the voluntary principle, he hastily published *A Discourse Concerning the Maintenance Due to those That Preach the Gospel*. He perceived that the clergy were suffering and said that they always had suffered, quoting John Cotton's apothegm, "There is nothing cheap in New England besides Milk and Ministers." But, he insisted, bad as the situation was, salaries must be settled only upon an agreement between minister and people; to claim a tenth is not only imperious, it is "in most places" to demand too much, and would, he warned the clergy, "expose themselves to censures." (Stoddard, having herded almost all the town into his church, was seeing to it that his elders and deacons, Pomeroy and Hawley, were extracting out of the rates the most princely salary any cleric outside Boston enjoyed.) Having made clear his adherence to free enterprise, Mather then launched into another denunciation: "Ministerial Work is not to be levell'd with Mechanic Labours, Merchandize, nor other more Liberal Imployments neither; the Practice of Physic, or the teaching of Phylosophy, not accepted." He was still attempting to rectify the abuse by moral persuasion; meanwhile, the bills of credit went down and the cost of living went up.

In 1725 another anonymous author (the problem had become so delicate that frank discussion had to appear anonymously) tried to deal with the root of the matter, and ominously entitled his discussion *Anti-Ministerial Objections Considered*. It is, in every implication, an acknowledgment that the campaign for raising salaries had by that date stirred up angry passions. The people answer, especially in "Country-Towns," by bargaining even closer with the poor candidate, on the open premise that "a Cheap Minister is the Best, let his Qualification for the Ministry be ever so mean." The youth accepts, having no alternative, little realizing what he will require when married and father of a family; a man needed a bare minimum, as of that year, of £100, but few were lucky enough to get that much. Surely, if the clergy are still to lead the community, they must have more than the "middling livers"; not only, like other men, do they have to provide for widows and children, but they have "to give more & better Entertainment in their Houses." Against this stood the contention of townsmen that the pay was what had been bargained for, that the war increased taxation, and finally that ministers did get as much as most "middling livers." What more were they worth? We find in one sentence a summary of the social change and its effect upon social philosophy when this author asks if it be not reasonable that the minister be recompensed "in some Proportion to what he himself might have gain'd in any other Business, he could have employed himself in?" Tidings of this sort were bound to reach pious students at Harvard and Yale and diminish their sense of vocation.

More and more of them discovered that they had no such calling; Samuel Sewall had been something of a prognostication, but he could still show that divine providence had specifically turned him from the pulpit by devolving upon him the administration of the estates of his father-in-law, John Hull. In the eighteenth century, slighter summons were heeded, most disturbingly by some who took a church and promptly discovered that the pay was insufficient. Young men like Thomas Phipps, Jonathan Remington, and so promising a luminary as John Read went into business or began to study law. The danger was visible as early as 1706: many youths, said Increase Mather, bred up at great expense by their parents, "do decline the Imployment; they are sensible they can get a better livelihood in another way." For these defections, the stinginess of the people again was blamed; but instead of bowing in shame before the charge, they ventured to whisper to each other in the tavern that it was none of their responsibility.

Still more lamentable was the situation in which those dedicated souls found themselves who tried to persevere. Many were forced to spend their weekdays in mundane and soul-destroying businesses, preparing their sermons hastily on Saturday evenings. Some of them were clever enough to succeed, like Christopher Toppan of Newbury or Ephraim Little of Plymouth, at making money in land speculations. But most of them, helpless Brahmin scholars, were miserable failures. They could not even furnish themselves with books, nor even read the few they brought from college, "their time is too much taken up in looking after their Families, that they may be kept from Pinching wants: and so many of them fall short of that Learning, that men of their Profession ought to have." The founders never supposed that a scholar stationed in a country town would give over scholarship; by 1717 it seemed to many leaders—notably Timothy Cutler, who at this point began to cogitate about the advantages of an episcopal system—that parsons were too much distracted from their proper work by worldly affairs. *Anti-Ministerial Objections Considered* regretted that they must take to the fields, but begged them to do even this rather than sue their people before the Quarter Session, "when that is likely effectually to ruine their Ministry." If clerical reports are to be believed, the land was full of parsons barely holding body and soul together, eking out a scanty income, clogged in their studies.

For this melancholy state of affairs, the clergy blamed the people. "I am persuaded," said Stoddard's son-in-law, William Williams, in a typical passage, "that the beggarly pinching way of bargaining with Ministers to get their Service as cheap as they can, hath been a provocation to God in this Land." For three generations, ministers had pointed out wherein the people, by their fornication, drunkenness, and gaudy apparel, incited divine retribution; so far the masses (except for an extremely rare recalcitrant) had mutely accepted the blame even when incapable of abstaining from fornication or rum. But was it their fault that ministers must plow or teach school? John Wise, we have noted, was one who disregarded the advice about not going to law; evidently (as far as can be made out) he aroused no hard feelings in Chebacco. But he of course was John Wise, and in 1721, fully as aware as the Mathers of the plight of the clergy, he dared to speak the thought of the people by saying that most accounts represented things as worse than they were. As a matter of fact, he declared (you get no hint of this in the customary jeremiad), most places have taken into consideration the depreciation of currency and have done something: "There has not been near so much Unrighteousness in the Country as some Men speak of." Furthermore, there is an ulterior motive in this universal clerical exhortation to raise the pay of parsons: it is insidious propaganda against the bills. To which Wise, and Wise alone, was able to reply, "Do we think these Reverend Men, don't find that they can make as good a Dinner on the Bills of Credit, as on Gold; and Silver?"

The great force of the inventory of sins compiled in 1679 was that it had given an objective account of the social situation. It was designed to excite the community to repentance, but it had aimed at elevating the entire body politic; it did not excoriate one group at the expense of another. Now, as the inexorable workings of the economy degraded ministers and compelled them to blister their hands on plows and rakes, the accusation of declension became, in pulpit after pulpit, a charge that the people were destroying the land by starving their shepherds. This was a very different use of the formula: it was not a baring of the general bosom but a demand, arrayed in the folds of the covenant, for higher wages. Only Wise dared, or could, print the people's answer: they had done the best they could. But if the masses could not print, they could mutter; when their grumblings reached clerical ears, the ministers took the fatal step of beginning to denounce what they called antiministerial sentiment. Vile words, they said, are being cast about, "of Priest-Craft, and Priest-Ridden, an ambitious and Designing Clergy." No doubt, since they published these phrases, the words were being spoken, but by publishing them the ministers not only acknowledged the fact but gave it currency. Fornication was a sin to which a man, overwhelmed by temptation, might yield even while knowing it a sin and despising it; antiministerial sentiment, when charged upon him by a minister whom he paid out of his taxes, was something in which he might take pride.

Was there no way, asked Timothy Cutler, whereby the General Court of Connecticut could collect rates without exposing the clergy to odium? In 1721 Jonathan Marsh told them that one could easily observe "a Spirit of Jealousy prevailing in the People of this Land against the Ministry of it." That the complaint should be especially clear in Connecticut, where *The Saybrook Platform* and the solidarity of the government made control more rigorous than in Massachusetts, proclaims that resistance was all the greater. In 1723 Eleazar Williams told the General Court that both in Connecticut and in "the Neighboring Governments" thousands were confirmed "in their Wicked and Groundless Jealousies concerning the Ministry, as if they had a design to get the power in their own hands; that they might lord it over God's heritage." In Massachusetts, Jabez Fitch, erstwhile tutor at Harvard, cast more light upon the sources of these clerical recriminations by deliberately removing from a poor church in Ipswich to a richer one in Portsmouth, and in 1724 telling why: bills of credit no longer serve for dealings upon the same terms as formerly, being used at face value only to pay ministers' salaries, which have "scarcely in any place, been raised in proportion to the differences between Bills of Credit & Money." Depreciation, for which nobody was responsible, created a struggle for power in every community between people (who could or would pay no more) and clergy (who demanded more); out of this contest arose animosities of a sort the founders had never envisaged. The effort of the clergy to reduce the masses to repentance was thus transformed into a cry for more money, and the jeremiad became a village haggle.

From this situation arose a suspicion, gradually becoming a settled conviction, that preachers of the jeremiad, when calling upon citizens to observe simplicity and sobriety in expenditures, were not so much expounding Scripture as supporting the restrictive policy of Wigglesworth and the "Court party," that they were trying to browbeat the people into going without the few available comforts in order to pocket the money themselves. If merchants would import less, preachers let themselves say, there would be less temptation because fewer items on which the populace could squander their pennies; hence less indulgence in sinful luxury, and therefore fewer judgments. But were these articles really or inherently sinful? Was it actually the way out of economic difficulty to import less? Was an economy of scarcity more holy than one of even moderate abundance? Might not the answer be, in both financial and moral terms, that prosperity required more rather than less imports? The one ministerial authority in whom the common man had any trust told him, in unforgettable words, that denunciations of trade and upbraiding of legitimate finery were improper themes for the pulpit. At this time, in even the

most contentious of towns, women still curtsied toward the pulpit as they
entered the meetinghouse and the minister was a figure of dignity. Still,
there is a subterranean development which would remain undecipherable
were it not for John Wise's habit of blurting out realities. He who had
confronted Andros and become thereby such a patriot as even Cotton
Mather could not denigrate, drew out the logic of his career in *A Word
of Comfort* with an unabashed defense of those articles of commerce which
contribute, in the long run, to material well-being:

> For working Wood, Iron, Brass, Leather, &c into Fine Coaches and Chariots,
> and Horses as Fine and Proud as they, suited to them; why were these made, &c?
> And turning glittering Earth, and glutinous matter of Worms, into Embroideries,
> &c? But to furnish a Generous People, that would Banish sordidness, and live
> Bright and Civil, with fine Accomplishments about them?

Orthodox jeremiads (strangely coinciding with advices of the Court party)
inculcated simple living; in the parsonage at Chebacco an old man wondered; he, who had lived in what our century would certainly consider the
plainest manner, agreed that were we to exist upon "Ground-Nuts and
Clams," to clothe ourselves in raw pelts, we might lower our expenses
and thus purchase less from England, just as amateur economists in the
pulpits told us. "But," said he, "if we intend to Live in any Garb, or
Port, as becomes a People of Religion, Civility, Trade and Industry, then
we must still supply our selves from the Great Fountain." I have no way,
lacking contemporaneous evidence (except such as appears in the previous
chapter), of gauging how these words fell upon New England ears. Possibly their economic insight was still strange doctrine, but in any event the
importations continued; works of wood, iron, brass, and leather and fab-
rics derived from glutinous worms were purchased somehow. Was there
no one beside John Wise, thinking his thoughts in solitude, to suggest that
a generous people, devoted at one and the same time to religion and civility, had a right to banish sordidness?

Wise was nowhere more radical, life-long radical that he was, than in arguing that luxury is not sinful. For as long as there was trade in these works
of wood, iron, brass, and leather, there were bound to be areas in what Benjamin Colman called "Trading and Seaport Towns" where men were
"apt to grow profane and lose their Manners," wherein clerical denunciation had progressively less effect, where antiministerial sentiment spawned.
"The Sea casts up the mire & dirt of profane swearing & cursing, of excessive drinking, rude speech and carriage among them." In country towns
antiministerial sentiment might be stigmatized as sin because the people were
theoretically in covenant to support their church, but the uncovenanted
profligacy of a seaport, such as Boston or Salem, was another matter. There
immoralists could not be reached by a jeremiad; they could not be subdued
unless the government would intervene, but a royal regime, even though
the Council were all saints, was more concerned with trade than with

morals. If John Wise's argument were to prevail—as in fact it was prevailing—the more ships that brought in luxurious manufactures, the more drunken sailors would swagger in the streets and blasphemous books be circulated among dissidents.

"That ever that Element," bewailed Cotton Mather (for whom all God's creation was beautiful), "should be so poisoning, so polluting!" The observation was older than the days of Plato: the sea is a school of vice. Sailors come ashore, to squander in days of riot what they get by months of hard service "abourd and abroad"; every time a ship paid off, Cotton Mather beheld them: "Filthy Speaking, Baudy Speaking, Unclean and Obscene Ribaldry." Every year he and his colleagues tried to exhort masters and crews: "Poor Sailours, will you never hearken to the Voice of Wisdom?" They seemed to be a peculiarly impervious lot.

Not only that; they sang their siren song in Boston and shrewd wenches perceived the economic opportunity. "What, shall there be any bawdy-houses in such a town as this!" For years the clergy referred darkly to taverns that served more than rum; in 1713 the admission became specific: "Let Harlots of this Place also be afraid, and fearfulness Surprise the Lewd Women of the Town; The Houses where some of them dwell, are too well known."

Nor was prostitution the worst of afflictions suffered by trading and seaport towns. Youths were constantly lured into piracy, many of whom had sat under the means of grace. Most of them "perished wonderfully" (an execution of pirates furnished the most suitable of occasions for a rousing jeremiad), but the contagion spread ashore: there was thievery in Boston. Time was when neither a lock nor a bolt had been required, and "I wish it had continued"; but during the fire of 1711, houses were looted: " 'Tis a Wickedness of very prodigious Elevation. O Monstrous Wretches! O Monsters of Wickedness!"

Prostitution and profanity were familiar and "natural" vices; but sailors of the eighteenth century were still more inventive, thus compelling the jeremiad to take account of "self-pollution, sodomy." In 1724 was published a seventy-page tract, *Onania, or the Heinous Sin of Self-pollution, and all its Frightful Consequences in both Sexes, Considered.* It called itself the tenth edition, an eleventh was deemed necessary in 1726; it accounts for many veiled passages in the sermons.

As I have suggested, we have few evidences that in the seventeenth century the populace did anything but cringe under the lash. In 1712 Judge Sewall was obliged to bind over to the Session a group who circulated a mock sermon "full of Monstrous profaneness and obscenity"; the next year, when reproving a drunkard with the admonition that every time he took a pot of rum he was selling the blood of Christ, Cotton Mather met an unexpected rejoinder, "Truly, Sir, when we are going to make our selves Drunk, we never think of that." Insubordination was mounting, and who could control it? At nine in the evening of February 6, 1714, Sewall was summoned by the watch to the tavern of John Wallis, where a number of citizens had made themselves gloriously drunk and were noisily toasting Queen Anne. To his solemn remonstrance they replied by toasting him (he took no notice). He demanded their names, which were freely given; one of them, Netmaker, reproached the province, "said they had not made one good Law." Another turned out to be Thomas Banister, long an inhabitant and freeholder, his family pillars of the Brattle Street Church. Sewall preferred his charges, only to discover how thorny had become the ways of the righteous: Netmaker proved to be secretary to General Sir Francis Nicholson, who raised a frightful furor because his servant was molested, while both Dudley and Lieutenant-Governor Tailer ostentatiously called upon Banister.

One Sabbath morning in 1717 there was found upon the door of the Old South this inscription:

> Good people, within this House, this very day,
> A Canting Crew will meet to fast, and pray.
> Just as the miser fasts with greedy mind, to spare;
> So the glutton fasts, to eat a greater share.
> But the sower-headed Presbyterians, to seem more holy,
> And their Canting Minister to punish sinfull foley.

Cant was the word that Royalists applied to Roundheads; the provincial clergy had encountered it in their reading, but until now it had not been hurled at them within their own precincts. In 1711 Cotton Mather sought to rally the spirits both of himself and his fellows with *The Right Way to Shake off a Viper*, which he felt was even more called for in 1720 when he published a second edition. No doubt he was oversensitive, but antiministerial sentiment was clearly mounting. Ministers must confront their foes with patience and forgiveness: "Embrace your Defamators, as affording you precious opportunities to exemplify a patience that shall glorify God"— which sentence, if it means anything, signifies that there were many defamators. Not, as we know, that Cotton Mather subsided into taciturnity: he was working out a new strategy, by which antiministerial sentiment might be woven into the expanding sins of the land, so that from it servants of the Lord should prosper: "By and by, they see rest from the Days of Defamation; they prove more serviceable than ever they were in their Lives before, and a pit is digged for the Wicked." New England was dedicated to an interest which maintained itself by the jeremiad; now there was a smouldering but as yet inchoate rebellion—not only among the "Yokeless, but by Professors of Godliness"—against that formulation. No longer capable of turning history into a pattern of affliction and repentance, of imposing its requirements upon sailors and harlots, that interest was obliged to contrive new pits for the wicked.

Certainly, there seemed no way in which the wicked could defend themselves except by dumbly persisting in wickedness. Ministers would not so doggedly have denounced the vices of trading and seaport towns had these not offered conspicuous exhibitions of unrepentance. Only occasionally did such recalcitrants strike back, as in the nailing of a libel on the door of the Old South: they had little opportunity and no weapons. Nevertheless, a few straws, recorded with distaste by officialdom, indicate what winds were blowing around less reputable corners. That individuals in those areas were gathering strength, Cotton Mather confessed in 1712 by calling them "Pied Pipers of Hamelen." So far, the pipers had no way of presenting their side of the story, wherefore they are lost to literature, but Cotton Mather could clearly see children of the saints dancing to hell behind them: "Our City is filled with Snares by those hateful Scorners of Goodness."

What, in all sobriety, could a scorner of goodness possibly contrive at that date? Certainly not open defiance; he could not stand up in public and assert, in the name of natural law, the right of a natural man to enjoy rum and harlots. There was only one way in which the reprobates might, even obliquely, mount their counterattack, and that was wit. In 1714, Boston had its first taste of it: somebody ventured to publish a series of heroic couplets entitled *The Origin of the Whale Bone-petticoat.* It was a pale imitation of a popular form, a satire upon the follies of the town, but in America amateur copies of European sophistication have cultural, not to say spiritual, references unknown to the capitals; in provincial New England, a castigation of the fad was bound to appear, no matter how much it aped the mode of London, a mock jeremiad and therefore an insult to Americanism. Nathaniel Ward had, long ago, employed Puritan rhetoric to make comedy out of women's foibles, but his manner was that of Renaissance satire, in which an exuberance of vocabulary excused him from seriousness of purpose without plunging him into frivolity. Since his time, the hoop skirt had come in for its share of clerical denunciation in the encompassing catalogue of depravities, but as a topic of discourse it was not considered funny; how then could it be treated lightly without the treatment amounting to more than satire, to a cryptic defiance of morality?

This little essay purported to find the origin of all absurdities in the sin of pride: the farthingale was invented to conceal an "Embrio," starched ruffs to hide ugly necks, pyramids on the head to heighten pigmy maids, and tiny muffs to show off fine arms. Who could protest against so righteous a fulmination—except that in thus purveying righteousness on the streets of Boston, the language of the streets happened to be employed? The hoop skirt originated in Versailles, where a French Belinda

> *suffered grievously by sad Mishap*
> *Which modern Empirics now call a Cl — p.*

Told by her physician that she must take a fortnight's cure, Belinda offers him ten thousand livres to keep her in society, whereupon he devises the skirt as a "circling Ambuscade to hide your stradling Gate." Wherefore, as all jeremiads would contend, women in Puritan Boston ought to reject the fashion of a French strumpet. Or at least they ought, as the jeremiads would not get around to saying, to hang plummets on the hems of their gowns,

> *That ev'ry saucy, ruffling, wanton Breeze,*
> *Mayn't toss up all, and shew your Knees*
> *As now it do's.*

Only one copy of this broadside survives—chastely catalogued in the British Museum—but it introduced New England to satirical pornography.

In this society, in what other form but that of an attack upon vices could wit venture? Was there any other subject for ridicule? Had even an anonymous versifier pretended that the sight of a girl's knees, the wind blowing up her skirts, was anything but shocking, there would have been no audience, even among those who relished the spectacle. But in the form of denunciation, it might be celebrated: could the ministers object? They could and did: such a vein of ridicule, said Cotton Mather, once given its head, will suffer no restraint. "The Flood-gates will be Set open, for an Irresistible Torrent of Abominations." Somewhere among drunken sailors and their doxies, out of reach of the town watch, lurked the old Adam, whom the ministers could pillory as a spirit of ridicule and try to silence before he spoke; but they could never rest in the assurance that he would not find a voice—or a publisher.

He came dangerously close to speaking in several of the financial tracts, most audibly in those of John Wise. Against him, until the middle of 1721, the ministers maintained, either through the passionateness of Cotton Mather or the judiciousness of Thomas Paine, that frugality, sobriety, simplicity were the regnant virtues. "Alas! Sinful Boston," exclaimed Increase Mather, "dost thou not see, that Poverty is coming on thee like an armed Man?" What should or could Boston do but acquiesce? On August 7, 1721, James Franklin brought out the first number of *The New-England Courant:* those elements in the town who did not want to acquiesce, those forbidden voices, at last had an organ, and through it an accumulated store of antiministerial sentiment found a long sought vent.

James Franklin was the son of a professing member of the Old South; unlike most of his class, tallow-maker Josiah Franklin had progressed from a mere owning of the covenant in 1685 to full communion in 1694. His sons dreamed of going to Harvard, but there were too many of them and there was no money. James managed to get to London and there learn the printer's trade, returning in 1717 with a font of type to the house on Union Street. Thirteen years previously, the postmaster, John Campbell, had started the first newspaper, the weekly *Boston News-Letter,* because he was in a position to intercept the latest (generally two or three months late) intelligences. That such a journal was even supported is part of the emergence of New England from colonial isolation into provinciality, even though the *News-Letter* consisted of nothing but extracts from London papers, of obituaries and of official proclamations. In 1719 a new postmaster commenced a rival, *The Boston Gazette,* no different in character, the printing of which was given to James Franklin, who therefore felt himself well enough established to afford an apprentice, and so signed indentures for Benjamin, his twelve-year-old brother. But in August 1720 the owner transferred the printing to another house, and James was reduced to living off such odd jobs—which were not many—as he or his industrious apprentice could scrape up. In London, James Franklin had learned of the revolution wrought in modern journalism by *The Spectator;* to him it appeared that Boston, with its sailors, harlots, and taverns, was ripe for a similar enterprise, that it might be amused by something more topical than a jeremiad. He and his friends entertained notions of mirth which extended beyond the limits set by Benjamin Colman: fancying themselves a set of American Roger de Coverleys, they issued the *Courant.*

Several of these associates were, as a matter of fact, Anglicans. One of them, John Checkley, born in Boston of old Puritan stock in 1680, had studied at Oxford, traveled on the Continent, and come back in 1710 with a collection of books and paintings to flaunt his adherence to the Established Church. While making his living as an apothecary, he published two books defending the Church of England, which had already (as we shall see) brought him into trouble with the authorities; but even worse, he fascinated a nephew of Cotton Mather, one Thomas Walter, who seemed so far lost as to invite his uncle's condemnation: however, the family influence prevailed and by 1720 Walter was securely installed as minister at Roxbury. Checkley wrote a manifesto for the first number—anonymously, of course, although the whole town recognized his hand. To our eyes it seems tame enough: should the *Courant* be told that it cannot keep company with the sages because its beard does not yet reach to its girdle, it will answer, "Barba non facit Philosophem"; out of consideration for other writers in the town, it promised to be as dull as they. Sophomoric though this seems, nevertheless it raised the standard of wit and, unlike the fugitive *Origin of the Whale Bone-petticoat,* was determined to carry on once a week.

A joke about the dullness of others might conceivably have been welcomed among such saints as were obliged to listen to Benjamin Wadsworth. But if among Franklin's associates were those who, like Checkley, had Anglican sympathies, or if he himself was suspect, then the most innocent of jibes was a threat to the reigning order. Walter had done penance for his friendship with Checkley by answering, in 1720, Checkley's attack on New England's theology; now it was expected of him—or so he assumed—that the challenge should be matched by the wit of New England's pulpit. He undertook the unequal combat by preparing *The Little-Compton Scourge: or, The Anti-Courant,* which James Franklin, having learned in London the game of publicity, delightedly published.

The student of today, compelled to read Walter's squib, sheds tears of anguish. However, it has its importance, if only because through it the clergy attempted to reply in kind to the *Courant,* or at least allowed Walter to do so for them; they appeared, for the first time, silly. The *Courant* entered the field at a moment when the community was divided over the issue of inoculation for the smallpox; it boldly and impudently took the anti-inoculation line, thus assuring itself of substantial popular support. On the side of inoculation were aligned the Mathers, Colman, and most of the clergy, but only a minority of the population; hence the first clerical rebuttal made discretion the worser part of valor by trying to make a joke. Actually, Walter did score a direct hit: he accused the *Courant* of coming into the world in the guise of "Mr. Bickerstaff," but pronounced it as much like him "as Lackey and Link Boy to Mr. Gentleman." Because it was written in a "native Stile," it was bound to be "very, very Dull," and so never to make good its pretensions.

This was exactly James Franklin's problem: could he, out of provincial America, muster a sufficient parade of wit to keep his sheet going? In his second number, on August 14, he acknowledged the difficulty by asking his friends to favor him "with some short Pieces, Serious; Sarcastick, Ludicrous, or otherways amusing; or sometimes professedly Dull (to accommodate some of his Acquaintance)." But at the same time, he had to promise that he would print nothing "reflecting on the Clergy (as such) of whatever Denomination." This was, in one sense, a gauge of battle, but in another it was Franklin's dilemma: could the secular wit of New England devise any method of becoming sarcastic or ludicrous except by parodying the jeremiad? Did either English literature or their own materials provide writers for the *Courant* with any other themes? How else compose even the most ephemeral squib? If not, how could they write at all without, if only by implication, reflecting upon the clergy, into whose preserve they were bound to venture?

For a while the *Courant* had the advantage that the populace sympathized with its fight against inoculation, but in the long run it was defeated, not because it took the wrong side in a scientific controversy but because it presumed to exercise a monopoly belonging to the clergy. By daring to berate the sins of seaport and trading towns in town language, it served as a vehicle for the retorts of those who had long been the targets of pulpit denunciation. While the town was seething with fear that the Mathers had exposed it to a smallpox epidemic, Checkley elected to tell how Thomas Walter spent a night in bed with two sisters of ill-repute. The death toll mounted, while James Franklin resolutely printed verses on the follies of women of fashion, and allowed "Amelia" to reply. In October the city buried 428 bodies, but Franklin kept up his game, informing a female correspondent,

> *Lucilius now*
> *Has an innocent Brow,*
> *His Caution to Batchellors shows it;*
> *But if sooner or Later*
> *He merits a Satyr*
> *You have not the Sense to compose it.*

There is something touching beyond words in these primitive efforts to sound the metropolitan tone; yet they are at least endeavors to erect some other standard than self-recrimination. On November 20 Franklin found his way to declaring by what rule he would deal out castigation: "to reform the present declining Age, and render it more polite and vertuous." Because he, with no more warrant than his press, without the sanction of a Harvard degree, took upon himself thus to reform the community, he was confronted in the street by a "Gentleman" (everybody knew this was Cotton Mather) who told him he was vilifying ministers.

James Franklin remains eternally transfixed in the malice of his brother's *Autobiography:* he beat his apprentice (thereby imparting to that youth a life-long aversion to arbitrary power) and was jealous when the boy won the esteem of the wits; in 1724, when the runaway Benjamin returned in opulence, he "receiv'd me not very frankly, look'd me all over, and turn'd to his work again." This is the grim and sullen James whom posterity knows, but a different personality—gay and courageous—is recorded in the *Courant.* On December 4 he told Cotton Mather that a newspaper-man gives both sides of a story, and quoted Joseph Addison that any attempt to reduce all men to a single standard of thinking is "absurd in Philosophy, impious in Religion, and Faction in the State." He proclaimed in New England the utterly novel doctrine that errors should be published rather than suppressed, because they less endanger the state when exposed than when circulated without opposition in private conversation.

To anathematize a Printer for publishing the different Opinions of Men, is as injudicious as it is wicked. To use Curses without a Cause, is to throw them away as if they were Nothing Worth, and to rob them of their Force when there is Occasion for them.

At the moment Cotton Mather was describing Boston as "a Town which Satan has taken a most wonderful Possession of," James Franklin was inviting all who had leisure and ability (were they enough?) "to speak their Minds with Freedom, Sense and Moderation, and their Pieces shall be welcome to a Place in my Paper." One could not respond to this invitation in the Boston of 1721 without bringing down upon his head anathemas, nor could anyone publish a *Courant* in this spirit without inevitably becoming a mouthpiece of every antiministerial sentiment.

Franklin did not improve his standing in the eyes of the respectable by publishing on December 11 the account of a man in Stonington who castrated himself and thus incensed "the looser Sort of the Female Tribe." No less shocking was a letter purporting to come from "Tom Penshallow" in "P———h" (Cotton Mather's good friend, his ally in the inoculation fight, was Samuel Penhallow of Portsmouth), which declared that the *Courant's* assertion of journalistic liberty was not calculated to a New Hampshire meridian. In January, Samuel Mather assumed unto himself the name "John Harvard" and over it published a letter in the *Gazette* which accused the *Courant* of being an enemy to the ministers and a destroyer of religion; by this time his father everywhere asserted that the enterprise was the work of "a Hell-Fire Club"—a charge he delivered, reported Franklin, "with as much Zeal as ever he discover'd in the Application of a Sermon on the most awakening Subject," which remark, with all its cunning, casts a white and glaring light not so much on what the jeremiad had become but upon what, as a rationale of the society, it had always been.

Franklin was in a position to throw such a barb because he consistently disavowed any hostility to the clergy as a caste. In general, he meekly attested, they are faithful and admirable: except that some of them have lately taken to dictating not the will of God but their private whims, and these things other men are not obliged to obey, "being good Protestants, & the Subjects of a King who allows us Liberty of Conscience." He took his life in his hands by calling rumor-mongering one of the arts by which Cotton Mather aspired to "reign Detractor General over the whole Province, and do all the Mischief his ill Nature prompts him to," but he saved his life by saying of Samuel Mather what many had often thought of the father yet never had a chance to speak: "It seems the venemous Itch of Scribbling is Hereditary." Whether he was right or wrong about inoculation, Franklin was ready to discuss; but as a layman says on January 22 to a minister in one of the *Courant's* many dialogues, the clergy are furious because laymen write or learn something beyond the bare minimum of getting to heaven; the clergyman thereupon laments that formerly nothing was transacted in Zion without clerical advice, but the layman stands his ground: "People are more Knowing and don't need advice." The cleric thinks it argument enough for inoculation that all the rakes are against it, to which the lay spokesman replies by merely publicizing the twist preachers had already given to the jeremiads: he is convinced that inoculation is from the devil precisely because all ministers are for it, since Satan "often makes use of good Men as Instruments to obtrude his Delusions on the world." Cotton Mather picked up this passage, left out the last clause and declared that Franklin had said that anything advocated by the ministers was, *ipso facto*, devilish; Franklin asked whether, should he hear Mather say from his pulpit, "The Fool hath said in his Heart, there is no God," and then should represent Mather as denying the existence of God, that could be called accurate reporting!

In January, Increase Mather wheeled into line the heaviest of clerical artillery: he longed for the fire-power he no longer could command—"I can well remember when the Civil Government would have taken an effectual Course to suppress such a Cursed Libel!"—but lacking that, he brought down upon the offending viper the concentrated fury of the covenant. (Would it work?) "I am afraid that some Awful Judgment will come upon this Land, and that the Wrath of God will arise, and there will be no Remedy." He committed himself to the certainty of his prediction: "I cannot but pity poor Franklin, who tho' but a Young Man, it may be

Speedily he must appear before the Judgment Seat of God." (This incantation had disposed of Dr. Noyes; surely Franklin was a thousand times more vulnerable?) However, until the covenant should take over, Increase told subscribers to the *Courant* that they should withdraw.

Not since the patient ass turned and remonstrated with the prophet Balaam had such a thing happened: an object singled out for total annihilation by "the oldest Minister in the Country" declined the honor! Franklin took the offensive, "if a profane Son of Corah, a Child of the Old Serpent, &c., may be allow'd to defend himself." He traded blow for blow:

> Here I may justly observe, that if I may lawfully print the Courants, then I may as lawfully get my Living by selling them; and the Doctor may as well publish an Advertisement to advise Persons not to buy Goods of any particular Merchant or Shopkeeper, as to advise them not to countenance the Courant. I desire him to consider how it would be taken, if upon a Misunderstanding, between any particular Minister and my self, I should publickly advise his People not to hear him, or contribute to his Support.

Who could have foreseen, only thirty years before, when the old charter went under, that the problem would be not church and state (because state was bound to become indifferent) but church and public opinion? To James Franklin, nothing was sacred, not even Harvard College, which he blamed for the scribblings of Samuel Mather and addressed in prayer, "From such Ministers as Thou art like to make, Libera nos Domine." All this time, the apprentice was in and out of the shop, mainly employed "to carry the papers thro' the streets to the customers." At the end of March, James Franklin found under his door an anonymous communication, evidently a response from one of the few with enough leisure and ability to accept his invitation to speak with freedom; on April 2, 1722, the *Courant* carried the first letter from "Silence Dogood."

In June, James Franklin was arrested for printing an allegation that the government had been lax in pursuit of a pirate, and spent three weeks in jail. In January 1723, when Shute had come to the final impasse with the House over his salary, just as he was about to retreat to England, there to bring down upon New England the vengeance not of Jehovah but of the Privy Council, James Franklin chose that moment to run, as a leading article, an attack upon hypocrisy which, at least on the surface, might have been extracted from any of a hundred jeremiads.

Hypocrisy, we have seen even the founders discovering, had its uses in New England; it proved against Presbyterians that Congregationalism was not absurdly perfectionist. But in the early years of the new century, were ministers to be believed, the land was full of it. "Nothing is more apparent," they were constantly proclaiming, "than that, the Religion of the Body (even) of Professors among us is sunk into a Lifeless Formality." No one was more profuse or ingenious upon this theme than Cotton Mather: "I know we have a sort of Good People, that have no Goodness in them. We flatter them, that they are to Live with us in Heaven, tho' none cou'd Live near them on Earth." The *Courant's* piece owed much to *The Spectator,* but more to the local pulpit; its burden was unexceptionable.

But to it violent exception was taken. The hypocrite, it said, makes a more than ordinary profession, is full of pious ejaculations, and is peculiarly prone to fall into serious and edifying discourse when time, place, and company are unfitting; he keeps up family religion, is strict in observing not only the Sabbath but the evenings before and after. In church, his grimaces and awkward gestures advertise how deeply he is taking the sermon to heart. And yet, in daily business, he and his kind are the greatest of cheats: "they will dissemble and lie, shuffle and whiffle, and if it be possible, they will overreach and defraud all who deal with them." Of all knaves, the pious one is worst, and will find in the end that publicans and harlots enter heaven before him. Are there such in New England? "Alas! it is to be fear'd the Number is not small. A Few such Men, have given Cause to Strangers (who have been bit by them) to complain of us Greatly." To this moral and patriotic essay, Franklin appended a verse from Ezekiel which had times without number done duty as the text for a jeremiad: "This is a Lamentation, and shall be for a Lamentation."

Whereupon the House of Representatives declared that the tendency of the *Courant* was to mock religion, injuriously to reflect on faithful ministers, and to affront His Majesty's government; the Council agreed, and James was forbidden to publish—the edict soon being changed to require that he publish nothing until he had carried it for approval to the Secretary of the province. The result, as the world knows, was that on February 11, 1723, the paper announced it had changed hands and was henceforth to be printed and published by Benjamin Franklin. "A very flimsy scheme it was," the latter would one day remark; it was the beginning of the end for James Franklin.

Wherein had James offended? He had, of course, built up a store of resentment among the clergy sufficient to ruin him, but as long as he openly contradicted them, they could not touch him. He undid himself when he presumed to exercise the ministerial function of berating the sins of the land, when he printed a secular jeremiad. He usurped their office of decrying hypocrisy. On January 14 he published a clever letter of advice, supposedly addressed to him by several friends. You must speak of religion only with honor, they tell him, and you must not cast reflections on ministers (if you do, they will use their great influence to get you suppressed). You must furthermore not quote from such scandalous writings as Butler's *Hudibras,* and above all not from the Bible, since men lose respect for Holy Writ when "droll'd on in Taverns and Coffee Houses." And you must, as you ought to know, not endanger the reputation of the people (and so supply Shute with ammunition), because while we do all confess that we have visibly declined and that apostasy has come upon us, yet fundamentally we are the most virtuous people in the world. Here James Franklin got in his subtlest dig: "It may be you will say, there has been more said and printed in some Sermons on this Head, than ever you published," to which his friends reply (making crystal clear why he was prosecuted), "There are many things good and proper in the Pulpit, which would be vile and wicked in a Courant." It was, in short, utterly inadmissible, by the logic of the jeremiad, that he fill his pages "with Religious Exhortations of any kind."

It is hard to tell from this distance, but there is every reason to guess that the *Courant's* profile of the hypocrite bore unmistakable resemblances to Cotton Mather. In the first issue under the new management, the apprentice who had wonderfully become master wrote a sort of retraction (he was preternaturally skilled in this sort of thing), promising to leave off acrimony and "Billingsgate Ribaldry," professing that henceforth the design would be "to entertain the Town with the most comical and diverting Incidents of Human Life, which in so large a Place as Boston will not fail of a universal Exemplification." Could unrepentance have kept to this courtly tone (learned out of imported periodicals), respectability might have been confounded, but James Franklin was an American and therefore an angry man. By April 8 he was back again with a deliberately calculated jeremiad, reviewing in sternest pulpit manner the full panoply of native sins: vice, immorality, profaneness, decay of godliness, pride, extravagance in dress, drunkenness, idleness, "the sweet sin of Fornication," swearing, oppression, and grinding the faces of the poor. There was not space enough—"The Catalogue would be black and Voluminous." But as to whether this misrepresented the country abroad, he had to say that the report of an ecclesiastical council recently held in a vain attempt to settle a vicious church squabble in Eastham—and blatantly published—was actually a greater "Satyr" on the ministry of New England than anything the gentle *Courant* would ever utter; had the *Courant* published this very account, "the Author must have lain under the charge of being a Member of the Hell-Fire Club."

Samuel Mather, speaking as "John Harvard," had accused the *Courant* of pilfering its articles from English journals; Franklin had answered that he and his friends possessed "Stock enough of their own to live on, and to entertain, inform and edify the Publick." From April to October of 1722 he could support this boast by producing, among other items, the Dogood Papers; but on September 30, 1723, he ran a mournful advertisement that he needed a likely lad for apprentice. Soon thereafter his stock of wit began to dwindle. The essays became dull and conventional, until they disappeared entirely and whole issues were composed of nothing but "Foreign Affairs." He filled pages with a series of "feature articles," on what happens in Rome upon the death of a pope or about the life and adventures of Jonathan Wild. With its 255th number, on June 25, 1726, the *Courant* collapsed; James Franklin removed to Rhode Island, where in the obscurity of 1735 Increase Mather's prediction was fulfilled.

But before he left, James Franklin struck one last blow. In the prospectus for February 11, 1723, Benjamin, trying to erase the impression of a hell-fire club, portrayed the editorial board as a genial and inoffensive group presided over by a jovial "Father Janus," their "perpetual Dictator." He bequeathed this creation, the first work of his imagination, to his brother; during the next years James tried to keep up his own courage by further skits about Father Janus. In the hour of defeat, 1726, he published a little "satyr" in heroic couplets, *The Life and Death of Old Father Janus, the vile Author of the late Wicked Courant*. He had failed, he insisted to the bitter end, because he castigated vice, censored immorality, and exposed "The gainful Secrets of the cheating trade"—wherefore he was called wicked. He had tried to do this in the name of wit, but without any title conferred by Harvard:

> *But what inflames his Guilt, he wrote Good Sense,*
> *Yet never at the College did Commence;*
> *And like a Felon, stole a loftier Fame*
> *Than some that in the List can show their Name.*

James Franklin was fleeing from Boston, carrying out of the colony his irreducible portion of antiministerial sentiment, but still insisted that without him the "golden" days of ignorance would return to the town.

That same year there died a tradesman, John Coney, member of the Brattle Street Church, at whose funeral William Cooper preached. Born in 1701, Coney was five years older than James's brother, and during the first year of the *Courant* he also was an apprentice; hence he too never commenced at Harvard, but he kept a journal wherein, according to Cooper's literary judgment, he showed "more of good Sense and Accuracy, than could be expected from one that had no greater Advantage of education." Indeed, it showed so much that Cooper was not ashamed to publish selections from it as an appendix to his own sermon, *The Service of God recommended to the Choice of Young People*. These were indeed degenerate times, but occasionally they afforded "some amiable Patterns of real and living Religion." Coney was unable to set off his piety by social station—"which sometimes makes a little Religion make a great show"—but he shone brightly "in a lower Degree of life." Hence his lack of education could be forgiven and his prose admired. There was nothing antiministerial about him; he was everything the pious and industrious apprentice should be, and it could be told to his credit that he much occupied himself with "transcribing valuable Passages out of the Authors that pleas'd him."

The other apprentice read much and also transcribed passages that pleased him: "Often I sat up in my room reading the greatest part of the night." He labored faithfully in his calling, skimping on his dinner so that he might read when left alone in the shop. He achieved in his boyish writing infinitely greater sense and accuracy than was to be expected from one who had no advantage of education.

Out of this industry and application came the Dogood Papers. They are, of course, amateurish imitations of *The Spectator*, as were other pieces James Franklin published over the signatures of Abigail Afterwit, Ann Careful, Betty Frugal, Fanny Mournful, and one Anthony de Potsherd, who wrote from Cuckold's Point. The eleven communications from Silence Dogood might well be as lost to all except antiquarian students of the *Courant* were it not that Benjamin Franklin wrote them; however, even though it is no longer possible to estimate them apart from what he became, I believe that any searcher of the records would linger over them even had the absconding apprentice been drowned in the Delaware. They are more than colonial apings of Addison and Steele; they come from the streets of a trading and seaport town, out of that world which the official mind regarded with abhorrence, out of the mire and the stews where antiministerial sentiment was generated. They speak for "Leather Apron men," and one of them accordingly was a pointed attack upon Harvard College.

The *Autobiography* tells us that by this time Benjamin had "become a real doubter in many points of religious doctrine," that he was evading public worship (in order to get more time for reading). In January of 1722, apprentice Coney was uneasy in his mind because he had failed to reprove a sinful companion, but after he spoke and exhorted, "my conscience was easy." There are various ways of speaking to others that relieve the conscience. John Wise had shown how he would do it: "For have not some (possibly in Jest-Earnest) said, What pity it is that Lying was a Sin, it being so necessary in our Trade?" The *Courant* called its efforts at reforming the town "Joco-Serious": the "joco" part of Benjamin's burlesque of Harvard is evident, but the seriousness is deep. Harvard, he said, is a rich man's college, where blockheads and dunces learn little more than how to carry themselves handsomely and to enter a room genteelly, "which might as well be acquir'd at a Dancing School." Students are beckoned into the temple of theology by "Pecunia"; they qualify themselves for Puritan pulpits by transcribing eloquent paragraphs out of Colman's favorite author, Archbishop Tillotson of the Church of England.

The leather-apron youth was playing for high stakes. Silence Dogood, like the *Courant* itself, was preëmpting the prerogative of berating the sins of the community: pride in apparel, feminine foibles, drunkenness, and above all hypocrisy. But if such as he were to denounce hypocrisy and folly, where then would he locate hypocrisy and who would become the foolish? If uneducated apprentices, instead of meekly accepting their place and searching their souls, were to take it upon themselves to lecture their betters, then the only weapon the clergy possessed, the jeremiad, was wrested from their hands and a social revolution threatened. The satire on Harvard stung, as we make out when we find that Samuel Mather, still calling himself "John Harvard," declared anew that the *Courant* plagiarized articles, and made fun of Silence Dogood's style. She had observed the tribe of students climbing to the throne of the temple, but the work proving troublesome, "they withdrew their Hands from the Plow." "Friend," exulted

John Harvard, "who ever heard of entering a Temple and ascending the Magnificent Steps of a Throne with a Plough in hand! O rare Allegory! Well done Rustic Couranto!" Thus rapped on the most sensitive of knuckles, Benjamin Franklin learned early to keep his metaphors unmixed, but he had nothing more to learn as to where he stood in relation to the orthodoxy of New England. On the morning of July 22, John Coney found himself in a dull frame of soul, but in the evening "God seem'd to make up then in some measure what I wanted in the day." The next morning, Silence Dogood declared that the commonwealth suffered more harm from hypocrites than from the openly profane, a fact which needed particularly to be explained to the clergy, since they frequently aggravated the condition by heaping praise upon hypocrites and then denouncing what they knew nothing about. "The Reason of this Blindness in the Clergy is, because they are honourably supported (as they ought to be) by their People, and see nor feel nothing of the Oppression which is obvious and burdensome to every one else." A group that was pressing by every means it could command for an increase in the tribute it levied upon the community had no difficulty perceiving the insult in this observation, or in sensing that here stood an enemy.

When Franklin then put on a solemn mien, the point of his charade was obvious. The gusto of his denunciation shows altogether too much affection for the vices, and a frank scorn of those who denounce what they are ignorant of. The natural man could not yet openly assert a right to be what nature made him, but he could make a shambles of the pious New England elegy; he could, even while frowning upon drunkenness, give it a sort of Rabelaisian scope: "boozey, cogey, tipsey, fox'd, merry, mellow, fuddl'd, groatable, Confoundedly cut, See two Moons . . ." With certain districts of this seaport town his acquaintance was not, like that of the tribe at Harvard learning out of Tillotson to denounce them, academic. At the moment pulpits were steeling themselves to whisper, with bated breath, the awful fact that prostitutes flourished in Zion, Franklin told of drunken sailors with their doxies on Boston Common, and of two nymphs "who, by throwing their Heads to Right and Left, at every one who pass'd by them, I concluded came out with no other Design than to revive the Spirit of Love in Disappointed Batchelors, and expose themselves to Sale to the first Bidder." While the clergy denounced "night-walkers" and called upon family government to keep young people at home, the apprentice allowed a man of the people, a shoemaker, to say to a noted rambler that he could foretell how many days her boots would last, but not the number of nights.

In this very year, Solomon Stoddard's grandson took his first pulpit, in New York where also could be encountered on summer evenings sailors with their doxies, where also shoes were worn out in the "more violent and irregular Service." Not, however, by observing such phenomena, let alone finding them amusing, did Jonathan Edwards learn how to revivify the jeremiad and to become a scourge of depravity. In those months he was exclusively occupied with a burning desire to be in everything a complete Christian; like John Coney, he thirsted after progress, striving night and day to perfect himself in holiness. Later, in *his* autobiography, he was to say, "My experience had not then taught me, as it has done since, my extreme feebleness and impotence, every manner of way; and the bottomless depths of secret corruption and deceit there was in my heart." If ever he noted that the wind lifted up hoop skirts, he did not record the fact; instead, on December 19 he made a resolution which henceforth was to bind him: "Never to speak evil of any except I have some particular call to it." The next February 11, Franklin created his mock-heroic Janus, whose fellowship aimed at the "propagation of Sense and good Manners among the docible Part of Mankind in his Majesty's Plantations."

Speculation as to what Benjamin Franklin might have become had he remained in Boston is fascinating. Every bit as unanswerable, but no less fascinating, is the question of which of the two, Franklin or Edwards, was the more precocious, and so which comes more directly and revealingly from the heart of New England culture. Both of them were trained in the same intellectual universe, amid a formalized rationale of the sins of the land. The complexion of his future, Franklin was always to say, could be known "to Him only in whose power it is to bless to us even our afflictions." Thus the jeremiad, which originally was a simple scheme for insuring unity, became a game at which several, or at least two, could play; the uses to which human depravity could be put depended upon what aspects of it the user had more experience with—whether he was taught at college magisterially to denounce it or was a leather-aproned apprentice among the denounced. In any event, the latter could see by 1723 that to stay would be to invite scrapes, and "that my indiscrete disputations about religion began to make me pointed at with horror by good people as an infidel or atheist." So one of the two archsymbols of New England emigrated.

With the demise of the *Courant*, the threat of wit receded, since there was no one to carry on the assault. The ministers went back to denouncing the sins of seaport towns (which did not diminish) and to trying (with no better luck) to get depreciated salaries raised. The sentiment which the Franklins had ventured to express shows itself here and there, but not until the ecclesiastical order was shattered by the oratory of Jonathan Edwards could it again come into the open. In that perspective, the *Courant*, pitiful as it was and failure though it became, is momentous; something over a century would still be needed before Dr. Holmes of Beacon Street could say that the worst affliction to fall upon a land is boredom, but the *Courant* had glimmerings of his perception. It grew out of disruptive forces that had long been gathering momentum; it was the first open effort to defy the norm, and though it did not succeed, it foretold a time when increasing complexity would of itself engender intellectual rebellion.

CHAPTER XXI

I_N

the spring of 1721, a hundred copies of Cotton
Mather's long awaited *The Christian Philosopher* reached Boston (the manuscript had been sent to London in 1715); he was as proud of it as of anything he ever did, and acquiesced in, if he did not actually compose, his
bookseller's advertisement, addressed to scholars and "Gentlemen of any
Education," declaring that the book contained the most copious collection
yet assembled of those discoveries in nature "which the Diligent Enquiries
of the Last Age have met withal," set forth in a plain style and with religious improvements, all to be had for ten shillings. That sense of "the Age"
which Colman made most articulate at the dawn of the new century grew
upon Cotton Mather as he himself waxed older; he knew that from every
side the Enlightenment threatened him, wherefore he increased his efforts
to capture it. Over every move he made during his last decade, particularly over the conflict into which he threw himself this year, hung the
specter of a sophistication or an illumination that might render all his learning—which was to say his very being—obsolete. Hence he devoured all the
latest books he could lay his hands on, even if he had to borrow them, and
concentrated with particular ferocity on bulletins concerning "natural philosophy."

He borrowed volumes of the *Transactions* of the Royal Society (to
which he had been elected a Fellow; because he was unable to sign the
book in London, his name did not yet appear in the printed list of members,
but that did not prohibit him from deluging that body with a variety of
ingenious "Curiosa Americana" on such subjects as rattlesnakes, the strength
of imagination, "An Horrid Snow," or from signing himself proudly
F.R.S.) from a recent arrival, Dr. William Douglass. This gentleman had
studied medicine at Edinburgh, Leyden, and Paris, and found his way to
Boston through the West Indies, to set up as the town's only professionally
trained "practitioner." In addition there were several who administered
"physick" on the basis of a few books and brute experience, as did so many
country ministers; one or two of these, notably Zabdiel Boylston, enjoyed
the courtesy title of Doctor. There were further a few apothecaries, like
Checkley or a weird tobacconist named John Williams, who concocted herb
remedies, and also the midwives. Douglass was the only one of these whose
library would contain such modern works as the *Transactions*, and for a

long time his were the only copies available. Hence, before Cotton Mather returned them, he took notes on his reading—as was his habit.

He particularly studied and digested two reports from Constantinople, one by Timonius and the other by Pylarinus, describing a method used by the Turks to impart, through artificial means, a mild case of smallpox and so to secure immunity; these accounts jibed in his mind with a fantastic story his slave, Onesimus, had told about a similar practice among the Negroes of North Africa. (He so strove to get Onesimus' story accurately that he tried to imitate the dialect orthographically.) After returning the books to Douglass, he wrote John Woodward, Professor of Physic at Gresham College, through whom he sent his own communications to the Royal Society, asking why this device was not more extensively used, because obviously thousands would give thousands of pounds to have the danger and horror of the disease well over; assuredly, he said, were he once more to find himself amid an epidemic, "I would immediately procure a Consult of our Physicians, to Introduce a Practice, which may be of so very happy a Tendency."

The smallpox had, of course, long been considered the most deadly of scourges in the arsenal of a covenanted Jehovah; He might at any moment discharge it upon a transgressing people, yet out of respect for the terms to which He had bound Himself, He would resort to it only upon the utmost provocation. The sins of the land had been great, and He had answered them with proportional severity, but except for a slight intimation in 1678, He had held this punishment in reserve. In September 1720—reading the signs carefully—Increase Mather warned New England that smallpox was the next in order; by the end of May 1721 cases were reported, and by June 6 the disease had become epidemic. On that day Cotton Mather sent a letter to all the practitioners, of whatever qualification (except, Douglass was to insist, to him), telling them the substance of his notes on Timonius and Pylarinus and suggesting that they give serious thought to this way of relief, although he advised them that it "be warily proceeded in." Only Boylston was persuaded, and his way of proceeding warily was to experiment upon his own child and upon two slaves.

Boston contained about 11,000 people; and in so compact a community word of such a venture would quickly become public property and be carried from Boston to the extremities of the settlement. By June 27 the epidemic had become serious, the population were on the verge of panic, and Governor Shute took his mind off the conflict with Elisha Cooke long enough to set in motion the great therapy by which New England traditionally encountered the judgments of heaven: he called for a day of fasting and humiliation, to be followed (if possible) by a rectification of such iniquities "as have stirred up the Anger of Heaven against us." Even this dread visitation would not be in vain, said the proclamation, if only it could be sanctified into a "Humbling and thorough Reformation of this whole Land."

This being the standard and (within reasonable limits) demonstrably efficacious method of contending with adversity, we can easily comprehend with what consternation good citizens learned that Dr. Boylston, egged on by Cotton Mather, was wantonly spreading the disease. The clamor became so loud that on July 17 Boylston addressed the town through the *Gazette*, explaining that the procedure was recommended by "Gentlemen of Figure and Learning," that furthermore it was agreeable to reason, and that the experiment performed in his own household, at his own risk, had proved successful. There had, indeed, been a bad moment when his little son's fever seemed serious, which, together "with the rage of the people, affrighted me," but now he could report that the narratives in the *Transactions* were fully substantiated. But a week later, on the twenty-fourth, Dr. Douglass asserted in the *News-Letter* that the method was untried and dangerous, that if it were to be attempted at all, the circumstances should be better regulated than Boylston had contrived, and that Boylston, plunging recklessly into something he did not understand, would poison the whole community.

The disease was spreading, more and more persons were dying, fear mounted to frenzy. Increase and Cotton Mather easily persuaded Thomas Prince, John Webb, and William Cooper (their henchmen in the Boston pulpit) to join with them and with Benjamin Colman (their one-time enemy) to publish a letter in the *Gazette* on July 31 in defense of Boylston: "We that have stood by and seen his tenderness, courage and skill in that hazardous Operation cannot enough value the Man and give praise to God." True, they acknowledged—and it was they who made this concession!—Boylston had not "the honour and advantage of an Academical Education," but he was not, on that account, to be pilloried throughout the town as "Illiterate, ignorant, &c." They wished, as for decades all jeremiads had pleaded, that men might treat each other with meekness instead of calling vile names, and insisted that inoculation was a means graciously bestowed by a kind providence. The rage and fear of the people now had a target: the result was the most outspoken, the most snarling, wave of anti-ministerial sentiment New England had yet witnessed, led and fomented by such able agitators as Douglass and Checkley, who, after August 7, could speak through an organ utterly unintimidated by ministerial prestige, James Franklin's *Courant*.

The printed documents and terse passages in newspapers give us, we may be sure, only a glimpse into the violence of passion aroused during the remainder of that year, while the death toll mounted. With the coming of winter, in December the disease was arrested; by February 1722, Boston was burying its average monthly quota of eighteen. By the next summer, controversy was dropped; the episode was virtually forgotten in the fascination of the struggle between the House and Governor Shute. Except, of course, that the Mathers were left with an implacable resolution to serve as instruments of divine vengeance upon the *Courant*.

The story of this epidemic inevitably looms large in histories of New England, particularly as it exerted an influence in Europe, or at least in England; it has been widely retold by historians of medicine, and most largely celebrated by those happy to have so rare an opportunity of defending the clergy. As posterity judges, the verdict of history supports the ministers; by contrast with their progressive and enlightened stand, Douglass, Checkley, and the *Courant* figure as credulous, unscientific, and reactionary.

Actually, the story loses all point if recounted out of a modern predilection for preventive medicine; it is of the greatest moment in the development not only of the New England mind but of the European mind simply because on June 6, 1721, when Cotton Mather urged the physicians to try this device, there was absolutely no reason to suppose, on any grounds which science or intelligence needed to respect, that his medical hypothesis was any more to be trusted than had been the theory of spectral evidence employed in 1692 by the Salem Court. At that time, the righteous sacrificed their victims to an untenable notion by hanging them—and Cotton Mather justified the executioners; here again were the same murderers, Mather at their head, deliberately wreaking their vengeance upon a society they could not dominate by infecting it with smallpox. Douglass and the *Courant* had reason, caution, sobriety, and scientific authority (as well as all the wit) on their side. By a lucky shot—almost, one might say, in the dark—Cotton Mather came up with an idea which all of us nowadays believe correct; he deserves much credit, and we cannot too much extol the heroism of Zabdiel Boylston. But what was really at issue in 1721-22, in the minds of participants, was not a long-range victory of science over credulity, but a more pressing question of prestige and authority. Only when examined in this purely contemporaneous (or should I say, social?) aspect does the episode have meaning as an important crisis.

Most commentators suppose that the strength of the opposition was a theological aversion to tampering with the will of God, that pious people believed they should depend for cure upon the providence which infected them, while they did nothing but pray. Regarded in this perspective, the battle is seen as one of the engagements in that warfare of science with theology which those ignorant of history suppose occupied the seventeenth and eighteenth centuries. There was, indeed, some such sentiment in New England: Adam Winthrop wrote his son that a Christian's first concern should be a new birth, which would mean a readiness for death, wherefore God might either preserve the saint from distemper or else give it to him gently "in the common way," but that the Almighty was more than apt to be so angered by the presumption of inoculation as to make it fatal. You will do well to consider, old Adam concluded, whether inoculation "does not look like placing your Refuge in means and creatures rather than in God." In England, we ought to note, this argument figured most prominently: one Edmund Massey preached on July 8, 1722, at St. Andrew's

Holborn that only atheists, scoffers, heathens, and unbelievers would so disdain dependence upon divine wisdom, whereas true believers refuse to alter the course of nature, and so bless God for every affliction He sends them, including the last agonies of the smallpox.

The utterly astonishing fact about the Boston affair (as far as we can recover it) is that this argument was not the center of the dispute—for the simple reason that in New England the debate had to be conducted within the social framework into which the covenant had been merged, or rather within that conception of communal destiny which had preëmpted the will of God. Here the issue was bound to be (as it could not be in England) whether this means could properly be employed in the face of an affliction patently pronounced upon the sins of the community. The six ministers who published their letter on July 31—the "conservative" Mathers along with "liberal" Colman—advanced onto dangerous ground when they asserted that this was not an impious measure because they were convinced, after consulting the opinions of men of both piety and learning, that it was *safe.* If any doubted, who should know better what constitutes profanity and impiety than the ministers of Boston! Because they certified the safety, therefore inoculation must be a means given in the providence of God, just like "bleeding, blistering and a Score more things in Medical Use." However, what this ringing pronouncement does not disclose is the fashion in which it evaded, in a way that would seem to honest men utterly dishonest, the real question.

There had never been any doubt in the providential doctrine of Western Christendom, either Catholic or Protestant, that man was required to use all the means he could command for extricating himself from any predicament into which he was *already* brought by the providence of God. The captain of a ship was expected, not only by maritime but by divine law, to utilize to the full his knowledge of seamanship and what he knew of the science of navigation to pilot his vessel through a storm with which the Almighty had encompassed him. Urian Oakes, at the end of Philip's War, gave the classic New England formulation to this doctrine in *The Sovereign Efficacy of Divine Providence:* the success of an undertaking is not determined "infallibly by the greatest Sufficiency of Men, or Second Causes," but by the counsel of God: the moral of his discourse was ostensibly an admonition to the military to be prepared for disappointment, but even he digressed so far as to note that God "hath given Creatures power to act: and Man, to act as a Cause by Counsel, and hath furnished him with active Abilities." Accordingly a local parson who did his town double duty as physician, just as did Gershom Bulkeley, William Hubbard, or Edward Taylor, might legitimately bleed or blister a parishioner fallen into a fever; but in 1721 the proposal of the metropolitan clergy was that physicians should anticipate the judgment of heaven, that they should deliberately give the affliction *in advance* of the divine judgment. These clerics asserted that this procedure was authentic solely and entirely because they, in their wisdoms, were persuaded that it was safe. Were they not, therefore, presuming to say that a problematical outcome was in fact to be determined (to use the venerable language of Urian Oakes) "infallibly by the greatest Sufficiency of Men"? Were they not arrogating to themselves precisely such an impious, not to say infectious, sufficiency? Were they not subordinating piety to their own self-righteousness? To accuse inoculation of blasphemy, they said, is a wild surmise, "and the Argument falls with the Hypothesis in our Schools." But if inoculation was really a fiendish way of spreading the pox—or if Mather and Boylston did not really possess the technique for employing it safely—the ministerial hypothesis would fall, and along with it would go, not only the lives of their deluded followers, but something even more precious, the right of the clergy to interpret and expound affliction as retribution.

In modern accounts, Dr. William Douglass is a reprehensible creature, despite the fact that he eventually became a historian to whom all historians are indebted. After the evidence was all in, he could accept inoculation; some writers exult over his recantation as though it should retrospectively discredit everything he said in 1721–22. But when his words of that period are more closely examined—when we remember what pressures he was then resisting—he may claim our admiration: in March 1722 he said what had all along been his guiding principle (and none can deny him), that he wished well to any method, "whether casually discovered, or ingeniously contrived by the Sons of Æsculapius." What Mather and Boylston were attempting was a rash, headstrong, and irregular procedure which, for all they knew or could know, was as likely to spread contagion as to check it; and for authorization they (or at any rate Cotton Mather) relied primarily upon their sanctimoniousness. Douglass utilized the *Courant* in August and September of 1721, not because he hated the ministry, but because as an honest scientist he believed inoculation "a dubious and dangerous Practice." There were no provable grounds for asserting its safety; it might very well slay not only the patient but everybody in his vicinity.

Therefore Douglass had full right to demand of the six ministers by what authority they fixed their case upon the "Safety of the faulted method of Inoculating the Small pox"? To which demand, the Mathers answered that they were eminently righteous. James Franklin (along with little brother Benjamin) may not have heard about the germ theory, but he could see the gaping fallacy in this logic: "We leave the World to judge," said the *Courant* on August 21, "whether any Mans Ipse dixit without any proof, ought to be sufficient to weigh down the Scale against sufficient Evidence, right reason, and the Safety and Welfare of a People."

Controversy over the bank had made New England painfully aware that the welfare of Zion was contested by country versus town; Dr. Noyes had dared to exploit that difference, for which effrontery Cotton Mather's

God struck him dead. A little over a year after his offense, eleven months after printer Gray had been censured for publishing a letter from the country, a still more anonymous author produced *A Letter from one in the Country, to his Friend in the City*, which widened the breach by giving (or purporting to give) the country's reaction to the latest metro folly (this publication resolutely spelled it "Inocculation"). Accordi the author, Boylston was no better than an apothecary, who nevertheie proceeded, without civil or professional warrant, to contaminate the corr munity—to commit, in short, exactly what every jeremiad held was the supreme violation of covenant. On November 14 a bomb was thrown into Cotton Mather's house; the writer deplored such a "riotous wicked disturbance," but the fact remained: "To spread a mortal Contagion, What is it but to cast abroad Arrows and Death? If a man should wilfully throw a Bomb into a Town, burn a House, or kill a man, ought he not to die?" This question was not, as were so many questions in New England oratory, merely rhetorical. Suppose Mather and the clergy were spreading destruction? Those accused of witchcraft had, in 1692, been hanged upon evidence much less incriminating.

Or suppose, this pamphlet continued, inoculation does save the inoculated? Have inoculators any proof that it will not also infect bystanders? By what right do they, in order to save their partisans, involve the rest? Cotton Mather learned this murderousness (at second-hand) from the Turks; let him now, in December 1721, confront the high tide of what he called antiministerial sentiment: "How shall we excuse our Mohemetan Missionaries, from being truly, tho' not designedly the cause of their death?" He and his obedient cohorts may be persuaded that their procedure is lawful: "shall they in this manner force it upon others?"

This is no mere outburst; behind it stood scientific authority. There was, to say the least, tobacconist John Williams, who may have written a peculiar English but who knew something of ordinary recipes; he could perceive that inoculation was obviously contrary to all received rules of "physick." And in January, William Douglass left off the satirical vein which the *Courant* had found strategic—which hitherto had been the only line of attack—and published a sober discussion, *Inoculation of the Small Pox as practised in Boston*. Two casual pieces in the *Transactions*, he said, do not constitute scientific authority, because most of the articles appearing therein are so obviously fantastic that were they to be taken seriously the world would be (as every student must agree) turned upside down. This problem calls for skill and circumspection, for those who can distinguish "between a Disease simply Epidemick and a Contagious Epidemical Distemper"; but neither Mather nor Boylston can tell the one from the other. As for what they did, he flatly reported (and meant what he said), "We soon found it infecting; many have dy'd of the Infection received from the Inoculated, whose Deaths in a great Measure lie at the Inoculators Doors." There precisely was the fundamental issue: did inoculation spread the plague? If it did, it was not "safe." If it was not safe, who then affronted the covenant God, and who then deserved to die?

Douglass was enough of a scientist to weigh all the consequences. Many of the inoculated might well recover, but was there any assurance that eventually they would not suffer from delayed reactions, from complications and debilitations that would shorten their lives? What proof to the contrary could Mather and Boylston offer? Possibly there is some good in the method—Douglass never categorically denied it—but nothing is to be gained by a "rash and bold Experiment." Douglass could not help remarking—although to his credit be it noted that he did not particularly stress—the incongruous position in which the clergy found themselves: having predicted the epidemic, they then devoted themselves to praying that God would put a stop to it; when He did not, they decided to employ a procedure which was not repentance, but which, for all they really knew, would multiply the affliction. They might call it an act of faith, but there was no precedent in their theology for this sort of taking-for-granted, for this degree of arrogant inference. To this contention Douglass clung, and thereby threatened the structure of society: inoculation is every bit as infectious as (possibly even more than) what the people called the "common way." Spokesmen for the dominant theory (into whose care even Governor Shute entrusted the management of the business by appointing a day of humiliation) had elected to stake their reputation for sanctity not upon the purity of their federal theology, but upon the accuracy of Cotton Mather's reading of two absurd articles in the *Transactions!*

In this situation, clerical defenders of inoculation needed to do only one thing: to stand firm upon Boylston's demonstrations and to adduce from them that inoculation was both successful and safe. Benjamin Colman nowhere so admirably exonerated the tone he brought into provincial culture as when he confined his argument, on November 23, 1721, in *Some Observations on the New Method of Receiving the Small-pox, by Ingrafting or Inoculation,* to precisely these limits. He knew what he was doing, for he dedicated this perspicacious discourse to President Leverett. At first he could hardly credit what Timonius and Pylarinus reported, but upon reflection, "the little Philosophy I am Master of led me into the apparent Reasons of the thing." The thing quickly became to his mind rational even though surprising; in simplicity of heart—he had the grace to say that this was his sole motive—he fell in with Cotton Mather's proposal. He never urged Boylston to proceed, but he had not the light to dissuade him (a typical Colman utterance). However, he could give the populace an accurate account (not, be it noted, in terms of the jeremiad), because he had been privileged to observe Boylston's experiment "from my house (which faces into the Doctors yard)." From that promontory he watched Boylston's child and the Negro children recover: "Their tongues were filled with laughter, and ours with Thanksgiving on their account," which was enough to enlist a sentimental Colman. His rhetorical passages were eminently more persuasive, if only for their sentimentality, than the stern edicts emanating from the North Church: he was wholly moved by what he himself had seen when, coming from the chambers of the dying, whom he was obliged to visit and to comfort, he returned to Boylston's house as one "passing out of darkness into light, or from a tempestuous Sea into a Calm Haven, or from a place of horror into a Garden of pleasure." By contrast with that which he was forced to behold, Boylston's hospital seemed full of ease and sweetness; out of this divination Colman hazarded what may be perhaps the most remarkable medical insight in the whole discussion, especially considering that it came from the one most humble about his scientific sophistication: it was not the inoculated who spread the infection, but such holy men as he, "call'd from day to day, to the many noxious Chambers, each of which have had poison eno' in 'em to have spread the Town over." We are frequently tempted to make Colman out a greater or more stalwart man than he ever was, but at this moment, in his quiet way he comes close to grandeur: in humility of spirit, he grasped the theory of contagion.

In fact, he ventured even further, thus putting the author of *The Christian Philosopher* on his mettle: there exist, Colman was informed, "Glasses" that have discovered in every pustule of the pox "a Multitude of Animalcula"; scientists tell us "that our common Infection is by swarms of these." He would call them "Animated Atoms, if I might so speak." If these things be, then was it not plausible that such "Animalcules," inhaled into the nostrils and throat, cause the distemper? Were this so, was it not further reasonable to conclude that to introduce a few of these creatures by incision would produce a milder form of the disease, since the number thus taken in would be fewer than by inhalation? "Because in this way not so many enter, nor immediately into such parts of hazard and distress, as in the nostrils, throats & inwards." However, Colman well knew that all this was sheer speculation; he would not commit the ministerial cause to a hypothesis: "I pretend not to argue, on Principles or Premises, which are themselves uncertain." Possibly he was, as Douglass declared him, ignorant; but of this much he was certain and to this he stood: he was a man of good will endeavoring the welfare of the people, and so he was not going "out of my line" by testifying to the success of Boylston's work. "This is a Care beseeming me, or any one else, if it be manag'd with modesty and decency." Colman's booklet is a fine, a truly magnificent, piece of writing. Had the Mathers restrained themselves to similar limits, they, with their curious prestige among posterity, would today receive the honor they almost deserve. But Colman did what they would not risk: he conceded that in such a crisis as an epidemic, the clergy do not necessarily speak with the absolute prerogative of an Old Testament prophet.

Boylston too was content to defend himself on empirical grounds. On January 15, 1722, he published in the *Gazette* a factual statement designed to silence rumors: the Mathers were also, had they only realized it, in a position once the epidemic died out to reap a similar credit. But their efforts revealed little of Colman's humanity or humility, although they did their best: Cotton ran in the *Gazette* for October 30, 1721, "A Faithful Account," and at the end of November, Increase published *Several Reasons Proving that Inoculating . . . the Small Pox, is a Lawful Practice,* to which Cotton appended *Sentiments on the Small Pox Inoculated.* These two communiqués, appearing as a single broadside, told of Boylston's achievement and proved that the Mathers, if only they tried, could for once tell an unvarnished tale. They needed to do no more.

But they could not let well enough alone. It was not so much that the habits of a lifetime persisted, but that spokesmen for a vested interest suddenly (for reasons they could not comprehend) become insecure were unable to let slide an opportunity to execrate anybody or everybody who opposed them. The *Courant* had insinuated that inoculation was the work of the Devil; now was the time to prove that those who entertained such thoughts blasphemed not only a wonderful work of God but God's devoted servants. All objections have come from profane quarters, said Increase Mather, and upon this proposition all the clergy are agreed, not only his son but also Solomon Stoddard and John Wise. The Mathers were experts in analysis of the tergiversations of original sin, but they could not comprehend James Franklin's simple argument that the Devil often makes use of good men like themselves; with a goodly amount of social solidarity organized behind them, they attempted to win more out of Boylston's cures than the cause of science. They tried to make them serve that unification of the clergy they had failed to achieve either through their associations or through the *Proposals.*

This left the opponents no alternative but to subordinate the scientific inquiry to the moral accusation, and to assert that to the best of their knowledge opposers were not blasphemous. Most of the critics might have been ready to admit, in the spring of 1722, that Boylston had proved his thesis; the vituperation of the Mathers made any such admission synonymous with a confession of infidelity. James Franklin, William Douglass, and the last adherent of Old Janus would have died rather than (at that moment) give an inch. Cotton Mather stood upon the most solid ground he had yet commanded, more solid than he was ever again to occupy, when he affirmed that the method had proved the most successful for which human reason dared ask, that it was everything "a Rational Mind can desire." He would have swept the board had he said no more: the provinces would have been obliged to bless God (and him) for their salvation. But he who had compulsively overplayed his hand in *The Wonders* was again the victim of his old neurosis; to his factual demonstration he was obliged to add that those who refused to submit their weak judgment to that "of the most able Divines in the Country" were violators of the Sixth Commandment. Thus he gave James Franklin an opportunity to prove the virtue of the *Courant* by demonstrating that even though it might be mistaken about inoculation, the Mathers had no call to levy against it the crushing cannonade of the jeremiad.

Matherian nerves were undoubtedly stretched taut. In December, Cotton noted that when he tried his utmost to make warnings out of the fact that the arrows of death were flying among his people, they failed to respond. Instead, the bomb thrown into his house on November 14 had carried a message: "Cotton Mather, You Dog, Dam you: I'l inoculate you with this, with a Pox to you." He was in ecstasy over the prospect of martyrdom, but also expended his venom upon the wicked printer and his accomplices who "every week publish a vile Paper to lessen and blacken the Ministers of the Town." His journals for the two years after February 1722 are missing (undoubtedly a gain for the chastity of the language), but the line his supporters had resolved to press, that which Thomas Walter had opened in the *Little-Compton Scourge,* appears in a letter, dated from Portsmouth, in the *Gazette* of February 5. It pays no attention to the facts, but harps upon the ignorance and malice of the *Courant,* picks up Samuel Mather's charge that James Franklin is destitute of wit, and so concludes that the *Courant* confesses its bankruptcy by exploiting inoculation because it has nothing else to write about. Later that month, Increase issued as a pamphlet the historical account he first had printed in the *Gazette;* to it he appended his compliments to Douglass, insisting that had an impudent New Englander gone to Scotland and there behaved as Douglass did in New England, the authorities would have stuck him in the pillory.

A year later, when the controversy was exhausted, Cotton Mather was to tell Dr. Hurin that the whole thing had been contrived by "a jacobite, or High-flying Party" who took up anti-inoculation in the hope of discrediting the established clergy. Possibly that was the only moral he ever drew from his experience. Which of the parties first resorted to mere calling of names we cannot tell, but of one thing we may be certain: when the Mathers announced that the board of the *Courant* was "Hell-Fire Club," and so tried to array against it the force of the national covenant, they let themselves in for the consequences. They obliged honest men who conscientiously differed from them to become antiministerial; by demanding that a scientific thesis be received entirely because its advocates were pious, they threw the ministerial character into the scales. Dr. Douglass tried to warn them: if they want such reasoning to prevail, "who knows but it may oblige some prophane Person to canvas that sort of Argument." To such a canvass, Jeremiahs should never expose themselves: if a prophet of doom once lets himself be critically scrutinized, he ceases to be a prophet. Douglass did his best to help the foolish clergy: "I think their Character ought to be sacred, and that they themselves ought not to give the least occasion to have it called in question." But the Mathers, wrapped in their egotism, paid no attention.

During the early months of the controversy, the *Gazette* appeared a meek mouthpiece for inoculators, while the *Courant* preserved at least the forms of impartiality by publishing a few pro-inoculation pieces and even, on September 4, a letter advising the editor to drop the subject because it is "a very insipid Theme to us, who have a most exquisitely nice and refin'd Tast." Not to be outdone, the *Gazette* asserted its independence by publishing on the same date a letter from "W. Anti-inoculator," who defended both the practitioners and the *Courant*. Some statements, he said, are persuasive, such as those appearing in the *Gazette*, but there was no excuse that persons who still have sincere doubts should be "Anathematized with vile horrid execrable Names, too foul for any Gentleman to pronounce, and which decency does not allow me here to repeat." Checkley's slur on Walter was in bad taste, but was not to be taken seriously; obviously the writer, "for some private reasons of his own might think that the Anti-Couranteer did not expect or desire any quarter," and in any event, the *Little-Compton Scourge* was bombast, a "loose wild pedantick School Boy performance," inviting any sort of rebuttal. But what this correspondent was truly worried about was the conduct of the clergy: their invective seemed to proceed from a more than human spitefulness, "from some Devil incarnate, under the Cloak of what Function I know not." They were in a furor because the *Courant* had twitted Cotton Mather's nephew; could they not understand that this kind of interchange is "a farce or comical sort of Amusement which these Two Gentlemen are pleased to oblige the Town withal, and give no body offence?" (However, while Cotton Mather was constitutionally incapable of appreciating sheer frippery, in this case his lack of humor was also a reflection of his sense of the seriousness of the situation: had the bomb exploded, it would have killed this same Thomas Walter, who at that moment was symbolizing his return from Checkley to orthodoxy by undergoing inoculation in the very chamber into which the engine, intended for Mather, was thrown.)

The physicians, pursued this letter, make themselves known, but the clergy publish anonymously; does not this fact prove that they have an ulterior motive? It is certainly a sign of wickedness when a man instead of using arguments resorts to calling names; why should the ministers, "with what unparaleld magisterial impudence," call upon the practitioners to clear themselves from an aspersion which, even to suppose the possibility of their guilt, "is worse than cutting of Throats"? In other words, by the time public opinion could find such a voice as this, factual arguments, even those of a Boylston, no longer had any effect; the debate had come to seem to such observers a dispute between, on the ministerial side, insufferable arrogance and, on the part of the physicians, a humane concern for the public welfare. Out of this conviction was fashioned the bomb thrown against Cotton Mather.

There is no other way to say it: the Mathers invited the charge. The wonder is that it took so long to find expression, but in January, with Douglass' *Inoculation of the Small Pox as Practised in Boston*, James Franklin's preface said it, once and for all: New England has suffered the ignominy of three "infatuations"—in 1659 the persecution of Quakers, "the hanging of those suspected of Witchcraft, about the Year 1691, &c., and Inoculation, or Self-procuring the Small Pox, in the year 1721." Skipping over chronological exactness, Franklin continued, "to speak like an Astronomer, or rather in the manner of Dr. C. M., Infatuation seems to return to us after a Period of about Thirty Years." The Mathers had insisted that opposition to inoculation was nothing but antiministerial sentiment; here they had the answer, full in the face. By now the people knew that the Quaker hangings were a disgrace, that the witchcraft trials were criminal and that the clergy had not sufficiently resisted them, that Cotton Mather had temporized. Nobody talked in public about witchcraft, not since Calef and Hale had published, but privately they had worked it out; James Franklin knew what the people thought, saw his chance, and thrust home. This explains the frenzy that amounts, in Mather's *Diary*, to sheer insanity.

By the spring of 1722, the disease was gone, Boylston's fame assured; partisans of Mather might still have imitated the tact of Colman and taken modest credit for the victory, while the *Courant* could be let to stew. But they were incapable of restraint or dignity. Cotton Mather tells us that he was supplying his friends with materials (as he had done against Brattle Street in 1700 or against Stoddard in 1708—from either of which defeats he ought to have learned better), and internal evidence suggests that he had more than an editorial hand in *A Vindication of the Ministers of Boston*, published on February 5. This work could do nothing but exclaim in utter astonishment that against faithful pastors such insults should be flung as might cause professed libertines to blush. If James Franklin was so soon able to produce a "character" of the hypocrite who was palpably Cotton Mather, it was in part because here Mather insisted upon assuming the pose: ministers are men of the most refined virtue, always ready to do good; their savory and entertaining conversation constantly discovers their inward goodness, and "Some of them have Great Names in distant lands." Cotton Mather was a genuine Fellow of the Royal Society, but against Douglass' aspersion he "disdains to draw his generous Pen for his own Vindication." The six clergymen had not "gone out of their line" by recommending inoculation: "When they saw their People dying about them . . . they did not cast off all bowells of compassion," and ought to be blessed as instruments of good rather than vilified.

With the urgency of the debate relaxed, the *Courant* might well have been in the toils had not the Matherian party thus given it the advantage. As early as November, James Franklin had seen the wisdom of shifting his attack from science to burlesque, and so constructed a parody of Cotton Mather's manner which few in his audience would fail to enjoy:

Hundreds of Lives are lost, I say Lost! because they would not come into the Practice of it. Never one dyed in this Way, and 'tis probable, more than probable, never will. O! our Brethren in the Country, be advis'd: Come into this Safe and Easy Practice.

What really stung in this little skit was not only that Mather's eloquence became absurd, but that the whole formula of the jeremiad, with its cosmic threats, was reduced to nonsense. Even as they attained their scientific triumph, the clerical party experienced a peculiar and utterly novel shyness about invoking the creaking machinery of the avenging covenant. Who could help them?

Isaac Greenwood, fresh from his Harvard degree, now rushed in where Walter had learned not to tread, and in *A Friendly Debate; or, a Dialogue between Academicus; and Sawny & Mundungus* tried to regain the field under the banner, not of Boylston and science, but of wit and insult. Douglass and Williams both spoke broad Scots, and the latter apparently managed to mangle the English language in a most bizarre manner; for several pages Greenwood amused himself, if not his readers, by imitating Douglass' accent, and we must adjust our sense of values to realize that, in a community where amusements were few and far between, such mimicry would seem hilarious: "Maister, ye ken vary weel, that I canno spak Englis." However, once Greenwood gives up this orthography, his dialogue does become more sprightly, as when he represents Douglass confessing defeat and trying to break off the discussion, to which Academicus says, "I perceive then, you are much of the Fellows mind, whose plea to his Indictment was; My Lord, I perceive 'tis a dirty Business, and I desire to hear no more on't." Yet most of the wit is nothing more than abuse: Cotton Mather has for years been a celebrated preacher and scholar and member of the Royal Society, while you, Dr. Douglass, "can't spell the Word Philosophy nor construe the word Hades," and all scribblers in the *Courant* are nought but "Leather Apron Men." Greenwood was so carried away by this argument that he committed himself to a full-dress defense of Mather's "Sense and Style." But in order to get into this topic, Greenwood had to let his Dr. Douglass say, "I don't like their whining Preaching, I can't profit by their canting Ministry." Greenwood let this statement appear in print so that he could refute it with the claim that Mather's prose forever charms all competent judges, and did not note that henceforth the adjectives "whining" and "canting" were a part of the public record.

In fact, the inadvertent admissions in this effort are much more striking than the feebleness of the wit. Not only does Greenwood let his Douglass blurt out about Mather's preaching what many had come to feel, but by leaving the solid ground of medicine for a tilt of abuse, he manages to rest his case upon that miserable definition of the issue which for the Mathers took precedence over the scientific: "There is a Number in this Town, who are irreversibly resolved, to destroy the Religion of the Country." By the

time Greenwood was finished, the point of the controversy was no longer
(and seems never to have been) the reliability of inoculation but entirely
the infidelity of physicians. These might well, by this time, have been
willing to admit that Mather had proved the best scientist of them all, but
Greenwood gave the game into their hands: maybe they had faltered professionally, yet they were the better Christians and the better mannered.

Douglass answered with dignity. If the inoculators wanted to fence at
wit, he was their man, for in this they were novices; by shifting from
their indisputable success to cheap ridicule, they threw away their advantage: they gave up all title "to correct Stile, Justness of Thought, and
Force of Argument." The only issue now up for debate was whether
the practitioners were meekly to let themselves be trodden on. Douglass
still believed that many would have lived had inoculation not spread infection, but when inoculators stoop to defend themselves by making fun of
the Scots dialect, not only do they fail as wits—which "they must impute
to their Ignorance of the Nature of a burlesque Satyr"—but they affront
a proud people and make themselves "Objects of the highest Resentment
of every native of the Country so abused and vilify'd"—which was a palpable hit because the Mathers fulsomely vaunted the Scotland-New England
axis. He stood his ground, the highly rational ground, that most things
printed in the *Transactions* are absurd, and that to encourage a headlong
rush into so dubious a business was exactly the same "Wickedness" the
clergy and judges had exhibited at Salem: "When a Man is not positive
of a Practice, it is natural and consistent for him to be cautious in the rash
and indiscreet Use of it."

Professing that he would, out of respect, say nothing against Increase,
Douglass turned the heat of his wrath upon Cotton Mather, so that the
student of this period, condemned to much reading of that worthy, experiences a certain glee, as may even the reader of this book, when at last
Mather's less winsome qualities finally get their just deserts. He, "the
Hero in this Farce of Calumny," must be used with "Philosophical Freedom." The *Vindication* is full of "Billingsgate Terms of Art" (a remark
that gives point to Benjamin Franklin's promise on February 11, 1723,
to eschew "Billingsgate Ribaldry"); its contribution to the discussion of
a serious topic is a hysterical charge of treason: "Are there no Degrees in
this Man's Censure? Are these his Philosophical Arguments and mild
Christian Rebukes?" Surely, Mather's own contributions to the *Transactions* are among the more ludicrous: is a man capable of such follies to be
accounted a good voucher for an experiment of fatal consequences? Mather
modestly acknowledged that he had read more books of physic than had
the physicians; as a matter of fact, he had, but there were now elements in the community less impressed by his scholarship than delighted
with Douglass' rejoinder: Mather may have swallowed innumerable volumes without chewing them, "but I know so much of his Constitution,
he is naturally troubled with indigestion." As for an ability to spell the

word philosophy and to construe Hades, "I suppose he Designs to be witty upon Couranto. Couranto can answer for himself"—which, as we have seen, Couranto could. But Douglass helped out the *Courant* in one all-important respect: even while supporting Boylston (who had no academic training) against Douglass with all his degrees and professional qualifications, the Matherians sneered at James Franklin for his lack of education: "Why should Gentlemen otherwise well qualified, be called illiterate, Ignorant, etc., because they did not idle away four years at the Colledge, as some of our learned Men have done." This sentence would be read in the shop of the two Franklins with both amusement and gratitude, as would also Douglass' conclusion. "May Dr. C. M., when he writes or causes to write, forbear Scurrilities," for these are a scandal to his profession. We stand upon the threshold of a new era when Douglass can beard Boston's high priest: "Let him keep close to Matter of Fact; railing is not reasoning in this country."

How far the debate had departed from the original terms, and what forces the Mathers had unleashed, is even better shown by another answer to Greenwood, the anonymous *A Friendly Debate; or, A Dialogue between Rusticus and Academicus,* in which the rustic mother-wit disposed of Harvard academicals. (Benjamin Franklin would be especially interested.) Dated from "the South Side of my Hay-Stack" and ironically dedicated to Cotton Mather, "Fellow of the Royal Society," it told the ministerial faction how, by heaping up reckless charges of infidelity and subversion, they had put themselves in the stupid position of having to be rescued by their enemies. Greenwood's fantastic indictment is a noise that "comes out of the North," and while the pastors of that institution continue to denounce everybody who disagrees with them in things indifferent, they will have to admit, when they cry that they are defrauded of the people's affection, that "their own Order have done more this Way than the Laity." Thereupon this pamphlet, in a refinement of cunning, struck Cotton Mather the cruelest blow he ever received: it quoted—thus giving the passage publicity in his own land, in his own city—that part of John Oldmixon's *The British Empire in America* which in 1708 had heaped derision upon the style of the *Magnalia* ("cramm'd with Punns, Anagrams, Acrosticks, Miracles and Prodigies") and had termed the whole book one of those "School Boys Exercises [of] Forty Years Ago." Thus supported, Rusticus addressed himself to Harvard College: leave off cant and stop imitating what was in fashion a century ago; cultivate instead a purity of language, "and let the Scoffers see that Religion needs no little Shifts and Arts to support it self," that divine truths can be most convincing "when they are express'd in Elegant and apt Phrases, free from the Poverty and Tautology of the present New-England Diction." Inoculators made sport of the weird language of Williams, and christened him Mundungus, but if all Harvard men write like "John Harvard" (who, we remember, disdainfully mocked the prose of Silence Dogood), they should "be doom'd to the Cellar of Mundungus, to perfect themselves in his Language."

Thus what had begun, under the shadow of pestilence, as a grim struggle for the mastery of New England's soul petered out, by the next spring, into a tiff about style. The later stages of the debate are crude: yet the fact that antiministerial sentiment, mobilized against inoculation, persisted by shifting the point of attack to language marks an epoch in the training of the mentality. We are, fortunately, able to divine something of the effect by watching the reaction of one of the youngest but most perceptive intelligences. Rusticus not only used Oldmixon to blast the great Mather's style, but even thumbed his nose at Mather's erudition: he would not pretend to determine "Whether much Learning has not made the Doctor mad, and rendered his Books of no Use to him." And joining Douglass in passionate resentment of Greenwood's sneer, he denied that contributors to the *Courant* were all "Leather Apron Men."

Benjamin Franklin tells us how assiduously he studied *The Spectator*, how he acquired his own limpid manner by rewriting its paragraphs. Rusticus answered Greenwood on March 9, 1722, and it was on April 2 that the first Dogood Paper appeared in the *Courant*. Mr. Spectator had introduced himself on March 1, 1711, with a gentle insinuation against the critical discernment of the age:

> I have observed, that a reader seldom peruses a book with pleasure, till he knows whether the writer of it be a black or a fair man, of a mild or choleric disposition, married or a bachelor, with other particulars of the like nature, that conduce very much to the right understanding of an author.

In the Bostonian context, there was also a problem, as this debate had made evident, about securing a hearing solely on merit, particularly if the writer happened to belong to the wrong caste. But this sixteen-year-old could see the superb opportunity in Addisonian urbanity:

> And since it is observed, that the Generality of People, now a days, are unwilling either to commend or dispraise what they read, until they are in some measure informed who or what the Author of it is, whether he be poor or rich, old or young, a Scollar or a Leather Apron Man, &c. and give their Opinion of the Performance, according to the Knowledge which they have of the Author's Circumstances . . .

The phrase undoubtedly was in general parlance before Greenwood used it and Rusticus objected to it. An aspiring young journalist would want to make his terms relevant to his audience: the artist in America, working with imported forms, always attempts at first to domesticate them by a mere substitution of terms; yet even so mechanical a recasting starts him on his way, and through it the issues of American life come to expression. For Addison the alternatives were black or fair, mild or choleric, married or unmarried; for Benjamin Franklin they were rich or poor, old or young, scholar or "Leather Apron Man." Thus he took upon himself that symbolic role he never thereafter would forget how to play, with which he could charm and conquer even Versailles.

On May 15 the selectmen finally forbade Boylston to perform any more inoculations, and Douglass got in his last licks by exulting in the *Courant* that this delusion was brought under control, in joyful contrast to that "Infatuation Thirty Years ago, after several had fallen Victims to the mistaken Notions of Dr M———r and other learned Clerks concerning Witchcraft." Yet Douglass knew, in so far as the technical issue was concerned, that the Mathers had proved their case. In February, Cotton and Boylston had collaborated in *Some Account of What is said of Inoculating and Transplanting the Small Pox*, in which (possibly Boylston exerted the restraining hand) vituperation was exchanged for clinical reporting. Boylston could quietly say that he had "succeeded well in all, even beyond Expectation." Had his friends always employed this tone, they would have won a smashing victory. "We are yet but Learners," he said, "and hope through Experience to grow more expert in our Practice." Cotton Mather, always aspiring to play to a larger theater than little Boston, now prepared a confident narrative and sent it to Jeremiah Dummer, who printed in London *An Account of the Method and Success of Inoculating the Small-Pox in Boston in New-England* and dedicated it to Sir Hans Sloane (to whom, in 1725, Benjamin Franklin was to address his earliest surviving letter). All new discoveries, moralized Dummer, are received at first with opposition, but truth is mighty and must prevail. In this version, even amid the confidence of success, Cotton Mather could not withhold a few scoffs against his opponents: the people "were scar'd (I cannot say) out of their wits"; he had never seen the Devil so let loose, but how shockingly such possessed persons dared to treat certain meritorious ministers of the Gospel, "I Leave unmention'd." Praying God to forgive them, he bethought himself that a European audience might not be interested in a provincial squabble, and so told his story simply and without hyperbole, thus materially assisting the cause of inoculation in Britain. Boylston, coming to London in 1726, there published *An Historical Account*, a model of objective reporting, which assures his stature in medical history. Another epidemic threatened Boston in 1730: William Douglass was the first to urge inoculation. His was the rugged Scots honesty compatible with admitting that he could be mistaken, just as he was to show in 1735 the intelligence to perform, in the "sore-throat" distemper, pioneer work in the diagnosis of scarlet fever. However, there is no evidence that he ever forgave Cotton Mather.

It may well seem, in the light of this great exoneration, that the frivolity of Rusticus was a weak rear-guard action; we may suppose that a Mather, emerging victorious, could stand before a contrite people more than ever empowered to tell them that they should yield to the informed judgment of their superiors, in inoculation and so in everything else, and hence should stay away from taverns and frolics just as he demanded of them. Actually the confirmation of his hunch had no such effect; the later stages of the debate show that in fact the clergy had been fought to a draw, and that this outcome, considering how great had been their initial advantage, was a mortal defeat. The conflict was a crisis within the culture, of which the ultimate effects were to be felt in other regions of the mind than those in which scientific verification mattered. What had been risked and what had not been regained was the covenant conception itself. Spokesmen for that national philosophy could never again authoritatively contend that what the people suffered was caused by their sins and that repentance alone, as directed by hierophants, could relieve them. The clergy themselves had introduced another method, and so brought a fatal confusion into the very center of their mystique.

The troubled author of *A Letter from one in the Country* wrote from the depths of the communal bewilderment: we recognize, he said, that ministers fulfill their proper function when they supplicate God to avert "the Judgment of the Small-pox," when they beg Him to intervene—on condition that the people profess their sins and promise to reform. Thus they had, times without number, helped the country to save itself, and thus they should have acted in this desperate emergency. Instead, these official intercessors, for some devious and inexplicable reason, refused to apply themselves in the time-tested manner, and "have been carrying about instruments of Inocculation and bottles of the poisonous Humour to Infect all those who were willing to submit to it." This most sincere of writers was profoundly disturbed: he beheld loving and considerate fathers insanely attempting to poison their children. "Can any man infect a Family in a Town in the Morning, and pray God in the Evening, that the Distemper may not spread?" The real perplexity behind this question could not be relieved by the assurance that inoculation was safe: if so, then the smallpox, which should be the most dread of judgments, became a mere annoyance, a ghost of a judgment. "And tho' we don't pray that it may not spread, Yet by praying for a blessing on this practice, we pray against the Judgment." Where, then, if this queer metaphysic were to prevail, would New England stand, with all its sins heavy upon it? What would be left of the very idea of correction? What could be the meaning of the country's sufferings, of its history? All of a sudden, therefore, the New England mind found itself, wholly within the circumference of its straightforward assumptions, entangled in contradictions.

An irreconcilable division was introduced, most concretely, into devout congregations: one party was confessing, according to the standard prescription, "Lord we have Sinned, and are afraid of thy Judgment . . . Let not this sore Disease spread further among us"; at the same moment, the other half was exulting, with equal sincerity, "Lord, we have Sinned & thy Judgments are upon us in sore Sickness; but we have (by thy Providence) found out a way to lighten it, give us thy blessing upon it, & then let it spread, the faster the better." But of this second sort, there was a most disturbing characteristic to be noted: in the assumed security of their method, in their contempt of fellow Christians not capable of substituting "Animalcules" for divine dispensations, they spoke like Pharisees; instead of praying for a nation suffering as one man because of common sins, they asked, "Let us have the benefit of this Invention, tho' others of thy people are so blind they will not see the benefit of it." For this reason they consigned the others to perish, in the phrase of the time, "in the common way" —whereupon the phrase took on new connotations, not providential but social or political.

Here was the predicament in which the intelligence of the community found itself by December of 1721: "Thus we are brought into a state of War, Sin and Contention in our very prayers, by carrying on this practice in such a lawless, unguarded manner." What had first been proposed for the good of the whole had proved, quite apart from its physiological effects, a means of evil; evil was piled upon evil the more it succeeded, and a social virtue became ambiguous. Instead of being humbled by affliction (as for a century was held to be the purport of all such distresses), instead of affliction teaching the people to treat each other with meekness and forgiveness, "are we not filled with contentions, and every wicked work?" Thus, by a self-styled country writer, the jeremiad was thrown back upon the city's Jeremiahs: "I pray God grant us Repentance, lest despising the Chastening of the Almighty, we provoke him to bring yet sorer Plagues upon us." By introducing into the covenant theory an unprecedented (and worse than that, a not yet explicitly avowed) criterion of utility, inoculators overturned—without quite knowing what they were doing—the corporate doctrine. In all innocence, they had imagined that they could save the people from smallpox by inoculating them, and that thus they would secure the people's gratitude!

Because these innovators also believed in the covenant doctrine, they were bound to aggravate their situation. In any European society, in England or France—which is to say, in some profane nation outside the covenant—there would inevitably be a percentage of scoffers, infidels, even atheists. Retribution upon these individuals would have to fall individually, it might even be postponed to the next world; their blasphemies would not of necessity involve the whole society, because an uncovenanted community has no responsibility for its members. In those regions, infidels might experiment with inoculation as with black magic without bringing down divine vengeance upon Christian compatriots. They would need to be called nothing more than what they had long been called, or had become accustomed to being called. But America was different: here there was no place for profane dissent. There was no social niche for the infidel. Once a scientific controversy was intruded into a dedicated community, religious supporters of reform had no choice but to pillory those who differed from them as scoffers and infidels, and to relegate them to perdition.

Or rather, once the guardians of society resolved on a course of action, there was no arena in which the scientific evidence could be debated in scientific terms: those who contradicted the pundits had to be stigmatized at once as traitors to the New England way of life. Nevertheless, thousands of good Americans (like this country author) knew in their hearts that they were utterly loyal to the ancient theory, that they were not infidels—or that if they were, then the founders also had been tragically mistaken and that every subsequent jeremiad was a lie.

William Cooper, Colman's stern colleague, realized better than the egotists of the North Church what was needed, and on December 18, 1721, issued *Letter to a Friend in the Country*, attempting to resolve the country's quandary. I know, he said, that God can preserve me from infection, but "when my Neighbours all round me are visited, I know of no Warrant that any particular Person has to expect an extraordinary Preservation." Some have taken New England's doctrine to mean that such a trust constitutes faith, but he flatly called it presumption (turning the tables on those who called inoculation just that). Yet was not this the very faith that a century of jeremiads had inculcated? No, said Cooper: of course, if you trust only the device, you will commit sin; but if you "principally" seek God in the use of this medical means, you may employ it. Let us remember that, although the smallpox is an affliction, yet it comes through second causes; in inoculation, we do no more than employ these. "What is there of the hand or power of Man in this Work, after the Incision is made and the matter apply'd? The Work is still left with God and we must wait upon Him for His actual Influence and Blessing." It was exactly as with the farmer: he must sow his seed, and then wait upon providence for the rain and sun.

The revolutionary implications in this recasting of the covenant theology, slight as the verbal changes may seem, is staggering. Probably Cooper was not aware of what he wrought; old distinctions had grown dim, and so he took the chance: he ventured to call for an exertion of man *before* the action of God, instead of arguing that human endeavor must, like repentance, be the fruit of instruction. He did not at this point realize, if ever he was to realize, that he had refashioned Calvinism into an activism more Pelagian than any seventeenth-century Arminianism had ever dreamed of. Yet if he was so oblivious, it was because he was deeply immersed in New England's peculiar experience: to the country man's argument that the thing must be bad because it produces factions, Cooper replied that the spirit of party is worse than any disease. He asked opponents to consider how many good things, as they well knew—such as the choice of a new minister or the erection of a church—excited animosities and engendered contention. He did not for a moment doubt the truth of predestination; nevertheless, God administers His decrees "with a Regard to Second Causes, or that Course of Nature which He has established." The founders had always asserted as much—but in a different social and cosmic setting. They had been vigorous men, ready to adventure their all, even while leaving the outcome to providence; yet they never quite said, as Cooper now did, that he who perishes in the use of inoculation enjoys the consolation of dying "in the Use of the most likely means, he knew of."

Cotton Mather was, we must admit, a more subtle intelligence than Cooper, but in several respects more obtuse; in this dispute he achieved nothing so gentle or so persuasive: the best he could say was that any Christian ought to understand how he might employ the available means and still thank God for the result—thus leaving hundreds in the land to wonder who, after all, was the Christian. There is a curious mixture of sanctions in Mather's argument, as there was a strange medley of ideas in his head. On the one hand, he appeals to stark empiricism: the thing is true because it is, and because it works; any reasonable man can see it. If my neighbor's house is on fire, and mine is "an Inch and half off" (as houses were in Boston), am I going to abide his saying, "Pray, sit still, My Neighbour, your House is not yet on Fire: the Almighty can preserve it"? Furthermore, on the level of ordinary economy, inoculation is profitable by the cheapest of considerations: it not only saves lives, but "some Time also, and some Charge (which some it may be, Consider) and the Health of the Town much sooner be restored." Mostly, Mather skirted around the great and fundamental point, yet once or twice he did plunge straight into it: with a sweep of his hand he would wipe away all theological scruples, and cry aloud, "EXPERIENCE! EXPERIENCE! 'tis to THEE that the Matter must be referr'd after all; a few Empiricks here, are worth all our Dogmatists."

And yet, perhaps in the very next moment, this superpragmatist would feel his mind gripped in the vise of the jeremiad; his rage against those who challenged his authority, who taunted him and so brought all God's lieutenants into disrepute, would compel him to maintain inoculation not at all upon experience but upon that dogmatic proposition by which the clergy had ruled and by which they must somehow continue to dominate, that it is the most imperative part of their duty "to go out of their way" both to remedy evils and to prescribe remedies for evil. Were they to subside into silence on the argument that they should not meddle with what the community ruled was beyond their ken or none of their business— above all if they were not to give directives in scientific matters, about which Cotton Mather knew more than the professionals—then the consequence would soon become evident: "Iniquity and every Abomination will break in among us, and bear down like a Torrent, all Virtue, and Religion before it." Spiritual plagues would follow the physical, the town would be wracked still more than it had ever suffered by the wrath of God; if such as Douglass and the *Courant* were to be tolerated in Boston, God would enact the utmost of his condemnations, the judgment a thousand times more terrible than smallpox itself: He would punish such unspeakable iniquity by depriving the city of its holy ministers.

CHAPTER XXII

A SECULAR STATE

T HESE
adventures of the mind and spirit, these disputes over
covenant, currency, and inoculation, were carried on in a world where
the horizon of consciousness was always delimited by two considerations.
On the frontier there was endless war, with a steady chronicle of massacre
and slaughter. In Boston (as to a lesser extent at Hartford) there was a
constant struggle by the House of Representatives to defend, or rather to
enlarge, those "English liberties" which the charters had bestowed. All the
while other matters were being debated, energies were persistently applied
either to the wars or to the political offensive.

In 1691 Cotton Mather said that men are taught by the light of nature to protect their lives, liberties, and properties against foreign injuries:
"The Steel will always Command the Gold; men can have no Right
secur'd unto them if they do not make sure of might." Later he may have
wished he had bitten off his tongue before he said such things, but he read
New England's problem in realistic terms. Both on the frontier and in the
chamber it was basically the same problem, of organizing enough might to
command rights. But by the early eighteenth century, as the campaigns
lengthened out and veterans of the one as of the other became absorbed in
the techniques of combat, the problem for the intellectual leaders came to be
this: what part could the religious interest have in either of these engrossing activities?

The Peace of Utrecht in 1713 brought some relief to the borders, but
the skirmishing continued and in the 1720's the fighting in Maine against
minions of Father Rasle was as bitter as any in the annals. John Wise
was so infatuated with the bills of credit as to claim that thanks to them
the colonies could wage war without financial strain, but he knew, as
did every parson, that communities did suffer "now and then the smart
of a Spur or Bullet, or in the Death of a particular Friend." Undoubtedly the common folk upon whom the burden and the horror fell found
sustenance in their religion. Many survivors told their story, creating in
the literature of Indian atrocities and captivities what might be called a
subsection of the theology of the covenant. The masterpiece of this genre
is John Williams' *The Redeemed Captive Returning to Zion*, published
in 1707 and in print for over a century. His objectivity would be monstrous were it not that he could view his ordeal as a sample of the cove-

nantal process. Routed out in the middle of a blizzard, their friends and
two of their children murdered, condemned to trudge three hundred
miles, the parson and his wife look back upon the desolation of their town
—and bethink themselves of their sins. She who had lain-in only a few
weeks before "never spake any discontented Word as to what had befal'n
us, but with suitable expressions justified God." In exhaustion she fell,
the savage slew her with a single stroke, "the tidings of which," wrote
her husband, "were very awful"; yet he summoned patience by reflecting
"That an Afflicting God was to be Glorifyed." Exchanged in 1706, he
told his tale in Boston, published it, and went back to Deerfield, where
in his last years he was frequently heard to mutter, "It was a dangerous
thing to be set in the Front of New England's sins."

Yet powerful as was the theology of the covenant, the monotonous
sameness of border warfare, leading always to the same "improvement,"
meant that there was a certain conventionality in the religious treatment.
The tomahawk might still be real, but the literature of it had become a
sterile type. In 1723 the minister and two children were butchered at
Rutland, two other infants were kidnapped; Israel Loring told survivors
that bereavements open the eye of faith: "It was Mercy that you had the
Children which now alas! You have not . . . Bless God for these and
be not unthankful." Every such disaster regularly inspired new jeremiads,
none being a more suitable occasion than the death of Captain Lovewell,
his chaplain Jonathan Frye, and most of his company at "Piggwacket"
in 1725. Thomas Symmes put it to the traditional use, but by then had
to confess that the artistic problem of using Indian war as a summons to
covenant repentance was more difficult than it had once been: "How
many calls have New-England had, from the Pulpit, and by the Press
also, from year to year: To Remember whence we are fallen and Repent
& do our First Works!" Instead of taking such admonitions to heart, people regard them as exhibitions, and are so critical of style and delivery
that they remain untouched by the content; they "either Humm or Hiss
the Preacher & his Performance pretty much as they stand affected to
him." They give him a vote of thanks ("and then he comes off mighty
well") or even print the discourse, "yet perhaps they don't put it in Practice."

Thus a noticeable callousness developed toward the theological significance of the subject matter of New England's most brutal and most per-
sistent contact with reality. To make capital out of this material, preachers had to spice their jeremiads with purple passages, and then with still
more lurid details, in the effort to keep up with a capacity to absorb (and
become bored with) horrors. You must not delay repenting and reforming, said Symmes, until "hearing the hideous yellings and Ejulations of
the Enemy, and the Groanings of Deadly wounded Men, & seeing them
lie all bath'd in their Gore." Yet the moment preachers gave thought to
such features of composition, they were aware that they had not always

been holding their audiences. Some people, Symmes predicted, instead of being at all moved by the sad tale of Lovewell, will object to too much detail: let them consider "the Different Taste of Readers, & consequently the extreme Difficulty, if not Impossibility of pleasing every Body." This was hardly a frame of mind in which one lifted up the voice of excoriation like a trumpet!

Furthermore, even his theologically improved version of the fight suggested that the real meaning of Indian warfare had become not the glory of the Lord but mere blood. Symmes tells of Lieutenant Robbins, wounded and dying on the ground, who begs his comrades to load his gun and leave him, "for says he, The Indians will come in the Morning to Scalp me, and I'll kill one more of 'em if I can." The bell that tolled for Robbins excited his fellow men not to a confession of sins but to the killing of more Indians. We are, as a matter of fact, given a remarkable sense of the scheme of life with which the masses had become accustomed to comprehending such an affair, for in May of 1725 James Franklin was hawking a ballad about Lovewell's fight, of which he assuredly sold more copies than did Symmes of the sermon:

> Our worthy Captain Lovewell among them there did die,
> They killed Lieut. Robbins and wounded good young Frye,
> Who was our English Chaplain, he many Indians slew,
> And some of them he scalp'd when bullets round him flew.

Or else there was a quite different frame of reference within which tragedy might now be set. Jonathan Frye had a sweetheart in Boxford, the daughter of a minister and presumably brought up within the covenant, yet her manner of lamentation was a far cry from the Reverend John Williams':

> Assist, ye muses, help my quill,
> Whilst floods of tears does down distill;
> Not from mine eyes alone, but all
> That hears the sad and doleful fall
> Of that young student, Mr. Frye,
> Who in his blooming youth did die.

Susanna Rogers probably had not read Benjamin Franklin's recipe for the New England elegy, but she followed it implicitly ("it will be best if he went away suddenly, being Kill'd, Drown'd or Frose to Death"); she at fourteen had entered as far into the era of sentimentalism as he at sixteen into that of rationalism, and for her, affliction had become as delicious as it was comic to him:

> A comely youth, and pious too;
> This I affirm, for him I knew.

One would be hard put to determine which of the two mentalities, hers or Franklin's, had become the more worldly, the more secular.

By the 1720's even clerical language takes on the tones of temporality when applied to the unending war. Cotton Mather lamented Captain Josiah Winslow as a valiant and good-natured gentleman fallen "in the Defence of a Country and a People, for which how many Brave Lives have been sacrificed!" But his friend Samuel Penhallow of Portsmouth published in 1726 the book which most astonishingly reveals how even piety itself had unwittingly accustomed itself to measure the conflict. To compare *The History of the Wars of New-England with the Eastern Indians* with what Increase Mather, fifty years before, made out of Philip's War is to perceive the nature and acceleration of the cultural evolution. Colman, in the preface, shows how urbanely border struggles could now be handled: New England does exhibit a likeness to Israel—"let it not seem vain" to say so! Providence has prospered the land, but to preserve it against complacency has left a few savages on its frontiers "to be pricks in ours ears, and thorns in our sides." He is happy to introduce this account "on principles both humane and religious," but has to confess that unfortunately for the human interest, chronicles of battle cannot offer much variety and therefore little entertainment; it is enough if the facts be accurate and the style familiar. This consciousness of style, which owed so much to Colman in the first place, is itself a symptom of an attitude toward the afflictions of Indian warfare which has only a dim sense that they come directly from the appointing hand of Jehovah. Here is what Penhallow makes of them, in a familiar and easy style:

As the milk white brows of the grave and ancient had no respect shown; so neither had the mournful cries of tender infants the least pity; for they triumphed at their misery, and applauded such as the skilfullest artists, who were most dextrous in contriving the greatest tortures; which was enough to turn the most stoical apathy into streams of mournful sympathy and compassion.

Being a friend of the Mathers, Penhallow would, of course, find morals in massacres; frontiersmen had cheated Indians, and upon them the war was a judgment. "In several instances" he could detect the finger of God. Yet he made no effort to fit the conflict, as Increase had done with Philip's War or Cotton with all New England's history, into a coherent pattern; instead, composition was for him an exercise—as when he says about the slaughter of two old men, "they were so infirm that I might say of them as Juvenal did of Priam, they had scarce blood enough left to tinge the knife of sacrifice." A man capable of writing in this fashion would still think of himself as religious, in the best tradition of the land, and so would not notice that a large part of his book is a hard-headed attack on New York for remaining neutral in order to preserve its own fur trade, for which reason, rather than because of the wrath of heaven, New England bore the brunt. While he mechanically called the land to repentance, the moral he found most memorable was this: "The charge of war was by this time so great, that every Indian we had killed or taken, cost the country at least a thousand pounds."

Meanwhile, in that other arena, the General Court, where the war-fare was less sanguinary but every bit as intense, learning to think about society in secular terms was even more positively inculcated. Clerical propagandists for the charter had found it strategic, we have seen, to stress secular advantages, the liberties and privileges. Having so committed themselves, they were obliged to continue praising the charter's immunities, its assurance that government would never again be the arbitrary "humour" Andros had made it. They tried hard to present the charter as a compact between the people of Massachusetts and the Crown, in which Parliament did not figure. Hence the two Cookes were plentifully supplied with slogans, to be used whenever a governor negated an election to the Council or to the speakership, or whenever he asked for his salary. Every year the struggle centered more and more sharply upon this contention: "They were as much Englishmen as those in England, and thought they had a right to all the privileges that the people of England had." Whenever asked to vote a fixed wage, the House became expert in responding: "It is the native right and privilege of English subjects by consent of Parliament from time to time to raise and dispose of such sums of money as the present exigency of affairs call for." Such thinking, such speaking, bore less and less relation to any theological covenant, even though the thinkers and speakers might be, in their theology, the most rigorous of conservatives. The Mathers had confidently expected that political conceptions would always be held subordinate to a superior definition of social aims, but after two or three decades of controversy, the charter became an end in itself, its designation of rights and privileges (or the definition read into them) proving a self-sufficient philosophy of the state, requiring no further elucidation in the language of theology.

The crucial year, once more, was 1720, when for the first time a political argument was staged in print which, even less than the currency debate, gave not a glance at the spiritual aspects. (Granted that by our logic the descent of the smallpox the next year seems fortuitous, to participants in the drama the concentration of crises in 1720 represented so logical a confronting of the several issues of society that an epidemic seemed almost inevitable.) The elder Cooke died in 1715; for the last ten years of his reign, his son kept in the background, apparently taking no part in public affairs but certainly being groomed. He stepped at once into his inheritance, both the large fortune (it is important to remember that this leader of Patriots was the wealthiest man in the colony) and the political machine. He was thoroughly in command by the next year, when the newly arrived Governor Shute declared open war by negating Cooke's election to the speakership. By 1720 the struggle had become so bitter that when Shute accused Cooke of preventing John Bridger, the king's officer in Maine, from preserving the great pines for the Royal Navy, the tribune of the people was obliged to take to the press. Like his cousin, the President of Harvard, the younger Cooke was rather a leader than an exhorter of

men, who, while he might cause others to write, had himself no vocation for
authorship. Still, what *Mr. Cooke's Just and Seasonable Vindication* lacks
in polish, it more than makes up in bluntness. The governor's party was
forced to reply, and *News from Robinson Cruso's Island* appeared anonymously, to which Cooke (or one of his henchmen) retorted with *Reflections upon Reflections.*

The satire in *News from Robinson Cruso's Island* is fairly banal, but the
book shares that virtue which, in this remarkable year, suddenly became so
admired: it aspires to be witty. Its point is that if Cooke and his crowd continue defying Governor Shute, they will bring the colonies "under a Parliamentary Cognizance," and that thus their agitation for liberties will betray
the country: "And it is not a little valiant talk over a bowl of Punch, that
will help you, when you have Undone Your selves." In his pamphlets,
Cooke argues that while Bridger is speculating in Maine lumber, he, noble
patriot, is saving the king's masts; he further insists that the House have
"an Indubitable Fundamental Right to Chuse their Speaker" and should
stand to their choice, "as became true and Faithfull Assertors of the Peoples
Liberties." Shute intimated (so Cooke says) that would Cooke apologize,
he might be speaker—a bribe which Cooke rejects with a fine show of indignation. The happiness or misery of a people, Cooke asserts without giving
thought to any religious scruple, depends "entirely" upon the enjoyment or
deprivation of their liberties; therefore the populace must know what rights
are theirs, and must "assert them against the Attempts of any in time to
come." This did not mean disloyalty, for the royal prerogative itself is designed for the good of the people—"when rightly used." His anonymous
opponent roars and bellows "like the Popes Bull," but the issue is clear: are
we to be frightened into tamely giving up our privileges "and so render our
selves obnoxious to the Curse of succeeding Generations?" Here, then, was
a covenant which extended, in its way, to the seed, but it decidedly was not
a Covenant of Grace.

When maintained as a secular conception, divorced from all religious
purpose, the philosophy of charter rights proved to have implications which
the Mathers in 1691 had not foreseen. It meant, as events worked out,
that the control of the press was an exercise of tyranny. In 1690 Benjamin
Harris attempted to supply Boston with a newspaper, which was promptly
suppressed as containing "reflections of a very high nature." Campbell's
News-Letter was avowedly published "by Authority," and in meekness and
dullness showed itself incapable of giving offense. The instructions issued to
all governors vested in them the power of licensing; Shute had every intention of using it, and so was happy to get from the General Court an act
arraigning "dissaffected" publications. At the moment the legislators were
willing to vote thus because they were shocked by John Checkley's edition
of Charles Leslie's *The Religion of Jesus Christ* and then by his own *Choice
Dialogues.* Under this law, Checkley was tried and fined. But when the
House prepared their remonstrance against Bridger, Shute invoked the

same rule and forbade them to publish a disaffected document; whereupon Cooke and his friends found themselves, to their own amazement, violent champions of freedom of the press. Immediately they added it to the catalogue of rights. Hence, though the Council ordered John Colman prosecuted for his *Distressed State* and Benjamin Gray for the *Letter to an Eminent Clergy-man*, the House would not coöperate, and suppression failed.

In March 1721 Shute specifically demanded a licensing act because of the many "Factious and Scandalous Papers Printed and Publickly Sold at Boston"; he was certain to lose, because he declared the power was his even without an act of the General Court, by "the King my Masters positive Command." The House coyly answered that the proper method of dealing with scandalous publications was for him as governor to prosecute authors or publishers in the common courts, and suggested that if Shute was sincere he get to work on those responsible for *News from Robinson Cruso's Island*, for it had shown the greatest disrespect to that pillar of the state, Elisha Cooke! As for passing a licensing act, the House perceived "the innumerable inconveniences and dangerous Circumstances this People might Labour under in a little Time" were governors allowed such authority. Hence Increase Mather could do nothing but lament the good old days when the state would have put a James Franklin in the stocks; the General Court did proceed against Franklin when he insulted their own dignity but, since they had committed the land to freedom, even their indictment failed to convince a grand jury. We cannot attribute to the Patriot party a deep or exalted devotion to this great principle, or indeed we hardly dare say that they were aware it was a principle; nevertheless, out of jealousy of the governor they conceived it and brought it forth. If they did not know quite what they had done, Silence Dogood told them on July 9 by publishing an extract from a London journal which declared, "Without Freedom of Thought, there can be no such Thing as Wisdom; and no such Thing as publick Liberty, without Freedom of Speech." The most righteous among the Representatives, those who most hated the *Courant*, would have to acknowledge that upon this piece of purely secular wisdom they and the antiministerial Silence Dogood were perforce agreed.

Among the many inducements the ministers had originally employed to make the new charter palatable was, we remember, that of religious liberty. Within thirty years they found themselves obliged to follow the implications of their action further than they ever intended. They had hoped to entrench themselves behind the Act of Toleration, treating it as an article in the compact between colony and Crown, which would then keep the colony from invasion by the Church of England and protect it against Anglicans in Parliament. Therefore they took every possible occasion to say that they, "like the vast Body of Non-Conformists," were the most loyal of peoples— to the king. To him "We are all Indebted, for the Recovery of those Liberties." But in the first years of the century, the number of Anglicans increased (their churches assisted by the Society for the Propagation of the Gospel), while Quakers and Baptists grew more obstreperous in the name of religious liberty. All too soon, the ministers were caught between the Devil and the deep-blue sea: while publishing against Baptist and Quaker errors, Cotton Mather had also, in 1710, to declare it a fundamental principle of this society "that no man may be persecuted because he is Conscientiously not of the same Religious Opinion, with those that are uppermost." Taking advantage of this sort of statement, a minority split off from the Newbury Church in 1712, and by calling themselves converts to the Church of England challenged exemption from the rates. Could those "uppermost" seriously pretend that the doctrine taught in their churches was "the pure Doctrine in the famous Articles of the Church of England," they might contend that such secessions were unnecessary, and so prevent interference from London. However, it also remained of the greatest importance that New England keep its allies among the English Dissenters, wherefore the Mathers continued loudly to proclaim themselves at one "with the United Brethren, the Protestant Dissenters in South-Britain." Simultaneously to keep up both these fronts, New England had to fall back upon telling its enemies, and then retelling itself, that the points in abstract theology on which the people of God agree are more numerous, and of vastly greater importance, than those on which they differ. Therefore all "persecution"—which was to say, political action on behalf of any one denomination— was a hellish monster which mankind "ought with an United Cry to chase off the Face of the Earth." But to persuade the Church of England, or friends among the Nonconformists, of the sincerity of such speeches, something more tangible was needed to show that its religious professions were fact. Cotton Mather most vividly perceived this necessity; he was capable of responding, even though he knew that extensions of the principle brought the New England Way face-to-face with a religious indifferentism in which it would become increasingly difficult for Congregational bodies to claim privileged status.

In 1718 the Baptist Church of Boston ordained Elisha Callender; Increase Mather gave the right hand of fellowship and Cotton preached the sermon, which he took care to print and to scatter abroad, *Brethren Dwelling Together in Unity*. He says that many of his friends were displeased; the discourse is as important, in its peculiar way, as the *Courant* or the financial pamphlets. Cotton attained the difficult feat of condemning Baptists' tenets and yet defending their right to be wrong: "There is no Escaping Church-tyranny, but by asserting the Right of private Judgment, for every Man in the Affairs of his own Salvation." If you impose anything but piety, you will soon be inventing ways to enforce what you impose; therefore, a state that gives advantages to any one faction, "exclusive of such as ought to be owned as our Brethren," is a persecutor. A great many in New England would not only be amazed upon hearing these words, but would ask Mather whether he was not describing himself; however, when he stood in Callender's pulpit, he was not addressing the Baptists in front of him, but the bishops and "high-flyers" in England. He was asking that he be done unto as he was doing unto Baptists. His motive may have been thinly disguised self-interest, but he did, at least on this occasion, go all the way to the end of that logic he and his father had introduced into the land when they accepted toleration along with the charter: "That Liberty of Conscience is the Native Right of Mankind; and that every Good Neighbour and Good Subject, has a Right unto his Life, and all the Comforts of it." Fully to pursue this truth meant a comprehensive repudiation of the past, and here Mather handsomely did disown the persecutions once inflicted upon Anabaptists. But suppose all New England brought itself to this pitch of liberalism; would not that mean eventually that civil authority was nothing but a secular power, never to be exercised in any religious sphere whatsoever? How could political theory be rephrased so that the essentially secularized character of an eighteenth-century state might be most conveniently recognized, and yet as much as possible of the old regime be preserved? Or, how could the administration of what had from the beginning been called, and still was called, a commonwealth be administered for the welfare of its citizens within the framework of the covenant? An obstinate governor might be an affliction upon the populace, but was moral repentance the way to curtail him?

It was still the function of the election preachers to answer these unanswerable questions, as it was also incumbent from time to time upon those who spoke to the Artillery Company. Thus some sixty or seventy discourses were delivered in Massachusetts and Connecticut between 1700 and 1730 (most of them printed) which strove to adjust the pious political premises to the empirical and impious fact. On all these occasions, the audience was composed of adherents of various factions; the orators, who loved decorum, generally aimed at the common denominator—although many of them, schooled in New England's acquired cult of indirection, managed by indirections to make their direction clear. Compared with the mighty sermons of the 1670's—with Stoughton's, Oakes's and Hubbard's—these are a dull lot; yet despite their caution and poverty of metaphor, they tell the story of a stalwart intellectual exertion, or at least of dogged persistence. Sometimes, indeed, the preachers simply could not face it, and took refuge in a conventional jeremiad, relaxing amid the conventionally sinful landscape; but many of them attempted still to render society intelligible to itself. These men were cudgeling their brains, trying to keep up with change; on the surface the decades between 1700 and 1730 seem the most static in New England's history and the sermons most placid, but underneath was a torrent of anxiety.

The basic proposition in the political doctrine of the founders was the fall of man: because of it, government was the badge of lost innocence, divinely instituted to keep sinful creatures from destroying each other. Therefore, the great Puritans had reasoned, the state must enforce the true faith, impose orthodoxy, and suppress dissent; but if nowadays that consequence had to be denied, could the first premise still hold? Can a secular state permit liberty of conscience without, if only by implication, denying that men are totally depraved? These theologians still maintained that men had fallen, and so were bound to regard government as a desperate necessity, but at the same time they were urging it not to be too vigorous about theological purity. To the extent that the state was tolerant and mainly concerned with prescriptive rights, it arose not out of sinfulness but out of a rational power wherewith mankind decided ends for themselves. Could the contradiction be resolved? If not, could it be concealed? Could a man continue to be a sincere Protestant were he to hide it?

Once more, the gnawing question: could anything of New England's original purpose—which was its uniqueness—be carried on when in place of the seventeenth-century authority had come a regime constructed upon Whig principles, in which the most vigorous elements, in Connecticut no less than in Massachusetts, were devoted to keeping executive authority on the short leash of an annual and insufficient salary? A start might be made by stating the recognized truth that, although such a government extends liberty to law-abiding Baptists and Anglicans, it must make certain that "Blasphemies, and attempts to poison People with Atheism, come not into the Catalogue of Things that may sue for a Toleration." Yet even this self-evident proposition had to be recast and suppression called for, not because blasphemies were intrinsically evil, but because they had harmful sociological effects: "Human Society has its Ligaments all destroy'd by such Things." The difficulty with this way of putting it was that John Colman, Dr. Douglass, James Franklin, could then reply that they were public benefactors, that therefore their divergences from church leaders did not constitute scandal. The spectacle of such men, along with country deacons who would not help raise the ministers' pay, along with rioting sailors and prostitutes on the Common, was enough to persuade clerical orators that the ancient premise must never be surrendered, that even a government of contract and of natural rights must be held to originate out of depravity. There was as little reason in an eighteenth-century universe as in an earlier one—if anything, less reason—to doubt that once authority was removed, "there would be no living one by another, the Weak would become a Prey to the Strong, and the Largest Societies would soon Disband, and come to nothing." To present the Massachusetts and Connecticut charters as rational compacts between the people and the king was all very well, but most ministerial theorists (outside Chebacco) were unwilling to contemplate a rational state of nature; surely not, for example, Nathaniel Stone, whose reaction to the crucial year of 1720 was that *Rulers are a Terror*, their primary duty being to damn up the stream of human depravity, "to prevent Sin from breaking out to that degree to deluge the World."

Hence there still were ways in which a chartered society could be reclaimed for the old system, still be theoretically imposed upon sinners as an ordinance of God. The infinite wisdom has never decreed one or another specific form (Calvin had said this, but there were satisfactions in repeating it), but whatever the constitution, while there are many arguments as to why magistrates should be obeyed, "the Supreme reason is, The Will of God." All power belongs in the first instance to Him, "but he has deputed and delegated Magistrates to act for him, and in subordination to him." A governor and his council might nod in sage agreement when the election speaker propounded this sentiment, and then note with amazement that it was also being applauded along the benches where sat Cooke's unruly crew. Having to affect neutrality, the ministers strove to preserve ancient platitudes to which none could take exception (they had become what in modern American parlance is called "key-noters"), but which they hoped might even yet be used to rescue their declining interest.

For if the institution of government remains a divine appointment, it will—of its own free volition—exert itself in the cause of piety and morality. "We may warn them from God, and set the terrors of eternal judgment before them," but there is little hope for concrete results "unless you can make the sword of justice to reach them." The state has a practical stake in these matters because, unless there be a reformation, there will come even more afflictions, with economic and financial consequences; you can see, said William Williams, that our sins by "a Natural as well as a Moral Causality make us Miserable." Men entrusted with power, no matter how the electorate is made up, ought to be godly; unconverted magistrates, Stoddard granted, may be of some use, "but other qualifications do no better supply the want of holiness, than a wooden Sword does supply the want of a Sword of Steel." In fact, reiteration of this plea—even in Connecticut, as by Joseph Moss in 1715, who said, "All Persons of Atheistical Principles, are unfit for Rulers . . . also all Irreligious Persons, who shew by their Practical Ungodliness, that they are Unacquainted with the Law of God"—was sometimes merely ritualistic; but the recurrence is a sign of clerical worry. The "practical" fact was that general courts were, whether godly or ungodly, utterly absorbed in military or political projects. It should never be thought enough, as Joseph Sewall asserted in 1724, that civil rulers simply administer ordinary moral rectitude: they must act from an inward principle of religion or all is lost.

These passages are shards and fragments of what had once been a magnificently coherent political philosophy; but in the sermons they are little more than pious hopes. No longer able to demand that governments impose uniformity or suppress heresy, parsons had to change the definition of their goal: by making it merely "piety" instead of the Congregational order, they sought to enlist politicians in the obvious. They were trying to show how general courts devoted to rights and privileges would necessarily be concerned, at the same time, about the most precious heritage of the land, its religion. Hence they made every effort to equate Christian piety with civil liberties. John Bulkley startlingly made this point at Hartford by quoting

Machiavelli (whom he called one of the first rank in wisdom): "We are a People, very tender of our Civil Interests, & jealous lest by any means they are invaded or taken from us." Colman's relaxed catholic spirit did not lead him to anything so dangerously "liberal" as to discourage legislators from passing laws to promote public worship; a seeking for the welfare of the people would entail, he said, enforcement of ordinances about the Sabbath—and doing something about the ministers' income. Stephen Hosmer told Connecticut in 1720 that good magistrates "Discountenance and Punish both Intruders, & such as Advance Damnable Doctrines, and endeavour to Subvert the Established Religion." They are duty bound, exclaimed Joseph Sewall, to compel people to attend public worship. (No young Franklins should be allowed to sulk in their rooms during the time of worship, reading subversive literature.)

Yet there was every danger that these things might be said too aggressively, that they might reflect upon the profession of religious liberty. Sometimes the speaker would forget and launch into a tirade better suited to 1670, but he could not forget for long. In 1728, Thomas Prince remembered that he was addressing Governor Burnet, who was no Dissenter, and so explained that compulsory church attendance did not mean a "groveling and limited" favoring of one denomination, that the state could be friendly to "every religious Company that professes their subjection to the Laws of God." The eagerness with which the New England of 1690 had adopted toleration (as a theory) proved a self-inflicted wound that could not be healed.

Difficult as was the task of reconciling zeal for the civil administration of piety with adherence to the principle of religious liberty, the preachers had a still more difficult balance to maintain. Almost all of them were, personally, sympathetic with the "Court" party—or at least, they had little love for the two Cookes. They could thus hardly avoid making their pleas for the support of their polity look like a covert offer to return the favor, to swing the pious citizenry to the side of prerogative. A governor in Massachusetts is immensely recompensed, said Stoddard, by the opportunity he here enjoys, beyond all other posts on earth, of good society and spiritual opportunities; yet even so (Stoddard turned toward the Representatives) governors should be honorably supported. Sermons constantly admonish the people not to elect Representatives merely for party reasons—the implication being clearly against the Patriots. Pemberton cracked the surface of good manners in 1710 by saying that no man of private station, "who can with a nod inflame and raise the multitude," has a right by crying upon corruption (as Cooke did against Dudley) to unsettle the community. Cotton Mather came in 1719 as openly as any cleric dared to the aid of Shute by telling the Patriots that their disaffection would alienate what were left of New England's friends in London and make them think us "fit for none but a Parliamentary Cognisance." (His phrase was to be used, the next year, against the younger Elisha Cooke.) Were Parliament ever thus to descend in fury upon the colonies, there was every reason to fear the consequences: as Mather virtually proclaimed, these would be more ecclesiastical than political. Cooke, we know, went recklessly ahead, fighting Shute so vigorously that by the first of January 1723 he forced the executive into an ignominiously secret flight from New England's shores.

The clergy may have hated Cooke, may have wrung their hands over the danger to which he was exposing them, but there was one sufficient reason why, even when Cooke seemed most objectionable, they could not as a body align themselves with the royal prerogative against the House: Cooke and his sort had captured the watchword, and no theologian dared any longer disown it. A people's "happiness" depended upon their standing for their liberties, wherefore the slightest surrender of privilege would be diminution of prosperity. Called upon, in their forensic capacity, to expound a political doctrine founded upon the lessons of 1689, the ministers were obliged to argue that the end of government is the welfare of the whole and to show how they had learned that "welfare" is a material conception. Pemberton had to qualify his reprimand of "popularity" by explaining that he did not deny the right of revolution, that he was no Tory nonresistant. In an effort to keep everything together, preachers would urge rulers to see that citizens "enjoy Tranquility and Peace, their due Rights and Liberties, both as Men and Christians: That Vertue and Religion, Learning, and Arts, Trade and Commerce may flourish together; and the Kingdom grow Wise and Rich, Potent and Renowned"—but it was impossible to disguise how preponderant in such an inventory were physical goods over spiritual. Pemberton might attack Cooke, but he had to subscribe to Cooke's motto: the civil aim is "the good and happiness of the people under their conduct," or more specifically, "the general happiness and prosperity." As Foxcroft was saying in 1727, if government encourages simultaneously both piety and trade, the result will be that "a People may have not barely a sufficiency for themselves, but be able to lend unto others." It would have been suicide for the clergy to put the cause of organized religion openly on the governor's side, for then the new and potent slogans would have been monopolized by those they had most cause to fear. Not daring to identify the aims of piety with those of the Court party, they had to make a concerted effort to join religion to the ideal of "happiness," despite the metaphysical, not to mention theological, difficulties created by their continued adherence to the conception of forcibly restrained depravity. There was every chance that their effort would fail, because only Elisha Cooke could speak the word "happiness" so as to make it sound as though he really meant what he said. Therefore when ministers also voiced the word, they found themselves manufacturing propaganda for him.

Among the many ambiguities which inform these election sermons is an incipient contradiction between what may be called their negative and their positive exhortations. To the extent that civil order is a bridle upon lust, its function is mainly negative; to the extent that it bears the responsibility for securing happiness, it must be active. In the original philosophy as we find it in John Winthrop, no such antinomy existed: the positive duty of inculcating righteousness, of furthering conversions, had not weakened the necessity for constraint: but Winthrop, we again remember, had defined the social goal as that which is good, just, and honest. In Whig doctrine, or at least in what New England Patriots deduced from the principles of 1689, the goal was reduced to mere happiness. Therefore another implication followed: man is quite competent to discover the content of happiness by the light of nature or reason, whereas the meaning of the good, just, and honest must be handed down from on high by authority. If man can make out for himself what constitutes his happiness, he cannot be altogether depraved: he has understanding, said Pemberton, by which he entertains ideas, passes judgment upon them, and so makes political decisions; therefore government must be "suited to the principles of reason, to the nature of man, and the ends of civil society." People must be ruled, but they "ought not to be broken by the force and weight of power." As soon as this consideration becomes dominant, while it may still be important for magistrates to know piety, it is of greater moment that they comprehend the history, constitution, customs of the people. All such secular wisdom assists them, said Timothy Cutler, in recognizing "wherein the Happiness of a Place doth consist." Again and again these sentences do not seem, verbally, to depart from the founders; yet the entire orientation has been reversed since the inheritors of these propositions are obliged to prove that the maxims of salvation are also engines of happiness.

A few things, it might appear, could be ventured without putting too great a strain upon older conceptions. Religion would not be reduced to a mere handmaid of happiness when ministers boasted that, through the incentive of the fear of God, it helped maintain law and order. Benjamin Colman most loved to toy with this double-edged contention, for here he felt that opposing tendencies were reconciled: the ministry directly serves for salvation, yet indirectly it also "abundantly serves to the peace and good Order of the World at the same time." Likewise, although the direct end of civil government is this same outward peace, tranquillity, and prosperity, yet because these are included within the religious aspiration, "it has also really a further Aim, Influence and Effect, even in the Religious and spiritual Good of its Subjects." Less subtle orators simply exclaimed concerning spiritual righteousness, "How well doth it become every Rational Creature! How Useful and Serviceable doth it render Persons in Societies." And several parsons, particularly in Connecticut, frequently assert one of the inestimable virtues of sanctity to be that it works against "levelism."

Yet the effort to praise religion out of these considerations, although it had precedent among the founders, was in constant danger, once social stability had become a qualification not for goodness but for happiness, of losing its moorings in the doctrine of original sin, of becoming a political or economic moralism, in which the criterion of utility would take precedence over holiness. Because religion teaches frugality it discourages expensive vices (which, said the hard-money men, all of them enemies of Cooke, are the source of all our woes, not because they are vicious but because they feed on English imports and so send specie out of the country). As soon as a minister had delivered himself of such a resounding platitude as this, "Thus by keeping the Outward Actions of Men in due Bounds and Channels, the Good of Human Society is Secured," he had an uncomfortable feeling that the good of society ought to consist in something more than what the constable can enforce better than the church. Still present was the idea, inherited from federal theologians, that a society is rewarded in this world. So piety was bound to become not just a check upon inordinate propensities, but "the best Friend to outward Prosperity." Before they quite realized what they were doing, a century after the founding, ministers were pleading for Christianity itself on the surprising ground that it "hath a natural tendency to promote civil Peace and Order; to make a People prosperous in their trade & business."

Since the founders were, outside their peculiar theological doctrines, good scholastics, they held that things which are naturally good for the creature, suitable to his place in the scale of being and adapted to his need, were legitimate and, in themselves, good: they joined with Milton in hailing wedded love. Such things, they believed, are temptations only when misused; vast compendia of all the sciences said this in a thousand ways, and nowhere is there a denial, in so many words, of what John Rogers said before Governor Dudley in 1706: "Righteousness taken in the Latitude of it, for the whole of Religion . . . comprehending all Divine & Social Virtues, has a natural tendency to promote Publick Happiness." Yet when preachers got the habit of going out of their way to stress this point, they showed their uneasiness; when they protest over and over again that piety has "an happy influence upon the prosperity of single persons, and whole societies," the apologetic tone is distinctly, often painfully, audible; or when a speaker pleads that "the Comfort and Quiet of our Consciences" are indissolubly joined to "the good of Humane Society" he shows himself nervous lest the two should at any moment part company. There is a constant reminder of how New England proves religion an asset for a people wresting civilization from the wilderness: the founders had no improved land or houses, said Colman, "But God it was that gave them Wisdom and Courage and Strength, a heart to subdue a waste Wilderness, and to fill it with Towns & Villages as it is this Day." Let piety then still be prized, and it will continue, as before, to make us rich and happy.

But it could never be enough, in this situation, to prove piety useful, to weigh it in the scales of economic felicity without also linking it to the philosophy of contractual or natural rights—because those were the most obvious instruments of happiness. Religion had to be made over, or at least redesigned, to demonstrate that by its innermost nature it signified a resolution to defend the privileges confirmed by William and Mary of blessed memory. Ministers might not admire Elisha Cooke, might wish that he and his Patriots would make less noise, attract less attention in England, but they could not admit that Protestantism was opposed to the principles Cooke upheld: "So dearly did our Fathers purchase, and thus highly did they prise, those Charter Privileges, and Religious Liberties. . ." Many may secretly have hankered—possibly all except Wise actually did—for the vanished days when liberty had meant the liberty of the masses to submit to the rule of the few divinely set over them, but to express publicly any such longing would be an invitation to the Church of England. Therefore the clergy did what they had to do: they glorified the Whig philosophy. Their election sermons continued to resound with the sins of the land and to call for reformation, to beseech the magistrates to help; but somewhere in the delivery the tone of voice would change, and there would be, for at least several paragraphs, an explanation that all power is limited "by the will of God, and right reason, by the general rules of government, and the particular laws stated in a land" (although a moment before the preacher might have been saying that the power is given of God). Orators would call upon the state to collect their salaries from a reluctant people, and then tell the statesmen, "God has not subjected the Lives, & Libertys of the Ruled, to the Arbitrary Will and Pleasure of the Rulers." They were willing to pay the price of survival: the great design of civilized society is "the Protection of Persons in the Undisturbed Enjoyment of those two grand Interests (viz. Religion & Property)"; they were ready even to elevate property to such an equality with religion, hoping thereby to assist the communities in retaining both. Yet since property called for a vigorous stand in behalf of rights of Englishmen, officials appointed by the Crown might well decide that the clerical offer of pious support in return for governmental favors was a deal not worth entertaining. Though the religious interest dreamed of making an alliance with the secularized state against demagogues like Cooke and immoralists like James Franklin, it was prevented from going beyond tentative overtures because it, too, by the process of history, was obliged to tell that state how rulers might not invade—"either by Secret Practices, or Open Violence"—the free enjoyment of the civil rights of life, liberty, and estate, "or if they do, they are of no force."

Here, it might be, another strategy would suggest itself: why not give over entirely attempting to identify the law of God with that which delimits and restrains, why not instead present the ecclesiastical system of New England as being (of course derived from the Bible) in effect the chief of those enumerated rights and privileges which are the natural, the inviolable possession of Englishmen, which were graciously confirmed by the charter, but could never have been treated other than with such respect? Were the clergy firmly to take this line, then every assertion against the Crown of provincial liberties would automatically become a defense of the church system. Perhaps, after all, the Patriot faction might prove the better staff to lean upon: it might repay clerical support by collecting salaries (for if boss Cooke decided ministers should have their wages raised, the wages would rise), and certainly it would resist encroachments by the Church of England. Was not the real logic of the situation something like this: could the clerical caste overcome their distaste for the vulgarity and recklessness of the Patriots, did they not stand to gain more by alliance with them than by trailing forlornly in the wake of the royal prerogative?

We can hardly say that any minister before 1730 frankly attempted this dangerous tack. The sturdy blasts of John Wise were too splenetic, or else too ebullient, to be of practical use to insurgents in their day-to-day struggle with the governor. But there is enough increase in the attention given to this possibility by some of the later preachers to suggest that it was recognized. John Bulkley in 1713 balanced the factors by saying that "all Civil Power is Derivative, comes from God," and that God has ordained subordination among men, and by then grafting onto this absolutism a vigorous assertion of the inviolability of rights and of the right of revolution. Two years later, Joseph Moss was even more explicit, and his discourse showing *That Frequent Reading and Studying the Scriptures . . . is Needful and Profitable for Rulers* belied its title by presenting the most radical political statement to be found outside the remarks attributed to Cooke or published by Wise. All civil rulers have their power limited, "and that by the boundaries of some Laws, that are the Laws of that Kingdom, State or Commonwealth," because just government is "founded originally in Compact or Agreement"; wherefore "none can make a just Claim to any Natural Original Right to rule over others (Family Rulers only excepted)," and "so Mankind never did nor will, Submit." Few before 1730 went so far as Moss (indeed, none was to venture quite so far until Mayhew and Charles Chauncy spoke, and even then many of their people were aghast), but several kept the ideas alive. John Hancock in 1722 declared that rulers must exert themselves for the good of the people and "defend their rights & liberties, and protect them in all their valuable Priviledges." Jeremiah Wise in 1729 praised "fixed Rules" and told the Court of Massachusetts, "God has not subjected, the Lives, Liberties or Properties of a People to the Pleasure of their Superiors."

Thus the clergy commenced, and continued, to make their contribution to what ultimately became the theory of the American Revolution. They were not altogether happy in their work, for they were of divided and contradictory minds. They wanted the state to be a divine ordinance executing their behest, but they had to accept contractualism. Their confusion bespeaks more than an inner tension in their ideology; it was the outward sign of their indecision between two factions struggling for power in the secular order. Were they to emphasize the first strain, they would be supporters of prerogative; were they to put the greater stress upon the second, they would become, will-they nill-they, subsidized pamphleteers for Patriotism. They had a peculiar motive for enhancing contractual rights, but it was sharply in conflict with their urge to preach, as more religiously acceptable, a code of submission, obedience, and social classification. If they were in the awkward position of appearing to bid for support from either faction, they were in effect trying to sell themselves to the higher bidder—or what was even worse, of seeking to convince each contestant that their influence was worth bidding for.

In this predicament, hampered at every turn, they were bound to break out of their dilemma by showing that they could still say something, some one thing, loud and clear, that they could still, as the time-honored phrase had it, raise their voices like trumpets. And what could this possibly be but that they also subscribed, with positive enthusiasm, to a conception that had become the hope and prospect of New England? They could not let themselves fall behind the others in advocating happiness. The end of every government, said even Joseph Sewall, must always be "the Good of Civil Societies & Communities of Men." This end, he would of course say, is subordinate to the glory of God, but immediately thereafter it is "the last End of all things."

CHAPTER XXIII

A TENDER PLANT

T HE
actions which Samuel Shute charged against New
England amounted, he said, to "continual encroachments on the few prerogatives left to the Crown." Royal agents heard nothing but what they
deemed treason in Boston; governors were called blockheads, and dead dogs
and cats were thrown into their coaches. The patient Jeremiah Dummer,
hearing these tales and rumors circulating in London, was constantly begging the General Court to lie, if only for a short time, low.

There was every reason to fear that because Cooke had badly overplayed
his hand the Parliamentary reprisal, at the mere thought of which Cotton
Mather trembled, might now be at hand. Yet once we go outside the journals of the House of Representatives and a few private diaries, we find very
little reflection in the published remains of the seriousness of the crisis. The
newspapers are as reticent as the election sermons are vague. This circumspection was calculated: the main topic of conversation, we gather from letters and other disclosures, was the worsening relations of these plantations
with the home government, but in formal utterances it was permissible to
speak only of New England's undying devotion to the Crown, to Hanover,
and to the Protestant succession, to sing the untroubled felicity of constitutionalism. Were public speech for even a moment to be relaxed, an accumulated store of grievances and hatreds would burst into the open, an eruption
which certainly would not help a delicate situation.

One source—perhaps the chief source—of this sullen disposition masked
by a fervent rhetoric of loyalty was the sad record of attempts at military
coöperation. Some scholars accuse the colonists of dragging their feet, of
failing to appreciate imperial requirements, of thinking only of self. But
many in the land—by no means all of them in Cooke's party—felt that
they had been consistently misused and humiliated. The fleet supposed to
aid Phips in 1692 went instead to the Indies, coming to Boston only after
it had become infected with the plague, which it discharged ashore. Two
New England companies were sent in 1702 to Jamaica and there wiped
out. In 1709, at great expense the colonies organized an army and kept it
in readiness all summer before the English government deigned to inform
them that the invasion had been diverted to Portugal; the British fleet,
which had been waiting in the harbor and consuming colonial provisions,
serenely sailed off, the whole futility costing New England £46,000. The

worst of indignities was the expedition against Quebec in 1711: the colonies were given short notice but worked hard; £40,000 of credit were issued, supplies impressed, and that year probably over one-fifth of all inhabitants capable of bearing arms were in service. To command this force, and to gamble with provincial lives, England sent two of the most incompetent and fatuous commanders out of the lush harvest of eighteenth-century favoritism. By sheer stupidity they managed to wreck the enterprise; the Royal Navy abandoned it, while the New Englanders, thanks to their pilots, barely saved themselves. And then the word soon came from London: the returned British were blaming this disaster upon Americans.

Cotton Mather, complicated soul that he was, had reasons for loving his country, and was as galled as any at these aspersions; but temperateness was laid upon him, as upon all public speakers, so that when referring to 1711 he would go only so far, and then ask, would you know the rest of the story? "Enquire into it, O Britons, at home. And let Justice take Place." Agent Dummer was a shrewder man: he was a master of patience and caution, but he comprehended well enough the British character to know that there come times in dealing with it when one must assume the offensive.

Whether Jeremiah Dummer really belongs in a history of the New England mind may be queried. Having added to his Harvard degree a training at Leyden, he had become, in respects which Cotton Mather could never understand, Europeanized. His return to Boston in 1704 had not been a success; in fact, his discourse on the Sabbath produced consternation, to the embarrassment of his patron, Increase Mather. Dummer soon returned to London with a sigh of relief, and there found himself, being chosen agent, entirely at home among the coffeehouses and other amenities. He kept his religious opinions to himself; yet, although in 1720 he scored a brilliant success by disputing for the cause of Protestantism at Saint Sulpice in Paris, displaying an impeccable Latin, he was more than suspected of infidelity. John Colman, having exhibited in his *Distressed State* an emancipated intelligence, was one of a few capable of asserting that Dummer's religion and morals might be anything he chose so long as he was diligent in affairs of the province. On that score, Dummer more than demonstrated his devotion to the cause, among such pitfalls as no American had yet learned to avoid, where none was again to pick his way so successfully until Franklin followed him. Among the hazards he ran, not the least was such constant grumbling from New England because he did not always achieve the impossible as would have discouraged any but one who, even among his mistresses, could remain the Puritan. If he was not, like his great successor, an apprentice himself, he was the son of John Hull's industrious apprentice; ingrained in him were those same virtues which make Franklin, who also lived most of his life outside the region, so strangely representative of its basic qualities.

Instead of employing Matherian innuendo, he in 1712 published *Letter to a Noble Lord*. It is gracious, but it firmly denies that colonials were responsible for the idiocies of Mrs. Masham's brother, General Jack Hill, and of Admiral Sir Hovenden Walker. Boston merchants did not, as accused, trade with the enemy, for they have too much honor and love of country— "whatever some People may say of 'em here, judging them I suppose by themselves." British dignitaries did not like to be so bearded; talk about revoking the charters, those foundations of colonial insolence, increased in the bureaus and salons of Whitehall, until in 1715 there seemed a real possibility that the government would commence upon the charters of the Carolinas, after which those of New England would certainly be dealt with.

At this moment Thomas Banister reached London, a year after his drinking bout that had so exasperated Judge Sewall. This episode suggests that he, although trained at Harvard and a prosperous merchant, was like Franklin more responsive to the influences of a seaport and trading town than to jeremiads. He heard what was afoot, and promptly came to the aid of his country by publishing *A Letter to the Right Honourable the Lords Commissioners of Trade and Plantations*. He argued that New England's liberties must be respected, but he brought into the light of day the point which election sermons strove to keep hidden, that these privileges are primarily to be evaluated in an economic context. We take several thousand pounds worth a year of your manufactures, he told the British, and pay for them in commodities you need, "and not one Article that increases your Luxury or unnecessary Expense." Londoners cast slurs upon the people as "Dissenters, Commonwealth's-Men, Anti-monarchical, and whatever else they please to call them," but do not understand that their variety of religions, which the Act of Toleration has encouraged, is a principal guarantee of colonial dependence. So great a diversity could "never form any Idea of a Combination to the Prejudice of the Land of our Fore-fathers." Hence not in the realm of religious ideas or of ecclesiastical tradition did danger lie, no matter how often preachers extolled Puritan founders or incautiously developed aggressive theses concerning limitation of power. The real issue was something other: at the moment, Banister put it, the colonies depend upon England for necessaries, and as long as they so rely upon her, will be dutiful: "But if the Nature of their trade, or great Duties on their Goods, destroy this Ballance, of Necessity they must make for themselves, and will, since they have Materials to work on." Banister had grown up amid a rationalization of the historic role of New England in terms of the religious bond, but he had acquired (or somebody taught him) another language. He suddenly makes explicit a reality that had long been taking form: as against England, New England's bargaining strength consisted not in its righteousness but its industrial potential. As the more humble scion of this trading town was to explain to the House of Commons in 1776, when the issue had had time to mature, it might almost any day become the pride of Americans to wear their old clothes over again (something the jeremiad could not induce them to do) until they were able to make new ones for themselves.

Fearful of that prospect, and incapable of comprehending the ideas taking shape in minds like Banister's and Dummer's, Cotton Mather could only beg the Patriots not to "provoke our King, and those under Him who have Power over us, to deal with us, as a People unworthy of our Distinguishing Liberties." But the Patriots would not relent; during the year 1720 provoking complaints piled up before the Lords Commissioners, including those from Bridger and from the Boston Collector of Customs. Then appeared what seemed the key to the conspiracy, Cooke's *Vindication*, which tried to involve Jeremiah Dummer by citing him in support of Cooke's thesis that Maine woods belonged to Massachusetts Bay by right of purchase, and therefore not to the Crown. A frantic letter was sent by Judge Sewall, begging Dummer not to let his rage against Cooke prevent him from saving the charter.

The years 1720–21 constitute the social and spiritual crisis in these colonies: the land bank, the *Courant*, smallpox, Cooke's campaign against Shute; on the other side of the water the situation was just as grave, for were the charter destroyed, New England would no longer have the liberty to indulge its newly devised pastimes. Dummer had been extremely worried in 1715, and evidently composed his major statement at that time; it is unthinkable that Banister, arriving fresh from Boston, would not at once have got in touch with him. When we consider that Banister wrote nothing else, and does not seem (from the glimpse Sewall gives of him) to be much of what the *Courant* called a "scribbler," there is reason to surmise that Dummer put him up to publishing, intending to hold his own fire for the psychological moment; he may even have helped Banister in the writing. At any rate, Dummer saw in 1721 that the moment had come, and so sent to the press *A Defence of the New-England Charters*, one of the few works of this period that boast a permanent place in American literature. The story of its appearance is ironical: it was to appear on September 12; on September 11 Dummer received news that the House, under Cooke's goading, had deprived him of the agency. He was soon restored, but the episode reveals into what a political as well as ideological morass the colonies had stumbled.

Dummer's *Defence*, in great contrast to the election sermons, is bold. But it could be bold because, aside from noting that the founders had been Puritans, it completely ignores the religious consideration. And even the founding appears not to have been for the city on a hill, but "to increase the nation's commerce and enlarge her dominions." The plantations cost Britain nothing, but have enriched her by their purchases despite the difficulty of obtaining bullion. This, and not a designation by Jehovah, is their reason for being. "The conclusion, that I would draw from these premises is this, THAT to strip the Country of their charters after the service has been so successfully performed, is abhorrent from all reason, equity and justice." Here, at long last was the secular measurement, here the ground upon which Americanized Puritans must learn to stand if they were to stand at all.

Dummer reinforced this interpretation with a masterful summary of what the people had performed in the wars, got in several sly digs at the incompetence of the British high command, and set forth, with a dignity that made more formidable his indignation, the cowardice by which New York saved itself at the expense of New England. Then he played his trump card: reciting everything it had accomplished, he compared New England of to-day, under a rule of liberty, with its abjectness under Andros, and so wrote one of those paragraphs which, as John Adams was to say, make the *Defence* a handbook of the Revolution:

And to compleat the oppression, when they, upon their trial claimed the privileges of Englishmen, they were scoffingly told, those things would not follow them to the ends of the earth. Unnatural insult; must the brave adventurer, who with hazard of his life and fortune, seeks out new climates to enrich his mother country, be denied those common rights, which his country-men enjoy at home in ease and indolence? Is he to be made miserable, and a slave by his own acquisitions? Is the labourer alone unworthy of his hire, and shall they only reap, who have neither sowed nor planted? Monstrous absurdity! Horrid inverted order!

This tract—or rather declamation— is weakest when pleading that the colonists do not flout the Navigation Acts—or that the many ought not to be blamed because of a few smugglers! But against the charge that they make laws contrary to those of England, it regains the highest ground: they have every right to legislate for their own conditions, and so to enact a few rules "various" from the English, but not therefore "repugnant." "Every country has circumstances peculiar to it self in respect of its soil, situation, inhabitants and commerce, to all which, convenient laws must, with the nicest care and judgment, be adapted." Englishmen, or at least undersecretaries, might object to the deduction of this conclusion from the given premises, but not one of them (and hardly anyone in New England) would challenge this relativity on the score that New England had once been committed to an absolute good, just, and honest. Therefore Dummer could enlist upon his side not only the economic history of colonization but the spirit of the age by asserting that true conformity to English law means simply that plantations be not subjected to arbitrary government. In that spirit also he could manifest his own character by adding that if ever they are so reduced, and they do not object, "I'll be no longer an advocate for them."

To be quite accurate, Dummer was not a prophet of the Revolution. The final portion of his *Defence* is an empassioned plea for continued dependence, with the result that in 1776 Tories were to invoke him no less than did Otis. But neither he nor the contemporaneous election sermonizers can be understood through a subsequent light. In the development of the American mind, Dummer's book is a landmark because it shifts the conception of America from the covenant to business. It justifies not only piety but liberty itself as a way of prospering, and in that fashion redefines the relation of America to Europe. "It were no difficult task," he blandly asserts, "to prove that London has risen out of the plantations, and not out of England." To them Britain owes her fleets, the increase of seamen, the improvement of her navigation: " 'tis their tobacco, sugar, fish, oil, logwood, and other commodities" that have enabled her to keep a favorable balance of trade and to make the figure she has cut for a century "in all parts of the commercial world." Not to the United Brethren nor even to the Glorious Revolution did Dummer appeal in trying to teach Englishmen their responsibilities, but to enlightened self-interest; with that irresistible argument he sought to prevent them from laying the rough hand of oppression on America. "The trade of a young plantation is like a tender plant": if it be abused, the plant will die. Yet throughout the book runs an unspoken implication: a people who had accomplished what Dummer paraded might find ways, if oppressed, of not dying.

This inference did not need to be explicitly stated; it was conveyed by the style itself. Splendid as is Dummer's marshaling of arguments, the greatest triumph of the *Defence* is literary. His admonition was doubly effective for being couched in good humor, for conspicuously allowing wit temporarily to drain off resentment: "So that I may say without being ludicrous, that it would not be more absurd to place two of his Majesty's beef-eaters to watch an infant in the cradle that it don't rise to cut its father's throat, than to guard these weak infant colonies to prevent their shaking off the British yoke." The skill of the prose foretells the day when the colonial mind, of which the New England was a component, having adapted European rhetoric to domestic "circumstances," would speak in so accomplished a manner as to astound the world. Assuredly, Dummer concludes,

they would reckon the loss of their privileges a greater calamity than if their houses were all in flames at once. Nor can they be justly blamed, the one being a reparable evil, but the other irreparable. Burnt houses may rise again out of their ashes, and even more beautiful than before, but 'tis to be feared that liberty, once lost, is lost forever.

It would be agreeable to add that Dummer's eloquence saved New England's charters, much as it would be gratifying to suppose that Milton's won freedom of the press. But the attack collapsed, not because of his representations, but merely because of confusion, rivalries, and brute inefficiency in the British civil service. This, however, should not prevent our savoring every word in the tribute John Adams paid to the *Defence:* "both for style and matter, one of our most classical American productions," which ought "to be read by every American who has learned to read."

To assist Dummer, the House sent Elisha Cooke to London, who proved, as Dummer knew he would, a disaster. The moderation of the "Explanatory Charter" of 1725 was due not to Cooke or even to Dummer, but as the latter said, to the "lazyness of the Ministry." Still, that in itself was something for a tender plant to take into consideration. William Burnet arrived as governor in March 1728, to take up the fight for salary where Shute had abandoned it in 1723. Before him Thomas Prince preached the election sermon: he told Burnet how frequently Increase Mather had taken delight in quoting his famous Whig father, then Bishop of Salisbury, that the charter of 1629 had been in effect "a Contract between the King and the First Planters," and that because the people had performed their part, "for the King to deprive their Posterity of the Priviledges therein granted to them, would carry a Face of Injustice in it." This was the most daring thrust an election preacher had so far attempted; whereupon the House refused Burnet a fixed salary in the name of their "undoubted rights as Englishmen." Burnet summoned the General Court to Salem and then to Cambridge, hoping to wean them from the influence of Boston's streets, but they insisted that they acted for, "and may be said to be the People." At the election of 1729 Jeremiah Wise, who inherited something from his father, preached on the limitation of power, and wove in as many quotations as possible from Bishop Burnet. Governor Burnet was not so much limited as powerless; his death in 1729 brought another armistice. A hundred years after the Great Migration, the House of Representatives, resembling nothing so much as a cat that had swallowed the canary, sat down to await the new governor, native-born and Harvard-trained Jonathan Belcher, who, it was expected, would show the proper reverence toward chartered liberties.

The House behaved even more arrogantly toward Burnet than they had against Shute. The reason was not far to seek: they knew by then that if the situation became too hot, Walpole would not stand by him. Examined in this perspective, the conduct of the Patriots appears something less than heroic. Their methods were crude, dirty, hypocritical. But the important fact is that they knew this, better than the moralists, then or later, who condemn them. They had actually to deal with one whose motto was to let sleeping dogs lie, and the whole ocean was between him and them: was there any reason why they should be the sleepers? They used slogans to play at ducks and drakes, frankly for their own interest. They manipulated English principles to resist English exploitation, until resentment mounted into contempt. If the Lords Commissioners meant what they said, let them come and collect the governor's salary. These provincials were possessed of the great secret: England was incapable of any such exertion. Illuminated by that new sort of assurance, the House made no more of a gesture toward pious standards than was required by listening patiently through an election sermon and voting the publication. Many if not most of the members were still professing communicants, but they were discovering a deeper identity.

This sense of their discovery is what makes Penhallow's history so striking a contrast to works of the Mathers. The crux of the difference is that he read (and quoted) Dummer's *Defence*. Penhallow had heard that "at home" New England was blamed for the debacle of 1711, but could find no reason "but what sprung from some capricious brains" for so slandering his country. We are not, he insisted, enemies to the Crown, and we are not foes to the Church of England. True, he did concede, remembering that he had been brought up on the jeremiad, "we have degenerated from the pious steps of our forefathers"; but the rest of the world should learn to take these extravagances in a New English way. Even so—in these quiet tones a new era opens—"I am bold to say, that as to number, there are as many sincere and good people in New-England, as in any one part of the world."

Nevertheless—self-accusation still had its uses. The day before the *Defence* was released, Jeremiah Dummer opened the letter that told him he was dismissed from his office; he sat down to his desk and promised to send copies of the forthcoming book to all members of the General Court who might still wish to see what he had written in their behalf. He expected no thanks, although it was a hard fate, while he was doing all in his power to obtain justice both for the province and for these gentlemen, that they should take pains to lessen and to expose him. "I wish they do not prejudice themselves by it in the end. It matters little what becomes of me." There is a curious echo in these sentences of the magnificent statement of Roger Williams to the town of Providence, that should he perish "in endeavoring after your temporal and spirituall peace," he would be content to perish: "It is but a shadow vanished, a bubble broke, a dream finished." However, that great dissident, never more the Puritan than when creating dissension, had been able to add, "Eternity will pay for it." Jeremiah Dummer could contemplate less enduring but more sensuous consolations for the discharge of his duty, such as the premier prophet of liberty had not counted upon or even desired. Still, Dummer wrote his resigned letter out of a strangely similar serenity: he too had been endeavoring after the temporal (and incidentally the spiritual) peace of his countrymen, and so could speak in the assurance that upon the morrow would appear in the bookstalls of London a novel species of jeremiad, in which the doctrine would be that no man is to be made miserable, nor to become a slave, because of his own acquisitions. Should this presumption be denied, he was to say, the universe will become a horrid inverted order.

BOOK IV

The Socialization of Piety

Righteous art thou, O Lord, when I plead with thee:
Yet let me talk with thee of thy judgments:
Wherefore doth the way of the wicked prosper?
Wherefore are all they happy that deal very treacherously?
Thou hast planted them, yea, and they have taken root:
They grow, yea, they bring forth fruit:
Thou art near in their mouth,
And far from their reins.
But thou, O Lord, knowest me:
Thou hast seen me, and tried mine heart toward thee:
Pull them out like sheep for the slaughter,
And prepare them for the day of slaughter.
How long shall the land mourn,
And the herbs of every field wither,
For the wickedness of them that dwell therein?

JEREMIAH 12:1–4

Wwwwww
HILE
the debate of Mathers, Stoddard, and Wise was
going on, all through political, financial, and medical crises, the clergy
still played their role of formulating communal thought. After 1700
printing was easier and cheaper; publication was available not merely for
full-dress performances like election sermons, but for slighter pieces—
ordination and funeral sermons, discourses on diverse topics, or occasional
meditations. Compared with 1660–1690, the literature of 1700–1730
is quantitatively immense. The leading figures were staggeringly prolific.
Despite failing powers, Increase Mather kept printers busy up to 1723;
Colman and Wadsworth let hardly a year go by without issuing at least
three or four items; the rising generation, especially those in Boston, took
to publishing with gusto—Thomas Foxcroft, Joseph Sewall, William
Cooper, Joshua Gee, John Webb, and above all Thomas Prince, who
from the moment of his ordination at the Old South in 1718 bade fair
to outpublish them all. President John Leverett was too busy with administration to find time for productive scholarship, but in the 1720's those
most closely identified with his "catholic" spirit brought out books in his
stead—Nathaniel Appleton, Ebenezer Gay, Edward Wigglesworth, and
"Johnny" Barnard. And up to the moment the quill dropped from his
hand, the peerless producer of the lot, Cotton Mather, never desisted from
what the *Courant* called scribbling; he left behind him, in 1728, the
longest bibliography yet achieved, or likely ever to be achieved, by an
American author.

Consequently, for these decades there exists, apart from tracts arising
out of specific controversy, a relatively large body of expression which is
not topical, which is concerned with general currents of thought and feeling.
This generation was the first who could, at least occasionally, escape the
clutch of the jeremiad, who could venture to experiment with new techniques and fresher forms. Meanwhile, English examples—whether journalistic or religious—instilled a self-consciousness about style which colonial efforts at imitation heightened. The seventeenth-century manner
became outmoded even among those most reverent of the founders; everyone realized that greater attention must be paid to elegance, grace, and
ease. The sermon was, inevitably, the literary type in which the clergy
still operated, but they found themselves free—indeed obliged—to modify

the rigid sequence of doctrine, reasons, and uses, to find variations more pleasing to wearied auditors. The plain style of the past seemed no longer plain, but gnarled, abstruse, metaphysical; it had now to be modulated.

In one sense this literature is, in tone and manner, a reflection of the cultural situation, responding more sensitively to shifts in taste than could formalized jeremiads. Because of printing, Thomas Symmes declared, the statesman, physician, gentleman, "the Mechanick, yea, the Ladies, as well as the Scholar, the Philosopher, the Christian and the Divine are furnished with agreeable libraries." With this sense of a diverse audience, and of the meanings of the word "agreeable," productions of 1710 or 1720 bespeak a climate of sensibility advanced by more than a century over that into which Increase Mather was born. Yet on the other hand, the change was almost entirely a matter of style and emphasis, not of ideas. No intellectual break with the past had yet been broached; officially the creed was untouched, the only acknowledged amendment being freedom of conscience—and that was artfully kept from disturbing foundations. The mental framework was still technologia and the covenant; cosmology might imperceptibly be altered from within, but it was not yet challenged from without. Appropriation of the new physical science (especially physics) raised no challenges to orthodoxy. In so far as it was a system of doctrine, of explicit propositions, the New England mind remained utterly unaffected by anything that had befallen it.

And yet, the world it purported to deal with had changed from decade to decade until the social setting of the eighteenth century presented at every point a radical contrast to that of Winthrop and Cotton. Hence, though the situation was directly reflected in tone and language, it was only obliquely, even obscurely, recognized in ideas. Most of the literature is not, like pamphlets about the land bank, modeled upon experience, yet it is dimly aware of remoteness. The entire output is defensive, apologetic, fundamentally disingenuous. It is the literature of a soceity poised upon the brink of an alteration for which few, if any, of its intellectuals are prepared. Though the analyst may, by patient dissection, discover in it more relevances to the environing society than in the limited output of 1660–1690, it is, paradoxically, far more evasive. It does not attack its material head-on; it shuffles, it is shocked or indignant, retreats into incantation, and repeats itself interminably. To read it intelligently, let alone sympathetically, one must bear in mind that in its pages effects have connections with their causes only underground. But if it be examined in that awareness, it may become an instructive lesson concerning the relation of literature to society.

For example, in that realm of social experience we call "the Protestant ethic," this literature abounds with exhortations to pious labor, continues to explain that profane work is sacred when done with a religious heart, that riches are bestowed by God, that "poverty is a great affliction, and Sin the cause of it." God has been especially good to us, because in New England He has made our business our pleasure, "and we do not come to it, as the Bear unto the stake." Idleness is the worst of vices, and time is to be redeemed. "Pardon me, if I say, any Honest Mechanicks really are more Honourable than Idle and Useless men of Honour." Recreations are to be used "for Sawces, but not for Meat," and the good old rule of weaned affections is unmodified: "You must Buy, and Trade, and Marry, and Weep & Care for these things, as if you did not." Prosperity normally follows sanctified labor, but losses can be a trial of faith, whereas frequently providence permits the most wicked to prosper in all outward things.

When John Cotton had announced these truths, he had not so much exhorted as he had prescribed a code that could be reinforced by calling upon civil government to impose a just price and inflict sumptuary laws. He did not preach, he dictated. A century later, ministers were pathetically pleading; even while repeating Cotton's words, they had to prove them. "The Protestant Religion hath not been set up scarce in any Nation, but it has made them, even in Temporals, within a very little while, Twice as Rich and as Great as they were before"; the Protestant succession has been worth eight million pounds sterling per annum to Great Britain! From 1689, when the Revolution permitted preachers to resume the seventeenth-century injunction, a steady transformation of the theme can be traced, wherein the religious spirit less and less figures as the cause of prosperity, and becomes instead a benediction upon the process, to be prized for the adventitious grace it bestows upon wealth, or for the consolation it extends to poverty. "As Temperance has a natural tendency to secure our Health and Ease," runs a characteristic passage (this by Foxcroft in 1719), "so Frugality, Fidelity, Justice, and the like Virtues are the surest method to promote our outward Prosperity." Whereas, "Art thou Poor and Low in the World? Religion will contribute to your Advancement. The diligent Hand maketh rich, and Religion tends to promote Industry." The exhortation itself shows that it is no longer delivered out of the majesty of an authoritative dictate, but out of an awareness that controversy is rending a competitive society. "If the Poor will but Work, they would make a better hand of it in this Country, than in almost any under the Cope of Heaven. What Pity 'tis, that such an Hive should have any Drones in it!" The unacknowledged admission is, in the opinion of the clerical commentator, that the poor no longer work hard enough; consequently religion is brought in, not as the arbiter of society, but as an economic nostrum. It has become, unwittingly, one among the several assets of a commonwealth.

Arising out of the same alteration of sentiment is a second plea, developing along with the first: once wealth has been gained, the prosperous should not forget the help they received from religion, and so should pay their debt. "It is but equal, that Humane Society should Receive Benefits from Us." The more the goal of a secular calling became defined, not as the

glory of God, but as "a Tendency to the Happiness of Mankind," the·
more religious spokesmen had to remind the successful that piety (and the
support of it) is an indispensable constituent of even the most temporal of
happinesses. "Gods blessing a people obliges them to be religious," said
Colman, and then added the observation which gives to even the very
phrases of John Cotton an odd ring when quoted in the context of this
period: "and yet how often is prosperity a means of a peoples Irreligion."
Repeated insistence upon the impiety of looking for success anywhere but
in the blessing of God, of ascribing it solely to prudence, means that
preachers knew of many who were thus impious. Even while propound-
ing this truism, Colman had to descend into the particulars of New England's history, to argue that since all depends on God, "so little reason
have the Town or Country to repine at their own, or to grudge one another's state." There, precisely, was the difficulty: how could ministers
extract from either town or country an expression of gratitude for divine
favor when each was busily accusing the other of causing its economic
distress?

Thus the very moment preachers inculcated the traditional doctrine that
Christians must live in their callings, and tried to remind them that those
profiting from their occupations should thank religion for their gains, they
found themselves urging acquiescence upon men who cherished grievances.
They poured fuel on the fires of antiministerial sentiment by addressing
various groups as though each was irrevocably appointed to a particular
place in a static edifice, when in fact each was fighting tooth and nail for
advantage. (Leather Apron Man, forsooth!) Here once more the New
England mind had inherited a concept it knew not how to surrender:
just as it strove to retain the doctrine that government is an ordinance of
God even while gradually accepting the philosophy of chartered rights, so
it clung to this primitive conception that gradations in society are divine
appointments, that a body politic is a hierarchy. Preachers still used "order"
to mean not civil peace but distinction of rank: "For the strength and glory
of a politick body, consists in a great measure in a variety of parts, fitted
to discharge the functions of their respective places, and in the proportion
of these parts to the whole, and one another." This precept, said Pemberton in 1714, "stands in opposition to pragmaticalness, impertinency, and
playing the Busy-body"; it forbids encroachments, especially of inferior
upon superior. Before 1730 this premise was never seriously called in question, even in the roughest political strife. No matter what experience suggested, ministers insisted that men are "fixed" in their class; the goodness
or even the justness of a rebellious action is no excuse: "if in the doing it
men break their Ranks, and step out of their Places, God will not be well
Pleased with them." With a single voice (except John Wise's) all this
literature condemns as licentious any "levelling Spirit that would have all
men alike."

Meanwhile, however, the social reality was anything but static. Not

only were new men coming up and old names going down—a phenomenon still as bewildering as it had been for theorists of the second generation—but the community had become an arena for conflict, amid which
no rational system of subordination could any longer be made out. Status
was not the same thing it had been, nor could it be treated as "fixed." For
if now there were class distinctions, these clearly were determined not by
any archetypal structure but quite simply by wealth got in competition; the
bases of all conceptions of order were threatened not by an insurgency of
levelers but by business rivals who sought to impoverish each other, or else
by Lords Commissioners for a Crown to which loyalty must constantly be
proclaimed. The clergy had made one union indissoluble: "Religion and
Property are the two great things that are dear unto a People that are
not abandoned of God." But it was one thing to preach a serene pattern
of manifold subordinations, and quite another to say, as did even Joseph
Moss for all his Whig principles, that rulers ought to be men of good
estate because the poor are "apt to be of mean and mercenary Spirits."
Welding the cause of religion to that of property might be a clever means
of obliging champions of property to protect the churches; but it also
meant that when spokesmen for religion undertook to instruct the people
in obedience, to urge upon them resignation to fixed status, they in effect
made Christianity a minion of property. In the name of piety, they required the poor to be content with poverty.

This was not what the original philosophy (with its sharply defined conception of social gradations) had ever intended, for that had centered upon
a conception of mutual obligation as well as of privilege. Over class lines
hovered the standard of the good, just, and honest; its distinctions were
never of rich against poor, but among degrees of culture, and it had not
been concerned whether John Cotton or Thomas Hooker possessed less
wealth than John Winthrop. In an entirely different frame of reference
the community had agreed in 1630 that as a matter of course Winthrops
and Dudleys should be rulers; in 1719 Cotton Mather was crying out
upon the sins of Boston, grieving that merchants should oppress the country,
or the country the town. "Who," he asked, "does the Oppression chiefly
fall upon?" and had to answer, "Not so much upon the Rich as upon the
Poor." Hence there sounded a peculiar hollowness in pompous assertions
that levelism was impious when all the while the poor were being told that
they were not qualified for rule because, lacking property, they were of
a mean and mercenary spirit. What a providential opportunity this provided an Elisha Cooke to increase his vast holdings by mobilizing the
propertyless?

The founders had been anything but democrats: yet leaders of the Great
Migration universally assumed that were God to bless the covenant of
the people, those whom Winthrop unhesitatingly called "the meaner sort"
would thrive more in New England than in old. Indeed, that the meaner
would advance, while those able to invest estates in the civic enterprise

stood to lose, was an axiomatic assumption of the men who took upon themselves the burden of command—a conception of *noblesse oblige* to which shrewd traders like John Hull and Samuel Sewall were still bound. But we have recorded with what a shock the second generation realized that somehow, despite the rich opportunities of land and sea, despite the ethic of pious labor, New England had a pauper class on its hands. Clerical theorists of the covenant then responded by denouncing those who ground the faces of the poor, excoriated capitalists, and sublimated consternation into redemption by suffering. For a generation or more, this eloquence carried the community; precisely because the jeremiad, by insistently arraigning social evils, never gave over the hope of rectification—never gave over expounding in concrete detail just what enormities would be chastized and what trials rewarded—it never saw poverty as the inescapable burden of the poor. It always said that, come the reformation, indigence would be abolished. Possibly in the last half of the century this formula continued to be effective because penury still stopped short of destitution. But early in the eighteenth century, the preachers themselves had to admit that oppression of the poor had become a habit, and by the wearisome repetition of their complaint confess that such injustices, being merely deplorable, would never be redressed. A certain cynicism crept into the forensic delivery, as preachers strove to find the lot of the poor not really so bad as their own lamentations had earlier pictured it. In New England, Cotton Mather learned to say, the poor—although greatly increased and much afflicted—are more comfortably provided for than elsewhere; they ought, instead of complaining, to say, "God hath not so dealt with the rest of the poor in our Nation, or scarce in any Nation." In 1719 Benjamin Colman stepped out of his pulpit to tell the town authorities that they should establish a regular market: the fathers, he admitted, had not seen this necessity, but "they were not quite enough Men of this world for us"; though they took great care for our minds and souls, they "were a little too Negligent of those mortal Bodies." A market would, he felt, improve virtue and good morals, but there was, he conceded, a danger that once goods were spread out in such display, the poor would be tempted to buy the best. To this objection he could answer only by revealing what had gradually become the tacit premise of clerical admonitions to that class:

They that are poorer in worldly state should and must give way to the Rich. Who but they ordinarily should buy the dearest and best of the kind? Providence means it for them. It is the Government of Heaven; let us submit to it. GOD has given into their hand more abundantly . . . Now & then we that are poorer may tast of the best too and be thankful. But we should be willing to live low, where God has set us.

Seldom did a cleric let himself speak so openly (the frankness of this statement needs to be balanced against the courtly sanity Colman exhibited in the smallpox argument). Nevertheless, the disguise wore progressively thinner; there wanted little wit indeed to perceive that commiseration from the pulpit, in the sign of an ordered and unalterable philosophy of society, meant only that the poor were poor.

"God is said to be the maker of the Rich and Poor" thus became the social content of official Puritanism. The poor should not repine, said Increase Mather, because though they be mean in the eye of the world ("it may be they go in Leather Cloathes"), they may by their piety prove blessings to society "and keep off destroying Judgments." Complacency was implied, on the one hand, by exhortations to the rich to give more abundantly to charity (in these years that word took on the restricted meaning unknown to John Winthrop) and by funereal praises of those who had devoted their estates to the poor (accompanied with shocked exclamations that there were some "unto whom God gave Riches, but they have not Willed so much as one Penny to the Poor, or to any Pious use"), and, on the other, by a number of works addressed, shamelessly, to the poor as an incurable class. By 1716 Cotton Mather deigned to tell them that "To Receive Alms, with such a lowly Mind, as becomes them who need them, is as great a Grace, as to Bestow them." They should thank God that He has commanded "us" to help: "Your Benefactor is but the Instrument of Heaven in what is done for you"; should you, after this bounty, become vicious, "or if you should Steal, as the Poor sometimes do," you will suffer spiritual pangs. Mather was not yet a Gradgrind, but he was closer to him than to the first legislators of the colonies; there was not yet an Oliver Twist to ask for more, but Mather tried to forestall him: beware of this, he warned the poor, if you cannot bear poverty on earth, "with a Submission of Soul to the Thing Appointed for you, 'tis very certain, your Preparation for Heaven, has but very Dark Symptoms upon it." As for the hope—or at least the expectation—that had stirred the meaner sort among the immigrants, that egalitarian prospect was postponed: "The Grave, the Grand Leveller, will quickly bring the Rich and the Poor to be upon Equal Terms; One shall not be upon Higher Ground than another, when Both are Laid under Ground." The language of these passages—of which there are thousands—shows the equanimity with which, along with mechanical admonitions against oppression, the inherited philosophy of class distinction had subsided into a single dimension. "If Great Things are carv'd out unto one person, and Small Things unto another, it is the Hand of Divine Providence that has the carving of them." Strangely enough, a few who went "in Leather Cloathes" were reluctant to submit to such carving.

Preachers regularly demanded reformation of the social sins upon pain of immediate judgment; but a smug acceptance of economic inequality in a system where lesser grades had no other function in the cosmos than to let their benefactors be instruments of heaven (and then to refrain from stealing) could not support convincing threats of retribution. The national covenant had been made with a society ordered in seried ranks, like a regiment going into battle; victory or defeat could be promised according to its courage and vigor. But with a class alignment resulting from depreciation or the high cost of imports, how could a covenant be framed? Piety might still serve to facilitate happiness, at least by teaching contentment to the impoverished; if so, although jeremiads could be reeled off by the yard, something else was needed, some new form of marketing religion in a bourgeois community.

In their new awareness that style was a virtue, New Englanders learned to use the adjective "nervous." Cotton Mather, whose addresses to the poor are among the most brutal, was in a hundred respects too neurotic a creature to be quite typical of his generation; yet, possibly because of that disability, he was the most hypersensitive to the slightest nuance. Twisted though his record of the epoch may be, it provides insights into tensions which his less nervous contemporaries, whose dullness preserved them from shocks he daily suffered, could not so vividly appreciate. They were obliged to follow his lead; he created the forms in which Puritan piety might organize itself into effective expression, in which it might prove its utility in a world where prices, wages, and civil rights had displaced the good, just, and honest.

In the spring of 1692 he stood on the pinnacle of success—or of what the New England priest and statesman would call success. The regime had emerged out of the Dominion with nothing lost; it was, if anything, strengthened by the charter. Because those features of the old order that had become obnoxious to England were removed, provincial orthodoxy had the field to itself. Increase's concessions were all acquisitions, power was in the right hands, to be rightly used. But for Cotton Mather, life thereafter was continuous and unrelenting defeat, beginning with the mortal stroke of witchcraft, coming down to the insults he had finally to endure from the *Courant*. Upon him, as perhaps upon no other man living through what Paul Hazard calls the crisis of the European conscience, fell the burden of that transition: every event—Harvard College, Brattle Street, Stoddard's defection, Dudley's rule and the Vetch affair, Wise's libel, Cooke's insurgence, the effrontery of the land bank, of the *Courant* and the anti-inoculationists, the shift of patriotism from piety to profit—left him shorn of power, of prestige, and of influence, thrown back upon himself, terrified and isolated.

However, he was not the man to break, or to admit defeat. The result of all this experience was a complicated series of psychological movements deep within him which were methods for healing internal wounds or for overcoming external reverses. The intellectual history of Cotton Mather exhibits a dual response, one inward and another outward—a retreat into imaginative triumph and a compensatory going forth into the world. Each of his gestures has a representative quality beyond its merely biographical significance; taken together, they are the pattern of mind imposed upon Puritanism by the ordeal of leaving the Middle Ages. Each is symbolic of the generation; the two are complementary and have meaning only in relation to each other.

For him as for his contemporaries, the covenant was still the basic conception, and was bound to be the innermost meaning both of nature and of economics. The jolt of external defeat forced him to seek for covenantal reassurances within. Under this compulsion he worked out his notion of "a particular faith"—of a promise given to the saint not for life as a whole, not for society, but for a specific occasion. Ransacking the federal theology for bits and pieces, he was driven to the furthest extreme of subjectivism ever to constrict the Puritan mind. He tried to preserve the covenant by atomizing it.

A particular faith, as Mather defined it, is an irradiation of the soul, a marvelous persuasion, a comfort, which comes at the moment of intense prayer "for this or that particular Smile of God." It is different from an ordinary expectation of a general good, such as for church or country, because it has to do with a concrete request by a particular individual, and is accompanied by "a Strong Impression made upon his mind, which Dissolves him in a Flood of Tears, and Assures him, Thou shalt have the Petition which thou Desirest of thy God." It is an impression borne upon him with as full a force as though it were "Articulately" pronounced. It is a psychological discharge, filling him with a heavenly glow, leaving him with the luster of an excellent spirit. But it is not mystical vision, neither is it settled confidence: it is merely a relieving of anxiety about some one worry. It is not granted to all, even to saints; to any one saint, it comes only intermittently. A believer cannot cause himself to have it, but on his knees, after a day of fasting and weeping, it may visit him. Precisely because it is finite and not general, it cannot be described to natural men, any more than an idea of color can be conveyed to those born blind.

This peculiar visitation frequently invigorated Cotton Mather, usually, he tells us, when he was prostrate in the dust of his study floor. Whether this signifies that the housekeeping of his various Mesdames Mather was remiss, or that they were not allowed to invade the study with so vulgar an object as the broom, is unknown; possibly it means that the experience was so ecstatic as to be expressible only in hyperbole. "What is the Meaning of this Operation? Whence comes it? Who gives it? How far is it akin to the Faith of Miracles? or, is it all a meer Delusion?" This last question is crucial: again and again practitioners of the method were deceived, none more cruelly than Mather himself, who several times received particular faiths, for instance, that his father would go to England and procure a charter for Harvard College. But to raise the question, "How do I know this operation from a Counterfeit?" only made the adventure of consciousness more exhilarating. In the search for a particular faith, saints who had come to take the Covenant of Grace for granted, who had become casehardened in convention, could recapture those ardors of soul the founders had experienced when translating the energies of conversion into theorems of ecclesiastical polity. And the beauty of it was that this ecstasy might be repeated indefinitely, out of an unending potency; from each success the believer could arise refreshed, as he could no longer be replenished by the institutionalized covenant of the nation.

Unwary seekers, hearing themselves cry aloud that God had heard them, have run abroad with nothing but a notion, "and made a very Formal and punctual Story upon it"; thereafter, the thing failing, "all the whole Particular Faith remains only to be Laugh'd at." Particularism is a dangerous business to trifle with (as Kierkegaard was to warn a later period); ordinary people should be content "with the Ordinary Satisfaction of Praying and so waiting for the Blessings of God," in comfortable uncertainty. But for those who have the courage, who can shut the door, go hungry, lie for hours in the dust, the reward is priceless: anxiety falls away, foes are rendered powerless, and in due time the one specific thing assured, whether it be a copy of the *Magnalia* or the death of Dr. Noyes, comes to pass exactly as promised.

Few of Mather's contemporaries were sufficiently brave or strenuous to venture as far as he into this labyrinth; some who tried it, despite his cautions, came to grief. An easier and more viable method for stimulating a flow of emotional juices was what he called "daily spiritualizing." He was initiated into this technique by reading a new type of Puritan literature invented after the Restoration, the chief exemplar being John Flavel's *Husbandry Spiritualized* of 1669. The Puritan mind was given to allegory, as Bunyan and (according to some) Hawthorne demonstrate; but Flavel's method was allegory turned inside out: instead of starting with abstract propositions and embodying them in figures like Ignorance or Giant Despair, he commenced from the outside, taking some observable fact—an operation on the farm—and by analyzing it as though it were already the given allegory, extracted from it the abstraction. The more ingenious, the more strained was the lesson taken out of the concrete, the better; this was not, like the particular faith, a private speech but a public. Neither was Flavel's method what the Ramist-trained founders meant by a metaphor or simile: he did not say that the fallen sinner was like a child lost at the fair, but concentrated upon a fragment of experience already provided, took it into his being, and there let it fructify into an exclamation or, as Cotton Mather liked to call it, an "ejaculation." (James Franklin's fatal sketch of the hypocrite has him constantly uttering ejaculations!)

Mather expounded the procedure: it is putting to highest uses the creatures who surround us, deriving from them not only spirituality "but also Ingenuity." It is to see heavenly light constantly descending in an earthly garment, it can be employed in all trades and occupations, in every act of life, even the meanest. "Emptying the Cistern of Nature" at a wall, Mather was joined by a dog, who did likewise; the spiritualization was immediate: "What mean, and vile Things are the Children of Men, in this mortal State! How much do our natural Necessities abase us, and place us in some regard, on the same Level with the very Dogs." To master this habit is to enjoy a double advantage: hungers of the spirit can be indefinitely fed—"Soul, snatch at all Handles for such Thoughts, and being Taught of God, thou will find them Innumerable, Innumerable"—and yet piety be kept alive in the midst of such distractions as modern society imposes upon citizens. These "little Fragments and Filings of our Golden Time" may be accumulated "in the Intervals of our Business." Although a more facile, and in that sense a more democratic method, daily spiritualizing, like the particular faith, is adapted to a universe in which the overriding concern has become the finite.

Hence reasons for the vogue of this plebeian typology in the society of the moment are not far to seek: it followed upon a disintegration of the political vision, when true saints had been forced into the shop and the closet. It was compensation for public failure, a way of living with a world that had become too much for them. Bunyan might still conceive the Christian pilgrimage as an epic drama and so make the visible universe subserve his allegory, just as the new Model Army could scatter Rupert's cavaliers; but later on, the universe proved obstinate and recalcitrant, demanding to be treated for what it was. Thrust back into the self, the trembling soul looked at first timorously upon the things amid which God had placed him, and then found that there might be joy in the excitements they aroused within him. In Mather's day the Puritan began to say, as Emily Dickinson would still say, "Better an *ignis fatuus* Than no illume at all." This sort of joyousness might or might not be shared, but it soothed the perceiver in great part because of the element contributed by his own ingenuity.

Cotton Mather assiduously practiced this genre, publishing monographs on how to spiritualize thunder, fair weather, winter, the fire, the techniques of sailors or hunters, summer, tempests, rainbows, rain. One of these expositions is revealingly entitled *Stimulator*. For an early work, *Winter Meditations* in 1693, old John Higginson wrote a preface, setting forth what he thought Mather was about: the works of God are the proper subjects of natural philosophy, but they may also be studied theologically in relation to the Final Cause which is God. But Higginson had not quite grasped the new idea: he was still thinking in terms of scholastic physics, whereas the point of Mather's treatment was not rational speculation upon the frame of the universe but a utilization of given objects for an ingenious gratification. He wanted to make them serve as "engines of piety," stimuli for "Ejaculatory" prayers. His most ambitious production in this vein was *Agricola*, in 1727, which was a redoing of Flavel for the New England landscape: three ministers attested the first edition, and the second was endorsed by Wadsworth and Colman, along with all the new recruits to Mather's party. "To Spiritualize the Common Actions of Life, and make a religious Improvement of worldly Affairs," the book said, "is an holy and happy Art." What it did not quite say was that by popularizing this art, certain pious ends might be won even though the saints no longer controlled the state; the endorsers hoped it would be acceptable "in a Country the Business of which is mostly Husbandry, and which has been famous for religious Husbandmen." It ought to be effective, because it is written "with that Fervour and Pungency which is so peculiar to the author." The clerical interest would not be lost, nor would commerce stifle piety, if New Englanders could be taught to see God in every thing, "from the Sun in the Firmament, to the Stone in the Pavement."

Had these inventions signified merely a surrender of the outer and political world, a retreat to contemplation, they would be easier to comprehend. But in psychological fact, their effect was the opposite: they were recoilings from society only for a new and more vigorous assault, they generated energies for conquest under an inspired change of tactics. A people who had become passive under the lash of jeremiads, who could no longer see the relevance of a national covenant to their daily grind of husbandry, fishing or merchandizing, could be stirred once more by direct admonitions of divinity through the things they constantly beheld:

> What is that thou seest there? Behold, A Cloud! A Cloud! Seest thou not a Cloud that looks big upon thee, and seems a lasting Storehouse for the Treasures of God! But how long will this Cloud continue there? Tis vanishing, Twill disappear, how suddenly!

However, before this method could work, one further purging of traditional hermeneutics was required: the foreground between the preacher and his audience had to be cleared of a litter of half-demolished scholasticisms. Technicians had to sweep these into the refuse bin along with the just price, along with those refined but now meaningless discriminations among the preliminary stages of humiliation, preparation, contrition, and implantation, which had formerly served to encourage but had lately done nothing but confuse and discourage. Mather struck the note as soon as Andros was removed: ministers must henceforth resolve to give the people not "Windy and Empty Speculations . . . but solemn and useful Admonitions, about Faith and Repentance." It is enough if New Englanders categorically deny that they are Arminians without entering into metaphysical niceties about the two covenants; thus they could get on with serving God. The "vitals" of Christianity, he was shrieking by 1702, are not opinions but righteousness: "To what purpose is it, for a man to Deny Free-will to Good in the Unregenerate if the man remain himself Unregenerate?"

In that spirit Mather early began, and strove all his life, to produce catechisms and creedal formulations of ever briefer compass, "adapted unto Children, and People of the lowest Capacity," striving to perfect an "Epitome" which would contain "the Substance of all the Sermons, that are ever Preached." He boasted at last that he had accommodated the cate-

chism to the rudest understanding, so that a bare yes or no would be adequate answer; he became so expert that he composed catechisms in French
—"S'appliquent principalement aux bonnes oeuvres"—and for Negroes and
Indians. Triumphantly in 1711 he so squeezed the sum and substance of
doctrine that it could be "Contrived into a single sheet." Of like nature
were his many handbooks of practical piety—*Family-Religion Excited and
Assisted*, or *Religion of the Closet*—some of which went through numerous editions, in his own lifetime and afterwards. His faction followed his
example, so that among them appears no such sustained theological disquisitions as was, for example, Stoddard's *Safety of Appearing* or even his less
technical *Guide to Christ*. Their opponents made some attempts: Colman
wrote at length but felicitously upon the incomprehensibility of God, and
students of Leverett, notably Appleton, produced essays on such topics as
the wisdom of God in the redemption of man; but Matherians wrote
characteristically upon *Morning Health No Security against the Sudden
Arrest of Death Before Night, The Duty of Every Man to be Always
Ready to Die*, or *A Discourse Concerning Kindness*.

We need not seek outside the circle of pressures arising within the society to account for this turning toward simplicity. However, the movement
was guided by English models; there also, leaders laboring under the
Clarendon Code were forced to keep the party alive by shoving aside
doctrinal hair-splitting and concentrating upon simple faith. Hundreds of
manuals produced for this purpose were reprinted in Boston, to join the
flow of domestic efforts. But as time went on, Mather and his friends came
to the marvelous discovery that by reacting merely to their own necessities
they had, all unknowingly, moved with the times; instead of rallying a
desperate hope, they were in the vanguard of progress. Chiefly through
Mather's far-flung correspondence, they learned of Francke and the great
work at Halle, and of corresponding manifestations in Holland, all seeking "to advance True, Real, Vital Piety," foretending "a Glorious Revival
of the Primitive." What had commenced in New England as a furtive
maneuver, a timid endeavor to rescue religion from sterility by methods
which, in the canons of the founders, seemed tawdry, proved to be a
providential falling in step with the progressive march of the century.

There has been awakened of late Years, in the Minds of Men, a vehement
Inclination to shake off those Religious Formalities, by which they do not find
themselves brought nearer to GOD; and to get more into a Real, Vital, Spiritual
Religion, and such as will have the Life of God in the Soul of Man, with a more
transforming Energy operating in it. Multitudes and Millions of People, are at this
Day, both among the Romanists and among the Protestants, thus disposed; and the
Disposition which is now too much imprisoned in Unrighteousness, will one Day
break forth with an astonishing Revolution upon the World.

Suddenly, out of the hesitations, confusions, out of the abject conviction
of inadequacy and of guilt, there was born in New England a new spirit,

a new Puritanism, toward which the society had blindly groped, toward which it was driven by frontier slaughter and political dissensions, by forces it had not understood. Old words took on vibrant meanings, particularly when spelled in capitals, and especially "PIETY." The astonishing revolution, with its charged sense of vitality and energy, aimed to conquer not the forms of government (to which it was indifferent) but the hearts of men, and so to achieve that social regeneration for which the jeremiad, captive to the intellectualism of the covenant, had pled in vain.

The time is not far off, exulted Cotton Mather, when, to the tune of "tremendous Concussions, and Convulsions, and Confusions upon the Nations," will be felt the approach of this purely pietistic power, when men shall be disentangled from the follies to which "Sectaries" have bound them, when "this Panting and Heaving Tendency to Reformation will beat down all before it," and nothing shall obstruct the Kingdom of God "from appearing in an Universal Reign of Holiness and Righteousness among the Nations." Sewall, Prince, Foxcroft, and Cooper joined—although not always with such Chiliastic assurance—in hailing the dawn of the century as an era in which piety, and piety alone, would accomplish the tendency of our spirits to reunion with God, would attain the goal to which the Reformation had aspired but been unable to reach because it had been hobbled with scholasticism.

What had been required, in the way of bombardment of their nerves, to excite within men this vision of the kingdom on earth, I have endeavored to relate. The most skeptical can understand how in the clanking days of the Roman Empire, to the sound of legions' tread, a voice had arisen saying that the kingdom is within; history is not amazed that in the turmoil of the English Civil Wars overheated imaginations had struck out for the Fifth Monarchy and attempted to enthrone purity. But the commotions of New England were not spectacular; ostensibly its history was a gradual evolution, from a charter government by saints to a charter expounded in the name of property rights. Where was the aggravation? It is no answer to say that all the leaders were, even if not quite so obviously as Cotton Mather, neurotics; the forces that wrought this transformation can be summarized: the growth of a capitalist economy, imperial interference, an enforced yielding to toleration, class struggles. The result can be given a name: Pietism. What had happened here was that, under the impact of the blows, mild as they may seem, of the repeal of the charter, of fragmentation in ecclesiastical and political theory, the human spirit sought for surcease. It found that life might yet be worth living if piety could still pervade society.

Obviously, one advantage of accepting a Pietistic point of view was that worries over diversity of sects became irrelevant; with the abandonment of that concern, the fissiparous era of Protestantism, with all its violence, would be closed. Could the creed be simplified and controversial articles dismissed as things man no longer has time or inclination to fight about, then no one formulation would remain standard. God "will form a New People of the Good Men, who shall Unite in Articles of their Goodness, and sweetly bear with one another in their Lesser Differences." If the essentials can be contracted into a single sheet, therein "all, that are Men of Understanding, will find Satisfaction." All mankind will agree "in the Grand Point of Practical Piety." Precisely there, in fact, was the thumbscrew turned every day upon spokesmen for New England: they did not want to yield to the Church of England, nor let Quakers and Baptists escape the rates, but how could they resist unless their own people stood firm? But to raise, in the eighteenth century, the banner of a sect, and to expect a busy population to come out of the woods, fields, and shops in order to fight and die for a denominational cause was absurd. How else, then, could they reorganize or recapture this society except by letting the covenant slide, by enlisting everybody in the army of "Practical Piety," and so solve the problem of religious liberty by playing down sectarian distinctions? If not only minority religious groups but factionalists of any sort could be convincingly shown the vision of vital religion, strife would come to a halt, antiministerial sentiment evaporate, and freedom of conscience become so much a matter of course that mere piety could administer an essential uniformity.

This would be feasible if, in dismissing unprofitable speculations in theology, the ancient controversy concerning dependence of good works upon election and true faith could also be forgotten. For generations, abstruse refinements about hypocrisy, preparation, and the abilities of half-way members had driven the community distracted. Was it not enough to say, once grace was identified with the all-inclusive term of piety, that good works are pious and that good men do them? Thereupon, preachers were no longer obliged to fritter away their energies proving that sanctification has no value except as a consequence of justification, but could call upon the wealthy to contribute to "charity," or upon the poor not to repine. Motives were still to be searched; but the criterion of acceptability was now perceived on every side: piety, as distinguished from the faith of the fathers, proved its worth by contributing, out of particular faiths and the spiritualization of occupations, to happiness.

The difficulty in describing the forces at work in the intellection of these years is to avoid overstatement: in 1700 Willard delivered a memorable speech on the theme that morality is not to be relied upon; periodically the most socially minded reverted to flat statements that those already adopted can do a good act. Cotton Mather frequently got far ahead of his most devoted disciples, who cautiously allocated portions of their writings to safeguarding their Calvinist orthodoxy. Yet herein lies precisely the point of this revolution: it was not enacted in the sphere of ideas, it did not challenge creeds or raise doctrinal heresies—it was staged in the heart and among the affections, and stressed old morals in new ways. We never dare say, wrote Increase Mather in 1710, that if men improve their natural abilities, grace will infallibly follow. No, not the furthest extension of the Half-Way Covenant ever explicitly came to that: still, "there will not one Sinner in all the Reprobate World, stand forth at the Day of Judgment, and say, Lord, Thou knowest I did all that possibly I could do, for the obtaining Grace, and for all that, Thou didst withhold it from me." However, in the first years of the Half-Way Covenant, sinners had not known precisely what they had to do to obtain grace. In 1706 Eliphalet Adams could give them the hint they long had been wanting: "since we are Set in Communities together, there are accordingly Social Virtues which must be Exercis'd toward each other." Out of his morbidly increasing awareness of this dimension, Cotton Mather led the way toward what we must call Pietism; although never admittedly surrendering a syllable of *The Westminster Confession*, he still wrote, in gratitude for his Doctor's Degree, to the University of Glasgow that Protestant scholarship had produced an honorable array of "Books full of matchless Reading and Criticism and Argument," but that the surest way of defending truth is to live it. "Light without Flame is the Scandal of our Protestant Profession, and would threaten the Ruine of it." In 1725, in a tract bearing another of his significant titles, *Vital Christianity*, he was straining to push the age along the road he foresaw: "our Faith its self will not be found good and profitable if Good Works do not follow upon it."

Out of this background of tension and introversion—out of, in brief, the implicit contradiction between Calvinism and the temper of the times —emerges the epochal treatise Cotton Mather published in 1710. Under its running title, *Essays to Do Good*, the book fully entitled *Bonifacius, an Essay upon the Good that is to be Devised and Designed by those Who Desire . . . to Do Good While they Live,* supplied the perfect slogan for a generation aware that Puritanism had somehow to kindle the flame without which its light was burning cold. In terms of the particular social and intellectual process we have laboriously traced, it is possibly the most important work in the early eighteenth century. It is not, like anything of Stoddard's, the expression of a militant segment of the country; it is not, like a work of John Wise's, original, nor is it, like Dummer's *Defence,* patriotic. Yet it comes straight out of the center of this culture and is profound because it discovers the greatest common denominator. Of all Mather's writings, it was by far the most popular, running through eighteen editions well into the nineteenth century, in all of which time it was not a curiosity but an "engine of piety." With diabolical cunning, Benjamin Franklin took unto himself the cognomen of Silence (since Cotton Mather was possessed, according to the *Courant,* of an irresistible itch for scribbling) Dogood, a blasphemy for which he did penance in his old age by confessing to Samuel Mather (the same who as "John Harvard" satirized the style of the Papers) that the *Essays* had an influence on his conduct through life, "for I have always set a greater value on the character of a doer of good than on any other kind of reputation; and if I have been, as you seem to think, a useful citizen, the public owes the advantage of it to that book."

The volume may owe something to a work of Baxter's published in 1682, but undoubtedly owes more to reports reaching New England around 1700–1710 about the formation in England of societies for the reformation of manners. These did, in fact, express in Britain aspirations of the sort Mather entertained: they were rallyings of the Nonconformist conscience in an effort to recapture, by nonpolitical means, moral territory lost to the Restoration, and precisely in these terms did the Mathers appreciate them: "A Flood of Debauchery and Profanity hath even overwhelmed the Land, and appears too strong yet, for the Societies of Reformation to conquer it: Tho' we have cause to bless God, for those Good Societies, and some Good that hath been done by them." Each year the two Mathers and their followers described, praised, and tried to organize such societies; the deeper they penetrated into this realm, the more they realized that here lay a formula for accord through which pious interests might yet dominate the community, a mechanism even more promising than had been the United Brethren and the associations. Exactly because the movement had no political affiliations it could more efficiently organize social pressures. "Why should not our Natural Affection to Society, be Sublimated into a Religious Affection, to Associate for the Interests of Religion?" Could a *Courant,* even though legally guaranteed freedom of expression, find an audience in a town so organized? The Matherian party, to be sure, did not abandon the jeremiad; instead, they took refuge in it whenever disappointments seemed more than they could bear, but in between these moments of dejection they did more than call for a spontaneous demonstration: they girded themselves to go out and get it. If all our exertions amount to no more than "For Sensible Persons in a Scattered way to discern and bewayl our Distresses, and not Unite in Endeavours that we may all get out of them; This will be but a poor Procedure." In sober fact, the *Essays* may be a more modern book than any of Stoddard's or Wise's: its exhortation is, "Sirs, You must Get up and be doing." The founders, we know, had been able to get up and do, but they were incapable of thus talking about it.

While the project may seem on the surface merely an elaborate scheme for minding other people's business, *Essays to Do Good* is fundamentally an effort to make society center upon the life of piety; were the enterprise to succeed, the life of politics and business (not to mention journalism) would become subordinate. Here is a prophecy of Protestant, small-town, Middle Western culture of the nineteenth century; the book hails the advent of Main Street, when the emergence of that way of life promised more than spiritual starvation. Indeed, some of the activities prescribed for these societies were enough, even in Mather's New England, to outrage their intended victims. He besought the groups to inform against blasphemers and swearers, to admonish misbehaving acquaintances, and to suppress "Base Houses." He called his methods "Unexceptionable," and so they would seem to all but their objects. Yet that was exactly what the whole doctrine needed, a sufficient number of the disreputable to be given the treatment. Not merely out of vanity did Cotton Mather devote pages of his book to the spite and insult the doer of good must expect to receive from ingrates for whom he exerts himself: this was a way of bracing others to do good though it killed them. He was arming them against what piety had now most to fear, not persecution and the stake, but "that way of Banter, and Scoffing, and Ridicule, or the Bart'lemew-Fair Method," which, unless countered, could more discourage goodness than fire and fagots. In the same devious manner, he girded the clergy to resist antiministerial sentiment and wheeled embattled societies into action by their side: "Your Salaries will be meaner than even those at Geneva. They will Neglect you; they will Oppress you; they will Defraud you, of what they have Engaged, and you have Expected"—but not if the minister, instructed by the *Essays*, founds in his town an energetic society for reformation of manners!

That Mather's program was not successful in chastening the opposition in country towns, or that despite his injunctions to do good congregations continued to do their pastors ill, is of less importance than the terms in which Mather addressed them. He constructed his analysis upon a list of social characteristics: what the doing of good means as concerns children, servants, and neighbors; how ministers, schoolmasters, physicians, ladies, lawyers should do good, and then how society should pool its resources into meetings for reformation of manners. In the end, all are woven together in a net of obligation, mutual responsibility, and involvement, from which escape is virtually impossible. They are not knit together as one man in Winthrop's sense, but tied into the pattern of a mutual aid society where the weight of each other's opinion becomes compulsive and that of public opinion irresistible. He instructs societies not to backbite or gossip, and by the same token shows that he would take such care to avoid dissension that any open deviation from the group would become supremely difficult: their discourse must be about "not the Disputable and Controversial Matters, but the Points of Practical Piety." Thus engines of piety would become engines of conformity; the man who would go aside by himself, into profanity or to Walden Pond, who would broach a controversial topic or refuse to be pawed by reforming institutions, would stand before the community automatically convicted of antisocial propensities. Against a society Cotton Mather had imbued with this presumption, James Franklin tried to make headway.

The book cannot altogether mask, even though it tries, the one weakness in the scheme: Mather has to discuss what good ought to be done by magistrates. He begs them to give preferment to men of virtue, to enforce laws, but the vagueness of his generalized appeal (in contrast to the bill of particulars, for instance, which he imposes on lawyers) shows that the

whole project is in fact intended to get along without them. In that sense
it is a farewell to the seventeenth century; but it is no less so in the realm
of theology. The first thing, in order to do good, is to be born again—but
the proposition that works follow grace is transformed: after warning that
we must not make good actions the "matter" of salvation, Mather rapidly
insists that the marks of true faith are to be found in an abundance of them,
that none does so many as he who has abandoned all pretences to merit.
But the old theology is left even further behind as, throughout the discussion, the real incentive to doing good is made a delicious, swooning joy
of the thing itself: "It is an Incomparable Pleasure," and a man "must
Embrace it with Rapture." There is not a single proposal here advanced
but what, well pursued, "would yield the mind a more Solid and Lasting
Satisfaction, than the Solution of all the Problems in Euclid."

These passages link the emotions discovered through an ecstatic rape
of a particular faith or through symbolizing the commonplace with the
drive manifested in organized benevolence. "O Rational, Immortal,
Heaven-born SOUL; Are thy wondrous Faculties capable of no Greater
Improvement, no better Employments?" The answer comes rolling back:
"Assume and Assert the Liberty of now and then Thinking on the Noblest
Question in the World; What Good may I do in the World?" What all
these tendencies have in common, that they are schemes for recovering
a lost world, Mather helps us to grasp by calling upon society to do good
for tradesmen by supplying them with spiritualized treatments of their base
occupations: "To spread the Nets of Salvation for men, in the ways of their
Personal Callings, and convey Good Thoughts unto them, in the terms
and Steps of their Daily Business, is a Real Service to the Interests of
Piety." Preachers are to serve the same purpose by livening up logical
sermons with ejaculations, and with even more: they will do most good
by letting people see them "Praying, and Weeping, and Striving." Joseph
Sewall, to take one example, soon gained such a reputation as the weeping
preacher as would, I am confident, have made Thomas Hooker retch.

Thus the book proposes that nets of salvation be spread throughout
society without the help of compulsive magistrates, of systematic theology,
or of even an established church. The whole pyramid of doing good comes
to its apex in the doing of good to the poor, and so in rescuing society
from itself; the organized bands might levy fines upon their members
for breach of manners, and so collect a tidy sum: "The Poor, the Poor
will be far the better for them!" The crown of delight, the exquisite joy
beyond joy which a man cannot express though he were master of seven
languages and had feasted upon all the curiosities of learning—the most
"Ravishing Satisfaction"—is to be found "in relieving the Distresses of a
Poor, Mean, Miserable Neighbour." To modern ears this appeal has become so (to say the least) conventionalized, we can hardly comprehend
the fervor with which it was first propounded; in 1719 Cotton Mather
gave another of his inimitable glimpses into the motive behind it: "My

Friends, Allow me to address you after this Manner: Associate your selves, O ye People, that he may not be broken in pieces."

For us, critical evaluation of the *Essays* seems to involve a contradiction: clearly the book is a response to, or a recognition of, a social change that has gone in the direction of competition, the open market, liberty of conscience and of religious indifference, of limitation of power by law and the inviolability of constitutional rights. All of those changes have been wrought within the society which now becomes the object of benevolence; yet the book and the movement are not concessions to this revolution, but a counterrevolution. The motto of do-good was not what young Franklin made of Dogood, a cry for freedom; it was a calculated plot for the reestablishment of unity. "Instead of contriving every one to enlarge his own Little Party, would Good Men Unite in promoting that Piety which all good Men in every Party confess to be the main Interest, the World would soon feel the Blessed Effects of such Associations." What could not be done by law or ecclesiastical censure could be done by the club, the fraternity, the lodge or the social class. "It is a remarkable Work of God," said Danforth, "to Unite the Hearts of good Men in determining what ought to be done for the Promoting of Religion." Mather's friends expressed it a thousand times: Cooper, for example, in 1716: "True Piety, as it will not let Men live to a bad end, so it can't but make them to live to some good end; and none are so Publicly Useful, such Universal Blessings as are the Pious and Godly." Colman was more suave, but he joined the crusade: men are formed for society and mutual dependence, and none is so destitute but what he "will find many an opportunity to serve the Publick, and contribute to the weal of his Country." You must labor, the chant continues, to be useful: always the recompense is subjective, this note being oratorically heightened with the years. "No Epicure can swim in such Delights, as the Man that is Useful wherever he comes, Useful to all about him." Why languish in a want of assurance? (None more agonized over the lack than Cotton Mather.) "My constant Counsil would be; be Fruitful: This is the way to be Joyful." Once more, out of the campaign comes the new-found American imperative: "Be up and be doing. Activity, Activity . . . This will be most likely to be followed and rewarded, with Triumphant Satisfaction."

In this spirit the ministers went forth to urge inoculation upon physicians: "A power to do good," they said, "not only gives a right to the doing of it, but makes the doing of it a Duty." Thus we comprehend the intransigence of the scorned and disreputable elements in the community, who set themselves against inoculation not out of scientific persuasion but because they would not be suffocated by being done good unto. (The *Courant*, we remember, was eventually suffocated.) In the background of this crusade for benevolence lay a history that explains the vehemence. The clergy of the 1670's had won, with the support of the state, a crushing victory; they beat down the pragmaticals and reduced their churches to submission over the Half-Way Covenant—and so drove pragmaticals out of the churches, or even into outer darkness. Hence, once the charter· was gone, when concerns outside the churches became more engrossing or amusing, became in fact the terms of survival, the clergy found that the entire area was an ecclesiastical desert. Without a repressive state, it could not be regulated for religious purposes; only the jeremiad could have effect there, and the jeremiad was wearing thin. Within the churches was, by clerical standards, such an apathy, let alone such bursts of anti-ministerial sentiment, as would eventuate in an even deeper torpor unless external stimuli could be applied. There seemed only one way in which both realms could be brought to heel: the clergy must go outside the churches, and bully pragmaticals into benevolent organizations.

They had the opportunity because society was still officially dominated by religious forms; there was opposition, but there was no outright intellectual challenge. Infidelity had to remain hidden. But an Increase Mather who had won the battle for the Half-Way Covenant would know that in 1720 he was a lesser, even though a more venerated man; his son, whose memory of the golden days was dim but who for one brief moment had drunk deep the wine of power, would see that if regal stature were ever again to be attained, he and his friends would have to create the kind of community they could command. An ability to retreat was a defense; hidden in his study, prostrate on the floor, dedication renewed itself, energies revived; but self can save self only up to a point—at least a Puritan self. Out of these crises of abnegation—a resource always available—arose a determination not simply to do a good turn daily, but to seize direction of forces ready to be directed. Who would, in this kind of world, know what qualities were needed for leadership? Surely not some magistrate of the John Winthrop variety, not such a warden of the frontier·as Solomon Stoddard's son, Colonel John, with an undisturbed self-esteem and an assumption that lower orders should automatically bow before his dignity. Along the borders, the Colonel was still a great man in that tradition, but in the older areas he was an anachronism; to enlist and discipline the eighteenth century called for one who sensed its failures, discouragements, and the harrowing ambiguities of a particular faith. Only he who in defeat had experienced the bewilderment within, but out of it was sustained by the certainty of ultimate—and not remote—final judgment, could save this society by making it do good unto itself. His was the duty of reducing those who, as his father put it, go in "Leather Cloathes" to consent that good be done to them and for them. It was not a "going out of his way" when he took the task upon him: it was his appointed way. If he could not conquer the rebellious, then nobody could; for he more than any other understood, out of inward terror, that this community had lost the art of defining the good, just, and honest. Cotton Mather could, and did: *Bonifacius.*

It was a rallying point; it proved for more than two centuries to be,

essentially, the stabilizing conception for vast segments of American Protestants. It was not revolutionary, nor did it call down upon an evolving
economy the wholesale condemnation of the covenant; therefore it was
not obstructionist, did not blame people for doing what they had to do,
and so relieved their anxiety. On the other hand, it was not quite a surrender of piety to business: it did not pronounce a blessing of heaven upon
millionaires while leaving the poor to die in the gutter. It was a social
gospel, not a gospel of wealth. It recognized evils, and proposed to do
something about them. The philosophy of do-good was not quite an apology
for the *status quo;* it was a discovery that the goals of the commonwealth
need not be settled by an inhumanly scholastic logic. The Christian problem
had (implicitly) ceased to be the transformation of spiritual energies into
a predetermined order of church and state; it had become (effectively)
how to gather up the abundant energies of the community for the attainment of ends arising out of complexity. Doing good was a method for
doing exactly this.

Would the ideology serve? A hundred years after Winthrop's *Modell
of Christian Charity* here was the issue, and it hung upon the transformed
meaning of the word "charity." In 1730, success was still in doubt. Meanwhile, there was another methodology that had received only a limited
trial; perhaps it needed more consideration. Suppose experiment were to
show that societies for reformation of manners would not work any greater
effects than had jeremiads? Suppose not only that the pragmaticals, even
when organized, remained obtuse, but that virtue itself found organization
only a deeper descent into the ambiguity that haunted the philosophy of a
nation in holy covenant? There remained the portent of Solomon Stoddard's harvests. He had forged quite a different weapon: contemptuous of
human ability to lift mankind by its bootstraps, he preached the stark terror
of judgment, not within the consolatory frame of a covenant, not for the
titillations of charity, but naked and uncovenanted. Much would depend, as
to which of these techniques should triumph over the other, upon what
Stoddard's grandson and successor might do, Stoddard being dead, out there
in the Valley.

THE
Mathers began to talk about do-good around the
year 1700. In that year Cotton Mather also published *Reasonable Religion*.
Not for ten years could he give to the social program the precision of *Boni-*
facius. In 1715 he sent to London the manuscript that waited until 1720
to appear as *The Christian Philosopher*, copies of which reached Boston on
the eve of the smallpox epidemic. Meanwhile, with the one hand he short-
ened the creed and spiritualized homely pursuits, and with the other produced such titles as *Reason Satisfied and Faith Established*, *A Man of*
Reason, and *Ignorantia Scientifica*. In 1720 Experience Mayhew published
A Discourse Shewing that God Dealeth with Men as with Reasonable
Creatures, and in 1723 Benjamin Colman announced, *God Deals with us*
as Rational Creatures. Sermons of Sewall, Prince, and Foxcroft burgeoned
with similar tributes to the charms of reason.

In one perspective, do-good originates entirely out of the exigencies of
New England society, owing little (except for English examples of reforming societies) to extraneous influences. Seldom is it explicitly connected with
recently acquired connotations of the word "reason," yet those most active
in advocating it are also those most sensitive to scientific rationalism. If the
two had no causal connection, at least they were not incompatible; behind
both looms a larger discovery: the preëminence of efficient over final causes
is the secret of successful method.

Nowhere is this intellectual entente between the two more illuminating
than in Cotton Mather's *Manuductio ad Ministerium*, ready at last for the
press in 1726. He had worked on it long and hard, and together with the
Magnalia, *Bonifacius*, and *The Christian Philosopher*, it justifies his place
in American literature. It was a last stand: his father was dead, he was
excluded from Harvard and dubious about Yale; he had lived much, and
he knew what had to be said to the clergy of New England were they to
succeed where he had failed. The book is a remarkable welding together of
precisely those elements in the intellectual situation out of which the New
England mind was obliged to make what coherence it could, out of which
Cotton hoped that the ministerial generations might regain their hegemony.

A minister must think constantly of death, he declares, in relentless contemplation of which he rises to the "Universal Discipline"—Mather's existential logic was never more powerful—which requires serving God by

doing and using those things that most glorify Him, or specifically, "Whatever contributes unto the Welfare of Mankind, and such a Relief of their Miseries, as may give the Children of Men better Opportunities to Glorify Him." Mather spells it out with concrete prescriptions, including the organization of societies for reformation; he demonstrates how a minister may spiritualize his activities, whether preaching, eating, sleeping or bathing, and confirms the regimen by a quotation from Francke, "a Professor in the Frederician University." The book, a last will and testament of New England's most ranging intellect, is a Pietist document, insisting that the principle of grace is preferable, not only to wealth, "but also to all Intellectual Accomplishments and Embellishments," preaching the vanity of knowledge and calling for an enhancement (to which the founders had not been prone) of the person of Christ. (He had seen, "in the Days of my Pilgrimage," that many celebrated sermons barely mentioned the Savior.) In this vision of simplified piety the basic maxims could at last be stated in a couple of pages, whereby all controversies might be, indeed, must be, reduced to "an Amicable and a Comfortable Period":

> But, if both Parties are agreed for that PIETY, which is the Main, and the Scope of all, how much Good may you do, if you can so Syringe the Odoriferous Water of the confessed MAXIMS upon them, that the Quarrelling Hives in the Loss of their Distinction may give over their Quarrels, and the Children of Jacob not fall out by the Way, or be so angry about the Way, seeing they are Brethren?

It is, in fact, a summation of the new mood, of what the battering of experience wrought upon the innermost psyche when the barrier of the covenant gave way: the pious soul, clinging to mere piety, tried to rescue mundane pursuits by spiritualizing them, and to redeem mankind by benevolence. At the heart of this gesture lies a pronounced anti-intellectualism—at least as regards scholastic disciplines of the former era—but, paradoxically, an enthusiastic welcome to newer forms of intellectual achievement, to the elegant style and to spontaneous reason. The Pietism—as for lack of a better word we are obliged to call it—of the early eighteenth century was not a rejection of the mind but a conscious endeavor to give to reason a larger part than hitherto it had played in the life of the spirit—in a confidence that it would serve, through the long run, "to propagate the PIETY of the everlasting Gospel."

The peculiar balance Cotton Mather struck in his last decade—by him imparted to his contemporaries—is demonstrated in the *Manuductio* by, on the one side, solemn commendation of the venerable manuals of Puritan theology and casuistry, and on the other, rejection of the intellectual disciplines out of which they had been written. He endorsed Alsted's *Encyclopaedia*—which from 1630 had served New England culture as "a North-West Passage" to all the sciences—made proper genuflections toward such venerable textbooks as Wollebius and Ames, Mastricht and Usher, and then declared that the best defense of truth is sincere piety. Without letting on that he was breaking with the past, he advised against "Squandering away your Time, on the RHETORIC" instead of observing "the Flowres and Airs of such Writings, as are most in Reputation for their Elegancy"; against having any truck with that "Vile Thing" called ethics, the content of which is better to be "learnt by a Wise Observation of what you see passes in the Conversation of Politer People"; and, most startlingly, against wasting effort "in that which goes under the Name of LOGIC." Formal logic supplies no more than provocations for altercation. In place of the long-cherished dialectic, conservative Mather set up another rule, in a passage which makes him perhaps the great innovator of his time:

> The Power and Process of Reason is Natural to the Soul of Man; And those Masters of Reason, who argue the most Rationally, and make the most Rational Researches into the true State of Things, and who take the most Reasonable Measures for their Conduct, and who in all things arrive to the most notable Discoveries, I pray, what sort of Logicians are they? Either they never once read a Page of any Burgesdicius, or else they have unlearnt and forgot all their Vulgar Logic.

He would allow students, if they must, to glance at modern simplifications, generally derived from Ramus, such as Milton or Watts or *Ars Cogitandi*, but he proclaims the dawn of an era by telling them they need consult such masters only as "Touch and Go."

Mather and his friends—all of them younger than he—were a long time coming to these conclusions; it is doubtful whether old Increase ever comprehended them, or approved them. But in Benjamin Colman there is a premonitory sense of the age which was confirmed thereafter by such returning pilgrims as Dummer and Thomas Prince; books crowded in, and lesser breeds, like the Franklins, challenged vested interests in the name of standards to which the world of literature and learning now universally paid tribute. "We that live in a remote American Wilderness," said Increase Mather in 1708—every word burning with chagrin—"may well be strangers to some considerable motions & transactions in other Parts of the World." This had to be said by him who, in London in 1689, had pleaded for the charter on the ground that in New England names like Burnet were as precious as any at home, who never was to be outdone, even by Colman, in saluting "that Eminent Man Dr. Tillotson, late A.B. of Canterbury." Yet student after student, not to mention an occasional minister, was experiencing what befell Samuel Johnson as he perused the collection sent to Yale by Jeremiah Dummer, where he encountered "the vast pleasure of reading the works of our best English poets, philosophers and divines," finding them "like a flood of day to his low state of mind." In 1715 Johnson inscribed on the margin of his manuscript technologia—that exercise in organizing the universe which every New England graduate, trained in logic, offered the faculty as proof of his literacy—that he had become wholly changed to "the New Learning." So orthodox a cleric as Eliphalet Adams at New London was, in 1708, copying issues of *The Spectator* into his private papers; in 1726 he sent his son William to Yale armed not only with Ramus but with Locke. Nathaniel Chauncy of Durham, grandson of President Chauncy, read William Wollaston's *The Religion of Nature Delineated*—which proved that even had there been no supernatural revelation, there would still be proofs of Christianity—and confessed, "I think I don't know any thing. Forty years I have been studying, and this book has told me more than I ever knew." (In London, in 1725, a destitute printer, Benjamin Franklin, set type on Wollaston's book, and was so repelled that he attempted to answer it, drawing upon standard New England ideology, with his one foray into naturalistic metaphysics: *A Dissertation on Liberty and Necessity*; before Franklin had decided that this sort of disputation was fruitless and tried to destroy his jejune assertion of determinism, Stoddard's grandson, encamped with that portion of Connecticut's college then resident at Wethersfield, was studying Locke's *Essay Concerning Human Understanding* with more joy than the greediest miser could find in gathering up handfuls of silver and gold.) Motions like these were, so far, isolated, disparate and fugitive; yet an organized and ostensibly invincible system of ideas is a sensitive plant, and displays a curious premonition of death the moment its roots are tampered with.

The magic word in the new mode was "Reason." As soon as the charter brought Boston closer to the orbit of London, New England heard that reason had become, as never before, the passport to respectability. For a while, after 1692, spokesmen like Cotton Mather continued to praise reason in the language of the founders: it was the faculty for apprehending truth as truth exists in objects, it was master of the passions. He was still using standard terminology as he demanded, in 1698, what more "Reasonable Provision" for the redemption of man could be conceivably devised than the Covenant of Grace. But *Reasonable Religion* in 1700 shows him making trial of the new tone—not that he deviates doctrinally from the founders, but that his very determination to prove "Did men Act Reasonably, they would Live Religiously" gives the adverb a fresh stress. Sin is, suddenly, violence against the principles of reason: " 'Tis a most Reasonable Thing, to Believe those Things, which oblige all men to Live Religiously." The notion of God springs from an innate faculty which is natural to the reason; the works of creation are enough to satisfy the reason of any man; it is plain to reason that the world had a beginning; by contemplating the work of providence, "Reason sayes, It must be ascribed to a God." Deism is, rationally speaking, a form of bestiality; some hearers admire what they call "Rational Preaching," but reason itself reasons that it needs "Scriptural Preaching." "The more of Gospel there is in our Preaching, the more of Reason there is in it. Scripture is Reason, in its highest elevation." The world of creatures is a system of "Heieroglyphics" to be interpreted by reason, and out of reasonable considerations New England should reform its abuses, its drunkenness, idleness, swearing, and profanation of the Sabbath.

Samuel Willard, whose mind was completely enclosed in the traditional rhetoric and logic, was at the same moment preaching in the Old South that hypocrisy is irrational, contrary to the sentiments of common reason, and reprehensible by the light of nature. What other was Mather saying? From the pulpit of Brattle Street, Colman was further drawing out implications of the rational configuration: "Did Religion only require of us . . . a meer belief, without the ordinary exercise of prudence and reason, or the use of proper means to defend our civil or sacred Rights; then indeed a Christian would be the most unmeet of all men to bear Arms." Seldom indeed did prophets of rationalism make the union quite so explicit, but we need not miss the point: relations with governors might be better in one year than in another, but steadily the consciousness grew that by emphasizing "the Verity & Rationality of the Christian Religion," rationality in every department of life, most of all in politics, was enhanced. In 1702 Increase Mather delivered *A Discourse Proving that the Christian Religion is the only True Religion,* the declared thesis being the necessity of divine revelation, but even he introduced his argument by setting forth the claims of natural religion to an extent he surely would have considered, forty years before, extreme. Again, nothing is said in so many words but what the founders might authorize: "If a man does consider the Works of Creation, his natural reason will tell him that there is a God." However, the accent is modified; even though Christians are no longer under the law as a covenant, still "The light of nature tells men these are very reasonable precepts." The Gospel requires such a holiness as pagan philosophers never taught; "nevertheless in their Writings we find excellent Morality." It must be acknowledged that natural men do possess remainders of the image of God, "appearing both in Theoretic, and Practical Principles: And thence some thing of a Natural Religion."

Increase would never pass beyond this point; still, he was conceding something to the necessities of evangelism. Unless men give credit to the principles of natural religion, he would say, they will never believe in revealed religion: this in itself prescribed a preliminary tuition in natural religion which the founders had never placed in so exactly chronological an order. His son would not, officially, go further; however, he was more fluent. In the midst of the enjoyments which God provides you, he told his people in 1703, you remain proud, vain, sensual: "Man, If there be one spark of Reason left in thy Soul, now let it revive"—and shine forth in reformation! The next year, at the election sermon Jonathan Russell announced, "Let our principles be Rational, those that are not Rational, are not Scriptural"; in 1710 Ebenezer Pemberton was stressing, what auditors had come to expect, that although God is paramount and his sovereignty unaccountable, "Yet he always exercises his supream authority according to the rules of the most consummate wisdom." The accommodation in sentences of this sort was not, let me repeat, a break with the past; it was merely a matter of "pronunciation." Little by little, the people became accustomed to hearing these things said with greater conviction—or with greater unction.

Up to a point, there was satisfaction in such statements: New England was not fanatical, crude, behind the times. It had always stood for scholarship, reasonableness, sobriety. The virtues of a rational disposition did not need to be grafted onto the native stock, they had always been there. But at the same time, intelligences began to stream across the Atlantic as early as the 1680's which were not always comforting: under "a pretence of Sobriety of Reason" there were those in Europe and England who became Socinians, people who "would not believe beyond Reason." By 1698 there were reports of "Epicurean Swine" who, in the name of reason, held that man "is nothing but a meer Lump of matter put into Motion." In the year of *Reasonable Religion*, Cotton Mather had to compose also *The Everlasting Gospel* to show that "Meer Natural Reason, without Revelation, both External and Internal Revelation, would never understand the Mystery of a Sinners being made Righteous." But anxiety increased as this rationalizing temper began to infect, not only disreputable elements on the fringe of the Christian community, but Nonconformity itself. Dissenters might expect that segments within the Church of England would learn to be content with "Harangues upon Moral Vertues" (although, of course, Tillotson was not such!), but when the remnant of the United Brethren split over the Trinity, when respectable heirs of the Presbyterians could no longer accept this irrationality, distress in New England became acute. Arianism led to Socinianism, which led to Deism, beyond which lay only the abyss of infidelity; were men like the Mathers, Colman, Pemberton to pose against the rational, tolerant—and constitutional—spirit out of which these heresies sprouted only a bare, dogmatic fiat of revelation? New England had never been of that mind: it had always assimilated doctrine within the nexus of a logical system. Could it claim the liberties and privileges of a liberal charter if it suddenly froze its religion in an authoritarianism that could not consist with the rational power of conducting its own affairs?

One line of strategy was available, broadly based in historic Christian theology and exemplified in New England's tradition, namely, the large scope given to man, even when fallen, to conduct his own affairs in politics and business; because he is still benighted, the defects of his reason are supplied by the Bible, in which he must believe, not because the content is reasonable, but because the testimonies are convincing. Thus he becomes rationally persuaded of irrational mysteries, such as the Trinity, because, in a phrase originated long before the Reformation, the truths of revelation may be above reason but are not contrary to it. On the whole, this was the line followed by Increase Mather, Wadsworth, and Colman. They were doing no more than paraphrasing the more scholastical terms of their elder and revered colleague, Samuel Willard. Great scope could be given the powers pertaining to the image of God which yet remain in fallen man, but at the same time God's absolute sovereignty could be so asserted as to reduce the creature to clay, to prevent his ever asking of the Potter, "What doest thou do?" This was Increase's last line of defense; mummified into the oldest and most venerable figure in the colonies, he pontifically delivered himself against ministers who set before men the good that will follow belief, and who then "say there needs no more; and that Men can change their own heart." Conversion still had to be something which only God could effect; a wonderful light had to dart into the dark soul, so that man "seeth things which once he never saw." Effusion is an infusion, and the dim light either of nature or reason is no sufficient guide to heaven.

Nobody could deny these propositions; but there were various ways of asserting them: Increase Mather uttered them with such dignity and restraint that, however contrary they were to the tendencies of the age, they had the solemn ring of universality. But angrier men like William Williams of Hatfield were less exalted; at the ordination of a cousin in Watertown in 1723, he preached and published upon *The Great Concern of Christians, and Especially of Ministers, to Preserve the Doctrine of Christ in its Purity.* He took the offensive against those who introduce into theology the idle speculations and philosophical niceties of heathen philosophers, asserted the absolute authority of Scripture, excoriated merely "external Reformations," and ran through the list of fundamental doctrines upon which there must be no yielding: the perfections of God, the doctrine of Christ, the Trinity, man's apostasy, utter inability, the nature and necessity of conversion, justifying faith, the resurrection, the last judgment and eternal recompense. "These, and other points of Faith, should be received, retained, & kept as a precious Treasure, or Depositum committed to their Trust for their own benefit & comfort, & for the service of succeeding Generations." Having roundly asserted this fundamentalism, Williams declared, "Faith is a reasonable act, it is upon such Pillars as these that it is supported."

Cotton Mather dutifully and voluminously published upon each and all of these doctrines; he gloated over letters from orthodox Nonconformists who thanked New England for support against Arians, Socinians and Deists. Indeed, New England should have savored immense gratification had it enjoyed real assurance, as Cotton Mather tried to asseverate, that "If the Groans of these Plantations complain, That they meet with some Difficulties from England, on Political Accounts, 'tis well that on Religious ones, we have some Compensations made unto us." He took pride in New England's intellectual appetite, and boasted that in addition to its native publications, the province "annually Vends (I suppose) Hundreds of Books published by Divines Beyond-Sea," often giving them a "Second Impression." Even as he speaks, however, he must denounce the "vile Pelagian Books, that from beyond-sea are vended among us," must lament not only that those who go abroad bring back, as the saying of the country had become, "Dutch Drunkenness, Spanish Pride, French Wantoness, and Italian Atheisme," but those corrupt ideas and corrupt books which "find our Children at home." Mather's simplifications of the creed were clearly not only gestures of Pietism, they were "preservatives" against the "wretched and foolish Pamphlets, which the Enemies of Grace of Souls industriously Scatter about the Country."

The chief danger of these books, he was the first to appreciate, was not their heresies but the "little Elegancies" for which they were applauded. By which he meant not so much works of men "who go under the Name of Deists" as manuals of rational piety (like *The Whole Duty of Man*); these, while seeming to condemn Arianism and Deism, propounded a faith no more than "historical," which merged Christianity with rational morality, and made the term "Preaching Christ" a reproach, pretending "that is the way to drive Rational Preaching, and Morality out of the World." Thus it was that John Checkley could rock the entire edifice in 1719, thrusting a lever into cracks already gaping, by having his protagonist in *Choice Dialogues* say that since his reason tells him to trust God's Scriptural promises, he will reject predestination, "and chearfully set about my Duty, without perplexing my self about his secret Decrees." In every manifestation, the new literature taught morality and doing good; but too often with a sinister implication: "That all the Vertue in the World, is but a Sham; and that a meer Trick, to Serve one's self." These calumnies, said Cotton Mather, are "beyond the reach of Satyr." He spoke out of a tradition rich in the depiction of hypocrisy, and therefore could fairly be hoist with his own petard, as James Franklin neatly did in his sketch of a Matherian Tartuffe.

There had been an earlier portent: the debacle in 1704 of Jeremiah Dummer's homecoming. It forecast the dilemma of a rational New England mind caught in shifting connotations of the word reason. Long before the migration, a method for demonstrating the coincidence of scholastic rationality and divine appointment had hinged upon the doctrine of the Sabbath; Shepard and Hooker discoursed upon it, as had the young Cotton Mather, who in 1689 pointed out that since the week consists of seven days, God has both naturally and supernaturally indicated that one day out of seven should be observed. Dummer wrote his dissertation, *De Jure Sabbati*, at Leyden and Utrecht—assuredly orthodox institutions—and came home to an enthusiastic reception by the Mathers and Sewall, preached and published his trial sermon—such a display of Continental erudition as none in the colonies was master of—*A Discourse on the Holiness of the Sabbathday*, and succeeded only in scandalizing the community.

Dummer attacked the problem of how the Sabbath was changed from Saturday to Sunday, concluding that the present designation of the first instead of the last day is wholly "positive"—that is, mere command—rather than inherently necessary. The unsophisticated modern mind may suppose this a "fundamentalist" revision, giving greater weight to revealed pronouncement than to rational induction from natural phenomena. Yet this irrationalism—rationally worked out—subtly made arbitrary determination more reasonable than even the law of nature, and so, in the name of judicious investigation, relegated the scholastic portion of traditional doctrine to limbo. By trying to make the Sabbath a peculiar appointment, he detached it from the realm of moral precepts which "are discoverable by the light of Nature"—thereby leaving New England with nothing more than a dogma to support its most cherished institution! By elevating the religious observance to the highest level of mere obedience to command, he made it, in effect, easier for disbelievers to flout it. By inflating the Sabbath (and with it all such "positive" conceptions as the Trinity) into an absolute decree, he turned all the lesser world of nature over to such maxims of philosophy and ethics as require no proof but reason. That a man naturally knows good or evil the fathers had frequently said; but they had also demanded submission to that which Winthrop called the good, just, and honest. Dummer opened up revolutionary vistas by saying, without the usual safeguards, "Men know by nature the Essential difference between good and evil," and then citing the most refined and exalted of heathen philosophers. New England was provincial, but it was clever enough to catch the sophistical in Dummer's sonorous conclusion that the Sabbath ought the more to be acquiesced in because reason does not primarily teach it to us, that we ought the more to subscribe "to the equity of it." Dummer made too great a parade of his authorities: Cicero, Selden, Grotius. And he openly declared that on this subject John Calvin erred by trying to identify decree and reason.

One of his clerical patrons was forced to tell him that his doctrine was "not calculated for the Meridian of New England"; out of the depths of his meditations, Edward Taylor of Westfield grieved that the son of his childhood friend should destroy the very bowels of practical piety by founding the Sabbath "onely upon humane institutions." This, he said—here letting us perceive the character of New England's struggle with the concept of rationality—opens the door to all merely positive inventions, such as the ceremonies of the Church of England. Dummer was a returned traveler, corrupted by Europe, frolicking with his fancy: "the Lord help against such aetheistical Poison."

The Mathers stood by him; Increase introduced the book, manfully demanding that for the honor of New England so erudite a man should not be forced to leave his country, and recommended him for a post at Harvard, with which motion Dudley agreed. The House of Representatives, the minions of Elisha Cooke, resisted; Dummer went off to England, there to serve New England by rationally defending its charters, just as, in 1723, Benjamin Franklin went to Philadelphia, there to serve mankind and himself by reasonably doing good.

Doctrinaires like William Williams might recite the articles which ministers must preserve, election orators might chant that government is an ordinance of God, and that therefore laws for enforcing the Sabbath and paying ministerial salaries should be obeyed; but just as some political speculators like Joseph Moss and John Bulkley realized that a larger explanation was required to prove a regime founded upon compact and constitutional rights to be still divine, so a few Christians perceived that the seductive language of modern heresy would not adequately be refuted by old-fashioned dogmatism. In general, it may be said, they were those most sensitive to literary criticism—Cotton Mather was the chiefest—most miserable at having to appear before the wide, wide world as backward colonials. Conscious of inadequacy, they were the most forward in cultivating the new mode of expression, hoping, by concentration upon language, to transform reason into a slogan for colonial orthodoxy without having to submit their beliefs any longer to the relentless scrutiny of formal rhetoric or of "vulgar logic."

Reason—" 'Tis a Noble Thing; a mighty Thing; 'Tis the glory of Man." Of course, man must not presume upon his reason to dictate methods to God; it should not be idolized above revelation. But it is not to be slighted, for, Cotton Mather says in 1721, as mankind grows more reasonable, the heresies of reason will be found irrational, and those "pitiful Cries of Priestcraft" will soon "no longer hold their Enchanting Efficacy." In this spirit, Mather did welcome the importation into New England of books by Scottish moralists, by Ferguson, Buchanan, and above all by Hutcheson, "who has taught us how to gather the Delicious Things that grow on the Tree of Life." Election sermons progressively devoted longer paragraphs to such propositions, as did Samuel Cheever's in 1712: "Sound reason will tell every man that there is no living where every man may do what he will without controll." God condescends (as Governor Dudley should) to debate with poor mortals so as to convince them of the equity and reasonableness of his demands. There might be some confusion as to just where the emphasis should be placed in this rising chorus of reasonableness, but that it was rising and that it had work to do, was evident: it had to combat "levelism," refute antiministerial sentiment, prove that Checkley, Anglicans, Deists were wrong, and rally the benevolent piety of New England, even while invigorating its resolution to defend chartered liberties, upon this magnificently rediscovered truth: "The Reason of Man under the Energy of these Principles, is ready to confess, Things that are Mathematically True; and as ready to confess things that are Morally Right." (All this while, Jonathan Edwards was pouring over the *Principia*, trying, with his rudimentary mathematics, to comprehend its scholia.)

Cotton Mather addressed himself to this whole mighty task in 1709, in *A Man of Reason*, the manuscript of which, being carried to France, was not recovered and published until 1718; the contrast between it and his first foray of 1700 indicates the deepening of his concern. There is now abroad, he said, a foolish and cursed opinion that all right and wrong are founded only upon some arbitrary compact of human society; there is even a pretense "that we have no Ideas in our minds, but what are introduced from abroad, by Observations." Puritan scholasticism of the previous century had hesitated before the problem of innate ideas; Mather tried to cut the Gordian knot, to assert that man is born with "a rich cluster of Ideas" which are only awakened by experience, that these, the innate principles of reason, as valid in ordinary life as are the inborn maxims of mathematics, furnish the foundations of morality. Therefore "the Voice of Reason, is the Voice of God."

The importance of *A Man of Reason* is not so much what it says—in the literature of religious rationalism it is utterly commonplace—but the eagerness it exhibits that somebody in New England should make a showing. Mather had probably not read Toland or even Samuel Clarke's *Discourse* of 1705; we know that he picked up his sense of their tenor largely from a monthly digest, *The History of the Works of the Learned,* and that out of these hints he fabricated his response. Here he found (if he needed to find surcease outside his own wit) the formula that nothing in Scripture is against reason, even though some things be beyond reason, and so pled that because it is reasonable to believe the Bible is revealed, it is reasonable to accept what the Bible teaches. Even while cautioning us not to trust too much to faculties broken by the fall, his celebration of rationality carries him— having decided reason is innate—to the pious conclusion which could give his program of benevolence a more solid foundation than *The Westminster Confession:* "a Rule engraven by the Hand of GOD, upon the Reason of Mankind" is what calls upon them to do good unto others. This ought particularly to be observed "in the Business which Men have with one another; their Traffic, their Commerce"; but compliance with it in these realms would also mean, not respect for irrational ceremonies, but "Respect unto the countenance of any Neighboring Churches." By the time Mather is finished, reason means, in short, the *Proposals* of 1705. "You have," he exclaimed in 1724, "all the Demonstrations which a Reasonable Mind can ask for, That you are not under the Dark Delusions of a False Religion." One and all, the clergy were trying, by these rhetorical passages, to make of reason such an appeal as would rouse the people against dangers to the system, such as would stimulate them to preserve that order by doing good, by helping the poor—and by not subscribing to the *Courant.*

Perhaps the greatest interest in these phrases of Mather's is what they reveal of the social connotations of his terms—and even more of how many former associations were lost. For the founders, reason had been a "faculty," the supreme, deciding power among man's several organs of operation—the will, imagination, common sense, memory, and passions. It was a function, not something with content; it was a way of perceiving, or extracting principles out of the things in which they are embedded, and arranging them in order (that is, in the ranks of the liberal arts). It was not, as it had become for Cotton Mather, "engraven." It originated nothing, because it was a photographic plate on which things were registered; it was a "discourse," exactly as for Hamlet:

O God! a beast, that wants discourse of reason,
Would have mourn'd longer.

Reason was that active comprehension of the cosmic system which both angels and men might share. In order that discourse might proceed accurately, that it might not make mistakes because deluded by the senses or seduced by the passions, it had to be controlled by logic. By the inexorable rules of dialectic it would extract intelligibles from things, place them in sequences, and apply them to circumstances. Reason for the founders, who were men of the Renaissance, was an ability to handle logic; apart from logic, reason was nothing. The line of logicians and scholars from whom the New Englanders descended, Richardson and Ames being the chief, had fixed this conception: since man is unable to receive wisdom by direct communication, God has placed it in things, from which it is radiated to the brain through the perceiving senses, as is the smell of a flower through the nostrils. It is "art" in the thing, "intelligence" in the mind, "science" when ordered by logic, and "prudence" when employed, whether for plowing a field, writing a sermon, or governing a plantation. This basic idea persisted throughout the century, at the end of which, in Samuel Willard's *Compleat Body*, it was still the content of the word "reason." The sciences being imprinted in the book of the creature, "from thence it is that Men's Reasoning Power Collects them, by observation and Experience." Reasoning was thus not a knowledge of self-evident propositions, but a "curious inquiry."

To trace the process by which this strict definition of reason as a function became transformed into the vaguer and more generalized usage of the eighteenth century would be to tell the entire intellectual history of Europe. Because for so much of the time New England was quarantined against radical influences, because its disciplines were for so long unchallenged, the Renaissance doctrine was there preserved in a purer form than elsewhere. Yet even in the 1680's, while Increase Mather was in England, tutors Brattle and Leverett became aware of the need for revision, and introduced Cartesian ideas into Harvard's logic, although this reform did not yet break up the hierarchy of the arts nor the assumption that all results of reason can be systematically tabulated in technologia. That "God hath ranked things in order, that there is a subordination of things one to another, and one under another" had not yet been shaken by what New England learned from Descartes.

In several quarters of Europe the shift in connotation was facilitated by a lessening sense of the sinfulness of man, and by a decreasing respect for formal logic. In fact, one might say that these two changes were one and the same: in the completely organized universe of the founders, sin was most precisely defined as that which prevents man from accurately employing logic. "Sin," as Increase Mather put it, "makes the Rational Soul to become a slave to the Sensual Soul in men." There was no epistemological problem in technologia, in the sense, that is, of there being any doubt that the idea in the mind is not a faithful image of the thing, because the assumption was that reason, governed and checked by logic, perceives an object "uti res est." But there was a discrepancy between subjective and objective, because sinful man refuses to profit by what he learns and thus perverts true art to egotistical ends. Reason became carnal, not because it was inherently corrupt but because it was perversely employed. Like all other faculties, it needed to be sanctified by grace; but when so regenerated, it received no new disclosures, no inward intuitions: it simply became logical, patiently able to make inferences and to frame heavenly conclusions. The main occupation of regenerated reason was, of course, drawing right inferences from the words of Scripture, but the implication always was that, when sanctified, it would also read aright the truths incarnated in physical objects. "Learn wee to use our Logick this way," President Chauncy had said, "and it will arm us for those combates wee meet withall in dealing with sin or Satan."

Officially speaking, the New England intellect did not yet mitigate the severity of innate depravity; sermon after sermon throughout our period returns with gusto to the theme, especially the jeremiads. The alteration in usage is a purely semantic evolution, which went on for years without registering itself in consciousness. It was certainly hastened by the new literature, by Tillotson and Addison, and even more by a freer and looser employment of the term by English Nonconformists. But it may also be viewed as a gradual response to the social situation, as part of an adjustment of discourse to an audience who no longer wanted the reasonable to convey a dialectical subordination of things, one to another, but rather a concept which would serve more efficiently in business or in the contest for political rights. There was no systematic logic required in the argument that the General Court should refuse Shute a permanent salary; that was self-evident common sense—that was the essence of "reason." John Wise was in advance of his contemporaries in granting right reason a large capacity of formulating its own premises and arguing from them rather than from externally given data. Others, as they became aware or even half-aware of what was happening, were more fearful. Although Jeremiah Dummer's intentions had been of the best, he showed what an uninhibited use of reason might come to: it would inevitably reëxamine the foundations of New England's order and raise embarrassing speculations concerning such sacred axioms as the coincidence of natural law and divine decree in the institution of the Sabbath. If reason were given royal rights, how could it be chastened, as in the past it had been, by the admonition that its "spiritual Opticks are strangely discoloured," by the requirement that it always subordinate its judgment concerning either what is or what is right to the cool arbitration of incorruptible dialectics?

Pascal had written, in the middle of the seventeenth century, that the heart has reasons which the reason knows not of. New Englanders did not hear of him for some time, but by 1710 Ebenezer Pemberton cited him, "one of the greatest masters of thought in the last age," to prove that there are two sets of thought for the regulation of conduct, one elevated by grace and the other merely natural. The fact that Pemberton or Mather could invoke Pascal indicates that they too had had their confidence shaken in what Pascal called the reason—in that systematic faculty which, instructed by logic, presumed to confront the universe directly, which under pretense of describing things as they are had invented a purely imaginative system. In their fashion, the colonials were also seeking for rational sanctions in what Joseph Sewall called "such noble and exalted Powers as to be capable of an Intelligent and Rational Service." The things a man knew were reasonable, not as conclusions of a syllogism, not out of distribution, disjunction, contradiction, antecedence, and consequence, but spontaneously —these reasons of the heart were to be relied upon if the righteous man was to be described, as Cotton Mather now did, as one who excels another "in his Doing of Good unto other Men." In short, the scholastic definition of reason had to be altered in practice, even though it hung on in the schools, so that preachers might declare, "Usefulness is Excellence."

Experience Mayhew has sometimes been adduced as the first avowed Arminian in New England; whatever he was to become in the stress of the Great Awakening, his *Discourse* of 1720 is a conventional argument for the federal theology, on the familiar ground that dealing through covenants is rational. The founders had said it a thousand times; as they had concluded, so did Mayhew: "In Order therefore unto Men's coming to their Right Minds," a supernatural change must be wrought by the Holy Ghost. What he does betray is the principal cause, among local influences, for New England's increasing emphasis upon rationality: God Himself deals with men as intelligent beings, eschewing compulsion and asking for a voluntary obedience; therefore, as in commerce or in politics, unless men deal with each other as reasonable creatures, "they could be no more said to obey God in their Motions, than Irrational Animals, and Creatures without Life, may be said to do." Since God never exercises His sovereignty in any way contrary to equity, neither should a royal governor! The Almighty Himself would have citizens, debtors, and ministers "expect to be dealt with accordingly, and would have others also observe it, in order to their treating of them in such a manner as is suitable to so noble a Species of Being as they are." Mayhew's doctrine as of 1720 was untroubled orthodoxy, yet in every implication that bore upon practical life, above all on the political, he managed to portray depraved man as capable of nobility.

Experience Mayhew's importance as a prophet of rationalism has been magnified, I suspect in great part because he was the father of Jonathan. A more neglected but possibly more ominous figure served in the frontier town of Colchester, Connecticut, and was, although he spelled his name John Bulkley, the son of Gershom Bulkeley. He displayed his heredity in his election sermon of 1713, *The Necessity of Religion in Societies*, by a particularly ferocious attack on levelers, as well as by citing Machiavelli with approval. There was nothing radical about his social thinking; on the contrary, he defended "the Publick, Instituted Worship of the Gospel" against all enemies, some of whom were to be found not "among the more Base and Vile" but "among those of Rank and Quality." Years later, Charles Chauncy said that Bulkley, along with Thomas Walter and Jeremiah Dummer, was the "first for extent and strength of genius and power New-England has ever yet produced"; though the prize might go to Dummer for quickness, brilliance, and wit, Bulkley was his superior "in regard of solidity and strength of argument." It is important to remember that Chauncy says this; Thomas Prince could not have agreed. For in this sermon, even while upholding the established order, Bulkley strongly insisted that religion is a reasonable service, that addresses made to the affections of listeners are easily erased, "whereas due Conviction of the reasonableness of Religion will abide with & have a permanent Influence upon them."

Colchester was an isolated spot—for lack of a horse, Bulkley once wrote, "I have endured a long confinement here in the wilderness, secluded (I had almost said) from the company of mankind." Yet he had an extraordinary library, much of it from his father, and in his successful pastorate evidently did all he could to further culture. At any rate, he encouraged a youth named Roger Wolcott to write poetry, and so interested the town weaver, one Joseph Dewey, in this genius that Dewey put up the money to pay for the publication at New London in 1725 of *Poetical Meditations*, for which Bulkley wrote a preface. This curious book enjoys a mild fame as the one self-consciously "literary" endeavor of the period, but it is much more fascinating when studied for its mingling of strains—reason, piety, social service, and would-be elegance. For example, trying to describe the deviousness of sin, the Connecticut poet, a century after Thomas Hooker, thus goes about it:

> *He that can trace a Ship making her way,*
> *Amidst the threatening Surges on the Sea,*
> *Or track a Towering Eagle in the Air,*
> *Or on a Rock find the Impression there*
> *Made by a Serpents Footsteps, Who Surveys*
> *The Subtile Intreagues that a Young Man lays,*
> *In his Sly Courtship of an harmless Maid,*
> *Whereby his Wanton Amours are convey'd*
> *Into her Breast; Tis he alone that can*
> *Find out the Cursed Policies of Man.*

Dewey, who footed the bill, took the last three pages to do good for the people of New England by telling them the proper way to prepare their cloth; a conscientious workman, he was shocked at the way they mishandled their material. Bulkley's preface has almost as little to do with the poetry; he hailed such useful arts as writing and printing, offered a brief observation on the distinction between wit as a putting together of things wherein there can be found congruity and "Judgment, or Clearness of reason" as an ability of mind "nicely to distinguish its Ideas the one from the other," and then announced what he already had made evident, that there was none among the whole number of mortals less qualified to evaluate verse than he. He did feel that an intelligent reader would here discern an uncommon vigor of mind exhibiting what a laudable ambition might make out of native talent, "tho' not Assisted with those Advantages of Education which some are favoured withal," whereupon he dropped his protégé, and took advantage of the subject of Wolcott's most ambitious effort, which was a versification of the mission of John Winthrop, Jr., for the Connecticut Charter, to launch into a disquisition proving that the English enjoy their title to the Indians' land by moral right, even if they never purchased it.

The contrast Bulkley proposes between wit and judgment was a commonplace of critical theory at the time, but had been given currency mainly by Hobbes. A man who read and quoted Machiavelli might just as easily be a student of Hobbes. Although he admitted that in some men wit and judgment might be combined, he doubted that this could happen very often, and as for himself, his preference was clearly for "the Great Man" as opposed to the poet, for he admired that clearness of reason which is not "misled by Similitude, and by Affinity to take one thing from another." It does seem a bit strange that at this late date anybody should still be worrying about title to the land, and perhaps there was simply a strain of crotchetiness in the Bulkleys. Yet it may be that he wanted to take this opportunity to do his sort of good for the country, to give it instruction not in the carding of wool but in the use of reason. The most arresting fact about the discourse is Bulkley's resort to an authority his father would not have respected, John Locke; his article is the first in New England in which Locke is extensively quoted and understood. By employing Locke's doctrine that a title to property is given by the mixing of labor with the raw material, Bulkley demonstrates that the lazy Indians never really owned the land in the first place, that the Yankees, by bringing it out of the state of nature, are the rightful possessors. In proceeding to this reassurance, he expounds the philosophy of contractualism and presents Connecticut's constitution as conforming to the terms prescribed by "that man of deep tho'ts." The solid rationalism of his argument is striking; religion figures primarily as a useful instrument of order, as he frankly addresses only those capable of thinking, not "the Multitude (who generally Speaking have too much Rubbish in their Brain to think of any thing with distinctness)."

Had Bulkley published more, he might have upset an unstable equilibrium. His only other utterance was an ordination sermon delivered in 1730, a year before his death, entitled *The Usefulness of Reveal'd Religion, to Preserve and Improve that which is Natural,* wherein revelation is ritualistically exalted above nature, and then all the heartfelt encomia are heaped upon the natural. At one point he must apologize for venturing upon "an Untrodden Path" (we think of John Wise), for using arguments many auditors may feel "improper and very aliene from what might be Expected." It is indeed hard to see how a Calvinist could go so far: defining natural religion as that attained by simple, uninstructed nature, from contemplation of the works of God in creation, Bulkley finds most of the doctrines of faith to be "no other than what Nature teaches," what we might have believed "had we never been assisted by Supernatural Revelation." Revelation in effect becomes valuable as a means of preserving and enforcing natural piety; there is no opposition between them, and whatever ethics are taught in the Bible, "Natural Religion recommends & enjoins." He would not be taken to mean that the clergy should preach only natural truth to a disregard of the evangelical, but still—"we must not so insist on these things, as to Neglect the other . . . and not allow them their due time and place in our Ministry." To deify the conclusions of natural religion, as do the Deists, would make earth a hell, but short of that, "There is an Intrinsick Goodness or Excellency in them as they all tend to advance our Nature, to make us better, more wise and good, and Consequently more happy."

Further north in the region of the Connecticut River, Stoddard's successor had also come to perceive that in a rational universe the word "excellency" took on a special importance, but whether it led so directly to happiness he wondered. He would wonder even more when Bulkley went on to remark that this admirable quality of "an Intrinsick or Inherent Goodness" could not be ascribed to pronouncements of the Bible, because these are not always good in and for themselves "but Good only because Commanded." Perhaps we appreciate at this point why Bulkley did not publish more; such ideas were not to be spoken aloud in Bulkley's New England of 1730 any more than in Dummer's of 1704. We hardly dare, out of Bulkley's brief bibliography, fashion him into a full-fledged rationalist, but he seems to be the nearest thing to it New England had yet produced. If he is, then it is interesting to notice what for him became the lesson of reason: not freedom but conformity. Regarded in the cold, clear light of "Judgment," the instituted religion of the land is "materially Consider'd, no other than the worship of Natural Religion"; wherefore those who oppose it have no excuse, either in nature or in reason! "What, does not Conscience tell you the truth of what is now asserted, that this Worship you thus Slight, Despise, Neglect, as to all the main parts of it, materially Considered, is no other than Natural Worship, that Worship which Nature tells you is intrinsically Good, and therefore of moral and perpetual Obligation?" At the end, Bulkley appears to be revivifying the injunction of the jeremiads, but he has come to it by an altogether different approach, in which the voluntarism of the covenant philosophy has been left behind. The federal conception has been consigned to that heap of rubbish which, in the brains of the multitude, keeps them from thinking with distinctness.

Assuredly, if Bulkley meant what these fragments suggest, he was ahead of his age—which is probably why Chauncy would ultimately rate him along with Dummer as the greatest of New England. But the tone of the whole society was changing with, all things considered, astonishing rapidity, as Sewall and Prince had to confess when they finally could bring out, in 1726, Samuel Willard's tremendous folio, *A Compleat Body of Divinity,* for which they had to apologize because modern taste would find Willard "less exact in his Philosophical Schemes and Principles" than it demands; his are indeed ancient and not suited to the present age, but we should excuse him because he never incorporated his schemes into piety itself, he used them only "as a Convenient means of ranking the various Creatures in a clearer and more conspicuous order, than if he had made no Divisions or form'd no Systems of them." Thus the logical structure of the mind and the universe—the content of technologia—which for the first Puritans had been absolutely identical with Christian doctrine, was detached from religion and admittedly, even though sadly, consigned to Bulkley's rubbish heap. And this by two of the most aggressive leaders of resurgent piety, who therefore found themselves handicapped by having to make clear, "in such things as these every Person is intirely left to his own Freedom without offence." After all, they noted, philosophical schemes change from age to age, but Christianity "will forever remain the same thro' all the successive Changes of Philosophy." We may justifiably doubt whether Willard himself (who after all died only nineteen years before his editors felt obliged thus to exonerate him) would have had the slightest conception of distinguishing his metaphysics from his Christianity, any more, let us say, than a liberal theologian of the early twentieth century can comprehend that an evolutionary progression of discovery may be something separate from the content of the Old Testament. One of Willard's reiterated themes had been from the beginning an axiom in the New England enterprise: the orderly frame of the human faculties is now full of confusion, wherefore "Reason is dejected at the feet of Sense; God is rejected, the Creature made Choice of." Cotton Mather, Mayhew, and Bulkley, not to mention Prince and Sewall, were still preaching the doctrine of original sin, but Cotton Mather's method of persuading men to avoid sinfulness had, even by 1717, abandoned Willard's clear and conspicuous order: they should manifestly embrace that religion "which the more accomplished any Men of Letters are in Literature, the more they reckon This the most valuable of all Accomplishments."

Here we may begin to apprehend the harm done to our historical thinking, let alone to our estimating of forces in our own day, by a facile labeling of Cotton Mather "conservative." Suppose it be admitted that changing philosophical schemes may from time to time be incorporated into Christianity, only to be expelled with the progressive revolutions in cosmological or psychological theory? What then is the essence of Christianity which, Mather's disciples assert, remains constant through all these periods? The great man, said Bulkley, is not misled by similitude, because he possesses clearness of reason. How then can he who preaches reasonable religion also inculcate the worship of, the imitation of, ancestors? How can he be a conservative?

The great fact is that in the same year *A Compleat Body* made its belated appearance, Cotton Mather published *Manuductio,* and emphatically rejected the logic that gives form and meaning to Willard's tome. To what purpose, Mather now demanded, should you "weave any more Cobwebs in your Brains?" The only useful trick learned in logic, that baneful curse of Aristotle, is the syllogism, but anybody knows that "all Syllogizing is only to confirm you in a Truth which you are already Owner of." Instead of trying to prove, let all tedious demonstration be cast aside, and let us put our trust in the simple cry: "O reasonable MAN!" do you not abuse and forfeit that which distinguishes you from the brute "if thou refuse a Life so agreeable to Reason?" Surely, in such an exclamation, Christianity was not merged with some changeable scheme of philosophy!

Few were altogether aware of the significance of this revolution in method. How far-reaching it actually was not even a Wise or a Bulkley could tell; yet in some strange manner, everybody knew what the central problem had become. If, as Sewall and Prince said, persons are left to their own freedom in speculation, was there any guarantee that the spontaneous reason, freed from the domination of an outworn logic, would support the propositions of the Bible? The Scripture was still there, of course, but once the traditional scheme of interpretation was discarded, once men read the book as "accomplished" men of letters, would they find in it the articles of *The Westminster Confession?* Jeremiah Dummer had extracted out of it a dangerous thesis about the Sabbath, and then had become, according to reliable reports, a complete infidel. The grandchildren of English Presbyterianism, studying the Bible by the light of reason, were becoming Arians; meanwhile Tindals, Tolands, and Blounts were proclaiming Christianity so much one with reason, so little mysterious, so coeval with the creation, that it was reduced (as Bulkley seemed to desire) to no more than natural religion. When Willard wrote, said his editors, "we were but just emerging out of those obscurities": but were we modernists in any brighter light, or was our footing more secure, once we were free of scholastic "Altercations and Logomachies" and found ourselves in an era of valuable accomplishments? Cotton Mather took his courage in his hands when, in his old age, he declared the innate principles of morality "as Plain, as Clear, as Undeniable, as any that are purely Mathematical." But suppose this premise should turn out to be just another logomachy, merely one more of those "Hypotheses subsisting only in the Imagination of Men," founded upon imperfect observations, "thrown out by others as unstable as they?" Suppose Christianity could be detached from its liaison with Ramist dialectic and its independence asserted, would it then, like a woman who must go from lover to lover, prove incapable of living its own life? The old logic may have been crabbed and have lacked elegance, it may have been sophistical, but it had once signified a secure intellectual ménage. If it was gone, to what awful prospect might not reason, left to itself, carry us? If that way-ward (at least in sinful humanity) faculty, which distinguishes humanity from the sinless brute, were no longer regulated by logic and confined to ex-tracting truth from concrete things or from the verses of Scripture, but was left free to wander the town over, with what imposters or profligates might it not take up? By what similitude or affinity might it not be misled? What commonplace or even vulgarity might it not try to spiritualize? What here-sies might it not conceive and wantonly give birth to? The modern per-suasion had become that innate moral principles were as clear as mathe-matical: but would reason submit to mathematics any more than to the syllogism? If the logic "learnt in our Colleges" had proved a stupid "Mo-rology" and reason alone was henceforth to be the sole guarantor of faith, who then was to guide this notoriously fallible faculty through the labyrinth of New England's sins?

CHAPTER XXVI

THE EXPERIMENTAL PHILOSOPHY

Cotton Mather led the way to the one prophet who could answer these questions, to "the Incomparable Sr. Isaac Newton." At a moment which without him would have been a disaster to the mind and spirit, he was given to mankind as though by an extraspecial interposition of providence. "Be sure," says the *Manuductio*, "The Experimental Philosophy is that, in which alone your Mind can be at all established." Mather never wrote a more considered sentence. Were the method to fail, were it to show itself just one more imaginary hypothesis, the prospect would be grim indeed, but Mather was certain—more certain than Winthrop had been about the covenant—that this philosophy was no mere theory. His confidence informs *The Christian Philosopher*, which he modestly recommended in the *Manuductio* and which he, along with many of his contemporaries, regarded as New England's major contribution to modern thought.

From the beginning, the Puritans had been hospitable to physical science. Obliged to study events in order to decipher the will of God, they welcomed the help of physics; the founders larded their sermons with illustrations borrowed from the Scholastic formulation. There was never in their minds any serious threat of conflict between natural causation and divine determination, partly because in Peripatetic science efficient causes were always subordinated to a final cause, but still more because their religious conviction was so strong that the notion of a purely naturalistic version of the universe was unthinkable. It was as easy for them to distinguish two sorts of causes in the fall of a tree or in an earthquake as it was, in their doctrine of the Sabbath, to reconcile the calendar with the resurrection of Christ.

However, although they conceived the world in Aristotelian terms, and though these do color their thinking, they never consciously made their theology dependent on them. Not that they were more enlightened than their age about Copernicus and Galileo, they were more indifferent. In the serried ranks of the liberal arts, physics stood by itself, a storehouse of metaphors for theological truths, but not directly involved in Biblical interpretation or the composition of sermons, as were grammar, rhetoric, and logic. In those disciplines, an error would have fatal consequences; but no spiritual truth was threatened if, let us say, scientists should come up with a new explanation for tides. In general the founders adhered to the logical system of Ramus, but in physics they were uncommitted; except for a few grumbles from conservatives like John Davenport (and even he thought scientific speculation infinitely less important than the issue presented by the Half-Way Covenant), New England seems to have accepted what it heard about the new physics with no visible distress.

As for participating more actively in the scientific advance than publishing essays in the almanacs, there was little opportunity in these remote plantations, and even less inclination. John Winthrop, Jr., was something of a virtuoso, kept up with advances in chemistry and medicine, and was well enough known to be a charter member of the Royal Society. He brought home a small telescope and gave it to Harvard; Thomas Brattle used it to record observations on the comet of 1680, which, when they reached Newton, helped him prove that the paths of comets are determined by the field of gravity. But Brattle had to write Flamsteed in 1703 that he had made little progress, "I am here all alone by myself, without a meet help in my Studies"; he knew of nobody in the colonies, he further reported in 1705, who applied himself to these subjects, and he could pretend to be no master but only a lover of them. "I never had any body to direct me, to assist me, or encourage me."

The mentality of early New England thus could not be distressed by the scientific revolution because it had no vital concern in such matters. Those people are in a perishing condition, Richard Mather had written, who have "none to speak unto them but Starrs, & trees, and the great book of the creatures, which is not sufficient for salvation, nor for saving faith." While an intellectual ought to learn what he could about the nature of things, still, Increase Mather commenced his career by saying, the sin of man has brought such confusion upon the natural world that, even though physicists do find rationalities in it, there is a "sad disorder even upon the frame of nature." A serious man should think and preach not about this present disorder but about the great day approaching "when all creatures shall be restored unto their right order and use, for which they were made at the first."

How his mind worked, and how he was thoroughly typical of his culture, is shown in his reflections on the comet Thomas Brattle observed in solitude. His *Kometographia* of 1683 achieved considerable fame and proves that Mather was far from ignorant about the latest investigations: he quotes the Royal Society, Kepler, Bacon, and Robert Hooke, and dismisses completely the "Peripatetick School." He is generous in praise of the "Learned Men, of these later times, wherein light in things natural as well as divine hath been admirably discovered," who have clarified so many mysteries with the help of mathematical instruments—although Mather was certain they would never get to the place where they could predict the arrival of comets. He was, however, agitated not by the discoveries but by the fact that people were misinterpreting them, were trying not to regard comets as voices of heaven foretelling approaching judgment; he took pains to show how they might, even by purely mechanical means, produce droughts, caterpillars, tempests, inundations, and epidemics, but whether or not they had such effects, he was convinced they were portents of God's displeasure. They proclaim "that flaming Vengeance is kindled, and burning in Heaven against a sinful World." This particular comet may be directed against some other region, but it would be well for New Englanders to consider whether it might be appointed for their benefit; women should give over wearing false locks and townsmen should come out of the taverns. A righteous God is wont "to discharge his Warning pieces before his Murdering pieces go off"; let science say what it will, the theological or moral meaning of the phenomenon was the same, and confirmed Mather's assurance "that ere this Century be expired, there will be very great Revolutions in the World."

This, however, had been back in the 1680's, when the approaching demise of the charter had seemed so catastrophic that an ultimate convulsion of the universe was bound immediately to follow. Increase could not get outside a Chiliastic attitude toward the order of nature. Although by 1711 he knew that instead of coming to an end with the seventeenth-century, the world had infinitely expanded its spatial limits; even so, he encouraged Christians to walk abroad in the night, to look up at the stars, and to think, "This Body of mine which is now walking here on the Earth, shall one Day walk above the Stars: For so it shall when after the Resurrection it shall be in that Heaven which is far above them." I know, he continued, that astronomers have their conjectures about the ends of space, "and they are but Conjectures." But for him it was enough to say that Scripture locates heaven geographically above the highest stars. Benjamin Colman was less literal, more at home among polite works, which he graciously employed for rhetorical embellishments; yet even he liked to distinguish between "science falsely so called" and "solid and substantial truth," the latter being morality and pious readings of the divine order, as opposed to mechanical laws. He had not the kind of intellect or interest that could be any "meet help" to his friend Thomas Brattle.

The great change quietly wrought in New England's ideas about the physical world had no real effect upon its formal system of ideas. Natural causes still coincided with supernatural determinations, the universe demonstrated the wisdom of God, but man's attention should be lifted above all this, to the life beyond or the heaven above. In 1705 Cotton Mather, preaching that the will of God is the reason why things are as they are, added, "There needs no Better Account for any thing than this." As Colman delighted to put it, "The glorious pattern here before us is God himself, and his will and precept is utter'd to us by every creature, that we also be not slothful in the reasonable and religious services, for which he has made us."

Meanwhile, in certain quarters, if only in that quarter which was the cranium of Cotton Mather, realization slowly dawned that the new physics was not merely a substitute for the Peripatetic, nor could it be utilized in exactly the same manner for mere subsidiary confirmation of theological propositions. Mather was no Pascal, but he was imaginative enough, or tormented enough, to realize along with Pascal that the experimental philosophy had opened up an infinity on either side of finite existence, that man was now poised between the mathematical extremes of microscope and telescope, that he no longer stood in the center of a symmetrical system, that he had become a thinking reed hemmed in by two massive enigmas. "By the Assistance of Microscopes," said Mather as early as 1690, "have I seen Animals of which many Hundreds would not Aequal a Grain of Sand," and thereafter was haunted by the specter of a minuteness beyond minuteness. It is indeed wondrous what we find out by microscopes: in a little body a thousand times smaller than a grain of sand can be folded up all parts of a plant or an animal—or a man. And yet our erect posture lifts our heads toward the stars, and "All this Globe is but as a Pins point, if compared with the Mighty Universe." We dare not guess at its dimensions, but were we among the stars, "we should utterly lose the sight of our Earth," this scene of the Christian drama. And all this vastness moves in unfailing order, so that he who knows the laws may predict an eclipse or even a comet. "If it should be so, that Every Fixed Star in all the Host of Heaven be a Sun, and the Center of a System not unequal to ours, to what Inconceivable Numbers do the Hosts arise." He would bravely try to behold the glory of God, but other words sometimes came: "Humane understanding tires, faints, is even Swallowed up."

In this moment of fright there came to him, as to other frightened men of piety, the *Principia* and the *Opticks*. Mather's first public reference to Newton seems to be 1711, when he used the law of gravity to show that, as weights raised toward heaven become lighter, so the self, if it would fly to heaven, must lessen. The next year, in *Thoughts for the Day of Rain* (a spiritualizing tract), he lets us see what the discovery of Newton actually meant to him, how thereafter the cause of piety, with its benevolent program and its newly learned techniques, was indissolubly bound up with Newtonian philosophy. Reviewing scientific theories concerning the rainbow, he proceeds through Descartes and Halley, until in a shout of joy he reaches the admirable Sir Isaac, "whom I may venture to call the Perpetual Dictator of the Learned World in the Principles of Natural Philosophy," the most sagacious reasoner who has ever shone among men— "and which is the Crown of all, The most Victorious Assertor of an Infinite God, that hath appeared in the bright Army of them that have driven the baffled Herd of Atheists away from the Tents of Humanity." Here, then was the savior of reason, who by perpetually dictating to it would keep it forever orthodox!

By 1713 he had accumulated a mountain of manuscript he called *Biblia*, which he spent his last years trying to get published; his prospectus, addressed to the learned of Europe, described it as a tree grown on the western side of the Atlantic, but "Gentlemen, the Fruits upon it, or at least the Seeds that produced them, were most of them, originally your own."

It would be an American contribution to the age of light now coming on; it would be orthodox Protestantism, yet acceptable to men of all persuasions, concentrating on the doing of good, enshrining the doctrine of the millennium: in natural philosophy it would be "Embellished with the Discoveries which our Days at Length have made of Things wherein the Glorious God of Nature calls for our Wonders & our Praises." Or, as he said of another effort, that while it would appear "A Philosophical Religion, yet it shall be Evangelical too, as to fear no Censure of a Vain Philosophy." This was what Newton provided, an escape from vanity. The cause of God and his churches in New England had suffered a succession of defeats, no whit mitigated by the humility of the jeremiad: the people had not reformed. Perhaps there was an element of vanity hidden in the abnegation, perhaps the physics had been too anthropomorphic. But in this presentation, religion, not to say humility, was safe, because "the more it is Examined by the more Pensive and Polite part of Mankind, the more it will be justified." Editors of the *Courant*, with the insulting figure of Old Janus presiding over the revels of their hell-fire club, calling him their perpetual dictator, were, obviously, neither pensive nor polite.

The Christian Philosopher was culled out of the *Biblia*; in content it is anything but original, most of it being a paraphrase of recent efforts toward making science religious: works of Boyle, Matthew Barker, Nehemiah Grew, George Cheyne, Fenelon, but particularly John Ray's *Wisdom of God Manifested in the Works of Creation* and William Derham's *Physico-Theology*, as well as *Transactions* of the Royal Society. All these sources were Newtonian; any of them would have subscribed to Mather's definition of the purpose, to prove "that Philosophy is no Enemy, but a mighty and wondrous Incentive to Religion." The book is an American plant, but the seeds were entirely European. However, its importance for American history does not demand that it be original. It had another function: to draw out the meaning of the revolution already imperceptibly wrought in New England, to demonstrate that in the experimental philosophy to which the mind had let itself become converted, the land had providentially been led to the bulwark of faith.

The virtually unobstructed advance of the new physics among orthodox Puritans in England and America owed everything to the terms in which it was advertised. After the founding of the Royal Society, as in the apologias of Sprat and Glanvil, the experimental method was presented as not only an assistance to piety but a practical benefit to mankind. While it made apparent the true pattern of God's universe, it would also devise instruments—thrice blessed—for improving agriculture, manufacture, and navigation, which would improve the lot (and increase the wealth) of those who labored faithfully in their callings. Thus it promised to do away, once and for all, with that opposition between acquisitiveness and piety which theology had striven in vain to reconcile. Those who opposed this philosophy, who like Butler ridiculed it or like Dryden denounced "philosophizing divines," were either profane scoffers or else obscurantists who cast up, where they belonged, in the Church of Rome. This body of wisdom was most serviceable for just those portions of society who, having become Nonconformists rather than Puritans, were concentrating upon profits instead of ecclesiastical conquest. Whether written by rationalistic Anglicans or by Dissenters, defenses of Newton always suggested that here at last was the synthesis which endless logical disputations, murderous battles, or even emigration to a city on the hill had failed to obtain. Cotton Mather caught the new vision; wherefore he, as much as any, turned America (including even such a perverse student of *Bonifacius* as Franklin) toward the program of social service according to an experimental method. All this while, patently enough, his intention was not to produce Detroit and the combustion engine, but to put down antiministerial sentiment, to preserve the New England church order. He believed that now he could present a religion beyond controversy, "which will challenge all possible Regards from the High, as well as the Low among the People," and so heal civil discord. Thus it would be, at one and the same time, philosophical and evangelical. Mather's is a curious way of backing into modernity; yet the charting of his crablike progress is one of the best methods for understanding how a middle-class, empirical, enterprising society could emerge out of an aristocratic, teleological order.

Viewed in this light, the great point of both *The Christian Philosopher* and the *Manuductio* (it appears more aggressively in the latter) is an explicit repudiation, not only of the scholastic arts of rhetoric and logic (even in the Ramist versions), but of the Peripatetic physics, which Mather now called jargon. "O Monstrous!" to think that there are still universities who kneel to Aristotle: no mortal has exercized such a tyranny over the human mind; even though "prodigious Cartloads of Stuff" have been written upon him, he remains unintelligible, "and forever in almost all things Unprofitable." These shackles Europe has begun to shake off "with fierce and long Struggles about it." With Aristotle dethroned, the first chapter of Genesis is no longer a "philosophical romance"—not, that is, when interpreted by "the Principles of our Perpetual Dictator."

Like every religious Newtonian, including Newton himself, Mather could now explain the operations of the universe—demonstrably and verifiably—by the laws of motion and of gravity; but most happily he could not, any more than Newton, explain gravity itself. "It must be religiously resolv'd into the immediate Will of our most wise Creator." No philosophical hypothesis could resolve it otherwise: it does not proceed from the nature of matter (thus Newtonian physics made an end to materialism), because the material efficacy of matter, being communicated only by immediate contact, cannot work at a distance. Gravity increases or diminishes reciprocally as the squares of the distance are increased or diminished, wherefore " 'Tis plain this Universal Force of Gravitation is the Effect of Divine Power and Virtue, by which the Operations of all material Agents are preserved." God is not only creator and first mover, but a continual influence without whom "the whole Movement would soon fall to pieces." The very "Vis inertiae" of matter, the weight and mass of its existence, is an implanted faculty; there is no cause, either for motion or for rest, except the omnipotent cause who preserves the being and faculties of every natural agent.

The natural world is therefore reasonable yet mysterious—and so infinitely susceptible of spiritualization. Meditation upon the techniques of fishing or husbandry is merely an application of scientific principles, nor is there need to be frightened either by minuteness or by infinite spaces. All motions are caused by some immaterial power exerting itself every moment upon every particle of matter. Comets themselves, reduced now from blazing stars "to a sort of Excentrical Planets," become objects of religious veneration when seen to serve the holy design of mathematical creation. (Mather was a bit reluctant to surrender comets to regularity, and tried hard to keep them among the catalogue of afflictions; he wrote a further meditation, not published until 1744, wherein he valiantly held to the best of both possibilities by reflecting that we don't yet know much about them because only recently have "final Causes"—he does not, of course, mean this in the Aristotlean sense—been cultivated "with that Care becoming so noble and useful a Part of Philosophy.") The moral was everywhere clear: "You cannot see any heavy Bodies descend, but you see the Glorious God at work." Or, as the *Manuductio* has it, "Child, See GOD in every Thing!" for "GOD is to Spirits, what Center is to Bodies." Piety being thus established—or reëstablished—it could face and survive the splintering of society, could sustain its identity even in an Age of Reason.

Cotton Mather was not a practicing scientist, but he read everything he could and tried his hand at collecting curiosities for the Royal Society, several of his eighty-two communications between 1712 and 1724 appearing in the *Transactions*, where they seem no more far-fetched than the average. He was elected a Fellow in 1713 (despite Checkley and Douglass), as was Paul Dudley in 1721; both of them published papers describing cross-fertilization of corn which are pioneer studies of hybridization. It appears from recent investigation that Mather was far ahead of his times in medicine, so that it was not mere chance that he had given thought to inoculation. The study of modern science in anything like a professional sense begins only with Thomas Robie, who, graduating from Harvard in 1708, served there as tutor from 1712 to 1723. The College procured a new telescope with which Robie made accurate observations upon eclipses; in 1719 he published a scientific report on a spectacular aurora borealis remarkable (like Dummer's *Defence*) for its slight emphasis upon any theological improvement. Robie proposed a natural explanation, and then announced that he would rest upon it "till somebody will give me, or I can find a better." He stands in striking contrast to Increase Mather's reactions to Halley's comet only four decades earlier: he would not attempt any prognostication, "for I have not so learned Philosophy or Divinity, as to be dismayed at the Signs of Heaven." To say even this much took courage; Robie had to protect himself: the sight was indeed surprising, nor did he doubt that there will be fearful demonstrations in the skies before the great and terrible day, "but I only mean that no Man should fright himself by supposing that dreadful things" would follow this illumination, "such as Famine, Sword or Sickness." Perhaps out of awareness that he had gone too far, he concealed his name and signed this portentous little book "Philos Sophiae."

Isaac Greenwood, who in the year of his graduation, 1721, came to Mather's side against the *Courant*, went to London in 1723 and there helped persuade Hollis to endow a chair of natural philosophy, of which he became the first incumbent. In 1726 he gave in Boston a course of public lectures "Illustrating and Confirming Sir Isaac Newton's Laws of Matter and Motion," for which subscribers paid four pounds. On April 7, 1731, he delivered *A Philosophical Discourse Concerning the Mutability and Changes of the Material World*, again expounding the incomparable Newton. Whether Greenwood any longer shared Mather's confidence that religion could be established on natural philosophy may be questioned, since he took conspicuous care to avoid moralizing. However, from Newtonian principles he felt it reasonable to infer that celestial bodies had a beginning and so would have an end. What a century had done to the New England mind he further demonstrated in reply to a question about what evidence natural philosophy might contribute toward the resurrection of the body: "Revivification is the joint Language of the Works of Nature." Certainly "Nature" is never at a stand; when one run of changes is out, another commences, so that a philosopher must be deaf to the united voice of all phenomena to imagine that a substance which has had, and is still capable of, life will not be put to the best possible use. To suppose that the soul shall be destroyed is "as repugnant to the Course of Nature, as that the Virtue and Attraction of Gravity and the other General Affections of Bodies should be destroyed in all those places where the Bodies themselves moulder and decay." Perhaps this was not so unqualified a support of Christian theology as Mather had anticipated, but such as it was, it at least had the virtue of modernity.

There is evidence that in the 1720's knowledge of the new physics became more widely diffused; Robie's almanac of 1720 expounded the planetary system, and in 1722 he received considerable amateur help in watching a solar eclipse. But the best evidence of what the infusion of science was doing to thought in general is the amount of space devoted to it in ordinary sermons, where Newtonian physics is employed not merely for metaphor (as Hooker and Cotton used the Aristotelian) but as the basis of doctrine. Thomas Prince is a good example: in his election sermon of 1728 he explains that created substance must depend on constant support of Him who made it, just as the operation of gravity requires a perpetual presence. "For all these curious and well adjusted Systems do intirely hold together and perform their Operations by virtue of certain new and prodigious Forces inspired every where in the same proportion into every Particle of Matter." If the minutest atom gets out of line, it will immediately be forced into its proper place, "and even there will be a constant Power exerted, in such a certain measure, to preserve it from wandering or being easily driven away." At this point, Prince checked himself from venturing further "into this surprizing Argument," but that he went so very far shows how great a determinant in both his political theory and his theology it had become. He had little notion of any dangerous implications, and would have been astonished could he have had a glimpse of the secret notebooks of Jonathan Edwards; but the first century of New England experience closed in a radiant confidence that "constant Power" was on the side of New England's creed.

Guardians of that creed had a providential chance to score their point, because on October 29, 1727, the land was shaken from end to end by an earthquake. Every church held a day of fasting and supplication, every preacher descanted upon the omen and called for repentance; twenty or more of their sermons were published. These show a remarkable unanimity; they are all, in a fashion, jeremiads, presenting the standard array of New England's sins. What, however, does make them revealing expressions of mood is the fact that one and all—including those disavowing any intent to speculate on natural causes—devote paragraphs, some of great length, to lectures on geology and to proving that, even after such second causes as caverns under the earth full of compressed steam are given their full due, God still works through them and by them. The sermons are efforts not only to make earthquakes serve as traditional instruments of reformation, but as means of confirming to the pious (including the preachers themselves) that the alliance between science and religion is salutary. In all of them appears something we may call whistling to keep up courage.

"Never did the City of Boston," cried Cotton Mather, "in the Ninety seven years that have rolled over it, see such a Night, as what we saw a few hours ago." The fear that seized upon the people, say several orators, was like that of a woman in travail. We are too apt to terminate our views in second causes, Prince announced, and then launched into scientific analysis, full of quotations from Boyle, about the power of gravity to hold together, or to cause to fly apart, "atoms." A short month later Cooper had to lament, "The Danger is that the Convictions will wear off, and the Purposes be broken." It is a sad fact that the shock of affliction does not change the heart; when the curb is taken off, corruption vents itself more fully: "And then as the Affliction was but a Curb, so the Deliverance commonly proves a Snare, and adds Fuel to the Flame." The experiential concussion seemed to be that this law of human behavior prevailed as universally in a Newtonian as in a scholastic universe. If nothing more in the realm of practical theology had been gained by shifting the physical bases, at least nothing had been lost. There was at least a hope that the mind might yet be taken off from mere second causes, that a further indoctrination in the experimental philosophy would finally convince it that a more intricate and elaborate mechanism of divine judgments should inspire a more awesome sense of the mighty and invisible cause which attends the minute atom as well as the great star, "moving them all in the most regular and intelligent manner." As long as this power could be invoked in the same manner as the God of the covenant had been, the failure of the people to reform demonstrated that original sin still prevailed in society, and so religion was safe. New England had moved into the Enlightenment, but not at the cost of breaking abruptly with its past. When God speaks through an earthquake, "Shall it not by all that have the Faculties of Reason in them rendring them capable of hearkening to it, be hearken'd to?" What a situation this society would have to deal with were the people, or any large percentage of them, ever to hearken and do something about it, the presiding doctrine had long since ceased to imagine; the important point was gained if, in a universe of modern physics, those whose function in the economy was to issue the unavailing summons still had their role demonstrably assigned them.

CHAPTER XXVII

THE DEATH OF AN IDEA

E BENEZER
Pemberton, graduating from Harvard in 1691, is,
along with his friend Colman, one of the few students upon whom it is
possible definitely to trace the influence of Leverett and Brattle. The de-
tection of ideological differences within this small society is hazardous,
first of all because the regnant theological creed was still unquestioned;
secondly, because differences were played down as much and as long as
possible (exactly as all mention of the split between Stoddard and the
Mathers was suppressed for years); thirdly, because the clerical caste,
despite divergent sentiments, were still solidly united upon major tenets.
Liberal or conservative, they all cherished a sense of the respect due their
order and were united in their detestation of the antiministerial sentiment
voiced by the *Courant* or by Checkley. Hence, one has to be thoroughly
steeped in the language of the time to appreciate how a nuance may betray an antagonism.

The difficulty of presenting a coherent story of the intellectual alignments is further complicated by personal relationships. In the vicinity of
Boston the leaders saw each other, or could see each other, every day;
there was too much vanity, jealousy, and sheer irascibility among Puritan
priests to prevent passions from flaring up in ways that had nothing to do
with opinions. Because Pemberton joined with the Brattles in inviting
Colman to return, he qualifies as a "liberal"; he had been serving at Harvard as librarian and tutor since 1693, until in 1700 Samuel Willard, evidently exercising diplomatic restraint, induced the Old South to elect him
colleague pastor, where he served until his death in 1717. Outwardly and
officially, he kept up proper relations with the Mathers; in private he broke
into storms of passion which seem to us neither liberal nor Christian, as
when "capering with his feet," he accused Judge Sewall of being such a
tool of the Mathers that were they to order him, Pemberton, shot, Sewall
would comply. He sided with Dudley in 1707 and told Sewall that Dudley
ought to humble Cotton Mather though it cost the Governor his head.
Cotton Mather paid tribute to Pemberton's abilities, but at his death secretly
reflected that because of his "strangely choleric and envious temper,"
Pemberton had prevented the Mathers from doing good.

Although passages can be selected from Pemberton's writings on such
subjects as political subordination, do-good, reason, and science, let alone

on topics like hypocrisy and the judgments of God, which are, in content at least, interchangeable with those by either Mather, one consistent thread does run through his story: he supported his colleague Willard in the theological truce which kept the Mathers out of the College; elected a Fellow in 1707, he then supported the election of Leverett. Thus the funeral sermon he delivered and published in that year upon Willard has to be closely read; on the surface it is conventional eulogy of a Puritan scholar, its chief point being the need for a learned ministry, upon which there could be no heartier concurrence than what came from the Matherian camp.

Cotton Mather had been sadly bitten in 1699 by the impostor Samuel May; as a result he renewed the old Puritan demand that sermons be well framed. The unanimity with which orators proclaimed this thesis during the next thirty years—decrying extempore sermons, exhorting magistrates and towns to support the schools, warning that if learning should fail the land would be reduced to primitive darkness—indicates that such a threat would submerge differences and create a united front. The threat was real. It was incarnate in the Baptists who protected Samuel May (although the Boston Church gradually became less obstreperous), in the Quakers who had to be tolerated, and in several native insurgents, of which the group in Connecticut led by John Rogers was the most annoying. Rogers, born in Milford in 1648, became converted in 1674 by Seventh-Day Baptists in Rhode Island, and thereafter developed a host of peculiarities on his own, all of them striking at the very foundations of New England churches and often, as in his doctrine of marriage, at the bases of common morality. He was a thorn in the side of the Connecticut magistracy, which kept him in jail off and on for a total of fifteen years, and once had him whipped with seventy-six lashes on the charge of blasphemy. He was Antinomianism in modern dress, preaching direct inspiration and a contempt of profane learning, but he attracted audiences because he denounced clerical salaries: in some towns this position was so popular that authorities had difficulty getting juries to convict him. Despite jail and the lash, he kept publishing, vaunting the superiority of learned ignorance to academic training. He caught the smallpox in Boston, and returned to New London to die in 1721, thus indicating how the judgment of God, in Newtonian times, overtook blasphemers who scorned science.

Among the masses, antiministerial sentiment seldom took such an openly schismatical form, but along with a reluctance to pay ministers more money there developed a tendency to consider official doctrine too abstruse to be worth paying anything for. It is a terrible abuse, said John Danforth in 1710, for any to say—thus testifying that some had said it—"If Knowing Sinners be the most Guilty, then let us know less, that we may be less Guilty." The more preaching was wedded to the concept of rationality and the more it depended upon science for proof, the more the value of learning had to be emphasized. In one sense, scientific rationality seemed a simplification of older disciplines, yet clerics trained in it oddly found themselves more remote from the language and conceptions of ordinary men than Hooker and Shepard had ever been. Those who have a smattering, said Danforth, are filled with self-conceit, which causes them to despise "those who are thorow-paced in those Sciences, and are indued with sincere love to the Publick Good." The clergy were contending relentlessly through these decades with a populace which, they felt, would pay more regard "to the popular, or to the cheap Preacher, than to the Man of solid Learning." They could not permit any division within their own ranks to show in the face of this danger: the General Court must care for our schools, said Colman, for New England is distinguished among all plantations for "Sobriety, Modesty and Literature"; zeal not according with knowledge, chimed in Foxcroft, "is but an erratic fire, that will often lead us into boggs & praecipices." Instead of taking pride in the new college, Connecticut citizens complained that there was already too much learning in the land; we had better, warned Timothy Cutler, err in the excess of that defect, because "the number of those favoured with a liberal Education don't seem to be too many."

Hence none of his colleagues could take offense when Pemberton employed the death of Willard to assert that granting liberty of prophesying to every ignorant intruder would overturn the order of the Gospel, that no mere smattering of knowledge should qualify a person for the office. "There must be a considerable acquaintance with the learned tongues, and liberal arts, which are subservient to divinity." People must not become bewildered "in the by-paths of simplicity." Although Pemberton experimented with sermons of a looser and more easy construction than Willard's, he stoutly praised Willard's devotion to system, his dexterity in confirming truths by incontestable arguments, and the fact that his discourses "were all elaborate, acute and judicious, smelt of the lamp, and had nothing mean in them."

Words often reveal more than they say. Pemberton's "mean," for instance. In 1718 Increase Mather painfully journeyed out to Cambridge to preach at the ordination of William Brattle's successor (where Brattle had not allowed him to preach at his own installation); it was his last chance to address the students, and he took the occasion to defend learning, reached back to the great sermon of President Chauncy in 1655 and to the resistance of English Puritans to William Dell. He explained that when the Reformers had attacked universities, these had been nothing "but Heathenism & Idolatry, with the Rixations of those called Schoolmen, who were much worse than their Master Peter Lombard." But such accusations are not to be levied against "Protestant Universities," such as Oxford, Cambridge, Dublin, the three in Scotland, or the two in New England. Ministers should be "elaborate," and should never come into the pulpit trusting to what comes next, "without any Premeditation or Dijudication." And yet in the foreword to the volume in which he published this, along with other sermons of the year, he boasted of them as "very mean, plain Ordinary Discourses," pointing out that comparison of them with his publications of fifty years before would show the style the same, because from his youth he had affected a plain Scriptural manner. "So have I lived, and so let me dye."

Therefore, when Pemberton represented Willard as a man of learning whose productions smelled of the lamp, there were passages in his praise which bespoke more his own ideal than his colleague's. Willard's style was "masculine, not perplexed," easy as well as strong, although, when the moment required, full of "Pathos and Pungency." This ability was related to the sanity of his mind: he did not set up a notion in his own head and then strain Scripture to conform to a preconceived scheme. While we all agree that zeal unregulated by knowledge is an unhallowed fire, by the same token we know that it must "be placed upon true catholick christianity; and not upon the religion of a party." It must be founded upon principles "which right reason, and the holy word of God will justifie; and not built upon unaccountable impulses, nor designed to serve the interests of any particular party." Some of Willard's teachings may be debatable, but to Pemberton they seemed "agreeable to the principles of right reason, and so clearly revealed in the infallible oracles of truth."

The founders said that the cause of religion rose or fell with that of "literature." There were slightly different accents in Pemberton's celebration of literature as something that has always been in highest esteem among "civilized nations," just as there was in Cutler's defense of the Connecticut college because it "Civilizeth Men, and Cultivateth Good Manners." Rudeness and barbarity, he said, "make Society less Pleasant and Delightful." In 1712 the Old South, in which Judge Sewall was the most powerful layman, was clearly disposed to elect Joseph Sewall as a colleague for whom Pemberton was conspicuously unenthusiastic. He called a meeting, commencing his written summons "Gentlemen"; many of those in favor of Joseph stayed away, affirming "they were not gentlemen." The cause of learning, to which all New England intellectuals were devoted, threatened to become not the cause of religion but of a party—if and when it was principally maintained by those whose standard was the "catholic" ideal of Leverett, the Brattles, and Colman.

For the Mathers, the decade following Increase's expulsion from Harvard was the darkest stage of their pilgrimage: Dudley barred them from political influence, Colman serenely went his way, Stoddard defied them, the *Proposals* failed, and Leverett captured the College. However, it is difficult to tell just what effect academic instruction does have upon students; probably under Willard's regime Harvard clung carefully to standard procedures and a conventional curriculum, with the result that it produced a generation who obviously responded more to intellectual influences from outside the College than to anything within. From those quarters they heard about the new prestige of reason and of revolutionary discoveries in physics, but the whisper of innovation was virtually drowned in the incessant boom of the old-fashioned jeremiad, the loudest sound emanating from the North Church. Under Willard's administration were graduated a group of the most vigorous youths, wholly uncontaminated by the catholic spirit of Colman, who sternly resisted the mollifying persuasives of William Brattle, who were eager to put their shoulders to the wheel of the covenant, and so to push the society into that universal reformation of manners they had been reared to expect. They were not children of Colman or of Stoddard, and certainly not of John Wise; for spiritual parentage they looked to the greatest intellectual in the land, to Cotton Mather.

A number of them got posts in Boston. Joseph Sewall, class of 1707, was ordained in 1712 at the Old South, Pemberton yielding gracefully; John Webb, class of 1708, entered the New North with Matherian assistance in 1714; Colman, trying hard not to be a man of party, welcomed to Brattle Street in 1716 the brilliant William Cooper, who, at his installation, insisted on delivering a doctrinal sermon in sharp contrast to Colman's catholic tone; in 1717 Thomas Foxcroft was imposed upon Wadsworth as colleague at the First Church; and in 1718, after the death of Pemberton, Joseph Sewall engineered the election at the Old South of his classmate Thomas Prince, who had distinguished himself in England in the manner of a young Increase Mather, of whose ordination Cotton Mather exultingly wrote that it gave him a companion with whom he might work more closely than with any upon earth; and in 1723, after the death of Increase, Joshua Gee—who had been graduated from Harvard in 1717, under the rule of Leverett but without being in the slightest touched by him—was installed as colleague to Cotton Mather at the North Church. In 1716 Increase was still announcing that he could see but little of Christ in recent sermons, but in 1718 he hailed a work of Webb's as an omen that some young ministers did after all have their hearts set upon the salvation of the rising generation. He was, he said in 1720, a natural father to the eldest of them, "and in some Sense a Father to the Two Next Eldest of them" [i.e., Colman and Wadsworth], but he pointedly rejoiced that just as he was going out of the world, "I shall Leave Ministers in Boston, who, I trust, will defend the Churches, when I shall Sleep with my Fathers." Increase died content, said his son, "when he saw given to the Churches of the City a Sewall, a Prince, a Webb, a Foxcroft, all singularly endeared unto him." With Thomas Walter rescued from the clutch of Checkley and installed in 1718 at Roxbury, with a few such stalwarts as Shurtleff and Father Moody in crucial outposts, from which they could be summoned periodically for lectures in Boston, the Mathers ended their days with as little reason to despair as any professional pessimists ever enjoyed.

However, there are a few names which conspicuously do not appear in Cotton Mather's lists, which do not figure in the many volumes this group produced in coöperation, or in the interlocking prefaces they wrote for each other's publications. John Barnard, graduated from Harvard in 1700, was for a time one of them, but he scandalized the community by playing cards at Port Royal in 1707, and in 1713 preached a sermon which struck Judge Sewall as "too much savoring of Arminianisme." Just as he does not appear in the literature of the Matherian group, neither does Edward Holyoke, who served as tutor at Harvard from 1712 until he became the colleague of Barnard at Marblehead in 1716. Nathaniel Appleton, nephew of Leverett, and ordained at Cambridge in 1718, is as little counted on as is Edward Wigglesworth, the "Hollisian Professor of Divinity." Likewise disregarded is Ebenezer Gay, installed at Hingham in 1718. Increase might be happy about the churches in Boston, but in 1719, announcing once more his approaching demise, he lamented over the Pelagians, Papists, Socinians, Arminians, Semi-Arminians of the age, "not to mention any New Methodists of our own Nation."

On what grounds did these two groups form their alignments? It is customary to call the Matherian connection "conservative" and the other "liberal." Unless, however, those adjectives are cautiously employed, they here are meaningless. Surely there was no real separation over science, on which the Mather following, under Cotton's leadership, was if anything more advanced than their opponents. Nor was it a split over the conception of reason: Foxcroft would call Tillotson "a Great Divine" as readily as Appleton, would proclaim that in Scripture there is nothing but what is agreeable to the genuine dictates of natural reason, and say that Christian obedience "is the exercise of our reasonable Powers and the exaltation of our rational Nature." Nor was it a matter of either one appropriating more than the other the tone of the eighteenth century: Cotton Mather made as much of the word "gentleman" as did Pemberton. Of William Waldron, the sympathetic minister at the New-Brick Church, he said that his education like his extraction was honourable, "A Gentlemanly Temper and Carriage was hence derived unto him; and much of the GENTLEMAN seen in his whole Behaviour." He praised young Winslow for his beautiful countenance, pleasant wit, sweet disposition and generous behavior, "Full of Life and full of Love to every one"; Foxcroft and Cooper constantly insisted that religion is incompatible with moroseness and gloom. And there is nothing to choose between the two factions in their professed adherence to the ideal of religious liberty.

Furthermore, both sides appear substantially at one in their conception of good style, in which are mingled devotion to the Puritan tradition of plainness with an appreciation of the graces of modernity. Few were so little influenced by the new as to remain exclusively faithful to the former, as did Increase Mather. In 1718 Foxcroft devoted a long section of *A Practical Discourse Relating to the Gospel-Ministry* to form and style, revealing that the example of Colman and the new prose had been fully exerted upon him; as far as the formal prescriptions go, his admonitions could be employed by either faction. The words should be acceptable, "so as at once to charm the ear, reach the mind, and touch the heart." Instead of the ancient logical method, he advocates "the rational, easy, natural" one, without "tumultuary perplextness, or a dry exactness." He wants no "Scholastical accuracy," and only the most intelligible of language, chosen for perspicuity "and easiness of expression," delivered "with a natural turn of speech, and in most entertaining images." Words should exhibit the most bright and clear idea of a truth, images keep their native purity and lively colors. Foxcroft's is still, at bottom, the Puritan ideal of communication to the generality, and so he remains loyal to plainness, but the criterion has become the "polite ear" and the "critical eye." Every phrase, every adjective is an acknowledgment that the prose of the age of Anne has conquered these provincials. Decency, neatness, elegance are virtues; defects are the loose, crude, and sordid. Every effort should be made, as always, to make the sermon efficacious, but not at the sacrifice of intellect: sound demonstration must support doctrines, there must be "a good blaze of tho't, a bright flame of reason." For a "good seasoning" to the whole, the voice should be tuned to a pleasing elocution, in the name of "grace." All this requires labor, wherefore illiterate emotionalism is utterly condemned.

Cotton Mather had gone in his youth to prose masters who taught him tricks he never could rid himself of; he suffered acutely when Oldmixon ridiculed the style of the *Magnalia* and treasured up his resentment for several lively paragraphs in the *Manuductio* against "the Humourists that set up for Criticks upon Style, as the most Unregardable Set of Mortals in the World." Yet he appreciated the trend and tried, especially in his last decade, to move toward simplicity and naturalness, confessing, "I am too liable to an Infirmity of Salting My Sentences . . . with Intermixtures of something or other that I have Read of." He cast aside, as we have seen, academic rhetoric, advised preachers to learn the language of the most polite, and held that every man should have his own style to distinguish him as much as his own gait. The essential thing was "always writing so as to give an Easy Conveyance unto your Idea's."

From the other side, Pemberton's instructions are all of the same tenor, even to identical adjectives. Style must be neither too labored nor too negligent, but "most expressive of the notions to be communicated"; wisdom requires that the manner be adapted to the audience, but in all cases it must be under the government of polite taste. He introduced a volume of Joseph Sewall's by calling attention to the perspicuity and justness of language, which should lend it relish for every serious and judicious reader. Upon Pemberton himself Colman pronounced a judgment which again conveys what had come to be the standard of the age: distinctness, exactness, lively images, strong and nervous, "truly eloquent and very argumentative." At Cotton Mather's funeral, Colman extolled his wit, fancy, invention, quickness of thought, ready apprehension.

Yet to take at random works by any two opponents is to see at once, in the very style, what sundered them. Here, for instance, is a typical bit of Foxcroft:

Think, with what smiling face & ravish't hearts we shall mount up to meet the Lord in the Air, with what transports we shall receive the Euge of our blessed Judge, with what triumphas we shall entertain the Congratulations of the holy Angels and our Fellow-Saints, and with what raptures of delight we shall shout forth our thankful Doxologies to the Great Redeemer, our judiciary sufferages to the Sentences post on the wicked World, and our Songs of holy exultation, glorying and triumphing over Satan, and all our accursed Adversaries.

And here is Appleton in characteristic vein:

As we are Men, i.e. rational Creatures, and as this is what distinguishes us from, and sets us above the Level of the brutish Creation; so if we would do Justice to our own Nature, we must have a peculiar regard for the superiour Powers with which we are endowed. If we would be just to our selves, we must be improving and advancing our rational Faculties, by getting a further knowledge of Things, especially of GOD and CHRIST, and of the way to eternal Life, as we have Opportunity. Moreover, if we would deal justly with our selves, we must endeavour to have all our inferiour Powers under the government of Reason. There is nothing in which we wrong or injure our selves more, than in suffering our Passions and Affections to usurp the Throne within us, and to tyrannize over the noble Powers of our Souls.

Or, again to select at random, here is Prince:

No! Your Hearts are the Principal and most Peculiar Things which God Regards; and they include and contain all others. The Preacher therefore does not say the Hand or Head, but Heart; Because by the possession of the Heart, God has all the members of the Soul and Body devoted to Him.

Whereas, Professor Wigglesworth practiced this mode:

I have hardly at all allow'd my self to address the Passions, or to write in the declamatory Strain, at least not so much as some might perhaps reasonably have expected on this occasion . . . I have study'd to preserve a due Moderation, and Temper; which the Laws of Civility & Christianity oblige to . . . And if any Expressions have happen'd to slip from me, that may seem a little too warm or harsh, I shall be sorry for it.

With these contrasts before us, we comprehend why Increase Mather, in his last days, cried again and again, "Sermons should not be meer Lectures of Morality," why Cotton declared that if Dissenters take to preaching in the manner of the Church of England it will be the end of them, and why their friends repeated these admonitions. Also, we understand who were their targets. Men like Gay, Appleton, and Wigglesworth were, of course, making formal profession of the same sentiments; the difference between the two was one of tone and manner, of tendency. Each grew out of the same background, each had developed under the same influences, and each still avowed devotion to the same creed, to the same orthodoxy.

Nonetheless, the cleavage was really fundamental and not merely a matter of style. Something more than divergence of pulpit manner thrust these Americans into opposing companies. Of this basic issue, the contrast in form is a symbol; but to find out precisely what it symbolized is not easy, because the difference must be defined not by what was said but by what was left unsaid.

It was almost enunciated in the contest over Harvard College. Pemberton and William Brattle died in 1717, Colman preaching a combined funeral sermon; President Leverett exerted himself through a political maneuver to get Appleton chosen to the Cambridge pulpit. It was no more than tactful, therefore, to ask Increase Mather for the ordination sermon; he observed the amenities to the extent of not calling names, but cut off his pound of flesh by admonishing Harvard students, as his "dying Advice," to try to assist the other academical society in Connecticut. He said that should Harvard deviate from the principles of its founders—making clear that he thought it had deviated—"the overthrow of the Churches shall proceed from thence." Joseph Sewall, as colleague of Pemberton, had also been obliged to preach at his funeral, and coyly induced Increase to write a preface for the published version, wherein that venerable man drove home the point that ministers are at best earthen vessels; younger ministers should hence beware of dashing against their fathers, of introducing innovations "as long as there be any that are Conscientiously concerned to maintain the Old Religion of New-England." Meanwhile Leverett saw to it that Appleton and Colman became Fellows of the Harvard Corporation, and so for the first time in his presidency had a friendly majority.

The next year, 1718, the College refused to give Ebenezer Pierpont his M.A., because, Tutor Nicholas Sever said, he was sending from the Roxbury school students improperly qualified, and so was obviously incompetent. For decades the degree of Master of Arts had been awarded automatically, and Bachelors had regularly acquired both it and a little cash by teaching school during the statutory period. This unprecedented action of the Corporation immediately became a political challenge, to which Pierpont responded by the equally unprecedented action of suing Sever in the civil courts. Behind him was mobilized an incongruous crew —the Dudleys, who were his friends in Roxbury, the Council, and, of course, the Mathers. Such a combination might ordinarily have thrown the Patriots into an opposite camp, but in this case they were swayed by theological hostility to Colman and Appleton. Besides, they saw it as a chance to bring the combination into their train, for even an alliance of Council, Dudleys, and Mathers could get nowhere without the House. In the midst of these obscure intrigues is to be made out the hatred of the younger Cooke for his cousin Leverett. He was certainly happy to have an opportunity of striking at the governor through anybody, including the President of Harvard; but possibly even deeper was the fact that he had a cousin to humiliate, for among New England families this motive takes precedence over all others.

The Corporation let Pierpont have his say in front of Governor Shute, where he performed so miserably that his case was thrown out; in Cambridge, the local court accordingly dismissed his suit against Sever. Leverett believed that this affair threatened the dissolution of the College, but the fight had only begun. At a meeting of the Overseers on November 12, Judge Sewall accused the President of omitting expositions of Scripture from meetings in the hall, and Paul Dudley joined in the charge. Cotton Mather, offering to support Shute against the Patriots, attempted to bargain with him in behalf of Pierpont; he even stooped to say that his "aged parent" permitted him thus to write to His Excellency.

That here was a truly vicious struggle, with no holds barred, is testified by the fact that in this same year, 1718, Cotton Mather persuaded Elihu Yale to turn his benefactions toward Connecticut. He and Prince also worked hard upon Thomas Hollis to divert in the same direction his intention of founding a professorship of divinity, or else to endow Prince's private collection of New England imprints so as to prevent its going someday into the profane library at Cambridge. The good Hollis, a Baptist, listened to a letter from the catholic Colman, and so persisted in giving his money to Harvard, although he could never get from the College an honest assurance that the professorship would be entirely undenominational. The Corporation would have assured him, but the Board of Overseers, where Judge Sewall was the power, would go no further, even when blessed with the gift, than requiring that the incumbent be "sound and orthodox." The Fellows of the Corporation chose Wigglesworth, who had been waiting for the post, in June 1721, and then were so frightened by the Board of Overseers that they went through the form of examining his theology and a second time elected him in January 1723. Hollis was never fully informed of these proceedings, and calmly wrote, "I doubt not but that they are pleased with my moneys." Probably nobody was in a position to tell him that as long as Wigglesworth was the professor, he need not worry too much about restrictions imposed by the Overseers, for Wigglesworth was capable of swearing allegiance to Ames's *Medulla* and to the divine right of infant baptism without allowing such un-catholic impositions to interfere with his moderate and civil instruction.

The crisis came in 1721—the year of the *Courant*, of inoculation, of the land bank, of *The Christian Philosopher:* two tutors, Sever and Welsteed, suddenly demanded seats on the Corporation. That body consisted of Leverett and the treasurer, John White, along with Wadsworth, Colman, Appleton, Joseph Stevens—and of Henry Flynt, who was a tutor but also a partisan of Leverett's. Behind the demand of Sever and Welsteed was the thrust of Judge Sewall and Paul Dudley; Leverett behaved heroically, and out of the contest there emerged, for the first time clearly, the distinction at Harvard, and ultimately for all American universities, between a governing body and the faculty. In the midst of this affair, Tutor Thomas Robie took his mind off his telescope long enough to note a report being spread about "That my Sermons were only Heathenish discourses, no better Christianity than was in Tully," wherefore he came to Leverett's aid by publishing one of them, dedicated to the President, which asserted that ministers should preach Christ and nothing but Him, but that they need not mention Him in every sentence. Stevens elected this moment to die; the Corporation tried to circumvent Judge Sewall by electing his son Joseph, but when the Overseers insisted upon a resident tutor, it neatly settled upon Robie. The Overseers sought for support in the House, and might have won a terrible victory had not Governor Shute, by this time thoroughly at odds with the Representatives, refused consent to a bill enlarging the Corporation. A royal governor and not the Overseers of Harvard College preserved the integrity, and so the independence, of the institution.

The fight went on, even though in 1723 Shute had fled; the Corporation signed themselves, in a petition to Lieutenant Governor Dummer, "Those of us, whose ejectment is so earnestly sought for." They developed the contention that resident tutors are not automatically members of the board, and won their case with the argument that tutors who through sloth or neglect of duties prove to be unworthy can never be expelled if they are also allowed to be governors. For a teaching faculty to make their own laws and vote their own salaries would be, said the Corporation, "contrary to the light of nature." Colman, Wadsworth, and Appleton, who knew themselves the object of the campaign, offered to resign, but Robie relieved them by withdrawing to private practice in Salem; the Corporation stood their ground and took Wigglesworth in his place. Judge Sewall, the Mathers, and their allies had to desist.

It is as nasty a story as any in the history of New England. We may get some insight into what these divisions signified from the operations of a committee appointed by the Board of Overseers in August 1723 to investigate the College—an early form of the inquest into un-American activities. Cotton Mather lent impetus—and animus—to the proceedings by making a series of inquiries: whether solid learning was kept up and Latin properly taught, whether tutors did not make students get by heart a deal of insipid stuff, whether the library was not full of Satanical books, the poisonous passages of which were not decried, or whether the tutors had ever spoken one word in defense of that church order "which is the distinguishing interest and beauty of the churches in this country." Was it not true, he asked—thinking of the little band he now had gathered around him in the Boston pulpits—that excellent young ministers have to declare that "before they came to be what they are, they found it necessary to lay aside the sentiments which they brought from the College with them." The committee of the Overseers brought in a report substantiating these charges, but by the time it was prepared, Dummer and the Council had come out in support of Wigglesworth. Even the most vindictive dared not push their charges too far. On May 3, 1724, President Leverett died in his sleep; the Overseers allowed Wigglesworth to enter the Corporation, and both factions prepared for a decisive battle over the presidency.

Leverett and his friends were a minority; they would have been completely routed and Harvard reconquered by the Mathers had not Shute saved them, in consequence of which the Council reluctantly came around. But Leverett's faction had courage enough not to wait upon salvation by the next royal governor, as Appleton proved by publishing a funeral oration on Leverett boldly entitled *A Great Man Fallen in Israel*. Considering the circumstances, it is one of the most gallant—and defiant—gestures in the period. Appleton sets forth a truly great man. While his pious conclusion affirms that "after all" true grace is requisite to greatness, on his way to that unexceptionable truism, the mold of catholic form has been so mirrored that Mathers and Joseph Sewalls could not fail to understand wherein by comparison they fell short. First of all, Leverett possessed a quick apprehension, which means "a promptness to receive ideas, when they are offered to our minds, without requiring a great deal of time and pains to have them beat into us." Then, he had a capacity of thinking clearly and distinctly, so that he could not only convey his thoughts clearly to others, but lay them together so as to pass good judgment upon them; he could tell what was true and what false, not being confined to "the narrow limits of Domestick Affairs," but ranging over general concerns. He was of an active temper, and because of such men—let *Bonifacius* take note!— "the most usefull discoveries, either in nature or art, have been produced." Leverett had magnanimity, enabling him to stem the current and stand against opposition; he would run the hazard of losing his friends, his estate, and indeed his very life in doing his duty. Yes, he had grace, but in him it enlightened the understanding, and so inclined the will to follow rational dictates, to regulate emotions. He studied all sorts of learning— philosophy, law, history, languages—but in addition he was a statesman, "few or none understanding the Times and Seasons, and what ought to be done, better than he." In this spirit, he was of a catholic mind. (Did any remember that in 1723, while the Overseers were trying to clog Hollis' gift, Cotton Mather had dedicated a book to Hollis, declaring a forceful subscription to rites of which conscience disapproves to be "a Mother of Abominations"?) Above all, deliberately concluded Appleton, this Leverett was a lover of his country and a true friend to these churches, who desired their flourishing "and was much concern'd at any thing that threatened their Overthrow or Injury"—even though he did not place religion so much in particular forms "as in those substantial and weighty matters of the Gospel." Under his administration the College increased in numbers, flourished in solid and "useful" learning. Let those who had hounded him, was the all-but-uttered moral, match this greatness if they can!

Had Mather and the investigating committee been able to charge Leverett's administration with specific doctrinal heresies, we might better understand the vehemence of the attack; however, besides finding discipline too lax, about all the accusers could say was that students were allowed to read subversive books. But when we examine publications of the minority, we quickly perceive their real offense: they gave little or no attention to the covenant, and generally ignored it completely. Hence they preached no jeremiads. Wigglesworth attested his orthodoxy by writing a proof of future torments; but he did not present hell as a threat of vengeance upon violators of the covenant: instead, he soberly pointed out that the prospect makes it "impossible for Reason to be at any Stand, which side to chuse," and that therefore dread of such punishment "is to be excited by a rational Expectation of it." The best illustration of the radical omission in the Harvard theology is Appleton's first ambitious work, *The Wisdom of God in the Redemption of Fallen Man:* this is quite orthodox Calvinism in that it preaches predestination and irresistible grace, but it never once mentions the covenants. It would have been impossible for any before this date—including a Stoddard who denied the existence of church covenant—to imagine that one could write even a paragraph on this topic without expounding the three Covenants, of Works, of Redemption, and of Grace, explaining how moral obedience was incorporated in the terms of a federal scheme of salvation by faith. Instead, Appleton commences with a definition of wisdom as that which proposes the most excellent of aims and subordinates other ends to it; what greater aim could God propose than to manifest His glory to all "Rational Creatures"? The problem faced by the Almighty is how, reasonably, He can manifest all His attributes simultaneously, which presents difficulties "insuperable to any created reason," but which divine wisdom achieves in Christianity—all without any resort whatsoever to the covenants. Worship of God does not take the form of consent to a bond, but simple understanding and admiration of that which—although in some sense mysterious—can, in so far as it is wise, be understood. Not the security of a covenanted promise makes the Christian, but intelligence:

> He that considers the Nature of true Wisdom, will find it a most excellent vertue; greatly, and above all to be desired. This is that which inriches, and enobles a Man, and makes him more excellent than his Neighbour. For as reason raises a Man above the level of Beasts: so wisdom raises one Man above another, makes him really a better Man in the sight of God, who is the best able judge in such a matter.

The fathers had been convinced that a learned ministry could not justify God's ways to man unless God condescended to confine Himself to terms; Appleton is quite content to confront an uncovenanted wisdom because of the inherently rational character of wisdom itself. For example, God took care that Christ should be sensibly proved the Messiah, "For unless he had given some evident proof, and demonstration of it, there would have been no sufficient grounds for any to believe in him," and what "more effectual way can we imagine could be taken, to convince Rational Creatures" than just the one God did adopt? So conversion is not a coming into the bond: God "begins with the Understanding, that being the leading and governing faculty, and makes use of this to incline & perswade the Will; and so the Man makes a rational Choice, and is persuaded from rational considerations."

In this same year Cooper is preaching, "Your Baptism is a bond upon you to early religion, and brings you under an indispensable engagement to walk in the truth"; therefore, "Beg of God that the entail mayn't be cut off." Or at a public lecture Webb proclaims the great concern of New England to be whether we "who are the Posterity of God's Covenant People" shall be cut off. The signs are that God is withdrawing—and out comes, in 1730, all the good old catalogue: profaneness, cursing, slandering, backbiting, injustice, oppression, rioting, drunkenness, lewdness, uncleanness, contempt for ecclesiastical ordinances. These, "Like an irresistible Torrent, threaten to Bury us in one common ruine." And so they will unless we repent and reform, by doing which we shall acquire the prosperity promised by covenant, because our fathers took care "to Entail the Priviledges and Blessings of the Covenant, to their Seed, in all succeeding Generations."

In virtually every utterance of the Matherian group, the federal theology thus survives. Striving with might and main to cling to that system so identified with the soil of New England, such New Englanders could not conceive what sort of personality would be left them were it discarded. Yet they, too, have embraced the cause of science, bowed to the slogan of rationality, founded society upon compact and constitutional rights, been forced to think of social problems in terms of depreciating currency and of imports and exports—and had the gauntlet of wit slapped across their faces. They have not lagged in cultivating elegance, politeness, ease, and graciousness. They know that Stoddard's denial of the church covenant has not been silenced; so far, neither he nor any from his empire had carried rejection of the covenant upwards into theology—but might not some among his disciples do just that? The vehemence of the attack upon Leverett and Harvard shows a basic insecurity among the so-called conservatives; they were captives of an idea, but they had also learned to accept, willingly or unwillingly, an array of ideas simply incompatible with their federalism. In trying to hold all together, they saw the covenant collapsing; out of their own instability, they turned in anger upon men like Wigglesworth and Appleton, who serenely dispensed with federalism and left New England naked before the Almighty.

From this inner tension flows a strain of oratory which the group perfected around 1710 or '20, of which the title of Increase Mather's *Now*

or Never is the Time for Men to make Sure of their Eternal Salvation is
sufficient characterization. Taking care to guarantee their orthodoxy by
occasional assertions of salvation irrespective of merit, they expend their
major effort on proving, by the rationality of the covenant, that men must
seize it now, must jump while they can, must not hang back because of
scruples or doubts, but must arouse themselves. While we are waiting upon
God, says Cotton Mather's *Stimulator*, "Our Importunity must be Vehement, be Violent, be Unpacifiable."

In the subtle logic of the founders, where an armory of precise technical
terms permitted the finest of distinctions, it had always seemed easy to distinguish the federal theology from Arminianism. The Mathers continued
to believe this possible: they do not propose a rational and moral duty alone,
they remember that the will is corrupt and requires grace in order to comply with the terms. But, with all that vocabulary consigned to vulgarity,
what remains of the covenant? "The Laws," said Timothy Woodbridge
in 1727, "are Wisely and Graciously suited to the state of man under his
Probation." What then is to prevent a rational man from taking up the
terms? Not so much original sin as more explicable influences—preoccu-
pation with business, poisonous books from abroad, taverns, laziness, or
a spreading doubt that the covenant ever existed. To counteract these de-
terrents, the covenant must be thrust harder, more violently upon the
people. They must be entreated with tears, they must be stimulated with
new tricks of speech, and above all they must be frightened with vivid
portrayals of eternal torment. Rational preaching within the framework
of the covenant, as contrasted with rational discourse outside it, must
become more and more emotional.

For this reason, then, the formal creed of the two groups could be the
same, and yet the result be a difference in connotation and practice as
wide as any between diametrically opposed philosophies. God treats with
men "as rational Agents, capable of deliberating, chusing and resolving,"
says Foxcroft; "He affords the best Means to enlighten their understand-
ings." Hence ours is a "reasonable Service." But if the concept of hell is,
as Wigglesworth contends, a rational inducement, is it not doubly so when
a sanction of the covenant? Therefore, the fear of hell should be pressed
upon men, not as a demonstration of wisdom, but as a present and agonizing danger. "The Threatnings of the Word which are messages of Evil to
guilty Sinners are a proper medium to use with them to restrain them
from Sin, inasmuch as they address one of the Passions of humane Nature,
and are a just Alarm to the Fears of Men." With Cotton Mather waving
the baton of reason, science, and the natural style, his chorus chanted the
terrors of damnation, striving to develop a rhetoric by which these could
be made most effective against Harvard's "superstition Education." None
of the group being very creative, they went as far as they were able, but
by 1730 needed instruction from a greater master of the word than any
they yet had listened to. "O Spectacle full of Horror!" exclaimed Cotton

Mather, "O Hard Heart, O Base Heart, that is not Affected with it!"
Until a greater should appear, this was the best these federalists could
achieve in the way of instilling terror.

In 1726 Cotton Mather boasted that there was not a single Arminian
in New England; by 1734, the Matherian party were to endorse a jeremiad of John White's that called Arminianism the great sin of the land,
while in Northampton Edwards commenced the feud with his Williams
cousins by preaching against it. White's speech clearly is aimed at men like
Appleton and Wigglesworth; Edwards' more metaphysical thrust might
equally be directed against what became the premises, even if unacknowledged, of the revivalistic technique of Matherian federalism: "My Brethren," as Cotton Mather illustrates it, "This is the Way. And now, what
remains to be endeavoured, is, To use a Sacred Violence upon you . . .
You are now to be excited unto an Action of the greatest Importance in
the World." Throughout these sermons the cry arises, come in while you
can, until one wonders with what brazenness they could still maintain this
was not Arminianism. Possibly because men like Appleton and the young
Charles Chauncy (whom the First Church forced Foxcroft to accept as
colleague in 1727) broadly intimated that by their lights such uninhibited
excitation was exactly that, the federalists were more and more eager to
brand as Arminian heretics all who would not cry aloud that covenant violations brought down afflictions on New England. "Be not surprised at it,"
Cotton Mather preached, "if I tell you, I must leave you Dead upon the
spot, before I have done with you." But Ebenezer Gay's first published discourse was entitled, *Ministers are Men of Like Passions with Others*.

The motions and countermotions over the choice of Leverett's successor
make a modern political caucus seem naïve. The Corporation offered the
post to Joseph Sewall, he being the most amenable of the opposition, and
his election would spike their biggest gun, the Judge his father. This might
also have split the group wide open; Cotton Mather was already putting in
his journals insulting estimates of Sewall's scholarship, but Sewall declined
and so regained Mather's love. Colman was then asked; he did not want
to leave the comfort of Brattle Street, and he knew that Leverett, having
invested not only health but all his fortune in the College, died bankrupt.
When the House refused to enlarge his salary, he refused. The next move
was the obvious one: William Wadsworth.

Although Wadsworth had for a time become an object of wrath because
he voted with Colman and Appleton, the opposition never held him so far
gone in treason as the others. In 1707 he had in fact opposed Leverett, and
throughout the later contest took care of his fences, offended nobody, and
retained the favor of the General Court, which was ready to vote him the
raise in salary they had refused Colman. He promptly conciliated everybody
by putting Sever on the Corporation; in return the General Court built him
Wadsworth House, which still today, although shorn of its lawn and
crowded upon by brick and steel, delights the eye.

Wadsworth was the ideal choice for more reasons than his agreeable—or should one say pliant?—character. For thirty years he had been publishing almost as much as Cotton Mather; he was rational, enlightened, unemotional. His doctrines were as unexceptional as his style, generally formulated in this wise: "Christians should indeavour to be blameless, harmless and without rebuke, in their whole carriage and behaviour among men in the world." Every word of this preaching, he practiced. But what qualified him to placate the enemies of Leverett, for all that he had stood beside Appleton, was that he had always expounded, and gave every indication of continuing to expound, the conventional theology. He wrote much upon baptism, explaining it as the seal upon the Covenant of Grace, and at immense length identified the duties expected of a Christian with the terms of the Covenant. In every covenant, "there are two Parties which stand Oblig'd and Ingag'd to each other"; God in the Gospel "offers Eternal Life and Glory to Sinners, if they'll Comply with such and such Termes and Articles." The promise extends to the seed, it contains both duties and benefits, and though there is no guarantee that outward prosperity is among the latter, still "while the Saints are on Earth, some outward supplies are needful for them; and God has by Covenant Promise ingaged to bestow outward Things, so far as he sees best for them." With this familiar, orthodox, undisturbing doctrine once more enthroned at Harvard, Appleton was checkmated, investigating committees could disband, and Cotton Mather die reasonably content. He had good hopes, he wrote Hollis, that Wadsworth would prove infinitely better than "the infamous drone, his predecessor." Cotton Mather meant that Wadsworth was safe. Matherians no longer needed to be alarmed, because Wadsworth had often written, "The Termes of this Covenant of Grace are most reasonable," and that since they are, "let nothing hinder thee from complying with them." Mather had striven to inject a little more life, a few more exclamations and apostrophes into his presentations of this idea, but it was, thus flatly stated, the sum and substance of his theology as well as that of those inestimable blessings, the pastors "whom our glorious LORD has of late years bestowed upon the Churches of Boston." He prophesied that "The whole Countrey will feel the sweet Influences, of more than seven Stars, that Irradiate its Metropolis." Hollis, a pious but a shrewd man, wrote back questioning how Mather dared give such a character to the deceased Leverett, and he always let it be clearly seen that he felt the greatest satisfaction with what he heard of Wigglesworth. He might have been able to tell Mather, or Mather might have realized for himself, that rhetorical hypodermics can keep a dying idea alive only so long. Wadsworth's ponderous solemnity, unrelieved either by wit or by worry, was a sign large enough for any to read—or at least for Edwards to read—that the covenant theology was out of place in the eighteenth century, not only because it was incompatible with the new rationality and with a Newtonian universe, but because it had become unendurably dull.

CHAPTER XXVIII

POLITY AS A FORM OF PATRIOTISM

BENJAMIN
Wadsworth proved a successful compromise presi-
dent, not only because of his pleasing personality and his covenant theology,
but even more because both factions, at the moment of his elevation, realized that they were equally threatened by the gathering strength of the
Church of England.

What America today knows as the Protestant Episcopal Church was not
then a dignified body above the storm of politics: instead, it was an instrument of imperial aggression, all the more dangerous because, despite a century of warfare and despite the empirical solution of the Act of Toleration,
Nonconformists had not yet reconciled themselves to the notion of being
minority sects existing on sufferance. Baptists and Quakers had been obliged
to secede, but orthodox Puritans never admitted to having withdrawn, and
still had a nostalgia for solidarity. In New England, the difficulty was particularly troublesome because the founders had expended so much ingenuity
in proving that their ecclesiastical order never was, and never could become,
Separatist. Theologically, New England always professed allegiance to the
Thirty-Nine Articles; never, by any act of its own, had it severed itself
from the national communion. By the end of the century, provincials were
painfully learning to call themselves Congregationalists (or in Connecticut,
Semi-Presbyterians), but even then merely in a descriptive sense, not—if
they could help it—with the implication that they had become a peculiar,
distinct, or merely local denomination. They still believed that the New
Testament showed their polity to be apostolic, and in their heart of hearts
remained convinced that it was no more than the most reformed portion of
the universal church. Even after the new charter obliged them to take advantage of exemptions allowed by the Act of Toleration, leaders of the
regime would never fully admit that they were outside the pale. They welcomed the Society for the Propagation of the Gospel in 1701, and then were
hurt and chagrined when that Society directed its energies to recovering
New England for episcopacy, in effect declaring it not yet gospelized. They
felt as might a Benedictine monastery invaded by Jesuits intent upon converting it to the true faith.

Complaining passages in the 1700's show more bewilderment than anger:
why treat us as heathen? But as the S.P.G. continued to afford financial
aid to Anglican groups—or, worse yet, to any rebels against the regime who

pretended to be Anglicans—the meaning of the assault became clear: certain forces in the Church of England were resolved to subdue New England. A people who had providentially escaped Presbyterian invasion in the 1640's, who had fended off Charles II and, after the brief ordeal of the Dominion, had received by a tolerant charter a confirmation of their ecclesiastical privileges, had now to face a more subtle form of penetration. Certainly this Episcopalian thrust would take immediate advantage of any cleavage among the Congregational churches; so, despite the depth and seriousness of the division, ranks had to be closed.

After 1698, when Bellomont arrived—for all that he was a gentle soul —the problem for the clergy became, as we have seen, how to present their polity to the world as, on the one hand, a group of Dissenters graciously allowed by the Act of 1689 to indulge their idiosyncrasies, and at the same time the legal equivalent of the Church of England, standing upon enduring rights and entitled to all the perquisites of an establishment. These churches, as Pemberton said in 1717, are not formed in all points like those of "the established church of South-Britain," yet they "have their constitution and priviledges secured to them, not barely, by an act of toleration, but a legal approbation and establishment." Hence they should be doubly secure, both as a tolerated minority and a ruling majority, because all their laws had been confirmed in the glorious reign of King William—until, that is, they had seriously to face the question of how they could simultaneously be both, or, had they to choose, upon which basis they would stake their case.

At first the problem seemed simplified by rallying, in the manner of Benjamin Colman, behind such moderate Anglicans as Tillotson, by stressing not forms but formulae of accord. In this spirit Leverett tried to conduct Harvard, with the result that his students reported in England that he was no enemy to the Church, while his opponents called him a crypto-Anglican. In the name of his motto "catholick," Colman wrote to friendly bishops that no other place could boast of such genuine freedom as "our little College." Although Bishop Kennet told him frankly that the S.P.G. was determined not to compromise but to conquer (the Society was pouring pounds into Stratford, Connecticut, out of which operated a vigorous group of converts), Colman desperately kept up the pretense that there was no real antagonism. For a while he received support from the Mathers, who insisted that as concerns the everlasting maxims of piety all good men—Anglicans, Scots, and New Englanders—are united. Cotton Mather sometimes worked this argument around to mean that a church which does *not* exclude profane persons is actually the one that has separated from Christianity, but he was still trying to prove that New England, by practicing Congregationalism, had never split off. At the same time, as when accepting his degree from Scotland, he insisted that this compliment to him was a symbol of the universal communion: "To Unite, not upon matters of Doubtful Disputation, but upon the Essentials and Substantials of Christianity, and Receive those whom Christ Receives."

Successfully to maintain this position required difficult acrobatics. It demanded, in the first place, that no doctrine taught in New England, either *The Westminster Confession* or the Covenant of Grace, be publicly treated as anything other than a more precise exposition of the Thirty-Nine Articles, a drawing out of consequences clearly contained within them; secondly, it meant that those Anglicans who insisted that the Church of England did teach a theology at variance with New England's be called interlopers, "Tory" perverters of a fundamentally Whig and Protestant institution truly exemplified by such as Tillotson and not at all by Sancroft or Dr. Sacheverell. But furthermore, it called for adroit skill in employing one or the other of New England's favorite lines of defense to suit the opponent of the moment, but never to press one so far as to leave the other out of sight: if the S.P.G. was on the march, New England must resist in the name of liberties allowed to all Dissenters; but if Quakers and Baptists demanded larger immunities, the New England Way must become the colonial version of the English Church, and be permitted to decide for itself how little it would allow to divergent minorities. Danger lay in following either argument to the exclusion of the other; success could be won only if both were maintained simultaneously, contradictory though they might logically seem.

This juggling act became precarious when Baptists and Quakers appealed to London, where they had powerful friends to whom the Lords of Trade would listen, not out of religious sympathy but in an eagerness to collect evidences of colonial insubordination. The difficulty became doubly terrifying as protests accumulated from Anglicans or from those who said they were. For New England to ask English support in keeping down King's Chapel or Trinity Church was to suppose that ministers of the Crown occupied (if with anything beyond place and preferment) with enforcing the Navigation Laws would let themselves be persuaded by New England's strange and wonderful dialectic to curtail their own co-religionists. In America, the people might be lulled into security by infallible demonstrations that the New England Way was at one and the same time a tolerated minority and yet the American segment of the Established Church, but that logic looked fairly wizened in Whitehall.

In the 1640's Massachusetts deliberately took the risk of punishing a Presbyterian Child, prepared to argue that the charter gave full authority, and, if that plea failed, to resist by force. The second charter obviously allowed the province no such power, but instead required freedom of conscience; furthermore, resistance by subjects so extravagantly loyal to Hanover and to the Protestant succession was unthinkable. The situation could be handled, if at all, only with diplomacy, unction, and duplicity. Religious liberty could be so conspicuously advertised as to conceal (for a time) how grudging and how minute were the concessions made to dissidents; cordial relations could be cultivated, or at least affected, with Whiggish or indifferent elements in the Church. If worst came to worst, trouble-making minorities, including Anglicans, could be accused of disturbing the peace, and be dealt with as Connecticut dealt with Rogerenes: they could be accused of rebelling against His Majesty King George, Defender of the Faith and head of the Church of England.

The problem of preserving coherence was aggravated by the conflict of Stoddard and the Mathers, which almost rent the seamless garment. It was worsened when Patriots and financiers, and ultimately Jeremiah Dummer, pushed religion aside and argued New England's case as being entirely secular—for in this context, why be concerned for religious uniformity at all? Meanwhile another worry had been growing with the years: ought all who contribute to maintaining the ministry be allowed a voice in the election of ministers? In 1700, Increase Mather resoundingly answered "NO." This would be against reason, for non-members are generally more than twice the membership; thus a minister might be chosen of whom not even one of the fraternity could in conscience approve. All our great reformers, "Prelatical ones excepted," have asserted limitation of the electorate. Yet Mather's language, his placing of reason before Scripture, shows him resisting an inexorable trend: the threefold division of communities into church, congregation, and town could not be sustained without either active support from the government or a continuing sense of the spiritual bases for these complicated distinctions. As the government became powerless or indifferent, people who could not remember the fine-spun arguments of 1662, but who knew that the character of their minister was a community concern, simply exerted mass pressure; parish and precinct dictated to the saints, so that in hundreds of communities Stoddard's reform was in effect accomplished, although not through clerical leadership. Cotton Mather had to yield one more step by advising churches in 1713 to "consult" the inhabitants, but still tried to hold the line by crying that if further invasions are made, the consequences will be fatal, "and may bring in an Imposition of Ministers, without any Election of the People at all." As the New England Way became, under the force of circumstances, less and less what the founders meant by Congregational, it lay the more vulnerable before the bishops.

By 1720, there seemed but one hope, only a synod could reëstablish unanimity. Without it, all other efforts, such as transforming the piety and appropriating science, even active societies for reformation, could not check the disintegration. Colman was asking for a synod as early as 1708: it alone could "make People know that there must and shall be some End to their Strifes and Discords." It is all very well to be tolerant, Cotton Mather found himself saying in 1712, to make "generous Allowances to others' prejudices," but for the "Children of this Country"—i.e., the dominant churches—to depart from the holy principles of their ancestors is to "challenge Thunderbolts." Yet how, with Stoddard undefeated and the *Proposals* moribund, could the advance of those superstitions "their Fathers would rather have died than complied with" be halted "except by the reasserting of a synod"?

In his mightier days, Increase Mather had written vociferously against the Prayer Book; in 1712 an Anglican divine looked up these works, and raised the question of New England's loyalty. Mather was on the spot and had to take notice. He stood all the ground he could: the Prayer Book is Popish, we left England in protest against it; while we are truly hospitable to all the righteous, still, for us to give up our polity would be a much greater sin and provocation "than in any other part of the World." There exactly was the question that would not down: if New England was a land of freedom, if churches that had never separated and were one in piety with England still managed an accommodation not only with differences among themselves but with the *de facto* existence of unscriptural customs, why was alteration or concession so much more fatal, and therefore so much more to be resisted, for it than for any other society? Obviously, to maintain this thesis, no one person could speak for the whole land; but a synod might if Mathers, Stoddard, Colman, Wise, Appleton, Bulkley could be gathered together and their differences resolved. A synod alone could recommit the land to its primitive clarity, affirm its stand against the church from which it had never departed and against the sects it tolerated, and so prevent conquest by "another Church-Government, not gathered out of the Word." "I am troubled," wrote Increase in 1716, "that I should differ from so many of the present Ministers in New-England, or rather that they differ from me." If, at the end of his life, he could again preside over a synod as he had in 1679, might he not get even Wise and Leverett, let alone Stoddard, to agree with him?

In 1719 John Checkley published Charles Leslie's *The Religion of Jesus* and followed it with his own *Choice Dialogues,* which were vigorous propaganda for the Church of England. The enemy was now definitely abroad; orthodox leaders therefore decided to impose an oath upon "disaffected" persons, and Checkley was fined, as we have seen, on the charge of disloyalty to his king. But this could not prevent the circulation of his *Dialogues,* in which a "Country-Man" (a forthright fellow, a true Yankee) has his native suspicions about predestination confirmed by a kindly minister who demonstrates, by reason, that there can be no such cruel doctrine in the justice of God. The alert rustic gets the point at once: there can be no sin without free will. "What a Jest wou'd it be in you, if you shou'd pretend to argue with me, to promise or threaten, to perswade me to do such a Thing, if you knew before-hand that it was impossible for me to do it?" The minister reviews, with fiendish irony, the many dilutions New England had filtered into its theology—preparation, hypocrisy, the Half-Way Covenant, owning the covenant—and concludes that Calvinism is incapable of knowing its own mind. "Thou ought to bless God," says the minister, "that you have been educated in the Church of England, where you have been instructed in the true Foundations of Christianity, which give all the Assurance that the Word and Promise of God can give." Thus analyzing the true import of the Seventeenth Article, the *Dialogues* decide that no Calvinist can honestly subscribe to it, that those who do not—the churches of New England, for example—are schismatical, and therefore stand on no other legal basis than that of tolerated Dissenters. In a foolish effort to disguise this fact, they pretend that their theology is compatible with the Articles; because they force themselves into this hypocrisy they, and not the Church protected by its ceremonies, start down the path that leads to Arianism and Socinianism.

This was the moment for Thomas Walter to repay his uncle the debt he owed for being rescued from Checkley's spell, particularly as one passage in the *Dialogues* was a patent thrust at remarks Cotton Mather delivered during Walter's ordination at Roxbury. Walter died in 1725 at the age of twenty-nine; he is chiefly remembered, if at all, for the book he published during the year of crisis, 1721, on *The Grounds and Rules of Musick Explained*, which was part of the effort on the part of the orthodox leaders to get the people to sing in unison so that their thoughts and feelings might thereby become better ordered. For it the Mathers and their group signed a preface, but the cause was such (as was inoculation) that Colman and Wadsworth must perforce join with them. We have some difficulty in making out just why Charles Chauncy, years later, would still rank Walter, along with Bulkley and Dummer, as one of the three first geniuses of New England; perhaps it was because when Chauncy was at Harvard (he was class of 1721), Walter had the reputation of being the most accomplished and witty of the recent graduates (his class was 1713). At any rate, he seemed to the younger man to "have almost an intuitive knowledge of every thing" (Chauncy was to acquire, in a long life, an extensive knowledge, but a less intuitive creature probably never existed); he was supposed, by long and intimate converse with Cotton Mather, to be already possessed of his uncle's vast erudition while still in his twenties, which would, of course, have given him a terrific head-start over all his contemporaries. However, we make out not only in the satires that appeared upon him in the *Courant* but in Chauncy's remembering how "he loved company and diversion," that despite his Matherian connection (or perhaps, to keep the perspective historically accurate, we should insist that the Matherian tie was no handicap for the acquisition of such a reputation), he figured to the provincial society as a man not only of learning but of polish, wit, and grace, one who could be as elegant as Colman but as orthodox as Joseph Sewall. So in his short career he succeeded in being adored by his uncle and admired by Charles Chauncy, and his early death was a sad loss for the cause of provincial unity.

All this explains why he was, as Checkley put it, "taggd" by a sort of grand committee of the Mather faction to deal both with Checkley and the *Courant*, for no other member of the group dared trust himself to a battle of wits. Signing himself "Christopher Whigg," he published *A Choice Dialogue between John Faustus A Conjurer and Jack Tory His Friend*, in which the subordinate devil conveys Satan's thanks to Checkley for what he has attempted, but then berates him for having bungled the job. Checkley has made a fatal error in attributing to New England theology doctrines that are nowhere taught; but worse than that, his grammar and style are crude. As in *The Little-Compton Scourge,* Walter tried to win by ridicule —and we have seen what floodgates he opened. For the New England churches, or rather for the elements gathered around the Mathers, to let themselves be thus defended against Anglicanism—for them to give Checkley the chance to answer in kind and to characterize Walter's prose as full of "many Billingsgate Flowers which has so delicately perfum'd the whole Piece"—is an awful commentary on their demoralization. Somehow, out of the charge that Checkley writes like a tinker, arises the double and dubious contention that New England does not impose strict predestination on believers and "that Calvin's Doctrine is the true ancient and primitive Doctrine of the Church of England."

The serious point behind this misguided buffoonery appears when we ask for what audience Walter wrote. He might have imagined that he could get help from ecclesiastical Whigs in England by smearing provincial Anglicans as Tories, just as Colman was also hoping when he preached at Joseph Dudley's funeral and praised this erstwhile lieutenant of Andros for being "in principle a Calvinist according to the manifest Doctrine of the Church of England in her Articles." But whether Colman and Walter deceived anybody but themselves may be doubted, and probably not themselves very successfully. The Mathers soon had to publish three letters to English Nonconformists in which they strove manfully but not convincingly to plead that the Dissenters, being true children of the Church, believe in liberty, but that as such they must expel Arians from their communion. "I hope, a Protestant may have leave to ask his Brother, how he understands this Rule, in certain important Articles, which must be for the main rightly understood." Liberty does not mean that we associate ourselves with the works of darkness. But then, if we and we alone comprehend the Articles aright, in spite of having for a hundred years kept up the dialectic of non-Separation, are we not fooling ourselves about being in reality parts of the national church? Have we not obviously sunk into that mire of schism which the founders despised, and are we anything better than a collection of crotchety sectaries?

The absolute need for control within the system was made excruciatingly evident in 1720 (again, the great crisis!) when the New North Church, in which the Mathers' ally John Webb was installed, invited Peter Thacher to move from Weymouth; not relishing the prospect of smoking "out his days in so much and so great obscurity," Thacher accepted. The issue was the same as in Davenport's call to Boston back in 1669: a metropolitan church was robbing a helpless rural body, in violation of all the canons of Congregationalism. The Mathers protested, and a minority of the church withdrew, but the rest ordained Thacher and there was nothing the Mathers could do but make the best of what they could not prevent

(Thacher joined his colleagues in endorsing Walter's treatise on music, but significantly enough, while the names of Sewall, Prince, Webb, Cooper follow immediately after those of the Mathers, and then come those of Wadsworth and Colman, Thacher's is the last). The Mathers lamented that the affair scandalized "Strangers, even they that are afar off" (reports about this inability of the system to prevent fission were undoubtedly hastened to the Bishop of London), and tried to assure the world that most of the churches more faithfully observed the order of the Gospel; but if so shining a light as Webb could defy it and get away with the deed, there was no guarantee that even in the area most under the Matherian thumb uniformity could be maintained. The hallmark of a sect, as contrasted with a church, was the uncontrollable dissidence of dissent. The prospect was melancholy when "the Corruptions of Men are grown so Head-Strong as to render it not Easy to propose a Method for Cure, in which the Remedy may not anon prove worse than the Malady." The conventional threats of divine wrath could indeed be summoned up, but something more immediate was required; it begins to look, wailed Cotton Mather, as though the sole distinction between the children of God and the seed of the serpent is that the former have an affection for and the latter an aversion against "the most Faithful and Painful and Useful Ministers in the Kingdom of our Savior." Only a synod could organize these ministers to resist the serpent, only a synod could save them. "Indeed," Increase moralized, "the more Councils & Synods are disregarded & slighted, so much the more disorder and confusion will (we fear) grow & prevail."

In 1722 the heavens opened and consternation rained down: the Rector of Yale, two tutors, and four neighboring ministers announced their conversion to the Church of England. They had read the books in Dummer's gift; they had compared these weighty arguments and noble styles with provincial sparseness, had meditated upon the disorders and confusion of Congregationalism, and perceived the strength, dignity, and majesty of apostolic succession. Nothing in Leverett's Harvard had been anywhere near so shocking. Obviously, poisonous books were rightly suspect, as the Overseers had declared. It was not enough to preach piety and organize societies; some action had to be taken, which meant repression and censorship. But an Anglican governor would not suppress Checkley or expurgate the Harvard library. A synod, only a synod might work.

After having his fling in the *Courant*, Checkley went to England and returned in September 1723 to issue *A Modest Proof of the Order & Government Settled by Christ and his Apostles in the Church*. The next February he reprinted Leslie's *A Short and Easie Method with the Deists*; this was basically a work of 1694, but it incorporated a later essay on qualifications for the sacrament, as well as several impertinent editorializings of Checkley's own. On March 16, with William Dummer presiding but Samuel Sewall the main instigator, the Council indicted this reprint as containing both vile insinuations against His Majesty and scandalous passages "reflecting on the ministers of the Gospel Established in this Province."

While Leverett was exhausting himself shielding the Corporation against the Overseers, events moved swiftly. Cutler arrived in Boston, now ordained an Anglican priest, to lend his fanatical energies to Checkley's cause. Edward Wigglesworth seized the opportunity to prove the loyalty of himself and his clique by publishing a refutation of Checkley, ostentatiously couched in the calmest of "catholic" terms and staking everything on historical evidence. Not to be outdone, Foxcroft joined in with another historical vindication. On May 3, 1724, Leverett died; while the presidency hung in the balance, while Cotton Mather, exulting in the elimination of "that unhappy Man," modestly expected that the door was opened for his doing singular service to the best of interests, Checkley was tried before the Court of Sessions upon a bill of indictment that accused him of statements false, feigned, malicious, wicked. Found guilty, he appealed to the Council, before which, Sewall and Paul Dudley (Leverett's enemies) on the bench, he appeared in November. John Read was his lawyer, and a jury of twelve citizens listened.

Checkley made a remarkable speech (published in 1730 in what may be a revised version) demanding how one who spoke for the Established Church could possibly be accused of insulting the king. As for himself, he was no Jacobite, and affirmed that no person had a better right to the crown than the present incumbent. He detested Deists, all of whom are (like one "Daniel de Foe") levelers and "range themselves in the natural State of Beasts, all independent, and no Government among them." Having thus obfuscated the issue and confused the jury, Checkley turned to the charge that he had scandalized the clergy, and contended that no faction of ministers in these plantations could so set up their own private way as to make "the Episcopal Churches to be Dissenters." As long as the king rules, the Church of England is the one here established. Invoking the opinion of the late Joseph Dudley—"by wise Men, deservedly acknowledged the wisest Man that ever was in the Country"—he proved out of Magna Charta and the laws of England that to pretend any other system to be an establishment would be a breach of the imperial union.

John Read graduated from Harvard in 1697, but after a checkered career in Connecticut came to Boston as virtually the sole practicing lawyer who might be called a professional. He was friendly with James Franklin's goat-footed gang and was suspected of Episcopalian sympathies; he was a great disappointment to the regime for whose service he had been educated. By the time he finished speaking for the defendant, the amateur jurists on the bench were as befuddled as the jury, and nobody wanted to risk his neck. Leslie's book had long since become a standard work, and so no innuendoes in it, he said, should be taken as applying to the present ministry of these remote regions. "I look upon it as dangerous to admit such power in an Innuendo as to make crimes and scandalls of such matters as are not so without an Innuendo." The renegade told them point blank: "For this is to make cruel and dangerous Engines for the punishment of the Innocent." The jury abjectly wilted: voting that Checkley had not insulted King George, they ruled that if Leslie's book was libelous, Checkley was guilty; but if the book was not, neither was he. At this point Cotton Mather realized the utter futility of those friendly gestures he and Colman had extended over the last twenty years: the Church of England is a foe, never to be placated, and "applied to Indirect Purposes of Civil Policies & Interests." Nobody wanted open warfare, but it was a clarification to know that henceforth New England was in a state of siege.

The judges, left with this decision of Solomon, collected their courage, pronounced the book a libel and fined Checkley fifty pounds, to be paid "to the King." Fully comprehending what a pyrrhic victory the Council gained for itself (and how embarrassing it would prove to Jeremiah Dummer), Checkley paid his fine. While the trial was pending, he wrote an answer to both Wigglesworth and Foxcroft; Jonathan Dickinson joined the fray from distant New Jersey, while Thomas Walter, again assisted by Uncle Cotton, attacked this "vile, horrid monstrous Book" in another piece of would-be wit, not quite designed to please the bishops, signed "Martin Marprelate." Perhaps, after all, the good old cause was not so forgotten in New England as the catholic propaganda pretended. In 1725 an anonymous *A Brief Account of the Revenues, Pomp and State of the Bishops, and other Clergy in the Church of England* brought the argument home to the people of New England in a language which, in that year of grace no less than in the year of Martin Marprelate, they would better understand than the judicious learning of Wigglesworth or the erudition of Foxcroft. Bishops revel in pomp and luxury, wherefore New Englanders who go over to that church in the hope of getting a cheaper ministry will be deceived. We turn off parsons with eighty or a hundred pounds: "Surely the scene will be surprisingly alter'd, if ever the Parsons come to receive their English Allowance." This might be a sad descent from the high intellectuality of primitive Congregationalism, but it was twenty times as effective in persuading American countrymen to be content with the election at Harvard of an unoffending and inexpensive Wadsworth. Besides, as Walter indirectly confessed by assuming the cognomens of Whig and Marprelate, there was a fundamental memory among the people which might easily be drawn into action, that once-upon-a-time their fathers had proved their mettle by refusing to pay revenues to lordly bishops.

But for the moment, Cotton Mather and his friends were caught in a cleft stick. He might urge the Council to prosecute that "wicked fellow" for his "execrable Books," but in Checkley's and Read's defense he saw what for years he had tried not to see: by prosecuting Anglicanism to the point of forcing a genuine theological controversy into the open, there was danger that the attack "may be anon improved unto our Disadvantage by a persecuting Adversary." The uneasiness that spread through New England after about 1710, that became a galloping consumption in 1720–21, heightened the feverishness of Mather's last years. His work resounds with shocked surprise that New England should be called intolerant, where "you might see a Godly Baptist, and Congregational, and Presbyterian, and Episcopalian, and Lutheran as well as Calvinist, all sitting down together at the same Table of the Lord." You must admire a people who so lovingly bear with one another's different sentiments; this is not quite utopia, yet "New-England has in it more than twice Seven times Seven such Golden Candlesticks." Why should such as they be molested?

In 1724 interference came. In Dartmouth and Tiverton the Congregationalists overreached themselves, in what they thought was a clever plot, by electing certain Quakers to the board of assessors; when these dissenters refused to collect the regular ministerial rates, the courts imprisoned them for dereliction of duty. They appealed to London, where the Society of Friends worked hard upon their case, and by special Orders in Council they were liberated. It took Massachusetts until 1729 to recognize in law this Quaker victory, and Connecticut even longer, but intolerance was beaten. And in March of 1725 Cotton Mather got the first wind of a plot brewing among the Anglicans to get a foot into Harvard; he applied his dying energies to awakening "the Men at the Helm," and carried to the Lord his final offerings, including the book he had long been working over, his last major utterance, *Ratio Disciplinae Fratrum Nov Anglorum*, which Thomas Prince assisted his failing powers in preparing for the printer.

While it was being made ready, on May 27, 1725, the convention of ministers stood at Thermopylæ. Considering, they said, the visible decay of piety, and the laudable example of their ancestors who had overcome immorality "in the way of general synods," they besought the General Court to let them assemble another. It had taken a century to work this revolution; here it is completed, all the more strikingly because at that moment the governorship was vacant and one of their own, William Dummer, was temporarily occupying the chair. To this executive and to the General Court did the heirs of Cotton and Hooker petition that they be allowed to meet in solemn conclave in order to inquire what are the miscarriages the judgment of heaven asks us to be sensible of, "and what may be the most evangelical and effectual expedients to put a stop unto those or the like miscarriages?" Cotton Mather's was the chief signature.

Dummer and the Council were ready to assent, but Patriots in the House were suspicious of clerical motives (the tenuous alliance formed against Leverett had broken down, once Wadsworth proved a tame cat), and held up their vote. While the splintered society thus failed to respond, the town's Anglican ministers, including the traitor Cutler, rushed news of the request to London. The Lords Justices immediately dispatched a reprimand to William Dummer for even having contemplated so insubordinate a transaction. His brother was reporting on September 1 the displeasure of Their Excellencies that the clergy "without the King's consent as Head of the

Church" should presume to take an action which set so bad a precedent for Dissenters in Britain. The Bishop of London did not want to give his own clergy a handle of complaint for lack of a convocation, so it was better that the clergy of the colonies reconcile themselves to being a "tolerated ministry." The Attorney General advised Dummer that such a synod would be in contempt of the Crown. *The Saybrook Platform* of course was not mentioned, for that was beneath contempt; neither was any official attention paid to Stoddard's reforms in the Valley. But in eastern New England, the *Proposals* had got nowhere, there was no hope for unity without a synod—and now mother England made clear that, despite the precious liberties Increase Mather was supposed to have won for it, this American orthodoxy could neither persecute others nor save itself. The lesson was instructive for the whole land, and even the entire seaboard: despite their Biblical scholarship, their loyalty to Hanover, their economic worth to the empire, their professed adherence to liberty, their constitutional guarantees, their sacrifices on the frontiers, these citizens—who had their differences— were told by portly gentlemen and luxurious prelates that they could not have a synod of their own.

The next blow was foreseeable: in 1727 the Anglican ministers in Boston—Cutler and Myles—commenced a dual assault; they appealed to London that Anglican churches be granted such exemptions as the Quakers had won in 1724, and then, upon perusing the charter of Harvard and finding therein that the "teaching elders" of Boston should sit among the Overseers, they demanded their place. Seventy Episcopalian citizens signed a petition in their behalf, serenely citing the language Colman had employed for twenty years, that Harvard was a "common nursery." Following upon the heels of synodical failure, this brazen stratagem could not have been more calculated to reunite the children of both Leverett and Mather—each of whom had every reason to dread the ordeal of a synod, but who now, excused from having to confront each other in that forum, could agree that Benjamin Wadsworth was the perfect symbol of colonial unity and self-respect.

Having been reared in the New England tradition, Cutler had learned at his father's knee the metaphysic of Non-separation. Therefore, at this late date, in such an uncannily altered guise, Puritan legitimacy came home to roost. To ward it off, leaders of New England Puritanism now had to put an end to the logic of their forefathers. The founders may well have meant that a teaching elder was also a minister of the Church of England, because New England had never separated; nevertheless, Harvard College did not belong to priests—or, if that were the issue, to any foreign power. It was New England's own. Logic was logic, but only up to a point.

Patriots, liberals, and revivalists, all alike rejoiced to hear the College's casuists explain that "teaching elder" did not mean either an ordained Anglican cleric or a Baptist parson, but only New England's sort of parson: "This is the known use and significations of them at the present day." Wigglesworth and Foxcroft were threshing ancient straw when demonstrating Congregationalism out of the New Testament; there was a certain tactical value in having such activity kept up, for it gave some semblance of legitimacy to the claim that Cutler and Myles be kept off the Board of Overseers. But legitimacy itself was not what it had been for the founders, the basis of an order; it was no more than a weapon to fence with, while the great fact was that Wigglesworth and Foxcroft, in this conjunction, sank their differences and stood together, making a united front against the penetration of Anglicans into Harvard Yard.

In the course of excluding them, Harvard College was enabled, or rather obliged, to issue a few pronouncements it might rather not have made. However, these were its only available defenses: "We account it [the] distinguishing honor to our College that the education there is free, without oaths or subscriptions to any particular sort of church order or discipline." (What a fortuitous godsend it has been for the tradition of academic freedom in this country that the uniformity of primitive New England being so self-evident, Harvard had never needed these "humane inventions.") The Corporation, of course, are Congregationalists, but according to their well-known principles of liberty, "sons of the Church of England are as welcome to the learning and academical honors as any of our own children." Posterity reads into these winged phrases implications not necessarily intended in 1727, but the authorities were forced to discover them in order to answer John Read's able, although highly legalistic, brief for the petitioners. The House, for once enchanted by the Corporation's eloquence, voted that Anglicans had never been intended by the charter's definition. One shudders to think what might have happened had Leverett still been President, but by meekness and neutrality Wadsworth served the cause of freedom in American education as greatly as did Leverett with his boldness. On June 16, 1730, a hundred years after Winthrop's coming ashore, Overseers who had hounded Leverett to his death flatly rejected Timothy Cutler. He might indeed appeal to England, but provincials could amuse themselves imagining just how much support he would ever get from Sir Robert Walpole.

While a fumbling Cotton Mather in 1726 was trying to arrange sheets of the *Ratio* in his study, a gust of wind scattered them in the garden and over the wood-pile, whence his young friend Thomas Prince, heedless of dignity, rescued them. Prince also read the proof. Both of them knew that the synod had been stifled, and that, as was to happen next year, orders would come from England specifically exempting Episcopalians from payment of rates. In a hundred respects, Mather is the most intransigent and impervious mind of his period, not to say the most nauseous human being, yet in others he is the most sensitive and perceptive, the clearest and most resolute. The importance of the *Ratio* becomes evident when it is compared with the monumental rationalizations of the founders—to whom his allegiance was groveling. Where those were vast logical structures projected into the empyrean, his is descriptive; where those were prophecies, his is history; where those were compacted of dichotomies, contradictions, and syllogisms, his is straight assertion that whether or not Whitehall permits these people to hold their synod, to their polity they will cling because—if for no other reason—it is their own.

"They," as he calls his people, have developed variety in "certain Modalities," but few are "Eccentric": they all disapprove of some "Deformities" in the Church of England, but "cannot see, why they may not claim to be Real, and even some of the Soundest Parts of the True Church of England, according to the Intention of the first Reformers." The "Doctrinal Articles" are more widely preached in New England than in any other nation, there is not one Arminian or Arian, yet complete liberty of conscience prevails. Mather makes no attempt to conceal that practices have developed contrary to the original theory: he acknowledges, for example, that noncommunicants now regularly vote in the choice of ministers. The most important part of an installation is the convocation, the assembly of Christians from the surrounding towns; Mather constantly emphasizes the social context. He makes no dogmatic claims for the church covenant, yet he eloquently proves it "Expedient, Profitable, Desireable." (We must link this sentence with the discovery he made during the smallpox debate of the conclusive authority of "EXPERIENCE.") He himself does not like prayers read out of a book, but he has learned to let Brattle Street have them. Children will be helped if they make a profession before approaching the Lord's Supper, but on this there can safely be allowed a difference of opinion! The really important thing—and the glory of New England—is that there be "A Charitable Consideration of nothing but PIETY in admitting to Evangelical Priviledges." They have had four great synods, all successful and all called by the magistrate, but they believe in their right to meet without his direction; these assemblies did not claim absolute power, being "nothing but some Wise and Good Men meeting together to advise the Churches." Such synods are no threat to the secular authority, nor do they require its assistance; New England cannot believe that any Protestant government "would upon a due Information, any more Forbid their Meeting, than they would any of the Religious Assemblies upheld in the Country." It is simply incomprehensible, as Mather put it in what must be a late insertion in his manuscript, for any to declare that the gathering of a synod "won't be for the Safety, of—God knows what!—Unaccountable!" This was not open defiance, but it was submission with as bad a grace as possible.

Lacking a synod, the colonial churches must get along with the ministerial convocation (which had no real authority), with imperfect associations (which outside the Connecticut Valley remained merely formal), with councils (which more often than not created further dissensions), or else with societies for improving manners (which could not reach into the recesses of seaports, or to the remoter areas of the godless frontier). There has indeed been much complaint of apostasy; some of their "Seers" have sad apprehensions "lest New England have now done the most that it was intended for." But, no matter how degenerate they become, they will never, never be convinced that among their sins is the want of episcopacy: "This is an Invention which the Churches of New England will probably continue Strangers to." All this being so, the folly becomes manifest of "those unreasonable Sons of Procrustes, the Narrow-soul'd and Imperious Bigots of Uniformity," who try to force the land back into the Church. Here Mather would not submit: his defiance is clear. On this point, the great "conservative" died, even more explicitly than Jeremiah Dummer a prophet of the Revolution.

We cannot call the *Ratio* an entirely candid book. Cutler and Myles would easily see through the pretense that synods are innocent assemblies, and would so inform London. But in one basic respect, it is the most honest thing Cotton Mather ever wrote: it says, by forthright implication, that these are a peculiar people, no longer pretending to be the model for Europe but, fully conscious of how they came to be what they are, resolved henceforth to be just that. They comfort themselves that, to the extent reason can prevail, the principles they profess will be more and more espoused, even though "their Methods and Customs be not any where else presently Conform'd unto." This is all they have left of the city on a hill, and the New Testament is seldom appealed to. Reason is a help, but reason now figures not so much as John Wise's cosmic rationality but rather as brute common sense. The book does not pontificate; in fact, it is wonderfully chastened in tone. But it tries to say—granting all that has gone wrong or that remains defective—here is a system, inaugurated with the best of intentions, tested and tried, that has learned much but has even more to learn, that has proved itself expedient and profitable, and therefore will ultimately appear, like America itself, admirable and imitable to a wide and blundering world.

EPILOGUE

Cursed be the day wherein I was born:
Let not the day wherin my mother bare me be blessed.
Cursed be the man who brought tidings to my father,
Saying, "A man child is born unto thee";
Making him very glad.
And let that man be as the cities which the Lord overthrew, and repented not:
And let him hear the cry in the morning, and the shouting at noontide;
Because he slew me not from the womb;
Or that my mother might have been my grave,
And her womb to be always great with me.
Wherefore came I forth out of the womb to see labour and sorrow,
That my days should be consumed with shame?

JEREMIAH 20:14–18

VALE ATQUE AVE

THIS
Aged Saint," said Colman at the funeral of Increase
Mather in 1723, "was a Father to us all." You will remember how, from
this very desk, he often told you "in the most solemn and affecting manner
of his Desires to depart." Leverett went the next year, and on September 30
an apoplexy felled Governor Gurdon Saltonstall, who since 1707 had ruled
Connecticut "to the great Satisfaction of all Wise, Good and Impartial
Men," and who, said his eulogist, had steered the College through the
hurricane of Cutler's betrayal. In 1725 both John Wise and Thomas
Symmes were gone, and Thomas Walter untimely languished "of that
English Disease, a Consumption." Declaring himself more than eager to
migrate to a more glorious world, Cotton Mather wrote the life of his
father, *Parentator*, keeping close to matter of fact, just as it was: "I am
not more fond of Obtaining any Testimony than that." He preached in
September of 1727 at the funeral of William Waldron, who had financed
the *Ratio*, the principles of which lay close to his heart, though even closer
was "that serious and solid and substantial Piety, whereto all is to be subordinate and subservient, and Generous and Catholick Desire to have the
terms of Salvation the Only Terms of Communion." Mather preached
that the wrath of Jehovah was manifested in the earthquake, and like his
colleagues lamented that the terror of it was so soon effaced. He delighted
now in boasting that Harvard College "forever indifferently Instructs and
Rewards all Scholars of whatever different Perswasions in Christianity
among us," and upon that note expired, February 13, 1728.

Samuel Danforth at Taunton, Peter Thacher at Milton had gone two
months before. Funeral sermons, as Foxcroft observed, are often too prodi-
gal, and a Christian of merely common size should not expect to see his
virtues erected in a printed monument; "But where there have been remarkable Excellencys, as to Evangelical Graces and Moral Virtues, here a
Distinction is due." In every church there were discourses on Cotton
Mather, three of which were printed. He was pious, said Joshua Gee,
but not affected; serious and grave, but neither morose nor austere; affable without meanness; and—what seems inconceivable to the student of
his *Diary*—"facetious without levity." In fact, throughout these encomia,
amid praise of piety, eloquence, zeal, and learning, Mather figures as the
paramount "gentleman." We who have peered into the maelstrom of his

innumerable controversies, wherein gentlemanly manners are barely discernible, have trouble imagining what a formidable figure he presented to his world, what a standard of scholarship and decorum he held up to a provincial culture. His works, Colman assures us, give a very imperfect representation of him, for it was his conversation, his familiar and occasional discourse, that disclosed the vastness of his knowledge and his spirit. He had, said Prince, the largest and richest collection of books in these ends of the earth, "which He was at all times ready to use in the most sudden and extempore manner": hence we were happy in having him "at our head." Colman agreed: Mather was "the first Minister in the Town, the first in Age, Gifts and in Grace." From the beginning of the country to this very day, no leader of these churches amassed so great a treasure of learning "and made so much use of it, to a variety of pious Intentions, as this our Rev. Brother and Father, Dr. Cotton Mather."

With Mather gone, Colman ruefully observed that he himself was left the oldest minister in the colony, which was indeed an astonishing thought to those who remembered the willowy youth of Brattle Street in 1700. He forgot, when he said this, Solomon Stoddard and one or two others in the Valley, but in 1729 the great Pope departed, as did the redeemed captive of Deerfield. In 1731 John Bulkley joined his father. The younger men had now fully taken over: Foxcroft, Prince, Sewall, Cooper, Webb and Gee were established, as were also Barnard, Appleton, Gay. Wadsworth had become a shadow. Jeremiah Dummer let business take care of itself and retreated to his country estate, where a visitor surprised him among his concubines, who fled the unexpected approach by leaping over each other's backs like frightened sheep. Samuel Sewall, exercising to the last his sense of the symbolic, stretched his life into the hundredth year of Massachusetts Bay, and died on New Year's Day, 1730.

The Puritan mind was not, as we commenced this volume by observing, anniversary-conscious. Elections and thanksgivings had been settled into a routine of time, but still memorializations of merely chronological recurrences smacked of superstition. If anybody in Plymouth noticed 1720, no record survives. But for a land which regarded its true beginning as 1630, the year 1730 was an occasion for taking stock. Foxcroft published *Observations, Historical and Practical, on the Rise and Primitive State of New-England*, while Thomas Prince delivered *The People of New-England Put in Mind of the Righteous Acts of the Lord*. Both present history within the frame of the covenant, both portray the covenanting fathers as men of ideal piety, both survey the mighty things God has wrought for His chosen people, the wonderful deliverances—and then both turn into jeremiads, castigating the declension, apostasy, ingratitude, and corruption in which a century now finds America.

They start from a profound conviction that New England was once the fulfillment of the Reformation: in England men stopped short out of base political calculations; that nation which since the Glorious Revolution has become, says Prince, a happy land of ease and liberty, was in 1630 an "Egypt." The founders took the written Word for their sole canon, and with tears and mortifications purchased those liberties "which too many among us at this day are so ready to make light of." The God of Israel conducted them over the hazardous ocean, prepared a sanctuary for them "here in this obscure Corner of the World. He took compassion on them for His covenant's sake, and they responded by entering "into a special, open, express and solemn Covenant with Him." (Preaching upon his dead father, Joseph Sewall reminded himself that as children are virtually in their parents before they are begotten, "so it hath pleased God to include Parents together with their Children in the Covenant.") Under the old charter, with "a mild and equal Administration of Civil Government," the colonies prospered so remarkably "that scarce any History affords a Parallel." Although originally a plantation for religion, Boston has become a thriving town, "God has been pleased to smile on our Merchandize and Navigation, Trade and Business."

Both Foxcroft and Prince notice, after attributing success to the presence of Christ, some of the secondary causes. These add up to a picture of religion as the main procurer of wealth: the piety of the founders had "a powerful Efficacy, as the best natural Means, to promote their Universal Prosperity." They prized their privileges, executed wholesome laws forcing iniquity to hide; "Virtue was triumphant, and Religion reign'd every where." True, Prince explains, the methods God used with us were not miraculous, as in the Old Testament, but they were so manifestly providential that we ought to be irrevocably committed "to this Divine Standard, both in Belief and Practice, both in Life and Worship: And Wo unto us, if we depart there from!" Of all these marvelous interventions on behalf of a sober, civil, quiet people, the greatest was that happy advancement of the illustrious house of Hanover to the British throne, "in which alone, under God, we Trust to Preserve our Constitution, Laws and Liberties."

These centennial discourses should be paeans of exultation, and indeed, carried away at moments by their theme, they do become just that. But in their "applications" they descend, as did Richard Mather in 1657, to sordid realities. "Alas! Are we not become as an Oak, whose Leaf fadeth, and the Stock thereof is ready to die in the Ground?" Our commerce is immense, but our seaport towns "are exceedingly exposed and deprav'd by the Powring in of Trade and Strangers." Even lamentation upon our sins has become a sin, inspiring busybodies to whisper things they ought not, to the "manifest Forfeiture of all Pretensions to a Spirit of Charity and Brotherly Kindness." We pretend, concludes Foxcroft, to "a catholick Spirit, as 'tis called," and profess principles more generous than those of the righteous founders: but—and here was the heart of New England's question, of its doubt about itself, of its unappeasable disquietude—"But alas, have we not very much lost our Zeal for the great Substantialities of Religion, as well as for peculiar Modalities?"

To review the publications of 1730 is to go through virtually nothing but a string of jeremiads; that promise of escape into new patterns of discussion which 1720–21 made so brilliant is already forgotten. The form is as stereotyped as when set by Higginson and Stoughton; the familiar catalogue of crimes and abuses, swelled by annual additions, is rehearsed as it had been for decades. The knowledge that these things have been said a hundred thousand times is very much present. Don't say, William Russell told Connecticut in the election sermon of May 14, 1730, that this has not been the cry of ministers for many years. But you, the people, do not respond: you listen stolidly, incredulously, you even scoff; you say, "we don't see but that we have been of late, & are at present, as Prosperous as ever, there is Peace & Plenty, & the Country flourisheth." The worldly and the proud had better watch out: "There is nothing in the Covenant God stands related to them in, to Secure them." Should the covenant fail, sinners might find themselves in the hands of an angry God, who might hold them, as it were, over the pit of hell like a loathsome spider. Who could say that He would lengthen out His patience forever?

Politically, things did not look so grim. God has raised up Jonathan Belcher, said Ebenezer Gay, "from among the Sons of New-England, and by the good hand of his Providence led into the highest Seat of Government here, One, who (we trust) will naturally care for our State and industriously seek the Welfare of his People." The parentheses might suggest a slight lack of confidence, but there was no doubt about the objective: it was that very civil liberty and industrious welfare in the midst of which, according to the jeremiads, the land was sinking to perdition.

Many times we have remarked that the first thirty years of the eighteenth century, so neglected by historians, seem externally placid, dull, uneventful. The forms of the culture were not seriously threatened; the financial problems seem slight in comparison with the modern, the political contests only faint premonitions of more shattering events. However, examined more closely, and from the inside, the period becomes a complex of tensions and anxieties, in which, in sober fact, the die was cast. The points of contrast and contradiction represented at one extreme by, let us say, Williams' *Redeemed Captive* and at the other by Dummer's *Defence*—by Mather's *Magnalia* and by the ballad on Lovewell, by Stoddard as opposed to Wise, Benjamin Franklin as against Thomas Prince, Joseph Sewall as against Appleton, *The Christian Philosopher* as measured against the *Courant*—make an intricate system of interacting stresses and strains which not only foretell explosions, but predict the manifold directions in which the fragments will fly. This society had become a time-bomb, packed with dynamite, the fuse burning close.

It was a parched land, crying for deliverance from the hold of ideas that had served their purpose and died. It had more than the rudiments of new conceptions, an abundance of abilities demanding expression. It was a part of Protestant civilization, and, as everywhere in that kingdom, the weight of the past had become stifling. For the revivification of great principles, religious or civil, an awakening was necessary. It was a problem not only for thought but even more for language. The covenant had accurately described reality for John Winthrop, and Richard Mather had framed enduring counsel within its confines; but now reality—all the complex, jostling reality of this anxious society—demanded new descriptions. Ideas relative to these facts had to be propounded, and in words that could make the relation overwhelmingly felt.

By the end of 1730 it was evident that everybody had spoken from whom ideas or words were apt to come, had indicated what he might or might not contribute to the solution. Or rather, all except one. The next spring it was known that Jonathan Edwards would come to the Harvard Commencement, and he was pressed to give the Thursday lecture. Solomon Stoddard's successor announced that he would speak on *God Glorified in the Work of Redemption, by the Greatness of Man's Dependence upon him, in the Whole of it*. That man must depend upon God in the work of the covenant was always a basic axiom of New England. That he should depend upon God in reforming the sins he committed in his independence was the premise of all jeremiads. Yet somehow, in a century of American experience, the greatness of man's dependency had unaccountably become a euphemism for the greatness of man. Possibly that was because this greatness had not yet been thoroughly considered in the whole of it.

BIBLIOGRAPHICAL NOTES

BIBLIOGRAPHICAL NOTES

PROLOGUE: RICHARD MATHER'S FAREWELL

Richard Mather's *A Farewel-Exhortation To the Church and People of Dorchester in New-England* was printed in Cambridge, 1657, the title page declaring that his "incitements" and "perswasions" were "needful to be Seriously considered of all in these declining times." The text of *The Cambridge Platform* and of *The Westminster Confession* as formulated by the Synod of 1648 is in Williston Walker, *The Creeds and Platforms of Congregationalism* (New York, 1893), pp. 157–237, 367–402. Cf. Perry Miller, *Orthodoxy in Massachusetts* (Cambridge, 1933). Symond's letter to Winthrop is in *Winthrop Papers* (Massachusetts Historical Society, 1929–1947), V, 125–127; Winthrop's "Arguments for the Plantation of New England," *ibid.*, I, 106–149; "A Modell of Christian Charity," *ibid.*, 282–295; his letter defending his policy about La Tour, *ibid.*, IV, 402–410. Bacon on rhetoric, *Works*, ed. Spedding (Boston, 1882), IX, 131; on felicity, *ibid.*, 150–152.

CHAPTER I: THE WRATH OF JEHOVAH

The history and practice of the day of humiliation is told in William DeLoss Love, *The Fast and Thanksgiving Days of New England* (Boston, 1895).

CHAPTER II: THE JEREMIAD

Proclamations for days of humiliation are found *passim* in *Records of the Governor and Company of the Massachusetts Bay*, ed. Nathaniel B. Shurtleff (5 volumes; Boston, 1853–54). There are also texts of similar edicts in the records of Connecticut, Plymouth, and New Haven, as well as in virtually all local or church histories. Increase Mather's *Brief History* was reprinted with annotations by S. G. Drake as *The History of King Philip's War* (Boston and Albany, 1864). For the Synod of 1679–80, see Williston Walker, *Creeds and Platforms*, pp. 409–440.

CHAPTER III: THE PROTESTANT ETHIC

Because I am not attempting to write a comprehensive social history, I have contented myself with random samplings from what is at best (for this period) fragmentary evidences. However, it is evident that from the end of the seventeenth century down at least to the close of the nineteenth, the history of New England's "mind" was written as much, if not more, by the actions of merchants and men of business as in the publications of theologians and politicians. I have relied most heavily upon the published records of the county courts (*Essex*, ed. George F. Dow, 8 volumes, Salem, 1911–12; *Suffolk*, ed. Zechariah Chafee, *Publications of the Colonial Society of Massachusetts*, Volumes XXIX, XXX, 1933). I have also drawn upon William B. Weeden, *Economic and Social History of New England* (2 volumes; Boston, 1890), and have been guided by Edmund S. Morgan, *The Puritan Family* (Boston Public Library, 1944), and a yet unpublished dissertation by Norman H. Dawes, "Social Classes in Seventeenth-Century New England" (Harvard University, 1941).

John Cotton's disquisition on business ethics, extracted from *The Way of Life* (London, 1641), is reprinted in Perry Miller and Thomas H. Johnson, *The Puritans* (New York, 1938), pp. 319–327. John Hull's "Diaries" are in *Transactions and Collections of the American Antiquarian Society*, III (1857), 109–316. Willard's funeral sermon on Hull is *The High Esteem Which God Hath of the Death of His Saints* (Boston, 1683). Edward Ward observed New England manners in *A Trip to New-England* (London, 1699), ed. G. P. Winship (Providence, 1905), pp. 38–39. For John Josselyn's comments, see *An Account of Two Voyages to New-England* (London, 1675; reprinted Boston, 1865), p. 129. The inventory of Thomas Turvill's melancholy estate is in Joshua Coffin, *A Sketch of the History of Newbury* (Boston, 1845), pp. 89–90. Dunton's remarks are in *Letters Written from New England*, ed. W. H. Whitmore (Boston, 1867), p. 71.

How late the pattern of the jeremiad persisted, and how consciously the old-line clergy were aware of its psychological function, appears in Emerson's quotation in 1845 from his grandmother at a time the Unitarians were opposing the practice of public humiliation: she "hated to hear of the opposition of clergymen and others to the Fast Day, for she thought our people had so few festivals and this was now well established; and the penitential form of the proclamation gives it a certain zest which the other holidays want" (*Journals*, VII, 47).

CHAPTER IV: THE EXPANDING LIMITS OF NATURAL ABILITY

Documents concerning the Synod of 1637 and the trial of Anne Hutchinson are collected in Charles Francis Adams, *Antinomianism in the Colony of Massachusetts Bay* (Boston, 1894). For Wheelwright, see Charles H. Bell, *John Wheelwright, His Writings* (Boston, 1876). Cotton's version of his part in the affair is also related in *A Reply to Mr. Williams his Examination*, reprinted in *Publications of the Narragansett Club* (Providence, 1866), Volume II.

CHAPTER V: HYPOCRISY

Of the early theorists, Thomas Hooker is most explicit upon the distinction of covenants: *The Faithful Covenanter* (London, 1644); *The Covenant of Grace Opened* (London, 1649); also *A Survey of the Summe of Church Discipline* (London, 1649), especially Part I, pp. 36 ff. Presbyterian charges of perfectionism in New England can be found in Samuel Rutherford, *A Survey of the Survey* (London, 1658) and Samuel Hudson, *A Vindication of the Essence* (London, 1650). Cotton's major counterattack is *Of the Holiness of Church-Members* (London, 1650).

CHAPTER VI: CHILDREN OF THE COVENANT

The most important statements of the original baptismal doctrine are: Thomas Cobbett, *A Just Vindication* (London, 1648); Peter Bulkeley, *The Gospel-Covenant* (London, 1651); John Cotton, *The Grounds and Ends of the Baptisme of the Children of the Faithful* (London, 1647); George Phillips, *A Reply to a Confutation* (London, 1645); Thomas Shepard, *The Church-Membership of Children* (Cambridge, 1663). Hooker's doubts and soul-searchings are confessed in the *Survey*, Part III, p. 12. Rutherford's accusation is from *A Survey of the Survey*, pp. 146 ff. For Dunster's defection, see Samuel Eliot Morison, *Harvard College in the Seventeenth Century* (Cambridge, 1936), pp. 298–320.

CHAPTER VII: HALF-WAY MEASURES

For the history, bibliography, and basic documents of the Half-Way Covenant, see Williston Walker, *Creeds and Platforms*, pp. 238–340, and Cotton Mather, *Magnalia Christi Americana* (London, 1702), Book V, Part III. For the history of the Hartford quarrel, see George L. Walker, *History of the First Church in Hartford* (Hartford, 1884). Eleazar Mather's letter to Davenport is in James R. Trumbull, *History of Northampton* (Northampton, 1893), I, 202.

CHAPTER VIII: REVIVALISM

For hints, which I have improved for all they are worth, as to the nature of the struggle between pastors and people over the Half-Way Covenant, see William Hubbard, *A General History of New-England* (*Collections of the Massachusetts Historical Society*, Second Series, Volumes V–VI), pp. 562, 570, 601. Outlines of the conflict can be deciphered in countless local histories, the authors of which—whether out of ignorance or malice—strive to conceal or at least to soften the asperity. Particularly useful are: Arthur B. Ellis, *History of the First Church in Boston* (Boston, 1881); *Records of the First Church at Dorchester* (Boston, 1891); Walter Eliot Thwing, *History of the First Church in Roxbury* (Boston, 1908). For the Connecticut story, see George L. Walker, *History of the First Church in Hartford*, and Benjamin Trumbull, *A Complete History of Connecticut* (New London, 1898); the whole episode of Pitkin's petition and its consequences needs further investigation. The outstanding piece of ecclesiastical history, which supplies us with the documents, is Hamilton A. Hill, *History of the Old South Church* (Boston, 1890). See also Thomas Hutchinson, *The History of the Colony of Massachusetts-Bay*, ed. Lawrence J. Mayo (Cambridge, 1936), I, 230–235. Davenport's *A Sermon Preach'd at the Election*, issued in Boston in 1670, is reprinted in *Publications of the Colonial Society of Massachusetts*, X (1907), 1–6. The petition of the ministers is in *Records of the Governor and Company*, IV, Part 2, 489–494. For advices of the Synod of 1679–80 concerning renewal of covenant, see Williston Walker, *Creeds and Platforms*, pp. 433–436.

CHAPTER IX: INTOLERANCE

For the issues involved in the petition of Dr. Child, see my *Orthodoxy in Massachusetts*. The basic documents in the duel of the General Court with the royal authority are in *Records of the Governor and Company* and in Thomas Hutchinson, *A Collection of Original Papers* (Boston, 1769). Coddington's rambling but magnificent letter to Bellingham was published in London, 1674, as *A Demonstration of True Love unto You the Rulers of the Colony of Massachusetts in New-England*.

CHAPTER X: PROPAGANDA

For Randolph, see *Edward Randolph*, ed. R. N. Toppan and A. T. S. Goodrich (7 volumes; Prince Society, 1898–1909). The standard histories—Hutchinson, Palfrey, and J. T. Adams—tell of the colonial struggle with England and of the loss of the Massachusetts charter. Evidence as to the size and concentration of what Randolph called the moderate party is so fugitive that I am obliged to warn the reader to regard my account as in large part sheer surmise. Still, unless we recognize the existence of this mentality, we can make little sense out of the events and the publications. For Dudley, see Everett Kimball, *The Public Life of Joseph Dudley* (New York, 1911).

CHAPTER XI: PROFILE OF A PROVINCIAL MENTALITY

The Andros regime is described by Viola F. Barnes, *The Dominion of New England* (New Haven, 1923). The major publications are in *The Andros Tracts*, ed. William H. Whitmore (3 volumes; Boston, 1868–1874). For the part played by the Mathers, see Kenneth B. Murdock, *Increase Mather* (Cambridge, Massachusetts, 1925).

Gershom Bulkeley's *The Peoples' Right to Election* is in *Collections of the Connecticut Historical Society*, I (1860), 57–75; *Will and Doom*, *ibid.*, III (1895), 69–269. *The Poetical Works of Edward Taylor* are edited by Thomas H. Johnson (New York, 1939). For the Ipswich protest, consult Thomas F. Waters, *Ipswich in the Massachusetts Bay Colony* (Ipswich, 1905). Wise's report on Quebec is in *Proceedings of the Massachusetts Historical Society*, XV (1902), 285–290. Cotton Mather's defense of the bills in 1691 was entitled *Some Considerations on the Bills of Credit*, and is reprinted in Andrew McFarland Davis, *Tracts Relating to the Currency of the Massachusetts Bay* (Boston, 1902).

The more telling of George Keith's attacks on Massachusetts during this period are: *A Refutation of Three Opposers of Truth* (Philadelphia, 1690); *Presbyterian and Independent Churches Brought to the Test* (Philadelphia, 1690); *The Pretended Antidote Proved Poyson* (Philadelphia, 1691); *A Serious Appeal to All the More Sober, Impartial & Iudicious People in New-England* (Philadelphia, 1692). To the second of these, Cotton Mather—reinforced by Allen, Moodey, and Willard—replied in *The Principles of the Protestant Religion Maintained* (Boston, 1690). Mather's sermon before Phips on June 9, 1692, outlining the new conception of religious freedom, is *Optanda* (Boston, 1692). The endorsement of Increase Mather by the English Dissenters, as well as an explanation of the importance he attached to his association with them, is found in Cotton Mather, *Parentator* (Boston, 1724), pp. 159–160. Cotton Mather's *Political Fables* are printed in *The Andros Tracts*, II, 324–332, and in Kenneth B. Murdock, *Selections from Cotton Mather*, pp. 363–371.

CHAPTER XII: SALVAGING THE COVENANT

Thomas Maule hoisted the clergy with their own petard in his delightful although none too coherent *Truth Held Forth and Maintained* (1695) and *New-England Persecutors Mauld With Their Own Weapons* (1697), both probably

printed in New York. In this and succeeding chapters I have been guided by
Susan M. Reed, *Church and State in Massachusetts Bay, 1691–1740* (Urbana,
Illinois, 1914). For the background of Matherian Chiliasm, see my "The End of
the World," *The William and Mary Quarterly*, VIII (1951), 171–192. William
King's verses appear in *The Original Works* (London, 1776), I, 221–222. Sewall's
hymn to Plum Island occurs in *Phaenomena quaedam Apocalyptica* (Boston,
1697).

CHAPTER XIII: THE JUDGMENT OF THE WITCHES

The bibliography on witchcraft, and on Salem in particular, is, of course, enor-
mous (see Miller and Johnson, *The Puritans*, pp. 826–827). The principal docu-
ments used in this chapter are conveniently assembled in George Lincoln Burr,
Narratives of the Witchcraft Cases (New York, 1914), and William E. Woodward,
Records of Salem Witchcraft (2 volumes; Roxbury, 1864). See also the analysis of
Cases of Conscience and *The Wonders of the Invisible World* by Thomas J.
Holmes in his *Bibliography* of Increase Mather (Cleveland, 1931) and of Cotton
Mather (Cambridge, 1940). Holmes's dissection of Cotton Mather's processes in
composing *The Wonders*—the desperate filling up of blank paper while awaiting
documents from Salem—marks an epoch in the study of Salem witchcraft; however, the book itself, in terms of "internal evidence," yields up the meaning which
for centuries has been staring scholars in the face. Perhaps too many of them have
written with inadequate understanding of how an author—or at any rate such a
nervous author as Cotton Mather—writes a book.

CHAPTER XIV: THE DILEMMA OF THE SACRAMENT

The background, as well as the text, of *The Heads of Agreement* is in Williston
Walker, *Creeds and Platforms*, pp. 440–462. Also helpful is Olive M. Griffiths,
Religion and Learning (Cambridge, England, 1935). The publications in this
controversy are numerous, and I would hesitate to advise other students to spend
as much of their lives in reading them as I have; still, there are rewards, and I do
believe that such a little book on the affair as I once planned is worth the doing.
The most important titles out of which I derive my brief discussion, in addition
to those I mention in the text, are: Vincent Alsop, *A Faithful Rebuke to a False
Report*, 1697; T. Beverly, *A True State of Gospel Truth*, 1693; Isaac Chauncy,
Neonomianism Unmask'd, 1692, 1693, and *A Rejoinder to Mr. Daniel Williams*,
1693; John Humfrey, *Mediocria*, 1695; Daniel Williams, *A Defence of Gospel-
Truth*, 1693.

CHAPTER XV: CONTENTION

The biographical facts about Stoddard I assembled, from the obvious sources, in
"Solomon Stoddard," *The Harvard Theological Review*, XXXIV (1941), 277–
320. Assuredly, more research upon him and his ministry ought to be undertaken.
For Benjamin Colman, see Clifford K. Shipton, *Sibley's Harvard Graduates*, IV
(1933), 120–137. Russell's letter to Increase Mather, March 28, 1681, is in *Collections of the Massachusetts Historical Society*, Fourth Series, VIII, 83–84. The

struggle for the control of Harvard College up to the election of Leverett is recounted in Samuel Eliot Morison, *Harvard College in the Seventeenth Century*, pp. 472–569. Cotton Mather's life of Mitchell, with Increase Mather's preface, is in all editions of the *Magnalia*. The documents connected with the founding of the Brattle Street Church are in Samuel K. Lothrop, *A History of the Church in Brattle Street* (Boston, 1851). Cotton Mather's staggering oration of July 4 is in his *Diary, Collections of the Massachusetts Historical Society*, Seventh Series, VII, 384–388.

CHAPTER XVI: THE FAILURE OF CENTRALIZATION

The history and text of the *Proposals* are in Williston Walker, *Creeds and Platforms*, pp. 463–496; of the *Saybrook Platform*, pp. 495–507.

CHAPTER XVII: THE UNRESOLVED DEBATE

The Dudley-Mather letters are in *Collections of the Massachusetts Historical Society*, First Series, III, 126–130, and the pamphlets, *ibid.*, Fifth Series, VI. Dudley's encounter with the farmers is sadly recorded in Sewall's *Diary, ibid.*, VI, 144 ff. The funeral orations on Stoddard are: William Williams, *The Death of a Prophet Lamented* (Boston, 1729); Benjamin Colman, *The Faithful Ministers of Christ Mindful of Their Own Death* (Boston, 1729). In the same year, Joseph Nash, otherwise unknown to fame, published *An Elegy Upon the Much Lamented Decease of the Reverend & Excellent Mr. Solomon Stoddard*.

CHAPTER XVIII: THE POISON OF WISE'S CURSED LIBEL

Colman's and Mather's oblique attacks on Wise are recorded by Sewall in his *Diary, Collections of the Massachusetts Historical Society*, Fifth Series, VII, 51. Cotton Mather's letter to Woodrow is in his *Diary, ibid.*, Seventh Series, VIII, 327. Wise's two volumes were reprinted in Boston, 1862. Whitaker's reference is from *A Confutation of Two Tracts* (Boston, 1774). Thomas Symmes's invocation of Wise appears in *Utile Dulci* (Boston, 1723), p. A2 verso.

CHAPTER XIX: A MEDIUM OF TRADE

Virtually all the pamphlets issued during this controversy are reprinted in Andrew McFarland Davis, *Colonial Currency Reprints* (4 volumes; Boston, 1910–1911); the major ones are also in his *Tracts Relating to the Currency*. The issues are analyzed, and the background expounded, in Joseph B. Felt, *An Historical Account of Massachusetts Currency* (Boston, 1839); Charles Jesse Bullock, *Essays on the Monetary History of the United States* (New York, 1900); Joseph Dorfman, *The Economic Mind in American Civilization* (New York, 1946). For the younger Elisha Cooke, see Shipton, *Sibley's Harvard Graduates*, IV, 349–356. The crucial years of 1720–1722 are copiously recounted in Hutchinson's *History*. Cotton Mather's involvement in the business gives a special interest to the sermon preached before Governor Shute on March 12, *Concio ad Populum* (Boston, 1719).

CHAPTER XX: ANTIMINISTERIAL SENTIMENT

The photostat copy of the British Museum's file of *The New-England Courant* in the library of the Massachusetts Historical Society contains ascriptions of authorship of most of the early articles in a hand believed to be that of Benjamin Franklin himself. Sewall's account of Banister's drinking party is in *Diary, Collections of the Massachusetts Historical Society*, Fifth Series, VI, 419–424; the versified squib on the Old South Church, III, 117. An outline of the fight over the *Courant* is in Clyde A. Duniway, *The Development of Freedom of the Press in Massachusetts* (New York, 1906).

CHAPTER XXI: THE JUDGMENT OF THE SMALLPOX

Increase Mather's *Several Reasons* (along with Cotton Mather's *Sentiments*) was reprinted with an introduction by George Lyman Kittredge (Cleveland, 1921) which guides the student through the labyrinth of the bibliography, although assisting him little as to the purport of the writings. For the issues themselves, see Reginald H. Fitz, "Zabdiel Boylston, Inoculator, and the Epidemic of Smallpox in Boston in 1821," *Johns Hopkins Hospital Bulletin*, XXII (1911), 315–327; Francis R. Packard, *History of Medicine in the United States* (2 volumes; New York, 1931), especially I, 76 ff.

CHAPTER XXII: A SECULAR STATE

Thomas Symmes's account is in *Lovewell Lamented* (Boston, 1725). James Franklin advertised the ballad for sale on May 3, 1725, but the first printing that now survives was in 1824; it appears in many collections, for example, R. P. Gray, *Songs and Ballads of the Maine Lumberjacks*. Susanna Rogers' elegy first sought the light in the *New England Historical and Genealogical Register*, XV (1861), 91. Penhallow's *History* is available in *Collections of the New Hampshire Historical Society*, Volume I (1824). For Checkley, see Edmund Slafter, *John Checkley* (2 volumes; Boston, 1897). Most of my quotations on political theory are from election sermons of 1700–1730, for a bibliography of which see Lindsay Swift, "The Massachusetts Election Sermons," *Publications of the Colonial Society of Massachusetts*, I (1895), 388–451, and Alice H. Baldwin, *The New England Clergy and the American Revolution* (Durham, North Carolina, 1928).

CHAPTER XXIII: A TENDER PLANT

For Jeremiah Dummer, see Shipton, *Sibley's Harvard Graduates*, IV, 454–468; for Thomas Banister, pp. 496–501. I am indebted to a yet unpublished dissertation on Dummer by Charles Sanford (Harvard University, 1951).

CHAPTER XXIV: DO–GOOD

Cotton Mather's most explicit exposition of what we call the Protestant ethic is *A Christian at His Calling* (Boston, 1701), but the theme runs through much of his vast production. In his works as in those of his colleagues, statements about the relation of piety to business are most apt to appear in funeral orations on wealthy merchants. Stepping down from his pulpit to discuss a purely economic matter, Benjamin Colman in *Some Reasons and Arguments offered to the Good People of Boston and Adjacent Places for the Setting up Markets in Boston* (1719) spoke with greater frankness, or at least with more objectivity, than the sermons generally exhibit. The conception of "particular faith" and its place both in Matherian and other thinking need deeper study; the basic text is Cotton Mather's *Parentator* (Boston, 1724), pp. 189–196. He wrestles with the problem throughout the *Diary*.

CHAPTER XXV: REASON

For Bulkley, see *Sibley's Harvard Graduates*, IV, 450–454. Cotton Mather's *Manuductio ad Ministerium*, edited by Thomas J. Holmes and Kenneth B. Murdock, is reprinted by the Facsimile Text Society (New York, 1937).

CHAPTER XXVI: THE EXPERIMENTAL PHILOSOPHY

As with the economic activity, I have not here attempted a precise history of all the actions of particular individuals. Obviously a complete history of New England's "mind" calls for a careful tabulation of every step, even of those made in loneliness and isolation, as were those of Thomas Brattle. I am here surveying the public record, and my concern is with the conception of science in general within the over-all architecture of thought, or perhaps only of opinion. Exact evaluation of the work of the few New Englanders engaged, under tremendous handicaps, in actual experimentation is still being studied by scholars far more competent than I, who have not yet synthesized their findings.

Only recently have scholars begun to appreciate the astonishing range and depth of Cotton Mather's scientific intelligence, particularly in medicine. On the last point we shall know more when Dr. Richard Shryock reports on Mather's manuscript "Bethesda." Meanwhile, see Otho T. Beall, Jr., "Cotton Mather, the First Significant Figure in American Medicine," *Bulletin of the History of Medicine*, XXVI (1952), 103–116. Also Henry R. Viets, *A Brief History of Medicine in Massachusetts* (Boston, 1930).

For the truly remarkable observations of Cotton Mather and Paul Dudley on plant hybridization, see Conway Zirkle, *The Beginnings of Plant Hybridization* (Philadelphia, 1935).

For the bibliography of Mather's correspondence with the Royal Society, see George Lyman Kittredge, "Cotton Mather's Scientific Communications to the Royal Society," *Proceedings of the American Antiquarian Society*, new series, XXVI (1916), 18–57; also, "Some Lost Works of Cotton Mather," *Proceedings of the Massachusetts Historical Society*, XLV (1912), 418–479. Also Thomas J. Holmes's *Cotton Mather*, pp. 199–208. Mather's sentence of 1690 concerning microscopes comes from *The Wonderful Works of God Commemorated*; however, in 1685, in *An Elegy on . . . the Reverend Mr. Nathanael Collins*, he had shown himself already familiar with microscopes. For *The Christian Philosopher*, see Theodore Hornberger, "Notes" in Thomas J. Holmes, *Cotton Mather*, pp. 133–138.

For a long time, modern commentators have been thrown off because so many of Mather's communications to the Society seem the products of credulity and superstition, not to say of a lurid imagination, rather than of anything remotely resembling the processes of scientific investigation. To modern eyes reports on monstrous births or about "horrid snows" hardly seem to qualify him as a scientist; however, this view forgets that his work was entirely in line with that of his contemporaries and certainly with that of most of the contributors to the *Transactions of the Royal Society*. Furthermore, it forgets what in fact was the state of "natural science" in the first decades of the eighteenth century, and out of what "modern" science grew.

To cite only a few of the recent studies which have been restoring the perspective for us, see: I. Bernard Cohen, *Some Early Tools of American Science* (Cambridge, 1950); Frederick G. Kilgour, "Thomas Robie," *Isis*, XXX (1939), 473–490; "The Rise of Scientific Activity in Colonial New England," *The Yale Journal of Biology and Medicine*, XXII (1949), 123–138; Frederick E. Brasch, "The Newtonian Epoch in the American Colonies," *Proceedings of the American Antiquarian Society*, new series, XLIX (1939), 314–333; John W. Streeter, "John Winthrop, Junior, and the Fifth Satellite of Jupiter," *Isis*, XXXIX (1948), 159–163; Theodore Hornberger, "The Date, the Source, and the Significance of Cotton Mather's Interest in Science," *American Literature*, IV (1935), 413–423; also his *Scientific Thought in the American Colleges* (Austin, Texas, 1945).

CHAPTER XXVII: THE DEATH OF AN IDEA

For Pemberton, see Shipton, *Sibley's Harvard Graduates*, IV, 107–113. For Rogers, see J. R. Bolles and A. B. Williams, *The Rogerenes*. Pemberton's *A Funeral Sermon on the Death of the Rev. Mr. Samuel Willard* (Boston, 1707) appears also in Pemberton's *Sermons and Discourses on Several Occasions* (London, 1727). Increase Mather's sermon at the ordination of Nathaniel Appleton is printed inconspicuously (on purpose?) as "The Work of the Ministry Described," the last of four items in *Practical Truths Plainly Delivered* (Boston, 1718). Until Samuel Eliot Morison can be induced to continue his account, we must for events after 1707 still depend on Josiah Quincy, *The History of Harvard* (2 volumes; Cambridge, 1840); for the administration of Leverett and the election of Wadsworth, this supplies enough of the original documentation to make sufficiently clear the lines of cleavage and the aims of the maneuvers.

CHAPTER XXVIII: POLITY AS A FORM OF PATRIOTISM

Cotton Mather's most brazen attempt to present the New England churches as essentially at one with the Presbyterianism of Scotland is his letter, printed in Boston, 1710, *To the University of Glasgow*. The gradual encroachments of halfway members and then of townsmen upon the control of the churches can be traced in a hundred local histories. Increase Mather's last stand against the rising tide is *The Order of the Gospel* (Boston, 1700), pp. 61–71; Cotton Mather began to capitulate in *Advice from the Watch-Tower* (Boston, 1713). For Thomas Walter, see Shipton, *Sibley's Harvard Graduates*, VI, 18–24. For the New North Church affair, see Thomas J. Holmes, *Increase Mather*, pp. 5–8; Chandler Robbins, *A History of the Second Church, or Old North, in Boston* (Boston, 1852), pp. 170–176, 306–309. Cotton Mather's principal utterance during this squabble was *A Vision in the Temple* (Boston, 1721).

EPILOGUE: VALE ATQUE AVE

Colman's funeral sermon on Increase Mather is *The Prophet's Death* (Boston, 1723). The printed orations on Cotton Mather are: Joshua Gee, *Israel's Mourning for Aaron's Death*; Benjamin Colman, *The Holy Walk and Glorious Translation of Blessed Enoch*; Thomas Prince, *The Departure of Elijah Lamented* (all in Boston, 1728). Joseph Sewall preached on his father, *The Orphan's Last Legacy* (Boston, 1730).

INDEX